Dictionary of Literary Biography

Dictionary of Literary Biography Documentary Series

8 *The Black Aesthetic Movement,* edited by Jeffrey Louis Decker (1991)

9 *American Writers of the Vietnam War: W. D. Ehrhart, Larry Heinemann, Tim O'Brien, Walter McDonald, John M. Del Vecchio,* edited by Ronald Baughman (1991)

10 *The Bloomsbury Group,* edited by Edward L. Bishop (1992)

11 *American Proletarian Culture: The Twenties and The Thirties,* edited by Jon Christian Suggs (1993)

12 *Southern Women Writers: Flannery O'Connor, Katherine Anne Porter, Eudora Welty,*

edited by Mary Ann Wimsatt and Karen L. Rood (1994)

13 *The House of Scribner, 1846–1904,* edited by John Delaney (1996)

14 *Four Women Writers for Children, 1868–1918,* edited by Caroline C. Hunt (1996)

15 *American Expatriate Writers: Paris in the Twenties,* edited by Matthew J. Bruccoli and Robert W. Trogdon (1997)

16 *The House of Scribner, 1905–1930,* edited by John Delaney (1997)

17 *The House of Scribner, 1931–1984,* edited by John Delaney (1998)

18 *British Poets of The Great War: Sassoon, Graves, Owen,* edited by Patrick Quinn (1999)

19 *James Dickey,* edited by Judith S. Baughman (1999)

See also DLB 210, 216, 219, 222, 224, 229, 237, 247, 253, 254, 263, 269, 273, 274, 280, 284, 288, 291, 294, 298, 301, 304, 308, 309, 315, 316, 320, 324, 338, 340, 343

Dictionary of Literary Biography Yearbooks

1980 edited by Karen L. Rood, Jean W. Ross, and Richard Ziegfeld (1981)

1981 edited by Karen L. Rood, Jean W. Ross, and Richard Ziegfeld (1982)

1982 edited by Richard Ziegfeld; associate editors: Jean W. Ross and Lynne C. Zeigler (1983)

1983 edited by Mary Bruccoli and Jean W. Ross; associate editor Richard Ziegfeld (1984)

1984 edited by Jean W. Ross (1985)

1985 edited by Jean W. Ross (1986)

1986 edited by J. M. Brook (1987)

1987 edited by J. M. Brook (1988)

1988 edited by J. M. Brook (1989)

1989 edited by J. M. Brook (1990)

1990 edited by James W. Hipp (1991)

1991 edited by James W. Hipp (1992)

1992 edited by James W. Hipp (1993)

1993 edited by James W. Hipp, contributing editor George Garrett (1994)

1994 edited by James W. Hipp, contributing editor George Garrett (1995)

1995 edited by James W. Hipp, contributing editor George Garrett (1996)

1996 edited by Samuel W. Bruce and L. Kay Webster, contributing editor George Garrett (1997)

1997 edited by Matthew J. Bruccoli and George Garrett, with the assistance of L. Kay Webster (1998)

1998 edited by Matthew J. Bruccoli, contributing editor George Garrett, with the assistance of D. W. Thomas (1999)

1999 edited by Matthew J. Bruccoli, contributing editor George Garrett, with the assistance of D. W. Thomas (2000)

2000 edited by Matthew J. Bruccoli, contributing editor George Garrett, with the assistance of George Parker Anderson (2001)

2001 edited by Matthew J. Bruccoli, contributing editor George Garrett, with the assistance of George Parker Anderson (2002)

2002 edited by Matthew J. Bruccoli and George Garrett; George Parker Anderson, Assistant Editor (2003)

Concise Series

Concise Dictionary of American Literary Biography, 7 volumes (1988–1999): *The New Consciousness, 1941–1968; Colonization to the American Renaissance, 1640–1865; Realism, Naturalism, and Local Color, 1865–1917; The Twenties, 1917–1929; The Age of Maturity, 1929–1941; Broadening Views, 1968–1988; Supplement: Modern Writers, 1900–1998.*

Concise Dictionary of British Literary Biography, 8 volumes (1991–1992): *Writers of the Middle Ages and Renaissance Before 1660; Writers of the Restoration and Eighteenth Century, 1660–1789; Writers of the Romantic Period, 1789–1832; Victorian Writers, 1832–1890; Late-Victorian and Edwardian Writers, 1890–1914; Modern Writers, 1914–1945; Writers After World War II, 1945–1960; Contemporary Writers, 1960 to Present.*

Concise Dictionary of World Literary Biography, 4 volumes (1999–2000): *Ancient Greek and Roman Writers; German Writers; African, Caribbean, and Latin American Writers; South Slavic and Eastern European Writers.*

American Radical and Reform Writers
Second Series

American Radical and Reform Writers
Second Series

Edited by
Hester Lee Furey
The Art Institute of Atlanta

A Bruccoli Clark Layman Book

GALE
CENGAGE Learning·

Detroit • New York • San Francisco • New Haven, Conn • Waterville, Maine • London

GALE
CENGAGE Learning

Dictionary of Literary Biography, Volume 345: American Radical and Reform Writers, Second Series
Hester Lee Furey

Founding Editor: Matthew J. Bruccoli

Advisory Board: John Baker,
 William Cagle, Patrick O'Connor,
 George Garrett, Trudier Harris,
 Alvin Kernan

Editorial Director: Richard Layman

For product information and technology assistance, contact us at
Gale Customer Support, 1-800-877-4253.

For permission to use material from this text or product,
submit all requests online at **www.cengage.com/permissions**
Further permissions questions can be emailed to
permissionrequest@cengage.com

While every effort has been made to ensure the reliability of the information presented in this publication, Gale, a part of Cengage Learning, does not guarantee the accuracy of the data contained herein. Gale accepts no payment for listing; and inclusion in the publication of any organization, agency, institution, publication, service, or individual does not imply endorsement of the editors or publisher. Errors brought to the attention of the publisher and verified to the satisfaction of the publisher will be corrected in future editions.

EDITORIAL DATA PRIVACY POLICY. Does this publication contain information about you as an individual? If so, for more information about our editorial date privacy policies, please see our Privacy Statement at www.gale.cengage.com

LIBRARY OF CONGRESS CATALOGING-IN-PUBLICATION DATA

American radical and reform writers. Second series / edited by Hester Lee Furey.
  p. cm. — (Dictionary of literary biography ; v. 345)
"A Bruccoli Clark Layman book."
Includes bibliographical references and index.
ISBN 978-0-7876-8163-0 (hardcover)
1. American literature—19th century—Bio-bibliography—Dictionaries. 2. Reformers—United States—Biography—Dictionaries. 3. American literature—20th century—Bio-bibliography—Dictionaries. 4. Social problems in literature—Dictionaries. 5. Authors, American—19th century—Biography—Dictionaries. 6. Authors, American—20th century—Biography—Dictionaries. 7. Radicals—United States—Biography—Dictionaries. 8. Protest literature, American—Dictionaries. 9. Radicalism in literature—Dictionaries. I. Furey, Hester Lee.

PR721.N56 2009
822'.80903—dc22
[B]
                            2008034754

ISBN-13: 978-0-7876-8163-0   ISBN-10: 0-7876-8163-6

Gale
27500 Drake Rd.
Farmington Hills, MI 48331-3535

Printed in the United States of America
2 3 4 5 6 7 12 11 10 09 08

For Family—consanguineous, legal, and other

Contents

Plan of the Series

. . . Almost the most prodigious asset of a country, and perhaps its most precious possession, is its native literary product—when that product is fine and noble and enduring.

Mark Twain*

The advisory board, the editors, and the publisher of the *Dictionary of Literary Biography* are joined in endorsing Mark Twain's declaration. The literature of a nation provides an inexhaustible resource of permanent worth. Our purpose is to make literature and its creators better understood and more accessible to students and the reading public, while satisfying the needs of teachers and researchers.

To meet these requirements, *literary biography* has been construed in terms of the author's achievement. The most important thing about a writer is his writing. Accordingly, the entries in *DLB* are career biographies, tracing the development of the author's canon and the evolution of his reputation.

The purpose of *DLB* is not only to provide reliable information in a usable format but also to place the figures in the larger perspective of literary history and to offer appraisals of their accomplishments by qualified scholars.

The publication plan for *DLB* resulted from two years of preparation. The project was proposed to Bruccoli Clark by Frederick G. Ruffner, president of the Gale Research Company, in November 1975. After specimen entries were prepared and typeset, an advisory board was formed to refine the entry format and develop the series rationale. In meetings held during 1976, the publisher, series editors, and advisory board approved the scheme for a comprehensive biographical dictionary of persons who contributed to literature. Editorial work on the first volume began in January 1977, and it was published in 1978. In order to make *DLB* more than a dictionary and to compile volumes that individually have claim to status as literary history, it was decided to organize volumes by topic, period, or genre. Each of these freestanding volumes provides a

From an unpublished section of Mark Twain's autobiography, copyright by the Mark Twain Company

biographical-bibliographical guide and overview for a particular area of literature. We are convinced that this organization—as opposed to a single alphabet method—constitutes a valuable innovation in the presentation of reference material. The volume plan necessarily requires many decisions for the placement and treatment of authors. Certain figures will be included in separate volumes, but with different entries emphasizing the aspect of his career appropriate to each volume. Ernest Hemingway, for example, is represented in *American Writers in Paris, 1920–1939* by an entry focusing on his expatriate apprenticeship; he is also in *American Novelists, 1910–1945* with an entry surveying his entire career, as well as in *American Short-Story Writers, 1910–1945, Second Series* with an entry concentrating on his short fiction. Each volume includes a cumulative index of the subject authors and articles.

Between 1981 and 2002 the series was augmented and updated by the *DLB Yearbooks*. There have also been nineteen *DLB Documentary Series* volumes, which provide illustrations, facsimiles, and biographical and critical source materials for figures, works, or groups judged to have particular interest for students. In 1999 the *Documentary Series* was incorporated into the *DLB* volume numbering system beginning with *DLB 210: Ernest Hemingway.*

We define literature as the *intellectual commerce of a nation:* not merely as belles lettres but as that ample and complex process by which ideas are generated, shaped, and transmitted. *DLB* entries are not limited to "creative writers" but extend to other figures who in their time and in their way influenced the mind of a people. Thus the series encompasses historians, journalists, publishers, book collectors, and screenwriters. By this means readers of *DLB* may be aided to perceive literature not as cult scripture in the keeping of intellectual high priests but firmly positioned at the center of a nation's life.

DLB includes the major writers appropriate to each volume and those standing in the ranks behind them. Scholarly and critical counsel has been sought in deciding which minor figures to include and how full their entries should be. Wherever possible, useful references are made to figures who do not warrant separate entries.

Each *DLB* volume has an expert volume editor responsible for planning the volume, selecting the figures for inclusion, and assigning the entries. Volume editors are also responsible for preparing, where appropriate, appendices surveying the major periodicals and literary and intellectual movements for their volumes, as well as lists of further readings. Work on the series as a whole is coordinated at the Bruccoli Clark Layman editorial center in Columbia, South Carolina, where the editorial staff is responsible for accuracy and utility of the published volumes.

One feature that distinguishes *DLB* is the illustration policy–its concern with the iconography of literature. Just as an author is influenced by his surroundings, so is the reader's understanding of the author enhanced by a knowledge of his environment. Therefore *DLB*

volumes include not only drawings, paintings, and photographs of authors, often depicting them at various stages in their careers, but also illustrations of their families and places where they lived. Title pages are regularly reproduced in facsimile along with dust jackets for modern authors. The dust jackets are a special feature of *DLB* because they often document better than anything else the way in which an author's work was perceived in its own time. Specimens of the writers' manuscripts and letters are included when feasible.

Samuel Johnson rightly decreed that "The chief glory of every people arises from its authors." The purpose of the *Dictionary of Literary Biography* is to compile literary history in the surest way available to us–by accurate and comprehensive treatment of the lives and work of those who contributed to it.

The *DLB* Advisory Board

Introduction

America's special status as the first modern country intentionally created by citizens rather than by rulers fired even writers and composers from the disenfranchised classes with a sense of entitlement to have their voices heard and their experiences known. They felt an obligation to persuade others that the society's unifying institutions should be changed, in varying degrees, to improve the quality of common life. This process of transformed identification and articulation began well before the country formally emerged. Among the earliest books of poetry created in North America were a collection of writings by a group of French-speaking freemen of color from New Orleans (Armand Lenusse's *Les Cenelles,* 1645) and the poems of Anne Bradstreet, a Puritan housewife living in Massachusetts whose memorable reflections on her writing included the lines from "The Prologue": "I am obnoxious to each carping tongue / Who says my hand a needle better fits" (*The Tenth Muse, Lately Sprung Up in America,* 1650).

The large percentage of American writers concerned with social change shaped the course of literary history in this country. Like the visual arts, literature of the United States passed through a long crisis of self-definition in which creators and critics struggled against a broad tendency to defer to European traditions and strove to balance authenticity of voice with broadly defined ideas of aesthetic merit. Certainly the prominence of social concerns in American writing accounts for the labeling of American literature as "social documents" in the earliest editions of such series as the Harvard Classics. American literature did not appear regularly in college curricula until the 1940s. Its presence in those course listings still did not indicate any sort of veneration or even acceptance, as more than 95 percent of colleges in the United States failed to require American literature for a bachelor's degree, and only about a quarter of them required English majors to study it (Shumway). In the mid twentieth century American literature reached a level of established recognition. Many scholars—notably Cary Nelson and Marcus Klein—have discussed the Cold War era–based value judgments that underwrote the American literary canon as it emerged in the 1950s and 1960s, and *Dictionary of Literary Biography 303: American Radical and Reform Writers, First Series* served implicitly as a response to those discussions. That volume makes a meaningful contribution to literary history by assembling information previously unavailable in mainstream reference books on American writers famously connected with the political Left.

The present volume takes up the work begun by the first, inviting readers to imagine American writing as a much broader, more passionately engaging set of interventions in a far-reaching range of debates than the highly selected canon of national literature previously allowed. The figures included here represent both more diverse and more specialized sets of interests than the somewhat oversimplified popular understanding of the term "left" brings to mind. The best-known leftist vision of social change in the western world has been articulated as the group of theories, loosely called communism, that flourished between the French Revolution and the mid 1970s. The connotation of the term communism tends to obscure the significance of leftist theories about political change and social design; communism, however, is simply one example of the Age of Reason's discursive attempts to resolve issues concerning human rights and the proper role of government. Cold War–era opposition to communism produced rhetoric that radically simplified the terms of debate, overestimating consensus on the Left, on the one hand, and ignoring the vital connections of American thinkers to discourses regarding social change on the other. Self-identified leftists in the United States have often found sources of inspiration in Ralph Waldo Emerson, Henry David Thoreau, Edward Bellamy, Henry George, Laurence Gronlund, William Morris, or Leo Tolstoy, rather than in Karl Marx and Friedrich Engels.

Whatever their formative influences, American radical and reform writers perform a great service for the reading public because they provide constant reminders of the poverty of what Ernest Hemingway called "all the dirty, easy labels" *(A Moveable Feast).* Their writing moves audiences because it resists such broad classifications as "left" or "right." Most American writers advocating political or social change have identified and studied ideas of value from more than one tradition of thought. Further, most of these writers synthesize and syncretize the elements of these thought systems in remarkable and unpredictable ways that make their personal development as writers difficult to summarize but profoundly rewarding to study. They present audiences with complex intellectual challenges because they dissent not only from mainstream assumptions and normative behavior models of their time but from predominating trends and discourses within social movements about which current readers might know very little.

In examining the legacies of this national literature, readers will quickly realize the limitations of simple binaries when applied to American political writing. In the end, the word "radical," for example, functions only as a modifier of something else; thus its meaning is relative: it tells the reader nothing outside of particular contexts. Studied in terms of behavior, radical writers in America appear to consider causes and outcomes, to question what it means to live well and righteously, to redefine what it means to make social progress or err grievously, and to weigh common behavior against beliefs about the value of human life. They take seriously the possibility that their entire society could be dead wrong. Very often, defining moments in the lives of radicals require decisions about hierarchies of concern and action. At such times some radicals become reformers, and some reformers become radicals.

Americans have inherited much of their extended political vocabulary from the time of the French Revolution. Old maps of the social, political, and economic terrain, plotting positions in terms of "right" and "left," came into being to describe a world in which empires exploited colonies, hereditary monarchies dominated most governments, universal suffrage was unthinkable, and the strong power of Christian churches over everyday life was unquestioned. These polarities do not translate to the twenty-first-century concepts of "Republican" and "Democrat." In the old world, a "republican"—someone who believed people had rights not granted by a divinely appointed sovereign, who wanted a government held accountable to a written contract (a constitution), who perhaps even believed in secular education and the value of science—was a leftist radical. The established powers viewed such a person as practically an anarchist, based on the philosophical assumptions that underlay his politics.

First, the republican was a leveler: he believed that middle-class commoners were the equals of the aristocrats and the clergy. Second, he undermined the authority of the church in many ways: he called into question the right of the king to rule; he called for limits on the power of the church over secular institutions; he thought that each man should be the keeper of his own conscience and by implication the governor of his own conduct. Finally, the logical extension of republican thought led to the idea that governments functioned to protect the rights of men, and that if they failed to do so, they could lose their moral authority and be overthrown in a righteous search for justice. The horrific end of the French Revolution provided a vivid lesson in what this might mean to Europeans. Once this last thought sank in, most Western European governments set hastily about establishing themselves as protectors of human rights: they abolished slavery and began to extend the right to vote to classes of people who had never before held it because they did not own property or have incomes and thus could not be taxed.

Almost immediately the definition of the rights-bearing individual began to expand, inaugurating the longest-lived social movement of the modern world, the extended civil rights movement. Despite the brutal repression of the fledgling British abolitionist movement during the 1790s, the British Empire emancipated its slaves gradually, first outlawing slavery in the British Isles, then paying slave owners and repositioning the former slaves into indentured servitude beginning in the 1830s.

The ability of the United States to move gracefully from a slave-based economy was made far less likely by its own inherent instability. Given that the war of 1812 was widely perceived as a second war of independence, the United States had experienced only about fifty years of self-rule by the beginning of the Civil War. The attendant anxieties of the Louisiana Purchase, the Great Awakening, and the Industrial Revolution added to the still-unsettled intellectual atmosphere. Local, not national, identification had predominated even after the scrapping of the Articles of Confederation and the ratification of the 1789 Constitution. In the mid nineteenth century, the fervor that had been associated with the Great Awakening expressed itself in a flowering of intentional communities, and radical universalism, spiritualism, and "free thought" suddenly presented unforeseen challenges to the limits of Christian belief in the sanctity of individual conscience. Radical thinkers in this period sometimes used religious discourse in the service of social causes such as the abolition of slavery or to justify unconventional living arrangements associated with their chosen community. The balance of power among the states themselves remained unstable until civil war imposed by force the dominance of the federal government.

In this environment, the issue of slavery loomed as the first great transformative crisis the country had to face after choosing independence. Many American radicals and reformers focused their energies on work with the abolitionist movement in the antebellum years. All agreed only on the common goal of abolishing slavery in the United States. Abolitionists reached no agreement among themselves regarding how to accomplish the goal or what would happen afterwards. Some advocated secession long before the Confederate states considered it but could not summon any significant support. A significant number of those who supported the abolition of slavery did not support war as a means to accomplish it. In their view the Civil War signaled a fundamental social failure, because the government resorted to force and would, they feared, apply it more quickly in the next challenge to its authority. Still others, while finding slavery intolerable, were not ready to accept African Americans or members of other ethnic minority groups as their equals.

Even abolitionists did not agree about how extensively the republican model should be applied. At the last meeting of the National Anti-Slavery Society in 1865, a disagreement erupted over whether to support the Fifteenth Amendment that outlawed voting-rights discrimination on the basis of race or previous condition of servitude but did not include gender as a category protected from discrimination. Many early feminists had supported abolition, trusting that when the time came to make constitutional changes affecting suffrage, their male colleagues would insist on universal suffrage as the only acceptable outcome. The argument that the amendment should be supported as it stood because it represented some progress prevailed. Lucy Stone and her husband led the women's-rights advocates who agreed; Susan B. Anthony and Elizabeth Cady Stanton vehemently disagreed, declaring that they would never again work for a cause other than woman suffrage. The two divisions foreswore allegiance with yet a third type of women's-rights supporter, personified in such characters as Victoria Woodhull, that both called a "free lover." The American woman-suffrage movement was not reunited until early in the twentieth century after most of the early leaders had died.

As these struggles occurred, radical thinkers motivated by the emerging field of social science began to re-evaluate the individual's capacity for self-governance and to think carefully about which aspects of the self could or should be regulated by external forces. While suffrage activists narrowed their focus to support a constitutional amendment giving the franchise to women, the despised "free lovers" and other reformers set about expanding the vision of the women's-rights movement. They wanted to understand the ways in which women could become more self-determining—and they wanted to understand how self-determination would affect the future of humanity. Notably, almost no one now remembered as a women's-rights activist of the nineteenth century supported the cause of birth control.

Anthony opposed it as a convenience that would allow married men to further exploit their wives sexually; Charlotte Perkins Gilman imagined that sexual reproduction would become obsolete and that all babies would be created in laboratories.

The radical roots of the birth-control movement grew from a combination of emerging theories related to social science, medicine, and free thought, another branch of republican philosophy that developed a wholly secular vision of the world to replace Christianity. While freethinkers respected the right of individuals to believe as they chose, they did not believe that the moral power of common life derived from the divine; rather, they argued that individuals should be guided by the dictates of reason and respect for each other's rights. Free lovers claimed to apply the insights of free thought to personal and intimate relationships. At that time the general public held contraception to be a disgusting intrusion into the sanctity of marital intimacy; hence woman-suffrage advocates strove to distance themselves from birth-control supporters. Frequently radicals proposed new ways of living based on their interpretations of human evolution and social science. Although Thomas Malthus had not approved of "unnatural" methods of population control, considering the "natural" population checks of war, famine, and pestilence to be sufficient, so-called Neo-Malthusians in England first advocated birth control when social scientists began to study global overpopulation and to consider the strain on resources in the future as technological advances extended the human life span.

In the United States, "free lovers" held no more unified an outlook than any other group of American writers on social issues, but most considered themselves feminists and argued for the necessity of sex education, frank discussions of sexual matters, liberalized divorce laws, and the practice of birth control to protect women. Many of their explanations of birth-control methods as well as their general understanding of human sexuality relied on unscientific and long-outdated ideas about the human body (such as the conviction that orgasm had debilitating effects). Such misconceptions are hardly surprising considering how few scientists attempted to study the subject of human sexuality before the 1950s.

Until the 1960s, most of the American activists historians call "sex radicals" were in reality marriage reformers, who, despite obscenity charges and prison sentences, often held conservative assumptions about the meaning of gender differences and about sexual activity itself. Whereas Anthony and Stanton had argued from a republican stance that marriage is a secular institution based on a contract and should be severable, Ezra and Angela Heywood argued that marriage, in its essence a holdover from primitive times, is necessarily a coercive, brutal imprisonment of women, who must trade sexual congress for economic support. Moses Harman believed that marriage conflicts with the best interests of society because women's mate selection for propagation is the vital and moral mechanism of human evolution. Most of these writers shared the belief of their contemporaries that most forms of sexual behavior other than heterosexual genital-to-genital intercourse were "perverse," "vicious," or "degraded." Almost all of them believed reproduction to be women's highest function (Sears). Most held that women were morally superior to men and that this trait manifested itself in part in women's "natural" distaste for sexual activity.

In the late nineteenth century, while some writers grappled with the language to express a complicated understanding of human nature in discourses about rights, the goal of reaching universal suffrage remained unmet. In the decades following the Civil War, as woman-suffrage activists built popular consensus state by state and their cause made advances, African Americans suffered devastating setbacks in the arena of civil rights. Just as there had been no consensus among abolitionists about how slavery should end and what should follow, going into the Civil War the government had no workable plan for building a functional and peaceful new society to replace the old one. When Reconstruction dragged on for more than ten years after the war's end, public officials at every level became demoralized and eventually abandoned the work, leaving basic questions undecided, citizens resentful, and the social fabric dangerously thin. Almost as soon as President Rutherford B. Hayes recalled federal troops from the South and dispatched them to break the series of railroad strikes that spread rapidly across the country in July 1877, reactionaries in the South took the opportunity to pass or strengthen discriminatory "black codes" that deprived African American citizens of almost every civil-rights advance of the past ten years. A conservative Supreme Court upheld these laws in the face of challenges or found the broadly interpreted advances in civil-rights law unconstitutional. Lynchings occurred with greater frequency, reaching a peak in 1892 and thereafter continuing at a declining rate into the 1960s. Rigid laws enforcing segregation and virtually prohibiting African American voting rights spread completely through the South, culminating in Louisiana's reduction of registered black male voters from 130,334 to 1,342 between 1896 and 1904 (Cotkin). African Americans began to migrate northward to primarily urban areas in such great numbers that by the 1960s the vast majority of blacks lived in cities in the North.

Economic leadership in the North experienced the most immediate salutary effects of the Civil War, and significant changes began to take place in the organization of labor as the Industrial Revolution matured. U.S. cities began to grow at a phenomenal rate; railroads supplied the technological wherewithal for commercial unification of the country; and financial giants took control of large portions of the industries in resource-rich Western states. Social activists turned their attention to effects of capitalism on the organization of work and the living conditions of growing numbers of workers, particularly as immigration reached unprecedented heights in the 1880s and 1890s. Regulation of labor had been left out of the Constitution; hence, that burden fell largely to the states until the 1930s. In consequence, a mass movement arose as workers began to demand rights beyond previous conceptions of human emancipation. Western nations enjoyed the highest standard of living in history, yet under industrialism many workers were did not experience the system's benefits.

Unions had existed in the United States from the days of the colonies, having developed from the old European craft guilds. Highly skilled tradesmen who spent years training in their profession wanted to protect their markets and the value of their labor. Usually such unions focused on a particular location and a specific skilled trade, and their names, such as the Journeymen Shoemakers of Philadelphia, reflected this. After the Civil War, however, industrial powers grew unchecked by federal labor law, and unions began to broaden their scope as workers attempted to bargain collectively with vastly more powerful employers for better wages, hours, or working conditions.

The first union to call itself "national," the National Labor Union, arose in Baltimore in 1866. In 1869 a secret organization called the Knights of Labor began in Philadelphia with the aim of organizing all workers, with particular outreach to unskilled laborers. Knights of Labor did not advocate general strikes like the European unions, but attempted to make inroads through strikes in particular industries. It organized women and African Americans and had broad social policies, some of which seemed clearly connected to the union's social mandate, such as its support of the Chinese Exclusion Acts and other anti-Asian legislation designed, it said, to protect the jobs of American laborers. Knights of Labor lobbied to raise the age of sexual consent, which ran as low as ten years of age in some states, and they attempted to improve public awareness of the causes of prostitution. The union became known to the general public during the Great Upheaval of 1877, when strikes against the railroads and related industries spread quickly across much of the United

States and federal troops for the first time in history intervened to stop a strike.

The United States experienced its first red scare in the 1880s. In Europe the rise of republicanism had been followed by the growth of a movement that focused on collective rights rather than individual ones and argued that the workers of the world should rule. In 1848, Karl Marx's *Communist Manifesto* declared the European revolutions of that year proof of communism's inevitable approach. Leftists themselves were not so easily convinced. The history of the Internationals illustrates that Marx, who was somewhat arbitrarily chosen to be the secretary of the First International (1864–1872), tried vainly to corral the revolutionary thinkers of Europe into ideological unity. The First International quickly splintered. The Second International (1889–1916) excluded anarchists, who held a series of their own congresses. Two new radical organizations inspired by the European leftists, the International Workingmen's Association (in America it became the International Working People's Association) and the Socialist Labor Party (largely anarchists), attracted many newly activist workers in the United States.

Anarchists and freethinkers argued that unjust authority rested on two props: force and "blind faith." One of the first assumptions of "blind faith," most anarchists still believe, is the widespread belief that, as Paul Ricoeur says, "the first right of a human being is to live in a state." Another is the idea that status-based relationships are natural and inevitable, perhaps even the will of God. On average, anarchists managed to combine a refusal to compromise politically with a greater spirit of philosophical generosity than most leftists could manage. Anarchists resisted orthodoxy. They disagreed with each other over questions of specific reforms and approaches no less than Socialists, but their disputes usually did not involve attempts to compel others to agree with them or to somehow purge opposing viewpoints from the community. Historically anarchists defined their struggle for human progress much more broadly than the Socialists or other radicals who focused only on labor, so anarchist activism spread across a wider array of concerns: education, freedom of the speech and press, art, birth control, gender discrimination, and secularism. Making what some consider the ultimate break with civilization, such thinkers viewed government as a monopoly of power, a bully, an obstacle in the path of human enlightenment. Consequently, their writing does not focus on policy changes or laws, but calls on individuals and communities to enact the changes they support. Their communities have been open to other experimental thinkers, such as single-taxers, health-food enthusiasts, promoters of psychoanalysis, free lovers, and dress reformers; hence many American radical writers have passed through anarchist environments.

By the time of the Haymarket Riot in May 1886, the membership of the Knights of Labor had grown to more than one million. Labor historians agree that the union declined after the Haymarket Riot, as the new, more conservative and hierarchical American Federation of Labor (AFL) siphoned away members from the skilled trades and as the more radical political elements were discredited during the anti-anarchist backlash that followed. During the 1890s, however, radical unionism experienced resurgence as the worst depression in national history developed and major strikes erupted in Homestead, Pennsylvania, and Pullman, Illinois. The newest phase of unionism emphasized trade unions—organizations of all workers within an industry, from the highly skilled to the casual day laborer. As railroads and related industries (such as mining and steel refining) exerted greater economic power, workers in those industries became the most influential in labor organization. Eugene V. Debs, the new leader of the American Railways Union, became more radical in his outlook, defying a Supreme Court injunction and facing a jail term after the Pullman strike. The United Mine Workers tried during the 1890s to organize all the employees in the country's mining industry. A far more militant organization called the Western Federation of Miners emerged in the Northwest and showed itself ready to meet the hired guns of industry owners in places like Cripple Creek, Colorado, with violence. WFM leaders—including a hard-rock miner named William "Big Bill" Haywood—were later tried and acquitted for the murder of the governor of Idaho in 1906–1907.

The Socialist Party of America was founded in 1901. Radicalism suffered minor legal setbacks after President William McKinley's assassination by an anarchist that year, but continued to attract participation as dedicated journalists called "muckrakers" by President Theodore Roosevelt drew attention to the excesses of the monopolies in the various industries. On 5 July 1905 representatives of various radical organizations concluded their meetings in Chicago to found the Industrial Workers of the World (IWW): Debs; Algie Simons, editor of the *International Socialist Review;* Terence V. Powderly, formerly of the Knights of Labor; Mother "Mary" Jones, associated with mining unions; Haywood, of the Western Federation of Miners; Daniel De Leon of the Socialist Labor Party; and others collaborated to create a union that was open to all workers, all races. More important, the IWW represented a radical departure from other U.S. unions in that it became anarcho-syndicalist; that is, it came to advocate direct action on the job site rather than working within the political system to address wrongs. That meant support for the general strike, sabotage if necessary, and ultimately worker takeover of the factories and industries.

In the years leading up to World War I, as woman suffrage spread state by state, usually in association with temperance measures, Lucy Stone's daughter, Alice Stone Blackwell, brokered an agreement between suffrage and temperance advocates to unify and thereby increase pressure on government officials to pass woman suffrage at the national level. By this time two factors virtually guaranteed success, despite opposition by influential leaders, including President Woodrow Wilson. First, the counter-example of the uncivilly disobedient British woman-suffrage movement suggested the threat of similar actions in the United States if demands were not met. Second, the phenomenal growth of altruism that peaked during the Progressive Era brought unprecedented levels of popular involvement in civic organizations, as well as support and philanthropy from the wealthiest members of society.

Sectarian disagreements among leftist factions began to simmer during this time. In its first years, the IWW had already thrown off leadership by socialists. Then the Socialist Party split between those who favored the new union (Haywood was still a party official in 1911) and those who adhered to a more traditional political mechanism of social change. The more conservative group disavowed sabotage and urged reliance on electoral politics as a means of gaining power. Within the IWW a new power struggle was emerging between the rank-and-file—those who declared to the sheriff's deputies of Everett, Washington, that "we ain't got no leaders. We're all leaders"—and Haywood, the charismatic communist leader who began to centralize, give top-down orders, and eventually fled to Moscow to avoid imprisonment for sedition.

Nonetheless, despite a red scare, the broader Left in the years up to 1917 experienced a greater degree of heterodoxy than any time before. Leftists spoke to and for the working class, the intellectuals, and the students, but they also tried to pitch their vision of revolution to everyone in the society, including the upper classes. By 1912, the center of the national political spectrum had moved so far left that many educated Americans identified themselves as socialists or progressives. Nearly one million people voted for Debs, the Socialist candidate for president, that year. According to Floyd Dell, in New York "the wartime years turned the Village into a melting-pot in which all group boundaries were dissolved. Artists, writers, intellectuals, liberals, radicals, IWWs, bohemians, well-to-do patrons, onlookers—all were hurled into a miscellaneous social melee in which earnestness and frivolity were thoroughly intermingled."

The Progressive Party platform alleged in 1912 that "an invisible government . . . not accountable to the people" had arisen within the republic and must itself be subjected to law. Progressives proposed to do that by increasing government regulation of the economic world; at the same time the party advocated government absorption of the functions of the privately developed social-welfare agencies that grew during the late nineteenth and early twentieth centuries in response to the needs of burgeoning urban populations that included millions of non-English-speaking immigrants. Following the lead of the German government under Prime Minister Otto Von Bismarck several decades earlier, Progressive officials co-opted selected pieces of the extended Left's agenda to improve social stability yet extend centralized power, creating a new branch of government—the bureaucracy. To pay for it, a constitutional amendment was passed to institute the federal income tax beginning in 1913.

The Great War dispelled the widespread sense of optimism Americans had enjoyed since recovering from the depression of the mid 1890s. The radical left began to feel the effects of the shifting tide first, and as awareness of America's probable involvement grew, antiwar sentiment spread and met a repression of phenomenal proportions. The files of the Department of Justice Bureau of Investigation (started in 1908) and Military Intelligence bespeak a massive crackdown on anyone suspected of harboring pro-German sentiments as well as anyone who spoke against American involvement in the war or against war for any reason. By the end of 1917 hundreds of periodical publishers had been denied mailing privileges. The earliest files are labeled the "Old German" files; after the Bolshevik Revolution of October/November 1917, authorities became convinced that dissenters from the war effort supported the spread of such a revolution to this country. The offices of every major radical organization were raided, and the courts issued mass indictments naming in some cases more than one hundred individuals as violators of the Espionage and Sedition Acts. In September 1919 the major representatives of the American Left splintered into three factions during a series of meetings in Chicago. By 1921 thousands of radicals of all stripes had been tried, imprisoned, deported, or otherwise persecuted.

Among the most moderate of such groups, Socialists emerged with the least damage. Having refused Vladimir Lenin's Twenty-One Points, the conditions for membership in the Communist International (called the Comintern), they began to work with other liberal groups, including the AFL, and in 1924 supported the Progressive Party's presidential candidate, Robert M. La Follette. By the end of the decade, their two great leaders, Debs and Victor Berger, had died; the party had weakened; and the Comintern's cultural policies, dictating more of a hard line against non-Communist leftists, had further polarized the American Left into Communists and non-Communists. Between the divisions over the Great War and the Bolshevik Revolution, the Red Scare and Palmer raids, the trials and deportations and prison sentences, the heterodox Left was lost, and only the ideologues of the Communist Party remained with any concentrated strength as a target for governmental authorities.

Thereafter, just as European governments had responded to the French Revolution with human-rights advances, after the Great War, progressive and totalitarian measures passed throughout the world hand in hand. In a dramatic reversal of many fundamental tenets of American politics to that point, Progressives began actively to engage in social engineering. Progressives and then the New Deal brought into the mainstream many ideas and programs that radicals had first proposed or advocated–the eight-hour day, birth control, the abolition of child labor, and federal regulation of labor including the legal establishment of collective bargaining. Anti-child-labor campaigns began to win more support, although the national laws to this end and support for shorter workdays failed repeatedly until the Great Depression, when unemployment peaked at a quarter of the adult workforce in the early 1930s. The federal government began to exert more influence over education as the number of children working decreased. Birth control became more acceptable for many reasons, not all of them having to do with human liberation and fulfillment.

Reforms in American government during these years invariably served a stabilizing function. Still, sometimes radical activity and reforms reinforced and built upon each other. Arguably, the race radicalism of the late 1910s and the influence of the Harlem Renaissance during the 1920s and 1930s laid the groundwork for the Roosevelt administration's appointment of the so-called Black Cabinet. Relatively conservative changes during the Depression still encouraged the hope of African Americans that full enfranchisement and equality lay within their reach. Many unpremeditated civil-rights advances burgeoned in the wake of World War II: the U.S. Army was the first federal institution to desegregate. Also, just as women's rights advanced significantly in Europe after the Great War killed an entire generation of young men, in the United States the deployment of the largest military force in the country's history incidentally led to economic advances for women. Beginning with the G.I. Bill of Rights in 1944, passed in part because the government did not want millions of men to re-enter the labor market at

once at the war's end and re-create the Great Depression, the universities opened and the middle class grew.

By the second half of the century the traditional constituencies of the main political parties in America shifted as many union members voted Republican in the 1950s and the Democratic Party supported the Civil Rights Act in the 1960s. In the 1960s and 1970s a broadly defined version of liberalism combined with some types of social determinism to form what Americans now call "identity politics." The proliferation of many New Left social movements and their combined counterculture during the 1960s had profound and lasting effects on the general population. Just as republican thought had spread and expanded after the French Revolution, so the discourse of racial equality resulted in laws that caused a massive reorganization of society as the mechanisms of segregation were dismantled piece by piece. Immediately, other politically and socially marginalized identity groups pointed to the model of unjust and illegitimate categorical discrimination to make claims for their own empowerment. Disaffection with traditional political parties grew, especially after the disruptive Democratic National Convention of 1968, the economic crisis of the 1970s, and the Watergate hearings of 1973. Many argue that in general Americans became more liberal on cultural matters during the 1960s and 1970s, as a wider range of unconventional behaviors and ideas became acceptable. By 1980, however, the center of the political mainstream moved definitively to the Right. In particular, support for a strengthened U.S. military presence throughout the world increased even as the decade ended with an apparent victory for the Right when the Soviet Bloc in Eastern Europe suddenly and anti-climactically lost power after decades of "Cold War."

The mechanisms of the electoral process have been subjected to extreme scrutiny for the last two national election cycles. A categorical entrenchment has seized the two dominant parties, who each seek to paint the other as extremist despite clear evidence that they are centrists with more in common than not. Since the phenomenal growth of American government in the early twentieth century, uncritical expansion of government authority seems to offer solutions to an ever-vaster array of problems on the one hand, while on the other, advocates of deregulation of business and reprivatization of social services justify support for corporate welfare while abandoning society's most vulnerable members. As most available ideas about social organization and empowerment tend to model from the top down, a sense of helplessness and passivity has grown among American citizens, many of whom no longer vote, read, or believe that they can have an effect on the future of common life.

For Americans, it is no longer a matter of abstract intellectual questions and philosophical goods, but a matter of survival to have as a resource thinkers who are unafraid to ask questions that go to the roots of society, to consider that conventional approaches to common problems might be wrong, to imagine alternatives. In this way American radical and reform writers perform a critical public service, because they keep asking these questions when other citizens back down. Such writers have not been afraid to risk acceptance, dignity, or their freedom as they confront power in pursuit of the common good.

Given their philosophical differences, the writers included in this volume share much in spirit. They try (with varying degrees of success) to look past the received knowledge of their own time, to face the unknown, to make their own decisions about what constitutes "the good," and to understand their own responsibilities in bringing it about. They are not heroic visionaries, but ordinary people who ask difficult questions and refuse to let themselves or others fail to seek answers. They try to avoid what George Orwell called "prefabricated" thought but do not find satisfaction in mere self-expression. Few of them held the same views their entire adult lives. Most are individuals whose life journeys and writing problems carried them across a wider area of political and social life than a single party identification encompasses. Many experienced conversions or grew to see the polarizing distinctions of their youth fade and new ones arise to take their place. All took to heart the relationship between the individual and the state and struggled to understand the mutual obligations of the two entities and the limits to which each might within rights act autonomously. Their writing addresses intermediate levels of relationship and community in novel and thought-provoking ways; they demonstrate to contemporary audiences that on such problems few lasting solutions have yet been reached.

The present volume represents a collective attempt to humanize a category of writers whose interests have sometimes prevented them from reaching a broad audience and to begin to assess the achievements of people who may have been recognized as activists but are seldom studied as writers. In many instances, no other intermediate-level biographical or bibliographical information existed prior to the entry in this volume. Readers should also be aware that many American radical and reform writers, especially many extraordinarily talented and productive writers of color, do not appear here because they already have entries in the *Dictionary of Literary Biography. American Radical and Reform Writers, Second Series,* does not make any identity- or politics-based attempt to be representative. Rather, this volume takes as its starting point a statement from the reference series' plan: "We define literature as the *intellectual commerce of a nation:* not merely as belles lettres but as that ample and complex process by which ideas are generated, shaped, and transmitted." Ultimately, these essays seek to stimulate a broad scholarly re-evaluation of all American writers–which might well begin with a review of their entries in earlier *DLB* volumes.

–*Hester L. Furey*

References:

George Cotkin, *Reluctant Modernism: American Thought and Culture 1880–1900* (New York: Twayne, 1992);

David DeLeon, *The American as Anarchist: Reflections on Indigenous Radicalism* (Baltimore & London: Johns Hopkins University Press, 1978);

Floyd Dell, "Rents Were Low in Greenwich Village," in *Greenwich Village Reader,* edited by June S. Sawyers (New York: Rowman & Littlefield, 2001);

Bruce Franklin, *Prison Literature in America: The Victim as Criminal and Artist,* third revised edition (New York & Oxford: Oxford University Press, 1989);

Ernest Hemingway, *A Moveable Feast* (New York: Scribners, 1964);

Marcus Klein, *Foreigners: The Making of American Literature, 1900–1940* (Chicago: University of Chicago Press, 1981);

Cary Nelson, *Repression and Recovery: Modern American Poetry and the Politics of Cultural Memory, 1910–1945* (Madison: University of Wisconsin Press, 1992);

Robert R. Palmer and Joel Colton, *A History of the Modern World since 1815,* eighth edition (New York: McGraw-Hill, 1995);

Hal Sears, *The Sex Radicals: Free Love in High Victorian America* (Lawrence, Kans.: Regents Press, 1977);

David R. Shumway, *Creating American Civilization: A Genealogy of American Literature as an Academic Discipline* (Minneapolis: University of Minnesota Press, 1994).

Acknowledgments

This book was produced by Bruccoli Clark Layman, Inc. Richard Layman was the in-house editor.

Production manager is Philip B. Dematteis.

Administrative support was provided by Carol A. Cheschi.

Accountant is Ann-Marie Holland.

Copyediting supervisor is Phyllis A. Avant. The copyediting staff includes Frederick C. Ingram and Rebecca Mayo. Freelance copyeditors are Brenda L.

Cabra, Jennifer Cooper, David C. King, and Katherine E. Macedon.

Pipeline manager is James F. Tidd Jr.

Permissions editor is Dickson Monk.

Office manager is Kathy Lawler Merlette.

Digital photographic copy work and photo editing was performed by Dickson Monk.

Systems manager is James Sellers.

Typesetting supervisor is Kathleen M. Flanagan. The typesetting staff includes Patricia M. Flanagan.

Library research was facilitated by the following librarians at the Thomas Cooper Library of the University of South Carolina: Elizabeth Sudduth and the rare-book department; circulation department head Tucker Taylor; reference department head Virginia W. Weathers; reference department staff Marilee Birchfield, Karen Brown, Mary Bull, Gerri Corson, Joshua Garris, Beki Gettys, Laura Ladwig, Tom Marcil, Bob Skinder, and Sharon Verba; interlibrary loan department head Marna Hostetler; and interlibrary loan staff Robert Amerson and Timothy Simmons.

Dictionary of Literary Biography® • Volume Three Hundred Forty-Five

American Radical and Reform Writers
Second Series

Dictionary of Literary Biography

Leonard Abbott

(20 May 1878 – 19 March 1953)

Stephen Malagodi
WLRN

BOOKS: *The Society of the Future* (Girard, Kans.: J. A. Wayland, 1898);

A Socialistic Wedding: Being the Account of the Marriage of George D. Herron and Carrie Rand (New York: Knickerbocker Press, 1901);

The Root of the Social Problem (New York: Socialistic Cooperative Publishing Association, 1904);

Ernest Howard Crosby: A Valuation and a Tribute (Westwood, Mass.: Ariel Press, 1907);

Sociology and Political Economy (New York: Current Literature Publishing, 1909).

OTHER: *Reminiscences of Walt Whitman, with Extracts from His Letters and Remarks on His Writings,* edited by William Sloane Kennedy, includes a contribution by Abbott (London: Alexander Gardner, 1896);

The Suppression of free speech in New York and in New Jersey: being a true account by eye witnesses of law-breaking by the Police Department of New York City, at Lexington Hall, on May 23, 1909, by the City Authorities of East Orange, at English's Hall, on June 8, 1909 . . . / together with the full text of the suppressed lecture by Emma Goldman and the addresses by Leonard Abbott and Alden Freeman at the Thomas Paine Centenary (East Orange, N.J.: Allied Printing, [1909?]);

Memorial of Moses Harman, October 12, 1830, January 30, 1910 [microform]; tributes by George Bernard Shaw, Bolton Hall, Leonard D. Abbott, Gilbert E. Roe, Juliet H. Severance, Theodore Schroeder, and many others. Moses Harman in prison (Chicago: American Journal of Eugenics, 1910);

Francisco Ferrer: His Life, Work and Martyrdom, edited by Abbott (New York: Francisco Ferrer Association, 1910);

Leonard Abbott, *circa 1905 (Paul Avrich,* An American Anarchist: The Life of Voltairine de Cleyre, *1978; Thomas Cooper Library, University of South Carolina)*

The Detroit Francisco Ferrer Modern School, edited by Abbott and William Thurston Brown (New York: Herold Press, 1912);

Joseph J. Cohen and Alexis C. Ferm, *The Modern School of Stelton: A Sketch* (Stelton, N.J.: Modern School Edition of North America, 1925), includes a contribution by Abbott Stelton;

Jack London, *London's Essays of Revolt*, edited, with an introduction, by Abbott (New York: Vanguard, 1926);

Masterworks of Government: Digests of Thirteen Great Classics, edited by Abbott (New York: Doubleday, 1947);

Masterworks of Economics: Digests of Ten Great Classics, edited by Abbott (Garden City: Doubleday, 1948);

"Reflections on Emma Goldman's Trial" and "Voltairine de Cleyre's Posthumous Book," in *Anarchy! An Anthology of Emma Goldman's Mother Earth,* edited, with commentary, by Peter Glassgold (Washington, D.C.: Counterpoint, 2001), pp. 140–143, 214–218.

SELECTED PERIODICAL PUBLICATIONS–
UNCOLLECTED: "William Morris Labour Church at Leek," *Book Buyer,* 15 (February 1898): 31–33;

"William Morris's Commonweal," *New England Magazine,* 20 (June 1899): 428–433;

"The Arts and Crafts Movement in England," *Arena,* 22 (September 1899): 398–403;

"Book Handicraft" *Chautauquan,* 30 (November 1899): 142–148;

"Ruskin as a Revolutionary," *Independent,* 52 (1 February 1900): 301–302;

"Socialist Movement in Massachusetts," *Outlook,* 64 (17 February 1900): 410–412;

"Coniston-Ruskin-Land," *Cosmopolitan,* 28 (March 1900): 501–506;

"The Socialist Movement in Mass.," *Outlook,* 65 (17 February 1901);

"Edwin Markham: Laureate of Labor," *Comrade,* 1 (1902);

"How I Became a Socialist," *Comrade* (October 1903);

"Two Spanish Painters of Genius," *Chautauquan,* 55 (August 1909): 478–491;

"Review: Carlo De Fornaro's *Diaz: the Czar of Mexico*," *Mother Earth,* 10 (December 1909);

"What Ferrer Taught in His Schools," *Current Literature,* 48 (January 1910): 64–68;

"A Priestess of Pity and Vengeance," *International* (New York), (August 1912); *Mother Earth* (September 1912);

"An Intellectual Giant," *Mother Earth* (December 1912);

"The Fight in Tarrytown and Its Tragic Outcome," *Mother Earth* (July 1914);

"The Sanger Case," *New York Times,* 25 July 1915, II, p. 14;

"Is William Sanger to Go to Jail? *Masses,* 6 (12 September 1915): 19;

"Jack London's One Great Contribution to American Literature," *Current Opinion,* 62 (January 1916);

"Birthday Greetings," *Blast,* 2 (15 January 1917): 6;

"War as a Test of Anti-Militarist Sincerity," *Blast,* 2 (1 June 1917): 2–3;

"The Triumph of Revolutionary Principles in Russia," *Social War Bulletin* (February 1918);

"The Anarchist Side of Walt Whitman," *Road to Freedom,* 2 (March 1926): 2–3;

"The Courage and Faith of Alexander Berkman," *Road to Freedom,* 7 (December 1930): 1–2;

"Edward Carpenter, A Radical Genius," *Road to Freedom,* 7 (September 1931);

"Emma Goldman: 'Daughter of the Dream,'" *Road to Freedom,* 8 (April 1932): 7;

"Voltairine de Cleyre," *American Freeman* (July 1949).

Leonard Abbott is almost completely unknown today, but during the early twentieth century he was involved in the establishment of enduring literary and political institutions. A devoted friend and associate of Emma Goldman, Abbott was one of the lesser-known American anarchists who survived the World War I–era Red Scare. Gentle, brilliant, and well-mannered, he commanded the deference and admiration of his peers and served in leadership positions within the anarchist movement. In many respects the concerns of his life and his writing typify the sensibilities of the many upper-class young people of the 1910s and 1920s who, in reaction against the excesses of unregulated industrial capitalism, involved themselves in social work and social movements to try to create better living conditions for all. As a literary figure he is noteworthy for his ties both to radical activists and to the mainstream writing establishment.

Leonard Dalton Abbott was born on 20 May 1878 in Liverpool, England. He was one of eight sons born to Lewis Lowe Abbott and Grace Van Dusen. When his son was born, Lewis Abbott was a metal merchant from Andover, Massachusetts, who represented U.S. firms in England. Raised in Liverpool, Leonard Abbott attended the Uppington School and Liverpool College, where he first encountered socialist thought and began attending socialist meetings. He met Edward Carpenter and corresponded with him until Carpenter's death in 1929. He also corresponded with William Morris and called on Russian scientist and anarchist Petr Kropotkin. During the 1890s Abbott's taste in literature was typical of the generation; he enjoyed the writings of Percy Bysshe Shelley, Walt Whitman, Oscar Wilde, Henry George, and Karl Marx. In 1896 he contributed to *Reminiscences of Walt Whitman, with Extracts from His Letters and Remarks on His Writings,* published by Alexander Gardner in London and later published in the United States by *Atlantic Monthly.*

When his family returned to the United States in 1897, Abbott settled in New York City, where he became active in various radical causes. His socialism derived from his study of Kropotkin, Morris, Carpenter, and the English Fabian socialists. His first pamphlet, *The Society of the Future* (1898), advocated public ownership of agriculture and industry, workers' cooperatives, and women's emancipation. He wrote: "Some of us are thoroughly dissatisfied with the life of today, its strife, its heartlessness, its artificiality, its shabbiness. We long to cast from our midst forever the black nightmare of poverty; we yearn for fellowship, for rest, for happiness." He was a member of the executive committee of the Socialist Party of America by age twenty-two. Cut off from family support because of his political beliefs, Abbott made his living principally as an editor.

The first phase of Abbott's writing career grew from his new socialism and his social contacts with a particular circle of literary celebrities. From 1899 to 1905 he worked as associate editor of *Literary Digest,* a weekly current-events magazine. Absorbing other popular magazines, such as *Current Opinion* and *Current Literature,* it reached a circulation of nearly two million during the 1920s and continued until 1938, when it was purchased by Time, Inc. His work at the *Literary Digest* brought Abbott into contact with many writers, including Ernest Crosby, the foremost American expert on Leo Tolstoy at that time. He and Crosby met Goldman in 1903. Abbott also published in a Chicago magazine called *The Socialist Spirit* and served on the editorial board of *The Comrade,* edited by John Spargo and George D. Herron, from 1901 to 1905, contributing many articles. Some scholars have claimed that its policy of valuing artistic considerations over doctrinaire politics made *The Comrade* the closest antecedent of *The Masses.* Later he joined Spargo and Herron in founding the Rand School of Social Science. In 1905 Abbott took the post of associate editor of *Current Literature,* which later became *Current Opinion,* and he remained there until 1925.

Affiliated with the Socialist Party, the Rand School was founded in 1906 and named after the philanthropist who endowed it, Carrie Rand. In these years Abbott's close friends included people who wanted to break free of conventional lifestyles. Rand and Herron were wed by William Thurston Brown in a socialist ceremony; Abbott attended the ceremony and made it the subject of another early publication. The school became a center for socialist activity in New York and attracted luminaries such as Max Eastman, Oswald Garrison Villard, A. Philip Randolph, Scott Nearing, Norman Thomas, and Charles Beard to its

faculty. It was finally closed in 1956 by the board of directors of the American Socialist Society. On a more personal level, however, Abbott remembered this as a period when "I played with the idea that I was myself homosexual" (Abbott letter to Thomas H. Bell). He also wrote in his letters that he had been greatly influenced at this time by "four homosexuals of genius (Whitman, Wilde, Carpenter, and George Sylvester Viereck)." Abbott knew Viereck from *Current Literature,* and some contemporaries believed they had a significant relationship. Later Viereck edited *The International,* to which Abbott frequently contributed.

Already Abbott was interested in education. In addition to his connection with the Rand School, Abbott numbered among the founders of the Intercollegiate Socialist Society (ISS) in 1905. An organization of university students and faculty, the ISS formed study and reading groups, organized rallies and lectures by leading socialists, and published book lists and pamphlets on socialist issues. Its supporters included luminaries such as lawyer Clarence Darrow and authors Jack London and William English Walling, who later became one of the founders of the NAACP. In 1921 the ISS changed its name to the League for Industrial Democracy, which continued to sponsor a student branch, the Student League for Industrial Democracy, which in January of 1960 became the Students for a Democratic Society (SDS).

Goldman's magazine, *Mother Earth,* began publication in 1906, and Abbott contributed from 1907 until the federal government suppressed it in 1917. Later, when Goldman's colleague Alexander Berkman began to publish *The Blast* in San Francisco, Abbott contributed to that publication as well. In 1909 escalating attacks by police on First-Amendment rights caused an increase of radical activity. Free-speech fights occurred all over the country. In New York the National Free Speech Committee, including Abbott, Voltairine de Cleyre, Eugene V. Debs, Darrow, and London, organized a mass protest meeting at Cooper Union on 30 June, and each of them addressed the audience.

The year 1910 was seminal for Abbott. In that year he served as president of the Thomas Paine National Historical Association. From 1910 through 1914 he also served as president of the Free Speech League, which formally incorporated in 1911. Its leading members included Abbott; Brand Whitlock, then mayor of Toledo, Ohio as vice president; author Lincoln Steffens; lawyer and single-tax supporter Bolton Hall; attorney Gilbert E. Roe, son-in-law of Robert M. La Follette; Dr. E. B. Foote; Hutchins Hapgood; and Theodore Schroeder. In this capacity Abbott became more closely associated with the IWW and other organizers of the unemployed, whose protests against low

Will Durant, principal, and pupils of the New York Modern School, 104 East Twelfth Street, 1912 (Paul Avrich, The Modern School Movement: Anarchism and Education in the United States, *1980; Thomas Cooper Library, University of South Carolina)*

pay, unemployment, hunger, and dangerous working conditions made up the majority of free-speech cases of the early 1910s. League members—most often Abbott and one other—monitored public-speaking events, visited chiefs of police, found attorneys to represent those arrested, and publicized violations of First-Amendment rights by public officials. The league remained active until the formation of the American Civil Liberties Union in 1920, which, many felt, was better positioned to undertake legal struggles in defense of free speech.

By 1910 Abbott had moved past socialism and became a fixture of the anarchist movement, inspired by Goldman and de Cleyre, whom he called "one of the strongest influences in my life" (Avrich, *Anarchist Voices*). He co-edited *The Free Comrade* with an anarchist poet

and summertime neighbor, J. William Lloyd, from 1910 to 1912. Sincerely interested in the arts and literature, in 1910 Abbott also cofounded the Poetry Society of America. Still operating in New York, the PSA is the oldest existing poetry organization in the United States. Its members have included W. H. Auden, Langston Hughes, Robert Frost, Marianne Moore, and Wallace Stevens.

Among anarchist historians Abbott is most often remembered as a founding member of the New York Ferrer Association, formed in 1910 after the execution of Francisco Ferrer, a Spanish anarchist and education reformer. Ferrer developed a system of "free" education, which he called "Modern Schools," as an alternative to the rigid education system then controlled by the

Catholic Church in Spain. Ferrer set up the first such school in Barcelona in 1901. Along with primary education, it incorporated adult education and a publishing house. The Barcelona school was eventually shut down by Spanish authorities in 1906, when Ferrer was implicated in a plot to assassinate King Alfonso. Ferrer's execution in 1909 set off worldwide protests and inspired the establishment of numerous "Modern Schools" in his memory. The Modern Schools of America were first established in New York, Chicago, and Philadelphia in 1911, and in Detroit, Seattle, Portland, and Salt Lake City by 1915.

In New York, Goldman, Berkman, Harry Kelly, and Abbott formed the Francisco Ferrer Association in 1910. Abbott served as the association's first president. The group opened the first Modern School in America in January 1911 at 6 St. Mark's Place, former home of James Fenimore Cooper, in Greenwich Village. One of several offerings of the Ferrer Center, the school at first claimed nine students, including Margaret Sanger's son, Stuart. The center included a publishing house, an adult-education center, and a community center. It soon moved to a new building on East 12th Street, and later to Harlem. Bayard Boyeson of Columbia University was the first director for the center, and Will Durant became principal of the school early in 1912. Alden Freeman, a wealthy homosexual with family connections to Standard Oil, paid many of the salaries.

As a center of radical activity, the school drew much attention. The beautiful poet Lola Ridge served as the secretary. The flamboyant Hippolyte Havel lived in the basement and published his journal *Revolt!* there. Famous figures such as Darrow and Man Ray gave lectures; literary icons gave readings and presented plays; musical ensembles offered concerts. Art classes with Robert Henri and George Bellows drew the largest groups; students came to study languages, psychology, or other subjects in the humanities. Abbott set up a weekly forum called "Radical Literature and the Great Libertarians," and in addition to guest lecturers, he spoke on radical writers including Maurice Maeterlinck and George Bernard Shaw. He wrote to de Cleyre asking for guidance on educational reform in 1911, saying that the group seemed to have gotten involved in the project without clear ideas about how to proceed; regardless, the school flourished.

Abbott was one of the "saints" (as Roger Baldwin called them) who ran the school and occasionally taught classes. At the end of his life he said that he regarded the school as his greatest accomplishment, although his children noted with some amusement in interviews that he did not enroll them there. Accounts of Abbott from his years at the Modern School tend to be vivid, such as Maurice Hollod's account of his recruitment by another student:

> He led me upstairs to a classroom. There was a long table with a group of kids around it. In the center was a tall man [Leonard Abbott] peering through a microscope at a drop of blood on a slide, explaining to the kids what they were seeing under the scope. I became so entranced that I made up my mind on the spot that I'd be going to this school. That was it! It opened my eyes to what a school could be *(Anarchist Voices)*.

Similarly, Ariel Durant recalled that she was skipping school in a park one day when she saw Cora Bennett Stephenson reading with a group of Modern School children, and that she jealously edged in among them and felt so happy to be one of them that she enrolled herself in the school the following day.

Memories of Abbott during these years emphasize the sweetness of his temperament. Other students remembered Abbott as "one of the most charming people in the world" or as one of "a special breed of wonderful people" *(Anarchist Voices)*. Still others characterized him as "the sort of man people turn to look at in the street. . . . extremely well-spoken; he never chose the wrong word, even in ordinary conversation. . . . charming, sincere, generous, and decent" (234–235). They remembered picking cherries at his house, or that he frequently carried flowers. Will Durant said in the *Dual Autobiography* (with his wife, Ariel, that

> We fell in love, as nearly all did, with the third leader [after Goldman and Berkman] of the Francisco Ferrer Association–Leonard Dalton Abbott. He was an Englishman by birth and manners, and had imbibed his anarchism not from the background of desperate revolt against czarist despotism but from the nonviolent libertarianism of William Morris. He was as handsome as a Pre-Raphaelite angel; indeed, we called him "the angel of the radical movement"; . . . I doubt if he ever raised his voice to anyone. He was always slow to condemn, always ready to listen, understand, and help. I have never met a finer man.

In June 1912 de Cleyre died. Abbott presided at one of the many memorials held throughout the country and joined a memorial committee that included Kelly, Joseph Kucera, Saul Yanovsky, Havel, and Perle McLeod. Together they selected de Cleyre's most significant published works for a collection. In 1913 Abbott met Rose Yuster at the Ferrer Center, and they lived together in a large house in the Bronx. Her sister, Marie, later became the proprietor of a famous Greenwich Village teashop, Romany Marie's. Rose Yuster had been married before, to Arthur Samuels, with whom she remained friendly to the end of her life.

Abbott and Yuster named their first child Voltairine, but she died in infancy in 1914.

Mother Earth published *The Selected Works of Voltairine de Cleyre* in late 1914. Abbott began to include de Cleyre's work in his radical literature classes at the Ferrer Center, and over the years he published several essays about her, beginning with a commentary on the new book in the October 1914 issue of *Mother Earth,* "Voltairine de Cleyre's Posthumous Book." De Cleyre's anarchist readers never reached consensus about her work and character, and many tried to portray her as a saint. Abbott himself later called her a "priestess of pity and vengeance." Margaret Marsh, a scholar of American anarchism, argued that of all the anarchists, "Only Leonard Abbott seemed willing to allow her humanness" (*Anarchist Women,* p. 149).

From its inception the Modern School published a newsletter. By 1912 the newsletter was transformed into the *Modern School Magazine.* Abbott wrote items for this publication regularly until about 1920. The Ferrer Center moved several times in its early years to accommodate its growing constituencies. Eventually it had a finished basement recreation area, first floor lecture hall, a second floor with classrooms, and a third floor with apartments it rented out. After the anarchist press called for revenge on the Rockefellers for the 20 April 1914 Ludlow Massacre at their mines in Colorado (the culminating episode of a protracted struggle in which many striking coal miners along with their wives and children were killed, with seventy-four dead on both sides by the time federal troops intervened at the end of April), a bomb intended for the Rockefeller mansion at Pocantico Hills, New York, accidentally went off on the apartment level of the Ferrer Center on 4 July 1914, killing four renters—Arthur Caron, Carl Hansen, and Charles Berg, along with Marie Chavez, an uninvolved renter of another apartment. Hosting one of his large July Fourth picnics at his summer home in Westfield, New Jersey, Abbott briefly sheltered Michael Murphy, who had shared an apartment with the men, before helping to arrange his speedy departure for Canada, but this is the only known instance of Abbott working in contravention to the law. He never advocated violence. A former student recalled that some of the more outspoken anarchists mocked him as "Sister Abbott" because he "couldn't harm a fly" (*Anarchist Voices,* p. 119).

The center was placed under constant federal and local police surveillance. At one point Abbott opened a letter to the Burns Detective Agency that was returned for insufficient postage, and he discovered that a man named Spivak, who had been working at the center, was a spy. Other spies were rumored to be on the premises. When two anarchists were accused of leaving bombs in St. Patrick's Cathedral and the Church of St. Alphonsus on 13 October 1914, the pressure on the school became overwhelming. Freeman withdrew his financial support, and for a while school officials devoted themselves to a series of plays, debates, and bazaars to raise money.

Abbott and Rose Yuster were married on 9 April 1915, persuaded by his parents, who offered to establish trust funds for their children. That year their son William Morris was born. About a month after the Abbott wedding, on 16 May, the Modern School relocated to rural Stelton, New Jersey, where Kelly, Abbott, and Joseph Cohen formed the Ferrer Colony Association. The association purchased land and resold it in small plots. The Ferrer Center itself remained in New York City until 1918.

In February 1916 the anarchists of the Ferrer Center confronted another challenge when Goldman was arrested for discussing contraception at the New Star Casino in New York City. Abbott presided at the protest meeting that followed at Carnegie Hall, and as one of Goldman's closest friends he found himself caught up in the waves of political and legal upheaval that followed one upon another in the next few years. Abbott wrote an essay, "Reflections on Emma Goldman's Trial," that appeared in the May 1916 issue of *Mother Earth.* Goldman spent fifteen days in the Queens County Jail.

Abbott's account of the trial reveals much about the perspective of New York radicals at the time and relies on interpretive conventions that radicals used with some success until the United States entered World War I. First and last he establishes the nobility of the defendant, arguing that she has been arrested only for speech, never for crimes, and that the speech acts had only charitable motives and formed part of "the heroic crusade against poverty and superstition to which she has devoted her life" (*Anarchy! An Anthology of Emma Goldman's Mother Earth*). Next Abbott surveys the courtroom, viewing it as a dramatic occasion rather than a legal one. He compares "the influx of liberals" to "a gust of fresh air . . . blown into a musty room," relying on another standard argument of the time, that the courts had become a kind of dead wood in society, no longer alive and responsive to the needs of living people or sensible of what justice might mean to them. Goldman herself employed this argument in her testimony—typically using the courtroom as another educational forum, since an anarchist's chances of acquittal were slim to none—when she made reference to a play by John Galsworthy to argue that "behind every so-called 'crime' is 'palpitating life.'" Abbott himself allows the judges a little more humanity: "It would have been interesting to know the real thoughts and feelings of the judges. They did not seem particularly proud of the job that they had to do" *(Anarchy!).*

Being himself an insider of the upper classes, Abbott observes at several points that the entire case could have been thrown out for technical violations on the part of the prosecution, but Goldman defended herself and did not make optimal use of the legal process. The next time she was arrested, in October of that year, friends prevailed upon her to employ the single-taxer Harry Weinberger as her attorney, and she was acquitted on technicalities (one being the inaccuracy of the actual charge brought against her). As an artifact of its time Abbott's account of the trial is remarkable for its innocence, perhaps a product of the insularity of the East Coast radicals or of the perseverance of optimism among U.S. radicals in general. He assumes that not much has changed since 1909 or 1910 and discusses the trial as though the event signifies only another free-speech fight. The larger context of World War I does not enter the picture.

By the time a year had passed, Abbott could no longer remain completely oblivious to the dangers of war to the country or to his immediate community; however, very few radicals had at this point a clear understanding of the scope of what was happening. After anarchists were arrested in connection with an explosion at the *Los Angeles Times* building, the offices of Berkman's magazine, *The Blast,* were raided twice, once in July and once in December 1916. *The Blast* and *Mother Earth,* like many antiwar periodicals, were denied postal privileges in 1917 after the United States entered World War I. In May 1917 Abbott formed the No-Conscription League with Goldman, Berkman, and Eleanor Fitzgerald. The group scheduled its first protest at the Harlem River Casino. Within a month it had distributed 100,000 manifestos denouncing forced military service. At a 4 June meeting Abbott was impressed by his friends' courage when members of the armed forces in the audience pelted the stage with light bulbs.

On 15 June, Goldman and Berkman were arrested and the office of *Mother Earth* raided. The arrests marked the real beginning of the World War I–era Red Scare. Abbott joined the New York Publicity Committee of the Alexander Berkman San Francisco Labor Defense. He was forcibly removed from the Federal Building after bail was set for Goldman and Berkman, because he strenuously objected to the authorities' decision to hold without charges a young man named Bales who had the bad luck to be in the *Mother Earth* office at the time of the raid. He wrote an account of their trial in July and was one of the defense witnesses. Again they refused representation. Goldman and Berkman eventually served two years in prison and were deported as a result of their activity against conscrip-

tion. Abbott concluded that their examples would strengthen the anarchist movement; he did not consider that the case was the start of a systematic attempt to eliminate war resisters in the United States.

Abbott also served on the board of advisers of the League for the Amnesty of Political Prisoners, along with Baldwin, Lucy Robins, Sanger, and Steffens. The following year, the seriousness of the situation for the New York anarchists with whom Abbott had made his cultural home became apparent. When U.S. troops landed in Soviet Russia early in 1918, the Frayhayt Group, an underground anarchist collective with many connections to the Ferrer Center, printed and distributed leaflets in English and Yiddish calling for a general strike. Military intelligence officers raided the group's headquarters and arrested and brutally beat the leaders, Jacob Abrams, Jacob Schwartz, Hyman Lachowsky, and Samuel Lipman. Mollie Steimer and Gabriel Prober were also arrested. Their group was the first to be prosecuted under the Sedition Act of 1918, and their trial began in October of that year. Schwartz died during the trial of injuries incurred during the beating, although police officials claimed that he was a victim of the influenza epidemic. After not much of a trial, Abrams, Lachowsky, and Lipman received sentences of twenty years in prison and $1,000 fines; Steimer was sentenced to fifteen years and a $500 fine. In response the League for the Amnesty of Political Prisoners produced a leaflet, *Is Opinion a Crime?* Although the Supreme Court upheld the conviction, Louis Brandeis and Oliver Wendell Holmes recorded a dissenting opinion. The group's attorney and the Political Prisoners Defense and Relief Committee arranged release on condition of deportation, but the group was divided at first about whether to accept the deal. Finally in November 1921 they agreed to be deported to Russia. Abbott was one of the speakers at their farewell dinner in New York.

By 1919, about one hundred families owned land at the Stelton Colony, and a few years afterward the group opened another colony at Lake Mohegan in New York. Abbott and Kelly began a monthly journal called *Freedom* ("A Journal of Constructive Anarchism") there in 1919, but it did not survive for long. Abbott's daughter, named after the Swedish women's rights author Ellen Key, was born in 1920, a year that marked another turning point in Abbott's life. His wife, Rose, was diagnosed with multiple sclerosis and suffered paralysis for ten years. Devoting himself to her entirely, Abbott ceased involvement in anarchist activities and began to suffer from depression. Many of his friends were in prison or in the process of being deported, and the broader radical movement was at an all-time low point. Abbott published sporadically in the anarchist journal *The Road to Freedom,* published by the Stelton Colony from 1924 to 1932 and edited by Havel, but beginning in the mid twenties Abbott's writing work moved back to the mainstream, more from necessity than by choice.

In 1925 financial matters were so bad for the Abbotts that he decided to sell the cottage at Westfield. After leaving *Current Opinion* magazine that year, Abbott edited *Physical Culture* and *Psychology* magazines from 1926 to 1927. Also in 1926 he wrote an introduction for and edited *London's Essays of Revolt,* published by Vanguard Press. In 1927 Abbott wrote in opposition to the execution of the Italian anarchists Nicola Sacco and Bartolomeo Vanzetti and briefly seemed to pull out of his melancholy, hoping up to the last minute for a reprieve. Afterward he wrote to Cohen, "I am obsessed by a sense of futility of all that I have done or tried to do" (Avrich, *The Modern School Movement,* p. 339). He continued to lecture on Tolstoy and other literary figures at the International Anarchist Open Forum in New York City. Despite his seeming connection with larger groups of people, he was more and more isolated, however. From 1929 to 1934 through the kindness of another old friend he found regular work as a staff writer and copyeditor for the *Encyclopedia Of Social Sciences.*

After the death of Rose Abbott on 21 December 1930, Abbott turned increasingly inward, with one notable exception. He had met Anna Strunsky in May 1903. When Macmillan published her collaboration with Jack London, *The Kempton-Wace Letters,* Gaylord Wilshire arranged a luncheon party for her in New York, and the guest list included William Dean Howells, Norman Hapgood, and Abbott. Strunsky and Abbott thereafter maintained a friendship through correspondence, and when Walling obtained a Mexican divorce from Strunsky in 1932, Abbott began to make romantic overtures to her. She was still grieving over her failed marriage and did not return his affections, although they remained friends. Much of his most poignant writing can be found in their correspondence. On 13 February 1926 he wrote a letter that summarized the end of his life: "My impulses are the same as they were when I first knew you (how sweet those days were!), but the War and Bolshevism have smashed that old world, & I find myself now in a world in which I cannot function" (Boylan, *Revolutionary Lives*).

During the Great Depression and World War II Abbott lived with his daughter, Ellen, in Greenwich Village and fretted over the difficulty of finding work. In 1934 he saw Goldman again when she was allowed to come back to New York for a ninety-day visit. From 1935 until 1939 he served as literary editor for the Federal Writers Project in Washington, D.C., a New Deal

program of Roosevelt's Work Progress Administration. He kept up a correspondence of varying degrees with his former comrades, including Alexis Ferm, Kelly, Schroeder, Ben Reitman, and Weinberger (the lawyer for the Frayhayt group). He joined Fitzgerald, Reitman, Weinberger, and Baldwin in organizing a seventieth-birthday tribute and fund for Goldman, who had finally made her way back to North America and was living in Toronto. After Goldman's death in 1940, some of them tried to raise money for a monument to her, to be placed in Chicago. In their letters they discussed writing their memoirs and the need for a comprehensive history of their active period. Weinberger thought Abbott should write it, but they could not raise the money to support him for a year. In these years Abbott considered writing a book on Whitman or a history of the anarchists, but between his depression and his struggles with money, he could not find the presence of mind to do either. In a 19 June 1940 letter to Reitman during this period, Abbott noted "I am in a state of (partially) suppressed irritation against everything. I have been out of a job for many months. I don't seem to be able to earn a dollar. My 25-year-old son, with two university degrees, is as helpless as a baby. . . . This damnable war seems to be spoiling everything" (Ben Reitman Papers, University of Illinois Chicago Circle). In 1947 Doubleday published his *Masterworks of Government: Digests of Thirteen Great Classics* and in 1948 his *Masterworks of Economics: Digests of Ten Great Classics.*

Abbott maintained a relationship with the Modern School, visiting his friends the Ferms and Havel from time to time. He chaired a twenty-fifth anniversary celebration committee in New York. His children also kept up lifelong connections with friends from the Modern School. Morris Abbott married Mirel, the daughter of Abbott's old friend Konrad Bercovici, in late 1952. Abbott died on 19 March 1953, at Montefiore Hospital in New York, at age seventy-four. Bercovici, writer and Modern Library editor Manuel Komroff, and Strunsky spoke at his funeral. In that same year the Modern School at Stelton finally closed, and the property was sold.

A few anarchist memorial essays appeared after Abbott's death, scattered throughout the remaining radical press, but in the political atmosphere of the 1950s, these did not spark any sort of interest. Paul Avrich interviewed Morris Abbott and devoted a chapter to Abbott in his *The Modern School Movement: Anarchism and Education in the United States* (1980). Leonard Abbott's writing accomplishments have not been assessed in any organized or comprehensive way; his essays have never been collected. Many of his colleagues, for example John Sloan, Carl Zigrosser, and Cohen, spoke fondly of him in memoirs. Will and Ariel Durant, in their 1977 *Dual Autobiography* said of Abbott,

> Amid a crowd of excitable spirits denouncing Western civilization and demanding a proletarian paradise, Leonard never, to our knowledge, uttered one bitter note, never hated, never advocated–though he could forgive–violence. He went his quiet way, teaching less by words than by the example of his patient understanding, tolerance and goodwill.

Durant said that Abbott told him at their last meeting, "I'm afraid . . . that we exaggerated the ability of men to endure freedom" (p. 40).

References:

Paul Avrich, *Anarchist Voices: An Oral History of Anarchism in America,* abridged edition (Princeton: Princeton University Press, 1995);

Avrich, *The Modern School Movement: Anarchism and Education in the United States* (Princeton: Princeton University Press, 1980);

James Boylan, *Revolutionary Lives: Anna Strunsky & William English Walling* (Amherst: University of Massachusetts Press, 1998): 31, 266, 270, 272;

Richard Drinnon, *Rebel in Paradise: A Biography of Emma Goldman* (Chicago: University of Chicago Press, 1961);

Will and Ariel Durant, *A Dual Autobiography* (New York: Simon & Schuster, 1977);

"Leonard Dalton Abbott, Editor, Publicist," *New York Times,* 20 March 1953, p. 23.

Papers:

Leonard Abbott's papers survive in a private collection in New York. Other manuscript resources for Abbott include the Stelton Modern School Archive–a collection that also includes half of Abbott's personal library–and the Elizabeth and Alexis Ferm Papers at Rutgers University and the Avrich Anarchist Archive, Library of Congress. Letters from Abbott survive in the following collections: Thomas H. Bell Papers, private collection, Los Angeles; Alexander Berkman and Emma Goldman Archives, International Institute of Social History, Amsterdam; Joseph Cohen Papers, Bund Archives of the Jewish Labor Movement, New York; Albert Mordell Papers, University of Pennsylvania; Ben Reitman Papers, University of Illinois at Chicago Special Collections; Lola Ridge Papers, Smith College; Rose Pastor Stokes Papers, Tamiment Library, New York University; Horace Traubel Papers, Library of Congress; Anna Strunsky Walling Papers, Yale University Library; Carl Zigrosser Papers, University of Pennsylvania. Abbott's letters to Eleanor Fitzgerald are among the Emma Goldman Papers, Tamiment Library, New York University.

Saul Alinsky

(30 January 1909 – 12 June 1972)

Andrew J. Waskey
Dalton State College

BOOKS: *Reveille for Radicals* (Chicago: University of Chicago Press, 1946);

John L. Lewis: An Unauthorized Biography (New York: Putnam, 1949);

Rules for Radicals: A Pragmatic Primer for Realistic Radicals (New York: Random House, 1971).

OTHER: "The Basis in the Social Sciences for Treatment of the Adult Offender," *National Conference of Social Work Yearbook* (Chicago: University of Chicago Press, 1938), pp. 714–724;

"Testimony Before Civil Rights Housing Hearing," Chicago, U.S. Commission on Civil Rights, 5 May 1959, public document;

"Citizen Participation and Community Organization in Planning and Urban Renewal" (Chicago: Industrial Areas Foundation, 1962);

"What is the Role of Community Organization in Bargaining with the Establishment for Health Care Service?" in J. C. Norman, ed., *Medicine in the Ghetto* (New York: Appleton-Century-Croft, 1968), pp. 291–299;

"The Double Revolution," in Wilton S. Dillon, ed., *The Cultural Drama: Modern Identities and Social Ferment* (Washington, D.C.: Smithsonian Institution Press, 1974), pp. 288–303.

SELECTED PERIODICAL PUBLICATIONS—
UNCOLLECTED: "A Sociological Technique in Clinical Criminology," *Proceedings of the Sixty-Fourth Annual Congress of the American Prison Association* (New York: American Prison Association, 1934), pp. 167–178;

"The Philosophical Implications of the Individualistic Approach in Criminology," *Proceedings of the Sixty-Seventh Annual Congress of the American Prison Association* (New York: American Prison Association, 1937);

"Community Analysis and Organization," *American Journal of Sociology,* 46 (May 1941): 797–808;

Saul Alinsky (P. David Finks, The Radical Vision of Saul Alinsky, *1984; Thomas Cooper Library, University of South Carolina)*

"Review of *Nowhere was Somewhere,* by Arthur E. Morgan," *American Sociological Review,* 12 (June 1947): 374;

"Fights of Bishop Sheil," *Catholic Digest,* August 1951, pp. 75–80;

"Power and Leadership," *Nation,* 192 (25 February 1961): 174–175;

"The Principles of Community Organization," *Presbyterian Interracial Council Newsletter* (1962);

"The War on Poverty: Political Pornography," *Journal of Social Issues,* January 1965, pp. 41–47;

"Of Means and Ends," *Union Seminary Quarterly,* 22 (January 1967): 108;

"The Poor and the Powerful," *Psychiatric Research Reports of the American Psychiatric Association,* 21 (January 1967): 22–82;

"A Plea for Help in Crisis: A Rejoinder," *International Journal of Psychiatry,* 4 (October 1967): 314–315;

"John L.: Something of a Man," *Nation,* 208 (30 June 1969): 827–828;

"Life in the Second City," *Nation,* 212 (19 April 1971): 507–508.

Saul Alinsky was a community organizer and activist who successfully mobilized more than two million people into organizations that enabled them to benefit themselves. He carried on the tradition of American radicals such as Samuel Adams and Thomas Paine. He had little if any use for ideologies other than American democracy—people directly involved in and controlling their own lives and destinies. University trained in the social sciences (archaeology, sociology, and criminology), he was an engaging and sympathetic storyteller and humorist. With an amazing ability to understand human vulnerability and fears and to see kindness and generosity where others did not, he listened and talked his way into the confidence of criminals, gangs, residents of marginal neighborhoods, labor, racial, and religious groups, and, at the end of his career, imagined that he could make life exciting again for the alienated middle class. With a host of unlikely allies, he founded the Industrial Areas Foundation in 1939. From the Great Depression, when he worked with the Congress of Industrial Organizations (CIO), through the social and political upheavals of the 1960s and early 1970s, Alinsky advised communities how best to reach consensus, engage in negotiation or protest, and attain their goals.

Saul David Alinsky was born on 30 January 1909, in Chicago, Illinois, in a tenement house. His father, Benjamin Alinsky, a tailor, and his mother, Sarah Tannenbaum, a seamstress, were Orthodox Jews recently emigrated from Russia. Sarah bore her husband a second son, who died in childhood. In addition, the household included Harry, Max, and Kay, children from the father's earlier marriage. About 1915 Benjamin Alinsky bought an apartment building in a nicer area on the West Side and moved his family into it. Benjamin and Sarah Alinsky divorced in 1922, soon after Saul's bar mitzvah. After the divorce the senior Alinsky moved to California and started a new family. Thereafter Saul spent most of his time in Chicago with his mother. His visits to California were lonely times because he was forced to stay at a boardinghouse and was denied admission to his father's new home and family.

During Alinsky's youth the poverty in Chicago's diverse ethnic groups produced neighborhood gangs who fought to protect their turf against other ethnic minorities. In the Jewish neighborhood where the Alinskys lived, the opportunity to mingle with gang members afforded Saul his first exposure to urban criminal behavior. Their primary enemies were Polish boys. A leg injury that kept him in bed for most of a year insulated Alinsky from violence and habituated him to study. As a small boy Alinsky was sent to the local "heder" (Jewish parochial school) where he learned the basics of Hebrew. He attended a succession of high schools, including Marshall High in Chicago, and eventually graduated from Hollywood High School in Los Angeles in 1925. He attended the University of Chicago from 1926 to 1930.

His undergraduate major was archaeology. He spent two summers working on digs in the Southwest. He also worked on excavations of Winnebago Indian burial sites near Chicago. After the stock-market crash of 1929 destroyed many of the great fortunes that had funded archaeological expeditions, he accepted a fully funded graduate fellowship in sociology, but not before he had his first experience in community organizing. He worked out a system of cheating a local restaurant chain by pretending to lose a ticket for coffee, then going to another location, eating a whole meal, and paying with the far less expensive ticket. By this method he and many other students ate well for about six months before the company changed its checkout procedure. Recalling the incident in a 1972 *Playboy* interview, he said that in hard times the right to eat trumps the right to make a profit.

At the time the University of Chicago was a world leader in the new field of urban sociology. Its professors included John Dewey and other groundbreaking thinkers, who became known as the "Chicago School." Professor Robert Ezra Park was Alinsky's favorite. From Park, a former journalist, Alinsky learned to think of cities as more than material geographic units. He soon saw them as systems—social organisms whose processes, growth, morbidity, and decay could be studied. Park believed the data derived by studying an urban area could be used to improve the urban ecology in which people lived. From another member of the

Alinsky (middle) on the Packinghouse Workers' picket line at the Chicago Union Stockyards, 17 January 1946 (Sanford D. Horwitt, Let Them Call Me Rebel: Saul Alinsky–His Life and Legacy, 1989; Thomas Cooper Library, University of South Carolina)

University of Chicago's sociology department, Professor Ernest K. Burgess, Alinsky learned how to do sociological fieldwork. With notebook in hand he went out into the streets of Chicago to study the people in neighborhoods and organizations. Soon he mastered the art of doing both nonparticipant- and participant-observer studies.

Burgess used the data collected by his students to create a working map of Chicago's dynamic life and works. The combination of natural ability and the great opportunity afforded by Chicago's ethnic and social diversity provided Alinsky with rich material for study. His undergraduate studies included a report on the operation of the public dance halls then the rage in Chicago. Alinsky eventually chose to study criminology and particularly organized crime in Chicago. At the time Al Capone's gang dominated the city's criminal underworld, operating openly and with impunity. Many people in the Depression era viewed the organization positively; Boy Scouts cheered for "Big Al" at

baseball games and other public events. The mob was an important economic and social institution in the city, supplying what many people wanted–prostitution, alcohol, and gambling.

The Capone gang made its headquarters at the Lexington Hotel. Alinsky began hanging around the area. Eventually, he won notice by the gang; he later claimed that gangsters had easily hurt feelings, and that he listened to their stories when their comrades had heard them too many times and were plainly bored with them. He was honest about the fact that he was a university student who wanted to study the gang, and eventually the leaders accepted him as an observer. He became acquainted with Capone's top lieutenant, Frank Nitti (known as "The Enforcer") and "Big Ed" Stash, Capone's top executioner. They openly discussed mob business with the young researcher, explaining to him, for example, why they paid high sums for out-of-town hit men when they already had many on the payroll. Alinsky said the mobsters thought he was unfeeling to ask such a question; the reason was that they did not want hit men to have to kill people they knew.

Eventually, Alinsky came to know crooked cops, judges, lawyers, politicians, as well as the mobsters' girlfriends, soldiers, and other hangers-on. His fieldwork was a criminologist's dream—it included fast money, cars, the company of women, plenty to eat and drink. But he also saw the dark side of the organization's power: the extortion, beatings, terror, brutality, and murder. From this experience he learned the importance of personal but nonjudgmental relationships with subjects. Alinsky never wrote his planned dissertation on this portion of his field research, however, because he had fallen in love with Helene Simon, a leader of a Chicago social workers' union, and needed a real job in order to get married. They were married on 9 June 1932.

In the 1930s Alinsky worked for the Institute of Juvenile Research (IJR), run by Clifford Shaw. The IJR had been originally organized to provide diagnostic studies of juvenile delinquents ordered by the juvenile courts. By the time Alinsky met Shaw, the IJR had grown into a unit of the Illinois Division of Criminology. For eight years Alinsky served on Shaw's staff producing basic empirical studies of juvenile delinquency. Once again he was studying people on the streets of Chicago, but this time it was juvenile gangs. He was assigned to the "42 Gang," an Italian gang in the Near West Side considered to be a "farm team" for the Capone organization. At first rejected by the 42 Gang, Alinsky eventually found an entry opportunity when he provided the mother of a gang member killed during a robbery with a photograph of her dead son. Thereafter he was accepted as a friend. For the next two years Alinsky worked with the gang. He was able to get fifteen gang members to write their own biographies. His interview technique was featured in an article he wrote for the American Prison Association.

Shaw advanced Alinsky's career by helping him get an assignment to the Joliet State Prison as a sociologist from 1933 to 1935. Serving on the prison's classification board, Alinsky interviewed each new arrival. His report included a detailed evaluation along with recommendations for an individualized rehabilitation program. Eventually, he discovered that his reports were never used for the intended purpose, and he became convinced that prisons do not rehabilitate people. He also came to believe that prisons have a dehumanizing effect on both the people who work in them and inmates. Later he noted that to a judge and jury the death penalty was an abstract matter, but the people who worked in the prisons and knew the prisoners and their families found that participating in executions was—except to the occasional sadist—a brutalizing and

horrific experience. The only defenses were drunkenness and desensitization. When he caught himself viewing a new inmate as simply a number and case to be processed, he knew it was time to leave.

All of Alinsky's criminology experience led him to develop radical views on the causes of criminal behavior in America. He rejected the earlier, religious-based view that corrupted souls or disordered personalities caused delinquency. Instead, he argued that the disorganization of American urban society generated antisocial behavior. In 1939 Alinsky returned to his job with the IJR to organize a unit of Shaw's Chicago Area Project (CAP). The program was a traditional juvenile recreation program for working with troubled youth. He soon found himself involved in organizing the neighborhood near Chicago's stockyards. "The Back of the Yards" was a notorious place, with nearly 100,000 people crammed into a relatively small area, rife with crime and disease. The neighborhood had not changed much since its portrayal in Upton Sinclair's novel *The Jungle* (1906), which led to the establishment of the Food and Drug Administration. For months Alinsky worked on his own with the CIO as a volunteer as it sought to organize the meatpacking industry. From its professional organizers he learned the techniques of mass organization. He mastered ways to raise money, recruit members, and deliver efficient mass communications.

During Alinsky's meandering around the Back of the Yards he met Joseph Meegan, a young high-school teacher. Meegan and his wife were active Roman Catholics, and his brother was a Chicago-area priest. Together the group organized the the Back of the Yards Council, gathering as many community organizations as possible into the neighborhood, including the churches, card clubs, veterans groups, business associations, local unions, ethnic clubs, and other organizations. Many of the groups were in conflict with each other—churches often reflected ethnic rivalries, and communists faced opposition from the church and from within the labor movement. The local communist leader, Herb March, faced armed attackers twice and once was shot. Although most Catholic clergy in the area inclined to conservatism, Alinsky won them over to progressive activism by comparing the communists to the old Capone organization. They were, he said, rising to meet a need. He actually thought the communists were doing good work, but he challenged the clergy to fulfill the needs of their parishioners and put the communists out of business if they thought them so objectionable.

Eventually, Alinsky was able to put together the local communist union organizer and the Roman Catholic bishop, Bernard J. "Bennie" Sheil, in a 14 July 1939 meeting to work out their differences for the mutual benefit of the people in the Back of the Yards. From that meeting was born the Back of the Yards Council, an organization dedicated to action for community improvement. At the same time the council overcame the opposition from the Roman Catholic priests that the meatpacking union had faced in its drive to organize the meat packers. The neighborhood groups decided to create a recreation center, start nutrition and disease-prevention programs for children, and support the Armour Packing Company workers' union. The meat-packing companies, seeing the new solidarity of the community with labor, capitulated and accepted union-organizing activity.

By this time Alinsky had developed the idea that urban slums were beset with problems because the people who lived in them were without hope; they were enslaved by a feeling of powerlessness. He also had concluded that traditional social-work practices were ineffective in the urban-slum environment because solutions to problems caused by urban poverty were dictated by people outside the slum community. Instead, Alinsky made it his goal to empower the urban poor. To achieve this goal he thought it necessary to create viable organizations that would enable people to assume control of their own lives. Creating organizations usually took about three years, he learned, and he usually found that the social-work establishment and the traditional power structure organized against him.

Alinsky's involvement in organizing the Back of the Yards Council caused him to part company with Shaw, effective 15 January 1940. Shaw believed that the work Alinsky was doing was outside the scope of the IJR. The Back of the Yards Council's successes made it the subject of significant national interest. With the help of Bishop Sheil, Alinsky created the Industrial Areas Foundation (IAF) in 1940 as a base for organizing neighborhoods after the model of Back of the Yards Council. In the fall of 1939 Sheil took Alinsky to New York to meet with Marshall Field III, grandson of the founder of the Marshall Field's Department Store. Field had decided to devote himself to philanthropy in 1936, founding the Field Foundation to promote social change. He became a contributing supporter of the IAF and recruited other wealthy contributors to aid Alinsky's work.

The IAF board of trustees included Sheil; Field; Briton I. Budd, president of Northern Utilities; Kathryn Lewis, daughter of John L. Lewis and secretary-treasurer of United Mine Workers, District 50; Stuyvesant Peabody, Illinois coal magnate; G. Howland Shaw of the U.S. State Department; and Judge Theodore Rosen of Philadelphia. Throughout his career, rich and powerful people aided Alinsky because they agreed

with his democratic methods and more especially with his goals. The IAF voted to raise $15,000 a year for five years and to hire Alinsky as its active organizer. The institutional support allowed him to promote the democratic way of life through community organization.

Soon afterward, Alinsky traveled to Kansas City, Kansas, to meet with representatives of the Armourdale district, a meatpacking-workers neighborhood built on the floodplain of the Kaw River across from the stockyards. Its residents were poor whites who had come to escape the problems of sharecropping in the cotton-growing areas of the South. Protestant, poor, and lacking many of the advantages of the Back of the Yards, the neighborhood had few resources with which to work. Upon his arrival Alinksy was arrested by the local police chief, who had been warned that a dangerous radical was coming to town. During his several confinements he began working on a book. Eventually, following long hours of conversation, he won over the police chief to the neighborhood's cause. The chief joined the Armourdale Community Council and became an active supporter, providing security when necessary. Despite Armourdale's poverty, both material and social, the Armourdale Community Council organized quickly. After several successes, it also gave the CIO an opening for organizing slaughterhouse workers into a meatpackers union. In 1951 Armourdale was swept away in a flood, but until then it made some modest success.

Alinsky's next organizing effort was in South St. Paul, Minnesota. A community council organized, but it never operated with much success, in part because Alinsky was able to make only a limited effort. An organizer could energize the community, but without enough involvement by the organizer over a significant period of time, the impact on the community proved minimal. Both Armourdale and South St. Paul developed organizational problems over the growing rumor, spread by the powerful meatpackers in the areas, that Alinsky was a communist. The FBI began investigating him in 1940 upon complaints from local authorities in Missouri and Minnesota. The South St. Paul project functioned quietly until the mid 1950s, when it quietly folded.

Saul and Helene Alinsky adopted a daughter, Kathryn, in the summer of 1941, and before the end of the war the Alinskys adopted another child, Lee David. When the United States entered World War II, Alinsky went to work for the War Manpower Board. His job was to improve morale. He was classified unfit for military service (4-F) because of a childhood injury and a thyroid condition. Instead of combat or espionage, which he hoped for, he traveled around the country selling war bonds for the Treasury Department. While

Alinsky (seated) interviewing John L. Lewis in 1948 (from Alinsky's John L. Lewis: An Unauthorized Biography, *1949; Thomas Cooper Library, University of South Carolina)*

in Hollywood, Alinsky not only promoted war-bond sales but also met Hollywood's actors and actresses, producers, and other executives, many of whom became his supporters and contributors in future years. Traveling to promote war-bond drives exposed Alinsky to vast areas of the United States and to its complexities. Alinsky's contempt for the field of criminology and professionals in it reached new heights during this period. He began thinking about the postwar organizing efforts he would make.

In the early 1940s James B. Conant, the president of Harvard, issued a series of essays calling for new American radicals to counter what he saw as a growing elitism in the universities and educational establishment. Scholars believe that Alinsky's *Reveille for Radicals* (1946), which became a best-seller, is a response to those essays. Most of the reviews of *Reveille for Radicals* were favorable, with the notable exceptions of the *New Republic,* the *Nation,* and *Commentary.* While working on the book, Alinsky met the French philosopher Jacques Maritain, a political refugee lecturing at the University of Chicago. Maritain arranged publication abroad, hoping that the book could lend vision to French democrats in their coming struggles with the French Communist Party.

The book divides into two parts: the first is a statement of philosophy, and the second is a description of numerous organizing tactics. Alinsky believed, contrary to the trends of the period, that the remedy for the ills of democracy was more democracy. He was aware that majorities oppress minorities; however, he presented a polarizing argument based on his distrust of liberals, whom he said "like people with their head" (but not their heart). Liberals also tend to rely too much, he thought, upon top-down change imposed by the federal government. To Alinsky many business tycoons were totalitarians who used goons and high-handed manipulations to destroy the democratic rights of employees and of citizens at large. Both liberals and business powers tried, he thought, to take power from the people and prevent them from participating in democratic processes. Alinsky argued that the better course lay in making it possible for people to take responsibility and make the desired changes in their own lives. Previously labor unions had offered a way to address this need, but by the end of the war, he argued, they had too big a stake in the capitalist system to retain any sort of oppositional power. Alinsky's commitment to practical reality, not to an ideologically driven dream-world, drove his incessant organizing. The next step, he thought, was the establishment of community organizations. Part two of *Reveille for Radicals* covered that topic in more detail.

After World War II, Alinsky organized campaigns in numerous places, with mixed success. He became involved in organizing efforts in New York City; Lackawanna, New York; and in several cities in California. The limited results were owing to four factors–insufficient funding to stay the course; a lack of experienced organizers; opposition, especially from the social-work establishment; and Alinsky's own foibles. He had difficulty sharing control of a campaign in a manner that allowed it to grow. In other instances his attempts at organizing failed because he had not become personally fully involved.

Recognizing his limitations, Alinsky turned his attention to recruitment and development for IAF. In California he discovered Fred Ross, an organizer close to Alinsky's age, who had had some success organizing the American Council on Race Relations. The program was about to shut down, however, and Ross sought a new area for his talents. With the support of Bishop Sheil and Alinsky, Ross met with Roman Catholic leaders in southern California. The endorsement gave a stamp of orthodoxy to Ross and enabled him to establish the Community Service Organization (CSO). Among the group's best-known causes was seeing that the beneficiaries of the GI Bill of Rights did not face discrimination on the basis of race, religion, or ethnic background, a project that flowed directly into integration of neighborhoods. One of the more-famous labor organizers later associated with CSO was Cesar Chavez. Ross and Chavez organized many CSO units in California to benefit the Mexican American population. Chavez later led the unionization of farmworkers in California. Despite opposition, the IAF obtained sufficient funding to operate in California. Many contributors were Hollywood professionals Alinsky had met during the war.

On Labor Day 1947 Helene Alinsky drowned in a boating accident in Lake Michigan after heroically rescuing two children. Alinsky, who was elsewhere at the time, was devastated. His grief led him to neglect his work and his children; he visited his wife's grave daily. His inability to act ended when a cemetery manager apologized for a mistake: his wife's tombstone had been placed over the wrong grave. Realizing that he had been grieving in the wrong place for too long, he began a healing project, his biography of John L. Lewis, intended as an advanced textbook for organizers. In 1949 Alinsky published *John L. Lewis: An Unauthorized Biography*. Well written and documented, the book nonetheless offended scholars because it depicted Lewis in

saintly terms. Writing the book had been therapeutic for Alinsky, however. He had met and was planning on marrying Babette Stiefel, whom he knew from the Chicago Public Housing Authority. He was preparing to return to organizing when she died suddenly of polio in the summer of 1950.

In the late 1940s and 1950s Alinsky was not alone in finding it easy to become demoralized. Radicals all over the country faced strong political opposition and economic threats (many were blacklisted and banned from practicing their professions) during the second red scare. The McCarthy era was in full force, and funding a man like Alinsky, who called himself a radical, posed significant political risks for individuals and foundations. As usual, Alinsky found support from a variety of quarters, this time conservative Republicans. Harriet "Happy" Macy, an IAF trustee, raised funds for him. Also the co-owners of the *Washington Post,* Agnes and Eugene Meyer, aided him financially, having been enthusiastic supporters of his work since the days of the Back of the Yards Council.

In 1952 Alinsky married Jean Graham. She was his opposite socially: Park Avenue Republican and WASP. Soon after their marriage she exhibited symptoms of multiple sclerosis. Their life together was happy, and together they went about the business of raising his two children. Many times he came to the aid of friends who were McCarthy victims, sending bail money to Myles Horton of the Highlander School in Tennessee and introducing Larry Adler, a harmonica player in a blacklisted duo, to his rich patrons, the Macys. In 1954 even Alinsky's friend Bishop Sheil was the victim of anticommunist hysteria, losing his position when he criticized Francis Cardinal Spellman for appearing with Senator Joseph McCarthy. The 1950s proved to be mixed years for Alinsky's writing. He planned a book on social organizing that he never completed. He taught a summer course at Catholic University in 1951 and wrote a play with television writer Robert Shayon, featuring a thinly disguised portrait of Alinsky as the title character of *Socrates McGuinness*. Also in the mid 1950s he wrote *Come Now,* a biography of Monsignor John O'Grady. Neither piece was ever published, and the play was performed only privately in Alinsky's new home in Chicago's Hyde Park neighborhood.

America experienced a transformation in character in the 1950s as newly prosperous people moved to the suburbs. The unions also changed, moving away from the Left politically. More important, they moved their headquarters away from their old industrial community neighborhoods, a mistake, Alinsky thought. Their ranks had supplied the cadres that were able to extend his organizing efforts. Now he turned to the

Alinsky in Woodlawn, on the Chicago South Side near the University of Chicago, where he organized the Temporary Woodlawn Association in 1961 (from his Let Them Call Me Rebel, *1989; Thomas Cooper Library, University of South Carolina)*

churches for help. The Protestant churches tended to move with their flocks to suburban locations, but the Roman Catholic churches tended to remain behind in the cities. Over the years of his career, churches more than any other institution supported Alinsky's work–almost always the Roman Catholic Church, and later in his career many Protestant churches. From time to time Jewish support also was forthcoming. After the founding of the state of Israel, however, most American Jewish aid went to its support and only small amounts to Alinsky's work.

Some churches opposed Alinsky. Until Vatican II and the advent of the Civil Rights Movement, Protestants tended to look on Alinsky as an operative for the Roman Catholic Church. After he became involved in organizing the black community in Chicago, he encountered opposition from leaders in the Presbyterian, Lutheran, and Evangelical Churches. In the Chicago Presbytery of the Presbyterian Church, however, younger ministers engineered the expulsion of its hostile executive. His replacement was committed to racial

issues. The Chicago organization also turned up the usual complex system of counter-intuitive allegiances and enmities. For example, despite Alinsky's espousal of liberal causes, he met with opposition in the late 1950s and early 1960s from liberals themselves, including the editors of *Christian Century,* a liberal Christian publication. The antagonism puzzled many at the time, but in retrospect it seemed related to ties between conservative Lutheran leadership and the personal-property interests of at least one member of the magazine's board.

Funding for Alinsky often came from the Emil Schartzhaupt Foundation (which gave a grant of $150,000 in 1953) and from Monsignor O'Grady of Catholic Charities. O'Grady and Alinsky collaborated in numerous ways and became close personal friends. O'Grady established and developed the National Conference of Catholic Charities. Alinsky also found an important ally in Samuel Cardinal Stritch. Later he became friends with Bishop (later Archbishop) Fulton Sheen, who proved a strong supporter. Other clerics who gave aid and comfort for his battles included Martin Luther King Jr. and O'Grady's protégé Nicholas von Hoffman, who became a significant organizer in Chicago's Puerto Rican and Italian neighborhoods.

In January 1961, at Cardinal Stritch's suggestion, Alinsky undertook to organize the neighborhood around the University of Chicago. He created the Temporary Woodlawn Organization (TWO) to oppose the urban renewal plans of the city and University of Chicago. This also put Alinsky in the awkward position of opposing the expansion plans of his alma mater. Alinsky believed that urban blacks were so downtrodden that the most important factor of their development, at first, was building a sense of hope. They could be mobilized much more effectively if they had a memory of success; then they could be led to do even more-daring things.

Inspired by Alinsky, TWO members next dared to be bused in a caravan to Chicago's City Hall to register to vote. Once registered, they attracted the interest of vote-seeking politicians, another source of morale reinforcement. The most infamous tactic that Alinsky used to further the goals of the Woodlawn Organization was a sit-in of restrooms at the Chicago O'Hare airport, which was soon teeming with desperate passengers unable to attend to their biological needs. This "sit-in" met with limited success in publicizing what Alinsky called Chicago's "severe, chronic color constipation" (Horwitt, *Let Them Call Me Rebel*).

In summer 1964 Alinsky went to Rochester, New York, following race riots there to organize workers at the Eastman Kodak Corporation, most of whom were African Americans. Eventually, FIGHT (Freedom, Integration, God, Honor, Today) was created to carry the battle to Rochester City Hall and to Eastman Kodak. Alinsky held that an important part of community organizing was the ability to identify and threaten those things sacred to the opposition; in Rochester he determined that the Rochester Symphony was the appropriate target. He proceeded to buy a block of orchestra seats. Confident that a company stool pigeon was in attendance at a meeting of the new organization, he displayed the block of tickets and announced that they were for FIGHT members. Since the event was such an important cultural experience for the community, he said, it would be fitting to have an all-bean preperformance dinner: Let nature take its course. When news of the plan reached Eastman Kodak and Rochester officials, they immediately capitulated to the group's demands. Alinsky bought shares of Eastman Kodak stock in order to be able to attend the stockholder's meeting. He also got proxies from the retirement funds of churches to threaten the management with removal. Most of Alinsky's organizing tactics were peaceful, lawful, clever, and in many cases successful.

Alinsky spent much of his energy after Rochester on developing an institute for training organizers in urban communities. He put less effort into community organization and more into crafting the future through people trained in his philosophy. During the hectic days of the Civil Rights Movement and the antiwar movement Alinsky tried with limited success to influence the new generation of radicals, to whom he did not feel very connected and for whom he had little patience. One such group was the Campaign Against Pollution/Citizens Action Program, formed in response to a Mike Royko column, which allied IAF trainees and former members of Students for a Democratic Society with property owners and small-businessmen to oppose the Chicago Crosstown Expressway.

The IAF continued to win large grants, including from Gordon Sherman of Midas, the muffler company, and from the Rockefeller Foundation. Alinsky began to enjoy positive attention from the mainstream press, who contrasted him favorably with the younger generation of radicals. He addressed Smithsonian Institution members on social protest in 1970, remarking in a question-and-answer session afterward that "you know you're in trouble when they start throwing cocktail parties for you" (Horwitt, *Let Them Call Me Rebel*). *Rules for Radicals* was published in 1971. Alinsky divorced Jean in 1969 and married Irene McGinnis in 1971. Together they toured in Asia, where he was amazed to discover readers familiar with his books.

An interviewer at *Playboy* noted with some amusement that he "looks like an accountant and talks like a stevedore." William F. Buckley, the conservative editor of the *National Review*, applauded Alinsky's organizational genius. Alinsky had a great talent for reading a situation and seeing ways to empower people to engage in successful nonviolent actions.

Alinsky died of a heart attack on 12 June 1972 in Carmel, California. In a lengthy interview with *Playboy* a few months before he died, he offered a synopsis of his career and his vision of his work:

> My critics are right when they call me an outside agitator. When a community, any kind of community, is hopeless and helpless, it requires somebody from outside to come in and stir things up. That's my job—to unsettle them, to make them start asking questions, to teach them to stop talking and start acting, because the fat cats in charge never hear with their ears, only through their rears.

Letters:

The Philosopher and the Provocateur: The Correspondence of Jacques Maritain and Saul Alinsky, edited by Bernard Doering (Notre Dame, Ind.: University of Notre Dame Press, 1994).

Interviews:

Marion Sanders, *The Professional Radical: Conversations with Saul Alinsky* (New York: Harper & Row, 1970);

Eric Norden, "Saul Alinsky Interview," *Playboy Magazine* (March 1972): 59–178.

References:

Robert Bailey Jr., *Radicals in Urban Politics: The Alinsky Approach* (Chicago: University of Chicago Press, 1972);

Kathryn Close, "Back of the Yards," *Survey Graphic,* 29 (1940): 612–615;

P. David Finks, *The Radical Vision of Saul Alinsky* (New York: Paulist Press, 1984);

Sanford D. Horwitt, *Let Them Call Me Rebel: Saul Alinsky, His Life and Legacy* (New York: Knopf, 1989);

Mary J. Kirklin and Lyle E. Franzen, *Community Organization Bibliography* (Chicago: Institute on the Church in Urban-Industrial Society in Chicago, 1973);

Charles F. Levine, "Alinsky–Conservative Wine in Radical Bottles," *American Behavioral Scientist,* 17 (1973): 279–284;

Dale Rogers Marshall, "Rules for Radicals: A Pragmatic Primer for Realistic Radicals," *American Political Science Review,* 70 (1976): 620–623;

Donald Reitzes, *The Alinsky Legacy* (Greenwich, Conn.: JAI Press, 1987).

Papers:

The most extensive collection of Saul Alinsky's papers is held by the Industrial Areas Foundation Alinsky Institute in Huntington, New York. The University of Illinois, Chicago campus, has several boxes donated by Alinsky in 1966. Alinsky correspondence is included in the papers of Monsignor John O'Grady, National Conference of Catholic Charities (NCCC), Catholic University, Washington, D.C., and the Rochester Board for Urban Ministry Papers, Rochester, New York.

Ray Stannard Baker
(David Grayson)
(17 April 1870 – 12 July 1946)

John D. Buenker
University of Wisconsin–Parkside

BOOKS: *The Boy's Book of Inventions: Stories of the Wonders of Modern Science* (New York: Doubleday & McClure, 1899; London & New York: Harper, 1900);

Our New Prosperity (New York: Doubleday & McClure, 1900);

Seen in Germany (New York: McClure, Phillips, 1901; London: Harper, 1902);

Boys' Second Book of Inventions (New York & London: McClure, Phillips, 1903);

Following the Color Line: An Account of Negro Citizenship in the American Democracy (New York & London: Doubleday, Page, 1908);

New Ideals in Healing (New York: Stokes, 1909; London: Laurie, 1909);

The Spiritual Unrest (New York: Stokes, 1910);

The Friendly Road (Garden City, N.Y.: Doubleday, Page, 1915; London: Melrose, 1921);

What Wilson Did at Paris (Garden City, N.Y.: Doubleday, Page, 1919);

The New Industrial Unrest: Reasons and Remedies (Garden City, N.Y.: Doubleday, Page, 1920);

Woodrow Wilson and World Settlement: Written from His Unpublished and Personal Material (Garden City, N.Y.: Doubleday, Page, 1922);

Versailles Treaty and After: An Interpretation of Woodrow Wilson's Work at Paris (New York: Doran, 1924);

A Day of Pleasant Bread (Garden City, N.Y.: Doubleday, Page, 1926);

Woodrow Wilson: Life and Letters, 8 volumes (Garden City, N.Y.: Doubleday, Page, 1927–1939; London: Heinemann, 1928–1939);

Native American: The Book of My Youth (New York: Scribners, 1941);

American Chronicle: The Autobiography of Ray Stannard Baker (New York: Scribners, 1945);

Muckraking: Three Landmark Articles, edited by Ellen F. Fitzpatrick (Boston: Bedford Books, 1994).

Ray Stannard Baker (George Grantham Bain Collection, Library of Congress)

As David Grayson

Adventures in Contentment (Garden City, N.Y. & London: Doubleday, Page, 1907);

Adventures in Friendship (Garden City, N.Y.: Doubleday, Page, 1910; London: Hodder & Stoughton, 1910);

Hempfield: A Novel (Garden City, N.Y.: Doubleday, Page, 1915; London: Hodder & Stoughton, 1916);

Great Possessions: A New Series of Adventures (Garden City, N.Y.: Doubleday, Page, 1917; London: Hodder & Stoughton, 1918);

Adventures in Understanding (Garden City, N.Y.: Doubleday, Page, 1925; London: Hodder & Stoughton, 1925);

Adventures in Solitude (Garden City, N.Y.: Doubleday, Doran, 1931; London: Hodder & Stoughton, 1932);

The Countrymen's Year (Garden City, N.Y.: Doubleday, Doran, 1936; London: Hodder & Stoughton, 1936);

Under My Elm: Country Discoveries and Reflections (Garden City, N.Y.: Doubleday, Doran, 1942).

Collections: *Adventures of David Grayson* (New York: Doubleday, Page, 1925);

David Grayson: Selected Essays (London: Harrap, 1926);

More Adventures with David Grayson (Garden City, N.Y.: Doubleday, 1946).

OTHER: *The Public Papers of Woodrow Wilson,* edited by Baker and William E. Dodd, 6 volumes (New York & London: Harper, 1925–1927).

Journalist, author, historian, social reformer, presidential confidant, and biographer, Ray Stannard Baker is noteworthy for his work as a muckraking journalist during the first decade of the twentieth century, his edition of the six-volume *The Public Papers of Woodrow Wilson* (1925–1927), and his eight-volume *Woodrow Wilson: Life and Letters* (1927–1939). A reporter for the Chicago *News-Record* during the 1890s, Baker gradually evolved into a muckraker and social critic as a result of his exposure to the underside of life in urban, industrial America. The apex of his muckraking career came with the publication of *Following the Color Line: An Account of Negro Citizenship in the American Democracy* in 1908, a book that forced tens of thousands of Americans to confront the country's racial divide. Beginning as a believer in individualism and laissez-faire, Baker eventually embraced collectivism, public regulation, and even government ownership. An admirer of Theodore Roosevelt and Robert La Follette, Baker became a confirmed disciple of Woodrow Wilson's New Freedom and a staunch advocate of the president's foreign policy, whether it be neutrality or intervention or support for the League of Nations. After World War I, Baker devoted his life to assuring what he regarded as Wilson's proper place in history.

Baker was an influential journalist and author with a gift for identifying and explicating the most critical issues and developments of his time. Testimonies to his energy, resourcefulness, dependability, judgment,

and clear and lively writing style abounded among his contemporaries and colleagues. Although not generally seen as an original or profound thinker, he was celebrated for his open mind and his sensitivity to what was going on around him. At bottom, he was an idealist and a reformer in pursuit of a more just society and of a creed by which to order his own life. In addition, under the pseudonym of David Grayson, Baker wrote eight novels in which he was able to express his deepest feelings about life without the constraints imposed by the canons of journalism. By the same token, however, Grayson's musings, intentionally or not, reveal much of the ambivalence and turmoil that roiled within Baker over the impact of modernization, industrialization, urbanization, and immigration. Grayson clearly was a manifestation of Baker's imaginative side, but that impulse was almost always held in check by the reporter's rational empiricism. In the end, Grayson was reduced to seeking such publishing outlets as *Reader's Digest.*

Baker was born on 17 April 1870 in Lansing, Michigan, the son of Joseph Stannard Baker, a Civil War veteran, and Alice Potter. When he was five years old, the family moved to St. Croix Falls in northwestern Wisconsin, where his father worked as a land agent. The descendant of New England pioneering stock, Baker often boasted that he had been brought up on the "last frontier." He later elaborated on the experiences of his early years in the first of two autobiographies: *Native American: The Book of My Youth* (1941). (A second autobiography, *American Chronicle: The Autobiography of Ray Stannard Baker,* published four years later, focuses almost entirely on his adult experiences. "I have had the rare experience of having in my own life passed through all the stages of American development," he wrote.)

Baker's mother died when he was thirteen. He supplemented his public-school education by reading in his parents' well-stocked library and was sufficiently advanced to be accepted into Michigan Agricultural College (later Michigan State University) in 1885 at the age of fifteen. He majored in the sciences, edited the school newspaper, and took courses in journalism. Upon graduation in 1889, he returned to St. Croix Falls to work in his father's land office. In January 1892 Baker enrolled in the University of Michigan law school, but dropped out after a few months to take a job as a reporter with the *Chicago News-Record.*

Baker's six years with the *News-Record* transformed him into an incisive social critic and an ardent social reformer. Shocked by the devastation that characterized the depression of 1893–1897, he later wrote that he was appalled by the "dizzying haste" with which the grandeur of the 1893 Columbian Exposition in Chicago gave way to "another pageant, somber and threatening" and "marked by unprecedented extremes of poverty, unemployment, unrest." He professed dismay at the spectacle of such enormous "human downfall after the magnificence and prodigality of the World's Fair that had so recently closed its doors" (*American Chronicle*). Assigned to cover the march of the unemployed led by Jacob Coxey from Massilon, Ohio, to Washington, D.C., in spring 1894 to demand federally funded public-works projects, Baker was converted to an understanding "that there could have been no such demonstration in a civilized country unless there was profound and deep-seated distress, disorganization, unrest, unhappiness behind it—and that the public would not be cheering the army and feeding it voluntarily without a recognition, however vague, that the conditions in the country warranted some such explosion" (*American Chronicle*). During that same period, Baker was shaken by the assassination of Chicago mayor Carter H. Harrison, the use of federal troops to break the Pullman Strike and the American Railway Union, and the vituperation heaped upon Illinois governor John Peter Altgeld for his pardoning of three anarchists convicted of the Haymarket bombing. He learned to approach a story directly, to write accurately and clearly, and to become, in his own words, "a special and editorial writer." Baker also began writing independently for periodicals, particularly *McClure's Magazine*. In 1896 he married Jessie Irene Beal, the daughter of a college botany professor, a union that eventually produced four children.

In 1898 Baker left Chicago for New York to join the staff of *McClure's Magazine*, which was in the vanguard of a new school of journalism that stressed social reality, accurate reporting, and human interest. As director of the syndication department, he wrote articles on scientific subjects that demonstrated his capacity for making such topics intelligible to a lay readership. In 1899 he synthesized his thoughts into his first book, *The Boy's Book of Inventions: Stories of the Wonders of Modern Science*. Over the next few years Baker turned out a steady stream of articles on subjects ranging from the Spanish-American War and American imperialism to sketches of such prominent figures as J. Pierpont Morgan and Roosevelt. He traveled widely, both in the United States and abroad, wrote numerous freelance articles in addition to those published in *McClure's*, and published three books: *Our New Prosperity* (1900), a study of the economic recovery from the depression of the 1890s; *Seen in Germany* (1901), a series of articles written during his travels in that country; and *Boys' Second Book of Inventions* (1903), another compilation of his writings on scientific topics. In recognition of his growing renown as a contributor to popular magazines,

Baker was invited to the White House for a conversation with Roosevelt on various social problems. At first captivated by Roosevelt's charismatic personality, Baker later became increasingly disenchanted with the president's lack of action on many of the issues the two discussed.

In 1903 Baker combined with Lincoln Steffens, Ida Tarbell, and other staff members at *McClure's* in organizing what quickly became a nationwide movement to expose antisocial behavior by business trusts, railroads, and political machines. The popularity of this engaged investigative journalism spread rapidly and was imitated by scores of other journalists, who were eventually stigmatized as "muckrakers" by Roosevelt. Baker's resentment over that negative label was one of the primary reasons for his disillusionment with the president, whom he had initially admired and respected.

As investigative journalists, the muckrakers rarely proposed solutions to the social evils that they encountered, but instead followed the belief that a thorough explication would rouse their readership to initiate reforms. As a moderate muckraker, Baker produced hard-hitting but judicious articles on the use of violence against nonstriking coal miners, employer abuse in the New York City garment industry, the excesses of trade unionism, the necessity of regulating railroad monopolies, and various nefarious practices of American politics. In 1910 he stirred up considerable controversy with the publication of *The Spiritual Unrest,* a critical investigation of the country's religious life.

After traveling extensively in the jim crow South in 1907, Baker wrote a series of articles on race relations in the United States that formed the basis for *Following the Color Line*. Although Baker was fiercely denounced for his graphic discussion of lynching, segregation, disfranchisement, poverty, and blatant discrimination, most modern-day critics have hailed the book for its balanced approach, comprehensive coverage, and penetrating insights. Actually Baker warmed to his task by researching and writing a series of articles on race relations in specific American locales and publishing them in various journals. One of these research trips took Baker to Georgia where he met with Joel Chandler Harris, creator of the "Uncle Remus" stories, who introduced him to several "ancient Negroes" who recounted tales of the violence that accompanied the end of Reconstruction, the disfranchisement of black voters, and the imposition of the jim crow system of legal segregation. Although Baker sometimes described the violence in graphic terms, he eventually acquiesced in the policy defined by *American Magazine* editor John S. Phillips: "For the sake of effect we must keep the interest and friendliness of southern readers. After all, they

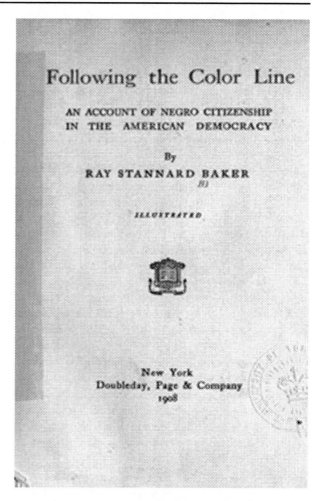

Frontispiece and title page for Baker's report on race relations in the South (Robarts Research Library, University of Toronto)

are the people whom we wish to reach and enlighten" (*American Chronicle*). Such an outlook squared well with Baker's own temperament and ideological outlook, which was essentially that of well-meaning Southern moderates and Northern philanthropists who sponsored the annual Conferences for Southern Education; he clearly preferred the strategy and tactics of Booker T. Washington over those of W. E. B. Du Bois.

Although Baker originally intended to limit his investigations to just a few Southern states, he eventually visited most of the states of the Confederacy, about a dozen large Northern cities, and several small communities just north of the Ohio River, between October 1906 and September 1908. Baker immersed himself in his subject matter—traveling, reading, collecting statistics, filling his notebooks with information and impressions, and retiring to East Lansing, Michigan, to ponder and compose. By the latter date, Baker had crafted more than a dozen substantial magazine articles, most of which were published individually. Sensing that he

was producing more than investigative journalism, Baker assured his father that he was "going to be able to do a real public service with these articles" (*Michigan Library Bulletin*). In the meantime, Baker signed a contract with Walter Hines Page of Doubleday, Page, and Company to produce a book-length synthesis of the various magazine articles. The result was a volume that is occasionally episodic and lacking in unity and focus but which deeply engages the reader and marries Baker's skills and insights as a historian and sociologist to those as a journalist. Although frequently superficial by modern-day standards, the book is the first to look at race relations in a national context, to give a clear description of how complex social relations contribute to racial violence, to reveal the actual dynamics of a lynch mob, to appraise the character of the Great Migration of African Americans to Northern cities, and to give a sympathetic account of Negro town life. True to the muckraker's code, however, Baker proffers no solutions beyond "time, growth, education, religion, thought"; "a gradual substitution of understanding and sympathy for blind repulsion and hatred" *(Following the Color Line)*. With all of its limitations, *Following the Color Line* was a pioneering study of the dynamics of race relations in the United States. Sociologist Rupert B. Vance described it as "the best account of race relations in the South during the period—one that reads like field notes for the future historian."

In 1906, Baker, Steffens, Tarbell, Phillips, and several other journalists collaborated on the purchase of *American Magazine,* declaring their intentions to publish material reflecting their own tastes that would be more constructive and less sensational than the norm at *McClure's.* They pledged that *American Magazine* would be "wholesome, hopeful, stimulating, uplifting, and . . . have a human interest on every page" *(American Chronicle).* The enterprise enjoyed substantial readership under Baker's editorship from 1906 until he resigned that post in 1915. By that point in his career, he had published more than two hundred articles on a variety of topics.

During the years of his editorship of *American Magazine* Baker began to write novels under the pseudonym of David Grayson. Grayson was actually his alter ego—a farmer-philosopher who extolled the virtues of rural and small-town life in contrast to the stark reality of the urban life in which Baker now resided. The nine Grayson novels, written between 1907 and 1942, enabled Baker to express the nostalgia he felt for his boyhood days in St. Croix Falls, Wisconsin, as well as the Emersonian idealism that he was at great pains to preserve in spite of constant exposure to the skepticism and cynicism that permeated the journalistic profession. He later confessed that his Grayson books "have been my life, rather than my work" *(American Chronicle).* The constant stream of letters that he received from readers convinced him that he was not alone in his search for a more idyllic and spiritually fulfilling existence. He moved his family to Amherst, Massachusetts, in 1910, establishing a rural retreat for the remainder of his life.

At the same time, he became increasingly involved in the reform politics of the Progressive Era, even flirting for a while with socialism. More comfortable with mainstream progressivism, Baker lauded Roosevelt, the Republican insurgents who revolted against President William Howard Taft and the "standpatters" in Congress, and Senator La Follette and his National Progressive Republican League in 1911. In the presidential election of 1912, he reluctantly voted for Democrat Wilson but was persuaded by the new president's successful New Freedom program and embraced it with enthusiasm. After reading Baker's account of his first meeting with Wilson in 1913, historian G. W. Johnson pronounced it to be "the story of a man who

found a leader, who devoted his whole life to them and burned himself out in their service." (Even so, Baker found it difficult to reconcile Wilson's progressivism with his administration's segregationist policies in the District of Columbia and the federal government.) When the war broke out in Europe in 1914, Baker came to see Wilson as the only hope for peace in the world. Grateful for Baker's support, the president appointed him a special agent of the State Department in Great Britain, France, and Italy in 1918. The following year, he was made director of the American delegation's press bureau at the Paris Peace Conference, enabling him to produce a steady flow of positive publicity for Wilson's Fourteen Points and League of Nations. When the conference ended in the spring of 1919, Baker hastily put together *What Wilson Did at Paris,* a tribute to what Baker believed to be the successful completion of his idol's labors. Three years later, he published the much more detailed three-volume *Woodrow Wilson and World Settlement,* in which Wilson emerges as a tragic leader repudiated by the very people whose prosperity and security he worked so diligently to guarantee and who literally sacrificed his life for that cause. Baker and historian William E. Dodd edited the six-volume *The Public Papers of Woodrow Wilson,* providing ready access to a well-organized compendium of the late president's official writings. For all of his fixation on Wilson, however, Baker still managed to turn out *The New Industrial Unrest: Reasons and Remedies* (1920), a cogent study of the labor-management strife that rocked American society at the conclusion of the war. He also wrote numerous newspaper and magazine articles and published two new books under his pseudonym Grayson: *Great Possessions: A New Series of Adventures* (1917) and *Adventures in Understanding* (1925).

For the next fifteen years, from 1925 to 1940, Baker was almost entirely consumed with the task of immortalizing Wilson in an eight-volume biography, complete with documents. Wilson himself had given Baker access to his papers before he left the White House in 1921, and in 1925 Edith Wilson selected him to write her husband's authorized biography. Baker meticulously plowed through the reams of the former president's personal papers, while interviewing many of Wilson's family members and associates and drafting detailed memoranda. He published the first two volumes of *Woodrow Wilson: Life and Letters* in 1927, and the remaining six were completed over the next twelve years. Even at that, Baker concluded the work with the armistice of 1918. Although he had already provided some coverage of the Paris Peace Conference and its aftermath, Baker made no effort to cover the tragic years of 1919 to 1924 when Wilson was in a constant state of physical and mental decline. The early volumes were enthusiastically received by critics and the public alike, but each succeeding volume encountered more criticism, owing in large measure to the fact that Wilson's reputation was being seriously undermined by the work of a new generation of revisionist historians who regarded American involvement in World War I as a mistake and blamed Wilson for his alleged inability to bring about an equitable peace and prevent a future war, which was clearly looming by the late 1930s. In spite of that, Baker received the Pulitzer Prize for biography in 1940, with World War II already under way.

Despite his seeming immersion in *Life and Letters,* Baker managed to produce three more volumes in the Grayson series: *Adventures in Solitude* (1931), *The Countrymen's Year* (1936), and *Under My Elm: Country Discoveries and Reflections* (1942). During the early 1940s, he published the two volumes of his autobiography: *Native American* and *American Chronicle.* Baker increasingly retreated to his home in Amherst where he spent hours working in the garden. During the winter of 1943–1944, he and his wife resided in Hollywood, where he served as a consultant on Darryl F. Zanuck's major motion picture *Wilson* (1944). Baker died in Amherst on 12 July 1946.

During the half century since his death, Ray Stannard Baker has all but disappeared from the history books, despite the many achievements of his long career. Along with Tarbell, Steffens, and a handful of others, he was a founder of investigative journalism. His dedication to the principle that the public will do what is right and necessary if properly informed is a cornerstone of democracy; he realized that "knowledge is power" long before anyone coined the phrase. For millions of mainstream white Americans of the day, Baker's *Following the Color Line* was their first exposure, from a source they could not easily dismiss, to the horrors of segregation, disfranchisement, and anti-Negro violence. Although his purported remedy of "time, growth, education, religion, thought" seems passive and ineffectual to modern-day activists, it remains basic to any permanent erasure of the color line. His David Grayson books, although bordering at times on nostalgia and wishful thinking, can be read also as an indirect critique of urban industrial society and as the foundation of a humanistic philosophy with which to counter

its excesses. Finally, his pioneering work on Wilson, although too uncritical and panegyrical, continues to be the best contemporary insight into Wilson's mind-set and provides scholars with an ideal starting point for additional research.

References:

Robert C. Bannister Jr., *Ray Stannard Baker: The Mind and Thought of a Progressive* (New Haven, Conn.: Yale University Press, 1966);

John G. Brooks, "Still the Muckrake," *Independent,* 60 (1906): 1030–1032;

David M. Chalmers, "Ray Stannard Baker's Search for Reform," *Journal of the History of Ideas,* 19 (1958): 422–424;

Bartlett C. Jones, "Ray Stannard Baker and the Progressive Dilemma," *Emory University Quarterly,* 17 (1961): 169–175;

Michael Kammen, *A Time to Every Purpose: The Four Seasons in American Culture* (Chapel Hill: University of North Carolina Press, 2004);

Peter Lyon, *Success Story: The Life and Times of S. S. McClure* (New York: Scribners, 1963);

"Ray Stannard Baker," *Michigan Library Bulletin,* 16 (1925): 30–33;

Daniel T. Rodgers, *Atlantic Crossings: Social Politics in a Progressive Age* (Cambridge, Mass.: Belknap Press of Harvard University Press, 1998);

John E. Semonche, *Ray Stannard Baker: A Quest for Democracy in Modern America, 1870–1918* (Chapel Hill: University of North Carolina Press, 1969);

Herbert Shapiro, "The Muckrakers and the Negroes," *Phylon,* 31 (1970): 76–88;

Harry H. Stein, "American Muckraking of Technology since 1900," *Journalism Quarterly,* 67 (1990): 401–409;

Harold S. Wilson, *McClure's Magazine and the Muckrakers* (Princeton, N.J.: Princeton University Press, 1970).

Papers:

The major collection of Ray Stannard Baker's papers are in the Library of Congress. There are also important collections at the Jones Library, Amherst, Massachusetts, and at Selley G. Mudd Library, Princeton University.

Roger Baldwin

(21 January 1884 – 26 August 1981)

Stephen E. Randoll
Saint Louis University

BOOKS: *Juvenile Courts and Probation,* by Bernard Flexner and Baldwin (New York: Century, 1914; London: Grant Richards, 1915);

Have You Free Speech? (New York: Methodist Federation for Social Service, 1923);

Liberty Under the Soviets (New York: Vanguard, 1928);

Should Alien Communists Be Deported for Their Opinions? Speech in Debate with Hamilton Fish, Jr., before the Boston Foreign Policy Association, March 4, 1931 (New York: American Civil Liberties Union, 1931);

Civil Liberties and Industrial Conflict, by Baldwin and Clarence B. Randall (Cambridge: Harvard University Press, 1938);

Democracy in Trade Unions, a Survey, with a Program of Action (New York: American Civil Liberties Union, 1943);

Human Rights, World Declaration and American Practice (New York: Public Affairs Committee, 1950);

Universal Civil Rights, What They Mean and How to Get Them (New York: American Civil Liberties Union, 1950);

The Prospects for Freedom (New York: American Ethical Union, 1952);

Universal Rights and American Practice (New York: American Civil Liberties Union, 1959);

John Haynes Holmes–Preacher and Prophet 1879–1964 (Boston, 1964);

Memorandum on the Origins of the ACLU (New York: American Civil Liberties Union, 1973).

OTHER: *The Truth About the I.W.W.,* edited by Baldwin (New York: National Civil Liberties Bureau, 1918);

A Year's Fight for Free Speech: The Work of the American Civil Liberties Union from Sept. 1921, to Jan. 1923 (New York: American Civil Liberties Union, 1923), prefatory note by Baldwin;

International Committee for Political Prisoners, *Letters from Russian Prisons: Consisting of Reprints of Documents by Political Prisoners in Soviet Prisons, Prison Camps and Exile, and Reprints of Affidavits Concerning Political Persecution in Soviet Russia, Official Statements by Soviet Authorities, Excerpts from Soviet Laws Pertaining to Civil Liberties, and Other Documents* (New York: A. & C. Boni, 1925; London: C. W. Daniel, 1925), introduction by Baldwin;

Kropotkin's Revolutionary Pamphlets: A Collection of Writings by Peter Kropotkin, edited, with an introduction, biographical sketch, and notes by Baldwin (New York: Vanguard, 1925);

"The Myth of Law and Order," in *Behold America!* edited by Samuel D. Schmalhausen (New York: Farrar & Rinehart, 1931);

Walter Nelles, *A Liberal in Wartime: The Education of Albert DeSilver* (New York: Norton, 1940), introduction by Baldwin;

"National Defense and the Restriction of Individual Liberties" by Baldwin, Robert E. Cushman, Edgar B. Tolman, and Adlai Stevenson, in *The Law School Conferences on Public Law,* 3–4 (Chicago: University of Chicago Press, 1940);

"Liberalism and the United Front," in *Whose Revolution? A Study of the Future Course of Liberalism in the United States,* edited by Irving DeWitt Talmadge (New York: Howell, Soskin, 1941);

The Rights of Man are Worth Defending (New York City: League for Adult Education, 1942), includes articles by Baldwin;

"American Liberties, 1947–1948," in *Art and Action: Tenth Anniversary Issue* (New York: Twice A Year Press, 1948);

A New Slavery: Forced Labor: The Communist Betrayal of Human Rights, edited by Baldwin (New York: Oceana, 1953);

"As the Executive Director," in *Pulse of Freedom: American Liberties, 1920–1970,* edited by Alan Reitman (New York: New American Library, 1976).

SELECTED PERIODICAL PUBLICATIONS–UNCOLLECTED: "Statistics Relating to Juvenile Delinquents," in *Proceedings of the National Conference*

Roger Baldwin, 1934 (Robert C. Cottrell, Roger Nash Baldwin and the American Civil Liberties Union, *2000; Thomas Cooper Library, University of South Carolina)*

of Charities and Corrections (Ft. Wayne, Ind.: Archer, 1910);

"The Saint Louis Pageant and Masque: Its Civic Meaning," *Survey,* 32 (11 April 1914): 52–53;

"St. Louis' Successful Fight for a Modern Charter," *National Municipal Review,* 3 (October 1914): 720–721, 724;

"The Use of Municipal Ownership to Abolish Trans-Mississippi Freight and Passenger Tolls," *National Municipal Review,* 4 (July 1915): 468–472;

"Conscience at the Bar," *Survey,* 41 (November 1918): 253;

"An Industrial Program After The War," *Proceedings of the National Conference of Social Work,* 45 (1918): 426–429;

"Social Work and Radical Economic Movements," *Proceedings of the National Conference of Social Work,* 45 (1918): 396–398;

"Freedom of Opinion," *Socialist Review,* 9 (August 1920): 115;

"The Immorality of Social Work," *World Tomorrow,* 5 (February 1922): 44–45;

"How Shall We Escape Private Property?" *World Tomorrow,* 5 (April 1922): 109–110;

"Where Are the Prewar Radicals?" *Survey,* 55 (1 February 1926): 560;

"While California's Governor Deliberates," *Unity,* 12 August 1929, pp. 329–330;

"Free Speech for Nazis?" *World Tomorrow,* 16 (November 1933): 613;

"Freedom in the U.S.A. and the U.S.S.R." *Soviet Russia Today,* 3 (September 1934): 11;

"Civil Liberties Comprise," *Social Work Year Book,* 5 (1939): 76–77;

"Conscience Under the Draft," *Nation* (9 August 1941): 114–116;

"Conscientious Objectors," *Nation* (12 October 1941): 326–328;

"Roger Baldwin Reviews the Japanese Evacuation Case," *Open Forum,* 19 (15 August 1942): 1–2;

"Japanese Americans and the Law," *Asia,* 42 (September 1942): 518–519;

"The Japanese Americans in Wartime," *American Mercury* (December 1944): 664–670;

"Of All the Literature on Gandhi," *Voice of India* (June 1946): 309;

"Reds and Rights," *Progressive,* 4 (June 1948): 5–6;

"Communist Conspirators and the Bill of Rights," *Progressive,* 5 (April 1949): 14;

"Norman Thomas: A Combative Life," *New Republic* (13 January 1968): 11–12;

"Recollections of a Life in Civil Liberties–I," *Civil Liberties Review,* 1 (Spring 1975): 39–63;

"Recollections of a Life in Civil Liberties–II: Russia, Communism, and United Fronts, 1920–1940," *Civil Liberties Review,* 2 (Fall 1975): 10–40;

"The ACLU and the FBI: 'They Never Stopped Watching Us,'" by Baldwin and Alan Westin, *Civil Liberties Review,* 4 (November–December 1977): 17–25.

Roger Baldwin is best known as the founder and longtime director of the American Civil Liberties Union. A Harvard graduate from an upper-class Boston family during the Progressive Era, Baldwin was influenced by the reform impulses of the day. He moved to St. Louis, started the Washington University sociology department, and became involved in juvenile reform work. During World War I, appalled at the restrictions on free speech imposed by the Wilson administration, Baldwin became director of the National Civil Liberties Bureau (NCLB), part of the American Union Against Militarism. After the war the NCLB became the American Civil Liberties Union (ACLU) with Baldwin as its director. In the two decades that followed Baldwin became more radical and involved the ACLU in liberal and left-wing causes, such as the Scopes Trial and the Sacco and Vanzetti trials. As he became disillusioned with communism after the purges in the Soviet Union in the late 1930s, Baldwin's criticisms of the Roosevelt administration during World War II were more muted than his previous criticisms of the Wilson administration. After the war Baldwin was eased out as ACLU director, but he continued to support international civil liberties causes actively, including assisting General Douglas MacArthur with the creation of the postwar Japanese constitution. Toward the end of his life Baldwin garnered numerous awards for his long-standing support of civil liberties, including the Presidential Medal of Freedom. He died at the age of ninety-seven, active almost to the very end.

Roger Nash Baldwin was born on 21 January 1884, the first of seven children of Frank Baldwin and Lucy Nash. The Baldwins and the Nashes were prominent Massachusetts families. Baldwin grew up with a sense of class consciousness in a family that associated only with the right sort of people. This upbringing also instilled a strong sense of noblesse oblige. He was raised in the Unitarian church and participated in its "Lend-a-Hand Society." His Boston social circle appreciated freethinkers, so Baldwin grew up admiring Henry David Thoreau, Ralph Waldo Emerson, John Brown, and Robert G. Ingersoll, among others. Baldwin developed an affinity for the rebel, the heretic, and the radical, and he identified himself as an aristocratic radical from an early age. This dualism, typically Bostonian, is inherently contradictory, a pattern characteristic of Baldwin throughout his life.

Baldwin graduated from Harvard in 1905. He was elected to the Institute of 1770 as a sophomore and joined the Memorial Society, the Signet, and Hasty Pudding. Involvement in reform efforts during the Progressive Era was quite respectable at Harvard, and Baldwin volunteered to teach at the Cambridge Social Union, which offered adult-education classes for workers. Baldwin gave piano lessons and lectures the first year. He became known for organizational skills; the next year he took charge of recruiting other students to serve as instructors. He also helped organize the Harvard Entertainment Troupers, who gave amateur performances for the poor in Boston. In his third year at Harvard, he joined an anthropological expedition to the American Southwest. The first stop was the 1904 St. Louis World's Fair, then on to New Mexico and Arizona, covering six hundred miles on horseback. Graduating in three years, Baldwin then began graduate studies in anthropology and philosophy, completing what he considered a pedestrian master's thesis in 1905.

After he left Harvard, Baldwin toured Europe with his mother and siblings. Upon completion of the trip, his parents separated but did not divorce. The family difficulties influenced Baldwin's next move. Louis Brandeis, then a prominent attorney, discussed a career in public service with Baldwin, and E. M. Grossman, a lawyer and Harvard alumnus, offered Baldwin a dual job with duties that included taking charge of a settlement house in St. Louis and establishing a department of sociology at Washington University. Baldwin accepted the position although he lacked any formal training in sociology. So he took a course in sociology the summer of 1906 at Harvard, became impressed with the work of Herbert Spencer, and that September headed off to St. Louis. Characteristically, Baldwin refused a full salary, working for expenses only.

In St. Louis, Baldwin again demonstrated his skill at creating and running organizations. His neighborhood work often brought him to the St. Louis Juvenile Court on behalf of the boys in his district. Judge George H. Williams, who looked for means of improving the treatment of delinquent and neglected children, recruited Baldwin as first chief probation officer for the juvenile court; another judge once insisted that he temporarily take custody of two children whose mothers were prostitutes and had abandoned them at an orphanage. Between meeting fellow radicals such as William Reedy, Emma Goldman, Frank and Kate O'Hare, and Anna Louise Strong (to whom he was briefly engaged) and battling against the childhood diseases that raged unchecked among the underprivileged populations he served, Baldwin managed to put together a professional staff and worked to coordinate the various child-welfare agencies in the city. This job took up so much of his time that Baldwin resigned his position at Washington University in 1909. In 1910 the

National Conference of Charities and Correction met in St. Louis. The statistics session featured Florence Kelley, Julia C. Lathrop, and Baldwin. His speech, "Statistics Relating to Juvenile Delinquents," contended that only those who threatened to become "habitual offenders" or those without the "capacity for normal moral conduct" should be categorized as delinquents ("Statistics," quoted in Cottrell biography).

Also in 1910 Baldwin became secretary of the Civic League, a good-government organization in St. Louis. Once again Baldwin refused a full salary for the position and turned down more-lucrative positions back East, preferring the opportunity to work toward reform in St. Louis. At this time Baldwin was a committed progressive, convinced reform could bring about "a pretty good society" (Lash interview, quoted in Cottrell, p. 37). The same year Baldwin and his close friend Gus Tuckerman, a former Episcopal priest, founded the St. Louis City Club. The club hosted lunches for businessmen and professionals and brought in outside speakers on important topics of the day. Baldwin helped bring in Theodore Roosevelt, William Howard Taft, Woodrow Wilson, and more-controversial speakers such as British suffragist leader Sylvia Pankhurst. In 1912 Baldwin learned the police had prevented birth-control advocate Margaret Sanger from speaking at a private hall. Baldwin persuaded her to hold her meeting in front of the hall as a protest, and he offered to chair the proceedings himself. Baldwin introduced Sanger to a small crowd of onlookers and a larger crowd of police. She engaged in her protest, and Baldwin found his first free-speech meeting "an exhilarating success as a matter of principle" (quoted in Cottrell, p. 43).

The year 1914 was eventful for Baldwin, one that changed him forever. At first he continued along the path he had chosen. With Louisville attorney Bernard Flexner, who had discussed juvenile justice at the 1910 National Charities and Correction conference, Baldwin collaborated on a textbook they published in 1914, *Juvenile Courts and Probation*. The two had sent out a lengthy questionnaire to major national figures in the field of juvenile justice, asking about effective treatments covering a variety of offenses both major and minor. Based in part on the responses, the authors contended that juvenile justice had to focus on making the child as good a member of society as possible. Punishment and probation had to be handled differently, and all social agencies' efforts had to emphasize providing "favorable influences" enabling the child "to maintain normal habits of life" (quoted in Cottrell, p. 33). The textbook came to be recommended by leading court authorities.

Baldwin helped push for and pass a new progressive city charter in 1914. Once St. Louis voters took the

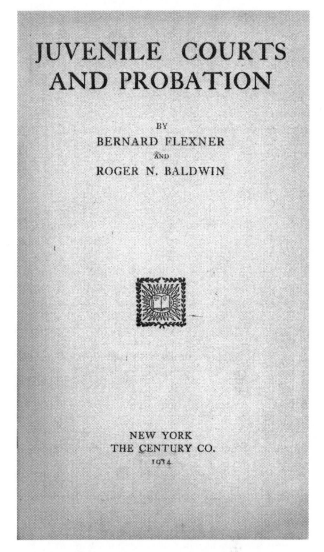

JUVENILE COURTS AND PROBATION

BY
BERNARD FLEXNER
AND
ROGER N. BALDWIN

NEW YORK
THE CENTURY CO.
1914

Title page for Baldwin's first book, co-authored with a Louisville attorney (Thomas Cooper Library, University of South Carolina)

initiative, however, the situation turned out quite differently than he expected. White neighborhood associations pushed for measures mandating segregated housing. That election took place in February 1916, with Baldwin leading the opposition. The voters passed the measure by almost three to one. Baldwin helped bring a test case in federal court, and a permanent injunction halted the measure. Private restrictive covenants to bring about residential segregation persisted, in spite of court rulings. The contest had its effect on Baldwin as well. He abandoned what he came to see as simple ideas about democracy and began looking to the courts to check "the prejudices of the majority" (quoted in Cottrell).

The war brought out Baldwin's pacifism and led him in a more radical direction. Even before the United

States entered the war in February 1917, Baldwin resigned all his offices in St. Louis and volunteered his services to the American Union Against Militarism (AUAM). Although he had previously turned down the position of secretary of the organization, assumed by radical feminist Crystal Eastman Fuller, when she became too ill to work, Baldwin accepted the post for the duration of the war and moved to New York, where the organization had its headquarters. When the United States entered the war in April 1917, AUAM became concerned about protecting the rights of conscientious objectors and safeguarding the civil liberties of those who opposed Wilson's policies. The modern civil-liberties movement stems from the actions of AUAM in attempting to safeguard civil liberties guaranteed by the Bill of Rights from state and federal action. The upper- and upper-middle-class background of the people in AUAM ensured that the public took the movement seriously, in part because its socially prominent members had access to high-ranking government officials, at least initially.

On 1 July 1917 AUAM announced the formation of a Civil Liberties Bureau (CLB) to serve as a clearinghouse for information pertaining to conscientious objectors, with Baldwin as its director. Baldwin sought to maintain his connections with government officials while at the same time pushing CLB to do more than simply distribute information among conscientious objectors. Baldwin began to advocate conscientious objection. Politically astute, he further urged that nonsocialists be prominent at conventions and made an appeal to patriotism to defuse the opposition. Baldwin wrote a letter to the *St. Louis Star,* published on 23 August 1917, noting how radical labor organizations wanted to end the fighting. He saw this as not just an antiwar stance, but even more that a "new internationalism will be established on a radical democratic basis" (Volume 3, ACLU papers; quoted in Cottrell). Baldwin increasingly saw Progressivism as inadequate and believed that the growth of democracy required more-radical structural change. Even as his attraction to radicalism grew, however, he still desired to maintain his connections to the Wilson administration.

On 1 October 1917 the civil liberties group formally separated from AUAM and soon took the name the National Civil Liberties Bureau (NCLB). The bureau took its cases from incidents reported by both the mainstream and the radical press and from individual correspondents' complaints. The board solicited legal counsel for each court case, publicized the issues, battled government officials, and helped raise defense funds. When the government prosecuted the International Workers of the World (IWW, also known as the Wobblies), the NCLB responded in April 1918 with a document titled *The Truth About the I.W.W.,* edited by Baldwin. Baldwin pointed out that the Wobblies were usually the objects, not the instigators, of violent attacks, and that the conspiracy trial of Wobbly leaders should be terminated because it could establish no overt acts of sedition. The NCLB and Baldwin in particular had already been under federal surveillance for some time, but then Baldwin and the organization began to offer more substantial support to IWW, providing office space for its legal defense team and intervening in its conflict with the postal authorities. The attention they drew from military intelligence and the Justice Department began then to intensify. On 31 August 1918 federal agents and members of the "American Protective League" (a self-appointed group of interested citizens with no federal authority) raided NCLB's office at the same time that the judge handed down sentences in the IWW case. On 12 September 1918 Baldwin refused to report for his physical as required under the Selective Service Act. He was arrested and kept in the Tombs, New York's old city jail, but, he later reported, was treated very well. Appearing before the court, Baldwin made a lengthy opening statement explaining his pacifism and his opposition to conscription. The *Nation* and the *Survey* published copies of his speech. On 30 October Baldwin was convicted of violating the Selective Service Act and sentenced to one year in prison, with credit for the time he had already spent in jail.

Moved to the Essex County Jail in Newark, New Jersey, Baldwin immediately began to organize his fellow prisoners. Having worked among the lower classes before, he won their friendship by working in the kitchens without complaint; at the same time, his upper-class manners invariably elicited deference from all who met him (except for his alcoholic boss, Bridget). He treated the Justice Department agent assigned to his case with unfailing kindness and humor. In May 1919, however, he was moved to the county prison in Caldwell, because the sheriff complained that he was spoiling the prisoners and converting them to socialism.

Shortly after his release from prison in July 1919, Baldwin married Madeleine Zabriskie Doty on 8 August. They had been engaged at the time of his trial, having known each other since 1913. She was thirty-nine, a journalist, lawyer, prison reformer, and feminist more famous at that time than Baldwin for her work with the Women's Peace Party and the Congress of the Women's International League for Peace and Freedom. Their combined families, who had been very supportive during Baldwin's prison term, joined him to meet her at the dock when she returned from Europe a week after his release. After a Greenwich Village–style ceremony performed by Norman Thomas, in which the couple eschewed the customary vows of fidelity and did not exchange rings, Baldwin went off to the Midwest, joining IWW and taking a series of laboring jobs for a few months to get a sense of what it was like to be a workingman. Bill Haywood, who was out on bail and knew Baldwin had worked in the kitchens in prison, urged him not to apply for jobs at any work camps where IWW members were employed. "Our boys like to eat good," he said (quoted in Cottrell).

Over the summer of 1919 twenty-six race riots had taken place in nineteen American cities. Antiradical investigations were heightened when J. Edgar Hoover established the Department of Justice General Intelligence Division. Hoover soon had index cards on 200,000 individuals. In November the Bureau of Investigation began the Palmer Raids (named for Attorney General A. Mitchell Palmer), and in December the Justice Department deported 249 aliens, including Goldman and Alexander Berkman. Once back in New York, Baldwin resumed his position as director of the NCLB. He was instrumental in renaming the NCLB the American Civil Liberties Union (ACLU). The change took place on 20 January 1920. The organization declared "all thought on matters of public concern should be freely expressed, without interference. Orderly social progress is promoted by unrestricted freedom of opinion" (quoted in Lamson).

The ACLU, Baldwin believed, would highlight civil liberties on a national basis. Ad hoc groups had periodically championed freedom of speech and press, but only Theodore Schroeder's Free Speech League, formed in 1902, had specifically defended free speech. Baldwin claimed Schroeder was too eccentric to work with and never invited him to join the ACLU. Baldwin was motivated in part by a desire to maintain leadership of the new organization. He included labor leaders and prowar liberals in the ACLU, along with holdovers from the NCLB. Its top levels hailed overwhelmingly from the American upper and middle classes. The activists were also few in number. Baldwin believed in keeping the organization small, limiting it to handpicked true believers whom he felt would best serve the cause of civil liberties.

Earlier, with the NCLB, Baldwin had worked behind the scenes. As ACLU director, he led aggressively, publicizing civil liberties and the new organization. He delivered public addresses and traveled widely. His first trip produced an article in the *Socialist Review* in August 1920 in which Baldwin argued that freedom of speech and of the press were under attack in the United States. The government sought to disable organized labor through the suppression of civil liberties. Baldwin felt that workers and farmers needed enough power to preserve their rights. They could not rely on the law for protection, he declared, because "legal rights are hollow

shams without the political and economic power to enforce them" (quoted in Cottrell). Merely invoking the Bill of Rights in a court or a legislature had proved insufficient to guarantee that people would not be arrested or imprisoned for criticizing the social order, promoting alternative arrangements, or noting corruption in government. People had to have the power to assert and defend their right to say and publish whatever they thought. Against concerted attacks by business against labor, this would not be easy. The first ACLU annual report suggested only radicals, the most militant farmers and workers, and a few liberals were "conscious of this condition and capable of outspoken resistance to it." Social progress required untrammeled freedom of opinion. The ACLU, therefore, made no distinction as to whose liberties it would defend. Even so, the report asserted that economic and political power was central to maintaining everyone's rights.

In the 1920s, while devoting the bulk of his time to the ACLU, Baldwin became involved in other organizations that connected him to the activities of a host of radical and reform groups. In 1921 he joined the board of the American Fund for Public Service, known as the Garland Fund. While on the board, Baldwin began to have misgivings about American communists' willingness to take direction from the party, rather than to act independently. Baldwin tried to present the Left as a united front, evoking the heterodox days before World War I. The communists continually undermined such efforts, and Baldwin found this of increasing concern. Still, in the April 1922 issue of *World Tomorrow,* Baldwin embraced the theory of communism as the ultimate goal for society. Even as Baldwin's own views moved further left, the ACLU under his leadership adopted an expansive view of civil liberties, defending the rights of anyone and any political perspective.

In fall 1922 Baldwin took part in the formation of the Labor Defense Council (LDC) as a member of its provisional national committee. By 1925 he had grown disillusioned with the group. It seemed to him that the LDC did not represent a united front of Wobblies, socialists, and anarchists; instead, the communist Workers' Party dominated the council. Baldwin also developed doubts about the communist stance toward civil liberties. When Edward Wentworth, the LDC chairman, admitted to Baldwin that he viewed the LDC as an adjunct of the party, Baldwin submitted his resignation from the organization. This action did not diminish his association with the Left or his belief that capitalism needed transformation to achieve its much-vaunted role as the best protector of democracy. Rather, he felt the party's dismissal of civil liberties would play into the hands of the opposition. He also disliked the pretense of independence. He was not opposed to communists

Roger Baldwin at an antiwar rally, Columbia University, 22 April 1935 (Robert C. Cottrell, Roger Nash Baldwin and the American Civil Liberties Union, *2000; Thomas Cooper Library, University of South Carolina)*

heading an agency for the defense of all parties; he just felt that such an organization should not pretend to be independent and nonpartisan.

In addition to his work with the ACLU, Baldwin became involved in promoting civil liberties and supporting workers' movements worldwide. He helped to establish the International Committee for Political Prisoners and the American League for India's Freedom. Through his connection with Haywood, who had fled to the Soviet Union, he became involved in planning the Kuzbas Autonomous Industrial Colony in the Ural Mountains (1922–1926). Kuzbas was the party leadership's concession to noncommunist leftists, mostly IWW members; the colony survived four years before being terminated from above. Like many leftists of his time, Baldwin tried to recognize the accomplishments of the fledgling social order even as he found himself repeatedly in conflict with communists.

The ACLU director believed he had demonstrated his own organization's political independence when he visited Paterson, New Jersey, where a walkout by eight thousand workers in the Associated Silk Workers had taken place late in 1924. Baldwin orchestrated a

public protest of the workers at city hall, which the police broke up. The publicity nonetheless resulted in management's agreement to meet the union's demands as well as prompting indictments of Baldwin and nine union leaders. They were convicted, but the New Jersey Court of Errors and Appeals overturned the convictions on appeal. Justice Samuel Kalisch wrote that he doubted that the gathering could have made a reasonable person fearful of a breach of the peace. *The New York Times* hailed the court decision as "the most sweeping First Amendment victory of the entire decade" ("There are Judges in Trenton," *New York Times,* 16 May 1928, p. 24).

In the 1920s and 1930s Baldwin negotiated a difficult path; his critics observed that he showed much more willingness to condemn the Soviet Union. Baldwin joined the board of the Russian Reconstruction Farms project and raised money to help develop Soviet agriculture.

In 1925 the so-called Monkey Trial of John Scopes in Tennessee led to far greater publicity for the ACLU, but Baldwin did not attend the trial that made his organization famous. He knew he would not be calling the shots for the ACLU at the trial; instead, the attorneys would decide on the tactics. He had objected to Clarence Darrow as defense counsel but had been overruled, and he found the circus-like atmosphere appalling. Instead, Baldwin stayed in New York, raising money and paying the organization's bills. His old friend from prison, Freddy Farnham, committed suicide that year, and Baldwin's marriage had all but legally ended. He went on a trip to Europe and visited the Soviet Union with friends for much of 1926. In an unpublished manuscript written upon his return to the United States, titled "Sabbatical Year of Study among the Down-trodden and Uplifters of Europe," Baldwin defended communism on economic grounds even when its methods "are not what seem to me to be the best" (Baldwin Papers, quoted in Cottrell).

The ACLU provided only peripheral help in two cases with which Baldwin was personally involved during the mid 1920s and early 1930s: those of Sacco and Vanzetti and the Scottsboro Boys. Baldwin contacted U.S. Prison commissioner Sanford Bates, an old acquaintance, in an effort to have Nicola Sacco transferred to the state penitentiary, as Sacco had undergone a nervous breakdown under the strain of the protracted legal proceedings and worries about his inability to support his family, and Sacco and Baldwin believed conditions at the penitentiary would be better. He also regularly corresponded with Bartolomeo Vanzetti and had occasional contact with their attorney Fred Moore about the case. When Moore resigned from the case in October 1924, Baldwin helped secure the services of William G. Thompson, a well-regarded Boston lawyer. After the 1927 executions of Sacco and Vanzetti, Baldwin became one of three trustees of a fund for the education of Sacco's son and daughter.

In his 1928 book, *Liberty Under The Soviets,* Baldwin wrote from his notes on the 1926 trip, and he tried to stress positive results in the Soviet Union despite his distaste for what communism was doing to leftist politics in the United States. While he gave an honest account of the dictatorial controls the Soviet regime put in place, Baldwin considered far more important the economic freedom of the working class and the abolition of a privileged class. He separated economic and political liberties, arguing one could occur without the other. Unlike Goldman, who had written *My Disillusionment with Russia* (1923) and discussed her criticisms of communism in conversation with Baldwin, he still clung to the idea that the Soviet Union was a dictatorship in the interests of the workers. Goldman considered Baldwin's position naive on this point. Others criticized Baldwin as a hypocrite or worse. Many found it disturbing that the champion of the First Amendment at home could defend an ever more repressive regime.

Yet, Baldwin's book gave expression to the attitudes of American liberals toward the Soviet Union.

He became personally involved in the Scottsboro case in the 1930s because the National Association for the Advancement of Colored People (NAACP), headed by the staunch anticommunist Walter White, could not afford consistent support for the defendants. One problem the defense confronted was that the Communist Party, through the International Labor Defense, provided counsel for the defendants. White did not want to put the NAACP at risk of defending young men accused of a terrible crime in the heart of segregationist Old Dixie, and he did not want to work with the communists at all. White hired Arthur Garfield Hays and Darrow, the defense attorneys from the Scopes case, but when the two ACLU lawyers discovered that communist attorneys were representing the defendants, they resigned in disgust. As a friend of both White and the two ACLU attorneys, Baldwin found himself in the middle of the dispute. He believed the ACLU had to support the defendants, even as he felt concerned that the Communist Party was merely trying to use the case for its own political advantage. Nevertheless, Baldwin worked on the Scottsboro Defense Committee with the communists, reasoning that he often worked with individuals whose motives were not pure. Baldwin spoke at mass meetings on the Scottsboro Boys' behalf and visited them in jail and after their release. When the first convictions were overturned and the defendants got a second trial, the ACLU attempted to secure expert counsel. In March 1933 that trial resulted in another conviction. The ultimate resolution of the case proved unsatisfactory; a third trial resulted in a plea bargain where four of the defendants were released and four received lengthy prison sentences. The final defendant was not released until 1950.

The ACLU took a narrow view of civil liberties and concentrated on cases that met that definition in the early years. So the ACLU did not contest Prohibition itself, for example, but concentrated on violations of the Bill of Rights resulting from the enforcement of Prohibition. The ACLU did involve itself in censorship issues, especially in obscenity cases. Baldwin personally argued that some things should remain private, and he focused more on protecting political speech rather than expressions of what he considered simply foul language. Even so, the ACLU board defended individuals against prior restraint, challenging censorship and calling for officials to have to prove charges of indecency.

The ACLU also focused on the courts as the best arena in which to defend civil liberties. The organization had as its stated goal upholding the Bill of Rights, and this tactical decision proved ultimately advantageous. The ACLU, often spurred by Baldwin, helped transform the field of constitutional law. Beginning with the *Gitlow* decision of 1925, which upheld freedom of speech and the press while reaffirming the conviction of communist leader Benjamin Gitlow, the ACLU proved instrumental in pushing the Supreme Court to rule more sections of the Bill of Rights as "fundamental." The organization's campaign continued through such cases as *Stromberg v. California* (1931), which protected symbolic speech from state encroachment, and *Near v. Minnesota* (1931), which disallowed the use of prior restraint against the press. In *Palko v. Connecticut* (1937) the ACLU claimed victory when the court declared basic rights such as freedom of speech, the press, religion, assembly, and the right to counsel guaranteed by the Fourteenth Amendment's due process clause. Similarly, the ACLU made progress for many free-speech issues with *Hague v. Congress of Industrial Organizations* (1939), in which the court ruled that public streets and parks were public forums shielded by the First Amendment. This reliance on the courts seems paradoxical, given Baldwin's increasing identification with the Left and his growing disdain for reform measures; yet, it was also in keeping with Baldwin's elitism and his long-standing willingness to rely on the courts to overcome injustice.

In 1931 an article elaborating Baldwin's leftist views appeared in a collection of essays titled *Behold America!* In it he referred to law and order as a myth and called democracy an illusion. He criticized parliaments, republican government, and civil codes as instruments of the ruling class that "fed the illusion that individual initiative could propel any man into the seats of power" (quoted in Cottrell). The United States, he thought, valued only the right to amass wealth, and the people could choose only between capitalist parties. As class tensions increased and capitalism faltered, he thought, the workers and the farmers would rise in opposition. When this struggle reached a successful conclusion, real equality before the law could exist. Until then, the more citizens are allowed the right to support even an open revolution, "the less violent will be the process of advance" (quoted in Cottrell). He viewed the ACLU's ultimate goal as working to stave off the wreckage that would result from a violent class struggle. And in the ACLU's annual report, Baldwin acknowledged that the Supreme Court displayed a liberal outlook regarding the First Amendment.

In an essay he published in *World Tomorrow*, Baldwin also countered criticism that the ACLU favored free speech only for communists by citing ACLU championship of free speech for Nazis. Baldwin believed Nazi (and KKK) propaganda could best be fought in the open, and that allowing these people to propound their doctrines would only cost them public support, while suppressing their speech made them martyrs and gave their fellow extremists some limited moral authority. Baldwin wrote, "Nazis can't live long in the open in America" (quoted in Cottrell). Allowing the Nazis to operate openly, in the ACLU's view, gave other citizens effective means of contesting the hatred they espoused. Baldwin consistently supported full legal protection for the expression of views and freedom of assembly for both the far Right and the far Left.

In September 1935 Baldwin and Madeleine Doty divorced in a Swiss court, having been estranged and living separately for more than ten years. On 6 March 1936 Baldwin married Evelyn ("Evie") Preston, a millionaire, in a Quaker ceremony that lacked legality under New Jersey law. Evie had two children from an earlier marriage, Roger and Carl. On 4 May 1937 Evie Baldwin gave birth to a daughter, Helen. Evie's wealth allowed the couple freedom of occupation.

In the second half of the decade Baldwin's political philosophy shifted. The show trials in Moscow revealed to Baldwin the dangers of dictatorship. Then the Nazi-Soviet pact of 1939 hit leftists "like a bombshell," in Baldwin's words (quoted in Cottrell). That two apparently ideologically opposed nations had allied against the democracies demonstrated for Baldwin, to the delight of his old friend Goldman, that the Soviets and, by extension, other communists could no longer be trusted.

This development placed the ACLU in a precarious position, because the ACLU had Communist Party members on its board of directors, people whose greatest loyalty lay with a party that did not support the ideal of civil liberties for its opponents. Civil liberties, after all, are meaningful only to the extent that they protect the rights of dissenters. The ACLU debated within its ranks whether those people should be voted off the board, and if so, whether the organization would be guilty of violating its own ideals. The board and the national committee passed a motion subsequently known as the 1940 Resolution, stating that those on the organization's governing committees and their staffs had to defend civil liberties consistently in all aspects and places. The resolution led to the resignation of Harry Ward as ACLU chairman and the "trial" of Elizabeth Gurley Flynn. Questioning whether Flynn's Communist Party membership disqualified her from the ACLU board, the board tied, 9-9, on the question of expulsion (Baldwin was not entitled to vote, as he was not officially a board member, but he was widely perceived as orchestrating the trial), and chairman John Haynes Holmes, a staunch anticommunist, broke the tie in favor of expulsion. The action provided a blueprint for the kind of red scare Baldwin had consistently opposed. This outcome meant that the man who had done more to protect First Amendment freedoms than anyone else would be blamed for devising a model to restrict those freedoms after the war. Flynn's expulsion has remained one of the most controversial actions in the history of the organization. For Baldwin it meant he had cast his lot with the anticommunists. He never viewed communists as trustworthy again, but he never called for the suspension of the civil liberties or political rights of American communists.

From the beginning of World War II, Baldwin defended the rights of fascists and anti-Semites to speak out in the United States. When *Nation* called for suppression of the fascist press, Baldwin wrote a letter to the magazine criticizing the proposal. He feared silencing a few fanatics would lead to the eventual suppression of all social criticism. Increasingly, though, Baldwin had to focus on the infringement of the rights of Japanese Americans rather than fascists. Many ACLU leaders accepted government policy including the internments, just making sure that procedural guarantees for the detainees were devised and carried out. When the actual evacuation order was issued, the ACLU chose to attack only the arbitrary nature of the order and its basis on national origin. In the ACLU annual report of 1943 Baldwin dissented from this view, noting fewer civil liberties violations in World War II than in World War I, but that the internment of Japanese Americans posed "the worst single invasion of citizens' liberties under war pressures" (ACLU, *Freedom in Wartime*). The ACLU had little involvement in either the Endo or the Korematsu landmark internment cases because the board was so divided. The December 1944 issue of the *American Mercury* featured an article by Baldwin arguing that the treatment of the Japanese Americans "stands as the blackest blot on our civil liberties record, . . . a record, incidentally, that has been, in most other instances, remarkably fine" ("Japanese Americans in Wartime"). Years later Baldwin admitted that he was ashamed of his own failure to challenge the ACLU board's reluctance to become involved in this situation, but he attributed his reluctance at the time to his efforts at compromising and holding the board together.

When the war ended, Baldwin accurately predicted the United States would shift to the Right. Red-baiting became a weapon of choice for members of both political parties. Groups such as the Chamber of Commerce, the FBI, and the House Committee on Un-American Activities (HCUA) not only promoted anticommunism but also advocated political purges. Baldwin warned that HCUA seemed eager to attack a broad set of targets including communists, liberals, and the CIO. His influence on the organization waned, however, as even the ACLU became more conservative. Baldwin's

A NEW SLAVERY

FORCED LABOR:
The Communist Betrayal of Human Rights

ROGER N. BALDWIN, Editor

Introduction by A. A. BERLE, Jr.

AN OCEANA PUBLICATION

Title page for Baldwin's 1953 collection of essays condemning forced labor in the Soviet Union (Thomas Cooper Library, University of South Carolina)

own anticommunism expressed during the war provided justification for the changing political scene. While Baldwin continued to enjoy a reputation as the nation's foremost defender of civil liberties, his radical fervor waned even as First Amendment freedoms underwent new attacks.

Then the government began to ask for ACLU participation in postwar reconstruction efforts. In January 1947 Baldwin was offered and accepted a position as adviser to General Douglas MacArthur as a consultant on civil liberties. He spent three months overseas and was pleased with the results. In a 1947 unpublished manuscript titled "Shogun and the Emperor," he praised MacArthur as a contemporary shogun engaged in "a crusade for democracy" (Baldwin Papers). The War Department requested that the ACLU send three individuals to undertake "an unofficial investigation of civil liberties" in Germany, and in late September 1948 Baldwin traveled to Germany. He sharply criticized cooperation with the Russians in Europe, contending, however, that Washington policymakers had to recognize "alliance with progressive forces, not the reactionaries, is the way to beat Communism" ("Can Democracy Succeed in Germany?" Baldwin Papers).

Once back home Baldwin wrote "Red and Rights" for *Progressive* magazine. He cautioned liberals against becoming caught up in the anticommunist mania and criticized the loyalty oath for federal employees, the HCUA hearings, and the Taft-Hartley Act. He continued to argue for First Amendment freedoms throughout the 1950s, recognizing the dangers inherent in witch hunts and investigative hearings. He also continued to defend the civil liberties of communists. Yet, many found this position difficult to reconcile with Baldwin's own insistence that communists could be denied employment in sensitive positions and the ACLU's exclusion of communists from its own leadership.

In October 1949 the ACLU board ousted Baldwin as executive director, announcing his retirement and giving him a new title as ACLU national chairman and responsibility for bringing civil liberties to the world. In fact, Baldwin had been relieved of his executive responsibilities at the ACLU. Younger members sought a mass membership for the organization, rather than the small, committed group Baldwin had always advocated, and the board members wanted to take power from Baldwin. When his retirement became official on 1 January 1950, Baldwin embarked on a new phase of his life.

During his retirement, he read newspapers and his extensive mail, and planned his day by phone. When the United Nations General Assembly was in session, he carried on discussions involving international civil liberties with the delegates in the morning, while in the afternoons he often went to the International League for the Rights of Man for consultations. Evenings he devoted to social occasions, with dignitaries and students often visiting him and Evie at their home in Greenwich Village. In 1953 Baldwin edited *A New Slavery,* a condemnation of forced labor in the Soviet Union. Baldwin now regretted his earlier optimism about the U.S.S.R. and, further, charged all the communist states with using forced labor, to which not even dictatorships in Spain or Latin America had resorted to retain power. Baldwin contended that communism posed a greater threat to the world than right-wing despotism. He visited South Vietnam in 1959 and sought to convince Ngo Dinh Diem to adopt democratic practices in an attempt to ward off the growing power of communism in Southeast Asia.

In June 1962 Evie Baldwin died of cancer. Baldwin's ex-wife, Madeleine Zabriskie Doty, died the following year. Unknown even to many of his friends, Baldwin had continued to assist Doty financially. He did not remarry, although he continued to maintain friendships with women. His children often remarked how much his spirits picked up when he was in the company of women, who helped to sustain him in his later years. Eventually, Baldwin lived with his daughter in their Greenwich Village house, along with her companion, Piero Mannoni, and their daughter, Francesca.

Although Baldwin had been involuntarily retired as ACLU director, he still sought to influence the direction of the organization. He attempted to mentor younger men and often sought interviews with those individuals he believed would be most influential on a particular issue, so that he could have a chance to contribute to their views. Baldwin found displeasing the growth of the organization, and he did not like its expanded emphasis on equal protection based on the Fourteenth Amendment. He felt the organization should focus on the First Amendment, due process, and equal treatment before the law. Nor was he pleased, as developments continued, with the organization's expanded support for gay rights and women's rights, feeling the ACLU should not "stray too far from the middle class." He believed once that occurred, "it's the beginning of the end for the ACLU" (quoted in Cottrell).

Baldwin had been a member of the advisory committee of the Congress of Racial Equality (CORE), but he resigned in September 1966 because he disapproved of its shifting emphasis to racial separateness, the right to self-defense, and black power. The CORE he stood for supported nonviolence, equality, and integration. In July 1967 he attended the third U.N. Conference for World Peace through Law. Baldwin emphasized respect for human rights, and asserted that without political freedom, economic justice, and rule by law, "world peace is an illusion." He also served as a visiting professor at Puerto Rico's public and most prestigious law school. In March 1968 the Fellowship of Reconciliation sponsored a Baldwin speech where he criticized the Vietnam War, which he saw as a civil war. Back home, he criticized the deplorable tactics of the student antiwar protesters, arguing that the failure of university administrators to deal adequately with student grievances led to protests and violations of the law. The ACLU, Baldwin asserted, supported student freedom and democracy in order to avoid such disasters.

On 6 December 1968 the International League for the Rights of Man awarded Baldwin its first Annual Human Rights Award. He had chaired the organization for twenty years and was by this point its honorary president. Many of Baldwin's old friends, including Norman Thomas and A. J. Muste, died in the next few years, and Baldwin began to focus his efforts on preserving the record of his work. He also prevented several biographies from being completed, most famously when Joseph P. Lash pressed too closely with questions about his sexual orientation and other matters Baldwin considered strictly private. Eventually, Peggy Lamson was able to complete a biography in 1976.

In April 1977 the decision of members of the American Nazi Party to march through Skokie, Illinois, and the resulting court case fostered a huge controversy, and thousands of members resigned from the ACLU in protest over the decision to allow the Nazis to march in the heavily Jewish suburb. Financial ruin threatened. Baldwin wrote a twelve-page essay defending the ACLU's support of free speech for Nazis, noting the ACLU had always been dedicated to defending the rights of all. He was surprised so many chose to resign "in protest over an extreme but traditional test of principle" ("Reflections on the Skokie Case," quoted in Cottrell). The ACLU had always backed free speech for unpopular groups, including Nazis, and American Jews had always backed the ACLU in its defense of such groups. Baldwin quoted Benjamin Franklin, who observed "Of course the abuses of free speech should be suppressed but to whom dare we entrust the power to do so?" (quoted in Cottrell).

In the next few years Baldwin struggled with illness but still managed to conduct filmed interviews. In May 1979 his daughter died, and following her death Baldwin found himself involved in a legal battle with Mannoni about the Greenwich Village property. In January 1981 a seriously ill Baldwin received the Medal of Freedom Award from President Jimmy Carter for his long-standing leadership in the field of civil rights. On 26 August 1981 Baldwin died at the age of ninety-seven in Ridgewood, New Jersey.

Baldwin's legacy is a complex one. While he changed positions throughout his life, starting as a reformer, then becoming a radical, and then a reformer

again, he remained always to the left of center in American politics. His organization nevertheless appealed to many who were more conservative than he because of its defense of civil liberties. At the same time, many on the Right considered the ACLU the enemy (and still do). Baldwin also had an elitist streak, striving for years to keep the ACLU small and select, rather than an organization with a large popular base. And the ACLU under Baldwin was not always so aggressive in the defense of civil liberties as its reputation suggested, especially during the 1940s and 1950s. But by the time he died, Roger Baldwin had been recognized as an icon of civil liberties in America, and the organization that he created continues.

Biographies:

Peggy Lamson, *Roger Baldwin: Founder of the American Civil Liberties Union: A Portrait* (Boston: Houghton Mifflin, 1976);

Robert C. Cottrell, *Roger Nash Baldwin and the American Civil Liberties Union* (New York: Columbia University Press, 2000);

Woody Klein, ed., *Liberties Lost: The Endangered Legacy of the ACLU* (New York: Praeger, 2006).

Papers:

Roger Baldwin's papers are catalogued with the Public Policy Papers, Department of Rare Books and Special Collections, Princeton University. They include many unpublished biographical manuscripts. The ACLU's papers reside at Princeton as well. Other Baldwin material may be found in the Peggy Lamson Collection on Roger Baldwin, Public Policy Papers, Department of Rare Books and Special Collections, Princeton University; in the Joseph P. Lash Papers, Franklin Delano Roosevelt Presidential Library, Hyde Park, New York; in the Columbia University Oral History Collection at Columbia University; and in the records of the Department of Justice and the Federal Bureau of Investigation, United States National Archives. The papers of his first wife, Madeleine Zabriskie Doty, are at Smith College.

Alison Bechdel

(10 September 1960 –   )

Edward Austin Hall

BOOKS: *Dykes to Watch Out For* (Ithaca, N.Y.: Firebrand, 1986);

More Dykes to Watch Out For (Ithaca, N.Y.: Firebrand, 1988);

New, Improved! Dykes to Watch Out For (Ithaca, N.Y.: Firebrand, 1990);

Dykes to Watch Out For: The Sequel (Ithaca, N.Y.: Firebrand, 1992);

Spawn of Dykes to Watch Out For (Ithaca, N.Y.: Firebrand, 1993);

Unnatural Dykes to Watch Out For (Ithaca, N.Y.: Firebrand, 1995);

Hot, Throbbing Dykes to Watch Out For (Ithaca, N.Y.: Firebrand, 1997);

The Indelible Alison Bechdel (Ithaca, N.Y.: Firebrand, 1998);

Split-Level Dykes to Watch Out For (Ithaca, N.Y.: Firebrand, 1998);

Post-Dykes to Watch Out For (Ithaca, N.Y.: Firebrand, 2000);

Dykes and Sundry Other Carbon-Based Life-Forms to Watch Out For (Los Angeles: Alyson, 2003);

Invasion of the Dykes to Watch Out For (New York: Alyson, 2005);

Fun Home: A Family Tragicomic (New York: Houghton Mifflin, 2005; London: Cape, 2006).

OTHER: "A Coupla Dykes Sittin' around Talkin' about AIDS," in *Strip AIDS USA,* edited by Trina Robbins, Bill Sienkiewicz, and Robert Triptow (San Francisco: Last Gasp, 1988);

Dykes to Watch Out for Calendar, annual (Ithaca, N.Y.: Firebrand, 1989–1996);

What Do Dogs Dream? by Louise Rafkin, illustrated by Bechdel (Kansas City, Mo.: Andrews McMeel, 1998);

What Do Cats Dream? by Rafkin, illustrated by Bechdel (Kansas City, Mo.: Andrews McMeel, 1999).

COLLECTIONS: *The Complete Dykes to Watch Out For* (New York: Quality Book Club, 1997);

Alison Bechdel (from the dust jacket for Fun Home: A Family Tragicomic, *2006)*

The Essential Dykes to Watch Out For (London: Cape, 2008; Boston: Houghton Mifflin, 2008).

Alison Bechdel is best known as the creator of the syndicated comic strip *Dykes to Watch Out For.* Its subject, the day-to-day lives of lesbians and the extended gay community, is a rarity in cartooning. Bechdel's candor in critiquing what she calls (in a 2003 interview no longer available on the Alyson Books website) "orthodox progressivism" distinguishes her among Left-leaning social observers, as well.

Alison Bechdel was born in Lock Haven, Pennsylvania, on 10 September 1960, the first of three children born to Bruce Allen Bechdel and Helen Fontana Bechdel. Both of Bechdel's parents taught high-school English, and Bruce Bechdel worked as funeral director at the family mortuary, as well. The Bechdels also had creative interests. She was an actress; he belonged to the Victorian Society of America and the board of directors for the Millbrook Playhouse. The couple reared Alison and her brothers, Christian and John, in a ten-room Victorian home in Beech Creek, Pennsylvania, and the family attended a Roman Catholic church in Lock Haven. From age three onward Bechdel drew, mostly pictures of people. Her childhood drawings settled into a distinct pattern: she drew only men. Specifically, she drew masculine figures, many bearded or mustachioed, many engaged in stereotypically aggressive male behavior, such as kicking sand into the face of a smaller man.

Bechdel left home in 1978 to attend Bard College at Simon's Rock Early College in Massachusetts. She received an associate of arts degree in 1979 and transferred to Oberlin College, where she realized that she was a lesbian. Before semester's end she had read Del Martin and Phyllis Lyon's nonfiction work *Lesbian/Woman* (1972) as well as Rita Mae Brown's *Rubyfruit Jungle* (1973) and Radclyffe Hall's *The Well of Loneliness* (1928). Bechdel came out at Oberlin during the winter-spring semester of 1980 and began a sexual relationship with a fellow student. Her reading of lesbian and feminist texts continued, and she swiftly became radicalized in her views. Bechdel says she decided "I wouldn't be kicked out of society—I'd leave of my own accord" (2003 interview, Alyson Books website).

Bechdel received her bachelor of arts degree from Oberlin in 1981, the year after her father, age forty-four, was killed in an automobile accident. She applied for admission to several graduate programs but was rejected by all. In August 1981 she attended her first Michigan Womyn's Music Festival. This multi-day outdoor festival, open only to women, made a deep impression on Bechdel. In a 2002 essay published in *The Advocate* and reproduced at the magazine's website, she wrote of her astonishment at the festival's total absence of men—a response to the broader feminist community's call for more woman-only space—and of her feeling that she was finally where she belonged.

Lacking any plan for her life beyond further schooling in art, Bechdel moved to New York City in 1981. She worked as a typist in the publishing industry and began to study martial arts. She explained, "I wanted to know how to fight and be strong. I stumbled into it through the Women's Center Karate Club" (2003 interview, <http://www.mountainpridemedia.org/oitm/issues/2003/02feb2003/fea03_abechdel.htm>, viewed 27 June 2008). At Manhattan's Oscar Wilde Memorial Bookshop she saw *Gay Comix 1,* edited by cartoonist Howard Cruse. This underground comic book caused Bechdel to rethink what cartoons and comic strips could be. The work by Cruse and others, including Roberta Gregory and Mary Wings, proved inspirational. Bechdel began to draw her own cartoons. In the margin of a 1982 letter she sketched a nude that she captioned, "Marianne, dissatisfied with the breakfast

brew." Bechdel labeled this cartoon "Dykes to Watch Out For, plate no. 27," despite its lack of numbered predecessors. Many similar cartoons followed. Eventually, a friend volunteering at *Womanews,* a monthly feminist newspaper, persuaded her to submit some drawings for publication. The first *Dykes to Watch Out For* single-frame cartoon appeared in the paper's July–August 1983 issue. Reader response was positive, so Bechdel started creating such a panel for each issue.

In 1984 Bechdel shifted from a single-panel format to the more common multi-panel comic strip. "Perils of a Midtown Dyke," the first such strip, depicts a Bechdel look-alike being chided by another woman for entering the ladies room. Some of the panels that follow offer suggested comebacks. They are labeled, successively, "political," "rude," and "lewd." During this period Bechdel broadened her enterprise to writing extended social commentary. Other early strips dealt with same-sex couples' issues, lesbian stereotypes, and commodification of politics. That same year Bechdel began to send the strip to other publications, and she found sufficient acceptance to allow her to move to part-time employment, augmented by freelance illustration jobs. Publisher Nancy Bereano, founder of Firebrand Books, offered to collect her work.

Bechdel relocated briefly in 1985 to Northampton, Massachusetts, where she worked at a food-bank warehouse and began offering readers postcards of her work; then she followed a lover to Minneapolis, Minnesota, where she worked as a production manager for a gay and lesbian newspaper, *Equal Time.* Firebrand Books published Bechdel's first collection of cartoons, *Dykes to Watch Out For,* in 1986. Late that year Bechdel created her last nonserial *Dykes to Watch Out For* strip. "Silly Putty Syndrome" featured Cleo Baldshein (an anagram for "Alison Bechdel"), a so-called "guerilla therapist."

Bechdel was captivated by *Wendel,* Cruse's serial strip for *The Advocate* that concerned a young gay man (its title character), his lover Ollie, and their friends, acquaintances, and associates. She began introducing recurring characters to *Dykes to Watch Out For* in January 1987. Mo (a nickname for Monica), her main character, was baldly autobiographical: "a young, white, middle-class, marginally employed lesbian-feminist" *(The Indelible Alison Bechdel).* Mo was also a bespectacled, androgynous neurotic. She shared that first serial strip with her friend Lois, a serial seducer of lesbians. Later came Clarice, a law student who had been Mo's first lover and remained her friend; Toni, Clarice's partner; Lois's housemates, Ginger, a graduate student in English, and Sparrow, a New-Age flake; Jezanna, proprietor of Madwimmin Books and employer of Mo; and Harriet, with whom Mo eventually became involved.

Front cover for Bechdel's first book (Thomas Cooper Library, University of South Carolina)

Story lines from the first serialized year of *Dykes to Watch Out For* incorporated such real-world events as the Iran-Contra scandal, the AIDS epidemic, and the 11 October 1987 March on Washington for lesbian and gay rights. Few other comic strips so much as referred to these politically charged topics and events. Bechdel's characters pondered them, argued over them, and even traveled to Washington to participate. They also dealt with the often-comic struggle between being socially engaged and submitting to the compromises nearly all adults must make, a struggle that Bechdel revisits regularly. In the 1987 strip Bechdel titled "Pride and Prejudice" Mo's response to a Catholic homosexual group, gay men's chorus singers, and lesbian investment bankers she sees at a Gay Pride march distills an ongoing concern of *Dykes to Watch Out For:* "Religion! Patriotism! Financial security! . . . We're conspiring in our own oppression!"

In the 1988 anthology *Strip AIDS USA* Bechdel shows a similar willingness to confront issues sidestepped by her fellow cartoonists. Bechdel's contribution featured Mo and Ginger discussing failure of the gay and lesbian communities to unite in the fight against AIDS. Also that year Bechdel sold a stand-alone cartoon entitled "A few things gay men have always wanted to know about lesbians (but were too afraid of being called sexist clods to ask)" to *The Advocate.* Its popularity led her to create a monthly strip for that magazine. *Servants to the Cause* concerned the staff of a fictitious gay and lesbian newspaper, the *Ten Percent Tribune.*

Bechdel's second book, *More Dykes to Watch Out For* (1988), established the cartoonist's practice of including new, long-form material that amplified the story line of her previously published strips. In this instance she showed Mo and Harriet's first night together, a daring move in the 1980s during the debate about pornography and sexuality among feminists. In 1989 the first *Dykes to Watch Out For* calendar (for 1990) appeared. Its twelve cartoons provided more adventures of Mo and friends and gave Bechdel a spin-off product. The calendar's August installment depicted several characters discussing positive and negative aspects of the annual Michigan Womyn's Music Festival, which Bechdel had attended since 1981.

A format change at *The Advocate* brought *Servants to the Cause* to an end in 1990, after nineteen monthly episodes. Because she was producing two episodes of *Dykes to Watch Out For* each month, plus one installment of the magazine strip, Bechdel felt relieved. A 1990 *Servants to the Cause* strip, reprinted in *The Indelible Alison Bechdel* (1998), uses a favorite Bechdel technique to question how progressive the gay and lesbian liberation movement (and media coverage of it) truly is: a news magazine being read at the *Ten Percent Tribune* office bears the headline "THE FUTURE OF STRAIGHT-LOOKING PROFESSIONAL WHITE GAY MEN IN AMERICA."

Bechdel quit her job at *Equal Time* the same year her strip perished. Again pursuing a relationship with a woman, she moved to Vermont in 1990; "I just follow women all over the country," she commented in an interview formerly posted on Lesbiannews.com. Her third collection of cartoons, *New, Improved! Dykes to Watch Out For,* appeared that year. It opens with an appalled, speechless Mo reading the strip's fictional newspaper *The Daily Distress,* whose headlines include "MORE AID TO DEATH SQUADS" and "HATE CRIMES ON RISE." Bechdel's own dismay at U.S. military action against Panama and its leader, Manuel Noriega, takes the form of fake headlines such as "FIND NORIEGA! WIN $1 MILLION!" The title sets the tone for Bechdel's parodies of commercial language and attitudes, such as the signage for a "Shop & Drop Megafoods" store: "Save on PESTICIDES! ADDITIVES!" and "We're open INCESSANTLY!" Strips in this volume also concern challenges to the academic literary canon, therapy, promiscuity, "coming out" anxieties, and same-sex marriage. The book won a 1990 Lambda Literary Award.

In 1991, Bechdel and Cruse collaborated on a *Village Voice* illustration depicting types of gay and lesbian Americans from successive decades. Of the finished piece Bechdel writes, "After seeing how my art practically disappeared next to Howard's, I started drawing thicker outlines" *(The Indelible Alison Bechdel).* Bechdel's fourth collection, *Dykes to Watch Out For: The Sequel* (1992), questions the cost of gay and lesbian assimilation into heterosexual culture and the impact of the contentious hearings to confirm Clarence Thomas to the U.S. Supreme Court. It won Bechdel a 1992 Lambda Award.

In 1992 Bechdel met Amy Rubin, who had studied dramaturgy at Syracuse University. They moved in together and settled in rural Vermont. That year Bechdel realized she had had her fill of the Michigan Womyn's Music Festival. In 1993 she created an autobiographical comic, "my own private michigan HELL," that enumerated all the ways she had come to despise attending the event. *Gay Comix* featured Bechdel's multi-page autobiographical comic "Coming Out Story" in 1993. Bechdel's fifth book also appeared that year. *Spawn of Dykes to Watch Out For* includes a long, original piece detailing the birth of a baby boy to the now-married Toni and her partner Clarice. Rafi is the strip's first recurring male character. This work brought the cartoonist her third Lambda Award. Bechdel's semi-autobiographical "Serial Monogamy," first published in *Dykes to Watch Out For: The Sequel,* was the only comic chosen for inclusion in *The Penguin Book of Lesbian Short Stories* (1994). Bunns and Noodle, Bechdel's parody of bookstore chain Barnes and Noble, and Bound-

ers (Borders) appear for the first time in *Unnatural Dykes to Watch Out For* (1995), which has many strips set at Mo's Madwimmin Books, whose existence is threatened by the chains. (Madwimmin itself is based on a venerable independent feminist bookseller in Minneapolis called Amazon Books. After the advent of the internet bookseller Amazon.com, the store changed its name to The Amazon Bookstore Cooperative.)

Bechdel produced her last *Dykes to Watch Out For* calendar (for 1997) in March 1996. She writes in *The Indelible Alison Bechdel* of the circumstances that led to her decision, "It became an annual ritual to essentially lose the month of March . . . in a crazed binge of all-night workfests." In 1997 Bechdel ceased all efforts toward merchandising her own ancillary products. Her onetime advertising flier had evolved into a twelve-page catalogue, and she found its ratio of work to returns discouraging.

Bechdel's seventh book, *Hot, Throbbing Dykes to Watch Out For,* also appeared in 1997, followed the next year by a memoir, *The Indelible Alison Bechdel,* and her eighth compilation of strips, *Split-Level Dykes to Watch Out For.* The latter two books both won 1998 Lambda Awards. *Split-Level Dykes to Watch Out For* includes a sex chat between Mo and her new lover Sydney that makes a mockery of academic jargon, questioning how free lesbians are once they have the freedom to marry, and Mo's epitaph for the gay and lesbian equality movement:

> What movement? This isn't a movement any more, it's a @#!*! closely-held corporation, run by a bunch of white, power-hungry marketing strategists who're packaging our lives into a commodity they can sell to pay their salaries!

Bechdel wrote a weeklong diary for the online magazine *Slate* in 1998 which detailed her creative process and how she dealt with her anxiety. Elsewhere she had revealed that she usually wrote the text for her cartoons entirely before drawing a line. In *Slate,* she describes the preparatory thirty minutes she spent prone in a "semi-conscious state" on 31 March 1998 and how helpful she finds having a line of dialogue to "perseverate on" during these near-trances.

Bechdel's tenth book, *Post-Dykes to Watch Out For* (2000), has her characters worrying over Taliban sexism in Afghanistan; a vodka ad on the back of a gay magazine declaring "ABSOLUT GLOBAL CAPITALISM"; headlines mourning the demise of two real-world feminist bookstores; and the cartoonist herself trying in vain to cope with the satiric potential of U.S. President Bill Clinton's impeachment. Sparrow, now involved with a man and identifying herself as a "bi-

Dust jacket for Bechdel's 2006 collection (Thomas Cooper Library, University of South Carolina)

dyke," says, "Identity is so much more complex and fluid than these rigid little categories of straight, gay, and bi can possibly reflect." A page later she is perplexed by the news of an acquaintance's transgendered status. Toni and Clarice contemplate opening up their marriage to other lovers.

Dykes and Sundry Other Carbon-Based Life-Forms to Watch Out For was published in 2003 by Alyson Books, following setbacks suffered by Bechdel's longtime publisher, Firebrand. The cartoonist's tenth collection of strips (which won a 2003 Lambda Award) opens with a headline in *The Ten Percent Tribune:* "VICTORY IN VERMONT: CIVIL UNIONS BILL PASSES." It ends with Jezanna's announcement that she is closing Madwimmin Books. In between, Bechdel depicts, without dialogue, her characters' experiences on 11 September 2001, when terrorists attacked the United States with hijacked jetliners.

Rubin proposed marriage to Bechdel on 14 February 2004. Perhaps predictably Bechdel's response

was, "OK. But what about our radical politics?" (*Dykes to Watch Out For* website). The two were wed in San Francisco on 24 February 2004, the same day that U.S. President George W. Bush called for a constitutional amendment banning the same-sex matrimonies that were flourishing at the time. Bechdel's twelfth book, *Invasion of the Dykes to Watch Out For* (2005) shows Mo in library school, Sydney in chemotherapy, and the nation at Code Orange.

In 2000, *Dykes to Watch Out For* was appearing in more than sixty publications internationally. Bechdel's fellow cartoon creator and onetime collaborator Harvey Pekar said, "You don't have to be gay or female to appreciate Bechdel's wit, thoughtful illustration and perceptiveness. Hers are thinkers' comics" ("Slice of Gay Life," <http://www.metroactive.com/papers/metro/08.08.96/comics-9632.html>, viewed 27 June 2008). Suzanne Wu, in the introduction to her interview with Bechdel for Swarthmore College's website (no longer available), called the strip "intricate, unexpected, maddening, convoluted and soap-operatic." Johanna Draper Carlson, at the Comicsworthreading.com website (no longer available), wrote, "Under all of this appealing and addictive soap opera, the series explores the fundamental question of how much a group not part of the mainstream should adapt their customs, including monogamy."

Bechdel has imbued the cartoon form with a rare humanity. In doing so she remade herself as well. As she stated in an interview on www.Alyson.com (no longer accessible): "over the past couple of years I morphed . . . from Mo into Sydney" (Sydney is Mo's acerbic academic lover, who loves to shop, struggles with debt, obsessively competes with her father, and questions every bit of progressive orthodoxy she encounters). In several interviews (formerly posted on the website of her publisher, Alyson Books) she referred to her memoir-in-progress about the experience of growing up with a "closeted father." That book, *Fun Home,* appeared in 2005, a quarter-century after Bruce Bechdel's death.

Alison Bechdel has candidly assessed and explicated her life (and the lives of her gay and lesbian coevals) through the lens of identity politics. She has also examined identity politics and fearlessly held up its triumphs and failings alike. She brings to bear the artistry with which she focuses on her own life, gender, and sexuality also on society at large. As Bechdel says of her medium in an interview with *Goblin Magazine,* "cartoons are harmless in a way, which is their true subversiveness."

References:

Dykes to Watch Out For: Life in a Box, Bechdel's website <http://www.dykestowatchoutfor.com/index.php> (viewed 27 June 2008);

Trina Robbins, "Watch Out for Alison Bechdel (She has the Secret to Superhuman Strength)," *Comics Journal* (September 2001);

Untitled Bechdel interview, *Goblin Magazine* <http://www.sonic.net/~goblin/9dyk.html> (accessed 21 May 2008).

Mary McLeod Bethune

(10 July 1875 – 17 May 1955)

Jennifer Harrison

BOOKS:

Editions and Collections: *Mary McLeod Bethune, Her Own Words of Inspiration,* edited by Florence Johnson Hicks (Washington, D.C.: Nuclassics and Science, 1975);

Mary McLeod Bethune: Building a Better World: Essays and Selected Documents, edited by Audrey Thomas McCluskey and Elaine M. Smith (Bloomington: Indiana University Press, 1999);

No Room for Despair: How to Cope in Troubled Times: Mary McLeod Bethune's Cold War Integration-Era Commentary, edited by Carolyn LaDelle Bennett (Baltimore: PublishAmerica, 2006).

OTHER: United States National Youth Administration, *The Tenth Youth,* foreword by Bethune (Washington, D.C.: U.S. Government Printing Office, 1940);

"Letter to George R. Arthur" and "A Century of Progress of Negro Women" in Gerda Lerner, ed., *Black Women in White America: A Documentary History* (New York: Pantheon, 1972), pp. 143–146, 579–584.

SELECTED PERIODICAL PUBLICATIONS–
UNCOLLECTED: "Letter to the Editor–City Officials Visit the Training School: Daytona Educational and Industrial Training School Honored with a Visit from Mayor Titus and the City Council," *Daytona Morning Journal,* 13 November 1915, p. 1;

"Letter to the Editor–To Help Negro Girls," *New York Times,* 18 April 1920;

"The Problems of the City Dweller," *Opportunity* (February 1925): 54–55;

"The Association for the Study of Negro Life and History: Its Contribution to Our Modern Life," *Journal of Negro History,* 20 (October 1935): 406–410;

"I'll Never Turn Back No More," *Opportunity* (November 1938): 324–326;

Mary McLeod Bethune (Benjamin Griffith Brawley, Women of Achievement, *1919; Thomas Cooper Library, University of South Carolina)*

"The Adaptation of the History of the Negro to the Capacity of the Child," *Journal of Negro History,* 24 (January 1939): 9–13;

"I Work with Youth," *The Brown American* (11 October 1939);

46

"We, Too, Are Americans!" *Pittsburgh Courier,* 17 January 1941, p. 8;

"Faith That Moved a Dump Heap," *Who, the Magazine about People* (June 1941): 32–35, 54;

"Pledge of Faith," *Quarterly Review of Higher Education among Negroes,* 11 (July 1943): 50–51;

"Army Erases Blot on the Escutcheon of Our Democracy," *Chicago Defender,* 12 February 1949;

"My Secret Talks With FDR," *Ebony* (April 1949): 42–51;

"Its Founder Takes Objective View of Women's National Council," *Chicago Defender,* 7 January 1950;

"The Privileges of a Democracy Are Not without Common Sense," *Chicago Defender,* 22 April 1950;

"The Negro in Retrospect and Prospect," *Journal of Negro History,* 36 (January 1951): 9–19;

"The Torch is Ours," *Journal of Negro History,* 36 (January 1951): 9–11;

"God Leads the Way, Mary," *Christian Century* (23 July 1952): 1–52, 85;

"Warns Against Violence or Hesitation at Integration," *Chicago Defender,* 2 October 1954;

"A Great People Hears Its Conscience Speak: Realizes Segregation Not Decent," *Chicago Defender,* 16 October 1954;

"Leader Recalls Pioneering Days When Organizing U.S. Women," *Chicago Defender,* 15 January 1955;

"Supreme Court's Desegregation Ruling Will Work, But We Must Have Patience About It," *Chicago Defender,* 22 January 1955;

"No Barrier Should Impede Progress of American People," *Chicago Defender,* 19 February 1955;

"Says Question of What Negroes Want Is Too Obvious for Answer," *Chicago Defender,* 5 March 1955;

"Ignorance, Root of Prejudice, Is Serious Foe of Democratic Living," *Chicago Defender,* 19 March 1955;

"Sees White South Resigning Itself to Integrated Life," *Chicago Defender,* 2 April 1955;

"Fair-Skinned, Blue Eyed, Blond Haired Walter White, Worker for Equal Justice," *Chicago Defender,* 9 April 1955;

"Negro Needs the Equality of the Unrestricted Ballot," *Chicago Defender,* 23 April 1955;

"Desegregation is Both a Human and National Problem," *Chicago Defender,* 14 May 1955.

Social and political activist Mary McLeod Bethune devoted her life's work to improving the lives of African Americans, and, in particular, African American women, through education and financial empowerment. Known as the "First Lady of the Struggle," she founded her own school, the Daytona Normal and Industrial Institute in 1904, later re-named Bethune-Cookman College after a 1923 merger, and she fulfilled social and political ambitions by creating the National Council of Negro Women (NCNW) and holding office in many national organizations. Her work, accomplished during an era of de facto segregation in the North and Jim-Crow laws in the South, helped African Americans by simultaneously making inroads against the race-based discrimination they faced and building their own support structures within the divided larger society. She has been called "the female Booker T. Washington," but she was far less accommodationist than that description would suggest; and, just as she approached politicians of more than one party to further her goals for social transformation, she considered and implemented the ideas of any leading black thinker that she thought might have merit. Bethune's public persona varied, and her biographers have noted that "she defies sociological categories and stereotypes." The poet Margaret Walker called her the "Great Amazon of God." Although she died at what historians consider the beginning of the modern Civil Rights Movement, Bethune earned a place among civil-rights thinkers with her determined and pragmatic approach to the problems she and other African Americans faced in her time.

Born on 10 July 1875, the fifteenth of seventeen children of Samuel and Patsy Macintosh McLeod, both former slaves, Mary Jane McLeod grew up working on a rice and cotton farm in rural South Carolina. Her childhood reflected in early form the determination for which she became known. By age nine she carried an adult workload picking cotton and helping her mother with housekeeping for the Wilson family (her mother's former "owners"). When she was eleven, the Mission Board of the Presbyterian Church opened a school for African American children in her area. Her family, though unusually affluent in that they owned their own farm, could afford to send only one child, and they chose "Janie." She learned to read and write in the one-room schoolhouse, worked in the late afternoons as before with her family, and did homework by the light of a kerosene lamp in the evenings. She then attended Scotia Seminary in North Carolina on a scholarship, and upon graduation in 1894 she entered Dwight Moody's Institute for Home and Foreign Missions in Chicago. She intended to go to Africa as a missionary, but when her petition was denied she returned to the South, teaching for a time at the mission school where she began her education.

While teaching at the Kendall Institute in Sumter, South Carolina, she met Albertus Bethune, a schoolteacher and store owner; they married in early May 1898, and their first and only child, Albertus McLeod Bethune, was born on 3 February 1899. The family

Bethune (right) on the New Negro Alliance picket line protesting hiring practices at a Washington, D.C., drugstore chain in the mid 1930s. With her is Roberta Child Hastie, mother of William Hastie, then dean of Howard University Law School (Mary McLeod Bethune: Building a Better World: Essays and Selected Documents, edited by Audrey Thomas McCluskey and Elaine M. Smith, 1999; Thomas Cooper Library, University of South Carolina).

which focused on both education and housekeeping skills. The inclusion of the term "Industrial" was more of a diplomatic nod to contemporary ideas about black education to gain support for her project than an actual expression of her educational focus. In any case, Bethune certainly needed the children to participate in the support and upkeep of the school, especially at first. Bethune scholar Audrey McCluskey has argued that "she understood the value of confirming America's sense of itself as a society fostered by hard work and fair play, especially when that confirmation came from the daughter of former slaves" (*Mary McLeod Bethune: Making a Better World*). Bethune's marriage did not long survive the move; her husband found the work available to him unsatisfactory and moved away, leaving their son with her, about 1907. Soon afterward she enrolled her son in a South Carolina boarding school.

During her years in Daytona, Bethune emphasized a strict code of conduct and a sense of morality as a central component of a successful life, a central theme that ran throughout her life. Having a keen sense of the importance of financial independence, she hoped that practical training would help her students earn money for their families, but more significantly she wanted them always to have a sense that they could support themselves, because a broader vision requires the ability to think beyond anxieties about survival. Originally a school with just five students, Bethune's school soon became a success, moving to a forty-two-acre campus with fourteen buildings and four hundred students within several years. The school became self-sufficient with its own farm and bakery, where Bethune herself worked.

Within several years of the school's opening, Bethune had become more than a teacher and school facilitator; she had become a public leader. In 1905 she campaigned against the sale of liquor in Daytona, since she felt alcohol consumption harmed the family structure. She began to offer outreach to the lumberyards and turpentine camps near Daytona, including Bible study and reading skills. She also courted public attention for the school, inviting wealthy residents and summer vacationers to tour it, and securing relationships with wealthy benefactors to ensure its continuation. At the same time, she did not neglect those who helped her run the school, the local black community that had sponsored her initial efforts. In 1911, with only two beds, she opened the first hospital to serve African Americans in the Daytona area.

Within ten years, the Daytona Normal and Industrial Institute as her school was renamed, became known nationally for its education of women. This recognition allowed Bethune to accept leadership roles in suffrage organizations. White women had been

moved to Savannah, Georgia, and then Bethune accepted a position teaching in Palatka, Florida, at a new mission school run by the Reverend C. J. Uggans. She sold life insurance to supplement their incomes. Although she taught for five years, she felt a sense of restlessness and a desire to assist others, particularly African American women. Upon learning that a railroad would be coming through the area, bringing an increase in the black population, she moved to Daytona in 1904, bought property, and established the Daytona Educational and Industrial School for Negro Girls,

involved in the suffrage movement for years, but the efforts of their black counterparts had often been thwarted. In 1912 Bethune joined the Equal Suffrage League, part of the National Association of Colored Women (NACW), because she felt that black women needed to have a significant voice. By 1917 she was elected president of the Florida Federation of Colored Women. Her son went to Morehouse College in Atlanta, and although she had given her marital status as "widow" on the 1910 census, her husband actually died in 1918.

Women won the vote when the 19th Amendment was ratified in 1920, and Bethune led a drive to register black voters in Daytona Beach. She went door-to-door in an attempt to raise money for the poll tax, and more specifically, she offered night classes so that African American voters could understand the literature on the topic for which they were voting. More than once the Ku Klux Klan marched past her doors. By the night before the 1920 election, she had registered one hundred voters, prompting a Klan demonstration that night. The next morning she led the one hundred voters to the polls. During these years she remarked to a white friend, "I don't know why they haven't killed me."

Bethune became a well-known public speaker, and she used speaking forums to campaign for the rights of disenfranchised African Americans. Her political activism in 1920 led to an executive position on the National Urban League's executive board, making her not only a representative from the South but also the only woman—and the only African American—on the board. After hearing W. E. B. DuBois speak about the difficulty of gaining access to libraries, she opened her school library to the general public. She had continued to make investments in real estate, business, and a growing stock portfolio. She was determined to expand her school, and eventually she was able to open a high school for adults. The institute became a coeducational college in 1923 when it merged with Cookman Institute in Jacksonville.

In 1924 she was a contender for the presidency of the National Association for the Advancement of Colored People (NAACP), running against Ida B. Wells, the famous anti-lynching activist. Instead, she became president of NACW, an office she held for two consecutive terms. Prior to becoming president of NACW, Bethune referred to herself as the "interpreter of my people," and she took this task seriously. She went on a public relations campaign to alert Americans about the purpose of the organization, and encouraged NACW members to examine at the deepest level their disposition to see matters in terms of individual or local concern, their understanding of the purpose of their

organization, and their own abilities as political actors. At the 1926 biennial convention in Oakland, California, Bethune noted that "this organization must assume an attitude toward all big questions involving the welfare of the nation, public right and especially the present and future of our race. . . . These questions are both national and international" ("President's Address, 1926," quoted in *Mary McLeod Bethune and Black Women's Political Activism*). Her efforts in professionalism resulted in a new headquarters as well as a reorganized program by the time she ended her second term in 1928.

Her coordination of the 1926 NACW national conference in Oakland elicited intense media coverage. The conference coincided with her NACW re-election campaign in which she led three hundred delegates by railway from Chicago to Oakland. The 1926 *New York Age* ran a headline that announced "300 Colored Women Travel Across Continent to California Chartering Biggest Pullman Equipment Ever Used by Transcontinental Women Travelers"; the article also announced her acceptance of a second term as NACW president. Bethune secured a place in the national spotlight, particularly significant during a time when the white-dominated press did not generally provide positive coverage of African Americans, particularly African American women. In addition, Bethune began to write columns for nationally distributed papers targeting African Americans, such as *National Notes* (1924–1928), the *Aframerican Women's Journal* (1940–1949), the *Chicago Defender* (16 October 1948–4 June 1955), and the *Pittsburgh Courier* (23 January 1937–18 June 1938).

Such positive publicity improved Bethune's standing to the extent that she began to have access to powerful figures in national affairs. Through her persistence and continued success, she became more than a token black female in public office; she secured the trust of federal officials. Her connections in the government also attracted the attention of the international press; in 1926 she called for a worldwide meeting of women of color. Her call for international support enabled Bethune to connect her organization's members to those of other organizations. The NACW began an affiliation with the Eurocentric International Council of Women (ICW), which resulted in a widespread support from sixty-five NACW executive members from twenty-two states at the 1925 ICW conference in Washington, D.C. Bethune toured Europe in 1927 as a representative of ICW. She recognized that international support, as well as support at home, would increase awareness of issues facing blacks, and black women in particular. She advocated turning the NACW into a unified organization, not one that concentrated simply on the grassroots level. This led to the creation of the new NACW headquarters, increasing the national, and

Bethune upon her return from Haiti, where she accepted the Order of Merit and Honor. She is holding a cane that belonged to President Roosevelt, given her by Eleanor Roosevelt (Mary McLeod Bethune: Building a Better World: Essays and Selected Documents, *edited by Audrey Thomas McCluskey and Elaine M. Smith, 1999; Thomas Cooper Library, University of South Carolina).*

international, component, and, in turn, the power of her own advocacy efforts as NCNW president. Bethune's skill in organization and ability to use public relations opportunities brought the concept of rights for black women to the forefront of national politics; the NCNW began with only eight organizations, and by 1949, when Bethune stepped down from the leadership position, it included twenty-two smaller organizations.

Bethune managed to establish relationships with government figures that transcended ideological differences. She first met Sara Roosevelt and her daughter-in-law Eleanor at a 1927 luncheon for the presidents of women's organizations given by the National Council of Women. A registered Republican, she met President Calvin Coolidge in 1928 and served on the White House Conference on Child Health and Protection at the request of President Herbert Hoover in 1930. In 1931 she attended President Hoover's Conference on Home Building and Home Ownership. During the 1930s she strengthened her friendship with the

Roosevelts. She became Special Advisor on Minority Affairs during President Franklin Roosevelt's terms in office, from 1935 to 1944. She created the NCNW in 1935. Eleanor Roosevelt's friendship and support became important to Bethune. Author and journalist Enoch Walters, in his 1987 book, *American Diary: A Personal History of the Black Press,* argued that the two shared so many personality traits that it was difficult to think of one without also thinking of the other. "Under a benevolent exterior," he noted, "each had a steeliness that emerged when confronted with opposition."

Bethune used this "steeliness" to her advantage as director of Negro Affairs between 1936 and 1944 in the National Youth Administration (NYA), an organization designed to offer youth between 16 and 24 better opportunities to find and secure work. Bethune felt that black issues should be a significant component of her NYA activities. She was one of a thirty-five-member panel on the NYA advisory committee, and this became a full-time staff position in June 1936. Historians estimate that the NYA assisted almost five million young people through its work-study programs, vocational training, and job-placement services. During the mid-to-late 1930s Bethune also chaired Roosevelt's special committee on Minority Affairs, informally known as the "Black Cabinet." This cabinet included federal appointees who shared a common bond of commitment to social and political change. Bethune lobbied on behalf of black interests, and while she was rarely successful, particularly in her attempts to acquire equal pay for African American employees at the federal level, she did occasionally achieve some success.

Bethune attended the National Conference on the Problems of Negroes and Negro Youth in 1937 and the April 1938 conference of the National Council of Negro Women hosted by Eleanor Roosevelt at the White House. In 1938 she became director of the NYA Division of Negro Affairs, the highest federal office held by a black woman to that date and one of only twenty high-level federal positions occupied by a woman. Bethune advocated solidarity and empowerment for women; her example communicated that black women should interest themselves in questions of national policy, because in that way they could gain positions of power. For the first time since Reconstruction, or since Bethune's birth, federal funding and national attention were being devoted to racial issues.

Her post within the federal government allowed her to facilitate positions for other African Americans at that level. She was especially passionate about the importance of cultivating black leaders. Roosevelt's so-called "Black Cabinet," with Bethune in a prominent position of authority, attempted to involve black youth in activities that would prepare them for higher-paying positions. She noted during a 25 May 1937 Minority Affairs committee meeting, "May I advise the committee that it does not matter how equipped your white supervision might be, or your white leadership; it is impossible for you to enter as sympathetically and understandingly, into the program of the Negro, as the Negro can do" (NYA Archives).

During her time in Washington, D.C., Bethune continued to use the press to build support from both black and white communities. In her columns for the *Pittsburgh Courier* between 1937 and 1938, and in the *Chicago Defender* from 1948 until her death in 1955, she focused on programmatic changes and expounded the importance of Roosevelt's New Deal programs. Rather than focusing on social injustice, she assumed that African Americans were entitled to positions of power and affluence in society, and she wrote as though audiences already agreed with her and that her vision must surely happen. After a tour of Los Angeles in October 1938, she commented, "I was greatly encouraged by the strides that Negroes are making in business." Historian H. Joyce Ross notes that "in the final analysis, Mrs. Bethune presented the public image of a woman who was so affable that even Southern whites could hardly be offended by her approach, but who, at the same time, clearly expressed a vision of racial equality."

Bethune's involvement with the NYA mirrored her involvement in education. While speaking at a regional NYA conference on work-study programs in black colleges on 6 September 1940 in Atlanta, she reviewed the NYA's accomplishments and told officials to "think . . . make up jobs and put them into motion. Get as many students as you can . . . make jobs . . . that will be helpful and stimulating and inspiring" (quoted in McCluskey and Smith, *Mary McLeod Bethune: Building a Better World*). Similarly, she advocated the pursuit of graduate and professional degrees. The student-aid program through the NYA allowed 150,000 black children the opportunity to go to high school and another 60,000 the opportunity to go to college and graduate school (Davis).

Concurrent with her educational goals for the NYA, Bethune continued her work with the NCNW, which provided women with a voice in the political realm. She said, "I am interested in women and believe in their possibilities. . . . We need a vision for larger things. . . . We need a united organization to open doors for women so that when it speaks, its power will be felt" (Smith). In a 1 January 1937 article in the *Courier,* she commented, "Today my eyes must really be sparkling with thrilling thoughts of the meeting in New York of the National Council of Negro Women of America. It was so gratifying to see the deepening interest of our women in the possibilities of our concerted thinking and acting on all fronts."

When President Roosevelt passed Executive Order 8802 on 25 June 1941 barring discrimination by government contractors, she was able to secure jobs for black youths that had not have been available to them previously. Bethune's efforts were thwarted by political restraints. Blacks in the Southern states, where the black population was significantly higher, often had no more representation than blacks in states such as Iowa or New Hampshire, where the population of blacks was significantly less. She was able to gain at least twenty-five assistant director jobs at state bureaus for African Americans. Ever resourceful when it came to financial considerations, she also found ways to allocate funds, through the creation of the Special Higher Education Fund, which increased to $609,000 within seven years.

She often invited Eleanor Roosevelt to join the board of trustees for Bethune-Cookman College in 1941; Bethune hoped that her presence and activism would provide further attention to her cause. Mrs. Roosevelt had first visited the campus as a keynote speaker for the thirty-fifth anniversary of the original Daytona Institute, and this in itself prompted speculation. By staying in Bethune's residence on campus, rather than in an all-white hotel off campus, Roosevelt prompted reaction in many white Southerners.

Bethune's career waned a bit during WWII, but she continued to turn to new activities. She resigned as president of Bethune-Cookman in 1942 to become closely involved in war efforts, particularly as part of her NYA activities. In 1942 she finally persuaded the U.S. War Department to allow black women to be commissioned as officers in the Women's Army Auxiliary Corps (WAAC). The male armed forces did not integrate racially until after the Battle of the Bulge and did not really end racially discriminatory policies until 1948, so Bethune's accomplishment was remarkably in advance of the national trend. In 1944 she joined the Women's Army for National Defense.

NYA activities ended with the last dispersal of federal funds in 1943, and the agency dissolved in January 1944. After the NYA disbanded, Bethune officially retired to Florida but continued to write and speak about civil rights issues and occasionally to make public appearances. From time to time rumors sprang up regarding her political ambitions; during her Washington years, a 1939 issue of the *Washington Afro-American* had contended that she planned to leave the NYA for a high-ranking position in the National Democratic Party. Bethune put down the rumors with a blunt reply: "I'm not in politics. My school comes first. I did not come here seeking this job, the job came seeking me. I carved

*Mary McLeod Bethune with James A. Colston, her successor as president of Bethune-Cookman College, January 1943 (*Mary McLeod Bethune: Building a Better World: Essays and Selected Documents, *edited by Audrey Thomas McCluskey and Elaine M. Smith, 1999; Thomas Cooper Library, University of South Carolina)*

out my job thirty-four years ago" (quoted in McCluskey, "We Specialize in the Wholly Impossible").

At the end of World War II, she joined two other African Americans, DuBois and Walter White, as part of a U.S. delegation to assist in the development of the United Nations charter in April 1945. Bethune continued serving as president of the NCNW until 1949. That year she received an honorary doctorate in humanities from Rollins College, the oldest recognized college in the state of Florida and the first Southern white college to give such an award to an African American. She received international recognition for her career as well; she was awarded the Medal of Honor and Merit from Haiti in 1949. She also represented President Harry Truman at the inauguration ceremonies for President William S. Tubman of Liberia in 1952, a final consummation of her dream from childhood to visit Africa. She received Liberia's highest honor, the Commander of the Order of the Star of Africa, during her visit.

Part of Bethune's success can be attributed to the fact that she sought both white involvement and white support in her efforts and community empowerment among African Americans. When she returned to Florida, she applied her political and social prowess to economic endeavors to help the local community in Daytona. She and a local Florida businessman, G. D. Rogers Sr., purchased beach property outside of Daytona, eventually promoting it as the Bethune Volusia Beach, and available not just to blacks but to anyone who chose to frequent the beach. She said of the beach, "its doors of opportunity and refreshment will be opened to all mankind" (Smith). She wanted the black community to join together and pursue economic prosperity, arguing that she refused to allow her skin color to be a "handicap." Bethune was, however, proud to be an African American, and while she considered equality to be an achievable goal, she never doubted the importance of "racial integrity," that is, the importance of the African American heritage. Comments to this effect, along with her involvement in suspect organizations, earned her the label of Communist in the McCarthy era of the 1950s. At one point she was told she could not speak at a public school in New Jersey because she was a Communist. The accusations were not pursued. Bethune had gone on record many times as a supporter of traditionally defined democratic societies. She had written, for example, in an article entitled "Certain Unalienable Rights," originally published in 1944, that "Under democracy, the Negro has the opportunity to work for an improvement in his status through the intelligent use of his vote, the creation of a more favorable public opinion, and the development of his native abilities" (Logan).

Eleanor Roosevelt spoke at the dedication in March 1953 of the Bethune Foundation, created by its namesake and to which she donated her house, furnishings, and papers. Bethune began keeping a diary in her mid teens, and she put together twenty-nine scrapbooks documenting her activities from 1936 to 1951. She began writing her autobiography in October 1952, an activity she seems to have contemplated sporadically over the years, as her papers contain many autobiographical fragments varying between 5 and 250 pages in length. She sometimes delegated her *Chicago Defender* column to ghostwriter Constance Daniel in these later years. Bethune often commented on her own personal faith, as well as her praise of beginning interracial community development and the small strides for equality for women. Her last column, published posthumously in 1955, encouraged blacks to apply pressure for "full citizenship."

Just before her fatal heart attack on 17 May 1955, Bethune published her "Last Will and Testament" in the August 1955 issue of *Ebony* magazine. Revealing the foundation of much of her work in religious oratory, each passage includes the beginning phrase, "I leave you . . ." indicating her attempt to bestow a sense of responsibility on the youth of America, as well as an understanding of equality on her readership. Her testament is one of hope and an emphasis on education, both of which were constant themes in her history. She wrote,

> I leave you love. Love builds. It is positive and helpful. It is more beneficial than hate. . . . I leave you hope. The Negro's growth will be great in the years to come. Yesterday, our ancestors endured the degradation of slavery, yet they retained their dignity. Today, we direct our economic and political strength toward winning a more abundant and secure life. Tomorrow, a new Negro, unhindered by race taboos and shackles, will benefit from more than 330 years of ceaseless striving and struggle. Theirs will be a better world. . . . I leave you the challenge of developing confidence in one another. As long as Negroes are hemmed into racial blocs by prejudice and pressure, it will be necessary for them to band together for economic betterment. . . . I leave you a thirst for education. Knowledge is the prime need of the hour. More and more, Negroes are taking full advantage of hard-won opportunities for learning, and the educational level of the Negro population is at its highest point in history. . . . I leave you a respect for the uses of power. . . . I leave you faith. . . . I leave you racial dignity. . . . I leave you a desire to live harmoniously with your fellow men. . . . I leave you finally a responsibility to our young people.

Noting that "we are a minority of 15 million living side by side with a white majority," she advocated the importance of attempting to build lives together with Americans of all races. This principle she specifically demonstrated in her association with Eleanor Roosevelt, which was a political relationship but also a genuine friendship based on mutual affection. She noted, however, "I would not exchange my color for all the wealth in the world, for had I been born white, I might not have been able to do all that I have done or yet hope to do."

Bethune's death in 1955 prompted an outpouring of sympathy and admiration. The *Pittsburgh Courier* praised her "indomitable soul." Poet Langston Hughes memorialized Bethune with a folksy anecdote that reveals much by what it does not acknowledge; for most of her life she traveled in a United States in which hotel rooms would not accept her business. In a Bethune-like gesture, Hughes chooses instead to acknowledge the generosity of those who provided her room and board:

> Colored people all along the eastern seaboard spread a feast whenever Mrs. Bethune passed along their way. Before Mrs. Bethune reached the wayside

home of any friend anywhere, the chickens, sensing that she was coming, went flying off frantically seeking a safe hiding place. They knew some necks would be wrung in her honor to make a heaping platter of southern fried chicken (McCluskey and Smith).

After Bethune's death, the foundation she had established was left without a powerful leader to secure funding. Almost twenty years later its financial problems were solved when Bethune gained additional recognition. On 10 July 1974, ninety-nine years after her birth, a statue in Lincoln Park in Washington, D.C., was dedicated in her honor, and in 1975 the National Park Service declared her home a National Historic Landmark. Her home state of South Carolina honors Bethune with a portrait in the capitol building in Columbia. Bethune-Cookman College survives as a testament to her vision of empowerment beyond racial and gender barriers.

Several times during Bethune's lifetime scholars attempted to write biographies of her. Frances Keyser wrote two hundred pages of a biography in the 1920s. Daniel M. Williams began but did not complete a biography in the 1940s. His records, including interviews with Bethune from 1946, survive in the Florida Memory Project, located at the Bureau of Archives and Records of the State of Florida. Catherine Owens Peare completed a biography with a foreword by Bethune, published by Vanguard in 1951, but Bethune later unsuccessfully sued Peare for misrepresenting her activities. Several biographical treatments appeared after her death, mostly heavily anecdotal accounts for children. Her papers, a goldmine of organizational and policy information in the period before the Civil Rights Movement, became available on microfilm in the late 1990s. Several graduate theses have addressed her work as an educator or civil rights activist. In the 1990s an outpouring of scholarship was devoted to her work; very little of it focused on her which though prolific writing, includes primarily essays, political statements, speeches, and correspondence. Although she spent decades writing and composing almost every day, Mary McLeod Bethune did not see herself as a writer; she wrote because life required it, because she was determined to solve the problems she and her contemporaries faced.

Bibliographies:

Selected Resources: Mary McLeod Bethune, compiled by the Black Christian Education Resources Center, Program Committee on Education for Christian Life and Mission, Division of Education and Ministry, National Council of Churches (New York: Black Christian Education Resources Center, 1974);

Carolyn LaDelle Bennett, *An Annotated Bibliography of Mary McLeod Bethune's Chicago Defender Columns, 1948–1955* (Lewiston, N.Y.: Edwin Mellen Press, 2001).

References:

Mary Frances Berry, "Twentieth Century Black Women in Education," *The Journal of Negro Education,* 51 (Summer 1982): 288–300;

Carol Sears Botsch, "Mary McLeod Bethune," University of South Carolina–Aiken Website <http://www.usca.edu/aasc/bethune.htm> (viewed 2 June 2008);

Joyce A. Hanson, *Mary McLeod Bethune and Black Women's Political Activism* (Columbia & London: University of Missouri Press, 2003);

Rayford W. Logan, ed., *What the Negro Wants* (Chapel Hill: University of North Carolina Press, 1944);

Mary McLeod Bethune Papers: The Bethune-Cookman College Collection, 1922–1955 (University Publications of America, 1995) <https://freud.psy.fsu/~women-studies/wsholdings.doc> (viewed 29 July 2008);

Audrey Thomas McCluskey, "'We Specialize in the Wholly Impossible': Black Women School Founders and Their Mission," *Signs,* 22 (Winter 1997): 403–427;

McCluskey, "Representing the Race: Mary McLeod Bethune and the Press in the Jim Crow Era," *The Western Journal of Black Studies,* 23 (Winter 1999): 236–256;

Catherine Owens Peare, *Mary McLeod Bethune* (New York: Vanguard, 1951);

Carol O. Perkins, "The Pragmatic Idealism of Mary McLeod Bethune," *Sage: A Scholarly Journal on Black Women,* 5 (1988): 30–36;

Tammy Lynn Pertillar, "Mary McLeod Bethune: Visionary Activist," *The Brown Quarterly,* 1 (1996) <http://brownvboard.org/brwnqurt/01-1/01-1b.htm> (viewed 2 June 2008);

H. Joyce Ross, "Mary McLeod Bethune and the National Youth Administration: A Case Study of Power Relationships in the Black Cabinet of Franklin D. Roosevelt," *The Journal of Negro History,* 60 (1975): 1–28;

"The Sacrifices and Achievements of African-American Women: Mary McLeod Bethune," *The Journal of Blacks in Higher Education* (31 August 2001): 35;

Elaine M. Smith, "Mary McLeod Bethune's 'Last Will and Testament': A Legacy For Race Vindication," *The Journal of Negro History,* 81 (1996): 105–122;

Smith, "Mary McLeod Bethune and the National Youth Administration," in *Clio Was a Woman: Studies in the History of American Women,* edited by Mabel E. Deutrich and Virginia C. Purdy (Washington, D.C.: Howard University Press, 1980): 149–177;

"Mary McLeod Bethune, Educator," The Florida Memory Project Online <http://www.floridamemory.com/OnlineClassroom/MaryBethune/> (viewed 2 June 2008);

Deborah Gray White, "Mining the Forgotten: Manuscript Sources for Black Women's History," *Journal of American History,* 74 (June 1987): 237–242.

Papers:

The papers of Mary McLeod Bethune reside in several repositories. The largest collection is at Bethune-Cookman College in Daytona Beach, Florida. The Amistad Research Center, Tulane University, New Orleans, has correspondence, diaries, speeches, and clipping files. The NYA papers are in the National Archives in Washington, D.C.; other Bethune items are in the archives of the National Association for the Advancement of Colored People, in the National Urban League Papers, the National Archives for Women's History, and the Records of the National Council of Negro Women in Washington, D.C. Smaller collections, mostly correspondence, survive in the personal papers of Bethune's colleagues and friends, including Eleanor and Franklin Roosevelt, Booker T. Washington, Charlotte Hawkins Brown, Nannie Helen Burroughs, Julius Rosenwald, Mary Church Terrell, and Aubrey Williams.

Murray Bookchin
(14 January 1921 – 30 July 2006)

Edward D. Melillo
Franklin Marshall College

BOOKS: *Our Synthetic Environment,* as Lewis Herber (New York: Knopf, 1962; London: Cape, 1963); as Bookchin, revised edition (New York: Harper & Row, 1974);

Crisis in Our Cities, as Herber (Englewood Cliffs, N.J.: Prentice-Hall, 1965);

Post-Scarcity Anarchism (Berkeley, Cal.: Ramparts Press, 1971);

Hip Culture: Six Essays on Its Revolutionary Potential (New York: Times Change Press, 1971);

The Limits of the City (New York: Harper & Row, 1974);

On Spontaneity and Organization (London: Soldarity, 1975);

The Spanish Anarchists: The Heroic Years, 1868–1936 (New York: Free Life Editions, 1977);

Toward an Ecological Society (Montreal and Buffalo, N.Y.: Black Rose Books, 1980);

The Ecology of Freedom: The Emergence and Dissolution of Hierarchy (Palo Alto, Cal.: Cheshire Books, 1982); revised edition (Montreal & New York: Black Rose Books, 1991);

Re-Enchanting Humanity: A Defense of the Human Spirit Against Antihumanism, Misanthropy, Mysticism, and Primitivism (New York: Black Rose Books, 1984; London & New York: Cassell, 1995);

The Modern Crisis (Philadelphia: New Society, ca. 1986); revised edition (Montreal: Black Rose Books, 1987);

The Philosophy of Social Ecology: Essays on Dialectical Naturalism (New York: Black Rose Books, 1987); revised edition (Montreal: Black Rose Books, 1995);

The Rise of Urbanization and the Decline of Citizenship (San Francisco: Sierra Club Books, 1987); revised and republished as *Urbanization Without Cities: The Rise and Decline of Citizenship* (Montreal: Black Rose Books, 1992);

Remaking Society: Pathways to a Green Future (Montreal: Black Rose Books, 1989);

Defending the Earth: A Dialogue between Murray Bookchin and Dave Foreman (Boston: South End Press, 1991);

Which Way for the Ecology Movement? (Edinburgh & San Francisco: AK Press, 1993);

Deep Ecology & Anarchism: A Polemic (London: Freedom Press, 1993);

*Murray Bookchin (*The Murray Bookchin Reader, *edited by Janet Biehl; London: Cassell, 1997; Thomas Cooper Library, University of South Carolina)*

To Remember Spain: The Anarchist and Syndicalist Revolution of 1936 (Edinburgh & San Francisco: AK Press, 1994);

Which Way for the Ecology Movement (San Francisco: AK Press, 1994);

Social Anarchism or Lifestyle Anarchism: An Unbridgeable Chasm (Edinburgh & San Francisco: AK Press, 1995);

From Urbanization to Cities: Toward a New Politics of Citizenship (London & New York: Cassell, 1995);

The Third Revolution: Popular Movements in the Revolutionary Era, 4 vols.; vols. 1 and 2 (London: Cassell,

55

1996–1999); vols. 3 and 4 (New York & London: Continuum International Publishing Group, 2004–2005);

The Politics of Social Ecology: Libertarian Municipalism, by Bookchin and Janet Biehl (Montreal: Black Rose Books, 1998);

Social Ecology and Communalism (Oakland, Cal.: AK Press, 2005).

COLLECTIONS: *The Murray Bookchin Reader,* edited by Janet Biehl (London: Cassell, 1997);

Anarchism, Marxism, and the Future of the Left: Interviews and Essays, 1993–1998 (Edinburgh & San Francisco: AK Press, 1999).

OTHER: Hans Thirring, *Energy for Man: Windmills to Nuclear Power,* introduction by Bookchin (New York: Harper & Row, 1969);

Ida Mett, *The Kronstadt Uprising, 1921,* introduction by Bookchin (Montreal: Black Rose Books/OurGeneration Press, 1971);

The Anarchist Collectives: Workers' Self-Management in the Spanish Revolution, 1936–1939, edited by Sam Dolgoff, introduction by Bookchin (Montreal: Black Rose Books, 1996).

SELECTED PERIODICAL PUBLICATIONS– UNCOLLECTED: "The Problem of Chemicals in Food," as Lewis Herber, *Contemporary Issues,* 12 (June–August 1952): 206–241;

"Stop the Bomb: An Appeal to the Reason of the American People," *Contemporary Issues,* 17 (1954): 60–66;

"Dangerous Environment of Man," as Herber, *Consumer Bulletin,* 45 (August 1962): 23–29;

"Desire and Need," *Anarchy* [U.K.], 7 (October 1967): 311–319;

"An Open Letter to Paul Goodman," *New York Times Magazine* (14 July 1968): 10;

"The Kronstadt Uprising: An Introduction," *Libertarian Analysis,* 1 (September 1971): 4–13;

"Murray Bookchin replies to [Edward] Abbey," *Utne Reader* (January–February 1988): 4–8;

"Libertarian Municipalism: An Overview," *Green Perspectives,* 24 (October 1991): 1–5;

"Intelligentsia and the New Intellectuals," *Alternative Forum,* 1 (Fall 1991): 1–8;

"Recovering Evolution: A Reply to Eckersley and Fox," *Journal of Political Ecology* [London & Athens], 1 (September–December 1992): 144–173;

"A New Politics of Confederalism," *Regeneration: A Magazine of Left Green Social Thought,* 4 (Fall 1992): 20–22;

"The Meaning of Confederalism," *Society and Nature,* 1 (1993): 41–54;

"The Ghost of Anarchosyndicalism," *Anarchist Studies,* 1 (Spring 1993): 3–24;

"Nationalism and the 'National Question,'" *Society and Nature,* 5 (1994);

"Reflections: An Overview of the Roots of Social Ecology," *Harbinger,* 3 (Spring 2003): 6–11.

From the 1950s until his death Murray Bookchin was a leading voice in the radical critique of the environmental and social contradictions underpinning modern society. As a founder of the social ecology movement, as well as an advocate for anarchist-libertarian politics of social change, Bookchin shaped the trajectories of Green movements throughout the world and influenced radical thinkers on both sides of the Atlantic. His multifaceted career as an activist, a teacher, and a writer was a prolific one. Bookchin's written work includes more than two hundred articles, two dozen books, and scores of published debates with his detractors and sympathizers. Despite the fact that many of Bookchin's ideas anticipated the well-publicized writings of such thinkers as Rachel Carson, E. F. Schumacher, and Barry Commoner, Bookchin's work has received little sustained attention from either academia or the mainstream press. His ideas earned him a considerable following in the United States, and they also met with significant success abroad. Bookchin's work has been translated into more than twenty languages, and he has developed an extensive readership throughout Western Europe, where he lectured for many decades. Additionally, Bookchin's research has helped stimulate crucial reforms in German food-and-drug legislation, his social activism has provided an organizing model for the transnational anti-nuclear movement, and his writings on Green politics have influenced the development of Europe's ecological Left.

Murray Bookchin was born in New York City to Nathan and Rose (Kaluskaya) Bookchin on 14 January 1921. His Jewish-immigrant parents had been revolutionaries in Russia during the Czarist period, well before the 1905 Revolution. As a teenager, Bookchin followed in his family's footsteps by joining the Young Communist League and becoming active in left-wing politics. During the Spanish civil war (1936–1939), Bookchin spoke at several New York rallies in support of the Abraham Lincoln Brigade. Although Bookchin was too young at the time to join the 2,800 American volunteers who traveled to Spain to defend the Spanish republic against the military insurgence led by General Francisco Franco, two of his older friends died fighting the fascists on the Madrid front. Bookchin's experiences during this period later informed his 1977 book, *The Spanish Anarchists: The Heroic Years, 1868–1936.*

While Europe teetered on the brink of total war, Bookchin turned his attention to working-class politics on the home front. His parents could not afford to send him to college, so Bookchin decided to take work as an apprentice electrician in Queens. Soon after completing his training he became a foundryman in northern New Jersey. During his four-year stint in heavy industry, Bookchin organized for the Congress of Industrial Organizations (CIO), gaining valuable experience on the front lines of the labor struggle. At the time, the CIO was heavily influenced by Communist politics, and many of Bookchin's comrades from the Young Communist League joined him in door-to-door union leaflet campaigns in the industrial towns of northern New Jersey.

Bookchin became disillusioned with Soviet Communism after the Moscow show trials of the late 1930s, the counter-revolutionary interventions of Comintern agents in Spain, and the Hitler-Stalin pact of 1939 exposed the authoritarian character of Stalinism. Despite his ideological break with the Communist Party, Bookchin's association with Trotskyism persisted until the end of World War II. After the war, his ties to all official Communist organizations withered. As he told interviewer David Vanek in the summer of 2000, "I hoped that the Second World War would end in revolutions, as the first war had, and became a Trotskyist. When the war ended without a revolution, I became disillusioned with orthodox Marxism and realized I had to rethink everything."

Bookchin returned from a tour of duty in World War II and immediately took a job as an assembly-line worker at General Motors. As an organizer for the United Auto Workers (UAW), he witnessed firsthand the rise of pro-business unionism and the compromises made by the reform-minded leadership of organized labor in the wake of the massive, three-month strike at GM in 1948. He felt deeply distressed at the decline of the shop-steward system and the increasing involvement of unelected company professionals in the union hierarchy during the tenure of UAW president Walter Reuther.

Bookchin's dismay at the bourgeoning accommodations between organized labor and big business accompanied his growing awareness of the environmental problems emanating from postwar industrial development. In 1952 Bookchin published a prescient essay on the risks of human exposure to man-made toxins. As he frequently pointed out, his treatment of this issue predated Carson's acclaimed warning about the hazards of the pesticide DDT, *Silent Spring* (1962), by ten years. Bookchin's essay, "The Problem of Chemicals in Food," appeared in the journal *Contemporary Issues* under the pseudonym Lewis Herber. "Within recent years," Bookchin warned his readers, "the rise of little known and even unknown infectious diseases, the increase of degenerative illnesses and finally the high incidence of cancer suggests some connection between the growing use of chemicals in food and human diseases." The year after Bookchin's article appeared, the German publisher Müller Verlag printed a translated version of the essay as a book. German environmental activists and consumer advocates adopted Bookchin's arguments in their campaign to alter German food-and-drug laws to make them more responsive to new, man-made health threats. A U.S. publisher also picked up on the startling revelations Bookchin's writings brought to light. Five months before the publication of *Silent Spring,* New York–based publisher Alfred A. Knopf printed Bookchin's findings under the title *Our Synthetic Environment.*

Bookchin's growing interest in environmental issues expanded rapidly with the rise of nuclear technologies. Throughout the 1950s and 1960s he became involved in campaigns to oppose nuclear weapons experiments and expose the presence of nuclear fallout throughout the world. In response to the testing of a hydrogen bomb in the Bikini Atoll in 1954, Bookchin wrote a fiery pamphlet entitled "Stop the Bomb: An Appeal to the Reason of the American People." Japan's largest daily newspaper immediately translated and published the full text of this essay on page three. "Stop the Bomb" also circulated widely in activist circles throughout the United States and Europe. Peace movement pioneer A. J. Muste later credited Bookchin's leaflet with changing his thinking on nuclear energy.

Shortly after he wrote "Stop the Bomb," Bookchin published a spate of articles in the German journal *Dinge der Zeit* and its English-language version, *Contemporary Issues,* under the pseudonyms M. S. Shiloh, Herber, Robert Keller, and Harry Ludd. During the 1950s and 1960s *Contemporary Issues* served as an ideological platform for the International Kommunisten Deutschlands (IKD), a group of exiled German radicals with whom Bookchin had connected in the political underground of McCarthy-era New York. The IKD espoused anti-Stalinist, left-libertarian politics and agitated for the airlifting of weapons to the partisans of the 1956 Hungarian uprising against Soviet control. Bookchin's discussions with IKD members helped him to move in new directions during the post-Communist period of his intellectual development.

During the decade in which he began to develop the social theory for which he became well known, Bookchin also became involved with the civil rights struggle and the women's movement. He served as an adviser to the Women's Strike for Peace (WSP) organization, which began in 1961. In 1963 and 1964 he helped to organize the campaign to stop the construction of a nuclear power plant in the Ravenswood neighborhood of Queens, New York. He joined a New York City chapter of the Congress of Racial Equality (CORE) during the "Mississippi Summer" voter-registration drive of 1964. These groups were involved in many protests that ended in confrontations with the police. Bookchin later recalled spending much of the mid 1960s in the Queens County Court House negotiating with prosecutors to drop or reduce charges against him and his fellow activists.

The mid 1960s proved to be a watershed period in Bookchin's thinking. In his experience the environmental and socio-economic issues involved in such campaigns as the Ravenswood action seemed inextricably intertwined. He drew upon his empirical experiences to outline a new mode of analyzing and transforming society, which appeared in a manifesto-like article in the journal *Comment*. His 1964 essay, "Ecology and Revolutionary Thought," proposed that human beings had entered an age of ecology. Bookchin argued that Renaissance thinkers had increasingly viewed their universe in mechanical terms, that the Victorians had employed Darwinian evolutionary theory as their model of understanding the world, and that a comprehensive understanding of the domination of nature and its commensurate effects would come to inform the most revolutionary thinking of the post–World War II era. He called his analysis of this new age "social ecology."

Although the concept of social ecology drew upon Marx and Engels's investigation of the alienated relationship between town and country under capitalism, Bookchin proposed a more general critique of all hierarchies and forms of domination. Influenced by the writings of anarchists such as Herbert Read and Peter Kropotkin, Bookchin contended that the destructive environmental effects of global capitalism emanated from the domination of human by human. Anthropogenic attempts to assert control over nature could never be abolished without addressing forms of human-to-human exploitation and dominance. Thus, he believed, ecological and social issues existed in intrinsic relation to one another and could not be treated in isolation. In 1965 Bookchin followed up on "Ecology and Revolutionary Thought" with a second essay, titled "Towards a Liberatory Technology," in which he called for a new eco-social order, to rely exclusively upon renewable energy sources such as solar, wind, hydroelectric, and geothermal power. In several subsequent interviews, he noted that his 1965 essay anticipated the conclusions at the heart of Schumacher's widely read treatise on nature, society, and technology, *Small Is Beautiful* (1973).

In the late 1960s Bookchin began his career in education, teaching courses at the Alternative University of New York, then part of City University of New York's Staten Island campus. The Alternative University was one of America's largest "free universities," offering classes to students from all socio-economic backgrounds. Bookchin quickly became an influential mentor for many of the young activists involved in the New Left. During the events of 1968 the New Left assumed an emphatically international temperament. In July of "the year of the barricades," Bookchin, his wife Bea, and their two children traveled to Paris and found themselves in the midst of student demonstrations on the Boulevard Saint-Michel. The area had been a hotbed of anti-government protests during the previous two months of popular unrest, and the neighborhood erupted in rioting once more during the Bookchin family's visit. Bookchin saw firsthand the violent police repression of the widespread demonstrations in France, and it made a deep impression on him. He also took to heart the successes and failures of the student movement and the reactionary attempts of the communist General Confederation of Labor (CGT) to prevent striking workers from allying with radical student groups. Bookchin later remarked in *Anarchism, Marxism, and the Future of the Left* (1999) that "The '68 events in Paris generated considerable controversy in the Left, and raised many issues that have yet to be sorted out: questions of organization, a public sphere, theory and practice, and the like."

Returning to the United States with these questions in mind, Bookchin engaged in sustained discussions with many of the student radicals involved in the campus-based movement Students for a Democratic Society (SDS). At the June 1969 SDS conference in Chicago, Bookchin and a collective of anarchists calling themselves "The Anarchos Group" distributed two thousand copies of a pamphlet titled "Listen Marxist" to the crowd of radicals in attendance. In "Listen Marxist," Bookchin attacked the orthodox communist idea that building a revolutionary vanguard organization to represent workers' interests was a necessary, or useful, step toward the transformation of society. He argued that such efforts not only reinforce hierarchical relations by creating further distinctions between leader and led, they also promote a heightened consciousness of identity through work. Instead, Bookchin argues, a genuine revolution in social relations would aim to end this feeling of working-class distinctiveness forever. According to Bookchin, Marx's nineteenth-century version of class struggle had become outdated, for humans must create revolution in society as a whole, not merely in the industrial workplace.

In the essay Bookchin targets, among others, the Progressive Labor Party (PL), the largest communist faction within SDS. According to Bookchin, the PL exemplified the dogmatic thinking that had precipitated the downfalls of previous broad-based, democratic social movements. Although SDS fragmented in the wake of the 1969 conference, Bookchin and his companions eventually circulated more than 100,000 copies of "Listen Marxist" to readers in the United States and Great Britain. One historian of the 1960s has called the pamphlet "a classic example of innovative New Left propaganda."

Bookchin reprinted "Listen Marxist" in his first widely circulated book, *Post-Scarcity Anarchism* (1971). The other essays contained therein focus predominantly on his efforts to elucidate the destructive relationship between hierarchical societies and nature. In the book's title essay, Bookchin writes that "the contradiction between the exploitative organization of society and the natural environment is beyond co-optation: the atmosphere, the waterways, the soil and the ecology required for human survival are not redeemable by reforms, concessions, or modifications of strategic policy." Instead, Bookchin contends, we need revolutionary measures to bring human relations with the earth into balance.

For such a radical change to occur, a new generation must develop modes of thought and practices heretofore unseen in history. Bookchin saw the immediate need to educate students on the concerns and methods of social ecology. In 1974 he and cultural anthropologist Daniel Chodorkoff founded the Institute for Social Ecology (ISE) in Plainfield, Vermont. With courses in sustainable agriculture, alternative technologies, political theory, and organizing strategies, the ISE became the headquarters for the development of social ecology. The ISE moved onto a forty-acre farm at nearby Goddard College in 1975 and was incorporated in 1981. At various times the institute has maintained cooperative agreements with Goddard and Burlington Colleges in Vermont and Prescott College in Prescott, Arizona.

The decade following the founding of the ISE emerged as Bookchin's most prolific. In 1974 Bookchin published *The Limits of the City,* an historical overview of the rise of the commercial metropolis. The book earned Bookchin critical praise in such publications as the *Toronto Star* and *Science and Society* and established him as a major social thinker. Although Bookchin never earned a college degree, he began teaching at Ramapo College of New Jersey in 1974. He was appointed full professor of social theory in 1977 and retired in 1981.

Bookchin applied his theories to his own grassroots organizing efforts. In the 1970s he and others founded the Vermont section of the Clamshell Alliance, a consensus-based group that opposed the construction of a nuclear reactor at Seabrook, New Hampshire, sixty miles north of Boston. In April 1977 more than 2,000 members of the alliance occupied the construction site. Police arrested

Dust jacket for the first edition of Bookchin's 1982 synthesis of ecology, anthropology, and political theory (Richland County Public Library)

1,414 of the activists and held them in National Guard armories for two weeks. As planned, those detained refused bail. The protestors viewed the demonstration as a success, because it created enough controversy over the power plant to delay its opening for fourteen years, and it initiated a new era of growth in the global anti-nuclear movement. In his role as one of the organizers of the demonstration, Bookchin educated fellow protesters in the use of affinity groups. These small, nonhierarchical units of five to twenty activists who coordinate direct action strategies are the tactical descendants of the *grupos de afinidad,* Spanish anarchists used in the late nineteenth and early twentieth centuries. Bookchin had studied the *grupos de afinidad* closely, and he helped to train fellow alliance members in their tactics. The Clamshell Alliance demonstration at Seabrook was the first protest in U.S. history to use the affinity group model, which developed into a favored option in the strategic repertoires of social movements.

Bookchin published *The Spanish Anarchists: The Heroic Years, 1868–1936* the year after the Seabrook protest. In the preface to the book's AK Press edition (1994), Bookchin recalled that he had originally taken on the project to inspire a new generation with the example of a group that fundamentally challenged the social relations structuring its world. As he saw it, contemporary progressive movements had much to learn from the study of ordinary citizens who had organized themselves to change the world. Bookchin followed this book with a collection of fourteen essays, *Toward an Ecological Society* (1980). Many of the pieces, including the title essay and the chapters "Spontaneity & Organization," "Self-Management and The New Technology," and "Marxism As Bourgeois Sociology" distilled Bookchin's thought over the previous two decades into a more accessible form.

In 1982 Bookchin published the book scholars consider his masterpiece, *The Ecology of Freedom: The Emergence and Dissolution of Hierarchy*. On the first page Bookchin again contends that "The domination of nature by man stems from the very real domination of human by human." From this proposition Bookchin casts a wide net, synthesizing the diverse approaches of ecology, anthropology, and political theory to demonstrate the historical rise and possible demise of exploitation. In *The Ecology of Freedom* Bookchin expresses uncompromising views on the need for radical solutions to the ecological and social problems facing the world in the late twentieth century. He criticizes the approaches of mainstream environmental organizations, arguing that such "partial 'solutions' serve merely as cosmetics to conceal the deep-seated nature of the ecological crisis. They thereby deflect public attention and theoretical insight from an adequate understanding of the depth and scope of the necessary changes." Bookchin also contends that men's oppression of nature and of women has been fundamentally interlinked throughout history. Eco-feminist thinkers, such as Ariel Salleh and Carolyn Merchant, later credited Bookchin with articulating a foundational principle for their work in his *The Ecology of Freedom*. The book received enthusiastic reviews in such publications as *The Nation, Telos, Library Journal, The San Francisco Chronicle,* and *The Village Voice*.

The same year he published *The Ecology of Freedom,* a 1982 documentary, *Anarchism in America,* featured Bookchin as it attempted to trace the historical roots of anarchism and dispel popular misconceptions about this enigmatic political tradition. In the autumn of 1982 Bookchin retired from his position at Ramapo College and returned to full-time involvement with programs at the ISE. Bookchin's work in the 1980s increasingly attacked what he referred to as "mystical thinking," which had emerged on both the Left and the Right in response to the ecological crisis. These arguments took shape in *Re-Enchanting Humanity: A Defense of the Human*

Spirit Against Antihumanism, Misanthropy, Mysticism, and Primitivism (1984).

One of the primary targets of Bookchin's scorn was the school of thought known as deep ecology. Norwegian philosopher Arne Naess (b. 1912) developed that concept in the early 1970s as a set of principles for transcending what he saw as superficial responses to contemporary environmental and social crises. Naess presented deep ecology in contrast to reformist environmentalism, or "shallow ecology," which he argued adopted both utilitarian and anthropocentric attitudes toward nature. Naess's philosophy opposed what he saw as the condescending relationship to the environment at the core of Judeo-Christian tradition. In *Ecology, Community and Lifestyle: Outline of an Ecosophy* (1989), Naess charged that "The arrogance of stewardship [found in the Bible] consists in the idea of superiority which underlies the thought that we exist to watch over nature like a highly respected middleman between the Creator and Creation."

While Bookchin ostensibly agreed with Naess's conclusions regarding the nature-stewardship tradition of Judeo-Christian spirituality, he took umbrage with the way many deep ecologists seemed to ignore the underlying socio-economic and authoritarian causes of environmental problems. Bookchin opposed in particular the worldviews of deep ecologists who based their concepts and proposals upon Native American belief systems, Goddess mythology, Zen Buddhism, Hinduism, Taoism, the pre-Socratics, and primitivism—all of which Bookchin dismissed as the uncritical veneration of pre-technological and pre-urban societies. Bookchin believes that this heterogeneous synthesis of nature worship and mystical philosophy serves only to focus people inward on strategies of personal transformation, thereby leaving unchallenged the exploitative external dimensions of hierarchical societies and what he calls "capitalism's grow-or-die imperative" ("Libertarian Municipalism: An Overview"). Leading exponents of deep ecology, including George Sessions, Warwick Fox, Joanna Macy, and Bill Devall, counter with the argument that Bookchin's approach to the ecological crisis is anthropocentric and obscures the basic equality of all beings.

These particular debates came to a head when Dave Foreman, cofounder of the radical environmental movement Earth First!, invoked deep ecology to justify his position that famine and disease serve as nature's way of reverting to harmonious equilibrium. In a 1987 interview with deep ecologist Bill Devall for the Australian journal *Simply Living,* Foreman contended, "The best thing would be to just let the people there [in Ethiopia] starve."

Likewise, in the May 1987 issue of the *Earth First! Journal* Christopher Manes, writing under the pseudonym "Miss Ann Thropy," stated, "If radical environmentalists were to invent a disease to bring human population back to ecological sanity, it would probably be something like AIDS." In the wake of such comments, a profoundly antihumanistic possibility inherent to a deep-ecology position seemed to be materializing.

Bookchin wasted no time in responding to these polemicists, characterizing their arguments as an "ideological toxic dump" and a "black hole of half-digested, ill-formed and half-baked ideas." Bookchin and Foreman debated their positions in public forums in the fall of 1989, and, at least in the short-term, Bookchin emerged the clear winner of the dispute. Foreman softened his stances on population issues considerably in the years immediately following the publication of *Defending the Earth: A Dialogue between Murray Bookchin and Dave Foreman* (1991).

During subsequent years Bookchin devoted much of his energy to defending his legacy within the environmental and anarchist-libertarian movements. A virtual cottage industry of Bookchin criticism surfaced in the mid 1990s, following a series of aggressive critiques of Bookchin and his work by former ISE faculty member John Clark. Although Clark edited a festschrift in honor of Bookchin's sixty-fifth birthday in 1986, *Renewing the Earth: The Promise of Social Ecology* (1990), and extolled the philosophical contributions of his former mentor in *The Encyclopedia of the American Left* (1992), Bookchin and Clark subsequently became estranged. After the board of the ISE asked Clark to leave the institution, Clark rapidly emerged as one of Bookchin's most vociferous critics. Clark wrote a series of journal articles, contributions to edited volumes, and conference papers accusing Bookchin of being "a theoretical bum," "an enraged autodidact," and a practitioner of "brain-dead dogmatism" and "ineptitude in philosophical analysis" ("Bookchin Agonistes" 20–23).

Bookchin also faced trenchant opposition from the writers of *Fifth Estate* and *Anarchy: A Journal of Desire Armed*, two U.S.-based anarchist journals whose contributors contend that Bookchin glorifies technology, uncritically venerates civilization, and dismisses the value of cultural resistance to authoritarianism. In this group, Robert C. Black has expressed the most overt antagonism toward Bookchin and his views. Black, a controversial figure in the underground publishing world, wrote a highly charged critique of Bookchin's personal background and theoretical arguments titled *Anarchy After Leftism* (1997). Black's book responded to provocative claims Bookchin made in *Social Anarchism or Lifestyle Anarchism: An Unbridgeable Chasm* (1995). In this highly polemical work, Bookchin contends that "For some two centuries, anarchism—a very ecumenical body of anti-authoritarian ideas—developed in the tension between two basically contradictory tendencies: a personalistic commitment to individual *autonomy*

and a collectivist commitment to social *freedom*. These tendencies have by no means been reconciled in the history of libertarian thought." Bookchin's preference for "social freedom" over "individual autonomy" irked Black, an ideological disciple of the German "egotist" philosopher Max Stirner. Black used his arguments in favor of individualism as a springboard for a wider attack on the phenomenon of patronizing and bureaucratic "leftism," into which he grouped social ecologists, making no attempt to disguise his contempt for Bookchin. In *Anarchy After Leftism*, Black derisively titled the first chapter, "Murray Bookchin, Grumpy Old Man" and grouped Bookchin with "the Neo-Conservative intellectuals . . . high-income, elderly Jewish ex-Marxists from New York City who ended up as journalists and/or academics."

Bookchin did not abstain from highly personal rebuttals, and a number of his detractors accused him of adopting a shrill and dogmatic tone in his replies to criticisms of his writings. Some of the critical responses to Bookchin's work and his replies are hard to trace, as the forums for these debates have often been hard-to-find journals. In addition, many of these exchanges were protracted, ranging over months, if not years. Nonetheless, the tremendous output from alternative media sources on Bookchin's work suggests his profound influence on contemporary social movements.

Independent of these debates, Bookchin spent the mid 1990s working out the particulars of his most salient contribution to contemporary social theory, a transformative politics he calls "libertarian municipalism." Inspired by grassroots political movements throughout history, Bookchin in this approach to reorganizing society replaces national statecraft with democratic decision-making processes at the local level. In *The Politics of Social Ecology: Libertarian Municipalism* (1998), Bookchin and Janet Biehl write of libertarian municipalism, "it advances . . . direct democracy—in which citizens in communities manage their own affairs through face-to-face processes of deliberation and decision-making, rather than have the State do it for them." Bookchin and other social ecologists have attempted to use democratic assemblies and voluntary confederations as models for the Green movement in the United States and throughout the world. To further this goal, the ISE helped organize the International Conference on the Politics of Social Ecology: Libertarian Municipalism in Lisbon, Portugal (1998) and a follow-up conference held on the ISE's campus in 1999.

In addition to developing new approaches to politics, Bookchin continued his work in philosophy. From the late 1990s onward his writings offer a reconsideration of currents in Marx's writings that he categorically rejected in earlier phases of his intellectual development. His philosophy of "dialectical naturalism," presented in the several revisions of *The Philosophy of Social Ecology: Essays on Dialectical Naturalism* (1987, rev. 1990 and 1995), draws upon the dialectical models of Hegel and Marx to formulate a way of analyzing the potential for relationships to develop beyond their present forms. According to Bookchin, dialectical thought provides us with rich ways of understanding humanity's relationship to the world and the possibilities for this relationship to change. "Dialectical causality is uniquely organic because it operates within a development—notably the degree of form, the way in which form is organized, the tensions or 'contradictions' to which its formal ensemble gives rise, and the metabolic self-maintenance and self-development of a thing or phenomenon." Bookchin contended that a dialectical approach to the study of nature "is, in effect, both a way of reasoning about causality in the form of a development and, simultaneously, an account of the objective world."

Bookchin also wrote retrospective assessments concerning the development of his ideas. Many of his statements in this regard reiterated his criticisms of the misguided motivations and tendencies he felt hindered the mainstream environmental movement and its offshoots. Bookchin summarized these troublesome systems of thought and his contrasting alternatives in an essay called "Reflections: An Overview of the Roots of Social Ecology" (2003). He wrote:

> Let me be quite outspoken: it was not an unbridled passion for wildlife, wilderness, organic food, primitivism, craft-like methods of production, villages (as against cities), 'localism,' a belief that 'small is beautiful'—not to speak of Asian mysticism, spiritualism, naturism, etcetera—that led me to formulate and promote social ecology. I was guided by the compelling—indeed, challenging—need to formulate a viable imperative that doomed capitalism to self-extinction.

Statements such as this one have led Bookchin's detractors to decry his self-righteous dismissal of non-Western traditions, critiques of modernity, and aesthetic motivations for environmental action. His supporters, however, have replied that social ecology has done a far better job than other contemporary social and ecological movements at overcoming contradictions between its theory and its practice.

Any retrospective analysis of Murray Bookchin's work is likely to include his vital role in pushing the Left to move from less-demanding critiques of capitalism and the state toward a more comprehensive opposition to domination in all of its manifestations. In his essay "Open Letter to the Ecology Movement," originally published as a special issue of the journal *Comment* (March 1980) and reprinted in *Toward an Ecological Soci-*ety, Bookchin articulated this indispensable enlargement of the terrain on which radical changes must occur: "Without changing the most molecular relationships in society—notably, those between men and women, adults and children, whites and other ethnic groups, heterosexuals and gays (the list, in fact, is considerable)—society will be riddled by domination even in socialistic 'classless' and 'non-exploitative' form."

At the end of his life, Bookchin lived in Plainfield, Vermont, with his companion of many years, Janet Biehl. Health complications related to diabetes limited his ability to travel, but he taught summer courses at the ISE, where he retained the position of director emeritus. Bookchin also served on the editorial advisory boards of *Anarchist Studies* and *Society and Nature*. He died at home on 30 July 2006 of heart failure at age eighty-five.

The Institute for Social Ecology has hosted more than three thousand students in its summer course and degree programs. Its publications have included a newsletter, *Left Green Perspectives,* and the journals *Democracy and Nature* and *Harbinger,* featuring articles on left-libertarian and Green issues in North America and Europe. The ISE maintains a website with information about its programs at the following address: <http://www.social-ecology.org/>.

Interview:

David Vanek, "Interview with Murray Bookchin," *Harbinger,* 2 (Summer 2000): 1.

References:

Robert C. Black, *Anarchy After Leftism* (Columbia, Mo.: C.A.L. Press, 1997);

John Clark, "Bookchin Agonistes: How Murray Bookchin's Attempts to Re-Enchant Humanity Become a Pugilistic Bacchanal," *Fifth Estate,* 32 (Summer 1997): 20–23;

Clark, ed., *Renewing the Earth: The Promise of Social Ecology* (London: Green Print, 1990);

Ulrike Heider, *Anarchism: Left, Right and Green* (San Francisco: City Lights Books, 1994);

Andrew Light, *Social Ecology After Bookchin* (New York & London: Guilford, 1998);

Peter Marshall, *Demanding the Impossible* (London: HarperCollins, 1992);

Brian Tokar, *The Green Alternative: Creating an Ecological Future* (San Pedro: R. & E. Miles, 1987);

David Watson, *Beyond Bookchin: Preface for a Future Social Ecology* (New York: Autonomedia, 1996);

Laura Westra, Bill E. Lawson, and Peter S. Wenz, *Faces of Environmental Racism: Confronting Issues of Global Justice,* second edition (Lanham, Md.: Rowman & Littlefield, 2001).

Ralph Chaplin

(30 August 1887 – 22 March 1961)

Mark W. Van Wienen
Northern Illinois University

BOOKS: *When the Leaves Come Out and Other Rebel Verses*
(Cleveland: By the author, 1917);

*The Centralia Conspiracy: The Truth About the Armistice Day
Tragedy* (Seattle: 1920); revised (Chicago: [IWW]
General Defense Committee, 1924);

Bars and Shadows: The Prison Poems of Ralph Chaplin (New
York: Leonard, 1922);

Somewhat Barbaric: A Selection of Poems, Lyrics and Sonnets
(Seattle: Dogwood, 1944);

*American Labor's Case Against Communism: How the Opera-
tions of Stalin's Red Quislings Look from INSIDE the
Labor Movement* (Seattle: Educator, 1947);

Wobbly: The Rough-and-Tumble Story of an American Radical
(Chicago: University of Chicago Press, 1948);

Only the Drums Remembered: A Memento for Leschi (Tacoma:
Dammier, 1960).

OTHER:
SONG LYRICS—SELECTED

Song of Separation, music by Rudolph von Liebich (Chicago: IWW, 1920);

Three Prison Sonnets, music by Marx Oberndorfer (New
York: Darch, 1922);

A Prisoner's Poem to His Little Son, music by Franz Beidel
(Chicago: International, [1922]).

BROADSIDES—SELECTED

"Maybe Pierrot . . . ," Case broadside 53, Newberry
Library, Chicago;

"A Campaign Song for Hoover," Case broadside 54,
Newberry Library, Chicago.

ILLUSTRATIONS—SELECTED

Mary E. Marcy, *Out of the Dump* (Chicago: Charles Kerr,
1909), illustrated by Chaplin;

"Twisting His Tail for Him!" *Solidarity* (26 August
1916): 1;

"John Farmer's First Lesson," *Solidarity* (2 September
1916): 1;

"Watchful Waiting," *Solidarity* (10 March 1917): 1;

"It's So Different in America!" *Solidarity* (28 July 1917):
1;

Ralph Chaplin, age twenty-two (from his Wobbly: The Rough-and-
Tumble Story of an American Radical, *1948)*

"Fellow Workers: Remember!" *Solidarity* (1 September
1917): 1.

SELECTED PERIODICAL PUBLICATIONS—
UNCOLLECTED:
POETRY

"The Red Feast, by a Paint Creek Miner," *International
Socialist Review,* 15 (October 1914): 196–197.

NONFICTION

"Violence in West Virginia," *International Socialist Review,*
13 (April 1913): 729–735;

"A Hunger 'Riot' in Chicago," *International Socialist Review,* 15 (March 1915): 517–519;

"Joe Hill's Funeral," *International Socialist Review,* 16 (January 1916): 400–405;

"The Deadly Parallel," *Solidarity* (24 March 1917): 1;

"'Overt Acts'–How Many?" and "Preparedness," *Solidarity* (24 March 1917): 2;

"Soldiers Are Wanted," *Solidarity* (26 May 1917): 2;

"Hats Off to the Rockford Rebels," *Solidarity* (14 July 1917): 2;

"Were You Drafted? Where the I.W.W. Stands on the Question of War," *Solidarity* (28 July 1917): 8;

"America's Bloodless Revolution Has Started," *Solidarity* (11 August 1917): 4;

"Why I Wrote 'Solidarity Forever,'" *American West* (January 1968): 19–27+.

Ralph Chaplin was a poet, journalist, illustrator, and activist in the radical labor movement from the first decade of the twentieth century into the 1940s. He was a leader in the Industrial Workers of the World (IWW) between 1914 and 1923, when his personal and literary fortune rose and fell with the fate of the union, and editor of the IWW's principal newspaper, *Solidarity,* in September 1917 when agents of the federal government raided the union's central offices. He was arrested along with the rest of the union's leadership on charges of wartime sedition, and in 1918 he was convicted on those charges and given a twenty-year sentence in federal prison. In court, the prosecution introduced his inflammatory poetry, editorials, and cartoons as evidence against the IWW. His prison poetry played a significant role in the IWW's drive for amnesty, which was granted for all its members still incarcerated in 1923. In subsequent years Chaplin became an ardent anticommunist in the labor movement. His writing and life, both during and after his deepest involvement with the IWW, reflect the social convictions of American radicals and the struggles of, and within, their movement in the first half of the twentieth century.

Chaplin was born in Ames, Kansas, to Clara (née Bradford) and Edgar Chaplin. Although he spent most of his working life in cities, his Kansas birthplace and his father's oft-expressed preference for life in the rural West left their mark on Chaplin, affecting his writings, philosophy, and personal commitments. Just as influential, however, was the Chaplin family's constant struggle to find gainful and lasting employment. Edgar Chaplin's family had been among the first white settlers west of the Republican River immediately after the Civil War, were reputed among the leading citizens in Cloud County, and steadily added to their land holdings over twenty years. When Edgar Chaplin lost an eye while breaking a colt, he was advised by a doctor to seek city employment. Selling his land at a tremendous discount during the depression of 1886, he arrived in Chicago wiped out financially, eventually finding work as a railway towerman. In the Pullman strike of 1894, Edgar Chaplin participated in a sympathy walkout and was subsequently blacklisted by all the major railroads. These events led to a series of increasingly unsatisfactory moves into the country for refuge and back into the city to seek work. The family spent a happy interlude of nearly a year with members of the Bradford family in Panora, Iowa. A much less successful stint with more Bradford relations in Dodge City, Kansas, followed a short period back in Chicago. Again in Chicago before finally locating steadier employment, Edgar Chaplin and his family became "migratory tenants." Ralph Chaplin recalls in his autobiography often moving "our dwindling load of furniture, including the old family organ, to still less expensive quarters."

In that autobiography, *Wobbly* (1948), the most complete source of information on the author, Chaplin reports his alliance with socialism by 1900. Converted to the cause by socialist pamphlets and soapbox speeches, he soon made speeches of his own, attended weekly meetings of the local socialist party, and sold copies of *Appeal to Reason,* the influential national weekly closely allied with the Socialist Party. Whether Chaplin was associating with the Socialist Labor Party or Eugene V. Debs's newly formed Social Democratic Party is not clear–the Socialist Party of America was not organized until 1901 by the merging of these two earlier parties–but in any case Chaplin considered himself a socialist at the very founding of its most important and durable organization. At midnight, 1 January 1900, the twelve-year-old Chaplin wrote in his notebook: "A new century is being born, the Century of Socialism."

Chaplin was an avid reader, taking on Charles Darwin, Thomas Huxley, and Herbert Spencer, as well as various socialist authors before that portentous proclamation in his notebook; sampling anarchists including Peter Kropotkin and Voltairine de Cleyre upon the recommendation of an itinerant anarcho-syndicalist lecturer; discovering the Chicago Public Library while at work at his first regularly paying job; and devouring Russian literature including Turgenev, Gorki, Dostoevski, Tolstoi, and Gogol at the suggestion of a coworker and Russian immigrant. In his testimony in the IWW's 1918 sedition trial–another important source of biographical information on the author–Chaplin stated that he left school at age fourteen before completing the seventh grade, moving directly from grade school into work as a commercial artist and to night school at the Chicago Art Institute and elsewhere. Commercial art, and particularly portrait painting, became his steadiest source of employment for the next thirty years. He was also thereby improving upon the artistic talents that soon made him so versatile and valuable as a radical propagandist. Meanwhile though, he entered into a highly competitive and fast-paced industrial job, in which artists were paid on a piecework basis for airbrushing color onto black-and-white photographs and mass producing decorative paintings. Starting around 1902 and continuing in Chicago until 1909, the teenage Chaplin worked his way up from apprentice to full-fledged studio artist. Along the way, he was thrown out of work when his first employer went bankrupt; he was fired upon the suggestion of a more senior artist resenting his ambition; and he briefly joined with other artists who attempted but failed in establishing their own cooperatively run studio.

During this same period, Chaplin continued to enlarge his acquaintance within the burgeoning reform and socialist movement. By 1905, at the latest, Chaplin had officially joined the Socialist Party. He met and argued socialism with Jane Addams. He made friends with Charles H. Kerr, the translator of the "Internationale" into English and publisher of the *International Socialist Review (ISR)*. Chaplin became a small stockholder in Kerr's Co-Operative Publishing Company, and by the time he had turned twenty-one, he was appointed to the board of directors. His teenage idols, however, were Jack London and Debs, both of whom he heard speak, and William "Big Bill" Haywood, whose activities in the Socialist Party and exploits in the Western Federation of Miners (WFM) Chaplin followed closely. Influenced by these examples, Chaplin viewed with suspicion more conventional party politicians such as Victor Berger and Morris Hillquit–"frustrated old businessmen or foxy young lawyers"–and respectable party theorists such as John Spargo, A. M. Simons, and Ernest Untermann–"petty-bourgeois characters . . . in a revolutionary proletarian movement" *(Wobbly)*. Along the same lines, Chaplin recalled gobbling up Upton Sinclair's *The Jungle* when it appeared serially in *Appeal to Reason* in 1905 but objecting to its "very inaccurate picture of the stockyards district which I knew so well" *(Wobbly)*.

Chaplin's increasingly outspoken affiliation with unskilled, unorganized, and exploited labor–coupled with his uneasy recognition that he himself had entered a highly skilled and white-collar, though highly individualistic and competitive, profession–led him to set out for a season in the harvest fields. The year was probably 1905. Arguably, this journey proved the key formative experience of his artistic career, if not his life: cementing his tie with the "jungle"-dwelling, migratory laborers that would soon be joining the IWW; hardening his contempt for members of the propertied classes and political and labor bureaucrats; awakening his fam-

ily affection for the open spaces of the West; and acquainting him with the hard-edged, working-class argot that informed his best and most famous poetry and songs. Having worked the sordid, crowded migratory labor market of West Madison Street in Chicago, a vast clearinghouse for jobs throughout the West on the railroads, in construction, logging, intercoastal shipping, and agricultural work, Chaplin and a fellow socialist laborer friend left Chicago for a construction job in East St. Louis, work that gave them access to the rails and a free ride on a freight train to Texas. There they joined the army of harvest laborers who followed the ripening crops, beginning in the Texas panhandle and working northward through Oklahoma, Kansas, Nebraska, and Minnesota, finally ending up in the fall in the Dakotas. His friend, "Blackie," continued north to pick grain in Canada; Chaplin proceeded to the West Coast to pick fruit and hops in Washington, Oregon, and northern California.

The migratory harvesters were among the most despised and marginal of American workers. When out of work, they typically slept in groups in hobo "jungles" and ate food gleaned from farmers' fields or even stolen outright from their gardens and henhouses. When they were working, the harvesters earned from $1.50 to $2.50 per day for between twelve and sixteen hours of work. Like the farmers themselves, they lived at the mercy of the weather, which could destroy crops and throw them out of work. The laborers were, in addition, vulnerable to the farmers who sometimes would not, or could not, pay the full wages they had promised; to law-enforcement officers and judges, who fined them and threatened them with jail time; and to fellow migrants–bootleggers, professional gamblers, and outright thieves–who worked to part them from their earnings. A fortunate, able-bodied, and savvy laborer could return to the city with enough money to live on until the next harvest season; other laborers returned to the city to eke out an existence on the streets and in flophouses. Not all, certainly, had the opportunity to return to families that would take them in and support them through the winter. Chaplin was not able to acquire a "winter stake," but he had certainly experienced the lot of an unskilled harvest laborer, and he returned home with the drafts of the first poems he published.

One of those poems, "The West Is Dead" (collected 1917), shows dramatically the degree to which Chaplin revised American mythologies of manifest destiny and upward mobility. Within a decade of Frederick Jackson Turner's proclamation that the frontier had been closed, Chaplin wrote bitterly that "Your fathers' world, for which they bled, / Is fenced and settled far and near." Moreover, even as the shift of American population away from farms and small towns toward cities

Front cover for Chaplin's first book, 1917, verses about the conditions faced by West Virginia miners (University of California Libraries)

was well under way, Chaplin remarked dourly: "Now dismal cities rise instead / And freedom is not there nor here— / What path is left for you to tread?" The poem goes so far as to question the ideology of the frontier mythology even for the "fathers' world," as the final stanza of the poem recounts that "Your fathers gained a crust of bread, / Their bones bleach on the lost frontier." Certainly, even as Chaplin's immediate experience revealed to him that the West now offered little opportunity for common workers, he knew that his father and mother had had their status as proud pioneers undermined by economic forces outside their control, and that city employment had not enabled them to recover their former, respectable status.

Returning to portrait painting in Chicago, Chaplin found himself working alongside Edith Medin, whom he knew from the studio at his first job. They

married in 1906, shortly after yet another disillusioning experience in the portrait business. Encouraged by his employer to buy stock in lieu of taking his full pay, and promised that in time he would be put in charge of a new studio as trade grew, Chaplin was rebuffed when he had reached the agreed-upon figure of $500 in stock; now, another young and ambitious artist was promised the partnership originally offered to Chaplin. Only through a lawsuit—and because he was underage—did Chaplin recover the money he had invested. Also this year, Haywood and other WFM leaders Charles Moyer and George Pettibone were abducted by the state of Colorado, transported across state lines, and charged and held in Idaho for the murder of former governor Frank Steunenberg, a bitter opponent of the WFM during his term. The case was a clear frame-up; when in 1907 Haywood was tried and acquitted of all charges and the other two defendants released without trial, Haywood made a triumphant speech in Chicago attended by Chaplin and some forty thousand other supporters. Days later, Ralph and Edith Chaplin met Haywood at the *ISR* offices and struck up an immediate and long-standing friendship.

Other events helped to draw the newly married Chaplins into closer alliance with the radical movement. Flush with enthusiasm for the socialist movement, Chaplin provided illustrations for many Charles Kerr publications free of charge: Edward Bellamy's *Parable of the Water Tank* (1910), Sinclair's *Prince Hagen* (1910), an entire series titled "Library of Science for the Workers," and even "a deck of Socialist playing cards" with radical jingles by *ISR* editor Mary Marcy. In the winter of 1907–1908 he graduated to part-time, paid employment at Kerr, his favorite assignment being the illustrations for London's *The Dream of Debs* (1912). Through his friends at *ISR* and Kerr, Chaplin learned of revolutionary activity in Mexico, where rebel armies were in the field fighting for the downfall of the Mexican general and dictator Porfirio Díaz. Both Ralph and Edith Chaplin traveled to Mexico to view the unfolding revolution firsthand, working in a studio of American artists and living in an apartment within earshot of an army barracks where rebels were frequently executed. They remained in Mexico for about a year, returning when they learned Edith was expecting a baby. Back in Chicago, Edith gave birth to a son in February 1910: Ivan, or "Vonnie," as his father called him. For the first time Ralph had success in unionizing workers in the portrait-painting industry. Improvements in camera technology had made color airbrushing a less skilled occupation; accordingly, the portrait companies lowered, then summarily slashed, the rates they paid their artists. The artists walked out spontaneously at the Chicago Portrait Company, then Chaplin's employer, and agreed to form a union. Leaders of the IWW were not interested in enrolling a union of no more than 350 members, but the group was given a charter by the American Federation of Labor (AFL). Christened the Commercial Portrait Artists Union of America, the union struck against the Chicago Portrait Company; leaders, such as first vice president Chaplin, were fired and the membership locked out. For his unionizing of commercial artists, Chaplin found himself blacklisted in Chicago. Desperately needing employment to support Vonnie and Edith until she could return to work, Chaplin applied for and received employment at a portrait and frame company in Huntington, West Virginia—just when a bitter labor dispute in the West Virginia coalfields was about to turn violent.

Chaplin's six months in the harvest fields had established his identification with the most marginal of American workers. The two years he spent in West Virginia persuaded him—for a time, and under the right circumstances—of the moral justification for violence in defense of mine workers. The poetry and journalism Chaplin produced during that period also established him as a nationally known poet and journalist of the radical labor movement.

When Chaplin and his family arrived in Huntington, West Virginia, in 1911, the coal miners were already on strike. In early 1912 officers of the principal union representing the strikers, the AFL-affiliated United Mine Workers (UMW), negotiated a settlement. But many of the rank and file in West Virginia rejected the terms and continued the strike; socialist-affiliated union leaders and "Mother" Jones came to West Virginia to lend their support. The mine owners hired additional security guards, evicted coal miners from their homes, and outfitted an armored train that attacked the tent camp where some of the miners and their families took shelter. Although Chaplin claimed in his 1918 trial testimony that he had resolved "for a while at least, I would take a rest; I would not mix up in strikes and socialism or anything else," he readily acknowledged that his sympathies could not remain unengaged. By the middle of 1912, if not earlier, he took a job as assistant editor and cartoonist at one of the local labor newspapers, the Huntington *Labor Star,* which was presently renamed the *Socialist and Labor Star.* Work there gave him no additional income and, indeed, compelled him to work only part-time at his portrait-painting job. It also threw him into the middle of strike activities. He wrote a sonnet, "Mine Guard," that struck a chord among the miners. Exploiting the coincidence that one of the socialist labor leaders was named John Brown, he wrote an editorial for the *Star* that compared this John Brown with the celebrated, militant abolitionist also linked to West Virginia. He spoke on the same platform with Mother Jones, urging the workers to consider joining the IWW in addition to the UMW—a plea for dual unionism that fell largely on deaf ears. He attempted to carry union literature into areas where martial law had been declared, was pummeled by a company thug, and thrown off the train. Fearing for his life, he kept clear of the roads and made a four-day walk home through the mountains. His poetry and articles written for the *Star* were reprinted not only in *ISR* but also in *The Masses,* and an additional article, "Violence in West Virginia," was written specifically for *ISR.* For readers outside West Virginia, Chaplin had become the primary conduit for news and commentary sympathetic to the strikers. Indeed, from the perspective of outside readers, Chaplin himself *became* one of the strikers, as the poems published in *ISR* appeared under the pseudonym of "A Paint Creek Miner."

The West Virginia poems rank among the most vigorous and virulent of all Chaplin's writing. The strike had turned violent on both sides, with workers arming themselves and attacking company guards, and both workers and guards carrying out murderous reprisals. Amid the chaos and with law enforcement backing the mine owners, Chaplin saw the policy of the West Virginia miners as a matter of justifiable self-defense. This perspective appears clearly in Chaplin's "When the Leaves Come Out," which was the title poem of his 1917 collection and refers to the miners' yearning for the better cover provided by spring foliage: "I will not watch the floating clouds that hover / Above the birds that warble on the wing; / I want to use this GUN from under cover— / O, Buddy, how I'm longing for the spring!" More elaborately, the long narrative poem "What Happened in the Hollow" describes the murder of a labor leader by a mine guard and the retribution of the leader's comrades, who confess under pressure from gun-brandishing militiamen only, "We 'lowed as how their friend got drunk and likely had a fall." Chaplin wrote these militant poems at widely differing levels of poetic diction as well: "The Kanawha Striker" throws the voice of a workingman into a Petrarchan sonnet. "Too Rotten Rank for Hell (Dedicated to the Journalistic Prostitutes of Capitalism)" employs rhyming couplets and quatrains, to be sure, but incorporates miners' slang—"stool" for a company-friendly worker, "yellow-leg pard" referring to a militiaman backing the mine guards—and descriptions bordering on the scatological for the "Newspaper-Truth-raper" who spoils the devil's vile brew of souls. Chaplin recalled having "scribbled" the poem as a furious response to the nonsocialist Huntington newspapers that ignored the evictions, beatings, and rape of miners and their dependents, instead choosing to blame the strikers for their troubles and praising the high character of the mine owners.

In Huntington not only was Chaplin's life under threat, but also all of the town's newspapers and the portrait company were underwater from spring floods. Chaplin and his family went to Cleveland in search of safety and work in spring 1913. There he took his first union card with the IWW and made his first appearances, a cartoon and an article, in the IWW's eastern organ, *Solidarity*. He continued to pay his dues with the IWW when, after just three months in Cleveland, the Chaplins moved on to Montreal, acceding to the encouragements of one of Ralph's artist friends transplanted there from Chicago. As would be the pattern until color photography rendered the Chaplins' profession obsolete, the family turned to commercial art to restore their financial footing, but again and again the labor movement called. While in Montreal, Chaplin observed firsthand the exuberant Canadian mobilization for World War I. A result was one of his most popular and controversial verses, "The Red Feast," first published in *ISR* under the pseudonym of "A Paint Creek Miner." The poem reveals the blend of coarse imagery and earnest revolutionary commitment that were the hallmarks of Chaplin's most memorable poems as an IWW member, or Wobbly. As Chaplin saw it, the recurrence of war was no more than the ongoing collusion of governments and capitalists, a theme he handled with no holds barred: "A bloody mass of high heaped human woe / For hungry vultures hovering on high . . . . / Black dogs, red muzzled, through the trenches go, / Where your wan, pallid features face the sky." *(ISR)* Drawing upon the argot of the "Internationale," the closing stanza urges struggle not between nations but by the working class against the propertied class: "Then you will find that 'nation' is a name, / And boundaries are things that don't exist; / That workers' interests, world-wide, are the same, / And ONE the ENEMY they must resist!"

Chaplin found the war mobilization in Canada disturbing; even more so was the vote of the German Social Democracy, then the largest socialist party in the world, in favor of war credits (government bonds issued to support the war). Chaplin remained a socialist in principle, but the German socialists' violation of international labor's pledge of the "general strike in time of war" helped to cement his already strong suspicion of socialist politicians; thereafter Chaplin's commitment would be to the IWW and against entangling alliances between unions and politicians, including the Communist Party and even the professional labor leaders who emerged in the 1930s. He required only a little urging from family members in Chicago to bring his family back to the city for more work there in portrait

studios—and more work in behalf of the radical labor movement. In January 1915 Chaplin participated in a hunger march protesting increases in food prices, driven up in the United States by increased wartime demand. In *Wobbly* Chaplin complained that the march was largely a partisan and unspontaneous affair arranged by Chicago anarchists. When reporting on the march in an *ISR* article in 1915, Chaplin also noted the listlessness of the affair, but then he attributed it rather to the malnutrition and innocence of the marchers, as contrasted with the well-fed energy and brutality of the police, who by violently breaking up a peaceful march claimed they had successfully quelled a "riot." In 1915, the only ax that Chaplin had to grind was with party theoreticians, as he argued that even a lackluster march was better than no action at all; it gave the crowd a taste of solidarity that might carry over to the shop when the marchers once again found employment. "Better any kind of action than inert theory," Chaplin concurred with his friends at *ISR*.

At about the same time as the hunger march, Chaplin completed a new song lyric that he had begun in West Virginia; he set it to the tune of "John Brown's Body" and gave it the title "Solidarity Forever." *(Wobbly)* Although less well known today than it was through most of the twentieth century, "Solidarity Forever" may still be "the greatest song yet produced by American labor," as Philip S. Foner called it in the 1960s. In the AFL-CIO's earlier *Songs of Work and Freedom*, it was hailed as "the most popular union song on the North American Continent. . . . If a union member knows only one song, it is almost sure to be this. It has become, in effect, the anthem of the labor movement." Such popularity might be attributed to the deep resonance of the tune to American ears (also used for the "Battle Hymn of the Republic") and the simplicity of the refrain: "Solidarity forever! / Solidarity forever! / Solidarity forever! / For the Union makes us strong." But the poem's verses do their own more complex and controversial cultural work as well: specifically singling out the ideology of individualism as the nemesis of industrial solidarity; subscribing to the Marxist slogan that the working classes and owning classes have nothing in common; declaring the primacy of productive labor over management or property-holding in the building of modern industry and, therefore, also proclaiming the principle of labor ownership and management of all industry. Ultimately, the power of labor to seize the means of production and thus "bring to birth the new world / From the ashes of the old" *(When the Leaves Come Out)*. Reflecting late in life upon the fame of his song, Chaplin attributed its success not to any particular sentiment or idea unique to his own imagination, but rather to the collective ideal of the "One Big

Union" and the fervor with which groups of Wobblies sang it ("Why I Wrote 'Solidarity Forever'").

Few song lyrics have such a colorful history of reception. Published in IWW's *Solidarity* in January 1915 and then *Songs of the Workers* in March 1916, the song soon became a Wobbly favorite. The union's songbook, familiarly known as the "Little Red Song Book," was itself remarkable, a collection of mostly satiric songs set to familiar popular and religious tunes that drew crowds to IWW street meetings and fostered esprit de corps among Wobblies. Among the songs in the IWW hymnal, however, "Solidarity Forever" played a singular role. It was one of the songs belted out by some 250 Wobblies arriving by steamer on 5 November 1916 at an Everett, Washington, dock in anticipation of a "free speech fight." That group provided the raw numbers necessary to challenge local restrictions on public assembly and free speech, passed to deter union organizing in the timber industry: they planned to speak on the streets, one after another, until the town jail was flooded by more lawbreakers than it could hold. Arriving at the dock, however, the IWWs met a large body of deputized townspeople who prevented them from coming ashore by opening fire; five IWW members and two of the deputies' own were killed before the boat could retreat into Puget Sound. The result was the last significant victory for the union until well after World War I: more than seventy Wobblies were held for some six months on murder charges, but only one was brought to trial and that defendant was acquitted of all charges. "Solidarity Forever" also helped to rally IWW spirits at some of the union's most devastating defeats. In a postwar confrontation in Centralia, Washington, IWWs used armed resistance to defend their union hall against members of the American Legion intending to ransack it. In the violent fracas that ensued, four of the Legionnaires were killed and one of the Wobblies hunted down, brutalized, and lynched; in the resulting trial, eight other Wobblies were convicted of second-degree murder and sentenced to twenty years. Upon their conviction, the eight defendants returned to their cells and sang "Solidarity Forever." In the 1930s while editing the IWW's western organ, the *Industrial Worker,* Chaplin bitterly fought Communist attempts to infiltrate labor unions. At one public meeting, Chaplin's anti-Stalinist remarks were greeted with jeers by young communists in attendance, who thereupon sought to drown him out by singing a truly revolutionary song—"Solidarity Forever."

Chaplin later claimed that he would have thought twice about sending the song out into the world, had he known in 1915 that it would have such an autonomous and wayward existence. In 1915, however, deeply and busily engaged in the activity of an ascendant IWW,

Chaplin did not reflect on questions of his literary legacy. In 1912, the IWW had for the first time organized workers successfully in the eastern United States, leading the successful Lawrence, Massachusetts, strike and reaping additional publicity benefit from the acquittal of the strike leaders, Joe Ettor and Arturo Giovannitti, charged with the murder of a striker killed by police. Results had been more mixed in 1913 in the Paterson, New Jersey, silk makers' strike, in which IWW members had orchestrated the "Paterson Pageant," a dramatization in Madison Square Garden, but the strike itself had been broken and added to an already-significant schism between the IWW and Socialist Party. (In 1913 Haywood was removed from the executive committee of the Socialist Party and effectively expelled.) But by the spring of 1915, the IWW was on the verge of its greatest period of constructive conflict and growth. IWW members founded the Agricultural Workers' Organization, which in the next two-plus years would become the IWW's most successful local by organizing midwestern harvest workers. In Chicago after the 1915 hunger march, Chaplin orchestrated the founding of an IWW local in the city, organizing workers at the McCormick Harvester Works, and in other industrial plants as far afield as Gary and Michigan City, Indiana. He became the closest confidant of Haywood; Haywood gave the eulogy at the funeral of Chaplin's mother in March 1915. Meanwhile, Joe Hill awaited his execution on murder charges in the Salt Lake City jail. Already the IWW's most prolific and popular songwriter, Hill was on the path that would make him an international cause célèbre and labor martyr. Although he had never met Hill, Chaplin was selected to be a member of the delegation that met the train carrying Hill's body and staged the great procession and funeral attended by some twenty-five to thirty thousand mourners through the streets of Chicago. His poem commemorating the execution of Hill—written, characteristically, on the day of the execution—appeared on the first page of *ISR* for December and was accompanied by a Chaplin illustration in which the firing squad consists of capitalist oligarchs, such as Henry Clay Frick and Utah governor William Spry.

If anyone could be an heir apparent to Joe Hill's Wobbly poet laureateship, it was almost certainly Ralph Chaplin. Chaplin's poems appeared with regularity in *Solidarity:* twelve between August 1914 and the end of 1915, including a vow to fight for the freedom of Hill, published while he was in prison and the drive for his amnesty was in full swing; "Harvest Song 1915" set to the most popular tune of the year, "I Never Raised My Boy to Be a Soldier"; and a raucous parody of socialist intellectuals, "The Prawblem Sawlver." During the same period, Chaplin made his initial appearances in

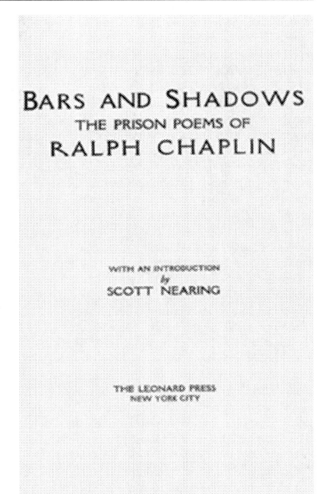

Frontispiece and title page for the 1922 volume written mostly while Chaplin was at Leavenworth Federal Penitentiary serving a twenty-year sentence, commuted after three years, for conspiring to obstruct the war effort (University of California Libraries)

the *Little Red Song Book,* with three lyrics in the edition printed in December 1914 and four in the next, appearing in March 1916. But Chaplin's talents and contributions differed distinctly from Hill's. "Solidarity Forever" excepted, Chaplin did not excel in fitting singable lyrics to tunes, as did Hill, and his satirical verses did not rollick with the wicked humor achieved in the best of Hill's work, such as "Casey Jones—The Union Scab," "Ta-ra-ra boom de-ay!," "Mr. Block," and "The Preacher and the Slave" (origin of the famous line, "You'll get pie in the sky when you die"). Whereas Hill wrote lyrics exclusively set to music, Chaplin was at his best writing verse alone. He could produce powerful work in several different registers: rebel poems filled with the rage and pity of proletarian life, often incorporating workers' slang, as in the "Paint Creek Miner" productions; poetic expostulations of IWW philosophy, writing sometimes verging on the pedantic but highly

persuasive when at its sincere and impassioned best, as in "Solidarity Forever"; and unapologetically romantic verse, certainly weaker writing judged by contemporary standards, and yet under the right circumstances—as in the prison poems soon to be written—poignant and effective in pleading the IWW's cause. Chaplin also served the IWW with skills in administration and editing in ways that Hill—save for his songs, an obscure and even mysterious rank-and-file Wobbly—never did. And his immense and professional talent for illustration transformed *Solidarity* and other IWW propaganda literature from the very first distinctive Chaplin visual design.

First came the Chaplin-originated "stickerettes." Adapted from the small, gum-backed "posterettes" then being used by commercial businesses, especially in Europe, for advertising, the IWW stickerettes featured Chaplin's pen-and-ink drawings and slogans propagandizing the IWW and were intended for posting by IWW members throughout the country on boxcars, lampposts, and even tools. Printed in batches of tens of thousands, the stickerettes were typically printed in revolutionary black and red; they were distributed in dozens of designs by the 1916 harvest season, during which some said that "every boxcar in the country carried with it at least one good argument in favor of joining the IWW" *(Wobbly)*. Recognized for his work on the stickerettes, in mid 1916 Chaplin accepted his first formal position in the IWW when he became director of publications, a step that required him to return to Cleveland where *Solidarity* was edited and published. There Chaplin's influence on the visual impact of *Solidarity* was immediate. Writing under the pseudonym "Bingo," Chaplin drew the traditional front-and-center cartoon nearly every week: ten cartoons between the middle of August and end of October. While in the past cartoon design in *Solidarity* had all too often been two-dimensional or, at best, rather busy, the Chaplin influence brought cleaner lines, dramatic imagery, and clear messages. For instance, a dragon representing the "STEEL TRUST" bears an immense bag of gold indicating its "$81,000,000 QUARTERLY DIVIDEND," but is sorely chagrined because an "I.W.W." workingman wearing wooden shoes has tied his willowy tail in knots and a black cat has torn holes in the bag. Or an "A.W.O." (Agricultural Workers Organization) harvest hand is taking a bearded, bespectacled, and clearly beleaguered "John Farmer" back to school, with lesson one of "I.W.W. Demands" written on the blackboard: "More wages / Shorter hours / Better conditions" and, more cryptically, "THE CAT LIKES CREAM." As Chaplin later explained in his IWW trial testimony, the black cats and the wooden shoes inserted into many of his stickerettes and cartoons were icons of sabotage, the latter alluding to the wooden shoes, or "sabots," that some French workers were said to have thrown into industrial machinery as they walked off the job, whereas the former was meant as a warning that "a little bad luck" might befall an employer who did not deal fairly with IWW workers.

Such references in Chaplin's work gave considerable fodder to federal prosecutors in the IWW's 1918 sedition trial. Not only in his stickerettes and cartoons did Chaplin refer to sabotage, but also in his poetry: a hymn to "Sabotage," set to the tune of the state song of Illinois, appeared in *When the Leaves Come Out*. Sabotage-inspired art in all three forms was introduced as evidence in the trial, although Chaplin, Haywood, and other defendants insisted that sabotage, as the IWW construed it, did not mean the destruction of property but rather inefficient or substandard work in retaliation for poor wages, and in fact the prosecution was not able to demonstrate a single incident of property destruction by any IWW member. Dangerous as Chaplin's work proved for himself and the union later, in early 1917 it led to his advancement in the IWW leadership. After a power struggle of some months between Ben Williams, the editor of *Solidarity,* and Haywood, Williams was removed from the editorship; *Solidarity* was moved from Cleveland to join the national headquarters in Chicago; and Chaplin became the new editor.

The period of Chaplin's greatest literary and artistic reputation followed, largely coinciding with the most tumultuous and perilous years of his life and the life of the IWW. From the time he stepped into the editorship of *Solidarity* in March 1917 until the day he left prison in 1923, Chaplin was admired and looked to for leadership in radical circles, while being reviled in conservative ones and considered by the U.S. government an enemy of the state. *When the Leaves Come Out and Other Rebel Verses* had come off the press in February. Another set of stickerettes had been prepared for the press in time for the 1917 harvest season. Major assignments arrived immediately after he occupied the *Solidarity* editor's chair. On 5 March 1917 the first of the Everett defendants went on trial–in effect, the test case for whether any of the Wobblies could be convicted for the death of the two deputies caught in the cross fire on the dock. Already the United States had broken off diplomatic relations with Germany; a declaration of war was imminent. Among Chaplin's editorials during that tense, uncertain March were two that tackled squarely the major issues from an IWW perspective. The first, "'Overt Acts'–How Many?" reflects on the fact that Germany was being denounced for its acts of aggression against American shipping interests, even while American business and its political and legal tools had committed numerous outrages against American labor, of which the incidents in Everett were merely the latest and most flagrant example. The second, "Preparedness," takes the theme then being intensely debated by the nation and applies it to the preparations of labor to "take your place with your fellow workers in the trenches of the industrial war–YOUR war." Especially addressing workers still outside the union, Chaplin hails the superiority of the fighting IWW: its refusal to sign contracts with the owning class, so that its members are free to strike whenever the occasion demands; its tactics of sabotage and "direct action" to thwart the capitalists at the point of production; its overall strategy of organizing "ALL the workers of ALL industries into ONE BIG UNION," rendering meaningful the threat of a general strike; its final objective of total victory for the working classes and the abolition of the "WAGE SYSTEM" so that each worker might "receive the full product of his labor."

The environment of the wartime mobilization was, in fact, rife with parallels both ironic and instructive regarding the IWW's situation. The Manichean struggle of the world war provided a rich environment to a revolutionary union that offered no quarter to capitalism, and so it was not merely ironic that the IWW found itself more popular and powerful than ever before in some of the industries most immediately necessary to the mobilization, such as agriculture, logging, and hard-metal mining. It was fitting, too, that visual and verbal parallelism became the central theme of Chaplin's seven-month tenure at *Solidarity*. The first of his succession of front-page cartoons, picturing cats waiting in a crowd outside a mouse hole labeled "The Everett Trial," was given the heading "Watchful Waiting," paralleling the IWW's situation with that of the nation waiting for Germany to tip its hand. For one issue later in March, Chaplin replaced the customary cartoon with "The Deadly Parallel," which in fact offered two parallels: a contrast between the IWW's declaration opposed to war with the AFL's recent pledge to support the coming war mobilization, and a comparison between the AFL's attitude and that of the European workers' parties in 1914, which had led to the killing of some ten million people. (Chaplin broke the numbers down into exact totals for the various combatants.) In June, the month of a military draft billed by the government as "selection from a nation that has volunteered *en masse*," Chaplin announced in *Solidarity* that "Soldiers Are Wanted," writing simultaneously in broad parody of the national mobilization and absolute earnestness about the IWW's efforts: "You are asked to enlist for the term of the war. . . . The I.W.W. will not compromise with any of the evils it fights against. It will make no separate peace with any of your enemies." In July, Chaplin offered a deadly parallel in cartoon form: responding to the forced transportation, earlier in the month, of striking IWW miners from Bisbee, Arizona, across the border into New Mexico, Chaplin drew a left-hand panel showing bayonet-wielding German soldiers rounding up Belgian workers for forced labor assignments in Germany, and a right-hand panel showing bayonet-wielding deputies loading American workers into cattle cars. Two weeks later, in August, Chaplin's grasp for historical parallels turned grandiose, as he announced in an editorial that recent strikes not only by IWW but also by AFL-affiliated and unaffiliated workers demonstrated that "America's Bloodless Revolution Has Started," aligning current events with the Glorious Revolution of late-seventeenth-century England. On September 1 Chaplin the cartoonist reworked the central iconic image of the U.S. war mobilization. Echoing the George Montgomery Flagg image of Uncle Sam demanding patriotic service with his index finger pointed outward at the viewer, itself a reworking of an earlier British recruiting poster, Chaplin drew a jailed workingman, his sleeves rolled up, right index finger outstretched past jail bars, and the caption addressing "Fellow Workers" to "Remember! We Are in Here for You; You Are Out There for Us."

Given that plainclothes investigators had been following the various IWW leaders for weeks, Chaplin had good reason to believe that the jailed figure in his cartoon would soon represent not only fellow IWWs but also himself. Indeed, the figure in the cartoon bears enough resemblance to Chaplin that it may well be a self-portrait and thus, also, an uncanny prophesy of his fate. On September 5 the IWW headquarters in Chicago was raided for evidence; for the rest of the month Chaplin, Haywood, and other leaders came to work in eerily uncluttered, virtually paperless offices until they were arrested on 25 September. The charges against Chaplin and more than one hundred others centered on an alleged conspiracy to obstruct the U.S. war effort. Ironically, on the matters of policy and programs most related to the indictments, Chaplin's actions had been relatively circumspect. The IWW leadership took no official stance on draft registration when the question was debated in July. Chaplin's editorial statement in *Solidarity* represented a compromise between the hopelessly deadlocked leaders. He advised that IWWs register for the draft but include with their signature the epithet "I.W.W. opposed to war." Yet from the outset, it was clear that the IWW was on trial not for any individual criminal acts of sabotage but for its ideology as a whole and its existence as an organization. And so the evidence did not feature the restraint of Chaplin's policy or of IWW actions in the field so much as editorials like Chaplin's "Hats Off to the Rockford Rebels," celebrating the decision of IWWs in Rockford, Illinois, to present themselves for arrest en masse instead of registering for the draft. In the same editorial, Chaplin had ridiculed the judge who sentenced the Rockford Wobblies to one year in prison, calling his remarks from the bench "stupidly vituperative" and classing him with "the eunuchs of Capitalism." The same judge, Kenesaw Mountain Landis, also presided over the Chicago trial, so it was hardly surprising that the first evidence presented there was Chaplin's "Hats Off" editorial.

Jail did not rein in Chaplin's fighting attitude nor rebellious writings—especially at first. The first poem Chaplin wrote in prison, later the lead poem in his collection of prison poetry, responds to incarceration much as Hill had in his famous final message: "Don't mourn. Organize." The poem's somber but stoic representations of death and imprisonment recall also the Haymarket anarchists, who had been executed in the same Cook County jail where the IWWs were held, and the vigilante lynching of Frank Little in Montana just days after his participation in the intra-IWW conscription debate. The poem's pity is reserved rather for the vast majority of the American public: "But rather mourn the apathetic throng– / The cowed and the meek– / Who see the world's great anguish and its wrong / And dare not speak." While awaiting trial in the fall and winter of 1917 and 1918, the IWW detainees also organized educational programs, entertainments, and a magazine, in all of which Chaplin participated. Only when the trial was about to begin were Haywood, Chaplin, and others permitted to raise bail and gain temporary release. The trial ran from April Fool's Day until the end of August 1918, at which time all 101 defendants who stood charged at its conclusion were convicted of all charges. The majority of the defendants received sentences of five or ten years in Leavenworth federal penitentiary; Chaplin and a smaller number of union leaders received the maximum sentence of twenty years. In his autobiography Chaplin fretted that he had let down his comrades by giving weak testimony in the trial; his lack of confidence as a speaker, in fact, comes up repeatedly in that book. But his brief remarks at the sentencing, though interrupted by Judge Landis, were as pointed as any of the defendants': "I have been convicted of an imaginary crime by a stupid jury," he exclaimed, and after interruption and admonishment from Judge Landis, "I am proud that I have climbed high enough for the lightning to strike me."

Chaplin was imprisoned in Leavenworth in two stretches. He began serving his sentence immediately in September 1918 but was released on bail, pending an appeal before the U.S. Supreme Court, at the end of July 1919. His appeal denied, he returned to Leavenworth in April 1921 and remained inside until June 1923, when he and several other IWWs agreed to terms proposed by President Harding and were granted clemency. His visibility both as an IWW and poet had never been higher. Like Arturo Giovannitti, whose celebrated collection *Arrows in the Gale* (1914) had been written while in jail after the Lawrence strike, Chaplin wrote most of the poems in his best-known collection, *Bars and Shadows* (1922), while in Leavenworth. While free on bond, he plunged back into IWW activity, mainly efforts to raise funds and public awareness for the IWW's ongoing legal defense. He made an extensive speaking tour, traveling through the Midwest, to Colorado, and to the West Coast, then doubling back to points east including Detroit, Cleveland, Boston, and Washington, D.C. He joined in fierce debates within the IWW over what attitude to take toward the Russian Revolution. Haywood, also free on bond, saw the Soviets as the Russian expression of their industrial unionism; Chaplin was more doubtful, agreeing with his

former colleagues at Kerr, Mary and Leslie Marcy, who feared Communist politicians and not industrial workers were in charge in Russia.

The significance of these ideological and organizational fissures had not yet fully emerged, however, and a certain degree of solidarity within the radical movement was virtually guaranteed by the postwar Red Scare. Chaplin's own energies focused on the latest sensational trial of IWW members for violence fomented by their opponents: the Centralia case. He witnessed the trial, held in Montesano, Washington, between 26 January and 13 March 1920, and he remained in Seattle for about a month after the guilty verdicts were handed down to write his exposé of the case, *The Centralia Conspiracy*. True to its genre, Chaplin's account of the case is strongly partisan, passing over fine points of law that were not entirely in the IWW's favor to portray the case as part of a larger class struggle and a further exhibit of the ongoing persecution of the radical labor movement. Chaplin made clear that the law permitted individuals to defend their property when their physical well-being was also threatened, as IWW members did when Legionnaires broke away from the 1919 Armistice Day parade, rushed their union hall, and broke down the door. Although he also acknowledged that several IWWs had armed themselves and taken up positions outside the union hall prior to the attack, he did not mention the thorny legal questions over whether a group might conspire in advance to defend property or whether individuals might take up positions outside the property being defended. Also he downplayed the fact that the jury showed some sympathy for the defendants, as the verdicts of second-degree murder showed that they had been moved by the IWW's self-defense arguments; indeed, the first reports in the IWW press described as a major victory the jury's refusal to follow the judge's orders either to convict for murder in the first degree or acquit. Chaplin's account highlighted, instead, the judge's prejudicial handling of the trial–for example, his refusal to admit as evidence the ransacking of the IWW's Everett union hall in 1918–and his handing down of unusually long sentences of twenty-five to forty years. But Chaplin's book served to combat other, wildly inaccurate accounts, charging that the Legionnaires had been ambushed while marching innocently in the parade. Chaplin gave the most plausible reason for the IWW members to stake out their own union hall: the IWW's previous hall in Centralia had been wrecked the year before, and a reprise was widely rumored around town to be planned for 11 November. The "Centralia Conspiracy" was not, Chaplin explained, the work of violent IWWs planning to overthrow decent society, but the concerted campaign of the timber interests, together with their political and social allies, to eliminate effective union representation and the chance at a fair deal for the timberworkers. A conspiracy of this sort was amply and accurately documented by Chaplin, with evidence ranging from Washington State's recently passed draconian criminal syndicalism laws specifically targeting the IWW to the resolution passed at the local Elks Club to "combat the IWW and kindred organizations," reported in the Centralia newspaper just days before the parade in the same article describing its route.

Chaplin's most vivid writing in *The Centralia Conspiracy* reveals both the persistence of his radical interpretation of labor relations and his ability to spin a good yarn. His extended exposition of conditions and events setting the stage for the Armistice Day confrontation stretched back to evocations of the forests primeval and the white settlement of the Northwest. Such themes helped Chaplin argue for the collective ownership of the forests—a human resource so basic that one might as readily justify private "ownership of the sunlight that warms us or . . . the air we breathe" as defend the private timber monopolies. Chaplin also thereby employed the mythology of the democratic and egalitarian westward expansion, which remained so potent for Chaplin via his father's homesteading experience in Kansas. The unmistakable core of Chaplin's narrative, however, is his account of the actions and fate of Wesley Everest, the discharged U.S. soldier who led the armed resistance originating from the union hall. By fleeing in plain sight of the Legionnaires, he may have saved the lives of others hiding in the union hall. Everest gunned down his closest pursuer and wounded others, and, after running out of ammunition, was seized by the Legionnaires and delivered to the city jail. He was mysteriously removed that night, had his genitals mutilated, and was hanged from the local bridge, his dead body riddled with bullets. In Chaplin's suspenseful telling of the story, Everest emerges as the central figure not only because in being lynched he joins a long line of American labor martyrs, and not only because in being an honorably discharged soldier his death becomes an ironic symbol of patriotism run amok, but also because in the face of insurmountable odds Everest went down fighting. Whether because of the compelling legal-defense issues involved or Chaplin's melodramatic narrative, *The Centralia Conspiracy* proved the most popular of Chaplin's Wobbly books; forty thousand copies, the entire first printing, were sold within a month of its release in 1920, and three more editions followed in the next several years.

Outside the realm of Western shoot-outs and vigilante justice, however, Chaplin found himself facing far less clear-cut situations. George Andreytchine, formerly the editor of the IWW's Bulgarian publications and recipient of a twenty-year prison sentence, jumped bail and fled to the U.S.S.R. at the invitation of the Comintern in early 1921. So did Haywood. Chaplin was invited also but stayed behind. His reservations about the Communists and the socialist experiment in Russia, coupled with family ties and a recently purchased home in the village of Lombard, Illinois, led him to refuse the offer. He joined the Workers (Communist) Party and attended its secret, second annual meeting, but subsequently he claimed to have done so mainly to follow up on party leaders' assurances (ultimately reneged upon) that Haywood's bondholders would be repaid. When Chaplin returned to Leavenworth in April 1921, rifts between the IWW class-war prisoners emerged and deepened. His differences with party leaders Earl Browder and Harrison George, both ardent supporters of the Soviet Union, centered on Communism but extended to a fierce rivalry in the prison handball league *(Wobbly)*. Differences between the political prisoners even entered into their singing of the "Internationale," in which the final line, "The Industrial Union shall be the human race," competed with a pro-Communist alternative, "The International Party shall be the human race." Yet, Chaplin complied with the request of an Everett comrade that he compose a sonnet dedicated to the U.S.S.R.'s five-year plan, its words to be cast in a bronze plaque and bolted to the fender of a tractor donated to the workers' republic.

Chaplin was a leader in pleading the case for clemency for the IWW's in Leavenworth. He was principal author of a lengthy open letter to President Harding. His son, Vonnie, joined a tour of the children of political prisoners. His 1922 collection of prison poems, *Bars and Shadows,* also played a prominent role in the drive for an early release. The book was published with the help of Scott Nearing, whose introduction named Chaplin's work "a contribution to the propaganda and the art of the new [socialist] culture." The assemblage of poems is considerably more complex than this description indicates, as the majority of the new poems were actually more traditional in form and conventionally romantic than those in *When the Leaves Come Out.* Five of the most radical verses in the collection are in fact reprinted from the earlier collection. These he joined with an additional number of explicitly radical poems, although Chaplin's style in these is no longer satire and invective, but an elevated diction and high socialist idealism. Among the many sonnets—fifteen of the twenty-five new poems—Chaplin offers some carefully crafted and pungent lines, as in "The Industrial Heretics," which concludes: "Today we face the awful test of fire—/ The prison, gallows, cross—but in the end / Your sons will call your children after us / And name their dogs from men you now admire!" Other lines offer themselves to *Poetry* editor Harriet Monroe's criticism rather too easily, as when she quotes from the final lines of "The Red Guard": "Pause and behold the earth made clean and pure– / Our earth, that you have drenched with blood and tears– / Then greet the crimson usurer of Day,– / The mighty Proletarian Dictature!" (*Poetry*, August 1922).

Arguably, Chaplin's more conventional romantic poems in the collection offered a more compelling case for clemency than those alluding to industrial unionism or the Soviet Union. Lachrymose lines dedicated to Edith–"And out there now with life's high dome above you / If you but knew how very much I love you– / If you but knew"–as well as to "My Little Son"–"that one stinging memory: / Your brave smile broken with a sob, / Your face pressed close to me"–offered nothing particularly original except that they were written by a class-war prisoner. Therein lay the key to their contribution to the clemency movement: a man so smitten with his wife and homesick for his child sounded no more like a dangerous enemy of the state than he did a sophisticated poet. These poems were most sought for reprinting, the ones set to music published by the IWW and International Publishers. Significantly, they also appealed most to mainstream reviewers of the collection, as one from the *Detroit News* notes the "bitter and terrible songs of the strike and the free speech fights of the past" but prefers those occasions when the poet "gives way to himself in poems that are true expressions of himself as an individual" (14 May 1922). The *New Republic* reviewer similarly comments that "One feels the essential humanity of the man, but one cannot be greatly moved by verse written in moments when passion has deteriorated into mere anger" (27 December 1922).

As the amnesty drive neared a successful conclusion, tensions between various radical factions, including some outside the penitentiary as well as those inside, came to a head. Indeed, the very terms of the clemency became the issue. Chaplin joined the group of IWWs willing to pledge, as a condition for their early release, that they would not break the law, would not encourage lawlessness in others, and would be loyal to the government. Others would accept only a general amnesty, and further charged the "clemency hounds" with a lack of solidarity in allowing their cases to be considered individually as opposed to demanding the release of the IWW inmates as a group. The critics of individual clemency argued that agreeing to Harding's terms would constitute an admission of guilt–a confession that the IWW leaders had in fact broken the law, advocated lawbreaking, and had shown disloyalty. But Chaplin found the inverse of this argument just as plau-

BY RALPH CHAPLIN

Wobbly

The Rough-and-Tumble Story
of an
American Radical

THE UNIVERSITY OF CHICAGO PRESS
CHICAGO, ILLINOIS

Title page for Chaplin's 1948 autobiography (Thomas Cooper Library, University of South Carolina)

sible: if the IWWs refused to pledge obedience to the law, then it would seem to imply that they *had* been disloyal and lawless all along–which they had strenuously denied at their trial–and, moreover, that they contemplated disloyalty and lawlessness upon their release. Forty-four other IWWs, more than half the number held at Leavenworth, joined Chaplin in accepting clemency with the presidential conditions. The rest of the IWW defendants were out of prison by the end of the year, their amnesty granted without conditions.

Had Chaplin remained in prison for the duration of his term, his identity as class-war prisoner, radical icon, and rebel poet would have been sealed; likewise had he died a martyr's death like Hill or Little. Instead he returned to Lombard, to his family and his easel. He returned also, though not immediately, to editorial positions in the labor press. Depending upon one's interpretation, Chaplin's subsequent life and career revealed him as 1) a patriotic American who grew to accept moderation; 2) a traitor to the working-class movement;

or 3) a defender of labor against Communist deceptions. In any case, although Chaplin enjoyed considerably less prominence as a labor activist and litterateur after 1923, his life and writing between 1923 and 1961 remain important for understanding the complexity of radical and reform traditions in the United States.

For a time Chaplin continued to work with a variety of left-wing movements. In spite of the friction between the IWWs released in June 1923 and those who demanded unconditional release, Chaplin participated actively in the drive to gain amnesty for them all. He accepted appointment to the legal-defense organization of the Communist Party, the International Labor Defense. Meanwhile, he entertained Debs at his home after Debs, too, had been released from federal prison, and he remained friendly with Carl Sandburg, who as a correspondent with the Chicago *Daily News* had given favorable coverage to the IWW during its sedition trial. His entire family socialized with Charles Kerr, Kerr's daughter Katherine Moore, and her family. But some IWWs who had gone to Russia to give aid to the revolution were coming home bitterly disappointed; other Wobblies numbered among the independent unionists killed in uprisings against the Bolsheviks. Chaplin's decisive break with the Communist Party came in 1929, when the *New Masses* editor asked Chaplin to review the posthumously published *Bill Haywood's Book,* and Chaplin complied with a piece that celebrated Haywood but charged that the autobiography had been carefully edited to conform to the Comintern line. When Chaplin refused to revise his review, the Communist-aligned *New Masses* refused to publish it.

During the 1920s Edith Chaplin continued to work in commercial art; she had worked in that profession throughout Ralph Chaplin's years in prison. He returned to that profession as well. Together they prospered in the growing economy of the decade. He also built an extravagant ornamental garden in his backyard in Lombard, which he had planned while still in Leavenworth. The tension between his continued connections with the radical movement and his bucolic life in Lombard had, in a way, been present in his collection *Bars and Shadows*—the romantic poems yearning for an unfettered family life coexisting uneasily with the raucous rebel verse and revolutionary sonnets. It appears still more clearly in a poem written in Leavenworth and left out of *Bars and Shadows,* "Maybe Pierrot," which Chaplin had printed privately and used as a Christmas card in 1932. Imprisoned because of his love for truth and beauty, the harlequin clown Pierrot blows bubbles that offer simultaneously an escape from the despair of imprisonment and the poetic ideal for which Pierrot has been imprisoned. The final section of the poem, "Pier-

rot Meets God," seems particularly at odds with Chaplin's revolutionary commitments expressed in *Bars and Shadows,* as Pierrot the speaker professes the common humanity of all people, "Knowing that every heart holds love and hate– / That every hand that tortures can caress . . ." and proclaims his ultimate allegiance to art: "not mad save in the ways of Art."

Still, both external circumstances and the Chaplins' connections to labor and radical causes kept them from settling comfortably into suburban life. The Great Depression devastated the art industry; the Chaplins lost their jobs and their home, and they moved in with a friend in Florida–not a Wobbly–from Chaplin's prison days. Chaplin again found work as an editor with the IWW, contrary to the assertions of several historians that he left the IWW in 1923 and never returned. From 1932 to 1936 he edited the IWW's western organ, *Industrial Worker,* vociferously opposing the influence of Communists within West Coast labor unions and preaching to a dwindling handful of adherents to the One Big Union. Briefly in 1937 he edited the *Voice of the Federation,* the paper of the Maritime Federation of the Pacific Coast, until the powerful CIO organizer Harry Bridges forced Chaplin out. In 1941–1945 he moved north to Seattle, where he edited *Labor Advocate;* there, too, he was an outspoken critic of Communist influence in the labor movement generally and the CIO particularly, and he was ultimately forced out because of that criticism.

Chaplin's opposition to Communism was readily assimilable to right-wing politics. His 1947 booklet, *American Labor's Case Against Communism: How the Operations of Stalin's Red Quislings Look from INSIDE the Labor Movement,* is in some ways indistinguishable from reactionary anti-Communist briefs of the McCarthy era, both in its lampooning cartoons and broadly drawn conspiracy theories. But whereas most anti-Communists had called for the merciless prosecution of the Wobblies, Chaplin's anti-Communism stemmed from a deep-rooted suspicion of centralized political authority, which he considered necessarily undemocratic. Like the rest of the Left, Chaplin hooted Herbert Hoover out of office in 1932. Still, the New Deal looked to him like an antidemocratic power grab, putting industrial as well as political power in the hands of bureaucrats instead of workers and encouraging workers to accept dependency upon the government rather than working cooperatively among themselves to make their own wealth. One new social development that he did approve of, the technocracy movement that flourished briefly in the 1930s, appealed to him for reasons that had everything to do with his mooring in the socialist and radical labor movements. Like socialism, technocracy predicted the eventual ruin of the profit system; like the IWW, it rejected political means to achieving industrial equality; like the vision of the Soviet Union that had beguiled Haywood, it proposed to build a new society in which engineers and workers, rather than politicians and capitalists, built industry. To Chaplin, the Communism that "bore from within" American labor organizations sought to replace democratic decision making with autocratic direction.

The consistency between Chaplin's fidelity to the IWW legacy and his utter rejection of Communism figure prominently in his 1948 autobiography, *Wobbly*. His repudiation of "The Red Feast," which sounded like "twaddle" to him when he heard an "enthusiastic young comrade" recite it in 1939, appears unable to make the very distinction between just and unjust wars that the comrade is charged with failing to make. But Chaplin's reassessment of his experience as an enemy of the state during World War I is striking both for its candor and thoughtfulness. In the United States, he was tried before a biased court and sent to prison for crimes he did not commit. Yet, in the United States, Chaplin argues, he also had opportunity to appeal, was allowed to go free on bond, and was freed by an act of presidential clemency after approximately three years in prison. In Russia, by way of contrast, IWWs and anarchists who sought to join the revolution but had dissented from the path taken by Lenin, Trotsky, and Stalin, had no such luxuries as due process or legal appeals; they were executed summarily, subjected to show trials, or exiled to indefinite terms of detention in the gulag. *Wobbly* contributed to a renewed interest in the history of the IWW. It was widely reviewed, with consideration of the book tending to remark upon the "mellowness" of Chaplin's radicalism (*Commonweal*, 22 October 1948) and the "soul-searing ideological growth of a serious, socially conscious person" (*Kirkus*, 1 July 1948). Such accounts verge on the triumphal, implicitly asserting that Chaplin's earlier radical views were youthful errors and that, with age and wisdom, Chaplin had discovered for himself the truth of American liberalism. Some of Chaplin's criticism of his youthful tendency for "fighting it out," contrasted with his subsequent "groping for a more rational type of labor relations," tends to support observations of this kind *(Wobbly)*. Such efforts to categorize Chaplin's response as liberal (and even conservative) miss, however, the nuances of his relationship with industrial unionism and radicalism generally, on display in *Wobbly*. As such, the autobiography stands in critical relationship to other autobiographies of the Left, including both books that strive for fidelity to one or another Communist Party line, such as *Bill Haywood's Book* or Joseph Freeman's *American Testament* (1938), and also books that attempt to repudiate radicalism along

with Communism, as does Granville Hicks's *Where We Came Out* (1954).

Relative to the obscurity and marginalization of Chaplin's work in the 1920s and 1930s, the 1940s provided a kind of renaissance in his literary career. Besides *Wobbly* and *American Labor's Case Against Communism* (originally written in the 1930s but unpublished at the time), he published in 1944 a volume of new and selected poetry, *Somewhat Barbaric*. The new poems in the collection confirm the more genteel and romantic direction taken in *Bars and Shadows* and "Maybe Pierrot." Out of step as this might be with the reigning orthodoxy of Modernism, the poems exhibit considerable technical polish and offer sometimes startling social observation. The effects can be unexpected, as when Chaplin's open-ended "That Corn May Grow" might suggest approval of anti-Communist witch-hunts as well as unrelenting war against European fascism: "Can there be peace? Can there be pardon? / Can there be argument or doubt? / We must make war in every garden / To keep the thistle out." But a poem such as "Pity Them!" indicates also how Chaplin sought to integrate his lifelong championing of the underdog with his more concerted efforts, later in life, to foster social harmony through cooperation instead of competition or conflict: "Pity the greedy who thrive on despair, / And pity a public too callous to care. . . . Pity the great and pity the small, / Pity them, pity them, pity them all."

At the conclusion of *Wobbly*, taking his story up to just after World War II, Chaplin reported that he and Edith had turned to religion, joining the Congregational church in Tacoma, Washington. In 1949 they converted to Roman Catholicism, and the Chaplins turned to the church increasingly for consolation after the death of their son, Vonnie, in 1950. Their religious conversion puts yet another ironic twist in the story of the erstwhile rebel poet and journalist: Ralph and Edith had insisted, over the protests of both their families, upon a civil union when they married in 1906. Yet, even as Chaplin's final published work, *Only the Drums Remembered: A Memento for Leschi* (1960), explores the affirmations of Christian theology, the poem maintains Chaplin's consistent advocacy of the down-and-out while also striking new progressive themes. Written to commemorate the execution of a nineteenth-century chief and war leader of the northwestern Nisqually tribe, Chaplin's tribute finds in its hero not only a martyr whose fight for the downtrodden and boldness in facing execution unmistakably echo Hill's, but also a figure generating sympathy for the rights of native peoples and advocating environmentalism. "The Sun a phantom in a fogged-out sky–," wrote Chaplin, "And Leschi's proud, white Mountain looking down, / Disdainfully upon the upstart town." Published in 1960, one year before his death, *Only the Drums Remembered* stands as a final testimony to the originality and courage of Chaplin's career centered in the home-grown, American radical tradition. He championed the rights of labor consistently and at times and in ways that were not popular or even fully understood. Sometimes, when Chaplin's life and work took their most idiosyncratic turns, it is difficult to discern whether he was behind or ahead of others in the social democratic movement.

References:

Melvin Dubofsky, *We Shall Be All: A History of the Industrial Workers of the World* (Chicago: Quadrangle, 1969);

Philip S. Foner, *History of the Labor Movement in the United States,* volume 4 (New York: International, 1965);

Leonard Levy, ed., *The Centralia Case: Three Views of the Armistice Day Tragedy at Centralia, Washington, November 11, 1919* (New York: Da Capo, 1971);

John McClelland Jr., *Wobbly War: The Centralia Story* (Tacoma: Washington State Historical Society, 1987);

Salvatore Salerno, *Red November, Black November: Culture and Community in the Industrial Workers of the World* (Albany: State University of New York Press, 1989);

John R. Salter Jr., "Reflections on Ralph Chaplin, the Wobblies, and Organizing in the Save the World Business–Then and Now," *Pacific Historian,* 30, 1 (1984): 5–19;

Gibbs M. Smith, *Joe Hill* (Salt Lake City: University of Utah Press, 1969);

Mark W. Van Wienen, *Partisans and Poets: The Political Work of American Poetry in the Great War* (New York: Cambridge University Press, 1997).

Papers:

There are two major repositories for Ralph Chaplin's papers. In the 1930s he gave most of his early papers to the Rare Books and Special Collections Library at the University of Michigan. Shortly before his death, Chaplin donated his later papers to the Washington State Historical Society, where he himself put them in a preliminary order that has largely been maintained. A third significant resource is the National Archives–Central Plains Region, Kansas City, Missouri, where Chaplin's prison file including some correspondence survives. Also of primary interest is the IWW archive at Wayne State University, Detroit, Michigan, which includes virtually a complete run of *Solidarity* and a transcript of the Chicago trial, *U.S. v. Haywood, et al* (1918).

Voltairine de Cleyre

(17 November 1866 – 20 June 1912)

Eugenia C. DeLamotte
Arizona State University

BOOKS: *The Drama of the Nineteenth Century* (Pittsburgh: R. Staley, n.d. [1888]);

In Defense of Emma Goldmann [sic] *and the Right of Expropriation* (Philadelphia: Privately printed by de Cleyre, 1894; London: Liberty Press, 1897);

The Past and Future of the Ladies' Liberal League (Philadelphia: Ladies' Liberal League, 1895);

Sex Slavery: A Lecture (Valley Falls, Kan.: Lucifer, 1899);

The Worm Turns (Philadelphia: Innes & Sons, 1900);

Crime and Punishment (Philadelphia: Social Science Club, 1903);

Det Anarkistiske Ideal [The Anarchist Ideal] (Christiania, Norway: Social-Demokraten, 1903);

McKinley's Assassination from the Anarchist Standpoint (New York: Mother Earth Publishing Association, 1907);

Anarchism and American Traditions (New York: Mother Earth Publishing Association, 1909);

The Dominant Idea (New York: Mother Earth Publishing Association, 1910);

The Mexican Revolt (New York: Mother Earth Publishing Association, 1911);

Direct Action (New York: Mother Earth Publishing Association, 1912);

Selected Works of Voltairine de Cleyre, edited by Alexander Berkman (New York: Mother Earth Publishing Association, 1914); republished as *Selected Works of Voltairine de Cleyre: Pioneer of Women's Liberation* (New York: Revisionist Press, 1972);

Selected Stories, edited by Cassius V. Cook (Seattle: Libertarian Magazine, 1916);

The First Mayday: The Haymarket Speeches 1895–1910, edited by Paul Avrich (Orkney: Cienfuegos Press / New York: Libertarian Book Club and Soil of Liberty, 1980);

Written in Red: Selected Poems, edited by Franklin Rosemont (Chicago: Charles H. Kerr, 1990);

Voltairine de Cleyre Archive, edited by Dana Ward <http://dwardmac.pitzer.edu/Anarchist_Archives/bright/Cleyre/Cleyrearchive.html> (accessed 18 June 2008);

Voltairine de Cleyre, 1891 (Eugenia C. DeLamotte, Gates of Freedom: Voltairine de Cleyre and the Revolution of the Mind, 2007; Thomas Cooper Library, University of South Carolina)

The Voltairine de Cleyre Reader, edited by A. J. Brigati (Oakland, Cal. & Edinburgh: AK Press, 2004);

Gates of Freedom: Voltairine de Cleyre and the Revolution of the Mind, With Selections from Her Writing, edited by Eugenia DeLamotte (Ann Arbor: University of Michigan Press, 2004);

Exquisite Rebel: The Essays of Voltairine de Cleyre—Feminist, Anarchist, Genius, edited by Sharon Presley and Crispin Sartwell with biographical essays by Presley, Sartwell, and Emma Goldman (Albany: State University of New York Press, 2005).

TRANSLATIONS: Jean Grave, *Moribund Society and Anarchy,* preface by de Cleyre (San Francisco: A. Isaak/Free Society Library, 1899);

Francisco Ferrer, *The Modern School* (New York: Mother Earth Publishing Association, 1909).

SELECTED PERIODICAL PUBLICATIONS–UNCOLLECTED: "The Philosophy of Selfishness and Metaphysical Ethics," *Open Court,* 5 (1891): 2871–2873;

"A Glance at Communism," *Twentieth Century* (1 September 1892);

"A Suggestion and Explanation," *Free Society* (San Francisco, Cal.) (3 June 1900);

"A Letter to Senator Hawley," *Free Society* (13 April 1902);

"Kristofer Hansteen," *Mother Earth,* 1 (May 1906): 52–56;

"Hugh O. Pentecost," *Mother Earth,* 2 (March 1907): 11–16;

"On Liberty," *Mother Earth,* 4 (July 1909): 151–154;

"Tour Impressions," *Mother Earth,* 5 (December 1910): 322–325; (January 1911): 360–363;

"The Commune is Risen," *Mother Earth,* 7 (March 1912): 10–14;

"Report of the Work of the Chicago Mexican Liberal Defense League," *Mother Earth,* 7 (April 1912): 60–62.

Voltairine de Cleyre was an American anarchist lecturer, essayist, poet, short-story writer, translator, and organizer during the first great flood tide of anarchism in the late nineteenth and early twentieth centuries. Known internationally among anarchists from Russia and Norway to Britain, France, Germany, Italy, Spain, and Mexico, she was noted among her contemporaries for the force and logic of her analyses as well as her insistence on living out her principles, a characteristic associated in particular with her widely publicized refusal to identify, testify against, or prosecute a man who shot her point-blank in 1902. Her refusal affirmed the fundamental tenets of anarchism: the view that governments, with all their institutions, are founded on and perpetuate violence; that the resources of the earth, which governments are designed to protect for a privileged few, belong by rights equally to everyone; that human liberty is the necessary precursor, not merely the result, of true social order, which must be based not on compulsion but on voluntary agreements in a decentralized society; and that such liberty can exist only in the absence of the state. De Cleyre's wide-ranging works bring these tenets of anarchist theory to bear on a range of subjects: economics, American history, literature, militarism, crime and punishment, evolution, education, and religion. Her most original contribution, however, was her anarchist analysis of women's oppression, set forth in a series of manifestos, short stories, and poems that establish her as a feminist theorist far in advance of her time. Since 1981, this aspect of her work has received the most attention both from historians and literary critics.

She was born Voltairine De Claire on 17 November 1866, in Leslie, Michigan. Her parents were Hector De Claire, a French-born socialist and admirer of eighteenth-century French philosopher Voltaire, for whom he named his daughter, and Harriet Billings De Claire, daughter of New England abolitionists. The family moved the next year to St. Johns, Michigan, where Voltairine grew up in extreme poverty, her father struggling to make a living as a tailor and her mother as a seamstress. In the early 1870s her father left, eventually moving to Port Huron, where Voltairine went to live with him in 1879 during her sister Adelaide's illness. In 1880 he sent her to a nearby Canadian convent boarding school run by Carmelite nuns, from which she graduated with a gold medal in 1883. Despite her academic success in French, piano, and writing, throughout her life she regarded this experience as a terrible incarceration, an encounter with authoritarianism that left her soul permanently scarred and determined her future course as a strenuous opponent of compulsion in any form.

She emerged from the convent as a proponent of free thought, also known as secularism, an eclectic movement whose adherents insisted on a rational, evidence-based approach to every topic, even the most sacrosanct. Tracing their heritage especially to Thomas Paine, author of *The Age of Reason* (1794), freethinkers followed him in advocating an absolute separation of church and state and in rejecting the authority of all organized religions. In addition, many questioned the institution of marriage, advocated rights for women and African Americans, insisted on the open discussion of sexuality and birth control, and upheld Darwin's theory of evolution against religious explanations of the Creation. After two years of living at home earning a meager income as a tutor in music, French, and calligraphy, De Claire moved to her aunt's house in Greenville, Michigan, where she began her career as a free-thought activist and wrote her first important poem, "The Burial of My Past Self" (1885), celebrating her triumphant resolution of the strenuous intellectual and spiritual struggles of her adolescence in the convent. In 1886 she left Greenville for an independent life in Grand Rapids, where she worked as a free-thought activist until early 1888, writing for and editing a free-thought periodical, *The Progressive Age,* and lecturing in nearby towns on the dangers of religious indoctrination. Her essay "Secular Education," which expounds on the importance of education free from religious authoritarianism, appeared in a major free thought journal, *The Truth Seeker,* in 1887. During this period she changed the spelling of her name to de Cleyre, perhaps as a final expression of "The Burial of My Past Self," an intellectual transformation she also celebrated in a diptych of poems in 1887, "The Christian's Faith" and "The Freethinker's Plea." Together these poems recapitulate the inner debates that resulted in her rejection of religion for free thought and set forth her creed as a freethinker. The first, in blank verse, presents Jesus in a sympathetic but tragic light, associating his offer of peace for all sufferers with an erroneous substitution of faith in the cross for transformative action in the world. Such transformative action is associated with the freethinker of the second poem, whose rejection of formal religion and embrace of the central moral imperative to do good in the world are presented in heroic couplets, an eighteenth-century form evoking the historical origins of free thought in such writers as Paine.

This early period of de Cleyre's free-thought writing and activism in 1886 and 1887 coincided with the unfolding of an historical drama that quickly shifted her commitment from free thought to anarchism. In early May 1886, Chicago anarchists rallied peacefully near Haymarket Square to protest recent police violence in a McCormick Harvester strike. Near the end of the event, 180 police suddenly marched on the protesters and ordered them to disperse. A bomb exploded, and police began firing in a chaotic scene in which they injured each other as well as protesters, causing fourteen or fifteen fatalities, including seven policemen. Although the perpetrator has never been conclusively identified, eight anarchists were sentenced—five to death and three to prison—not for throwing the bomb, which was demonstrated to have been impossible in every case, but for advocating ideas that could have inspired the perpetrator. The judge instructed the jury that the state was obliged neither to identify the perpetrator nor prove the defendants' influence on him. The trial became internationally notorious, drawing widespread interest in anarchist ideas and sympathy for the five men who became known as the Haymarket Martyrs: Albert Parsons, August Spies, George Engel, and Adolph Fischer, executed on 11 November 1887, and Louis Lingg, who committed suicide in his cell the day before. Initially swept into the popular cry for vengeance, de Cleyre felt convinced by the time of the executions that the trial was a farce (a judgment subsequently confirmed by Illinois governor John P. Altgeld's extensive investigation resulting in the pardon of the remaining three imprisoned anarchists in 1893). Further, she concluded that justice is not possible under law. Her medi-

tations on the Haymarket incident, her subsequent study of anarchist writings, a brief espousal of socialism after she heard Clarence Darrow speak in December 1887, and her loss of a debate in which she took the socialist side against a brilliant anarchist resulted in her embrace of anarchist activism as her lifework by early 1888.

The new trajectory of her work appears clearly in three poems of 1889. "At the Grave in Waldheim," an elegy for the Haymarket Martyrs buried in Waldheim Cemetery in Chicago, moves from an image of the peace of death, the martyrs quiet in their shrouds, to a resolution that such martyrdom will end and tyranny be crushed throughout the world. "Betrayed" is the dramatic monologue of a mother who has murdered her child to spare it the consequences of its illegitimate birth, including the starvation that will result from her inability as a fallen woman to find work. The poem details the tragedy of the mother's collapse under the burden of her social condition, but also her angry defiance of the executioners and her prophecy that the winds of injustice will finally issue in the whirlwind of an avenging storm, an "hour of parturition" that is close at hand. This vision of injustice as a sowing of violent seeds that must inevitably produce a violent harvest returns as a theme throughout de Cleyre's lifework, especially her poetry; although she was personally drawn to pacifism and saw violent responses to violence as the futile perpetuation of a tragic cycle, she invariably sympathized with those in whom the pressures of injustice created a need to strike back by force, and many of her images of storms and natural disasters exult the inevitability of a day of reckoning for oppressors. Such an image dominates the third important poem of 1889, "The Hurricane." It opens on a muted seascape compared to the as-yet-muted discontents of the oppressed, then moves gradually through a gathering storm toward the climax, when the voice of the people, compared to the voice of God, speaks in the thunder of the sea finally flooding across the wall that has contained it.

Later in 1889 de Cleyre moved to Philadelphia, where she began carving out a meager livelihood by tutoring the Jewish immigrants among whom she formed her strongest emotional ties over the coming years. Despite long hours teaching, she inaugurated a vigorous career of writing, speaking, and organizing on behalf of anarchism. An important early synthesis of the new trajectory of her work was her February 1890 lecture for the freethinking Boston Secular Society, "The Economic Tendency of Freethought," which begins with a "text," as she says, from Thomas Paine and then departs from his influence to trace a logical path from free thought to anarchism, the path she her-

No. 517 N. Randolph St.
Aug 2, 1906

My dear Alex:—

Do you really want to go to Russia? Crazy need not stand in your way. But I don't want you to go to Russia. I don't see why. I think Russia is fighting for something we can have no part in. I know you are thinking, "in what have I a part?" Yes I too, I have no part in things, in the last analysis. In the last analysis it is life itself I hate — not a fat bourgeois. Life, life this fiendish thing which brings millions of little creatures forth mercilessly, only to hunger, pain, madness. There is not a day when the sufferings of the little waif animals in the street, does not create in one a bitter rage against life. And this thing called indifferently "broadness" and "tolerance", is the refuge we take from too much feeling: it is a voluntary stunning of the nerves, as an escape from the terrible tension: I can't, I can't, I simply can't endure the agony of

First page of a letter from de Cleyre to Alexander Berkman in the year he and Emma Goldman founded Mother Earth *(Paul Avrich,* An American Anarchist: The Life of Voltairine de Cleyre, *1978; Thomas Cooper Library, University of South Carolina)*

self had followed, beginning with freethinkers' contempt for blind allegiance to authority. Arguing that failing to question the authority of the state amounts to reinstating a different version of the equally arbitrary authority of a non-existent God, she urged her audience to move beyond "dead issues" associated with religion and politics and to recognize that the important question is now economic: how to end control of one portion of humanity over another by ensuring equal access to the resources of the earth, which belong by rights to all. The climax of the lecture vigorously affirms a recent accusation made by the eminent Catholic official Henry Edward Cardinal Manning, who had warned that free thought leads to the subversion of the current social order. De Cleyre agrees, but describes the current state in scathing detail as a mere parody of order, a nightmare of economic inequality. A pageant of images reinforces the point: miners suffer through the winter while the owners' pockets fill; a barefoot tramp faces arrest for stealing shoes; six families live together in five rooms; a young girl must choose between working six twelve-hour days a week for $5 or marrying a man she dislikes but who can support her financially. De Cleyre calls for the complete subversion of such "order"–the destruction of every institution, including marriage, that makes one person a master and the other a serf.

De Cleyre's personal and philosophical opposition to marriage, including any domestic arrangements resembling it, continued throughout her lifetime, although she had lovers in keeping with her views as an adherent of sex radicalism, a movement rooted in freethinkers' insistence on an open approach to questions of sexuality, monogamy, and birth control, as well as a woman's right to say no to sex in any circumstances. As a result of one of these sex-radical liaisons, she gave birth in 1890 to her only child, Harry Elliott. The father was James Elliott, a free thinker de Cleyre had met on her first visit to Philadelphia and with whom she remained friends for many years after Harry's birth, which seems nonetheless to have ended their romantic involvement. De Cleyre held Elliott accountable for the pregnancy and regarded their son as his responsibility after the birth as well. Harry was born in June; in November de Cleyre arrived in Kansas, where she remained to lecture and write for a year before returning to Philadelphia. In Kansas she was associated with the prominent feminist Matilda Joslyn Gage's Woman's National Liberal Union (WNLU). De Cleyre had spoken at the first convention of the WNLU in Washington, D.C., in February of 1890, and she wrote her first letter to her mother from Kansas on WNLU stationery. In Kansas she grew close to a group of anarchists and freethinkers associated with Moses Harman's sex-radical publication *Lucifer, the Light-Bearer*. She returned to Phil-

adelphia in 1891 and lived in the same rooming house where Elliott and his mother raised Harry, until Elliott and Harry moved to a nearby neighborhood in 1894.

From 1890 to 1896 de Cleyre produced four of her most important feminist manifestos, as well as "The Fruit of the Sacrifice" (a powerful eulogy to the Haymarket Martyrs) and a set of lectures and essays explicating her central anarchist positions. De Cleyre's analyses of women's oppression are now regarded as belonging to a wider movement that historian Margaret S. Marsh has designated as "anarchist feminism," and it is customary to refer to de Cleyre as an anarchist feminist. In her day, however, the term "feminist" was a relatively recent invention and, in the eyes of such anarchists as Emma Goldman and de Cleyre, would have been regarded as having a much narrower application than it came to have in the wake of renewed feminist activism in the 1970s and thereafter. In particular, the theorists of de Cleyre's day who are now termed anarchist feminists saw most of their feminist contemporaries' intense focus on the question of women's suffrage as completely irrelevant to fundamental questions of women's freedom. Anarchists rejected participation in the political process, including the ballot box, because they saw any participation in state institutions as counter to their goals of replacing all governments entirely with other forms of social order–decentralized associations, for example, linked freely by common agreement and ever changing.

The first of de Cleyre's anarchist feminist manifestos, the lecture "Sex Slavery" (1890), responded to the imprisonment of Harman on an obscenity charge for the use of the word "penis" in *Lucifer*. The offense involved a letter to the editor detailing the suffering of a woman who was maritally raped shortly after the birth of a child and nearly died; de Cleyre centered her argument on the irony that it was legal for a man to stab his wife almost to death with an organ it was illegal to name in certain publications. In the lecture de Cleyre attacks marriage as a worldwide institution of imprisonment for women, maintained by an ideological and economic collusion of the church and state; to win moral authority for the coercive institution, these entities represent the obscenity of women's degradation as a form of virtue. Slaves in the antebellum United States fled to Canada, de Cleyre argues, but women have nowhere to flee; they must fight where they stand, and their ability to control their bodies is the key to freedom. In one of the many statements that give her rhetoric the edge more commonly associated with the 1970s, she announces, "The question of souls is old–we demand our bodies now." She defines the only remedy for the situation as liberty, and here as always she argues, like Paine, that liberty must simply be taken, not requested.

This idea underlies her second feminist manifesto of this period, one of the lectures she delivered on her trip to Kansas after Harry's birth. Titled "The Gates of Freedom" and published in *Lucifer* in 1891, it takes as its opening text a line from James Russell Lowell's anti-slavery poem "The Present Crisis": "They have rights who dare maintain them." Lowell's poem attacked supposed truth seekers who look back fondly on the great iconoclastic heroes and issues of the past, failing to see that they must move forward in the present, on current issues. De Cleyre applies the lesson to her modern-day audience of freethinkers at a Liberal Convention, attacking those who would create a new world without revising old views on women and appealing to women to stand up for their liberty—to insist on entering the gates of freedom. In particular she targets the argument that women's subordination—their current economic status as property, their bodies sold in exchange for the "protection" of a man—results naturally and inevitably from evolution and therefore must simply be accepted. Evolutionary theory was critical to free thought and to anarchist theory; it formed, for example, the foundation for the ethical theory of Russian revolutionary Petr Kropotkin, a leading figure of international anarchism whose work profoundly influenced de Cleyre. Evolutionary theory also underlay anarchists' assaults on the church, which they customarily paired with the state as one of the twin authoritarian obstacles to human freedom. De Cleyre thus faced the task in this lecture of claiming evolution as a support for anarchist feminism while at the same time rendering it untenable as a basis for sexist oppression.

She does so by arguing that justice, like evolution, is progressive: whatever the evolutionary benefits of women's subordination in the past, women deserve their rights in the present. The era when mere muscular strength conferred evolutionary advantage in the struggle for survival has ended. What matters in the modern world is not sheer physical power but brains—the ability to invent. She admits that women may be inferior in this regard because they have not had an equal opportunity to develop intellectually, not for any essential inability. Similarly, she finds that the objection that women must stay home and care for children has become irrelevant; in time child care will be given over to those especially qualified for it, experts who may well not be the parents. Currently, she argues, the marriage contract secures the sale of a woman's body, a situation to which many women themselves do not object because during the long period when their subordination may well have been evolutionarily adaptive, submission became part of their moral natures, an unconscious part of their intellect. Women's consciousness is changing, however, and their new sense of their

servitude signals an evolutionary change: current agitation over the woman question itself shows that current gender arrangements no longer carry adaptive benefits for the species. What may have been the justice of the past is not necessarily justice today. She concludes the lecture with an allusion to Olive Schreiner's feminist allegory, "Three Dreams in a Desert" (collected 1891), which describes a woman almost buried in the desert sand, bound for long ages to a man in a mutually incomprehensible physical dependency based on the importance of physical strength, but finally cut loose by the knife of mechanical invention. De Cleyre offers her audience a vision to fit between the end of this allegorical tableau, when the woman finally rises to her knees, and Schreiner's final tableau, which describes a woman's arrival at a river she must cross to reach the Land of Freedom. Between these two dreams, de Cleyre places the figure of a gigantic woman, alone on an American prairie beneath the gray morning sky, looking around her with apprehension, but also with a sense of the largeness of the space now available to her.

The impassioned commitment to women's equality expressed in these two manifestos of the early 1890s manifested itself, on de Cleyre's return to Philadelphia, in her participation in a new women's group from 1892 until the late 1890s. Her lecture and article "The Past and Future of the Ladies' Liberal League" (1895–1896) details its history and recounts with scathing wit the difficulties anarchist and freethinking feminists encountered in their struggles for equality even within social revolutionary movements. The group, which de Cleyre says she did not help to found but joined soon after it was organized, began as an offshoot of the male-dominated Friendship Liberal League, which conceived it as a ladies' auxiliary specializing in fund-raisers, but with no control over the funds. Scoffing at this plan as a version of church ice-cream socials and bazaars—a damning analogy for her audience, opposed to organized religion—de Cleyre describes the "ladies'" resistance to their assigned roles, exulting in their "non-submission, insubordination, rebellion, revolt, revolution, whatever name you please which expresses non-acquiescence to injustice." This revolt, she says, results from the natural impulse of the upward-climbing sap in a flower. This metaphor, taken from Kropotkin's *Anarchist Morality* (1897), suggests de Cleyre's desire to associate women's rebellion against their subordinate status with what Kropotkin defined as the highest version of morality: a vast expansion of life; a tremendous, overflowing, transformative energy. De Cleyre's use of this passage locates her description of the Ladies' Liberal League as a contribution to anarchist ethical theory just as "The Gates of Freedom" expanded anarchist evolutionary theory.

De Cleyre saw what Kropotkin termed "plenitude of existence, the free development of all [one's] faculties," as the deepest necessity of the individual life, and throughout this period her feminist theorizing of the constraints on women's ability to achieve such inner freedom coincided with her own struggles to forge sexual relationships based on anarchist conceptions of liberty. She experienced one of the most difficult such struggles in her tortured relationship with a younger anarchist she tutored in English, Samuel Gordon. She became involved with Gordon in 1893 and was still working to free herself from him emotionally as late as 1900, when she wrote her sister that she had to resign herself to not seeing him very much due to his desire for what would amount to marriage. In the early days of their affair he lived with her for a time, an experience that seems to have confirmed her opposition to any such domestic relationships as involving the dangers of what she described in an 1897 letter to him as "married slavery"–"the tortures of owning and being owned." For de Cleyre and Gordon, these tortures involved arguments so intense that after one of them they both took poison. De Cleyre, who lived on the edge of extreme poverty, financed Gordon's medical school education and railed against his subsequent criticism of her for her supposed financial impracticality; she became angry as well at what she regarded his increasing materialism and abandonment of his earlier anarchist idealism.

In an 1893 letter de Cleyre described to her mother her own earlier temptation, at an extreme emotional low point, to marry a man named Bentley, not for love but for the economic security he could provide, which would have given her more time for her work. Describing her mental state at the time as "degraded" and "disgraceful," she affirmed clearly her renunciation of the whole idea of economic dependency and explained her ideal domestic arrangements. Traditional homes, she said, should be replaced with huge communal shared spaces: palaces, "spacious grounds," theaters, sculpture, libraries, and swimming rooms, but with a private individual place for each resident's exclusive use.

De Cleyre's relationship with Gordon had reached its period of most intense crisis at the time of de Cleyre's publication of her final feminist manifesto of this period, "The Case of Woman vs. Orthodoxy" (1896). In it she expands further on the question of why women have accepted their subordination, and predicts even more emphatically a vast, imminent change in gender arrangements. She derives her argument from an analysis of historical changes in the material conditions of women's lives, beginning with an historicizing of women's roles as represented in the Bible. These

"sometimes nauseating accounts of the behavior of women in ancient times in Judah" she attributes to the pressure of material hardships so extreme that women were forced to take the command to be fruitful and multiply as their highest goal, in a society that nonetheless meted out horrific (and unequal) punishments to women who committed adultery. In a long, blasphemous, sarcastic paraphrase of King Solomon's praise of the perfect woman, she attacks the Bible as a major ideological foundation of women's oppression. This foundation she regards as now crumbling in the wake of changes in women's economic conditions brought about by the industrial revolution: "the factory is laughing at the church; and the modern woman, who grasps her own self-hood, is laughing at the priest." As terrible as the factory system is, its material effects have been translated into new conceptions of gender, and the old chains binding women can never be reforged. Alluding to the publication of this article at Easter-time, de Cleyre ends with a secular celebration of the Resurrection, invoking the spirits of rebellious women of the past and anticipating a great "time of transfiguration" for women.

De Cleyre's feminist writings of this period tie inextricably to the development of her anarchist theory more generally, as two other crucial articles of this period illustrate. The first, "The Philosophy of Selfishness and Metaphysical Ethics" (1891), she wrote in the same year as "The Gates of Freedom." In it she attacked an individualist version of anarchism that her readers would have associated with the influence of German philosopher Max Stirner on American anarchist contributors to Benjamin Tucker's influential periodical *Liberty*. Stirner, whose views are sometimes labeled "philosophical egotism," focused on the central importance of the individual ego; de Cleyre saw this as dangerously and erroneously making the self the center of every issue. While she defined herself in the early 1890s as an individualist anarchist (a label she soon rejected), especially in contradistinction to communist anarchism, the version of individualism she embraced grew not from philosophical egotism but from the economic analyses of Dyer Lum, one of her most important anarchist mentors, possibly also a lover, from their meeting in 1888 to his suicide in 1893. Lum's version of individualist anarchism emphasized mutualism and cooperation, looking to groups–workers' organizations and federations–as the basis for social revolution.

De Cleyre thought of this revolution in terms of the collective reclaiming of the world's resources by the dispossessed, a view she expressed in a passionate defense of one of the leading anarchists of the period, Goldman, after Goldman's arrest for a speech in 1893. Goldman had urged the unemployed to ask for work

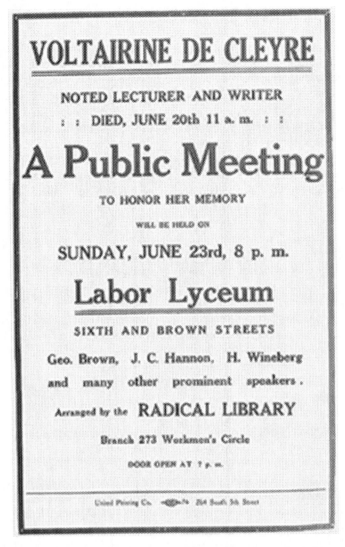

Poster advertising a memorial for de Cleyre in Philadelphia three days after her death (Sharon Presley and Crispin Sartwell, Exquisite Rebel: The Essays of Voltairine de Cleyre: Feminist, Anarchist, Genius, *2005; Thomas Cooper Library, University of South Carolina)*

and, if denied, to ask for bread, and then, if denied, simply to take the bread. De Cleyre's "In Defense of Emma Goldmann [*sic*]: The Right of Expropriation," published in the anarchist *Herald of Revolt* that same year, provides an excellent example of an ironic rhetorical style that characterizes much of her writing. Pointing out that a certain "seditious person" (Jesus) took corn from another person's field and also directed his disciples simply to take a colt when he needed one, she sets up the unifying thread of the speech, an analogy between Goldman and Jesus, which she eventually transforms into an analogy between "the immortal Race-Christ" and all the dispossessed. Describing Jesus as a "man who set the right of Property beneath his foot," she compares the accusation against him—"he stirreth up the people"—with that directed against Gold-

man. If she herself were giving advice to her auditors, de Cleyre says, she would tell them the bread is theirs by rights; it belongs to those who worked to produce the wheat, worked in the mills to turn it into flour, worked in the mines to get the fuel to bake it, forged the iron to make the ovens, and stood all night tending the machines. The authorities fear the power of the producers to take back what they have made, she argues. She concludes with a quotation from an English poet she much admired, Algernon Charles Swinburne, whose "Before a Crucifix" presages liberation theology and compares the oppressed people to the buried Christ. "And what man, or what angel known / Shall roll back the sepulchral stone?" he asks. In the presence of Goldman's courage, de Cleyre says, we may feel that the stone has indeed been rolled back.

Throughout the 1890s, de Cleyre made a strenuous effort to affirm the unconquerable force of the people in the face of the bitterest oppressions. In 1896 a bomb exploded at a Corpus Christi festival in Spain, and the government imprisoned three hundred anarchists, together with many supposed sympathizers, in the fortress of Montjuich. The prisoners described their tortures in letters smuggled out by sympathizers and circulated among anarchists internationally. De Cleyre read them with horror. In response she initiated and became the guiding light of a protest movement in Philadelphia, distributing pamphlets and working to involve Congress to pressure the Spanish government on the issue. Such work, undertaken on top of her usual writing and lecturing, as well as a tutoring schedule that sometimes lasted far into the night, exacerbated the chronic nose and throat infections from which she suffered throughout her adult life. In 1897 she sought to improve her health and broaden her anarchist horizons by visiting Europe, where she already had a small circle of friends she had met on their visits to America.

This visit proved transformative in many ways. First, it confirmed de Cleyre internationally as an important American anarchist, through her many lectures in London and Glasgow, where she spoke, sometimes to audiences of more than a thousand, on the broad economic questions of anarchism, "The Woman Question," the differences between European and American anarchism, and the nature of her own anarchist commitments and views. The latter she described in "Why I am an Anarchist," in which she identified her ultimate impulse toward anarchism with her early sense of the "cramped" circle into which women's subordination forces them. Second, the visit introduced her to a broad international group of anarchists, including Kropotkin; the famous French anarchist Louise Michel; French anarchist Jean Grave, whose book *Moribund Society and Anarchy* she arranged to translate; and Fernando Tarrida del Mármol, whose conception of "anarchy without adjectives"—an attempt to move beyond the fragmentation of anarchism into such hyphenated splinter groups as individualist-, communist-, mutualist-, and socialist-anarchists—Paul Avrich has identified as one of the most important influences on de Cleyre. Avrich observes that by 1900 she had become "the leading apostle of tolerance" in the American anarchist movement (*An American Anarchist: The Life of Voltairine de Cleyre*, 1978).

Third, in London, de Cleyre met some of the Spanish anarchists recently released from Montjuich. They spoke in a dramatic meeting at Trafalgar Square and later in private homes showed the scars from their tortures. In response, a young Italian anarchist, Michele Angiolillo, rushed off to Spain and assassinated the prime minister responsible for the atrocities. At his execution he cried out "Germinal!"—the title of Émile Zola's anarchist novel of 1885. Zola's final image of the seeds of revolution bursting through the sod—a metaphor for the impending rebellion of the miners whose desperate lives he had described in relentlessly raw naturalistic detail throughout the novel—inspired anarchists all over the world, including de Cleyre. She took "Germinal" as the title and organizing principle of one of her most powerful poems, written in 1897 soon after the assassination and published as the lead poem in her 1900 collection, *The Worm Turns*. She based one of her most powerful short stories, "The Heart of Angiolillo," on this event as well. In it she merged anarchist feminism with her response to Montjuich, recounting a double story of the tortures of the anarchists and a young woman's oppression in a supposedly sex-radical domestic arrangement with an anarchist man whose thoughtless exploitation of her labor is literally killing her. De Cleyre's fictionalized character Angiolillo sees into the heart of this relationship and, in love with Effie, the oppressed young woman, himself, offers her a rescue, which she rejects. How can they even speak of personal problems in the face of the wider issues of the world, Effie asks—the tortures of Montjuich? Inspired to vengeance by their conversation, Angiolillo leaves for Spain. In a dream that fuses the question of her own domestic oppression with the oppression of the Spanish anarchists, Effie sees the tortures and the execution, hears the ringing echoes of Angiolillo's final cry, calls out that she will kiss him now, and wakes wondering what responsibility she bears in this situation. By superimposing a critique of traditional ideas of romance and domesticity on her analysis of the oppression of the Spanish anarchists, which she relates both to the class system and to religious ideology, de Cleyre presents in this story her most elaborate exploration of the interlocking relations between women's private oppressions and the systemic violence of the state.

On her return to the United States, de Cleyre resumed her grueling schedule of writing, teaching, and organizing in Philadelphia, as well as lecturing in Kansas and in Chicago, where she customarily gave some of her fieriest speeches at the annual commemorations of the Haymarket Martyrs' executions. In 1899 she became briefly involved with a Russian anarchist named Nahum Berman, who died impoverished and mentally ill the next year. Inspired in part by his dedication, which she described as admirable but almost fanatical, she organized the Social Science Club, identified by Avrich as the "leading anarchist group in Philadelphia" by 1901. She expressed her anarchist hopes for a coming social revolution in the poem she wrote on 1 January of that year to celebrate the turn of the new century, "Ave et Vale" ("Hail and Farewell"). In it she describes angrily the injustices of the present day and looks forward to their eradication in the next century, confidently anticipating a massive international general strike as the event that will initiate justice throughout the world.

The poem pictures this strike as imminent, but de Cleyre always regarded education as the key to rallying workers around the idea of direct expropriation of the resources to which they were entitled. Thus in the same year, 1901, she plunged into a new organizing effort aimed at significantly expanding the anarchist movement in Philadelphia. This project became much more challenging in the aftermath of President William McKinley's assassination on 6 September by Leon Czolgosz, who allegedly identified himself to police as an anarchist. (His brief contacts with anarchists had led them to conclude that though he was not an anarchist, he was some kind of spy.) After the assassination, Goldman, whom he had visited at one of her lectures and who was vilified in the press as an influence on him, said that his act was not anarchism and that if he admired her ideas he had chosen "the wrong way of showing it." In general, anarchists of this period deplored individual violence as a means to their ends, which they saw as achievable through mass revolutionary actions but not terrorism. They repudiated Czolgosz's act, regarding him as a disturbed and tragic product of oppression. Anarchists all over the United States became the targets of violence, and organizing efforts such as de Cleyre's suffered from renewed public perceptions, dating back to the Haymarket incident and subsequent red scare, that anarchism itself was a violent movement. De Cleyre's article of 1907, "McKinley's Assassination from the Anarchist Standpoint," explained her own position on the subject, which was that Czolgosz's act erupted from the state violence perpetrated by McKinley himself, his hands red with the blood of the recent imperialist war on the Philippines: *"The hells of capitalism create the desperate; the desperate act,— desperately!"* Whether Czolgosz was an anarchist could not be determined, she said; he was "A child of the great darkness, a spectre out of the abyss!" *(An American Anarchist)*.

In January 1902 de Cleyre published "A Rocket of Iron," a short story focused on the relation between "the hells of capitalism" and the revolutionary consciousness they can produce. Indebted in its opening paragraphs to Zola's descriptions of the machines in the mines in *Germinal,* it asks what the hammers of the forge produce as they beat on the screaming iron and answers that "Frankenstein makes his monster." At the center of the scene appears the protagonist, with a chiseled face on which these hammers must also have been

beating. Suddenly a rocket of iron explodes from the furnace, creating a storm of sparks in which two workers are killed and another maimed. The protagonist carries his friend outside, and the narrator-observer catches in his otherwise calm face a glimpse of some inner furnace, some newly shaped resolution. His work has already made him ill of tuberculosis, and he will die before he can act. Even so, the story implies that whatever the intended act, it would have been forged in the hells of capitalism, perhaps a violent revolt against the violence of the system.

In December 1902 de Cleyre had her own, more personal encounter with violence when a desperately impoverished and mentally disturbed former student, Herman Helcher, accosted her as she was boarding a streetcar and shot her point-blank three times. In keeping with her opposition to any state institutions, including the criminal-justice system, she identified him only as a man she knew, refusing to say he was the one who shot her. She persisted in refusing to press charges or testify against him and as soon as she was able issued an appeal to anarchist comrades for funds on his behalf ("Appeal for Herman Helcher"). She explained to the newspapers that Helcher was mentally ill and that the world would be free of violence if society were organized to permit everyone a "normal life." The violence of government produces such violence as Helcher's, she argued; as in the case of Czolgosz, she saw Helcher as one of those driven to desperation by the current social order.

These views found expression in one of de Cleyre's most important lectures, "Crime and Punishment," delivered first in Philadelphia on 15 March 1903 to an audience of twelve hundred. In it she argued for the abolition of prisons, which function as schools of crime and render prisoners desperate and embittered; characterizing the idea of punishment as "savage," she said that social energies would be better directed toward the goal of freeing humanity from the oppressions that create criminality in the first place. She gave the lecture again in Glasgow and London the next year on a second trip to Europe, where she also visited Norway and experienced a brief rejuvenation, including an exhilarating mountain hike, after her recent physical ordeal. Back in the United States, she found her general health worsening significantly, as a sinus infection produced a middle-ear infection that left her with a permanent roaring in her ears. Hospitalized twice from July 1904 until January 1905 and then struggling to recover for many months after, she attempted suicide at one point, but finally recovered by 1906, the year in which Goldman and Alexander Berkman founded *Mother Earth,* the major publisher of de Cleyre's work during her last great productive period, between 1906 and her death in 1912.

In 1906 de Cleyre's son turned fifteen, the age at which, according to some accounts, he discovered that she was his mother, and the point at which de Cleyre first mentions him in her extant letters. She had given him a weekly allowance from the time he was ten and at one time also undertook to teach him piano; thus it is not clear how far to credit the idea that he did not know of their relationship. Whenever he may have learned of it, by all accounts he became one of de Cleyre's greatest admirers, taking her last name, talking of her admiringly, and later naming his first daughter Voltairine. His reports of what he learned from her, including the little-known fact that her friend Dyer Lum provided Haymarket prisoner Lingg with the means to commit suicide, imply at least some long conversations—and in this case on a matter de Cleyre would have perhaps regarded as confidential. De Cleyre's letters to Berkman in July 1906 and her mother in May 1907 reveal that Harry was boarding with her; the former tells of a wonderful midnight trip to Valley Forge with "my youngster"; the latter recounts his excitement about a new machine. De Cleyre sought to enhance this interest by contributing to Harry's brief effort to get a technical education, which, to her distress, he abandoned.

The letters to Berkman formed part of a long correspondence initiated by de Cleyre in 1893 when he was in prison for assaulting capitalist Henry Clay Frick during the Homestead Strike of 1892. De Cleyre, who told him she could not determine the moral status of his action but was impressed that he had at least acted on his convictions, began writing to him in prison; when he was released in 1906 she met him and strengthened their friendship, which grew as she offered extensive editorial and organizational advice throughout the composition of his classic, *Prison Memoirs of an Anarchist* (1912). At the same time, she wrote for Goldman's *Mother Earth*. In it she published her last feminist manifesto, "They Who Marry Do Ill"; "On Liberty," a call for agitation on behalf of the right to free speech during a wave of repression; a much-anthologized essay, "Anarchism and American Traditions," describing anarchism as a logical outgrowth of American revolutionary thought; "Francisco Ferrer," related to the movement of the Spanish anarchist educator; a translation of Ferrer's essay "The Modern School"; "The Chain Gang," the short story Goldman considered de Cleyre's fictional masterpiece; an influential essay on the relationship between ideas and material reality, "The Dominant Idea"; and a set of articles centering on questions of violence—its causes and consequences and the appropriate methods of ending it. Among these are her responses to recent activities in the labor movement and to the Mex-

ican Revolution, a cause into which she poured her energies during the last year of her life. Also in *Mother Earth* during this period, de Cleyre published two important corrections to some of her contemporaries' misconceptions of her anarchist position: a clarification in December of 1907 that she was not, and had never been, an anarchist communist, as had been recently reported, but was simply an anarchist without any economic label, and a statement in 1910 that she was not a Tolstoyan pacifist, as advertised recently on one of her lecture tours.

De Cleyre's last feminist manifesto, "They Who Marry Do Ill," extends and codifies her earlier thinking on women's oppression. Delivered as a lecture in 1907 and published in 1908, it preserves de Cleyre's half of a debate against an opponent who argued the other side: "They Who Marry Do Well." In a scathing summary of all of her earlier animadversions against any kind of dependent relationship between women and men, de Cleyre defines marriage—which she opposed absolutely—as including not merely unions legally blessed by religion or state but also any kind of contractual or noncontractual arrangement whereby men and women, whether in monogamy, polygamy, or polyandry, agree to live together. Any such arrangement at all endangers individual freedom, especially that of women, whose psychological, economic, and sexual oppressions she sees as underwritten by the institution of marriage. Beginning by claiming a critical role for "consciousness" in human evolution—a claim harking back to her earlier feminist manifestos—she admits the evolutionary role of marriage in a previous social order that must now be surpassed because it originated in a class system rather than in the current tendency toward concern for the creation and sustenance of free individuals. Freedom remained her key criterion here as in everything she wrote: she believed that liberty was the important issue, not whether some people found happiness in marriage.

The question of liberty, this time in the context of freedom of speech, arose forcefully in 1909 in Philadelphia, when de Cleyre was arrested at a rally of the unemployed that turned into a riot. Her offense was having advocated immediate, universal expropriation, by the workers, of all the means of production: land, mines, factories. After her acquittal when the prosecution did not produce a witness against her, she worked relentlessly, and finally successfully, for the release of others arrested in the same incident. In the wake of other such attacks on free speech, de Cleyre produced one of her most impressive lectures, "On Liberty," later that year. Published in *Mother Earth* in 1909 and reprinted in July 1912, it argues that the only way to maintain the right of free speech is to speak, and to resist actively any restraints on free speech, even the speech of those with whom one passionately disagrees. Beginning with a humorous story of a police visit to her house in a search for seditious materials, during which they tossed aside her book of revolutionary poetry, *The Worm Turns,* as irrelevant (clearly a book about worms), she builds to a climax in which she says that she herself will stand for the right to speech even of those editors who call for the lynching of anarchists. Deploring the public apathy to which she attributes the current wave of repression, de Cleyre nonetheless insists that "The worm, when trodden, will turn"–that in a "lightning-like clarification," the masses, finally overfull of tyranny, will discover they have spines and need no longer crawl (*Mother Earth,* July 1909).

The possibility of such revolutionary consciousness–where it originates; how to inspire and sustain it–absorbed de Cleyre in this last period of her life. Part of her strategy, in an American context, had always been to educate her audiences to see that anarchism fit squarely in the context of American intellectual and political traditions. Her 1908 publication of "Anarchism and American Traditions" concentrated on restoring a sense of the revolutionary nature of the American War of Independence in the face of the "shameless falsification of all acts of rebellion" in public-school curricula, whose goal–far from that of the founding fathers–is to glorify government. Americans, she argued, have confused the idea of "revolution" with the armies and battles of the American Revolution, not understanding that "the real Revolution" occurred in "a change in political institutions" based on the concept of "equal liberty," and that the revolutionaries themselves were profoundly distrustful of government, which Paine identified as "at best a necessary evil, at worst an intolerable one." Railing against the imperialist goals of the current U.S. government and pointing out that Jefferson reduced, instead of expanding, the standing army during his administration, she calls for an end to the standing army and to government itself. In place of government she envisions a decentralized society consisting of thousands of independent, self-reliant communities. Once again, she sees a general expropriation of the world's resources by ordinary people as the means of initiating such a society, which will be born when people overcome their "awe of government," and act to create true liberty.

The foundations of such actions, in de Cleyre's view, included a growing, overwhelming sense of oppression on the part of the dispossessed; the inevitability that even the worm will turn. The impetus toward such actions also included education: the act in which de Cleyre most consistently engaged in her lectures, speeches, and essays. One of her most stirring essays

during this last period of her career responded to the 1909 execution of Ferrer, founder of the Modern School movement, who emphasized the humane cultivation of children's rational and physical faculties, taught the scientific method and the theory of evolution, and rejected church involvement in education. He was arrested for his supposed involvement in a workers' rebellion in which some convents were burned, but de Cleyre argued in her 1910 lecture "Francisco Ferrer" (published as a pamphlet by *Mother Earth* the next year), that he was actually executed because his educational philosophy was capable of producing a more fundamental rebellion against church and state authority. The lecture turns on two images. One depicts Ferrer as an agent of the "thorough educational enlightenment" that must form the basis of any permanent social revolution. She couples this with a double image of the Virgin Mary. The first Mary represents the wealth and corruption of the Church as the gorgeous statue of the Virgin of Toledo–glittering, against the background of the most grinding poverty, with her $25,000 crown, $10,000 worth of bracelets, 85,000 pearls, and thousands of precious jewels. The second, a more obscure figure, "Our Lady of Pain," or "Our Lady of Hunger," hovers in silence but with a potential to take matters into her own hands if oppression becomes unbearable. If she and her children do not get relief from poverty and starvation, she will finally "set her own lights in the darkness." These lights work in counterpoint to two other images–the flames of the burning convents, symbol of violent revolution, and the "circle of light" that Ferrer briefly lit, with his Modern School, in the darkness of Catholic superstition.

As this counterpoint of images reveals, even de Cleyre's nonfiction often relies heavily on literary devices, an indication of the more strictly literary ambitions she felt she never had enough time to pursue. Even so, her production of poetry and fiction was impressive. In 1907 she published one of her best stories in *Mother Earth.* "The Chain Gang" offers a tight, evocative description of the songs of convicts laboring on a hot clay road in Georgia, where de Cleyre had traveled recently in an attempt to improve her health. The story, almost a prose poem, bespeaks her admiration for Edgar Allan Poe's "Philosophy of Composition" (1850), which urged poets to create "unity of effect." De Cleyre in this final phase of her career refined her skills at this technique, which shaped not only "Francisco Ferrer" and "The Chain Gang" but also her essay "The Dominant Idea," published in *Mother Earth* in May and June of 1910. Opening with an image of a dead morning-glory vine blooming at midnight in a storm, perhaps a further elaboration of Kropotkin's metaphor of the rising sap, the essay rejects materialist analyses of history that discredit the force of ideas, celebrates the power of ideas to change material reality, attacks the "dominant idea" of her own era—a materialist focus on things, expressed in increasing commercialism and a military imperialism designed to secure world markets for the sale of more and more unnecessary commodities—and calls for anarchists' commitment to ideas that will bring about social revolution.

Despite her accomplishments in these years, de Cleyre wrote her close friends of feelings of depression and emotional emptiness, worrying that she had nothing to say, that the force of her commitment to anarchism was waning, and that the whole movement had become too theoretical. She told her old friend Mary Hansen in December 1909 that she had felt "bankrupt" for the past two years. Eventually she decided to leave Philadelphia, where she had spent almost all of her adult life, and move to Chicago, another center of anarchist activism. It is typical of de Cleyre's periods of depression and burnout that she planned her route to Chicago as a vigorous one-month lecture tour through New York City, upstate New York, Cleveland, Toledo, and Detroit. Her "Tour Impressions," recounted in two installments in *Mother Earth* for December 1910 and January 1911, record part of her disillusionment with the direction of the American anarchist movement during this period; she complained of the predominantly middle- and professional-class composition of her audiences and a corresponding distancing of the movement from its working-class basis and responsibilities. Her first report concluded forcefully that the anarchist movement was taking the wrong path, an accusation to which Goldman reacted with a defensive rebuttal, arguing that historically the more privileged classes have had important roles to play in revolutionary movements. Behind the acrimony lay Goldman's recognition, perhaps, of an implicit attack on her own popular and charismatic lecture style, which attracted huge audiences but earned de Cleyre's disapproval for being too extemporaneous and repetitious, lacking the kind of organized content she believed necessary in a solid educational groundwork for social transformation.

One aspect of de Cleyre's work in the last phase of her career takes shape in a more relentless engagement with the question of violence: the violence she saw as endemic to all government, expressed in the oppressions of a fundamentally unequal society; the violence such systemic violence inevitably produces in those whom oppression makes desperate; and the question of a more reasoned "forcible resistance" to that violence, as in the Mexican Revolution or some labor-union tactics that involved the destruction of property

De Cleyre's tombstone, Waldheim Cemetery, Chicago (Exquisite Rebel: The Essays of Voltairine de Cleyre—Feminist, Anarchist, Genius, *edited by Sharon Presley and Crispin Sartwell, 2005; Thomas Cooper Library, University of South Carolina*)

and, in one notable case, the unintentional destruction of life.

At the end of her life, de Cleyre had become jaded about her "theory-rotted" fellow radicals, whom she considered too absorbed in ideas and too far removed from the process of making a revolution. She felt that she had made a mistake in moving to Chicago, and she considered returning to Philadelphia or even moving to Los Angeles, to be closer to the news about Mexico. She saw the Mexican Revolution as representing a benchmark of human progress: whereas all other revolutions had focused on political issues and rights, this one was primarily economic. It was the one happy note of her last two years. In the opening of *The Mexican Revolt* (1911) de Cleyre scans contemporary newspapers for reportage of the event and finds all, even the "revolutionary elements" silent; she interprets this as a sign of how little the extended radical movement has to offer, from Single-Taxers, who might have been assumed to have some interest in questions of land use, to the union of socialism and politics, "that old Blue-beard husband of so many fine young wives." Express-ing some fear that the instability of the provisional government in Mexico will inspire U.S. intervention, she nonetheless applauds it, for however long it may last, and concludes "Hail to the Mexican Revolution, victorious or defeated! And hail to the next that rises!" She became involved in the North American support network and took a post as Chicago correspondent for *Regeneracion*. In this work she met her last lover, Joseph Kucera, a Bohemian machinist who wrote for *Volne' Listy*. She began to study Spanish, but by September 1911 she was too ill even for a visit to Los Angeles.

Her last pamphlet, *Direct Action* (1912), picks up where *The Mexican Revolt* leaves off. De Cleyre first roughed out this thesis in a speech delivered on 21 Jan-uary 1912. Direct action, she argues, has come to mean individual acts of violence. More properly, she believes, it denotes enacting or being the change one wishes to happen without asking permission or going through third parties. People make change, she argues: laws do not. Most people believe in direct action, she says, but they also believe in indirect action, being contradictory creatures. The only people who really believe only in direct action are adherents to nonviolence, because they alone do not rely upon the coercive power of the state to force others to do their will. "For the basis of all polit-ical power is coercion," she states yet again, "even when the State does good things, it finally rests on a club, a gun, or a prison, for its power to carry them through."

Reviewing historical instances of conflict between conscience and state power in the United States and reiterating anarchist interpretations of the Civil War as a struggle between two forms of slavery, of which the greater had won, she uses the opportunity to comment on the developing split in the Socialist Party, then in the process of expelling its more radical left wing. Lauding William D. Haywood and Frank Bohn of the Industrial Workers of the World (IWW)–two of the chief radicals being expelled–as the political heirs of the Under-ground Railroad, she notes that reformers have done commendable things and may have been driven by a larger vision, but they cannot be accused, other than the IWW, of trying to solve "the social war." Ranging back through the history of labor organizations, she illustrates in each case how the ideology of individual-ism and the tendency of individuals to see the world in terms of personal problems have prevented optimal effi-ciency. In particular she focuses on strike-related vio-lence as an example of deterministic forces at work. No one rationally chooses to be part of this violence, she

observes, but "they do these things, through the harsh logic of a situation which they did not create, but which forces them to these attacks in order to make good on their struggle to live, or else go down the bottomless descent into poverty, that lets Death find them in the poorhouse hospital, the city street, or the river-slime."

Her final example in American history of the pov-erty of political action is the eight-hour day, which had been the law in Illinois since 1871 but was not enforced until well after her death (when it became a federal law in 1938). She also notes that laws can be manipulated, as in the case of antitrust laws being used against labor organizations. Finally, she argues, the greatest evil of reliance on the state and political action is that it habitu-ates people to inaction and dependency, "teaches them to rely on someone else to do for them what they alone can do for themselves." The general strike, the appro-priation of the means of production and the wealth of the world by the workers who made it all possible, are the only way to bring an end to the social war, which will otherwise continue "because Life cries to live, and Property denies its freedom to live; and Life will not submit. And should not submit." *Direct Action* provides a retrospective summary of de Cleyre's development as a thinker. Stimulated by her disgust with her comrades in North America and her hopes for progress in Mexico, the pamphlet implicitly traces her development as an anarchist.

De Cleyre appeared in public for the last time at an anarchist Red Cross benefit to give a poetry reading on 14 April 1912. Three days later her doctor found that her chronic sinus problems had spread again to the middle ear. The infection reached her brain, and she underwent surgery twice. Afterward she lost the ability to speak, and Harry de Cleyre and Nathan Navro trav-eled from Philadelphia to stay with her. She remained in the hospital in Chicago nine weeks in all, dying on 20 June 1912. More than two thousand people attended her funeral when she was buried three days later at Waldheim Cemetery in Forest Park, Illinois, near the graves of the Haymarket Martyrs. Memorial services were also held in Philadelphia and New York, and in July *Mother Earth* devoted an issue to her memory. That autumn a group of her friends began to compile her *Selected Works* for publication; they finished the volume in 1914.

After de Cleyre's death, the London anarchist periodical *Herald of Revolt* published a memorial edition that included one of her most interesting works of fic-tion, a feminist story titled "The White Room." The room of the title is an artist's painstaking tribute to his wife, created secretly over a period of fifteen years and filled with objects, all white or silver, that evoke his exalted conception of her white, angelic, Scandinavian purity. As he prepares this surprise gift in a house by a river, spending most of his time there, her horizons are bounded by the tenement where they were forced to live in his earlier, impoverished days. Just at the moment the artist's great surprise is finally ready, he returns home to find that his wife has fled in desperation, leaving a note that she can no longer tolerate her bleak situation and will not be back. The artist finds her drunk in the streets and takes her to the white room, laying her on the small white bed. Horrified by what seems to be a charnel house, she cries out against all the whiteness and dies. The husband, realizing his mistake too late, buries her with no white headstone, under violets and carnations. The story attacks late-nineteenth-century ideas of womanly virtue not only as erroneous but also as deadly; the white room is a metaphor for the artist's mistaken idealistic conception of his wife, his insistence on imagining her true nature in isolation from genuine contact with her.

Despite the brevity of de Cleyre's career, she produced a prolific body of work in a variety of genres: poems, dramatic monologues, stories, speeches, essays, translations, journalism, and letters. All of this work she dedicated to educating both anarchists and non-anarchists on the subject of what she regarded as the one great remedy for human misery—liberty. Her work celebrates the possibilities of a new and genuine decentralized social order, free of the violence on which every government inevitably depends, and founded on a just distribution of the earth's resources. In "The Chain Gang" and "Crime and Punishment" she applied these principles to an analysis of the justice system; in "On Liberty," to the question of free speech and a free press; in "McKinley's Assassination from an Anarchist Standpoint," and "A Rocket of Iron," to the sources of violence; in "The Right of Expropriation," "Our Present Attitude," and "Direct Action" to the question of methods; in "The Economic Tendency of Freethought," "Why I am an Anarchist," "Anarchism," "Anarchism and American Traditions," "The Making of an Anarchist," and many other such works, to a fundamental exposition of the social and economic principles of anarchism; in "Germinal," "The Hurricane," the poems of *The Worm Turns,* the Haymarket speeches, "Events are the True Schoolmasters," "The Modern School," "Francisco Ferrer," "The Mexican Revolution," and "The Commune is Risen," to the possibilities of social revolution. In a movement often splintered into contentious factions she spoke consistently for tolerance, reconciliation, and a mutual focus on the key issue of human freedom. In "Anarchism," de Cleyre urged her audience to "go free, go free beyond the bounds of what *fear* and *custom* call the 'possible.'" Over the course of her career

she sought to draw her audiences into transcending conventional boundaries of the imagination.

De Cleyre's anarchism also distanced her completely from the narrow focus on suffrage that characterized many of her feminist contemporaries, freeing her to write more broadly about the sources of women's oppression and their possibilities for liberation. She produced a far-ranging body of anarchist feminist theory that addressed such issues as the question of women's ownership of their bodies; the effect of evolution on women's social status, economic status, and consciousness; the relation between women's revolt against oppression and the foundations of ethical theory; the influence of changes in women's material condition on their desire and ability to liberate themselves; the role of the church in oppressing women; and the often unacknowledged role traditional gender expectations play even in social-revolutionary movements such as freethought, sex radicalism, and anarchism. A small group of her contemporaries touched on some of these issues. Matilda Joslyn Gage, Lillie Devereux Blake, and Elizabeth Cady Stanton analyzed the relation between women's oppression and religious orthodoxy, for example, and de Cleyre's anarchist comrade Goldman wrote about sexual freedom as a source of liberation for women. Even so, hardly a feminist writer before Simone de Beauvoir touched on such a wide range of questions related to women's oppression or integrated them so coherently into an overarching social, ethical, psychological, and economic framework. Voltairine de Cleyre's anarchist-feminist manifestos—"Sex Slavery," "The Gates of Freedom," "The Past and Future of the Ladies' Liberal League," "The Case of Woman vs. Orthodoxy," and "They Who Marry Do Ill"—in addition to "The Heart of Angiolillo," such poems as "Betrayed," "Mary Wollstonecraft," and "Bastard Born," and occasional pieces in *Lucifer* addressing such issues as romantic love ("The Death of Love," 1901) or prostitution ("The Hopelessly Fallen," 1902), constitute perhaps the most original contribution to progressive feminist thought made by anyone of her generation. Taken together, they anticipate many of the themes and directions of the "Second Wave" of feminism in the United States by more than a half a century.

Biographies:

Emma Goldman, *Voltairine de Cleyre* (Berkeley Heights, N.J.: Oriole Press, 1932); reprinted in *Exquisite Rebel: The Essays of Voltairine de Cleyre—Feminist, Anarchist, Genius,* edited by Sharon Presley and Crispin Sartwell (Albany: State University of New York Press, 2005), pp. 29–44;

Paul Avrich, *An American Anarchist: The Life of Voltairine de Cleyre* (Princeton, N.J.: Princeton University Press, 1978).

References:

Paul Avrich, *The Haymarket Tragedy* (Princeton, N.J.: Princeton University Press, 1984);

Leila R. Brammer, *Excluded from Suffrage History: Matilda Joslyn Gage, Nineteenth-Century American Feminist* (Westport, Conn.: Greenwood Press, 2000);

Marshall G. Brown and Gordon Stein, *Freethought in the United States: A Descriptive Bibliography* (Westport, Conn.: Greenwood Press, 1978);

Henry David, *The History of the Haymarket Affair: A Study in the American Social-Revolutionary and Labor Movements* (New York: Farrar & Rinehart, 1936);

Margaret S. Marsh, *Anarchist Women 1870–1920* (Philadelphia: Temple University Press, 1981);

Wendy McElroy, introduction, *Freedom, Feminism, and the State: An Overview of Individualist Feminism,* second edition (New York: Holmes & Meier, 1991), pp. 3–26;

Catherine Helen Palczewski, "Voltairine de Cleyre," *Women Public Speakers in the United States, 1800–1925: A Bio-Critical Sourcebook,* edited by Karlyn Kohrs Campbell (Westport, Conn.: Greenwood Press, 1993), pp. 143–155;

Palczewski, "Voltairine de Cleyre," *American National Biography,* edited by John A. Garraty and Mark C. Carnes, volume 6 (New York: Oxford University Press, 1999), pp. 329–330;

Palczewski, "Voltairine de Cleyre: Sexual Slavery and Sexual Pleasure in the Nineteenth Century," *NWSA* 7 (Fall 1995): 54–68;

Franklin Rosemont, introduction, *Written in Red: Selected Poems,* by de Cleyre (Chicago: Charles H. Kerr, 1990), pp. 5–12;

Hal D. Sears, *The Sex Radicals: Free Love in High Victorian America* (Lawrence: The Regents Press of Kansas, 1977);

Sidney Warren, *American Freethought, 1860–1914* (New York: Columbia University Press, 1943);

Alice Wexler, *Emma Goldman: An Intimate Life* (New York: Pantheon, 1984);

Emile Zola, *Germinal,* 1885, translated by Stanley and Eleanor Hochman (New York: Signet, 1981).

Papers:

Most of Voltairine de Cleyre's papers are in the Labadie Collection at the University of Michigan and the Joseph Ishill Collection at the Houghton Library, Harvard University. Others may be found in the Ishill Papers at the University of Florida in Gainesville and the Alexander Berkman Archive at the International Institute of Social History in Amsterdam. A few individual letters are located in the Bund Archives of the Jewish Labor Movement in New York, the Archives of Labor History and Urban Affairs at Wayne State University in Detroit, the Tamiment Collection at New York University, and the Benjamin Tucker Papers in the New York Public Library. Some private collections contain additional materials: the Thomas H. Bell Papers in Los Angeles, the Leonard D. Abbott Papers in New York, the Moses and Lillian Harman Papers in San Francisco, the Harry Kelly Papers in New York, and the William Wess papers in London.

Daniel De Leon
(14 December 1852 – 11 May 1914)

James J. Kopp
Lewis & Clark College

BOOKS: *To Business Men: A Specimen of Mr. Blaine's Diplomacy: Is He a Safe Man to Trust as President?* (New York, 1884);

Reform or Revolution: Address Delivered Under the Auspices of the People's Union, at Wells' Memorial Hall, Boston, Jan. 26th, 1896 (Boston: Daniel De Leon, 1896);

What Means This Strike? Address Delivered by Daniel De Leon in the City Hall of New Bedford, Mass., February 11, 1898 (New York: National Executive Committee, Socialist Labor Party, 1898);

Money (New York: New York Labor News, 1900);

A Debate on the Tactics of the S.T. & L.A. Toward Trade Unions Between Daniel De Leon of the Socialist Labor Party and Job Harriman of the Social Democratic Party Held at New Haven, Conn., November 25, 1900 (New York: Socialist Co-Operative Publishing, 1900);

Socialism versus Anarchism: An Address Delivered in Paine Memorial Hall, Boston, Mass., Sunday Afternoon, October 13, 1901, Under the Auspices of Section Boston of the Socialist Labor Party (New York: New York Labor News, 1901);

Two Pages from Roman History: Plebs Leaders and Labor Leaders and The Warning of the Gracchi (New York: New York Labor News, 1903);

The Burning Question of Trades Unionism: A Lecture Delivered at Newark, N.J., April 21, 1904 (New York: New York Labor News, 1904);

Flashlights of the Amsterdam International Socialist Congress (New York: New York Labor News, 1904);

The Preamble of the Industrial Workers of the World. Address Delivered at Union Temple, Minneapolis, Minn., July Tenth, 1905 (New York: New York Labor News, 1905); republished as *Socialist Reconstruction of Society: The Industrial Vote* (New York: Socialist Labor Party, 1912);

As to Politics. And a Discussion Upon the Relative Importance of Political Action and of Classconscious [sic] Economic Action, and the Urgent Necessity of Both (New York: New York Labor News Press, 1907);

Marx on Mallock, or Facts vs. Fiction. An Address Delivered in Maennerchor Hall, New York, Tuesday, January 21,

Daniel De Leon, 1915 (frontispiece for As To Politics, *1915: Robarts Research Library, University of Toronto)*

1908, under the Auspices of Section New York, Socialist Labor Party (New York: New York Labor News, 1908);

Unity: An Address Delivered by Daniel De Leon At New Pythagoras Hall New York, February 21, 1908 (New York: New York Labor News, 1908);

Abolition of Poverty: Socialist Versus Ultramontane Economics and Politics (New York: New York Labor News, 1911);

Berger's Hits and Misses at the Called Session of the Sixty-Second Congress, April–October; A Symposium of Economic, Political, Sociological, Tactical and Historic Live Topics (New York: New York Labor News, 1911);

republished as *Revolutionary Socialism in U.S. Congress: "Parliamentary Idiocy" vs. Marxian Socialism* (New York: New York Labor News, 1931) and *A Socialist in Congress: His Conduct and Responsibilities: "Parliamentary Idiocy" vs. Marxian Socialism* (1963);

Watson on the Gridiron; or, Bourgeois Theories Dissected and Hung Up To Dry: A Political-Economic Discussion Between Thomas E. Watson, Editor of "The Jeffersonian" and "Watson's Jeffersonian Magazine," and Daniel De Leon, Editor of "The Daily People." (New York: New York Labor News, 1911); republished as *A Decadent Jeffersonian on the Socialist Gridiron* (New York: New York Labor News, 1935) and *Evolution of a Liberal: From Reform to Action* (New York: New York Labor News, 1965);

Woman's Suffrage: An Address Delivered by Daniel De Leon, Under the Auspices of the Socialist Women of Greater New York (New York: New York Labor News, 1911); republished as *The Ballot and the Class Struggle* (New York: New York Labor News, 1933);

De Leon–Carmody Debate: Individualism vs. Socialism (New York: New York Labor News, 1912); republished as *Socialism vs. "Individualism"–Debate: Daniel De Leon vs. Thomas F. Carmody, Troy, N.Y., April 14, 1912;*

Father Gassoniana, or, Jesuit "Sociology" and "Economics" at the Bar of Science and History: the Effort of Religio-Politics and Economics to Shield Terrestrial Capitalism Shivered (New York: New York Labor News, 1912);

Fifteen Questions Asked by the Providence, R.I., "Visitor," Representing the Roman Catholic Political Machine, Answered by Daniel De Leon Representing the Socialist Labor Party (New York: National Executive Committee, Socialist Labor Party, 1914);

Vulgar Economy; or, A Critical Analyst of Marx Analyzed (New York: National Executive Committee, Socialist Labor Party, 1914);

De Leon–Berry Debate on Solution of the Trust Problem, Held Before the University Extension Society, Philadelphia, January 27, 1913 (New York: National Executive Committee, Socialist Labor Party, 1915); republished as *Capitalism vs. Socialism* (New York: New York Labor News, 1938);

Industrial Unionism. Also An Address on the Same Subject Delivered at Grand Central Palace, New York, Sunday, Dec. 10, 1905, by Eugene V. Debs (New York: New York Labor News, 1919);

Industrial Unionism: Selected Editorials (New York: National Executive Committee, Socialist Labor Party, 1920);

James Madison and Karl Marx: A Contrast and a Similarity (New York: National Executive Committee, Socialist Labor Party, 1920);

Anti-Semitism: Its Cause and Cure (New York: National Executive Committee, Socialist Labor Party, 1921);

Ten Canons of the Proletariat Revolution: A Revolutionary Decalogue (New York: New York Labor News, 1923);

Russia in Revolution: Selected Editorials (New York: New York Labor News, 1927);

Ultramontanism–Roman Catholic Political Machine in Action: Selected Editorials by Daniel De Leon (New York: New York Labor News, 1928); republished as *The Vatican in Politics: Ultramontanism* (1948);

Party Ownership of the Press: Historic Documents Relating to the Establishing of the Principles Involved (New York: New York Labor News, 1931);

Marxian Science and the Colleges (New York: New York Labor News, 1932);

Americanism (New York: Industrial Union Party, 1935);

Capitalism Means War! (New York: New York Labor News, 1941);

Socialist Landmarks: Four Addresses (New York: New York Labor News, 1952).

Collections: *Speeches and Editorials,* 2 volumes (New York: New York Labor News, 1900);

Over 600 works by De Leon are available on the Daniel De Leon Internet Archive (DDLIA), a mirror site of the Marxists Internet Archive, available at <http://www.marxists.org/archive/deleon/pdf/index.htm> (viewed 20 June 2008).

TRANSLATIONS: Karl Kautsky, *The Capitalist Class* (New York: New York Labor News, 1894);

Karl Marx, *The Eighteenth Brumaire of Louis Napoleon* (New York: International Publishing, 1898);

August Bebel, *Woman Under Socialism* (New York: New York Labor News, 1904);

Ferdinand Lassalle, *Franz von Sickingen: A Tragedy in Five Acts* (New York: New York Labor News, 1904);

Eugène Sue, *The Mysteries of the People: or, History of a Proletarian Family Across the Ages* (New York: New York Labor News, 1904–1911);

Marx, *The Gotha Program* (New York: National Executive Committee, Socialist Labor Party, 1922);

Friedrich Engels, *The Revolutionary Act* (New York: Labor News, 1922).

SELECTED PERIODICAL PUBLICATIONS–UNCOLLECTED: "Should the Jews Celebrate Christmas?" *Reformer and Jewish Times,* 14 February 1879, p. 5;

"The Conference at Berlin on the West-African Question," *Political Science Quarterly,* 1 (March 1886): 103–139;

"The Voice of Madison," *Nationalist,* 1 (August 1889), pp. 120–124;

"The Eleventh Census Conspiracy," *Nationalist,* 2 (February 1890): 85–90;

"Nationalism–Aspirations That Gave It Birth and Forces That Give It Strength," *Workman's Advocate,* 15 March 1890;

"Prof. De Leon Replies to Geo. K. Lloyd–He Never Was a Land Taxer," *Workman's Advocate,* 22 March 1890;

"Edward Bellamy," *People,* 8 (29 May 1898): 2.

A dominant voice in the American socialist movement in the last decade of the nineteenth century and until his death in 1914, Daniel De Leon was a prolific writer of pamphlets, speeches, lectures, and editorials. These works not only capture his views on Marxist socialism but also provide documentation of the ongoing labor struggles of this period and of the socialist movement during this critical time in its formation in the United States. He also translated into English important leftist texts by Karl Marx, August Bebel, and Karl Kautsky. His numerous contributions reflect his evolving views in a career encompassing involvement in a broad array of labor and socialist groups: the Union Labor Party, the Nationalist Movement, the Knights of Labor, the Socialist Labor Party, and the International Workers of the World (IWW). In his personal journey through increasingly more-radical organizations, De Leon wrote speeches and editorials that served as inspiration for followers of his ideals and equally as fuel for controversy and dissension among other labor and socialist leaders of the time such as Samuel Gompers, Morris Hillquit, and James Connolly.

Daniel De Leon was born on 14 December 1852 on the island of Curaçao in the Dutch West Indies. His father, Salomon De Leon, was a physician, and his mother, Sarah Jesurun De Leon, came from a wealthy family. Both parents descended from Sephardic Jews who were forced to leave Spain and ended up in the Netherlands. Salomon De Leon came to Curaçao as a surgeon in the Dutch colonial army and left the island in 1857 to pursue his medical profession, leaving the five-year-old Daniel to be cared for and educated by his mother and a scholarly uncle, Anjel Jesurun. When Salomon died in 1865, the family decided to send Daniel the following year to Germany to further his education and to be treated for chronic health problems. In Germany, De Leon studied the classics, geography, and languages. He returned to Curaçao in the late 1860s and in 1870 moved with his mother to Amsterdam, where he enrolled in the Athenaeum Illustre to study medicine. Prior to completing his course of study he once again returned to Curaçao with his mother in October 1872. Within the next year he departed for New York to join other relatives; his mother later joined him.

During this time De Leon served as associate editor for a newspaper supporting the Cuban independence movement. His focus, however, was still scholarly, and in 1874 he took a position at the Thomas B. Harrington School in Westchester, New York, to teach Greek, Latin, and mathematics. In 1876 he enrolled in the Columbia College School of Law, and he received his law degree in 1878. Later that year he moved to Brownsville, Texas, to practice law and remained there until 1882. The first substantial instance of De Leon's reform interests appeared when his lengthy letter, "Should the Jews Celebrate Christmas?" was published in *Reformer and Jewish Times* on 14 February 1879.

In 1882 De Leon moved his law office to New York City, and he returned to Curaçao briefly to wed Sarah Lobo, the sixteen-year-old daughter of a prominent Jewish family. The couple returned to New York, and the following year De Leon accepted the first of two three-year appointments as a lecturer in the School of Political Science at Columbia College. At this time he gave up his law practice. Also in 1883, the first of four De Leon children was born, a son named Salomon (Solon). A second son, Grover Cleveland, was born in 1885. Sarah died in 1887 while giving birth to twin boys who also died, and the same year the one-and-a-half-year-old Grover died. The seemingly stable life of the young academic moved abruptly into personal tragedy, and this series of events set the tone for the rest of De Leon's tumultuous career.

His career interests already had begun to shift by the time his young wife and three children died. Although he was successful as a lecturer at Columbia and published a scholarly article in the inaugural issue of the *Political Science Quarterly* in March 1886 ("The Conference at Berlin on the West-African Question"), a more active role in the political arena seemed promising to him. He participated in the 1884 presidential campaign of Grover Cleveland as a Republican Independent and produced a pamphlet attacking Cleveland's opponent, James G. Blaine, *To Business Men: A Specimen of Mr. Blaine's Diplomacy: Is He a Safe Man to Trust as President?* In 1886 he was active in the New York City mayoral campaign of Henry George, the United Labor candidate. De Leon found intriguing George's *Progress and Poverty* (1879) and his single-tax concept, which argued the only form of taxation should be on land, which would solve the economic problems of the country, limit the control of the monopolistic landowners, and open up land for laborers. Although De Leon soon moved away from the single-tax idea, the experience

Fragment of a note from De Leon to Socialist Labor Party activist Olive M. Johnson, 1904 (from her Daniel De Leon:
American Socialist Pathfinder, *1923; University of Georgia Libraries)*

served as his means to enter politics more actively. Numerous strikes and protests occurred in the United States in 1886, including several in New York City. The most significant labor-related event of that year occurred in Chicago, leading to the infamous Haymarket Riot, which influenced many forthcoming leaders of the labor movement and socialism in America, including De Leon. After George's defeat in the New York election, De Leon split with the United Labor Party but continued to seek a more active role in politics and labor affairs.

In 1888 he became a member of a local assembly in New York of the Knights of Labor. De Leon read the utopian novel, *Looking Backward 2000–1887,* published early that year. This work by Edward Bellamy centers on a nationalized industry that serves as the basis for a utopia. Although Bellamy did not call his scheme socialism, De Leon found the nature of the organization in *Looking Backward* appealing, as did many reformers of the period. De Leon became an avid advocate of the movement, named Nationalism, that grew out of the interest in Bellamy's book. He joined a local Nationalist Club and assisted in forming others. He spoke frequently on the ideals of the Nationalist movement, and, perhaps most significant, he wrote for the publications of the movement, including the monthly magazine, *The Nationalist.* Outside the letter De Leon wrote in 1879 and the anti-Blaine pamphlet in 1884, his contributions to *The Nationalist* offer the first real glimpse into his devel-

oping philosophy. In his essay "The Voice of Madison," published in the August 1889 issue, De Leon suggests that James Madison, an "earnest and profound thinker," foresaw some of the perils that existed in the late 1880s. According to De Leon, Madison "described in the not too distant future a serious conflict between the class with and the class without property; the fated collapse of the system of suffrage he had helped to rear; and, consequently, the distinct outlines of a grave national problem." De Leon expands the issue to economic and social situations and believes that Madison, along with Karl Marx, provides a solution to societal problems: "That the wisdom of the Revolutionary Fathers and their teachings are not lost upon their successors, the appearance and growth of the Nationalist movement demonstrates. The voice of Madison has reached our generation. The patriots in the revolution now impending and equally important with that of a hundred years ago will be on hand." The introduction of Marx into the discussion, not typical of most other followers of Bellamy, represents De Leon's personal intellectual development. After De Leon's death, the Socialist Labor Party combined and published two of his essays as *James Madison and Karl Marx: A Contrast and a Similarity* (1920).

By late 1889 De Leon was rapidly moving toward Marxist socialism, seeing the gradual and less radical nature of Nationalism as ineffective. He continued to acknowledge Bellamy's broad influence among social activists. When Bellamy died in 1898, De Leon paid tribute to him in an editorial. Noting that Bellamy "departed company with the organized Socialist Movement of the country, and, in our opinion fell into tactical errors," he nonetheless labels him a "striking figure in the Social Struggle of our day and our country." De Leon also cited Bellamy in some of his later writings, such as *Fifteen Questions* (1914), De Leon's "Socialist Answers to Fifteen Questions Asked by the Providence, R.I., 'Visitor.'"

De Leon's move into politics in the mid 1880s and his increasing and visible support of labor created tensions at Columbia College, where he still worked as a lecturer in the political-science department. When his second three-year appointment ended in 1889, and the promised professorship was not forthcoming, De Leon left the college, clearing his way to become more fully engaged in reform activities. By this time he was moving quickly toward the ideals of Marxist socialism. He completed that step when he joined the Socialist Labor Party (SLP) in September 1890. The SLP, first called the Working Men's Party of the United States, had been organized in 1876, and it was the only national-level socialist movement in the nation. The party was disorganized and largely dominated by Europeans when De Leon joined in late 1890. He sought to provide some structure to the organization and to bring a more American flavor to the Marxist core of the party. The existing leadership welcomed him for his education, political experience, and status as an American (although foreign born), and De Leon quickly rose to a position of power within the organization. He used this influence to make some important connections between the socialist message and trade unionism, and, most important, he developed a program of propaganda to carry forth the message of the SLP and socialism in general. He achieved this through the establishment of a new newspaper for the organization, *The People* (later the *Daily People*).

When De Leon joined the SLP, it had two newspapers—the German language *Der Sozialist* and the four-page English *Workman's Advocate*. He had contributed to the *Workman's Advocate* prior to becoming a member of the SLP, including a piece in the 15 March 1890 issue on "Nationalism—Aspirations That Gave It Birth and Forces That Give It Strength." He also countered accusations that he was a Single-Taxer in a piece on 22 March 1890 ("Prof. De Leon Replies to Geo. K. Lloyd—He Never Was a Land Taxer"). Despite writing for the *Workman's Advocate,* De Leon wanted a more substantial English-language organ, without advertisements, that would carry forth not just the SLP message but his message. He received funding from the organization, and in April 1891 *The*

People appeared. Initially the editor was Lucien Sanial but De Leon took over later that year as editor, a position he maintained until his death in 1914. A substantial portion of De Leon's written contributions appeared initially as editorials in *The People*. Several of these were later published separately as well by the New York Labor News Company (NYLN), a party-owned publishing house established in 1887. The NYLN became the principal publisher of De Leon's works throughout his life and for most of the twentieth century, including several editions of the compilations of his *Speeches and Editorials* (first published in 1900 and reprinted numerous times in the next seventy years).

De Leon's interest in bringing the socialist message to the American people also inspired him to provide translations of significant works by European socialists. He translated Marx's *The Eighteenth Brumaire of Louis Napoleon* (1898). He also translated Friedrich Engels's *The Revolutionary Act* (1922), August Bebel's *Woman Under Socialism* (1904), and works by Karl Kautsky. De Leon also translated literary works, including the multivolume French work by Eugène Sue, *The Mysteries of the People* (1904–1911), and *Franz von Sickingen* (1904), a play by Ferdinand Lassalle. The inclusion of plays and novels in his translations was consistent with his ideal of educating the working class in the United States.

Also of importance in De Leon's propaganda initiative was meeting directly with audiences to deliver his personal message and that of the SLP (which merged over time). At the same time that he started *The People,* De Leon embarked on a national speaking tour to raise public awareness of the SLP, whose membership expanded in terms of number and geography as a result of this tour. Along with his editorials, De Leon's speeches constitute a large portion of the works published under his name during his lifetime and after.

Besides spreading the message of socialism and the SLP, De Leon's speaking tour of 1891 led him to the woman who became his second wife. Bertha Canary was a schoolteacher in Independence, Kansas, fourteen years younger than De Leon, and he called upon her at the suggestion of an acquaintance. The following year the two were married in New York. They had five children over the next eleven years; in 1903 a three-year-old son died of an overdose of quinine during a malaria outbreak.

De Leon rose rapidly to the leadership of the SLP, and in the election of 1891 he ran as the SLP candidate for governor of New York. He was soundly defeated, but he received thirteen thousand votes, more than any socialist candidate to date. The following year the SLP candidate for president, Simon Wing, appeared on the ballot in several states and received over twenty-one thousand votes, indicating a rising interest in the party. Membership increased, as did circulation of *The People,* and De Leon came to be viewed by many as the champion of the socialist cause in the United States.

The formal entry into politics by the SLP seemed a natural move for the organization, and for De Leon it offered a way to merge the interests of socialists and trade unionists. Some in the trade unions were wary of the revolutionary rhetoric and tendencies of the SLP, particularly its leader. De Leon had used his role in the radical New York chapter of the Knights of Labor (KOL), which he joined in 1888, to gain control of the national organization by 1893. At the General Assembly of the KOL that year De Leon aided in deposing Terence V. Powderly, leader of the KOL since 1879 and more conservative than De Leon. This change in leadership set in motion a series of events that ultimately led to De Leon's own ouster from the KOL in 1895. At the same time, the other major trade union organization, the American Federation of Labor (AFL), grew uneasy with the political activities of the SLP. The AFL president, Samuel Gompers, rejected socialism outright, arguing that unions should stay out of politics. Several internal maneuvers in the early 1890s highlighted the growing conflict between the AFL and the SLP, and, although Gompers was temporarily removed as the AFL president, he returned to power in 1895 with a stronger resolve to oppose De Leon and the SLP.

Throughout all of these events De Leon adopted a more radical position as he felt the Knights of Labor, the AFL, and other organizations were moving away from what he considered the true socialist cause of the rights of workers and the abolition of the wage system. In late 1895 he established the Socialist Trade and Labor Alliance (STLA) as a means to strengthen the bond between socialists and labor, but the formation of this body only fueled the fires of opposition to De Leon and in some respects weakened the revolutionary platform that he sought to establish. Yet, De Leon carried on with a renewed vigor in defining the goals of socialism in America. In January 1896 he gave a speech that many consider the first of his "great quartet of 'primary' lessons in Marxism and its corollaries." Titled *Reform or Revolution,* the speech was subsequently transcribed and printed numerous times, as well as translated into several languages. In it De Leon systematically outlines the distinction between reform, which he sees as leading nowhere, and revolution, the true means of effecting change. In the process he minces no words in identifying what he labels as fake movements. He includes the single-tax movement as one "of these charlatan booms that only helped still more to dispirit people in the end." He charges that "ignoramuses" took hold of the KOL and the AFL, and he views the SLP as the only reputable cause. The argument took on particular importance at its first delivery because the Boston audience to which he spoke was considering reorganizing. The style and tone of *Reform or Revolution* document a new level of radical thought for De Leon, one that he continued to develop over the next decade.

He delivered the next major speech that reflects this development in the city hall of New Bedford, Massachusetts, on 11 February 1898. *What Means This Strike?* provides background for the development of socialism and emphatically instructs the striking men and women in attendance that "the aim of all intelligent class conscious workingmen must be the overthrow of the system of private ownership in the tools of production because that system keeps them in wage slavery." De Leon again presents the SLP and the Socialist Labor and Trade Alliance as the only vehicles for achieving this goal. This speech, often considered De Leon's strongest, was published and reprinted numerous times, including a 1940 edition that also contains a resolution on strikes by the Executive Committee of the SLP reaffirming the points raised by De Leon in the 1898 address.

The tone of De Leon's speeches and the revolutionary focus of the SLP under his leadership stirred dissension within the organization itself. A faction evolved that supported reform and links with trade unions, and it sought to oust De Leon. This attempt was unsuccessful, but it resulted in a split in the organization in 1899. A group led by the lawyer Morris Hillquit departed from the SLP and established the Socialist Party of America (SPA) in 1901, developing stronger ties with the trade unions. De Leon and a diminished group remained with the SLP, but others deserted the organization in the next few years. Rather than diminishing De Leon's revolutionary agenda, these activities seemed to him to offer a challenge to pursue even more-radical tactics.

Evidence of that further development in his thought appears in a speech he delivered at Newark, New Jersey, on 21 April 1904, titled *The Burning Question of Trades Unionism.* De Leon uses a dialogic method to illustrate the pros and cons of trade-union membership, and through this process comes to the conclusion that trade unions are almost part of the natural order of society. Further, he argues that such organizations should act as the vehicles of revolution, but other forces restrict them, most notably the power of the capitalists in control. The labor movement needs a revolutionary arm to lead the working class in the revolt against wage slavery. Such an approach, he notes, "implies struggle, dauntless struggle against, and war to the knife with that combination of ignoramuses, ripened into reprobates—the labor fakir who seeks to coin the helplessness of the proletariat into cash for himself, and the 'intellectual' (God save the mark!) who has so superficial a knowledge of things that the mission of Unionism is a closed book for him." The speech anticipated the development of a revolutionary arm of the trade-union movement that appeared in late June and early July 1905 with the formation of the Industrial Workers of the World (IWW), commonly known as the Wobblies. De Leon's influence, including the impact of *The Burning Question of Trades Unionism,* on the formation of the IWW is widely recognized.

The fourth speech in the "great quartet of 'primary' lessons" delivered by De Leon was made on 10 July 1905 in Minneapolis as part of a speaking tour in the Midwest following the IWW convention. Initially titled *The Preamble of the International Workers of the World,* the speech subsequently was published as *Socialist Reconstruction of Society* (1912), and, like many of De Leon's works, was reprinted numerous times. In this speech De Leon utilizes the preamble of the IWW to illustrate three basic points: 1) poverty and affluence will co-exist as long as the wage system is in place; 2) "The working class and the employing class have nothing in common"; 3) the workers must come together in a political way in the struggle against wage slavery, but they should have no formal affiliation with any party. The first two points largely reiterate accepted Marxist beliefs, which De Leon supports with facts and figures. The third point, labeled the "political clause," presented a new factor, one that had caused heated debate at the IWW convention. Although De Leon based his point of nonaffiliation on Marxist principles, the issue continued to elicit controversy. Typically, however, the objections of others did not deter De Leon from espousing the need for political power separated from other party organizations. This position increasingly alienated him from the anarchists and syndicalists within the IWW in addition to those who already opposed him in the SPA.

For De Leon this political element essentially provided the final piece in what became known as his Theory of Socialist Industrial Unionism. He based this theory on the assumption that the revolution against wage slavery should be peaceful, centering on civil debate, winning power through elections, and establishing a cohesive socialist industrial union to ensure economic and political stability for the masses. This idea was the culmination of over twenty years of his thoughts about a democratic and peaceful American revolution. He saw the IWW as the means to that end. His vision did not correspond, however, to the type of revolution many others in the IWW envisioned. From

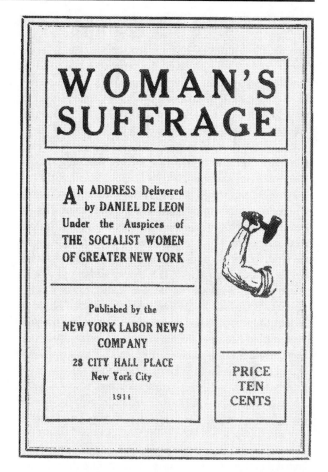

Front cover for the publication of De Leon's lecture republished in 1933 as The Ballot and the Class Struggle *(Thomas Cooper Library, University of South Carolina)*

1906 to 1908 oral and written objections and criticisms assailed De Leon's scheme and, in particular, those points expounding the political clause. Several of these objections appeared as letters written to *The People* by individuals, as De Leon labels them, "who advocated the dropping of political action altogether." De Leon compiled these letters and his responses into a pamphlet titled *As to Politics* (1907) that, he explains, "is intended to furnish in compact form the information whereby to arrive at the correct facts wherewith to reach the goals of the Socialist Commonwealth." Despite his efforts to counter the opposing views, at the fourth convention of the IWW in 1908 a move was undertaken to remove the political clause. De Leon attended the convention but was denied a seat, and the IWW deleted the controversial clause. Later that year the IWW split into factions, with the De Leon supporters forming the Detroit IWW later known as the Workers' International Industrial Union. But this organization proved ineffective in moving toward the goals De Leon envisioned.

The split of the IWW in late 1908 derailed the last significant vehicle for De Leon's broader socialist agenda. He continued to carry forth his message for the last years of his life through the means he had used for two decades—writing editorials and delivering speeches. In these years he remained prolific in the number of contributions he made and the diversity of topics covered. In May 1909 he delivered a speech titled "Woman's Suffrage" to the Socialist Women of Greater New York. This address subsequently was published as *The Ballot and the Class Struggle* (1933). Also in 1909 he used the *Daily People* as the forum for responding to attacks on socialism by Tom Watson, editor of *The Jeffersonian* and *Watson's Jeffersonian Magazine*. These articles were compiled into a pamphlet initially titled *Watson on the Gridiron* (1911) and later as *A Decadent Jeffersonian on the Socialist Gridiron* (1935). De Leon addressed a wide range of topics related to the U.S. Congress in a series of thirty editorials in the *Daily People* in 1911. These he brought together in the pamphlet, *Berger's Hits and Misses at the Called Session of the Sixty-Second Congress, April–October; A Symposium of Economic, Political, Sociological, Tactical and Historic Live Topics* (1911), later published as *Revolutionary Socialism in U.S. Congress: "Parliamentary Idiocy" vs. Marxian Socialism* (1931). In 1913, the year before he died, he focused on the institution of his alma mater in a series of open letters to Charles Chase of Columbia University published in the *Daily People; Marxian Science and the Colleges* (1932) was published after De Leon's death.

One of the best summaries of De Leon's socialistic views appears in his last major writing project. When the Roman Catholic newspaper, the *Providence Visitor,* of Providence, Rhode Island, issued a series of questions related to socialism in its 12 September 1913 issue, the editor included the statement, "The next time you hear a Socialist soap-box orator you might interest him in the following list of questions." For De Leon this challenge provided an opportunity to respond to the "Ultramontanists," and despite declining health he answered the questions in a document that summarizes the concepts of socialism as well as the development of his own views on the subject. *Fifteen Questions* went through numerous reprints and continues to serve as a primary document in the examination of American socialism. De Leon reputedly was developing his own set of questions to submit to *Providence Visitor* when he died on 11 May 1914.

De Leon's death came in the first year of World War I, which initiated a series of international events that would have disturbed his views of a peaceful, nonviolent solution to the ills of society. The publishers of the *New York Labor News* compensated for De Leon's absence by carrying forth his message. They reprinted many of the speeches and pamphlets produced in his lifetime and compiled other contributions he made into several publications. From *Ultramontanism—Roman Catholic Political Machine in Action* (1928) and *Anti-Semitism: Its Cause and Cure* (1921), to *Capitalism Means War!* (1941) and *James Madison and Karl Marx,* they thus kept alive many of his views for decades after his death. Daniel De Leon's career encompassed involvement in such reform organizations as the Urban Labor Party, the Nationalist Movement, the Knights of Labor, the Socialist Labor Party, and the Industrial Workers of the World. The nature of De Leon's beliefs, as well as his own self-assured style, elicited from his leftist and labor contemporaries expressions of the highest respect as well as vicious verbal assaults. The debate about his contributions and personal style continued after his death and remains a part of the "enigma of Daniel De Leon," as one biographer, Stephen Coleman, describes it. Some followers praised De Leon; for example, Arnold Peterson wrote a series of pamphlets describing De Leon as "social architect," "internationalist," "pioneer socialist editor," and "the uncompromising." Other contemporaries viewed him with less admiration, such as Connolly, who labeled him a "scoundrel"; Bill Haywood, who saw De Leon as "the theorizing professor"; and Gompers, who accused De Leon of being a Pinkerton agent during labor strikes of 1898. These widely divergent views of De Leon suggest the complexity of the man and his writings.

Bibliographies:

Joseph Carlton Borden, *A Bibliographical List of the Writings of Daniel De Leon* (New York: School of Library Service, Columbia University, 1936);

Oakley C. Johnson, *Writings By and About Daniel De Leon: A Bibliography* (New York: American Institute for Marxist Studies, 1966).

Biographies:

Olive M. Johnson, *Daniel De Leon: American Socialist Pathfinder* (New York: New York Labor News, 1923);

Carl Reeve, *The Life and Times of Daniel De Leon* (New York: AIMS, 1972);

L. Glen Seretan, *Daniel De Leon: The Odyssey of an American Marxist* (Cambridge: Harvard University Press, 1979);

Stephen Coleman, *Daniel De Leon* (Manchester and New York: Manchester University Press, 1990).

References:

Don K. McKee, "Daniel De Leon: A Reappraisal," *Labor History,* 1 (Fall 1960): 264–297;

L. Glen Seretan, "Daniel De Leon As American," *Wisconsin Magazine of History,* 61 (1978): 210–233;

Seretan, "Daniel De Leon, 'Wandering Jew' of American Socialism: An Interpretative Analysis," *American Jewish Historical Quarterly,* 45 (March 1976): 245–256;

Seretan, "The Personal Style and Political Methods of Daniel De Leon: A Reconsideration," *Labor History,* 14 (Spring 1973): 163–201;

James Stevenson, "Daniel De Leon and European Socialism, 1890–1914," *Science & Society,* 44 (1980): 199–223;

James D. Young, "Daniel De Leon and Anglo-American Socialism," *Labor History,* 17 (Summer 1976): 329–350.

Papers:

There are no known collected personal papers of Daniel De Leon. Microfilm of the records of the Socialist Labor Party, including information on De Leon, can be viewed at the Wisconsin Historical Society. A published guide, "The Papers of the Socialist Labor Party," is available for this collection. De Leon items can be found in other collections at the Wisconsin Historical Society, including the Matheson-Connolly Correspondence (1902–1914) and the Borden bibliographical list. Information on his experiences at Columbia College and his early political activities survives in the Columbiana Collection at Columbia University.

Barbara Deming

(23 July 1917 – 2 August 1984)

Kurt R. Kessinger

BOOKS: *Prison Notes* (New York: Grossman, 1966);

Running Away from Myself—A Dream Portrait of America Drawn from the Films of the '40s (New York: Grossman, 1969);

Wash Us and Comb Us (New York: Grossman, 1972);

We Cannot Live without Our Lives (New York: Grossman, 1974);

Remembering Who We Are (Tallahassee: Pagoda, 1981);

Prisons That Could Not Hold, edited by Sky Vanderlinde, with an introduction by Grace Paley (San Francisco: Spinsters Ink, 1985);

A Humming under My Feet: A Book of Travail (London: Women's Press, 1985);

I Change, I Change: Poems by Barbara Deming, edited, with an introduction, by Judith McDaniel (Norwich, Vt.: New Victoria, 1996).

Collections: *Revolution and Equilibrium* (New York: Grossman, 1971);

We Are All Part of One Another: A Barbara Deming Reader, edited by Jane Meyerding, with a foreword by Barbara Smith (Philadelphia: New Society Publishers, 1984);

Prisons That Could Not Hold, edited by Joan E. Biren (San Francisco: Spinsters Ink, 1985).

SELECTED PERIODICAL PUBLICATIONS–UNCOLLECTED: "John Osborne's War Against the Philistines," *Hudson Review,* 11 (Fall 1958): 41–49;

"Remembering Who We Are: An Open Letter to Susan Saxe," graphics by Laurie McLaughlin, *Quest,* 4 (Summer 1977): 52–74.

By the time Barbara Deming discovered her political calling to nonviolent activism in 1960 at the age of forty-three, she was a talented but struggling writer who had published poetry, movie reviews, and theater criticism in various literary journals and popular magazines. She is primarily known, however, for what she wrote in the last twenty-four years of her life. Passionately dedicated to nonviolent activism, she engaged in and wrote about a variety of pacifist actions supporting both domestic and international causes during the 1960s: unilateral nuclear disarmament, improved U.S.-Cuban relations, the Civil Rights Movement, and the end of the Vietnam War. In the early 1970s she shifted her attention to the women's movement. Mostly published in *The Nation* and *Liberation* magazines, her writings helped define the debate about tactics among both leftists and feminists throughout the 1960s and 1970s, and because they stress respect for all people regardless of politics or sexual orientation, they have remained primers on coalition building.

Barbara Deming was born on 23 July 1917 in New York City to Harold Deming, a Republican lawyer and domineering father, and Katherine Burritt, an open-minded professional singer and descendant of Elihu Burritt (1810–1879), an abolitionist and advocate of nonviolent activism during the Civil War. She had one older and two younger brothers. All the Deming children attended the Friends Seminary on East Sixteenth Street in New York City. Barbara Deming attended from 1923 until 1934, when she entered Bennington College, Vermont's new liberal arts college. At the Friends Seminary, Deming lived in a nonsectarian environment that stressed community, dignity, and respect for others. These values are at the heart of the Quaker tradition of pacifism in America and later grounded Deming's politics of the 1960s and 1970s.

While Deming was a teenager and young adult, family dynamics rather than her pacifist ancestor or her Quaker schooling had the most influence on her. Her father, as the family patriarch, dictated his children's career paths, requiring them to become financially independent once educated. He wanted his daughter to become a teacher, an acceptable career choice for a young, educated, upper-middle-class woman. Deming, opposing his will, desired to be a writer. Her rebellion began a father-daughter conflict she later called in the November 1978 issue of *Ms.* magazine "probably the most crucial struggle I had waged in early life." She majored in literature and drama at Bennington College, graduating with a B.A. in 1938, but her father blocked

Barbara Deming (in front of window) in Albany, Georgia, 1964 (from Prison Notes, *1966; Thomas Cooper Library, University of South Carolina)*

her from attending graduate school at Louisiana State University, where she was to assist Robert Penn Warren with *The Southern Review*. Instead, her father insisted that she attend Case Western Reserve University in Cleveland, Ohio, where she continued studying the arts, receiving a master's degree in drama and theater in 1941. During the summers of 1938 and 1939 she was codirector of Bennington Stock Theatre and spent the summers of 1941 and 1942 as a teaching fellow at the Bennington School of Arts. After she graduated from Case, her father suggested Deming support herself as an editor or art critic.

Deming's desire to become a writer was partially nourished when she was a teenager by the artistic community in and around a family-owned home in New City, a rural area just northwest of the Hudson River and New York City. Here her neighbors included sculptor Henry Varnum Poor; writer Bessie Breuer and her daughter and painter, Anne Poor; photographer Consuelo Kanaga; poet E. E. Cummings; poet Edna St. Vincent Millay; and, most important, Norma Millay. Deming fell deeply in love with Norma Millay, and her

earliest poetry passionately celebrates this love. Her mother's open-minded attitude toward homosexuality also played a part: it gave Deming a family member in whom she could confide. Despite her mother's support and her own wish to be remembered primarily as a poet, Deming struggled to publish her poems. Her first published poem, "Listen/cats love eyes" appeared in *New Directions* in 1936. From the late 1940s through the 1950s her poetry appeared sporadically in the literary journals and magazines *Chimera, Wakes 8, Perspective, The Paris Review, The New Yorker,* and *Voices.* In the 1960s she published even fewer poems, most in the political magazines *The Nation* and *Liberation.*

Much of Deming's poetry has become available to readers only since 1996, when Judith McDaniel published the manuscript Deming left at her death, *I Change, I Change.* The manuscript breaks into eight parts, chronologically arranged from 1933 to 1984, with all but one named after women Deming loved: Norma, Casey, Emmie, Vida, Annie, Mary, and Jane. The one section not so named, South Mountain Road, focuses on her life at New City while she was earning her master's degree. In one short poem from this section, she describes household etiquette so strict under her father's rule that "One must be a poet only in one's own room." This clash between repressive rules and open artistic self-expression reflects the struggle Deming faced throughout her life as a lesbian artist living in a homophobic society. One of her poetic strategies was self-effacement: while at Bennington she tried replacing female pronouns with male ones, resulting in love poems that even she realized were insincere. Her other strategy was to retreat, to keep her poetry secret by confining it to "a room of one's own." Just as her father knew nothing of his daughter's love affair with Norma Millay, Deming kept most of her love poetry, and thereby much of her personal life, out of the public's eye, fearing parental and social disapproval.

Between the years 1942 and 1959 Deming's public life followed the compromised career path suggested by her father. From 1942 to 1944 she worked at New York's Museum of Modern Art, analyzing motion pictures for the Library of Congress national film library project. By 1950 she had turned her observations while working on the project into what became *Running Away from Myself—A Dream Portrait of America Drawn from the Films of the '40s* (1969), a series of critiques. In the decade that followed Deming published the short stories, "Giro" in *The New Yorker* (1953) and "The Siege" in *Charm* (1954). In addition, she occasionally wrote movie reviews for *Vogue* and published two literary essays toward the end of the decade: "John Osborne's War Against the Philistines" in *The Hudson Review* (1958) and "The World of Hamlet" in *The Tulane Drama Review* (1959).

In *Running Away from Myself* and her two journal articles, Deming reveals an adherence to a realistic theory of art that she would eventually find compatible with nonviolent activism. Her analysis remains focused on an "impulse . . . with which every man is acquainted": the often self-destructive inability of humans to face "unpleasant truths" (Jane Meyerding, *We Are All Part of One Another*, 1984). The movies of the 1940s encourage this behavior by constantly replacing truthful representations that question the status quo with the blind comfort of wish fulfillment. Jean Gabin in the 1944 movie *The Imposter* undergoes an implausible metamorphosis from a criminal on death row to a French war hero by assuming a dead soldier's identity: what begins as fairly realistic examination of criminal opportunism during wartime becomes a celebration of the common man pulling himself up by "his" bootstraps.

In her analysis of John Osborne's play, *Look Back in Anger* (1956), Deming faults the playwright for avoiding truthful representation. She argues that his "hero,"

Jimmy Porter, lacks Hamlet's ability to reflect on the wisdom of those actions of his that create a living hell for himself and those he loves. Without this ability, the audience feels no sympathy for Jimmy, and Osborne's desire to wake his middle-class audience from their complacent slumber falls on deaf ears. Both screenwriters and playwrights fail to produce works that Deming calls art, since art never fails in its awareness of "the actual subject" being represented. *Hamlet* is art, in contrast, because William Shakespeare remains aware of his actual subject: Hamlet's refusal to accept the truth of the treasonous world he finds himself in, despite his inability to ignore it.

Deming's incisive critiques of movies and drama reflect her own artistic struggles to clearly apprehend the "actual subject" she wanted to represent. In 1940 Deming fell in love with Vida Ginsberg, whom she had met while attending Bennington. Their relationship lasted until 1947, when Vida left for Salzburg, Austria. In the love poems Deming writes during this time, she disguises her passion for Ginsberg with so much imagery that reading them is like observing a masque: one is aware of the participants, but does not know their actual identities nor quite comprehend their relationship to one another. Because of this oblique presentation, the passion conveyed is a diminished one, especially compared to her letters to Ginsberg, which McDaniel describes in the introduction to *I Change, I Change* as having a "richness and nervous trajectory" the poems lack.

Deming's insecurity about speaking openly in her art about her relationships with other women carried into the next decade. In 1950 and 1951 she toured Europe on an inheritance from her aunt Eleanor. While there, she ran into and fell in love with her friend from her teenage years, the painter Anne Poor, who was living and working in Anticoli, Italy. Deming's travels, her futile pursuit of Poor who did not reciprocate her love, and her lonely struggle to maintain her self-respect as a lesbian provide the subjects of her only book of narrative prose, *A Humming under My Feet: A Book of Travail* (1985). Deming began this work in 1952 when she was thirty-five and newly returned from Europe, but shelved the project for twenty years, discouraged by the way several of her friends responded to a draft of her first chapter. In the chapter's original version, "A Book of Travail," first published in Deming's collection of short stories, *Wash Us and Comb Us* (1972), she again conceals the name of the woman she loves. In its opening address, Deming casts herself as an Odysseus and Poor as a Penelope working at cross-purposes: "You weave . . . in my absence, no images of a future in which our figures are joined. Nevertheless it is you I go seeking." In the "story" that follows, Deming recounts a boat trip she took with three other friends to the Greek island, Mykonos, that begins idyllically but ends with a frank depiction of her "date-rape" by the island's doctor. At the time, this material was too personal and explicit for her friends' tastes. As Deming recounts thirty-two years later in the foreword to her book, "they were embarrassed for me"; one even asked her to switch her pronouns from the first to third person. She then admits, however, that without a developed "feminist consciousness," she not only lacked the conviction she needed to trust and persist in her own artistic impulses but also the ability to convey a clear "sense of what was really happening in the story" (*A Humming under My Feet*).

The long process of Deming becoming a fully conscious nonviolent radical feminist began in the mid 1950s. In 1954 her father died, and shortly thereafter Deming fell in love with Poor's friend, the painter Mary Meigs. With Meigs, Deming finally started feeling more comfortable with her sexuality. Unlike the women Deming had fallen in love with previously, Meigs had consciously chosen lesbianism. Shortly after their meeting, Deming moved into Meigs' house in Wellfleet, Massachusetts, where she lived for the next fifteen years. From 1954 until 1959 Deming and Meigs lived an apolitical life common to many artists at the time, primarily because Deming felt unable to reconcile politics with her artistic philosophy. To Deming engaging in politics would be to "become less truthful, keep less of a grasp on the *complexity* of truth" ("Barbara Deming: The Rage of a Pacifist"). Then she took two life-transforming trips: one to India with Meigs in 1959, the other to Cuba in 1960.

After returning from India, Deming began reading the writings of Mohandas Karamchand Gandhi. In Gandhi's work on nonviolent activism, she came across a concept central to his political thought, satyagraha, which allowed her to bridge the gap between art and politics. Translated both as nonviolent action and "clinging to truth," this Sanskrit term is similar to the Society of Friends' description of nonviolent action as "speaking truth to power." It immediately appealed both to Deming's Quaker background and her artistic philosophy: "I recognized at once that I was a pacifist" ("Barbara Deming: The Rage of a Pacifist"). Her trip to Cuba the following year brought her face-to-face with her unthinking acceptance of common myths about the American state, such as its generosity precluding any act of imperialism. In Havana on vacation with Breuer, Henry Varnum Poor, and Anne Poor one year after Fidel Castro had overthrown the dictator Fulgencio Batista, Deming experienced "the profound shock of discovering the gap that lay between what I had been told was happening there, and happening between our two countries, and what I now learned for myself was

happening" (*Revolution and Equilibrium*). Part of Deming's education came from talking with the Cuban people. They told her about daily firebomb raids carried out by planes stationed at Florida airfields, and complained that the U.S. government provided political asylum to members of Batista's regime responsible for torturing and murdering numerous Cubans. She was also educated by an impromptu interview she had with Castro when she accosted him on the sidewalk outside the famous Sevilla Biltmore Hotel. Wanting to question him about a recent speech in which he suggested American involvement in the explosion of the *La Coubre,* a munitions ship heading to Cuba from Belgium, Deming came away from the hour-long discussion convinced that Castro was a leader concerned about his people's welfare, not the warmonger a hostile American press had made him out to be.

The immediate result of Deming's experience in Cuba was to make politics her "art." Her first piece of journalism, "Dialogues in Cuba," appeared in the May 1960 issue of the leftist magazine, *The Nation*. Shortly thereafter, Deming joined the Committee for Nonviolent Action (CNVA), a political organization dedicated to Gandhian nonviolent action that at the time primarily dedicated itself to unilateral disarmament. She spent the summer and fall protesting the construction of the Polaris nuclear submarine in New London, Connecticut. While there, she and Meigs also appeared at the Peacemakers annual conference held in a rented house at nearby Waterford, Connecticut, lured by an advertisement of their training program on the back page of *Liberation,* the pacifist monthly magazine for which Deming would soon be writing. In *The Nation* article that describes her summer and fall, "The Peacemakers" (December 1960), she identifies a trait of nonviolent activists that anticipates the youth movement of the mid to late 1960s: having on moral grounds rejected unjust and immoral laws and the uninformed opinion of the majority that supports them, they have acquired a fearless freedom and spontaneity of action. Their commitment to Gandhian nonviolence made them all the more uninhibited and morally determined, since "no ordinary misgivings about injuring another person need dilute their resolution and make them hesitate" (*Revolution and Equilibrium*).

Such freedom and spontaneity struck a chord with Deming, who had rebelled against her father's rules and continued to struggle against the constraints of a homophobic society. As she later realized, with the CNVA she had found a community that allowed her to fight her personal anger as an oppressed woman and lesbian "by analogy," struggling to free others from oppression because of an inarticulate feeling that she was oppressed herself. Taking literally Gandhi's vision of nonviolent action as a journey in which one seeks and dramatizes the truth of one's convictions, the CNVA primarily organized peace walks. In May 1961 Deming participated in the San Francisco to Moscow Walk for Peace, joining it for a week as it reached Uniontown, Pennsylvania. It began in San Francisco on 1 December 1960 with ten walkers, and reached Red Square, Moscow, in October 1961 with thirty-one. In the two articles she wrote for *The Nation* describing the action, she answers the often-posed question "why they walk" in strictly Gandhian terms. As a physical act, walking in and of itself would convey the truth of the peace walkers' cause. As she recalls one participant saying: "It would be much better . . . to have everyone on the road at all times, *walking*. . . . The walk itself would communicate their message." Another participant describes the walk as a spiritual journey, as "a long walk in the sense of a serious conversation with oneself" (*Revolution and Equilibrium*).

If these early articles for *The Nation* show Deming well on her way to becoming one of the 1960s' leading American theorists of nonviolent action, they also reveal that she used the articles themselves to reenact the Gandhian search for truth that would become a hallmark of her expository style. In both articles, she describes her initial ambivalence about joining the peace-movement community. As she meets members of the Peacemakers for the first time, Deming's upper-middle-class background comes to the fore: she notes with disfavor the bare, dilapidated rental house, and like other reporters, is put off by the Peacemakers' sloppy, dirty clothes. When accompanying the peace walkers through Pennsylvania, she again mentions the disrespectful appearance of some, and even uses the lighthearted attitude on the part of others to question their moral commitment to the walk. At one point during a Peacemakers' training session, Deming makes her doubts about fitting in explicit: "I am the daughter of a well-to-do Republican lawyer: 'What am I doing here? This is talk of revolution.'" Each of these derogatory observations, however, always precedes a correction once she attends to the truth behind the appearance. She comes to see the decrepit meeting place and the disheveled appearance of the Peacemakers as signs of a voluntary poverty that gives them more freedom to act spontaneously; a blonde girl whom Deming initially accuses of treating the peace walk as a lark because she sings a silly song becomes an image of penitence as she labors up a hill with only a poncho protecting herself and her guitar. Immediately after Deming questions her presence among revolutionaries at the Peacemakers' meeting, she remembers: "the methods to which they were committed. . . . their rejection of secrecy; their

careful advance notice to their adversary of all their plans" (*Revolution and Equilibrium*).

Deming found the CNVA and Peacemakers appealing in their inclusiveness. Membership was open to anyone, regardless of religious affiliation or economic background, who practiced nonviolence. For that reason Deming found it obvious that CNVA concerns connected to the Civil Rights Movement. The organization itself did not immediately agree, and Deming took up the discussion in her account of the Nashville, Tennessee, to Washington, D.C., walk for peace, "Southern Peace Walk: Two Issues or One?" The 1962 Nashville to Washington, D.C., peace walk was one of three coordinated walks organized by Bradford Lyttle, national secretary of the CNVA. The other two started in Chicago and New Hampshire, and CNVA planned for all three walks to arrive simultaneously at the Pentagon for a day of protest. Because the Nashville walk began in the South, CNVA leadership decided that it would be integrated; they also decided, however, to have the walkers focus only on nuclear disarmament. To Deming, who understood the disarmament and civil rights struggles as linked, not only by similar nonviolent tactics but also by the recognition that all human beings should be treated with respect, the CNVA's decision did not make sense.

In her account Deming illustrates how combining the peace and civil rights movements strengthens both. The march began with a moment of forced nonrecognition on the peace walkers' part. At the time the youth arm of the Civil Rights Movement, the Student Nonviolent Coordinating Committee (SNCC) formed in Raleigh, North Carolina, in 1960, was staging a sit-in demonstration at a Nashville Simple Simon's restaurant. Deming recounts how she and her companions passed by without so much as a "pause in our marching," and how "unnatural" that felt to all of them. Shortly thereafter, while engaged in a meeting at Scarritt College for Christian Workers, the peace walkers heard lectures by two leaders of the SNCC, James Lawson and Metz Rollins, who pointed out the common ground of the two movements. As they walked through the Tennessee countryside, the peace walkers sheltered for the night in both white and black churches, faced constant death threats from Southern segregationists, and were joined by more and more black student integrationists, until, Deming reports, as they walk through Lebanon, Tennessee, "more of us were black than white" (*Revolution and Equilibrium*). She concludes her account by describing a near violent nighttime encounter with eight local young workingmen, who after pelting them and the church they were staying in with rocks, came out of hiding and talked with the peace walkers into the early morning hours. Deming credited the presence of the black man in her group, Robert Gore, with making these young men attend to the walkers' message of peace. As she saw it, his black skin made clear to all involved in the conversation that "the issue of war and peace remains fundamentally the issue of whether or not one is going to be willing to respect one's fellow man" *(Revolution and Equilibrium)*.

With the exception of a poem published in 1961, "Southern Peace Walk: Two Issues or One?" marks the beginning of Deming's association with *Liberation* magazine, which lasted from 1962 until 1975. Its editorial board at the time consisted of leading figures of the American radical peace movement, including Dave Dellinger and A. J. Muste. Dellinger led "the Mobilization," a national antiwar coalition during the Vietnam War, and was indicted as one of the Chicago Eight for helping to organize demonstrations at the 1968 Democratic National Convention. Involved in nonviolent antiwar and labor activism since World War I, Muste participated in the Fellowship of Reconciliation (FOR), the War Resisters League, the CNVA, and Peacemakers and helped found *Liberation* in 1956. Contributors to the magazine included Linus Pauling, Erich Fromm, Martin Luther King Jr., Nat Hentoff, Noam Chomsky, and Howard Zinn. Among such company Deming found a comfortable fit: most were of her generation and considered intellectuals in their respective fields.

Deming quickly emerged as a prominent voice within the magazine and the peace movement in general. By November 1962 she was listed as an associate editor of *Liberation*. Her essay in that issue, "Courage for the New Age: The Council of Correspondence" defends David Reisman and H. Stuart Hughes, two of the founding members of the Council of Correspondence, from charges made by the editors of *Life* magazine that they were "cowards and defeatists" for urging unilateral disarmament and "Gandhian nonviolent resistance to armed communism" *(Revolution and Equilibrium)*. Just before Christmas she attended the House Committee on Un-American Activities (HCUA) hearings where she witnessed committeemen assailing the members of the loosely organized Women Strike for Peace (WISP) with charges of communism.

In February 1963 Deming's essay, "Needed: A New Declaration of Independence," appeared. In it Deming takes issue with a speech President John F. Kennedy gave on 23 October 1962 regarding the Cuban missile crisis. She questions Kennedy's assertion that it is part of the American character to take courageous risks, even if these risks mean an all-out nuclear war, killing millions throughout the world not party to the conflict. Deming argues that Americans must face the unpleasant reality that they no longer exist in isolation from the rest of the world: telecommunications and

the certain global impact of nuclear war have made them part of a worldwide community. Americans' nationalism and their reliance on military power to enforce their will, in consequence, must give way to an idea of a world community that uses nonviolent action to solve disputes. Only in this way, she argues, can the United States make its actions consistent with its own Declaration of Independence, which declares that one of the self-evident, inalienable rights of all people is the right to life.

Whether applied locally, nationally, or internationally, this idea that "we are all part of one another" remained a constant theme in Deming's writings and politics for the rest of her life, giving her the conviction necessary to fight injustice and inhumanity wherever she found it. During the spring of 1963 Deming wrote in *Liberation* and *The Nation*, led a training session in nonviolent action at a WISP conference held at Urbana, Illinois, and on 6 May began a six-day incarceration in the Birmingham, Alabama, jail for joining blacks in a civil rights demonstration. Characteristically, she identifies not only with the demonstrators' demand "to be treated like humans beings ('that's what it boils down to, that's all we ask')," but also by the end of her imprisonment, with the poor, ill white women with whom she was jailed *(Revolution and Equilibrium)*. Like the demonstrators both inside and outside the jail, these women were, she thought, the victims of a social system that treated them as less than human.

In January 1964 Deming was imprisoned again, this time for twenty-seven days in the Albany, Georgia, city jail for participating in another integrated peace walk organized by Lyttle. Starting in Quebec City, Canada, on 26 May 1963, the walkers reached Rome, New York, by 7 July, and Georgia by the fall. Deming joined them in Georgia in October. On 7 November in the town of Griffin, about thirty-five miles south of Atlanta, most of the twenty-three walkers, consisting of three black men, fourteen white men, and six white women, were arrested and jailed for parading without a permit and resisting police. While holding them in custody, Georgia Bureau of Investigation agents repeatedly shocked the peace walkers with cattle prods for sitting down in noncooperation. Deming avoided arrest initially only because she had gone north for the day. Shortly afterward, the walkers were briefly jailed in Macon, this time Deming along with them.

Then on 23 December a nearly two-month struggle between the peace walkers and Albany, Georgia, authorities began with the first of two imprisonments, both over the same issue: the right to walk through the town's business district and pass out leaflets. Fearing any kind of demonstration through the business district would set a precedent for black civil-rights groups, Lau-

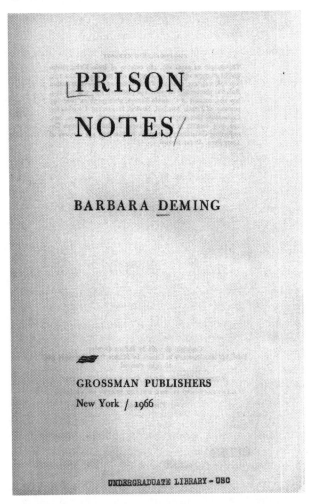

PRISON
NOTES

BARBARA DEMING

GROSSMAN PUBLISHERS
New York / 1966

Title page for Deming's first book, an account of her days in the Albany, Georgia, jail for passing out leaflets supporting a civil-rights peace march (Thomas Cooper Library, University of South Carolina)

rie Pritchett, the Albany police chief, jailed the walkers. For twenty-four days those in jail fasted, while Deming provided support from the outside. Eleven days after their release on 16 January 1964, the walkers attempted a second pass through Albany's business district and were rearrested, Deming among them once again. Finally, on 22 February, after most of them had fasted for over three weeks, the peace walkers were released by the Albany authorities and allowed to pass through the downtown business district distributing leaflets.

Deming's account of her experiences in the Albany city jail, *Prison Notes,* first appeared as a nine-part memoir published in *Liberation* between August 1964 and January 1966 and then in book form later in 1966. Written from notes she took on toilet paper and mailed to CNVA members working for the walkers' release, her first book offers both an exposé of Southern bigotry

and a moving testament to her own transformation while imprisoned. To her, "putting a man in jail remains essentially the act of wishing that man out of existence," essentially an act of violence. Doing so, a society uses prisons to ignore its "unpleasant truths," locking away "people with whom it has been unable to cope, whom it has been unable to sustain." The repeated imprisonment of the peace walkers reveals the absurdity of such violence and the ultimate impotence of a bigoted society. By their noncooperation with authorities, Deming argues, the demonstrators assert their right to exist, "refusing to allow them the godlike sense that their will alone exists. . . . We also make it inconvenient for them, and we make it expensive. It costs the city something to put us up in jail. When we fast, there are also medical expenses" *(Prison Notes).* The city of Albany spent $500 a day during the demonstrators' first imprisonment.

Prison Notes contains Deming's last extensive examination of American race relations. In May 1965 she became an editor at *Liberation* and, along with her CNVA colleagues, increasingly turned her attention to the Vietnam War. In 1966 she joined Muste, Lyttle, Sherry Miller, Karl Meyer, and Bill Davidson on a trip to Saigon where they engaged in a nonviolent protest against the war. Then, anticipating Jane Fonda's more notorious 1972 trip by six years, Deming toured Hanoi and the surrounding countryside with three other women from December 1966 to January 1967, observing the destruction of civilian areas by American bombers. Upon returning to the states, she went on a speaking tour to enlighten the public about America's involvement in Vietnam. The uproar her talk, "The Temptations of Power," created in the local press near her Wellfleet home ranged from bemused toleration to outright excoriation; all who commented, however, confirmed Deming's conviction that most Americans were unwilling to believe their government could do wrong, despite eyewitness reports to the contrary. On 28 April 1967 she accepted the Ninth Annual Peace Award of the War Resisters League at its forty-fourth annual dinner in honor of her nonviolent activism in support of civil rights and peace.

In February 1968 she published the essay which, along with *Prison Notes,* helped cement Deming's reputation as one of the major theorists of American nonviolent protest. "On Revolution and Equilibrium" summarizes Deming's response to leftist organizations, such as the Students for a Democratic Society (SDS) and the Black Panthers, which in the late 1960s became increasingly enamored with violence as a legitimate means to effect social change. *Liberation* magazine paired it with Régis Debray's "Declaration at His Court Martial in Camiri, Bolivia, November, 1967," creating a special issue that captures this moment of transition within the American Left. A professor of philosophy at the University of Havana, friend of Che Guevara, and author of *Revolution in the Revolution: Armed Struggle and Political Struggle in Latin America* (1967), a book that became a field manual for Latin American guerillas, Debray was in Bolivia when Guevara was captured and executed in 1967 and was tried and convicted of collaborating with Guevara and his guerillas. In his "Declaration" Debray contrasts the violence of the state, which oppresses, with the violence of guerillas, which because it liberates, he believes offers a justified means to an end.

Deming takes issue not only with Debray but also with proponents of violent revolution such as Algerian psychologist Frantz Fanon, SDS president Carl Oglesby, and Stokely Carmichael. Using their own analyses of the effects of "liberating" violence on the revolutionaries involved, Deming points out that what ensues is a "vertigo" that dooms revolutions to failure as the oppressors become the oppressed and the inhumanity that revolution was supposed to end continues. Nonviolent action, in contrast, breaks this cycle by focusing on the action, not the person. In what is now known as the "doctrine of 'the two hands,'" Deming argues that if revolutionaries respect the lives of all human beings, "the antagonist cannot take the interference with his actions personally, because his person is not threatened, and he is forced to begin to acknowledge the grievance against him." Thus, a nonviolent revolutionary has "as it were two hands upon him—the one calming him, making him ask questions, as the other makes him move." Only through the "two hands" of nonviolent action in revolutionary struggles, Deming believes, can people establish an "equilibrium between self-assertion and respect for others" and ensure true social progress *(Revolution and Equilibrium)*.

Despite Deming's forceful argument, the events of 1968 indicated that the views of Deming, Dellinger, and Muste (who died the previous fall) were quickly becoming unpopular. With the student uprisings in Paris, the assassination of Martin Luther King Jr. and subsequent race riots, and the violence at the Democratic National Convention in Chicago at which young Tom Hayden declared nonviolence dead, the new Left began to embrace violence as a legitimate means of social change. That summer Deming participated in one of her last nonviolent actions of the decade, living for three weeks in Resurrection City, an encampment of poor people in Washington, D.C., conceived by the Southern Christian Leadership Coalition.

During this year Deming also met Jane Verlaine, an acquaintance from Bennington College, and fell in love. From 1954 Deming had continued to live with Mary Meigs at Wellfleet even as the two became increasingly estranged from one another. Deming's political commitments kept her away from home for long periods of time; Meigs, feeling neglected, fell in love with Marie-Claire Blais, a Canadian writer who moved in with them at Wellfleet. When she met Verlaine in 1968, Deming had been in a stressful love triangle for six years; Verlaine had recently separated and was seeking a divorce from her husband. Deming's plans to share a house in Monticello, New York, with Verlaine and her two children were obstructed by Oscar Verlaine, who threatened to sue for custody of the children, arguing that the relationship with Deming proved Verlaine an unfit parent.

These struggles finally forced Deming to face the truth of her own oppression, both as a woman and a lesbian. Eventually, she did move in with Verlaine and the two children in 1969, began to withdraw from active participation in the peace movement, and concentrated on turning her written work into books. The study of 1940s films written twenty years previously, *Running Away from Myself—A Dream Portrait of America Drawn from the Films of the '40s,* was published in 1969. Although still a contributor to *Liberation,* in 1970 she resigned from her editorial position. In 1971, as if to signal the end of an era in American radical dissent and in her own life, she published *Revolution and Equilibrium,* a collection of her essays and speeches of the 1960s. The same year she began sorting through the short stories she had written, both published and unpublished, and this work became the collection *Wash Us and Comb Us.*

Her colleagues in the antiwar movement noticed her withdrawal from active political life and complained. One in particular, Ray Robinson, a black man who was jailed with Deming and others in Albany, Georgia, asked her in a letter: "Barbara, what are you doing now? What?" In her reply, Deming "comes out." To Ray's complaint that as a powerless black man in a segregated, racist society, he has "been to the bottom, the complete bottom" she replies that over the last two years she has also been to the bottom: "the bottom of being a homosexual" (*We Cannot Live without Our Lives,* 1974). Her battles against social injustice had become personal, and for the first time Deming faced her own anger at feeling powerless at the hands of a male-dominated society.

The first public indication of Deming's developing feminist consciousness came in a speech she wrote in 1971 but never personally delivered. While she traveled in September to the War Resisters' League national conference in Athens, Georgia, the car she was riding in crashed as she slept in the backseat. She sustained injuries so severe that she remained in a body cast for almost a year and suffered from double vision for more than two years. Her speech, "On Anger," was delivered by a friend and published in the November 1971 issue of *Liberation*. In this speech, Deming applies her previous analysis of violence in "On Revolution and Equilibrium" to the women's movement, expressing her fear that the rage women feel at their oppression by men will result in a similar self-defeating vertigo. Drawing on her personal experiences and emotions as a woman for the first time, she admits to an anger that seems out of character with her earlier writings: "I have to acknowledge that in many moments of anger I have, in effect, wished a man dead—wished him not there for me to cope with." She calls this impulse the "anger of affliction." For the women's movement, or any revolutionary movement, to effect meaningful social change, this anger must become "transmuted" into an "anger of determination," one that nonviolently demands both change and respect for oneself and others. Just as she confronted her own anger, she urges her audience to face their "own most seemingly personal anger" more effectively and to persuade those prone to violent anger to use peaceful and constructive means *(We Cannot Live without Our Lives)*.

After her release from the hospital, Deming continued to engage feminists and the Left with new insights and debate in personal letters and magazine articles. These she then gathered into mixed-genre collections. *We Cannot Live without Our Lives* (1974) contains letters, speeches, poems, memorials, and essays, including "On Anger," her letters to Robinson, and a letter to Arthur Kinoy. A teacher of law at Rutgers University who had defended the Rosenbergs, Southern civil-rights organizers, and antiwar protesters, Kinoy had proposed a "People's Party" at the heart of which would be "an understanding of the 'unique quality'" of the American black Civil Rights Movement. In her reply, "Women and the People's Party" (later retitled "You Are Forgetting Women"), Deming chides Kinoy for overlooking the women's struggle. Drawing on Sheila Rowbotham's *Women, Resistance, & Revolution* (1972) and Shulamith Firestone's *The Dialectic of Sex* (1970), Deming critiques the male-dominated, Marxist Left, arguing that the up-to-now unrecognized sexual class system is the original class system upon which all other exploitative systems are based; consequently, the sexual class system and the artificial gender differences upon which it depends must be eliminated before any attempt to eliminate economic class systems can be successful. Women, she says, need an alternative space for uninhibited communication outside patriarchal social structures that prevent them from expressing themselves without reserve. For Deming, men also must "begin to desert patriarchal space" if communication between men and women is to continue productively.

Deming's feminist critique of the Marxist Left and her separatist position proved too radical for *Liberation*'s editors, who in 1973 refused to print her letter until Kinoy himself insisted. In January 1975 Deming severed her official relationship with the magazine, requesting that it no longer list her as an associate. With the magazine no longer advocating radical nonviolence and unreceptive to feminism, she no longer shared "the political vision of the editors." With the exception of an occasional letter to the editor in *Liberation* defending radical feminists, Deming once again struggled to publish her work. Deming, Andrea Dworkin, Leah Fritz, and Karla Jay stopped writing for *WIN (Win Peace and Freedom Through Nonviolent Action)* when the magazine rejected their proposal for a special issue on radical feminist and antiwar activist Jane Alpert. Deming's piece "Seeing Us As We Are Not" was also rejected by *Lesbian Tide, Ms.,* and *Off Our Backs*. The War Resisters League finally published it in 1979 as a pamphlet.

In 1976 Deming and Verlaine moved to Sugarloaf Key, Florida, hoping to improve Deming's health. Here she collected the letters and essays she wrote between 1975 and 1977, along with her complete correspondence with Kinoy, in her self-published *Remembering Who We Are* (1981). Primarily a series of dialogues, the book includes the voices of those within the Left and the women's movements who do not share her views, creating a complex dissonance with her own voice that illustrates her nonviolent activist stance. In each reply, she treats her recipient with respect while disagreeing with elements of his or her politics. Her tone remains one of mutual exploration rather than ideological narrowness, one that genuinely attempts to connect with the other person and continue the dialogue. As in the 1960s, Deming concerns herself with building coalitions with other classes of the oppressed, with men as well as women. In "To Fear Jane Alpert Is To Fear Ourselves— A Letter to Susan Sherman," she encourages feminists to share with her a more complex but more truthful perception of men that patriarchy tries to deny: as both oppressors and oppressed, both "tyrant" and "comrade," divided from themselves as well as from women. Only by maintaining this "double vision" on all levels will feminists be able to realize a world in which they have full participation and selfhood. Double vision allows them, in the nonviolent tradition, to "abandon the concept of naming enemies" and instead begin "naming behavior that is oppressive, naming abuse of power, that is held unfairly and must be destroyed, but naming no *person* . . . whom we are willing to destroy."

Despite persistent poor health since the auto accident, Deming continued to work nonviolently for unification of the peace and women's movements, which she considered synonymous. She participated in her last peace walk as part of the Seneca Women's Peace Encampment on 30 July 1983. The New York City Women's Pentagon Action's Feminist Walk began in Seneca Falls, New York, with its intended end point the Women's Peace Encampment in Romulus. The intended twelve-mile walk, a celebration of feminists of America's past, came to an abrupt end after just over two miles in Waterloo, where an angry mob blocked the walkers' way out of town at the Waterloo bridge. In an attempt to calm the crowd and to emphasize their constitutional rights, the women sat down and refused to move. Deming and fifty-three other women were arrested for "disorderly conduct" and held in the Inter-laken Junior High School cafeteria, where, in the spirit of nonviolent protest, they "refused to cooperate in any way." Five days later, on 3 August, the charges against them were dropped.

During the last year of Deming's life *We Are All Part of One Another: A Barbara Deming Reader* was published. This collection encompasses her most important writings from 1940 through 1981. She died at age sixty-seven on 2 August 1984 of ovarian cancer, surrounded by a circle of friends at the Sugarloaf Key home she shared with Verlaine. She left two recently completed book manuscripts at the time of her death. *Prisons That Could Not Hold* (1985) combines her previously published *Prison Notes* with three dialogues concerning the Seneca's Women's Peace Encampment, a letter, an interview of her by the Boston Women's Video Collective, and the "Statement of the Waterloo fifty-four." Also published that year was the completed treatment of her year in Europe in the early 1950s, *A Humming under My Feet: A Book of Travail*. Now openly addressed to the woman she fell in love with while in Europe and all her "lesbian sisters," the book asks readers once again to maintain a double vision: one of Deming as a thirty-three-year-old character struggling with her sexual identity and self-respect, and one of Deming as a sixty-year-old author with a "developed feminist consciousness" that allows her to finally "make sense of what was really happening" in the story she tells.

Despite her importance to the peace movement of the 1960s, Deming and her writings on nonviolent activism received scant critical and scholarly attention after her death. The combined circumstances of her last years alienated her from many civil-rights and antiwar activists of the 1970s. Until her death she defended herself against charges of "man hating" because of her insistence on women communicating in their own space

and her belief that all men oppress all women. Hence, she remained on the margins of feminism as well. Nevertheless, feminists have preserved her memory and her commitment to peace for people of all classes, colors, and sexual orientation. Near the end of the 1970s, Deming founded Money for Women. Renamed the Money for Women/Barbara Deming Memorial Fund after her death, it awards grants and loans up to $1,000 to feminist artists whose work focuses on women's issues or advocates peace and justice. More recently, Judith McDaniel, the executor of Deming's literary estate, published a collection of her poetry, *I Change, I Change,* as well as a biographical essay in the collection *Impossible to Hold: Women and Culture in the 1960s,* edited by Avital H. Bloch and Lauri Umansky (2005).

The inscription on Barbara Deming's award from the War Resisters League speaks for all who knew her well: "With pride and affection for one whose gentleness intimidates the mighty. In Albany, Georgia, in Saigon, in Hanoi, she has quietly risked a compassion that reached across the lines of violence. She has gained from her risks. We have gained from her example" (*Liberation,* May–June 1967).

References:

Anonymous, "Nonviolence and Police Brutality: A Document," *Liberation,* 8 (November 1963): 9–17;

Régis Debray, "Declaration at his Court Martial in Camiri, Bolivia, November 1967," *Liberation,* 12 (February 1968): 22–37;

Leah Fritz, "Barbara Deming: The Rage of a Pacifist," *Ms.,* 7 (November 1978): 97–101;

Lamen Hoover, "Barbara Deming–She's a Real Shocker," *Liberation,* 9 (February 1967): 32–38;

Judith McDaniel, "Shaping the Sixties: The Emergence of Barbara Deming," in *Impossible to Hold: Women and Culture in the 1960s,* edited by Avital H. Bloch and Lauri Umansky (New York: New York University Press, 2005), pp. 196–216;

Staughton and Alice Lynd, eds., *Nonviolence in America: A Documentary History* (Maryknoll, N.Y.: Orbis, 1995).

Papers:

The Barbara Deming Archives are located at two libraries: the Schlesinger Women's History Library at Radcliffe College holds the main body of her work; the Muger Library at Boston College also houses some papers written during the time of *Prison Notes*. Each is catalogued and available to scholars and researchers.

Crystal Eastman

(25 June 1881 – 8 July 1928)

John D. Buenker
University of Wisconsin–Parkside

BOOKS: *"Employers' Liability," A Criticism Based on Facts* (New York: American Association for Labor Legislation, 1909);

Work Accidents and the Law (New York: Charities Publication Committee, 1910);

The Effect of Industrial Fatalities Upon the Home (New York: American Association for Labor Legislation, 1915);

The Mexican-American League (New York: Mexican-American Peace Committee, 1916).

Editions and Collections: *Toward The Great Change: Crystal and Max Eastman On Feminism, Antimilitarism, and Revolution,* edited by Blanche Wiesen Cook (New York: Garland, 1976);

Crystal Eastman on Women and Revolution, edited by Cook (New York: Oxford, 1978).

OTHER: "Address at a Hearing of the House Judiciary Committee, March 3, 1914," in *History of Woman Suffrage,* volumes 5–6, edited by Ida Husted Harper (New York: National American Woman Suffrage Association, 1922).

SELECTED PERIODICAL PUBLICATIONS– UNCOLLECED: "Charles Haag," *Charities and the Commons,* 17 (5 January 1907): 615–617;

"Non-Partisan Mayor," *Charities and the Commons,* 19 (2 November 1907): 953–954;

"Employers' Liability in Pennsylvania," *Charities and the Commons,* 19 (7 March 1908): 1671–1672;

"Year's Work Accidents and Their Cost," *Charities and the Commons,* 21 (6 March 1909): 1143–1174;

"Now I Dare to Admit It," *Survey,* 35 (9 October 1915): 46–47.

Lawyer, journalist, social reformer, socialist, suffragist, free-speech advocate, birth-control crusader, and peace-movement pioneer, Crystal Eastman was the epitome of the "new woman" who captured so much attention during the Gilded Age and Progressive Era. One of the nation's most respected authorities on workplace

Crystal Eastman (Library of Congress)

accidents, employers' liability, and workers' compensation, Eastman was instrumental in writing New York State's first version of a workers' compensation program. The list of organizations and institutions that she helped found includes the Congressional Union for Woman Suffrage, the National Woman's Party, the National Women's Peace Party, the Women's International League for Peace and Freedom, the American Association for Labor Legislation, the American Union Against Militarism, the Civil Liberties Bureau, and the American Civil Liberties Union. She also drafted the first Equal Rights Amendment and crusaded for access to birth control, a "mother's endowment" to supply economic support for needy mothers and children, and equality between men and women in personal relationships. Along with her brother Max, Eastman edited the *Liberator* (successor to the *Masses*), a monthly magazine dedicated to keeping socialists around the world informed about each other's activities.

Catherine Crystal Eastman was born in Glenora, New York, on 25 June 1881, the only daughter of Samuel Elijah Eastman, a Congregationalist minister, and Annis (Bertha) Ford Eastman. Crystal Eastman had three brothers, two older and one younger: Morgan, Anstice (Ford), and Max. Crystal's lifelong collaborator, Max, was born in 1883 in Canandaigua, New York. The next year Crystal and the oldest child, Morgan, came down with scarlet fever. Morgan died, sending Bertha Eastman into a prolonged depression. In 1886 Samuel Eastman began to have health problems that necessitated a temporary break from work. Bertha Eastman first took a job teaching, but eventually she began to preach. By 1889 she was the first woman in the state of New York to be ordained in her denomination, although she had only a two-year degree from Oberlin and no formal theological training. Bertha Eastman was highly regarded as a progressive thinker and eloquent speaker. In 1893 she attended the World's Congress of Representative Women in Chicago and delivered a paper on "The Home and Its Foundations."

In 1894, after years of moving frequently, the family moved to Elmira, New York, when Samuel and Bertha Eastman became associate pastors of the Park Church, a nationally renowned center for progressive, nondenominational Christianity headed by Thomas Beecher. A social center as well as a place of worship, Park Church covered an entire city block and included such amenities as a free library, pool and billiard tables, a dance hall, and a playroom for children. Samuel Langhorne Clemens and his wife attended Park Church, and Bertha Eastman wrote the funeral oration for him that her husband delivered. The Eastmans became joint pastors after Beecher's death.

The Eastman household included many foster brothers and sisters, whom Bertha insisted on taking in over the years, including the twin sons of her deceased sister; it also included Bertha's best friend, Mary Landen, and Bertha's mother, Catherine Stehley, who had separated from Bertha's father. Thanks to their immediate and extended families, and the larger church community presided over by their parents, the Eastman children grew up in an environment that fostered intellectual curiosity, self-confidence, personal moral responsibility, and a knack for balancing work and play. Chores were distributed among the various children on a gender-neutral basis, with girls expected to hoe the garden and clean the stable. Eastman later wrote that her grounding in feminism was due primarily to her mother's influence, but she also credited her father for encouraging and supporting her ideas. On one occasion, when his daughter was twelve, Samuel Eastman defended her right to wear short skirts while riding her pony around Elmira. After she and Max had gone to college, Samuel yielded to her sixteen-point brief in support of a petition written by Max and his "Apostles of Nakedness" to allow girls to remove their stockings while swimming.

Also beginning in the summer of 1894, Crystal Eastman's thirteenth year, the extended family began to spend the warmer months in cabins on various lakes in the surrounding area, where they spent time planting, picking, canning, and marketing fruits and vegetables. They attended Sunday-evening concerts and a semi-weekly "Supposium" at which everyone could present an idea and respond to questions and criticisms. When she was fifteen, Eastman delivered a paper titled "Women" at a summer symposium organized by her mother in which she proclaimed that the only formula for happiness was to cultivate an absorbing interest in life that did not depend upon any particular person. "No woman who allows husband and children to absorb her whole time and interest," the young Eastman insisted, "is safe against disaster" (Cook, *Crystal Eastman on Women and Revolution*). In 1898 the Eastmans bought a farm on Seneca Lake.

Crystal Eastman entered Vassar College in the fall of 1899. After graduating in 1903, she taught briefly at the Elmira Free Academy (to help Max raise the money for his senior year's tuition at Williams College) before moving to New York City. Their mother began attending Harvard Summer School that year. Crystal Eastman did some graduate work in political economy at Columbia University and then moved to New York University School of Law, where she finished second in her class in 1907, the same year that her mother convinced the Park Church membership to change denominations from Congregational to Unitarian. In New York City Eastman worked at night managing a recreation center and often ate at the Settlement House. She became friends with other feminists, including two lawyers, Ida Rauh and Jessie Ashley, and the well-known suffrage activist Inez Milholland. She shared rooms with a social worker, Madeleine Doty, who later married Roger Baldwin. Rauh occasionally lived with them for short periods.

During these years away from home, Eastman remained intensely involved in the life of her family. Her brother Max later remembered her from this period as "my dearest friend" and regretted that despite his great admiration for her "I did not keep her as close as possible. I did not keep anyone near" *(Enjoyment of Living)*. She wrote letters scolding him for not seeking summer work when their parents needed new clothes, and she introduced him to her New York City friends and pushed him to become involved in social reform. In the summer months at home she watched over his activities with an attentiveness equal to their mother's, praising his studiousness but mocking his verse writing. He credited his sister with getting him involved in political activism and keeping his interest focused on the social problem. History has remembered him as the political activist, but his memoirs make it clear that she was the radical, whereas he was a literary man.

Shortly after Crystal Eastman graduated from Law School and was admitted to the bar, Paul Underwood Kellogg, director of the prestigious Pittsburgh Survey project, engaged her as an investigator. The survey was sponsored by the social-work journal Kellogg edited, *Charities and the Commons* (which in 1909 became the *Survey*), funded by the Russell Sage Foundation. In 1908 and 1909 Eastman conducted the first in-depth sociological investigation of industrial accidents ever undertaken. When Max Eastman came to Columbia to do graduate work in philosophy in 1908, the Eastmans took the first of a series of apartments together in or near Greenwich Village. Their brother Ford was interning at City Hospital. Max recalled that while Crystal was away doing research, he hardly left Columbia, but that when she returned to town, he found himself swept up in activity.

In 1910 Crystal Eastman published her findings in *Work Accidents and the Law,* the second of the six volumes that eventually resulted from the survey. The federal government had been collecting labor statistics for just over twenty years at that time, so her study was especially important. Combining skills learned in graduate and law schools, Eastman produced a tightly organized, cogently argued, meticulously documented study that served as a model for the research monograph that became one of the hallmarks of Progressive Era reform. Using as source material the coroner and hospital reports of a year's industrial fatalities and of three months' industrial injuries in Allegheny County, Pennsylvania, supplemented with interviews of victims, survivors, relatives, medical personnel, and witnesses, she developed over one thousand case studies that offered a judicious blend of scientific objectivity and humanitarian sensitivity. For each case, Eastman and her staff compiled a dossier that included the circumstances of the accident, the nature and extent of the injury, the family responsibilities of the killed or injured worker, how large his income, what provision he had made for misfortune, how great the financial loss suffered by his family, what share of the loss was shouldered by his employer and by what means it was adjusted, and what was the effect of the accident on the economic life of his family. While acknowledging that her methodology would not yield "a complete view of the industrial accident situation," she asserted that this "small cross-section from the very heart and center of the problem" would render "a practical exposition of the problem as it exists today in American industrial communities."

The book itself divides into three major sections: the causes of work accidents by industry; the economic cost of work-accidents; and the history of attempts to enact and enforce employers' liability acts. The first state law addressing workmen's compensation had been passed in Baltimore in 1902, and no federal labor laws of any kind yet existed. Eastman begins with the legal basis of her study: "it is a fundamental doctrine of the civil law," she states, "that if a loss is to be suffered he who is at fault shall suffer it." Her claims build always on specific cases, and she does not seek immoderate outcomes. The book is a progressive classic, supporting "interference" based on complex considerations. To buttress her argument, Eastman and her staff included an impressive array of charts, tables, diagrams, and illustrations; and the volume is liberally illustrated with photographs, many taken by Lewis Hine for the survey, others from the companies' public-relations files.

In 1909 New York Governor Charles Evans Hughes appointed Eastman as the first woman member of the State Commission on Employer's Liability and Causes of Industrial Accidents. In that capacity, she eventually drafted one of the first statewide workers' compensation laws in the country. The writer's entire family began to be involved in feminist issues in the years that she produced this book. In 1909 Crystal Eastman had urged Max to form a Men's League for Women's Suffrage. In 1910 she famously invited an Australian Broadway star (a tank diver) to come to Greenwich Village to speak on feminism. In January 1910 she presented an early version of *Employers' Liability* at the annual meeting of the New York Bar Association in Rochester.

Bertha Eastman, plagued by religious doubts after her studies at Harvard, had begun undergoing Freudian therapy and had intensified her activity in the suffrage movement. She determined to leave Park Church altogether in the summer of 1910, and in October she suffered a fatal cerebral hemorrhage. Late in 1910 Crystal Eastman became engaged to Milwaukee-based insurance agent Wallace "Bennie" Benedict. The rest of the family was not altogether pleased with Crystal's decision, and when she became ill and moved back home briefly in February 1911 before her marriage, her brother Max commented in a letter that perhaps her decision had brought on the illness. She wrote back that after they both had "experimented," they might live together again in a few years. Shortly after she married "Bennie" in May 1911, Max married Ida Rauh, her sometime law-school roommate.

In Milwaukee Crystal Eastman undertook the task of heading the campaign for the passage of a state-wide referendum in favor of woman suffrage. Along with several younger members of the Wisconsin Political Equality League, Eastman openly courted the support of the state's ethnic working-class voters, especially adherents of the Milwaukee Federation of Trade Unions, the Wisconsin Federation of Labor, and the Social Democratic Party (SDP), which had gained effective control of Milwaukee's city and county governments in the 1910 elections. As Prohibition and woman suffrage had generally won all the same states, Eastman and her cohorts found that they had to work diligently to undermine the notion that woman suffrage would inevitably lead to the prohibition of alcoholic beverages. This point was especially important because the ethnic populations that predominated in Milwaukee had a record of opposing Prohibition statutes. The suffrage activists distributed campaign flyers in German, Polish, Czech-Slovak, Yiddish, Italian, Norwegian, and Swedish, and, along with the Americanization Committee of the Wisconsin Woman Suffrage Association and the Daughters of the American Revolution, drew up a plan for the Americanization of aliens that involved classes, books, movies, slide shows, patriotic meetings, and even visits to individual families.

These energetic and innovative methods notwithstanding, the 1912 Wisconsin woman suffrage referendum received only 27 percent of the votes cast statewide and about one-third of those tallied in Milwaukee. In her postelection report to the Political Equality League titled "Why We Lost in Wisconsin," Eastman lamented that the suffragists had once again overestimated what the Socialist vote would accomplish. While she believed that most SDP members voted for equal suffrage, Eastman declared that most of the party's sympathizers did not. She also blamed the pervasive influence of the German-American Alliance and the Brewer's Association, as well as the failure of the suffragists to attract the large Scandinavian vote. Privately, she and fellow Socialists Meta Berger and Maud McCreery worried that the popular identification of socialism and suffrage had done serious damage to the latter cause. Although Eastman did not participate in the eventual success of woman suffrage in Wisconsin in 1919, Wisconsin Woman Suffrage Association president Theodora Youmans later credited her with devising what became a winning strategy.

Eastman's brother Max Eastman (Library of Congress)

A social group emerged about 1912 that came to have great significance in Eastman's life. Heterodoxy began with about twenty members, including Henrietta Rodman, Marie Jenney Howe, and Mary Heaton Vorse, as a New York City luncheon club whose meetings allowed members to discuss issues public and personal without reserve. The club included women from a wide variety of occupations and political perspectives, sharing only an interest in the advancement of women, a fervent belief in the power of free speech, and a respect for each other's privacy—the latter so absolute that knowledge of the club was nearly lost to history. Its members almost without exception became famous, however, and since the 1970s feminist scholars have been able to reconstruct some of its history. Eastman eventually became a member of this club, as she spent more and more time away from her husband until at last she moved back to New York and into a communal living situation that included her brother and some of their mutual friends.

This moment in history marked a high point in radical activities in the United States. Max Eastman became the editor of the *Masses* in 1912, and under his direction the magazine became a cultural phenomenon, attracting contributions from top-notch visual artists and almost every radical writer of note. Despite the Wisconsin suffrage defeat, Crystal Eastman had been able to prove her mettle as an energetic and innovative political campaigner to go along with her already excellent reputation as a meticulous researcher, writer, and speaker. During this period Eastman published articles in such prestigious reform journals as *The Nation, The New Republic, The Outlook,* and *The Survey.* When President Woodrow Wilson created the United States Commission on Industrial Relations in 1913, under the direction of fiery labor lawyer Frank P. Walsh, Eastman was appointed as an investigating attorney. In an era when very few women served as government appointees, she received some notice in the press for this role.

Later that same year she served as a delegate to the Seventh Congress of the International Woman Suffrage Alliance in Budapest, where she formed lasting relationships with Aletta Jacobs (who later started the first birth-control clinic in Holland), Emmeline Pethick-Lawrence of England, and Hungary's Rosika Schwimmer. Back in the United States, Eastman joined with Alice Paul and Lucy Burns to form the Congressional Union for Woman Suffrage, an organization of younger and more-cosmopolitan suffragists than the average member of North American Woman Suffrage Alliance who attempted to introduce the more militant methods used by the Women's Social and Political Union in Great Britain. These tactics included mass demonstrations and daily picketing of the White House, an activity that led to the arrest of nearly 500 suffragists for "loitering" and 168 others for "obstructing traffic" over the next few years.

During the Progressive era, women began to mobilize and involve themselves in civic affairs to an unprecedented degree. The General Federation of Women's Clubs had more than 800,000 dues-paying members by 1914, and other groups such as the Women's Christian Temperance Union and the Women's Relief Corps claimed between 150,000 and 350,000 members each. When the Great War began in August 1914, women from suffragist and other social-reform groups began to take account of how many members supported peace. At the end of August 1914, 1,500 women participated in a peace march down Fifth Avenue in New York. In 1914 Eastman joined Jane Addams, Lillian Wald, Paul Kellogg, and publisher (of *The Nation*) Oswald Garrison Villard in establishing the American Union Against Militarism (AUAM) to oppose American entry into the war. AUAM also campaigned against conscription, the arms trade, and imperialism in Latin America. Wald became the president; Eastman was chief counsel and secretary for the organization.

By January 1915, Eastman joined with Addams, Wald, and Carrie Chapman Catt in urging members of twenty-six women's groups to convene and form a women's peace organization. More than three thousand women, including Addams, Wald, Mary McDowell, Florence Kelley, Alice Hamilton, Anna Howard Shaw, Belle La Follette, Fanny Garrison Villard, Emily Balch, Jeanette Rankin, Edith and Grace Abbott, Vorse, Catt, Freda Kirchwey, and Sophonisba Breckenridge, met in the ballroom of the New Willard Hotel in Washington, D.C., to form the Women's Peace Party (WPP). The organization emerged as one of the most outspoken opponents of the war, sending representatives to the April 1915 Peace Congress at the Hague. Many members of Heterodoxy joined; the Great War was the single greatest challenge to the club's ability to honor the principle for which it was named. A few women, including Rheta Childe Dorr and Charlotte Perkins Gilman, left the club because they supported the war. As a rule club members were so adamantly against the war that, for example, Elsie Clews Parsons would not allow anyone into her home wearing a uniform, including her husband. Until 1919 Eastman served as president of the more radical New York branch of the WPP; Addams served as national president. Over time a division between the outspokenly radical local group and the larger organization became pronounced. In 1921 the party was reconstituted as the Women's International League for Peace and Freedom, which is now the nation's oldest surviving women's peace organization.

Eastman finally filed for divorce from Benedict in 1915. To emphasize her conviction that the reception of alimony was an admission of women's financial dependency upon men, she refused to accept any. That same year Eastman published *The Effect of Industrial Fatalities Upon the Home,* which dealt with the terrible financial impact that the death of husbands as breadwinners had upon their wives and children. Over the next few years, Eastman collaborated with Emma Goldman in drives to legalize birth-control methods and prostitution and to protect free speech during wartime.

1916 proved an eventful and trying year for Eastman, who found herself in the midst of several developing fracture lines among radical activists. That year Eastman and the AUAM joined with other intellectuals in opposing U.S. intervention in Mexico and enjoyed a measure of success. Eastman organized a private mediation session at which AFL officials and the representatives of sixty Mexican labor unions met to discuss how best to avoid war and protect the gains of the recent Mexican Revolution, and afterward she convened a press conference in Washington, D.C., that prompted President Wilson to turn the matter over to a Joint High Commission. Eastman commented then that "people acting directly—not through their governments or diplomats or armies—stopped that war, and can stop all wars if enough of them will act together and act quickly"

("Suggestions to the AUAM for 1916–1917"). In the same year, however, her old friend and colleague, former New York Governor Charles Evans Hughes, ran against Wilson on a pro-war, pro-woman suffrage ticket, and many suffragette friends of Eastman decided to work for his campaign. As a leader of AUAM, Eastman wound up supporting Wilson, who said he supported peace but opposed woman suffrage. Her dear friend from law school, Inez Milholland, died suddenly after a lecture in which she had implicitly rebuked Eastman for her choice. The two had been close over the years because Milholland had married Eugen Boissevain, Max Eastman's sometime roommate and a constant feature of the Eastman communal living arrangements over the next few years. Crystal Eastman arranged a large memorial service for Milholland in New York.

Also in 1916, she married Walter Fuller, a British poet and fellow antiwar activist, with whom she had been living for some time. Fuller had been a contributor to the New York WPP's controversial "War Against War" exhibit, and he later became corresponding secretary for the British National Council of Civil Liberties. While Eastman was pregnant with Jeffrey, their first child (born 19 March 1917), she enlisted her friend Roger Baldwin, a social worker from St. Louis, to take on some of her responsibilities in the AUAM. More conflicts with her Women's Peace Party colleagues developed when Eastman's New York branch began in January 1917 to issue a newsletter called *Four Lights*. Although Eastman did not edit the newsletter, her cohorts in the larger organization, particularly Addams and Wald, attributed its polarizing and uncompromising tone and content to her, because she headed the branch that published it. The more-conservative leaders felt *Four Lights* stepped beyond its mandate as a party organ because it decried the St. Louis race riots and expressed support for the March 1917 Russian Revolution. Alan Dawley has compared the wartime schism in feminist ranks, represented by Anna Howard Shaw and Crystal Eastman, to the divide between the ideologies and groups represented in the labor movement by Samuel Gompers and Eugene Debs (*Struggles for Justice: Social Responsibility and the Liberal State,* 1991). Finally, an outspoken advocate of civil liberties and of the rights of dissenters and conscientious objectors during wartime, Eastman joined Baldwin and Norman Thomas to establish the National Civil Liberties Bureau in April 1917, the month in which the United States entered World War I; some of her AUAM colleagues, including Addams, Kellogg, Villard, and Wald, began to distance themselves from her despite the broader reconciliations that occurred following Wilson's breach of trust with his pacifist supporters. Especially once war had been declared, they preferred discreet meetings with congressional committees and the president to the sort of public confrontation that Eastman had come to represent.

While the war continued, Eastman, like most antiwar progressives, spent much of her time attacking American involvement, on the one hand, and defending her right to do so, on the other, particularly in light of the Espionage and Sedition Acts passed by Congress to suppress dissent. In these years Eastman also numbered among the founders of the People's Council of America for Peace and Democracy, begun in 1917, a loosely defined alliance of pacifists that included labor, the Left, and farmers. After the federal Post Office Department succeeded in killing off the *Masses* by refusing it necessary mailing privileges beginning in August 1917, Crystal Eastman and her brother Max raised $30,000 and invested a significant percentage of their own incomes to operate the *Liberator,* a magazine of radical literary and political ideas. The magazine published information about socialist movements throughout the world and was the first to break the news that the Allies had invaded Russia in 1918.

As managing editor Crystal Eastman recruited Claude McKay to write for the *Liberator,* and there he first published his well-known poem written in response to the post–World War I race riots, "If We Must Die." Many white women on the Left found McKay difficult; however, by his own account he formed an instant friendship with Eastman, whom he remembered as "embodying in her personality that daring freedom of thought and action–all that was fundamentally fine, noble and genuine in American democracy" (*A Long Way from Home*). Only she, Elsa von Freytag Loringhoven, and Sylvia Pankhurst won his approval. Later McKay became an associate editor of the magazine.

Eastman helped organize the first Feminist Congress in the United States in March 1919. Occasionally she joined Max on his pro-Russian lecture tour, and in Cleveland Labor Temple, menaced by vigilantes, they had to hide in a storage closet for two hours. She visited Hungary to meet the leaders of Bela Kun's nominally socialist revolution in the summer of that year, and she covered the story for the *Liberator.* She returned with pneumonia, terribly ill, as she reported in her articles, with a heightened awareness of American prosperity and wastefulness compared to the deprivations of Eastern Europe. All of these activities gained Eastman and her colleagues the enmity of superpatriotic groups and of Attorney General A. Mitchell Palmer and his special assistant J. Edgar Hoover, who ruthlessly enforced the Espionage and Sedition laws–first against antiwar activists and then against suspected communists, anarchists, and other radicals. At the same time, the Left itself continued to splinter.

Although Eastman escaped prosecution or arrest, the Bureau of Investigation and the Justice Department monitored her activities and mail. Her reputation was severely damaged, and she was blacklisted by several organizations that had previously hailed her as a champion of social justice. Refusing to be intimidated, Eastman continued to work with Addams, Kelley, Wald, Kellogg, Villard, and others in the organization that later became the American Civil Liberties Union, which dedicated itself to defending First Amendment rights, guaranteeing equal protection and due process of the law, and asserting the right of privacy. She continued to write for Villard's *The Nation* and for *Equal Rights,* a journal established by Alice Paul.

In 1921 Eastman, Paul, and other leaders of the National Woman's Party drafted an Equal Rights Amendment to the United States Constitution, which provided that "Equality of Rights under the law shall not be denied or abridged by the United States or any state on account of sex." In embracing this position, they and other advanced feminists parted company with the mainstream social feminist movement that feared that its adoption would invalidate the panoply of women's protective legislation that had been enacted in most states during the Progressive Era. In March 1921 Eastman resigned from the Civil Liberties Bureau, exhausted and again in bad health.

In 1922, following the premature birth of her daughter Annis Fuller, Eastman finally slowed down and began to be more careful of her health. She was already suffering high blood pressure, a bad heart, and nephritis, a frequently misdiagnosed disease of the kidneys. Fuller returned to England to look for better work when Annis was three months old. Between the medical expenses and the loss of their salaries–Eastman had made $90 per week as joint editor of the *Liberator,* and Fuller had edited *The Freeman* for about $50 per week–the couple faced severe financial difficulties. Eastman secured work for her husband at the *Survey Graphic,* but he wanted to remain in England, so she agreed to go, thinking that a quieter life might be good for her and that she could write a book on women. He began a literary agency with Charles Hallinan. Eastman moved to England in 1923. By coincidence she was leaving at the same time that McKay was departing for Russia. Unable to meet him for dinner as promised, she left a note on his door that he carried with him for much of the rest of his life and later gave to her children. She had previously provided him with letters of introduction to leftists in England and Russia.

In 1923 the National Women's Party persuaded a Republican congressman and senator to introduce the "Lucretia Mott Amendment"–an equal rights amendment–in congress, a ritual that was repeated every session of congress until 1972 when it was finally adopted by that body and submitted to the states for ratification. Typically, Eastman proclaimed "This is a fight worth fighting even if it takes ten years." The summer of 1924 she spent in the United States as the secretary of a committee of the National Woman's Party helping to coordinate the Women for Congress Campaign, unaware that her career as she originally conceived it was for all intents and purposes over.

Eastman found herself frantically searching for work. She had some income from renting her houses in Croton and Greenwich Village, but she could not bear not to work. For the next four years she and her two small children commuted regularly between the two countries and France as she searched for employment and an occasional respite from their embattled lives. Instead of writing for broadly defined political reform groups or retreating to write the book that she planned, Eastman became a freelance features writer, contributing to the *Daily Herald* and *Time and Tide,* a feminist journal. *Equal Rights* continued to publish her work in the United States. In England she established close friendships with Lady Rhondda, Lady Astor, and Rebecca West, and took part in the activities of two militant feminist groups, the Six Point Group and the Open Door Council.

Eastman's essential sense of decency, intellectual honesty, and optimism probably prevented her from realizing the extent to which her inability to find work in the United States was due to an organized blacklisting campaign. Even her old mentor Paul Kellogg was unable to help, for reasons that he stated sensitively but firmly. There were, he wrote in response to her request for employment "practical difficulties in making a fresh start that it does no good to minimize." The United States, he insisted, "is not as tolerant as England; we still have a lot of beating up of bugaboos, and you will get a touch of that in any public work . . . and your various espousals–such as the Woman's Party–would not help in some of the few quarters where industrial research is still carried on, etc" *(Crystal Eastman on Women and Revolution).*

When Max Eastman began to make his way home after an extended visit to the Soviet Union, he stopped in London to visit, and later another of Eastman's extended bohemian families vacationed together in the south of France. After five years of what was essentially a commuter marriage, Crystal Eastman decided to make the best of a bad situation by writing about it–for pay. In an article titled "Marriage Under Two Roofs," which she penned for *Cosmopolitan* magazine, Eastman presented a somewhat fictionalized and firmly cheerful account of the difficulties of trying to keep marriage, family, and career together. She made an original proposal there that heterosexual couples might find their physical relationships more rewarding if they maintained separate residences. Despite all the strain of instability, she reflected, "For the usual modern type, the complex, sensitive, highly organized city dweller, man or woman, marriage can become such a constant invasion of his very self that it amounts sometimes to torture" (*Crystal Eastman on Women and Revolution*).

The cheerful tone belied her determination to return to the United States even if it meant permanent separation from her husband. She convinced him to join her after she found permanent work. Shortly before Fuller died of a stroke in September 1927, Eastman returned to the United States. *The Nation* had offered her a temporary job of organizing its tenth-anniversary celebration, and Kellogg had at last agreed to help her find work in the health-insurance field; she had an idea that she might work on child welfare, a subject in which the federal government was beginning to show interest. She was in very poor health, however, and spent months at Battle Creek, Michigan, undergoing treatment before dying of a brain hemorrhage on 8 July 1928 at her brother Ford's home in Erie, Pennsylvania. Her friends from the AUAM and WPP, Agnes Brown Leach and Henry Goddard Leach, adopted her children.

In an obituary for Eastman in *The Nation* on 8 August 1928, Freda Kirchwey proclaimed that she

> brushed against many other lives, and wherever she moved she carried with her the breath of courage and a contagious belief in the coming triumph of freedom and decent human relations. These were her religion. Her strength, her beauty, her vitality and enthusiasm, her rich and compelling personality—these she threw with reckless vigor into every cause that promised a finer life to the world (*Crystal Eastman on Women and Revolution*).

Another friend wrote, "She was for thousands a symbol of what the free woman might be." Known for her vigorous spirit and stirring oratory, Eastman strove to extend the scope of female power and achievement, in her words, beyond all "preconceived ideas of what was fit or proper or possible." Standing six feet tall and of statuesque build, she frequently intimidated her opponents by what African American poet McKay called "her magnificent presence" (*A Long Way from Home*). Child-welfare advocate John Spargo recalled that she "always seemed the most intelligent person in the room."

As the Great War and the cultural retractions that followed the war brought an end to the ideal that she embodied, however, Eastman found herself living in a world that no longer had a place for her. Despite her

Cover of the journal edited by Crystal and Max Eastman from 1917 to 1921 (University of California Libraries)

impressive achievements, Eastman virtually disappeared from the history books within a half century of her death in 1928. In the 1970s her works and her reputation at last began to be rehabilitated by feminist historians who came to recognize Eastman as one of the seminal thinkers of their discipline.

At first the scholarship struggled with issues of establishing Eastman's legitimacy as an object of study. Writing in 1972, cultural historian June Sochen presented Eastman as exemplary of a small group of Greenwich Village feminists whose goal was transformation of society, not simply more rights for women. As both idealists and practical reformers, Sochen argued, Eastman and a small band of Greenwich Village feminists "wove an elaborate picture of the new world at the same time they tried to chip away at the old one," and whose "breadth of vision . . . optimism, and enthusiasm never deserted them, even when their defeat was apparent" (*The New Woman*). In contrast to the broader suffrage movement that had narrowed its focus over time, their commitment to women's rights was coupled with a conviction that socialism was inevitable in America, that pacifism was a viable position for the United States during World War I, and that the Bolshevik Revolution was the first act in the eventual triumph of a worldwide utopian society. Despite her interest in these women as early radical feminists, Sochen relied upon an unexamined literary history handed down from primary sources from the era whose authors viewed Eastman and her friends as less significant than themselves—most notably Eastman's brother and his friends, who had profound ambivalence about this generation of women for reasons of their own, as Ellen Kay Trimberger later illustrated in her study of the memoirs of Max Eastman, Floyd Dell, and Hutchins Hapgood, "Feminism, Men, and Modern Love: Greenwich Village, 1900–1925." Margaret C. Jones has also documented in *Heretics & Hellraisers: Women Contributors to the* Masses, *1911–1917,* that historians of the *Masses* have in general created an inaccurate understanding of the contents of the magazine through their exclusive attention to the male personalities of that periodical.

Another limit of Sochen's work relates to the fact that much of 1970s feminist scholarship and activism emerged from the new Left, which had a predilection for constructing critical narratives about the "failures" of the old Left without taking into account such historical facts as the astonishing breadth and power of the post–World War I era Red scare. Without discussing these events at all, Sochen remarked that "by 1920 Village feminists found themselves without Village organizations to articulate their views" *(The New Woman).* She concluded that their views must have been too far removed from reality.

These factors led Sochen to overstate the case and make errors about the group's publication success and social impact. Sochen argued that Eastman "had no audience for her views; the unpublished nature of her writing attests to the fact that that the publishers did not consider her concerns worthy of print" *(Movers and Shakers,* pp. 48–49). Less than two decades later, however, historian Blanche Wiessen Cook provided evidence that "almost everything Crystal Eastman wrote was published" *(Crystal Eastman on Women and Revolution).*

After a decade of collecting Eastman's diverse publications in newspapers and magazines, Cook established that Eastman had "an enthusiastic and dedicated audience," wrote "boldly and well," and was "paid sufficiently well to live for several years largely on that income." In 1976 Cook included more than sixty articles written by Crystal Eastman in an anthology titled *Toward the Great Change: Crystal and Max Eastman on Feminism, Antimilitarism, and Revolution.* Two years later Cook gathered together more than one hundred additional articles for inclusion in an anthology titled *Crystal Eastman and Revolution* and arranged under several

rubrics: Feminist Theory and Progress, Creating Feminist Life-Styles; Woman's Place—Beyond the Home, a Feminist Conception of Criminal Law; Organizing an International Socialist Feminist Future; There Is No Protection without Equality; Against Imperial Warfare: The Woman's Peace Party and the American Union Against Militarism; and From Reform to Socialist Revolution.

Also in 1976 Judith Schwarz came across a scrapbook labeled "Heterodoxy to Marie" in the Inez Haynes Irwin Papers at the Schlesinger Library at Radcliffe College, and another line of investigation began to be opened in the study of Eastman and her contemporaries. Still, however, since the 1970s ended, few doctoral theses or scholarly studies have moved past the most basic biographical work on these women and their writing. Some legal scholars—most notably Sylvia Law and John Fabian Witt—have written about Eastman. New York University named a law school fellowship and a faculty chair in Eastman's honor. Crystal Eastman secured a place in the National Women's Hall of Fame in Seneca Falls, New York, in 2000.

References:

Blanche Wiesen Cook, "Biographer and Subject: A Critical Connection," in *Between Women: Biographers, Novelists, Critics, Teachers, and Artists Write about Their Own Work on Women,* edited by Carol Asher, Louise De Salvo, and Sara Ruddick (Boston: Beacon, 1984), pp. 397–411;

Cook, "Female Support Networks and Political Activism: Lillian Wald, Crystal Eastman, Emma Goldman," *Chrysalis,* 3 (1977): 43–61;

Max Eastman, *Enjoyment of Living* (New York & London: Harper, 1948);

Eastman, *Love and Revolution: My Journey Through an Epoch* (New York: Random House, 1964);

Sylvia A. Law, "Crystal Eastman: N.Y.U. Law Graduate," *New York University Law Review,* 66 (1991): 1963–1994;

Claude McKay, *A Long Way from Home* (New York: Furman, 1937);

Judith Schwarz, *Radical Feminists of Heterodoxy: Greenwich Village 1912–1940,* revised edition (Norwich, Vt.: New Victoria, 1986);

June Sochen, *Movers and Shakers: American Women Thinkers and Activists, 1900–1970* (New York: Quadrangle, 1973);

Sochen, *The New Woman: Feminism in Greenwich Village, 1910–1920* (New York: Quadrangle, 1972);

Christine Stansell, *American Moderns: Bohemian New York and the Creation of a New Century* (New York: Metropolitan Books/Holt, 2000).

Papers:

Crystal Eastman's papers reside at Harvard University. Her voluminous correspondence with her mother and her brother Max is housed at the Schlesinger Library at Radcliffe College. Other correspondence with her brother is in the Max Eastman Collection at the Lilly Library at Indiana University. Her correspondence with Paul Kellogg is in the *Survey* papers in the Social Welfare History Archives at the University of Minnesota. Many of her letters and other writings during World War I are in the papers of the Women's Peace Party, the People's Council, and Emily Green Balch, all of which are located in the Swarthmore College Peace Collection. Correspondence with Oswald Villard survives in the American Union Against Militarism Collection, also at Swarthmore. Letters relating to the National Woman's Party are in that organization's papers in the Library of Congress. Eastman's correspondence with Lillian Wald is in the Lillian Wald papers at the New York Public Library and Columbia University. Many items written by Crystal Eastman survive in the National Archives, in the records of the Federal Bureau of Investigation and the Justice Department.

Amitai Etzioni

(4 January 1929 –)

Jessica Handler

Art Institute of Atlanta

BOOKS: *A Diary of a Commando Soldier* [in Hebrew] (Jerusalem: Achiasof, 1952);

A Comparative Analysis of Complex Organizations (New York: Free Press of Glencoe, 1961); revised and enlarged edition (New York: Free Press, 1975);

The Hard Way to Peace: A New Strategy (New York: Collier, 1962);

Winning without War (Garden City, N.Y.: Doubleday, 1964);

Modern Organizations (Englewood Cliffs, N.J.: Prentice-Hall, 1964);

The Moon-Doggle: Domestic and International Implications of the Space Race (Garden City, N.Y.: Doubleday, 1964);

Political Unification: A Comparative Study of Leaders and Forces (New York: Holt, Rinehart & Winston, 1965);

Studies in Social Change (New York: Holt, Rinehart & Winston, 1966);

Alternative Ways to Democracy: The Example of Israel (Jerusalem: Hebrew University, 1966);

The Active Society: A Theory of Societal and Political Processes (London: Collier-Macmillan; New York: Free Press, 1968);

A Sociological Reader on Complex Organizations, compiled by Etzioni (New York: Holt, Rinehart & Winston, 1969);

Post-Secondary Education and the Disadvantaged: A Policy Study, by Carolyn O. Atkinson and Etzioni (New York: Center for Policy Research, 1969);

Comparative Perspectives: Theories and Methods, edited by Etzioni and Frederick L. DuBow (Boston: Little, Brown, 1970);

Demonstration Democracy (New York: Gordon & Breach, 1970);

Technological Shortcuts to Social Change, by Etzioni and Richard Remp (New York: Russell Sage Foundation, 1972);

Genetic Fix: New Opportunities and Dangers for You, Your Child and the Nation (New York: Macmillan, 1973); reprinted as *Genetic Fix: The Next Technological Revolution* (New York: Harper & Row, 1975);

Amitai Etzioni (from the dust jacket for The Moral Dimension: Toward a New Economics, *1988; Thomas Cooper Library, University of South Carolina)*

A Comparative Analysis of Complex Organizations: On Power, Involvement, and Their Correlates (New York: Free Press, 1975);

Social Problems (Englewood Cliffs, N.J.: Prentice-Hall, 1976);

The Organizational Structure of the Kibbutz (New York: Arno, 1980);

Perspectives on Productivity: A Global View, by Louis Harris & Associates and Etzioni (Stevens Point, Wis.: Sentry Insurance, 1981);

An Immodest Agenda: Rebuilding America before the Twenty-First Century (New York: New Press, 1983);

Capital Corruption: The New Attack on American Democracy (San Diego: Harcourt Brace Jovanovich, 1984);

Organizations in Society, by Etzioni and Edward Gross (Englewood Cliffs, N.J.: Prentice-Hall, 1985);

The Moral Dimension: Toward a New Economics (New York: Free Press; London: Collier-Macmillan, 1988);

A Responsive Society: Collected Essays on Guiding Deliberate Social Change (San Francisco: Jossey-Bass, 1991);

Public Policy in a New Key (New Brunswick: Transaction Publishers, 1993);

The Spirit of Community: Rights, Responsibilities, and the Communitarian Agenda (New York: Crown, 1993);

The New Golden Rule: Community and Morality in a Democratic Society (New York: Basic Books, 1996);

The Limits of Privacy (New York: Basic Books, 1999);

Martin Buber und die Kommunitarische Idee (Wien: Picus, 1999);

Essays in Socio-Economics (Berlin & New York: Springer, 1999);

The Third Way to a Good Society (London: Demos, 2000);

The Monochrome Society (Princeton, N.J.: Princeton University Press, 2001);

Next: The Road to the Good Society (New York: Basic Books, 2001);

My Brother's Keeper: A Memoir and a Message (Lanham, Md.: Rowman & Littlefield, 2003);

The Common Good (Cambridge, U.K. & Malden, Mass.: Polity, 2004);

From Empire to Community: A New Approach to International Relations (New York: Palgrave Macmillan, 2004);

How Patriotic Is the Patriot Act? Freedom Versus Security in the Age of Terrorism (New York: Routledge, 2004);

Security First: For a Muscular, Moral Foreign Policy (New York: Free Press, 2007).

OTHER: *Complex Organizations: A Sociological Reader,* edited by Etzioni (New York: Holt, Rinehart & Winston, 1961);

Social Change: Sources, Patterns and Consequences, edited by Etzioni and Eva Etzioni-Halevy (New York: Basic Books, 1964);

International Political Communities: an Anthology, edited by Etzioni (Garden City, N.Y.: Anchor, 1966);

Anatomies of America: Sociological Perspectives, edited by Etzioni and Philip Ehrensaft (New York: Macmillan, 1969);

Readings on Modern Organizations, compiled by Etzioni (Englewood Cliffs, N.J.: Prentice-Hall, 1969);

The Semi-Professions and Their Organization: Teachers, Nurses, Social Workers, edited by Etzioni (New York: Free Press, 1969);

Societal Guidance: A New Approach to Social Problems, edited by Sarajane Heidt and Etzioni (New York: Crowell, 1969);

Comparative Perspectives: Theories and Methods, edited by Etzioni and Frederick L. DuBow, with introduction by Etzioni (Boston: Little, Brown, 1970);

Macrosociology: Research and Theory, edited by James S. Coleman, Etzioni, and John Porter (Boston: Allyn & Bacon, 1970);

Social Profile: U.S.A. Today, introduced by Etzioni (New York: Van Nostrand Reinhold, 1970);

War and Its Prevention, edited by Etzioni and Martin Wenglinsky (New York: Harper & Row, 1970);

Policy Research, edited by Etzioni (Leiden: Brill, 1978);

Socio-Economics: Toward a New Synthesis, edited by Etzioni and Paul R. Lawrence (Armonk, N.Y.: M. E. Sharpe, 1991);

New Communitarian Thinking: Persons, Virtues, Institutions, and Communities, edited by Etzioni (Charlottesville: University Press of Virginia, 1995);

Rights and the Common Good: The Communitarian Perspective, compiled by Etzioni (New York: St. Martin's Press, 1995);

Repentance: A Comparative Perspective, edited by Etzioni and David E. Carney (Lanham, Md.: Rowman & Littlefield, 1997);

The Essential Communitarian Reader, edited by Etzioni (Lanham, Md.: Rowman & Littlefield, 1998);

Civic Repentance, edited by Etzioni (Lanham, Md.: Rowman & Littlefield, 1999);

Rights vs. Public Safety after 9/11: America in the Age of Terrorism, edited by Etzioni and Jason H. Marsh (Lanham, Md.: Rowman & Littlefield, 2003);

Voluntary Simplicity: Responding to Consumer Culture, edited by Daniel Doherty and Etzioni (Lanham, Md.: Rowman & Littlefield, 2003);

The Communitarian Reader: Beyond the Essentials, edited by Etzioni, Andrew Volmert, and Elanit Rothschild (Lanham, Md.: Rowman & Littlefield, 2004);

We Are What We Celebrate: Understanding Holidays and Rituals, edited by Etzioni and Jared Bloom (New York: New York University Press, 2004);

Public Intellectuals: An Endangered Species? edited by Etzioni and Alyssa Bowditch (Lanham, Md.: Rowman & Littlefield, 2006).

Amitai Etzioni (né Werner Falk) is a sociologist, university professor, and writer generally considered the founder of the Responsive Communitarian Movement, or communitarianism, a mid-twentieth-century Western social movement. This movement proposes that a careful balance of individual liberty and planned social order provides the foundation for a society that functions well, as Etzioni expressed in his book, *The New Golden Rule* (1996). The communitarian outlook derives from ideas that have sources in the Bible and in classical antiquity. Modern communitarians, however, devote themselves to rethinking the concept of mutual aid, and as such they divide into two approaches, philosophical (holding that community is prior to the individual and rejecting the individualistic assumptions classical of liberalism) and ideological (combining Left-leaning ideas on economics with relatively conservative social-policy positions). Identifying with the second approach, Etzioni traces his commitment to activism from the Jewish Underground before the founding of the State of Israel. His intellectual prominence began with the groundbreaking study of organizations he wrote after he began teaching in the sociology department at Columbia University in 1958. In the next decade he wrote studies of various aspects of the Cold War (such as the nuclear-arms race and the space program) and the world governance potential of such entities as the North Atlantic Treaty Organization (NATO) and the United Nations. Balancing academic and popular interests, Etzioni then began to explore how Americans could create an actively self-determining and ethically sound society, using analyses of public-policy topics such as genetic selection, child care, and HIV testing. His journal, *The Responsive Community,* and the conferences he organized to generate dialogue and policy on these issues have engaged politicians as well as academics. Etzioni was a visiting scholar at the Brookings Institute in 1978 and served afterward in the White House as an adviser to President Jimmy Carter. Richard Posner's 2001 book, *Public Intellectuals: A Study of Decline,* listed him among the top one hundred American intellectuals. Etzioni believes that a public intellectual's mission is to think in an unorthodox manner—specifically, to examine societal assumptions and relationships that are otherwise taken for granted.

Amitai Etzioni was born Werner Falk in Cologne, Germany, on 4 January 1929, to Willi Falk and Gertrude Hannauer Falk. In 1933 his father left Germany for London, ostensibly to attend a course, although his true intent was to escape the growing Nazi threat. Etzioni's mother soon followed, leaving their child in the care of grandparents and an aunt. In his autobiography, *My Brother's Keeper: A Memoir and a Message* (2003), Etzioni recalls spankings by his guardians, which generated his "lifelong rejection" of violence. A relative transported Falk out of Germany when he was five years old and reunited him with his parents in Athens, Greece. The Falk family lived in Greece for approximately one year, waiting to immigrate to what was then Palestine.

In the winter of 1937 they moved to Palestine, where they stayed with relatives in the city of Haifa.

There Falk was enrolled in primary school, although at the time he spoke no Hebrew. The principal of his school advised Falk's mother to teach her son to introduce himself by his Hebrew name, given at his *bris* and recorded in the family Bible left behind during the flight from the Nazis. The Hebrew name was forgotten, although they later recalled that it was "Abraham." In response to the principal's request, Falk chose "Amitai," reflecting the Hebrew word "Emet," meaning "truth." Amitai Falk and his parents moved from Haifa to the village of Herzliya Gimmel, and shortly afterward his parents began a cooperative farm, called Kfar Schmaryahu, with friends. The cooperative farm introduced Falk, then seven years old, to concepts that he later included in the communitarian movement. While the farm was not a developed form of communalism, as in a kibbutz, the question of free enterprise versus government did come into play.

In 1941 Falk's father joined the Jewish Brigade, a unit of volunteer soldiers from then Palestine within the British army. Gertrude Falk enrolled her son in a boarding school called Ben Shemen. His classmates included future Israeli prime minister Shimon Peres. Etzioni graduated from Ben Shemen in 1944 and recalls in his autobiography that he "arrived at Ben Shemen a little German boy" and left the school as a "young Israeli." He attended a technical high school, enrolling at the age of fifteen, but his attentions were focused on participating in the activities of the Jewish Underground against the British blockade of European refugees. Willi and Gertrude Falk, like many members of the Jewish community, opened their home to *olim*—refugees—and the young Falk served as a lookout, alerting neighbors to the presence of British police. This experience developed in him a taste for "action and service." Against his parents' wishes, he dropped out of high school and joined the Palmach, the commando unit of Hagana. Amitai Falk took the name Etzioni while serving in the Palmach. In 1946 Falk's unit learned that the British police had found a file listing their names and identification documents. Given a few hours to decide on a new name, Falk chose "Etzioni" (deriving from Hebrew words for tree and Israel) as his surname, the pen name under which he had written for the Ben Shemen student paper.

Etzioni served in the Hagana until 1949. Toward the end of his service he was encouraged by a commander to write a rebuttal to a newspaper's inaccurate account of a battle in which Etzioni's unit fought. This article, "How It Really Was," was included in his first book, *A Diary of a Commando Soldier* (1952). Etzioni later assessed this work as "sophomoric." Originally written in Hebrew, *A Diary of a Commando Soldier* has not been translated into English. Nevertheless, Etzioni found that he enjoyed being a public voice. After serving in the military he briefly worked for an Israeli newspaper, then attempted to enroll in Hebrew University in 1950. Without a high-school diploma, he was required to take external qualifying exams. At this time he learned that Martin Buber was seeking students to participate in an institute he had founded, the Israeli Institute for Adult Education. Buber's influence on Etzioni was profound: not only did the Institute provide a framework for him to take the entrance exams for Hebrew University, but also the academic and intellectual stimulation helped complete Etzioni's evolution from teenage soldier to thinker. Buber introduced Etzioni to a form of communitarian philosophy as well as to his "I and Thou" philosophy. Buber's classrooms also introduced Etzioni to the study of economics, which, with sociology, came to guide his views of communities and individual responsibilities.

Etzioni attended Hebrew University, majoring in sociology with a minor in economics. While there, Etzioni met and married a fellow student, Hava ("Eva") Horowitz in 1953. The following year he earned his bachelor's degree. He went on to complete his master's degree from Hebrew University in 1956, focusing on sociology and philosophy. In January 1957 he moved to Berkeley, California. Hava soon followed. Their son Ethan was born just before Etzioni earned his Ph.D. Etzioni finished his dissertation during the first half of 1958. During this time, his work as a research assistant to sociologist Seymour Martin Lipset helped pay his way through school. Through his association with Lipset, Etzioni moved into his first academic position, as an assistant professor of sociology at Columbia University, beginning with the 1958–1959 academic year.

Etzioni's first forays into the role of public intellectual, distilling arguments for the public, rather than the academic or scientific voice directed only at colleagues, began at Columbia as he expressed his personal and intellectual interest in the then-nascent peace movement. Writing a review of the movie *Hiroshima, Mon Amour* in 1959, Etzioni commented on the sociological aspects of the movie rather than the film technique or the acting; he discussed the implications of the interracial love affair in the plot and the social consequences of hatred, which in this case added up to nuclear destruction. Etzioni claims that his colleagues considered this work driven by "value judgments" rather than objective science. Because he believed that society requires public intellectuals "to think big thoughts, challenge assumptions society takes for granted . . . and suggest new directions," Etzioni made the choice to fulfill two roles: to contribute as an academic and to "do

Etzioni in 1947 as a commando for Hagana, the Jewish defense organization in Palestine before the creation of the State of Israel (from My Brother's Keeper: A Memoir and a Message, *2003; Thomas Cooper Library, University of South Carolina)*

peace," as well *(My Brother's Keeper)*. In October 1962 he called Martin Buber, who had written a translation of the Old Testament for Pope John XXIII, and persuaded him to ask the pope to issue a statement asking President John F. Kennedy and Soviet premier Nikita Krushchev both to back away from the Cuban missile crisis. In 1963 Etzioni joined the National Board of Americans for Democratic Action, an independent liberal lobbying group that supported the Civil Rights Movement.

Etzioni's books *The Hard Way to Peace* (1962) and *Winning without War* (1964) reflected his worldview and self-perception as activist rather than bystander. In an article written for the *Washington Post* (28 June 1964), Etzioni made public his opposition to the war in Vietnam, arguing that the conflict was primarily a war of national liberation, not a communist threat, and that the United States should stop supporting dictators. In *The Hard Way to Peace,* a discussion of disarmament, Etzioni first undertook his signature move of seeking "a third way" for an answer. This book makes the case for "gradualism" in dismantling the arms races between the

United States and the Soviet Union. *Winning without War* continues that discussion, proposing "cooling off" gestures and improved communication between the countries involved in the Cold War, acts that Etzioni believed would lead to mutually agreed-upon arms reductions *(My Brother's Keeper)*. In 1964 Etzioni published a book critical of another aspect of the Cold War–Project Apollo and the space race. This book, *The Moon-Doggle* (1964), argued that the United States should direct the financial and intellectual resources it had allocated for space exploration to improving America's inner cities and developing ways to combat poverty, pollution, and disease. Etzioni targeted *The Moon-Doggle* to fellow citizens rather than academics, again prompting academic criticism of his approach. A review of the book in *The Journal of Politics* criticized Etzioni's nonscientific use of social directives such as "should" and "ought" *(My Brother's Keeper)*.

In 1964 Amitai and Hava Etzioni divorced. She returned to Israel, as she had long wished to, with their two sons. Ethan and Oren Etzioni visited their father in the United States during the summers, and Etzioni traveled to Israel to spend Passovers with them. He later summed up the divorce as "one of my gravest personal failures" because it entailed long separations from his sons *(My Brother's Keeper)*. Later that year Etzioni married Minerva Morales, a visiting scholar from Mexico whom he had met at a 1964 Columbia University peace seminar for faculty and U.N. diplomats. She converted to Judaism and, once their son Michael was born, stopped teaching and became a full-time homemaker. From 1965 to 1966 Etzioni took a year's leave from Columbia University to accept a residency at the Center for Advanced Studies in Behavior Sciences near Stanford University in Palo Alto, California. During this period, working at what he called a "dream think tank," Etzioni drafted the nearly seven-hundred-page manuscript that became *The Active Society,* published in 1968. In the preface Etzioni states:

> The modern period ended with the radical transformation of the technologies of communication, knowledge, and energy that followed World War II. A central characteristic of the modern period has been continued increase in the efficacy of the technology of production which poses a growing challenge to the primacy of the values these means are supposed to serve. The post-modern period, the onset of which may be set at 1945, will witness either a greater threat to the status of these values by the surging technologies or a reassertion of their normative priority. Which alternative prevails will determine whether society is to be the servant or the master of the instruments it creates. The active society, one that is master of itself, is an option the post-modern period opens. An exploration of the con-

ditions under which this option might be exercised is the subject of this endeavor.

Etzioni has commented that he considers *The Active Society* his best academic work. The book continued the social and ethical discussion he undertook in his earlier work, examining the question of how technology and modern life free individuals to live anonymously, thereby leading to deterioration of the social fabric and increased isolation. He notes that "[The books] . . . concerned protecting our values from being overwhelmed by the means we forged to serve them," a conundrum Etzioni likens to that of the Sorcerer's Apprentice. The publication of *The Active Society* led to his promotion to full professor at Columbia.

In Etzioni's position as professor he proved disappointing to the leaders of student movements, who at first asked him to speak at building occupations and rallies, but stopped when he told them they were wrong to disrupt educational institutions and were discrediting their movement by supporting violence. In 1968 he also founded the Center for Policy Research, focused on bridging the divide between academic research and policy makers in government. He turned his sociologist's eye to the emerging science of bioengineering in 1969. He was already the father of three sons (Ethan and Oren with his first wife and Michael with second wife Minerva) and eventually had two more sons, David (born in 1969) and Benjamin (born in 1974). The Etzionis began to consult physicians to determine whether they could have a daughter. Medical advice proved unreliable, and Etzioni began to examine the "what if" quotient of his question. If gender selection were easily accomplished, he wondered whether parents (and societies) would seek to have more male children than female. If a society had more boys, he questioned whether it would become more aggressive, and whether a scarcity of females would increase their value. In "Sex Control, Science and Society," published in *Science* magazine in October 1969, Etzioni discussed his findings regarding the societal and moral effects of gender selection, specifically his conclusion that given the opportunity to select the gender of offspring, parents in the United States would generate a 7 percent "surplus" of boys over girls.

The article surpassed all his other publications in the amount of public attention it attracted. Etzioni became chair of the sociology department at Columbia University that year and held that position until 1971. In 1972 the FBI began an in-depth yet error-ridden investigation of him that he later discovered when he requested his file under the Freedom of Information Act. His name was added to the Nixon blacklist, which he reflected "included some of the people I respected most, such as Senator Gary Hart, Madeleine Albright, James Baldwin, Ben Bradlee, David Brinkley, Ralph Nader, Paul Samuelson, and Stansfield Turner" *(My Brother's Keeper)*. In 1972 he was invited to a medical conference in Paris, where he learned about appalling experiments routinely conducted on children. Following discussions among conference participants about the possible role of the World Health Organization and other international bodies in shaping policy on such matters, Etzioni expanded the essay into his 1973 book *Genetic Fix,* nominated for a National Book Award in 1974 and lauded by one critic as the "*Silent Spring* of biomedical research." Despite the book's success, the issues it raised did not elicit governmental action (in the form of a bioethics commission) until the mid 1980s. The 1970s still proved rewarding to Etzioni, changing him from a political outsider to an insider. Proud of his track record in anticipating developments in policy matters by more than a decade, Etzioni has frequently recommended that nations would benefit from keeping a kind of "scorecard" assessing how well their public intellectuals forecast the social future. An article on this subject led to an invitation to a 1976 dinner with some members of Congress, hosted by then-Congressman Al Gore Jr. Shortly afterward he met and befriended financier and social activist George Soros. Etzioni became a member of Soros's World Future Society and has given keynote addresses at its conferences as well as publishing in its journal, *The Futurist.*

In 1978, determined to improve his sense of history, Etzioni spent a year as a guest scholar at the Brookings Institution, which brought him to Washington and increased, with that proximity, his interest in public-policy issues. He wrote a paper examining the sources of the strength of the United States' economy in the years between 1820 and 1920, identifying seven requirements of a well-run economy: low-cost transportation of people and goods and an inspiring sense of moral purpose ranked foremost among them. He called the solution "reindustrialization." The following year, he was invited to join the Carter White House as a senior adviser, an experience that he found disappointing, as it exposed him to what he perceived as dishonesty, tactical maneuvering, and, above all, unnecessary inefficiency in the political arena. The position with the White House broadened his contacts with lower-level government officials, however, many of whom were interested in his ideas. It also provoked him into thinking about new subjects, such as the proper deployment of voluntary organizations, whose involvement in processing immigrants and refugees began to come under increasing government supervision in 1979. More comically, Etzioni reflected that a major lesson of his work with the Carter administration was "don't meet the

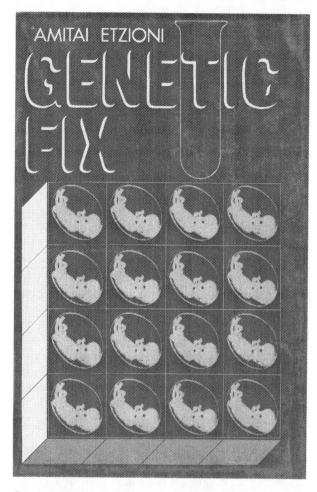

Dust jacket for Etzioni's 1973 book, exposing biogenetic experimentation on children (Richland County Public Library)

press," whose members rivaled the FBI for inaccuracy *(My Brother's Keeper)*. He noted how easy it was to violate laws and ethics while simply trying to do one's job.

In 1980 Etzioni left Columbia University to accept the position of University Professor at George Washington University, resulting in a change in lifestyle and location that suited his family and his professional life, as he had begun to spend increasing time serving on academic and public-policy boards. His family joined him in Washington, D.C. At the nation's capital he found himself in a position to notice political maneuvering that had escaped his notice in the past. For example, the U.S. Sentencing Commission sought his support for uniform sentencing guidelines, pointing to gross inequities in judgments concerning individuals' crimes and liberties. Once Congress passed legislation in favor of this change, the commission began to look into corporate crime and penalties. Finding that corporate entities with revenues in the billions of dollars hardly ever received fines of more than $10,000 no matter what their crimes, the commission brought public attention to the issue. Initially powerful corporate lobbies pressured the commission to backpedal; but even as penalties started to rise, Etzioni noted that punishments had seemingly no deterrent effect, because the corporations held a disproportionate financial sway in congressional districts and races. In 1983 Etzioni published *An Immodest Agenda,* building on the work he had begun in his Brookings paper to propose strategies for moral and economic renewal in the United States, and in 1984 his *Capital Corruption* addressed the power of corporate lobbies and campaign finance reform.

Minerva Etzioni was killed in an automobile accident on 20 December 1985. In his autobiography, Etzioni states that he "did not function well" for several years after her death, a period in which he lost initiative and was depressed. He was briefly cheered when in 1986 President Ronald Reagan suggested to Soviet leader Mikhail Gorbachev that they mutually coordinate a reversal of the arms race, and Gorbachev agreed. Still, as he felt that the Reagan administration issued empty talk about family values while it intentionally ran up a deficit to prevent Democratic successors from being able to fund social programs, his enthusiasm was limited. He sold their home in the suburbs in 1987. The two older sons were away at college, and Benjamin went to a boarding school.

Etzioni accepted an invitation to fill the Thomas Henry Carroll Ford Foundation Professorship at Harvard Business School, which he held until 1989. During his two years at Harvard, he expanded his interest in economics and sociology, or socioeconomics. In his 1988 book *The Moral Dimension: Toward a New Economics,* he attempted to reconcile a communitarian vision of social and moral good with the neoclassical model shared by most procapitalist economists. In 1989 he founded the International Society for the Advancement of Socioeconomics and served as its first president. For the next decade, communitarianism enjoyed a peak period of popularity.

In March 1990 Etzioni invited a group of scholars and policy makers to George Washington University for a bipartisan discussion of what he saw as a failing in America's social infrastructure: the emphasis on individual rights, he thought, outweighed a sense of social responsibility. Some of the issues he and his colleagues discussed at this and other early meetings in the development of responsive communitarianism included endorsement of strong, two-parent families, HIV testing and the responsibility to inform sexual partners of HIV-positive status, and the necessity of community service. Some of the first endorsers of the Responsive Communitarian Platform, issued in 1991, included Orlando Patterson, Albert Shanker, Newton Minow,

and John W. Gardner (President Lyndon Johnson's secretary of Health, Education, and Welfare). Two key individuals involved in drafting the platform were Mary Ann Glendon, an expert in family law and a close associate of Etzioni at the Communitarian Network, and William Galston, an adviser to presidential candidate Walter Mondale. The quarterly journal *The Responsive Community: Rights and Responsibilities* was launched in 1991 with Etzioni as editor. (He served in this position until 2004.) The journal, he writes, "tries to serve both the academic master and the public" (*My Brother's Keeper*). Also in 1991 Etzioni married Washington, D.C., physician Pat Kellogg.

After initiating the Communitarian Network in 1993, Etzioni accepted an invitation to discuss responsive communitarianism with members of the Senate as well as Bill Clinton, Bob Dole, and George H. W. Bush, and Helmut Kohl and Tony Blair, among other world leaders. Clinton informed the press that Etzioni was the person he admired most. The movement met with detractors, however. Feminist leader Betty Friedan, a personal friend of Etzioni for more than thirty years, called it an "effort to get women back in the kitchen" (*My Brother's Keeper*). Ira Glasser, director of the American Civil Liberties Union, described the communitarian philosophy as "mushy and simplistic" in an interview with *U.S. News and World Report*. Others suggested that communitarians naively celebrated "belonging" while irresponsibly disregarding the multitudes of historical examples casting excessive communal identity in an unfavorable light. To the last point, members of the movement have responded that modern communities differ significantly from old, fixed communities based on geography, class, and relatively homogenous ethnic and national identities. Modern communities, they say, are much more fluid; people in general have more mobility; and the members belong to more than one community at a time, thereby having an entirely new effect. Traditional societies that demanded such great sacrifices of individuals have become relatively rare, and few Western communitarians desire monolithic authoritarian structures. Rather, the movement encourages active participation in the life of communities and creation of consensus about the values shared by members.

From 1994 to 1995 Etzioni was the president of the American Sociological Association. Beginning in 1994, he organized annual White House conferences on character education, meetings where several hundred educators gathered. Keynote speakers since the first meeting have included Bill Clinton, Hillary Rodham Clinton, Gore, and Joseph Lieberman. In the last decade of the twentieth century, the Communitarian

Etzioni with President Jimmy Carter, whose administration he joined as a senior adviser in 1979 (from My Brother's Keeper: A Memoir and a Message, *2003; Thomas Cooper Library, University of South Carolina)*

movement used publications, broadcast media, and public speaking to bring public attention to the tension between individual rights and social responsibility in situations such as drug and alcohol testing for public-transit workers, sobriety checkpoints on public roads, voluntary disarmament of individual citizens, and stricter American divorce laws. Etzioni believes that some sacrifice of personal liberties may be necessary to counteract what he perceives as rampant selfishness and the resulting damage to the social fabric in the years following the 1960s. He presents the Responsive Communitarian Movement as a solution to the problems endemic to a Western society that he sees as increasingly self-involved and isolating.

Etzioni's 1999 book *The Limits of Privacy* advanced an argument that more-effective surveillance was becoming necessary to adapt to a changing political climate. Less than two months after the 11 September 2001 terrorist attacks on the Pentagon and the World Trade Center, the U.S. Congress passed H. R. 3162, known as the U.S.A. PATRIOT Act (Uniting and Strengthening America by Providing Appropriate Tools Required to Intercept and Obstruct Terrorism). The legislation, which in part reincorporated some earlier antiterrorism acts, was passed to "deter and punish terrorist acts in the United States and around the world, [and] to enhance law enforcement investigatory tools, and for other purposes." The PATRIOT Act, in protecting the rights and civil liberties of Americans, calls for a variety of law-enforcement efforts, including enhanced surveillance procedures and immigration provisions and protecting national borders. Like other public intellectuals, organizations, and private citizens, Etzioni joined in the post-9/11 discourse. In the years immediately following the tragedy, Etzioni extended the communitarian discussion to consider the role of the PATRIOT Act, identity cards, and Americans' approach to "recalibration" of their rights. In 2004 he brought the Responsive Communitarian perspective to the discussion of the U.S.A. PATRIOT Act in his book *How Patriotic Is the Patriot Act? Freedom Versus Security in the Age of Terrorism:*

Americans should share the commitment to find a middle course, a third way, between those who are committed to shore up our liberties but [are] blind to the needs of public safety, and those who in the name of security never met a right that they were not willing to curtail to give authorities a freer hand. . . . Charting the middle course . . . is both where the reasonable deliberations and moral considerations direct us.

Etzioni "takes it for granted" in *How Patriotic Is the Patriot Act?* that terrorist attacks will become both more common and more severe, and that in response Americans must protect their rights and freedoms. As in earlier work, he acknowledges that rights and freedoms have a "basic tension between them."

Etzioni identifies cellular telephones, the Internet, and data encryption as "liberalizing technologies" *(How Patriotic Is the Patriot Act?)*. These advances in socialization and communication have expanded individual choice and liberty, but have also outpaced governmental authorities' abilities to engage legally in activities such as intercepting communications. Courts and technologies, he says, have simply not kept up with each other. Etzioni claims that the PATRIOT Act makes a move toward leveling that playing field. In the 2004 book, Etzioni calls some policies in the U.S.A PATRIOT Act reasonable, while others, such as military tribunals, give him pause. As before, he writes for the nonacademic reader, taking a tone that encourages the common reader's ease. On the topic of surveillance of electronic mail—a policy that he believes falls under the "reasonable" heading—Etzioni writes that "law enforcement authorities have finally been allowed to catch up with the particular technological features of e-mail. Anybody who sees a civil rights violation here should have his or her vision checked." On the subject of national identity cards, Etzioni points out that drivers' licenses already serve this function. In the absence of a driver's license, he thinks, a green card will suffice. From the communitarian perspective he suggests that digitized, searchable birth and death records will serve the community's safety in a post-9/11 world, as will requiring department of motor vehicle employees to verify the authenticity of the social security number of each applicant for a driver's license. The Fourth Amendment to the U.S. Constitution, Etzioni writes, "refers to people's right not to be subjected to unreasonable search and seizure, hence recognizing a category of searches [fully] compatible with the Constitution; those that are reasonable." A reasonable search serves a compelling public interest, such as public health or safety.

Etzioni has been a critic of the Bush administration, however, and in June 2004 his article "Iraq's Sham Sovereignty" was featured on the website of thinking-peace.com along with articles by Greg Palast, Molly Ivins, Katha Pollitt, Gore, and Michael Moore. In this piece Etzioni argues that U.S. credibility will be worth no more than "a three-dinar bill" if President George Bush does not drop what he called elsewhere "hyper-optimistic" rhetoric about the role of the United States in Iraq, admit the hard facts about its presence in that country, particularly given the cost, and resume a more cooperative relationship with the United Nations *(From Empire to Community)*. The previous month Etzioni's book *From Empire to Community: A New Approach to International Relations* had been published. In it he made a return to more theoretical concerns about world government, reminiscent of his work from the 1960s, applying his "middle way" approach to global divisions.

Applying the lessons of Vietnam to contemporary conflicts, he noted that Western institutions, such as the International Monetary Fund and the World Bank, have frequently urged radical and speedy economic change upon Eastern societies, and, when such social engineering has failed, Western countries resorted to force, with very few good results. He observed that the West's idea of the good society tends to be fairly limited, focused on autonomy, creating wealth, and free markets. As beneficial as these goals might be, many people in the world center their lives around other sources of meaning, and the deep roots of a stable society usually grow from trust and shared values rather than competition and consumption, he noted. Instead, he argues, Westerners are the ones who need to adapt, because "we are all better off when we hold back, when we apply less power than we command, in order to win the collaboration of others and build institutions that will serve us in the longer run."

In 2008 Etzioni is director of the Institute for Communitarian Policy Studies at George Washington University in Washington, D.C. He sits on many editorial boards, including those of the *Journal of Peace Research, Administrative Science Review, Psychiatry and Social Science,* and *Social Policy.* He has written for reference works such as *Encyclopedia Hebraica* and *International Encyclopedia of Social Science,* and he contributes monthly columns to *Human Behavior* and *Psychology Today.* Etzioni has written more than twenty books and roughly five hundred articles for periodical publications and edited collections, many outside his academic field of specialty. A list of more than 360 of his articles is posted on the website of George Washington University on its Communitarian Network page (http://www.gwu.edu/~ccps/). He has won many honors, including a Guggenheim Fellowship, the John P. McGovern Award in Behavioral Sciences (2001), the Sociological Practice Association's Outstanding Contribution Award, and the Officer's Cross of the Order of Merit of the Federal Republic of Germany.

Critics have charged that Etzioni is egotistical, elitist, and too certain of his opinions. More often, Etzioni has confused and frustrated scholars and partisans because his ideas combine moral values that most U.S. citizens see as contradictory or residing in mutually exclusive categories. He considers community, located in a series of institutions and relationships somewhere between atomized individuals and formalized government structures, the appropriate site for sorting out and articulating collective ideas of the good. Conceiving of rights as emerging within a shifting set of relational frameworks rather than as absolute and unchanging, Etzioni also finds repulsive the idea of moral dictates handed down from a federal government. As such, his work offends both individualists and statists. He works with politicians from both of the major political parties, and as such has been both acclaimed and reviled as a representative of what some commentators have called "the radical middle." The Communitarian Network's platform concludes with the statement:

> We do not claim to have the answers to all that troubles America these days. However, we are heartened by the groundswell of support that our initial efforts have brought to the communitarian perspective. If more and more Americans come forward and join together to form active communities that seek to reinvigorate the moral and social order, we will be able to deal better with many of our communities' problems while reducing our reliance on governmental regulation, controls, and force.

References:

"Amitai Etzioni," Etzioni website <http://www.amitai-etzioni.org> (accessed 15 July 2006);

Gerrit Antonides, Wil Arts, and W. Fred van Raaij, eds., *The Consumption of Time and the Timing of Consumption: Toward a New Behavioral and Socio-Economics: Contributions in Honor of Amitai Etzioni: Proceedings of the International Colloquium, Amsterdam, 6–8 November 1990* (Amsterdam & New York: North-Holland, 1991);

"The Communitarian Network: For Individual Rights and Social Responsibility," The George Washington University, <http://www.gwu.edu/~ccps/platformtext.html> (accessed 8 August 2006);

David Sciulli, ed., *Macro Socio-Economics: From Theory to Activism* [Festschrift for Amitai Etzioni] (Armonk, N.Y. : M. E. Sharpe, 1996).

Papers:

The Amitai Etzioni Papers, 1918–1986 (bulk 1968–1984), are at the Library of Congress.

Benjamin Orange Flower

(19 October 1859 – 24 December 1918)

Karen Holleran

BOOKS AND PAMPHLETS: *Lessons Learned from Other Lives* (Boston: Spectator, 1889);

Fashion's Slaves (Boston: Arena, 1892);

Charles Darwin: His Life, and What the World Owes to Him, by Flower and T. B. Wakeman (Buffalo, N.Y.: H. L. Green, Office of the Freethinkers' Magazine, 1893);

First Ten Years of Queen Victoria's Reign (Trenton, N.J.: A. Brandt, 1893);

Civilization's Inferno; or, Studies in the Social Cellar (Boston: Arena, 1893);

The Menace of Medical Monopoly (Boston: National Constitutional Liberty League, 1894);

The New Time: A Plea for the Union of the Moral Forces for Practical Progress (Boston: Arena, 1894);

Gerald Massey: Poet, Prophet, and Mystic (New York: Arena, 1895);

The Century of Sir Thomas More (Boston: Arena, 1896);

Whittier: Prophet, Seer and Man (Boston: Arena, 1896);

Guiseppe Mazzini (New York: Alliance, 1903);

How England Averted a Revolution of Force: a Survey of the Social Agitation of the First Ten Years of Queen Victoria's Reign (Trenton, N.J.: Brandt, 1903);

Twenty-Five Years of Bribery and Corrupt Practises; or, The Railroads, the Law-makers, the People (New York: N.p., 1904);

The Vital Issue in the Present Battle for a Great American Art: An Editorial Sketch and a Conversation with Frank Edwin Elwell (Trenton, N.J.: Albert Brandt, 1905);

In Defense of Free Speech: Five Essays from The Arena (New York: Free Speech League, 1908);

Christian Science as a Religious Belief and a Therapeutic Agent (Boston: Twentieth Century, 1909);

Faith and Works of Christian Science (Boston: N.p., 1909);

The Bubonic Plague (New York: National League for Medical Freedom, 1910);

The Menace of a National Health Bureau (N.p., 1910);

The Compulsory Medical Inspection of School Children (Boston: Sherman, French, 1911);

Progressive Men, Women, and Movements of the Past Twenty-five Years (Boston: The New Arena, 1914);

From The Arena, *June 1891 (Mullins Library, University of Arkansas)*

The Patriot's Manual, dealing with the irrepressible conflict between two mutually exclusive world theories of government: a compendium of facts, historical data, reasons and present-day chronicles, showing why every friend of fundamental democracy must oppose politico-ecclesiastical Romanism in its un-American campaign to make America "dominantly Catholic" (Fort Scott, Kans.: Free Press Defense League, 1915);

Story of the Menace trial: A brief sketch of this historical case with Reports of the Masterly address by Hon. J. L. McNatt and Hon. J. I. Sheppard (Aurora, Mo.: United States Publishing, 1916);

Righting The People's Wrongs: A Lesson from History of Our Own Times (Cincinnati: The Standard, 1917).

OTHER: Will Allen Dromgoole, *The Heart of Old Hickory and Other Stories of Tennessee,* preface by Flower (Boston: Page, 1895);

James Gowdy Clark, *Poems and Songs,* introduction by Flower (Columbus, Ohio: Champlin Printing, 1898).

SELECTED PERIODICAL PUBLICATIONS–UNCOLLECTED: "The American Postmaster-General and the 'Kreutzer Sonata,'" *Arena,* 2 (October 1890): 540;

"Carroll D. Wright on Divorce," *Arena,* 5 (December 1891): 136;

"Uninvited Poverty," *Arena,* 5 (March 1892): 523;

"The Burning of Negroes in the South," *Arena,* 6 (April 1892): 630;

"Low Ethical Ideals in Our Higher Educational Centers," *Arena,* 7 (February 1893): 371;

"A Pilgrimage and a Vision, Social Contrasts in Boston," *Arena,* 7 (March 1893): 422;

"Pure Democracy versus Government Favoritism," *Arena,* 8 (July 1893): 260;

"Well-Springs of Present-Day Immorality," *Arena,* 8 (August 1893): 394;

"The New Education and the Public Schools," *Arena,* 8 (September 1893): 511;

"The Coming Religion," *Arena,* 8 (October 1893): 647–656;

"Jesus or Caesar," *Arena,* 9 (March 1894): 522;

"Joaquin Miller's Book *The Building of the City Beautiful,*" *Arena,* 9 (March 1894): 553;

"Labor Colonies, etc., for the Unemployed–Emergency Measures Which would have Maintained Self-Respecting Manhood," *Arena,* 9 (May 1894): 822;

"Social Ideals of Victor Hugo," *Arena,* 10 (June 1894): 104;

"Justice for Japan," *Arena,* 10 (July 1894): 225;

"Fostering the Savage in the Young," *Arena,* 10 (August 1894): 422;

"Plutocracy's Bastiles–Moneyed Militarism in the United States," *Arena,* 10 (October 1894): 601;

"In the Psychic Realm," *Arena,* 10 (October 1894): 684–691;

"Social Conditions as Feeders of Immorality," *Arena,* 11 (February 1895): 399;

"Prostitution within the Marriage Bond," *Arena,* 13 (June 1895): 59;

"Henry L. Call's Book *The Coming Revolution,*" *Arena,* 13 (June 1895): 138;

"The Right of the Child considered in the Light of Heredity and Prenatal Influence," *Arena,* 13 (July 1895): 243–262;

"Hazen S. Pingree's Successful Experiment for the Maintenance of Self-Respecting Manhood in Detroit," *Arena,* 15 (March 1896): 544;

"The Educational Value of Instructive and Artistic Entertainments which appeal to the Non-theatre-going Public," *Arena,* 15 (April 1896): 726–740;

"Some Eastern Conservative Authorities Who Are Championing the Cause of Free Silver," *Arena,* 16 (July 1896): 208;

"Sketch of Jay Cooke," *Arena,* 16 (July 1896): 211–218;

"Simon Pokagon, an Interesting Representative of a Vanishing Race," *Arena,* 16 (July 1896): 240–250;

"America's Wealth Creators in Current Cartoons," *Arena,* 16 (July 1896): 298–304;

"Gold Power, Transformation of the Republic into a Plutocracy," *Arena,* 16 (August 1896): 338;

"Peril of Encouraging the Persecuting Spirit," *Arena,* 16 (October 1896): 752–756;

"William Morris and Some of His Later Works," *Arena,* 17 (December 1896): 42–52;

"How to Increase National Wealth by the Employment of Paralysed Industry," *Arena,* 18 (August 1897): 200;

"The Latest Social Vision," *Arena,* 18 (October 1897): 517;

"Practical Measures for Promoting Manhood and Preventing Crime," *Arena,* 18 (November 1897): 673–680;

"Foreign Policy of the United States," *National Magazine, an Illustrated American Monthly,* 8 (1898): 430;

"Spanish-American War, Justifiable," *National Magazine, an Illustrated American Monthly,* 8 (1898): 513;

"Universal Peace, The Czar's Project," *National Magazine, an Illustrated American Monthly,* 9 (1898–1899): 180;

"The Corporations against the People," *Arena,* 19 (February 1898): 218;

"The Exiled Christ in Christian Russia," *Arena,* 19 (March 1898): 388–396;

"Brookline, Mass.; A Model Town under the Referendum," *Arena,* 19 (April 1898): 505;

"Restrictive Medical Legislation and the Public Weal," *Arena,* 19 (June 1898): 781;

"The Proposed Federation of the Anglo-Saxon Nations," *Arena,* 20 (August 1898): 223;

"The Genesis, Aim, and Scope of the World's Unity League–Interview," *Arena,* 24 (November 1900): 529;

"Wilhelm Liebknecht, 1826–1900," *Arena*, 24 (November 1900): 545;

"Toussaint l'Ouverture (1743–1803), Liberator of Hayti–the Greatest Black Man known to History," *Arena*, 24 (December 1900): 573;

"The Passing of the South African Republics," *Arena*, 24 (December 1900): 649;

"Crime and the Treatment of Criminals," *Arena*, 24 (December 1900): 653;

"The Last Century as a Utilitarian Age," *Arena*, 25 (March 1901): 271;

"Philippine Islands, An Army of Wealth Creators vs. an Army of Destruction," *Arena*, 25 (May 1901): 521;

"The United States as a World Power Yesterday and Today," *Arena*, 25 (May 1901): 547;

"William T. Stead on England's Crime in South Africa," *Arena*, 25 (June 1901): 634;

"Municipal Progress in England and America," *Arena*, 25 (June 1901): 663;

"Henry Demarest Lloyd's 'Newest England,'" *Arena*, 26 (July 1901): 100;

"A New England Poet of the Common Life," *Arena*, 26 (October 1901): 391;

"Power of the Ideal over Individual and National Life," *Arena*, 26 (October 1901): 417;

"The Assassination of President McKinley and the Aftermath," *Arena*, 26 (November 1901): 532;

"Science as a Handmaid of National Prosperity," *Arena*, 26 (December 1901): 650;

"The Automobile as the Servant of Civilization," *Arena*, 27 (January 1902): 93;

"A Prophet-Poet of the Fraternal State," *Arena*, 27 (April 1902): 391;

"Problem of Crime in the 20th Century," *Arena*, 27 (1902): 199;

"Co-operation, Key-note of the Present Revolutionary Movement," *Arena*, 28 (1902): 84;

"The Present Status of Co-operation in the Old World," *Arena*, 28 (August 1902): 202;

"The Divine Quest of the Fraternal State," *Arena*, 28 (August 1902): 152; (October): 398 (November): 481;

"Child Labor–The Cry of the Children," *Arena*, 28 (September 1902): 305;

"Fraternal Movements of the Present; Socialism, Single Tax, Cooperation," *Arena*, 29 (1903): 31;

"The Case against Trusts and Combinations," *Arena*, 29 (1903): 644; 30: 200;

"Trusts, Relation to Individual Welfare and National Integrity," *Arena*, 29 (1903): 414;

"Robert Browning Settlement, London; the Story of a Victorious Social Experiment," *Arena*, 29 (1903): 616;

"Germany and her Subject Races," *Arena*, 30 (1903): 93;

"The Rise of Anarchy in Europe and the United States," *Arena*, 30 (1903): 305;

"Street Railroads and the Public," *Arena*, 31 (1904): 417;

"Why America sympathizes with Japan," *Arena*, 31 (1904): 518;

"Autocratic and Bureaucratic Usurpations of Legislative Functions by Executive Officials," *Arena*, 31 (1904): 629;

"Movement for an Endowed National Art Theater for America," *Arena*, 31 (1904): 641;

"Dorothea L. Dix, and the Treatment of the Insane Poor in Massachusetts Sixty Years Ago," *Arena*, 32 (1904): 535;

"History of the Tweed Ring in N.Y. City," *Arena*, 33 (1905): 270;

"Ryan Walker, a Cartoonist of Social Protest," *Arena*, 33 (1905): 393;

"Homer Davenport, Cartoonist," *Arena*, 34 (1905): 58;

"Miss Tarbell's History of Standard Oil Co.," *Arena*, 34 (1905): 436;

"Great Insurance Companies as Fountain-heads of Corruption," *Arena*, 34 (1905): 514;

"Tolstoi on the Land Question" *Arena*, 34 (1905): 631;

"Markham, Poet-prophet of Democracy," *Arena*, 35 (1906): 143;

"Mayor Tom Johnson on Municipal Control of Vice," *Arena*, 35 (1906): 400.

Journalist and radical reformer, alternately hailed as "Father of the Muckrakers" or the "Jacob Riis of Boston," Benjamin Orange Flower believed that education could prompt social cooperation. Relying upon a religious model of sin and redemption, he believed that people needed to acknowledge the problems of society and re-awaken their social conscience. Flower held that as a person became more educated, his awareness of the consequences of his own actions improved and brought about an increase in his desire for social reform. He was most famous as the editor of a critical review, *The Arena*, but he also ran a paper called the *American Spectator*, developed several other newspapers and magazines–namely, the *Coming Age*, the *New Time*, and the *Twentieth Century Magazine*–and ran a publishing company. In his news stories and books, Flower exposed social wrongs and challenged widely held assumptions about the world. In literary history he is a figure of minor significance, a precursor of more-famous journalists devoted to exposing social problems, and an early supporter of American realists such as Hamlin Garland, Frank Norris, and James A. Herne. Flower wrote almost one thousand book reviews that, while not remarkable for their own sake, provide an index to the concerns and opinions of the growing middle-class readership of the time.

Benjamin Orange Flower was born 19 October 1859 in Albion, Illinois, to Albert and Elizabeth Flower. The family moved to Evansville, Indiana, and Flower grew up and attended schools there, one of which was housed in a building on his father's farm. Flower suffered from chronic illness and spent a lot of time reading. Raised in a family of Disciples of Christ preachers, he was expected to follow his father and older brother George by training for the ministry. His other brother, Richard Flower, pursued a profession in medicine. Flower spent a year at the University of Kentucky and then briefly attended Transylvania University Bible School in Lexington, Kentucky. As it turned out, he chose to preach to and educate his readers using journalism. After a short time working as a minister in Owensboro, Kentucky, Flower left the ministry in 1880 and, with a friend in Albion, started a newsletter entitled the *Egyptian Republican,* which became the temperance weekly *American Sentinel* (1880–1881).

At this time, Dr. Richard Flower opened a hospital in Boston and asked his brother Benjamin to assist him in managing it. Selling out his share in the *American Sentinel* after eight months, Flower traveled to Boston, where he was shocked and repulsed by the inner-city poverty and what he considered devolution of social structure. Flower was enraged by the slum conditions in which the lower class struggled to survive, while the middle and upper classes, he said, refused to acknowledge the struggle or even the existence of the people in the slums. His first work to treat a socially sensitive topic, *Civilization's Inferno; or, Studies in the Social Cellar* (1893), grew from a series of investigations into the lives of Boston's lower classes, particularly those below the working class (in, for example, the red light district). After touring for a few hours with a police officer through the squalid, crime-ridden neighborhoods associated with these people, Flower reported in florid and dramatic language that there was "No need to wander into other worlds for hells of God's creating. Man has made an underworld, before which the most daring imagination of poet or seer staggers." Flower's horror at his discoveries expressed the moral outrage he hoped to evoke, but also reflected the prejudices and fears he shared with his genteel target audience. Appalled to find the races living together in the worst neighborhoods, he chooses a Creole prostitute as his text, "her companion a low-browed, thick-necked Negro," and builds a sermon about "Ismaelites of our nineteenth-century civilization." "In this child of a dark fate," he argues, "we see a type of thousands of poor girls. . . . to them birth was a calamity, life a bitter curse, death their sweetest heritage."

Next Flower spent some time in Philadelphia working as the secretary of a doctor, but he returned to Boston. In September 1885 he married Hattie Cloud, and in 1886 he took control of the journal the *American Spectator.* In December 1889 Flower merged the *American Spectator* with a new magazine he had founded, *The Arena.* He took the name from a quotation from Herne that appeared on each issue: "We do not take possession of our ideas but are possessed by them. / They master us and force us into the arena, / Where like gladiators, we must fight for them." Flower took his causes to the public with his controversial new magazine. He edited the magazine himself from 1889 to 1896 and again from 1904 to 1909.

The Arena emerged amid the development of popular magazines that began in the early 1880s, appearing somewhat in reaction to the old, established, and primarily literary magazines—*Harper's, Scribner's, Century,* and the *Atlantic*—about the same time as *Ladies' Home Journal, Cosmopolitan,* and *Munsey's,* and just before *McClure's, Everybody's,* and *Pearson's.* The growth of these publications mirrored a phenomenal increase in the numbers of Americans buying and reading magazines. Historians of journalism believe *The Arena's* top circulation ran somewhere between 70,000 and 100,000 per issue during the mid to late 1890s, although most of the time it was below 30,000.

In September 1890 Flower began to sell books, beginning with the announcement that Benjamin R. Tucker's translations, books by Ignatius Donnelly, and his own first book, *Lessons Learned from Other Lives* (1889) were available from *The Arena* publishing company. He began to publish books in November of that year, beginning with Helen H. Gardener's *Is This Your Son, My Lord?* One of his most significant literary publications was Hamlin Garland's *Main-Travelled Roads* (1891). *The Arena* provided funding for many of Garland's research trips to the South and West as well. For the next six years the supplemental material advertising books for sale and books he had published ran between fourteen and thirty pages each issue, and by the end of that time Flower had published roughly 206 books and pamphlets on a variety of topics. Believing in the inherent value of heterodoxy, he published writings from reformers, radicals, intellectuals, clergy, and anyone whose views he thought interesting.

Roughly half of each issue was devoted to political, economic, and social issues; the other half addressed culture and science. The timing of *The Arena's* highest circulation coincided with the 1892 opening of Ellis Island to process the millions of immigrants whose presence then transformed the cities and industrial areas, the height of racially-motivated lynchings the same year, the economic panic and depression beginning in 1893 as homelessness and unemployment reached unprecedented levels, and the Pullman

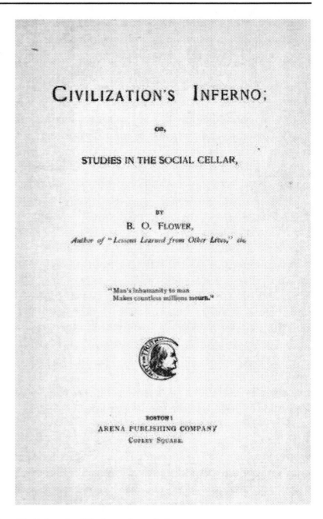

*Illustrated title page and title page for Flower's sociological study of the lower classes in Boston
(Thomas Cooper Library, University of South Carolina)*

strike of 1894 that focused the nation's attention on labor abuses. Flower created a political magazine that confronted problems of social democracy, women's rights, deplorable living conditions, sweatshops, and corruption. Scholars calculate that at least one-third of the content of the magazine dealt with such controversial issues at any given time. Convinced that the United States faced an impending crisis of world-shattering proportions and that it would emerge transformed spiritually and in political matters, Flower wanted to make the American public aware of what he considered the real problems; he attributed most of them to lack of education and the need for social reform. Like many other reformers, he borrowed freely from biblical language and the lexicon of the ministry to explain these ideas, telling readers that they must choose between Jesus and Caesar, for example, or describing various aspects of industrial capitalism as "Mammon-worship."

The crux of his social reform was unity; therefore, he did not usually name corporations and individuals who had violated moral laws. He did support the wave of urban reforms put forward by the middle classes in the 1890s, although he was just as likely to support far more radical measures, such as federally funded public works projects to support the unemployed—ideas now more closely associated with the 1930s. He kept an open mind about which political approach was best, entertaining ideas from populists, single-taxers, cooperatives, socialists, and anarchists as well as moderates of all kinds. Gaining readers and support to his causes by 1893, Flower started the Union for Practical Progress, a loosely-connected organization composed of local Arena clubs. In so doing he absorbed the Union for Concerted Moral Effort founded by Frank and Walter Vrooman of New York. The Arena clubs served as forums to discuss issues of concern, but they also lobbied officeholders, distributed literature, generated subscriptions to *The Arena,* and, for a time, offered correspondence courses as part of a People's University. Flower boasted of some fifty clubs in the organization by the end of 1894, and scholars believe that ultimately the number moved closer to seventy; but as he turned to other interests, the clubs were absorbed by civic welfare organizations.

In 1896 Flower hailed populism as the savior of the republic, endorsing William Jennings Bryan in the presidential election and working fervently for his campaign. During that year *The Arena* went into bankruptcy, and Flower, in ill health again, temporarily stepped down from editorship. Originally a year's subscription to the magazine had been costly for the time ($5 per year), but as part of the bankruptcy proceedings the price was reduced to $2.50 per year. While John Ridpath edited *The Arena,* Flower and Frederick U. Adams formed a new magazine in Chicago, the *New Time.* The new project ran from June 1897 through the end of 1898, and then Flower merged the old and new publications. In 1899 he started yet another periodical, the *Coming Age.* After that magazine also merged with *The Arena,* he again became active on the editorial staff. He returned as editor in chief of *The Arena* in 1904.

Other *Arena* editors (John Clark Ridpath, 1896–1898; Paul Tyner, 1898–1899; John Emery McLean, 1899–1904) concurred with Flower's idea to use the magazine's pages to deliver truths the capitalist-funded press hesitated to publish and to explore multiple sides of social issues with as few advance conclusions as possible. Flower favored the symposium format, offering a variety of viewpoints on topics of current concern, such as tenements and settlement houses, prostitution and age of consent laws, changing ideas of child-rearing, and lynching. The editors of *The Arena* believed that the more educated the masses were about corruption and inequalities, the more readily they would cooperate and join reform efforts. Muckraking journalism, later perfected in *McClure's,* was born in *The Arena.*

During these years Flower also developed an interest in psychic research and its acceptance in the scientific field. He published articles in the spiritualist press, studied the work of Mary Baker Eddy and her followers with keen interest, and opened his magazine's pages to writers of all backgrounds with an interest in psychical research or spiritualist philosophy. Many spiritualists of the time had varied practical interests connected to social welfare movements, including vegetarianism, dress reform for women, birth control, alternative education, labor organization or opposition to child labor, changes in the medical profession, as well as involvement in more-common political causes. Often spiritualist writers wove together the tenets of the reform movements with arguments in support of spiritualism—whether couched in broadly universalist terms of the

kinship and divinity of all people or more specifically issued as the supposed utterances of some influential representative of the dead. Flower's interest in the history of religious dissent, his lifelong health problems, and fascination with alternative healing may best explain this connection.

In the decade of the 1890s alternative religious movements proliferated, and it was common for political radicals or reformers to develop at least a passing relationship with one or another such movement. In the summer of 1899 Christian Socialist William Dwight Porter Bliss called a convention in Buffalo, New York, that brought together a motley assemblage of religious and political reformers to discuss the powerful monopolies, corruption and reform at the municipal level, alternative taxation methods, public or government ownership of utilities, and world government. Flower attended, and he supported the group's decision to form a new Social Reform Union not allied with any existing political group rather than to begin a new party. The group fell apart within a year, however, divided over the issue of voting in the presidential election for Eugene V. Debs or William Jennings Bryan. Flower voted for Bryan.

Flower was among the first writers to dwell on talk of an "invisible empire" pulling the strings of the world's elected governments, a line of discourse that by 1912 found its way into the Progressive Party's official platform. To uncover and provide solutions for the problems associated with unfair trade practices had numbered among Flower's original reasons for starting *The Arena.* He and Ridpath believed that questions of whether U.S. debts should be paid in gold or silver, manipulation of tariffs, and even support for wars or the emergence of newly independent nations somehow linked to conspiracies among international bankers and government officials who owned stock or shares in the bankers' enterprises. Meanwhile, they pointed out, in a supposedly prosperous country, a tenth of New York's dead were paupers and had to be buried in Potter's Field. Whole countries were being reduced to virtual slavery, they said, and the United States' citizens should not believe themselves immune. Nonetheless, adhering to their policy of representing multiple views, they published material by such writers as Frank Parsons advocating government ownership of utilities.

The Arena had begun the trend of muckraking, but the landscape of the popular press changed so much in one and a half decades that by 1909 a dismayed surveyor of the scene found only four liberal magazines left to express any criticism of big business whatsoever: *The Arena,* the *American, Everybody's,* and *McClure's.* When *The Arena* folded later that year, Flower founded and edited the *Twentieth Century Magazine* (October 1909–November 1911), which presented to the reading audience the problems caused by special privilege, the inequitable divisions of wealth, and ignorance. He continued to address the social ills of the day without fear of government intrusion or censorship. More often, he began to challenge the medical establishment consistently and to endorse Christian Science, although he himself was not a practitioner. In 1914 Flower published *Progressive Men, Women, and Movements of the Past Twenty-five Years.* In this book he offered an overview of the contents of *The Arena,* tracing economic, social, philosophical, political, and corporate movements during the preceding quarter century.

Living by his philosophy that people, especially reformers, need to be optimistic about the future outcomes of society, he confronted issues with a renewed vigor. Flower's interest in the psychic world sustained an optimistic image of the future despite the beginning of the Great War. His spiritualism was a holdover from the previous century, but Flower's failure to understand the significance of world events was in every way representative of his generation. United States radicals and reformers of his era were so caught up in their own causes and activities that few of them foresaw the war or how completely it was to change their lives. Accordingly, Flower's last two writing and publishing enterprises reflected the out-of-date concerns of an alternative religion whose popularity had peaked just as he emerged onto the national scene two decades before. With World War I spiritualism all but vanished from the mainstream press. After campaigning for reform of social customs and governmental practices for most of his life, Flower directed his energies toward enlightening the public about other conspiracies that he believed threatened their liberty. He spent the last years of his life attacking the medical profession's growing monopoly in the area of healing, on the one hand, and what he perceived as the evils of Roman Catholicism, on the other. He believed that the pope had caused the Great War, and he became the president of the Menace Publishing Company of Aurora, Missouri. Under its auspices he edited and published the *Menace* (circulation 1.4 million) and brought out a new edition of *How England Averted a Revolution of Force* (originally published in 1911) reflecting his altered views. The *Menace* was tried for sending obscene matter–meaning antipapal libel–through the mails in January 1916. The trial, held in Joplin, Missouri, lasted four days and resulted in an acquittal for the editors. On 24 December 1918, Benjamin Flower passed away in Boston.

Flower's contemporaries admired him personally and as a journalist, but he and his magazine, *The Arena,* do not feature prominently in current accounts of the turn of the century or progressive era. His writing style remained consistent throughout his career; the focus of his interest, by contrast, shifted frequently. Very few scholars have written about Flower. In 1939 Fred Carleton Mabee Jr. wrote a master's thesis about Flower and *The Arena*'s early

years at Columbia University. Howard Cline wrote a Harvard history honors thesis on Flower in 1939 called "The Mechanics of Dissent." In 1940 David Howard Dickason wrote a thesis at Columbia University on Flower's contribution to critical opinion in the United States. In the next few years some articles by Cline appeared in *Journalism Quarterly.* By 1942 Flower was beginning to be studied as a sort of backdrop to the literary output of his contemporaries. Again in the late 1960s and early 1970s a double flurry of interest surrounding urban renewal and Ralph Nader and the new muckrakers earned Flower an appearance in selected studies of socially conscious journalists.

References:

Edwin M. Bacon, ed., *Men of Progress: One Thousand Biographical Sketches and Portraits of Leaders in Business and Professional Life* (Boston: New England Magazine, 1896), p. 131;

Howard F. Cline, "Benjamin Orange Flower and *The Arena* 1889–1909," *Journalism Quarterly,* 17 (June 1940): 139–150;

David H. Dickason, "Benjamin Orange Flower, Patron of the Realists,"*American Literature,* 14 (May 1942): 148–156;

Roy P. Fairfield, "Benjamin Orange Flower: Father of the Muckrakers," *American Literature,* 22 (November 1950): 272–282;

Peter J. Frederick, *Knights of the Golden Rule: The Intellectual As Christian Social Reformer in the 1890s* (Lexington: University Press of Kentucky, 1976), pp. 3–27;

C. C. Regier, *The Era of the Muckraker* (Chapel Hill: University of North Carolina Press, 1932; Gloucester, Mass.: Peter Smith, 1957);

Roger Stoddard, "Vanity and Reform: B. O. Flower's *Arena* Publishing Company Boston, 1890–1896. With a Bibliographical List of *Arena* Imprints," *Papers of the Bibliographical Society,* 76 (1982): 273–337.

Papers:

Letters from B. O. Flower survive in the personal papers of many of his reform-minded contemporaries, most notably in the following collections: Francis Ellingwood Abbot Family Papers 1815–1940, Andover-Harvard Theological Library; Marion Butler Papers 1862–1938, Manuscripts Department, Wilson Library, University of North Carolina, Chapel Hill; Hamlin Garland Collection, Rare Books and Manuscripts, Doheny Memorial Library, University of Southern California; George Herron Collection, Hoover Library, Stanford University; Henry Demarest Lloyd Papers, State Historical Society of Wisconsin, Madison; Edwin Markham Archive, Horrmann Library, Wagner College; and Horace and Anne Montgomerie Traubel Papers, Library of Congress.

Matilda Joslyn Gage

(24 March 1826 – 18 March 1898)

Sue Boland
Matilda Joslyn Gage Foundation

BOOK: *Woman, Church and State: A Historical Account of the Status of Woman though the Christian Ages: With Reminiscences of the Matriarchate* (Chicago: Charles H. Kerr, 1893).

TRACTS AND CIRCULARS: *Speech of Mrs. M. E. J. Gage at the Woman's Rights Convention Held at Syracuse, September, 1852,* Woman's Rights Tract No. 7 (Syracuse: Master's Print, 1852);

Woman as Inventor, Woman Suffrage Tract No. 1 (Fayetteville, N.Y.: F. A. Darling, Printer, 1870);

Woman's Rights Catechism (N.p., 1871);

Arguments before the Committee on the District of Columbia of the United States Senate and House of Representatives upon the Centennial Woman Suffrage Memorial of the Women Citizens of this Nation—Introduced in the U.S. Senate by Hon. A. A. Sargent, of California, January 25, 1876 and in the House of Representatives, by Hon. S. S. Cox, of New York, March 31, 1876, Asking for Equal Suffrage for Men and Women in the District of Columbia, by Mrs. Matilda Joslyn Gage, President of the National Woman Suffrage Association, and by Mrs. Sara J. Spencer, Secretary of the District of Columbia Woman Franchise Association (Washington, D.C.: Gibson Brothers, Printers, 1876);

Address of the National Woman Suffrage Association to the National Republican Convention, Philadelphia, Pa., June 10, 1876 (Philadelphia: s.n., 1876);

Address of the National Woman Suffrage Association to the National Democratic Convention, to be Held at St. Louis, Missouri, June 27, 1876, by Gage and Elizabeth Cady Stanton (Philadelphia: s.n., 1876);

Declaration of the Rights of Women, by Gage and Stanton (Philadelphia: s.n., 1876);

Who Planned the Tennessee Campaign of 1862? Or, Anna Ella Carroll vs. Ulysses S. Grant, National Citizen Tract No. 1 (N.p., 1880);

Protest Against the Unjust Interpretation of the Constitution Presented on Behalf of the Women of the United States by

From History of Woman Suffrage, *volume 1, 1848–1861, edited by Gage, Elizabeth Cady Stanton, and Susan B. Anthony (Rochester, N.Y.: Susan B. Anthony, 1887; Robarts Research Library, University of Toronto)*

Officers of the National Woman Suffrage Association (N.p., 17 September 1887);

Plan of work for 1888, issued by the Executive Committee of the National Woman Suffrage Association, Matilda Joslyn Gage, Chairman of the Executive Committee (N.p., 30 April 1888);

Woman, Church, and State (Chicago: Charles H. Kerr, 1893);

"Woman as an Inventor," reprint of Gage's article in *The North American Review,* 1883 (Fayetteville, N.Y.: The Matilda Joslyn Gage Foundation, 2003);

The Dangers of the Hour, Reprint of the speech of Matilda Joslyn Gage at the Woman's National Liberal Union Convention, February 24, 1890 (Fayetteville, N.Y.: The Matilda Joslyn Gage Foundation, 2004).

OTHER: "Decade Speech: On the Progress of Education and Industrial Avocations for Women," in *A History of the National Woman's Rights Movement, for Twenty Years, With the Proceedings of the Decade Meeting held at Apollo Hall, October 20, 1870, from 1850 to 1870, with an Appendix Containing the History of the Movement During the Winter of 1871, in the National Capitol,* compiled by Paulina Wright Davis (New York: Journeymen Printers' Co-Operative Association, 1871);

"Speech of Matilda Joslyn Gage in Canandaigua and Sixteen Other Towns of Ontario County, previous to Miss Anthony's Trial, June 17th, 1873: The United States on Trial; not Susan B. Anthony," in *An Account of the Proceedings on the Trial of Susan B. Anthony, on the Charge of Illegal Voting, at the Presidential Election in November 1872* (Rochester, N.Y.: Daily Democrat and Chronicle, 1874);

"Woman's Rights," *Condensed American Cyclopedia,* volume 1 (New York: Appleton, 1877);

"Address of Mrs. Gage," *Proceedings and Addresses at the Freethinker's Convention Held at Watkins, N.Y., August 22d, 23d, 24th, and 25th, 1878* (New York: D. M. Bennett, 1878), pp. 44–45;

History of Woman Suffrage, volume 1, 1848–1861, edited by Gage, Elizabeth Cady Stanton, and Susan B. Anthony (New York: Fowler & Wells, 1881);

History of Woman Suffrage, volume 2, 1861–1876, edited by Gage, Stanton, and Anthony (New York: Fowler & Wells, 1882);

"Letter to the 16th National Washington Convention," *National Woman Suffrage Association Proceedings* (March 1884): 68–70;

History of Woman Suffrage, volume 3, 1876–1885, edited by Gage, Stanton, and Anthony (Rochester, N.Y.: Susan B. Anthony, 1887);

"Woman in the Early Christian Church," *Report of the International Council of Women, Assembled by the National Woman Suffrage Association, Washington, D.C., U.S. of America, March 25 to April 1, 1888* (Washington, D.C.: Rufus H. Darby, Printer, 1888);

"Remarks during the Conference of the Pioneers," *Report of the International Council of Women, Assembled by the National Woman Suffrage Association, Washington, D.C., U.S. of America, March 25 to April 1, 1888* (Washington, D.C.: Rufus H. Darby, Printer, 1888);

Report of the convention for organization, February 24th and 25th, 1890. Woman's National Liberal Union (Syracuse, N.Y.: Masters & Stone, 1890);

"What the Church Has Not Done for Woman," *The Truth Seeker Annual and Freethinkers' Almanac* (New York: Truth Seeker, 1895), pp. 46–54;

"Comments on Kings" in *The Woman's Bible,* by Stanton and the Revising Committee (Seattle: Coalition Task Force on Women and Religion: 1974, ca. 1895–1898), pp. 66–71;

"Comments on Revelation," in *The Woman's Bible,* by Stanton and the Revising Committee (Seattle: Coalition Task Force on Women and Religion: 1974, ca. 1895–1898): 176–179, 181–183;

"The Dangers of the Hour," in Karlyn Kohrs Campbell, ed., *Man Cannot Speak for Her,* volume 2 (Westport, Conn.: Praeger, 1989), pp. 339–370.

SELECTED PERIODICAL PUBLICATIONS–UNCOLLECTED:

POETRY

"A Fable of the Trees," *Golden Age* (13 June 1874): 6.

FICTION

"The Walking-Fern," *Appletons' Journal* (May 1877): 442–453.

NONFICTION

"The Women's Rights Question" (signed M.), *Daily Star* (17 November 1852): 2;

"The Women's Rights Question–Concluded," (signed M.), *Daily Star* (18 November 1852): 2;

"The Woman's Rights Question," *Carson League* (Syracuse) (13 January 1853): 1;

"The Woman's Rights Question," *Carson League* (20 January 1853): 1;

"Woman and her Wages" (signed M.), *Central New Yorker* (1854);

"A Few Thoughts on Passing Events" (signed M.), *Sibyl* (November 1860);

Mrs. M. E. Gage's Address in "Flag Presentation to the Third Onondaga Regiment," *Onondaga Standard* (28 August 1862): 3;

"The Woman's National Covenant" (signed A Woman), *[Syracuse] Daily Journal* (May 1864): 4;

"Colors and Their Meaning," *Continental Monthly* (August 1864): 199–207;

"Is Woman Her Own?" (signed Matilda E. J. Gage), *Revolution* (9 April 1868): 215;

"The Cotton Gin Invented by A Woman" (signed M. E. Joslyn Gage), *Revolution* (30 April 1868): 259;

"Woman An Inventor, Article II" (signed M. E. Joslyn Gage), *Revolution* (21 May 1868): 311;

"Husbands Not Wanted" (signed Joslyn), *Revolution* (11 June 1868): 364;

"Spiritual Philosophy" (signed Mrs. M. E. G. *[sic]* Gage), *Revolution* (3 September 1868): 133;

"Woman An Inventor, Article III" (signed M. E. Joslyn Gage), *Revolution* (17 September 1868): 165–166;

"Woman An Inventor, No. IV" (signed M. E. Joslyn Gage), *Revolution* (14 January 1869): 17–19;

"Letter [from Fayetteville]" (signed M. E. J. Gage), *Revolution* (14 January 1869): 20;

"Opportunity of Development," *Woman's Advocate*, 1 (January–June 1869): 255–258;

"Letter from New York," *Weekly Recorder* (20 May 1869): 2;

"Letter from New York," *Weekly Recorder* (27 May 1869): 2;

"Works of Art in Astor Library," *Weekly Recorder* (10 June 1869, 17 June 1869);

"Appeal to the Friends of Woman's Suffrage in the State of New York" (signed M. E. Joslyn Gage), *Revolution* (17 June 1869): 377–378;

"Woman as Inventor: Article Fifth–Mythology" (signed Mrs. M. E. Joslyn Gage), *Revolution* (21 October 1869): 242–243;

"Letter from Mrs. Gage [from Fayetteville]," *Revolution* (9 December 1869): 364;

"Letter from Mrs. Gage [from Fayetteville]," *Revolution* (6 January 1870): 4;

"The Washington Convention" (signed Mrs. M. E. J. Gage), *Revolution* (13 January 1870): 20;

"The Moral Aspect," *Revolution* (10 February 1870): 91–92;

"Colorado" (signed M.E.J.G.), *Revolution* (17 February 1870): 106;

"Onondago *[sic]* County" (signed M.E.J.G.), *Revolution* (24 February 1870): 122–121;

"My Dear Miss Anthony [50th birthday letter]" (signed Matilda E. Joslyn Gage), *Revolution* (24 February 1870): 125–126;

"Onondaga Co., N.Y." (signed M.E.J.G.), *Revolution* (3 March 1870): 140;

"New York State Suffrage Association Lectures" (signed M.), *Revolution* (7 April 1870): 213;

"Richmond Letters–No. 1" (signed M.E.J.G.), *Weekly Recorder* (12 May 1870): 1;

"Richmond Letters–No. 2" (signed M.E.J.G.), *Weekly Recorder* (12 May 1870): 2;

"Richmond Letters–No. 3" (signed M.E.J.G.), *Weekly Recorder* (19 May 1870);

"Richmond Letters–No. 4" (signed M.E.J.G.), *Weekly Recorder* (26 May 1870): 1;

"Richmond Letters–No. 5" (signed M.E.J.G.), *Weekly Recorder* (2 June 1870): 1;

"Richmond Letters–No. 6" (signed M.E.J.G.), *Weekly Recorder* (9 June 1870): 1;

"Down the St. Lawrence, Lakes Champlain and George," *Weekly Recorder* (11 August 1870, 18 August 1870);

"The Other Side," *Golden Age* (1 April 1871): 56–57;

"Woman's Rights Catechism," *Weekly Recorder* (27 July 1871): 2;

"Women Tax Payers," *Weekly Recorder* (3 August 1871);

"Letter from Mrs. Gage [from Saratoga]," *Weekly Recorder* (31 August 1871): 2;

"Letter from Mrs. Matilda Joslyn Gage [from Saratoga]," *[San Francisco] Pioneer* (21 September 1871);

"Correspondence of The Pioneer" (signed Martha Joslyn Gage), *Pioneer* (September 1871);

"Letter from Mrs. Matilda Joslyn Gage [from Saratoga]," *Pioneer* (October 1871);

"The Mother of His Children" (signed Mary Joslyn Gage), *Pioneer* (9 November 1871);

"All Along the Line," *Weekly Recorder* (16 November 1871): 2;

"Letter from Mrs. Gage [from Cicero, New York]," *[Syracuse] Daily Standard* (16 November 1871): 4;

"Woman Suffrage: The National Convention at Washington–Letter from Mrs. Matilda Joslyn Gage," *Standard* (19 January 1872): 2;

"Mrs. Gage at the National Woman's Suffrage Convention," *Weekly Recorder* (25 January 1872): 2;

"Letter from Washington," *Standard* (1 February 1872): 2;

"The Outlook for Woman," *Golden Age* (10 February 1872);

"Letter from Washington" (signed Mr. Josleyn *[sic]* Gage), *Standard* (19 February 1872): 2;

"Letter from Matilda Joslyn Gage," *New Northwest* (Portland, Oregon) (8 March 1872);

"Women in Ancient Times," *New Northwest* (22 March 1872);

"Speech of Matilda Joslyn Gage: Centralized Power vs. State Rights," *Woman's Campaign* (February 1873);

"The Woman's Anti-Whisky Crusade," *Golden Age* (21 March 1874): 60–62;

"The Albany Law Journal on Susan B. Anthony's Case," *[Syracuse] Daily Journal* (30 July 1874): 3;

"Sea-Side Notes" (signed Joslyn), *Weekly Recorder* (August 1874);

"Seaside Loiterings" (signed M.J.G.), *Syracuse Sunday Courier* (August 1874);

"Green Corn Dance of the Onondagas" (signed Alcor), *Evening Mail* (September–December 1874, date unknown);

"The Remnant of the Five Nations," *New York Evening Post* (24 September 1875);

"Miss Gifford's Bust of Samuel J. May," *Golden Age* (25 September 1875) 9;

"The Onondaga Indians," *Evening Post* (3 November 1875);

"Presidential Suffrage," with Lillie Devereux Blake and Clemence S. Lozier, M.D., *Weekly Recorder* (9 December 1875): 3;

"National Woman Suffrage Convention," *Weekly Recorder* (13 January 1876): 3;

"Woman Suffrage: Argument in Its Favor before the Judiciary Committee of the Assembly" [Albany] *Daily Knickerbocker* (19 January 1876);

"Washington Gossip" (signed Joslyn), *[New York] Evening Post* (12 February 1876);

"Letter from Mrs. Gage [from New York]," *Weekly Recorder* (24 February 1876): 3;

"Msickquatash *[sic]*," (unaccredited), *Appletons' Journal* (26 February 1876): 278–279;

"Letter from Mrs. Gage: Washington This Winter," *Weekly Recorder* (2 March 1876): 3;

"Letter from Mrs. Gage [from Philadelphia]: About the Centennial," *Weekly Recorder* (9 March 1876): 3;

"Centennial Letter from Mrs. Gage: Carpenter's Hall, Philadelphia," *Weekly Recorder* (16 March 1876): 3;

"Centennial Letter No. 3: The Women's Pavilion," *Weekly Recorder* (23 March 1876): 3;

"Woman A Mystery," *Appletons' Journal* (29 April 1876): 565–567;

"Burning the White Dog," *Appletons' Journal* (13 May 1876): 628–629;

"Women's Industries and Inventions," *Golden Dawn* (1876);

"Centennial Letter," *Weekly Recorder* (8 June 1876): 2;

"Our Exposition Letter," *Weekly Recorder* (15 June 1876): 2;

"Circular: National Woman Suffrage Parlors," *Ballot Box* (Toledo) (July 1876): 4;

"An Incident of the Centennial Fourth" (signed Joslyn), *[New York] Evening Post* (July 1876);

"Woman's Declaration of Rights," by Gage and Elizabeth Cady Stanton, *Ballot Box* (August 1876): 5;

"Woman Suffrage Pioneer: Mrs. Paulina Wright Davis," *Weekly Recorder* (14 September 1876): 5;

"Letter from Mrs. Gage [from Tenafly, New Jersey about the Centennial Exposition]," *Weekly Recorder* (16 November 1876): 3;

"Matilda Joslyn Gage on the Right of Habeas Corpus," *Ballot Box* (November 1876): 1;

"Appeal for a Sixteenth Amendment," by Gage and Stanton, *Ballot Box* (December 1876): 1;

"Woman Suffrage" (unaccredited), *Weekly Recorder* (15 February 1877): 3;

"Sixteenth Amendment: New Appeal," by Gage and Stanton, *Ballot Box* (April 1877): 2;

"National Woman Suffrage Convention–May, 1877," *Ballot Box* (May 1877): 2;

"Address to the Voters and Legislators of New York, May, 1877," *Ballot Box* (August 1877): 1;

"The Right of Indians to Vote," *Ballot Box* (January 1878): 2;

"Cleopatra's Needles," *Appletons' Journal* (January–February 1878): 86–88;

"Prospectus: The National Citizen and Ballot Box," *National Citizen and Ballot Box* (Syracuse) (May 1878): 1;

"United States Rights and State Rights," *National Citizen and Ballot Box* (May 1878): 2;

"Indian Citizenship," *National Citizen and Ballot Box* (May 1878): 2;

"What the South Needs," *National Citizen and Ballot Box* (June 1878): 2;

"Wadleigh's Report," *National Citizen and Ballot Box* (July 1878): 2;

"Woman's Rights Under the Law," *Weekly Recorder* (18 July 1878): 3;

"The Clergy Against Us," *National Citizen and Ballot Box* (August 1878): 4;

"Theological Christianity," *National Citizen and Ballot Box* (September 1878): 2;

"Woman vs. the Labor Party," *National Citizen and Ballot Box* (October 1878): 2;

"Universal Suffrage–'Too Much Suffrage,'" *National Citizen and Ballot Box* (November 1878): 2;

"The Utah Question Once More,'" *National Citizen and Ballot Box* (December 1878): 2;

"All the Rights I Want," *National Citizen and Ballot Box* (January 1879): 2;

"Women Without a Country," *National Citizen and Ballot Box* (March 1879): 4;

"The Brand of the Slave," *National Citizen and Ballot Box* (May 1879): 2;

"How I Decorated on the Fourth," *National Citizen and Ballot Box* (July 1879): 2;

"A Nation or a Confederacy–Which?" *National Citizen and Ballot Box* (August 1879): 2;

"Two Kinds of Centralization" *National Citizen and Ballot Box* (October 1879): 2;

"Anna Ella Carroll vs. Ulysses S. Grant," *National Citizen and Ballot Box* (November 1879): 2;

"A Lost Opportunity," *National Citizen and Ballot Box* (December 1879): 2;

"New York Woman Suffrage Boom," *National Citizen and Ballot Box* (March 1880): 2;

"Call to the 12th Annual Convention," *Woman's Exponent* (Salt Lake City) (1 April 1880);

"A World of Work," *National Citizen and Ballot Box* (May 1880): 2;

"Women Rebels," *National Citizen and Ballot Box* (May 1880): 3;

"Old Times and New: Woman Always a Slave," *National Citizen and Ballot Box* (May 1880): 3;

"The National Woman Suffrage Association and the National Republican Nominating Convention," *National Citizen and Ballot Box* (June 1880): 4;

"Woman Idolaters," *National Citizen and Ballot Box* (August 1880): 2;

"Professed Friends," *National Citizen and Ballot Box* (August 1880): 2;

"Men's Translations of the Bible," *National Citizen and Ballot Box* (September 1880): 2;

"For Neither Party," *National Citizen and Ballot Box* (September 1880): 2;

"To Women—School Suffrage," *Weekly Recorder* (23 September 1880): 2;

"Woman's School Suffrage," *Weekly Recorder* (30 September 1880): 3;

"Intimidation of New York Women," *National Citizen and Ballot Box* (October 1880): 2;

"School Suffrage in Fayetteville," *National Citizen and Ballot Box* (October 1880): 2;

"Women Voters of New York," *National Citizen and Ballot Box* (November 1880): 2;

"Persons and Things," *National Citizen and Ballot Box* (January 1881): 2;

"Russia and Liberty," *National Citizen and Ballot Box* (April 1881): 2;

"The Political Outlook," *National Citizen and Ballot Box* (July 1881): 2;

"God in the Constitution," *National Citizen and Ballot Box* (October 1881): 2;

"Women School Voters," *Weekly Recorder* (6 October 1881): 3;

"Mrs. Vice President Gage's Letter," *Omaha Republican* (28 September 1882);

"Woman as an Inventor" (signed M. J. Gage), *North American Review* (New York) (May 1883): 478–489;

"Self-Government," *Dio Lewis' Monthly* (Boston) (February 1884): 198–200;

"The Influence of Social Conditions upon the Health of Women," *Pittsburgh Commercial Gazette* (April 1885);

"The Church, Science, and Woman," *Index* (29 April 1886);

"Woman's Right to Vote," *Weekly Recorder* (28 October 1886);

"The Foundation of Sovereignty," *Woman's Tribune* (Beatrice, Nebraska) (April 1887): 52;

"Law in the Family," *Woman's Tribune* (31 March 1888);

"Letter from Mrs. Gage," *Woman's Tribune* (18 August 1888);

"The Matriarchate," *Open Court*, 2 (1888–1889): 1480–1481;

"Liberal Woman's Convention," *Liberal Thinker* (Syracuse) (January 1890): 1;

"An Impending Crisis," *Liberal Thinker* (January 1890): 2;

"The Ecclesiastical Machine," *Liberal Thinker* (January 1890): 2;

"A Few Sayings of Women," *Liberal Thinker* (January 1890): 3;

"To Liberal Women," *Freethinkers' Magazine* (January 1890): 50–51;

"The Woman's Convention," *Freethinkers' Magazine* (February 1890): 106;

"Woman's National Liberal Union," *Freethinkers' Magazine* (May 1890): 262–265;

"The Church and Public Schools," *Freethinkers' Magazine* (July 1890): 420;

"The Matriarchate; or, Woman in the Past," *Twentieth Century* (25 December 1890): 3–4;

"Women Bankers," *Weekly Recorder* (November 1894);

"Revelation," *Hermetist* (December 1897): 104–106.

Matilda Joslyn Gage was a leader of the nineteenth-century women's-rights movement and a top officer in the National Woman Suffrage Association for twenty years. Having been effectively ignored by historians for her radical views, she has gradually been restored to a place of prominence alongside Susan B. Anthony and Elizabeth Cady Stanton. But Gage's life work focused on much more than votes for women. She and her husband, Henry, were abolitionists who opened their home as a stop on the Underground Railroad. Some scholars now believe Gage was influenced by the gender-equity concepts of the traditional Haudenosaunee (Iroquois) Native American culture of upstate New York. She in turn passed on a vision of a utopian society and female leadership to her son-in-law, L. Frank Baum, author of *The Wonderful Wizard of Oz* (1900). Gage was also a noted critic of Christian churches and the effects of religious patriarchy on women throughout history. She spent the later years of her life working to maintain separation of church and state in the United States.

Born on 24 March 1826, Matilda Electa Joslyn was the only child of Dr. Hezekiah and Helen Leslie Joslyn of Cicero, north of Syracuse, New York. Her religious parents attended the local Baptist church but also investigated the teachings of Andrew Campbell and Emanuel Swedenborg. Gage later said that her father taught her the most important lesson of all—to think for herself. Hezekiah Joslyn was a founding member of the antislavery Liberty Party, in 1840, and the words "an early abolitionist" are engraved on his tombstone. Matilda grew up immersed in social activism, cir-

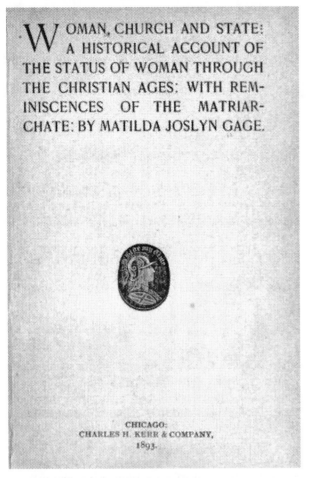

Title page for Gage's book, in which she accuses Christianity of oppressing women (University of California Libraries)

culating petitions and attending meetings and rallies throughout central New York, then a hotbed of antislavery activity. After a brief formal education at the Clinton Liberal Institute in Clinton, New York, she applied to medical school, wanting to become a physician like her father, but her application was denied because she was a woman.

In 1845 Matilda married Henry Hill Gage, a dry-goods merchant, and moved to Syracuse and later to Manlius, in the eastern part of Onondaga County, New York. When the Gages saw that the Erie Canal would bring a business boom to the nearby village of Fayetteville, they bought a home in 1854 on the main road and added on a large Greek-revival facade. Matilda and Henry Gage had five children: Helen Leslie, Thomas Clarkson, Charles Henry (who died in infancy), Julia Louise, and Maud. Matilda Joslyn Gage did not cease activism because she had a family. In the early 1850s she signed a document stating that she would not obey the Fugitive Slave Law. When Reverend Jermain

Loguen, the African American leader of the Syracuse branch of the Underground Railroad, came to her village looking for aid, the Gages agreed to shelter freedom seekers, in violation of federal law, subjecting themselves to a possible $1,000 fine and six months in prison for each fugitive hidden in their home. Several of the Gages' neighbors and fellow members of the Fayetteville Baptist Church were also active abolitionists.

Because of the births of children in 1848, 1850, and 1851, Gage did not attend a major woman's-rights meeting until the Third National Woman's Rights Convention, held in Syracuse in 1852. Although not used to public speaking and naive about parliamentary procedure, Gage's speech so impressed convention president Lucretia Mott that she recommended it be printed as a woman's-rights tract. This tract was one of seven printed in 1853, with other esteemed authors such as Reverend Samuel J. May, Wendell Phillips, Abby Kelley Foster, and Clarina Nichols.

Despite having young children and caring for her parents, Gage was active in both woman suffrage and abolition. She spent the 1850s and 1860s writing, attending conventions, lecturing on women's rights throughout upstate New York, gathering hundreds of signatures on petitions, and researching history. In 1868 Gage started making a national name for herself through articles published in Anthony's newspaper, *Revolution*. Parker Pillsbury, co-editor of the *Revolution* with Stanton, praised Gage's talents, using a biblical metaphor typical of the time: "The harvest waits her sickle in a thousand fields. Let her be called" (*Revolution*, 25 February 1869).

Gage answered the call. She was a founding member of the National Woman Suffrage Association (NWSA) in 1869 and named to the advisory counsel. The NWSA was born amid controversy over the Fourteenth and Fifteenth Amendments, which gave the rights of citizenship and the right to vote to African American men. Stanton, Pillsbury, and Anthony were adamant that women should not work for any amendment that enfranchised more men and no women. Many abolitionists who had been active in the NWSA parent organization, the American Equal Rights Association, were not willing to work for woman suffrage. Some joined the rival American Woman Suffrage Association (AWSA), centered in Boston and headed by Lucy Stone, who did support the Fifteenth Amendment. The women and men of the conservative AWSA were appalled by Stanton's liberal view of divorce and the NWSA's 1870 association with Victoria Woodhull, a notorious "free lover."

Gage's first contribution to the NWSA was to call for a New York State convention and undertake the mammoth task of organizing the state suffrage association, creating a model. She asked for the name and address of every person in the state who was in favor of woman suffrage. She taught women how to create local societies at the town and county level, which reported to the state association, which reported to the NWSA. Assistance in the form of speakers and tracts flowed from the NWSA down to the state and local organizations. Gage spent the next decade at the top level of the New York State Woman Suffrage Association while also holding top offices at the national level, the only person to do so during the 1870s. She spoke numerous times in Albany before legislative committees and at rallies in New York City, working for a wide variety of women's-rights bills. In 1882, with Governor Alonzo Cornell's support, the New York senate came within eleven votes of passing a woman-suffrage bill that had been passed by the assembly. But achievements on the state level were never the primary goal—they served to further the national agenda. Gage was also the author of the NWSA strategy of working towards an amendment to the U.S. Constitution, which would have been bolstered by the passage of suffrage in New York, the national leader in population, arts, culture, business, and finance for the second half of the nineteenth century.

From 1870 to 1872 Gage worked her way up in the NWSA, learning the ropes and assisting with arrangements for the twice-yearly conventions. After Anthony almost lost control to Woodhull's Equal Rights Party at the May 1872 convention, Gage was promoted to chair of the executive committee, a powerful behind-the-scenes position. For the next ten years, she traded the top offices with Anthony and Stanton. Stanton was most often president, but it was an honorary title, as she spent most of the 1870s on the lecture circuit and only reluctantly attended conventions or wrote materials when Anthony insisted. Likewise, Anthony also had to spend quite a bit of time lecturing to support herself and work off a large debt from the failed *Revolution*. Correspondence indicates that Gage and Anthony consulted each other to determine strategy—assessing the political climate in Washington and how to access the power brokers, which points to emphasize in their arguments for suffrage, and what work should be done by suffragists in the field. Gage traveled to Rochester many times, and Anthony visited the Gage home in Fayetteville so often that the Gage children called the guest room "The Susan B. Anthony Room." Anthony's signature remains inscribed on a windowpane of an upstairs room.

Gage often spoke at and presided over the semi-annual NWSA conventions, which she and Anthony organized with the help of local suffrage affiliates. Twice, when Anthony could not be present, Gage ran the convention entirely on her own. Gage and her fellow suffragists met with platform committees during political-party conventions and testified before numerous congressional committees, pleading for protection of women's voting rights. On two occasions, Gage, Anthony, and Stanton met with President Rutherford B. Hayes at the White House.

Matilda Joslyn Gage was a prolific writer. Because Anthony believed herself a poor writer, Gage often wrote calls and resolutions for conventions, statements of NWSA policy, and petitions to Congress. She wrote articles on a variety of topics for newspapers and magazines across the country. But she excelled in crafting arguments for woman suffrage. In 1871 Gage wrote "The Woman's Rights Catechism," one of the most important documents of this phase of the movement. Short and to the point, the Catechism's question-and-answer format takes an average person through an analysis of women's natural right to vote as citizens in a democracy. Of all the claims made in favor of woman suffrage—including variations on the theme that women were the moral guardians of society who would outlaw liquor traffic and other antisocial behavior—Gage's arguments best stand the test of time. She was regarded as the NWSA's most logical thinker.

When Anthony was arrested for voting in 1872, Gage was the only suffrage leader to stand by her during the trial. She and Anthony canvassed the county where the trial was held, Gage giving her speech "The United States on Trial, Not Susan B. Anthony." Gage defined the woman suffrage debate as the power of the United States versus the political rights of citizens, the chief of which being the ballot, and said that the question addressed by Anthony's trial was not simply whether women should vote but whether the Constitution held the supreme authority in the nation.

In 1874 the Supreme Court ruled in *Minor v. Happersett* that citizenship did not guarantee suffrage and that states had jurisdiction over their voting laws, not the federal government. Gage examined the law and found that, on the contrary, the federal government had created eight classes of new voters, most notably African American men who had been recently enfranchised by the Fourteenth and Fifteenth Amendments. She argued that voting was the primary right on which all other rights depended; therefore, voting rights had to be protected by a strong, centralized government. The NWSA strategy became to convince Congress of the need for national protection of women's right to vote by a sixteenth amendment to the constitution. By contrast, the AWSA was primarily appealing to states for suffrage. Gage knew that if states could give women the vote, they could also take it away or make voting difficult. In a post–Civil War era in which the debate of national rights versus states' rights was still raging, Gage repeatedly spoke and wrote throughout the 1870s and 1880s about national protection for U.S. citizens' rights.

Gage and Anthony were determined to use the nation's one-hundredth birthday celebration as an occasion to demand justice for women. Gage's foresight, writing, and organizing skills were employed to take advantage of this historical moment. In 1876 she was president of the NWSA and the New York State association, handling the January Washington convention and pushing the New York State legislature to allow women to vote for presidential electors. (The Constitution grants states the power to create presidential electors.) In May, Gage took on a new title within the NWSA—chair of the campaign committee, which placed her fully in charge of the centennial activities. She set up NWSA parlors in Philadelphia to take advantage of the nearly ten million visitors to the Centennial Exposition. Gage wrote an important appeal to the Republican nominating convention, the former abolition party, which had given women a sliver of a plank in its 1872 platform. She hoped that the Republicans would increase their support of women's rights in 1876. Gage and Stanton also wrote an address to the Democratic nominating convention and a "Declaration of Rights of Women." When they were refused even a brief time to present the declaration in the official ceremonies in Philadelphia on 4 July 1876, Gage and Anthony, along with three other women, risked arrest to disrupt the celebration and present their declaration to Vice President Thomas W. Ferry in front of thousands of people at Independence Hall. Gage felt it was important to "place on record for the daughters of 1976, the fact that their mothers of 1876 had thus asserted their equality of rights, and thus impeached the government of today for its injustice towards women" (*The Ballot Box*, August 1876).

Newspapers were an important means of communication for nineteenth-century reformers, with each other and the public. Gage and Anthony supported *The Ballot Box*, the newspaper of the Toledo, Ohio, Woman Suffrage Association; but it was local in scope, and they longed for a newspaper devoted to the NWSA, as the *Woman's Journal* was to the AWSA. In April 1878 *The Ballot Box* was transferred to Gage as editor and publisher, with Anthony and Stanton as corresponding editors, and renamed *The National Citizen and Ballot Box*. Under Gage's direction, the monthly paper was just as fiery and radical as the *Revolution* had been. Her motto was "the pen is mightier than the sword," and Gage wielded her pen like a sword, cutting down anyone who did not see the logic of woman's total equality. Her first issue created controversy, as Gage pledged to "make those women discontented who are now content"

("Prospectus," *The National Citizen and Ballot Box*, May 1878). When Governor Robinson of New York refused to sign a bill allowing women to vote for and run in school-board elections, Gage and the state association used *The National Citizen* as a vehicle for defeating him and electing a governor who did sign the bill. Gage and others, such as Lillie Devereux Blake, informed women of their new voting rights and how to organize. Despite harassment, thousands of women voted and several women were elected to public office across New York State in 1880, proving that women did want to vote.

Gage reluctantly gave up *The National Citizen* in October 1881 to concentrate on finishing the *History of Woman Suffrage* with co-editors Stanton and Anthony. Despite its many faults, the *History of Woman Suffrage* remains a monumental achievement—the primary source for information on the woman suffrage movement, much of which would have been lost without the efforts of these three women. They edited the first three volumes sporadically from 1876 to 1886, facing an enormous job of gathering, sorting, and condensing the mountain of papers that they had saved over the years and requested from other suffragists. Much of *History of Woman Suffrage* consists of speeches and previously published materials, such as newspaper articles, letters, and congressional reports, gathered from hundreds of people, spanning more than forty years of suffrage activity. Gage and Stanton wrote introductions and original material to tie these items together, in addition to several original chapters, while Anthony secured a publisher. Several women wrote chapters on their state suffrage organizations, and they are often identified either with a byline or an acknowledgment by the unidentified authors (Gage and/or Stanton).

Many historians have described Gage's role as that of a research aide, secondary to Stanton and Anthony's roles, based on Ida Husted Harper's description of Stanton and Anthony's work at Stanton's home in Tenafly, New Jersey. As Mary Corey has discovered, however, correspondence among the three women indicates that Gage played an equal role in the writing and editing, doing much of the work at her home in Fayetteville, New York. Of the chapters in which Stanton or Gage have a byline, Stanton wrote 86 pages, all reminiscences. Gage was the sole author of 110 pages: "Preceding Causes," "Woman, Church and State," "Women in Newspapers," and "Women during the Civil War"—chapters replete with research and historical analysis. The remaining 338 pages of unaccredited original material were written by Gage and Stanton in collaboration. Evidence suggests that Gage was the primary writer on at least 44 and perhaps as many as 174 of these pages, certainly her fair share; yet her role has been overshadowed by the famous friendship between Stanton and Anthony.

Gage was known in her own time as the foremost historian of this stage of the women's movement; she chronicled the forward progress of women in her time for future generations and researched the past for women's achievements and their oppression. She brought to light obscure facts about women. Gage ran a column in *The National Citizen* called "Women Past and Present" in which she documented the accomplishments of women. In *Woman as Inventor* (1870) and "Woman as an Inventor" (1883), she wrote of Isis, so revered by the people of Egypt for her gifts of invention that she was exalted to the status of goddess. Gage cited example after example of women inventors, culminating in her assertion that Catherine Littlefield Greene, not Eli Whitney, had invented the cotton gin, a machine that had a profound social and economic impact in the nineteenth century. In *Who Planned the Tennessee Campaign of 1862?* (1880) Gage defends Anna Ella Carroll, who was attempting to receive official recognition from the U.S. government for her role in planning successful Union military strategy during the Civil War. Gage loved the emerging field of Egyptology, and her lecture on ancient Egypt and its female rulers was one of her most popular. She did not have the advantage of a college education, but she read voraciously and investigated new ideas with great enthusiasm. The accumulation of years of research resulted in Gage's masterpiece, *Woman, Church and State* (1893), in which she chronicles the history of women since the beginning of time, focusing on the oppression of the Church.

Gage was interested in the status of women in cultures untainted by Christianity. She wrote several newspaper articles about the Haudenosaunee and the Six Nations of the Iroquois Confederacy—Seneca, Cayuga, Onondaga, Oneida, Mohawk, and Tuscarora. These nations, who continue to live in upstate New York, have a matrilineal structure in which husbands move into the longhouse of their wife's family, and children belong to their mother's clan. In traditional Haudenosaunee culture, women were respected: they owned property, grew the crops, and played an important role in religious ceremonies and government—in almost every aspect the complete opposite of nineteenth-century Euro-American women. Gage wrote, "The division of power between the sexes in this Indian republic was nearly equal . . . never was justice more perfect, never civilization higher" ("The Remnant of the Five Nations," *The New York Evening Post*, 24 September 1875). Gage was adopted into the Wolf Clan of the Mohawk Nation in 1893, given the name Ka-ron-ien-ha-wi, or Sky Carrier, and considered for voting rights in her adopted nation. In that same year, in her birth

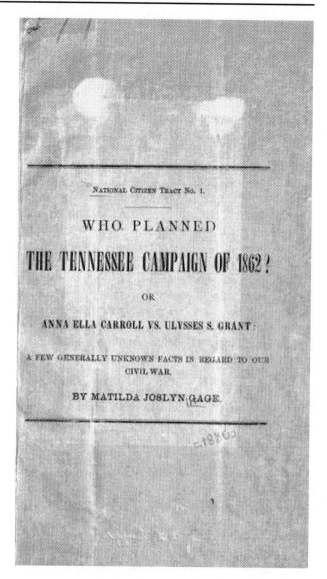

Cover for the 1880 tract in which Gage argues that a woman deserves credit for planning Union military strategy during the Civil War (University of California Libraries)

nation, she was arrested for registering to vote for school commissioner. Gage expert Sally Roesch Wagner believes that Gage, Stanton, and Lucretia Mott were inspired by knowing Native American women who already possessed the rights that the suffragists were struggling to obtain.

Gage's most important contribution to the long-term goal of women's equality was to place the issue of woman's religious freedom front and center on the woman-suffrage platform. Gage, Stanton, and other early feminist theorists struggled to understand how and why women had become second-class citizens so they could uproot the problem at its source. The prevailing belief at the time was that custom and tradition had kept women down, but Protestant Christianity and its civilizing forces throughout the world were gradually elevating women to a position closer to men. The women of the NWSA's rival organization, the AWSA, believed this theory and used the Bible to support woman suffrage. While the idea of women interpreting the Bible for themselves was in itself a radical concept, the AWSA's hope of Christianity being the savior of women's equality relied on a very old concept—basing human rights on the authority of God. By the middle of the 1870s, Gage had rejected the authority of God as revealed through the Bible and felt all humans were a revelation of the divine, given the authority to think for themselves. Once freed from the restraint of an invisible masculine deity, Gage was able to see with new eyes. As she studied the history of women, she came to an earth-shattering conclusion: the church was the source of women's oppression, both directly and through the church's considerable influence upon society, government, and the family. Islam and Judaism were also to blame, she thought, as well as any patriarchal religion, but Christianity had done the most damage, particularly in the United States.

Mainstream Christianity had provided the most vocal opposition to women's equality. Ministers and priests preached sermons against the cause, stating that woman suffrage would disrupt the family and upset the balance of society and nature as ordained by God. They appealed to the Bible to support the idea of separate "spheres" of activity for the sexes. Paul's command for "the women to keep silent" helped support women's subordination. Furthermore, the civil laws of the United States were based on canon law. Because "the two shall become one," and the "one" was defined as the man or the "head" of the household, nineteenth-century law treated a married woman as a nonperson, not even allowed to sign a legal document without her husband's permission. Although property rights gradually changed on the state level through the nineteenth century, women often had no legal right to their earnings or property. Marital rape was legal; spousal abuse was legal within limits. A father could specify the guardianship of his children, even an unborn child, in his will. Upon his death, the children could be legally taken from the mother. If a woman left her husband, she could lose her children forever. Single women were not much better off. Viewed as "unnatural" for being unwed, a single woman had few opportunities for education or satisfying work. Very few jobs available to women paid enough so that a woman might support herself.

When it came to bringing up the issue of religious freedom for women, Gage's timing was perfect. One of the NWSA's biggest conventions was its thirtieth anniversary celebration of the Seneca Falls convention, held in Rochester in 1878. Gage served as chair of the committee on resolutions and wrote two important and controversial resolutions: 1) the first duty of woman is self-development, so she should reject Christianity's teachings of self-sacrifice and obedience; and 2) women should interpret the Bible for themselves and free themselves from superstition and the authority of the church. These resolutions passed after a lengthy debate and brought months of criticism upon the NWSA, especially from ministers and the AWSA.

Radical ideas about religion were not new, but debating the role of religion within the woman-suffrage arena was something that had not been done in many years. Gage, Anthony, and Stanton believed the major obstacle to woman's emancipation was that centuries of male dominance had made women unable to feel worthy of freedom and therefore unwilling to work for their rights. Gage called it "the brand of the slave"; that is, she thought women were so beaten down that they accepted slavery as their natural condition. Gage and Stanton believed the basis of male oppression lay in the teachings of Christianity, which told women that they were inferior, created to serve men; that they had brought sin into the world through Eve; and that their greatest power, that of creating life, was a curse. In defending her resolutions, Gage said that the false ideas of Christianity had so restricted women's spiritual and intellectual development that women had to learn independence of action and freedom of thought before they could be expected to work for their political rights. By this point in her life, in her fifties, Gage had completely rejected all personal belief in Christianity and become involved in the Freethought movement, although she remained a spiritual person, professing a belief in "the Church invisible."

During the years 1882–1886, Gage needed to care for her ill husband (who died in September 1884) and several family members who had serious illnesses. Gage enjoyed her grandchildren immensely and alternated between staying with her children's families and having them come to live with her in the big house in Fayetteville. She was often hampered in her women's-rights work by a lack of money and a need to deal with business concerns and investments. But she remained active in the New York Woman Suffrage Association and the NWSA, holding (as did Anthony) the title of NWSA vice president at large, attending conventions when she could, and continuing to write. In 1884 Gage was an elector-at-large for the Equal Rights Party, which had nominated Belva Lockwood for president. At the cold and rainy dedication of the Statue of Liberty in 1886, Gage, Blake, and other women from the New York State association sailed around Bedloe's

Island with banners flying, in an open, smelly cattle barge (the only ship they could afford to rent) to protest the hypocrisy of freedom being depicted by a woman in a country where no woman was free.

During 1887 Gage worked on arrangements for the meeting of the International Council of Women (ICW), a job for which she has never received proper credit. Held in Washington, D.C., in April 1888, the ICW meeting drew women leaders from all over the world. It was a huge success, and thousands of people attended its receptions and speeches. Gage was honored as a "pioneer" of woman suffrage along with Anthony, Stanton, Lucy Stone, Frances E. Willard, Julia Ward Howe, Isabella Beecher Hooker, and Clara Barton, "the most eminent galaxy of women ever assembled upon one platform" (*History of Woman Suffrage*, IV). On Easter Sunday, Gage gave a groundbreaking speech titled "Woman in the Early Christian Church," which addressed the feminine nature of God, a theme added at the last minute when Gage saw the pious nature of the Christian women at the ICW.

Gage and Stanton were outspoken critics of both Christian representatives' actions and the foundation of Christianity itself, seeing it as a system built upon Eve's "sin," which necessitated a savior. "I regard the Church as the basic principle of immorality in the world, and the most prolific source of pauperism, of crime, and of injustice to women," Gage told a reporter ("Freedom of Women," *The Washington Critic*, 22 February 1890). The two women were in accord philosophically, and Stanton promised they would work together on this issue for the rest of their lives, despite the public image it fostered of suffragists being "infidels" and "heretics."

Anthony was uncomfortable with Gage and Stanton's radical position, because she saw the suffrage movement and indeed her own life's work in terms of a single goal: the vote. Anthony believed that a divided movement could not succeed. She was also eager to use the skills of the charismatic Willard, president of the rapidly growing Women's Christian Temperance Union and a member of the AWSA. Despite the huge differences between the NWSA and the AWSA, and knowing that many national members disliked prohibitionists because they wanted to put God into the Constitution and destroy religious freedom, Anthony engineered a merger of the two organizations behind Gage's back to form the National American Woman Suffrage Association (NAWSA) in 1889. She then asked Stanton to become president of the new organization, which Stanton accepted before sailing to Europe, leaving Anthony to preside in her absence.

Gage was furious. Not only had Stanton turned into a "Benedict Arnold" (as she wrote to her son) and betrayed her promise to work against the church, but also Gage felt that Anthony had ruined the women's-rights movement by aligning it with conservative Christian women. Gage called Willard "the most dangerous person in America" in an 11 March 1890 letter to Harriet Robinson because of Willard's goal, stated in her annual address to the WCTU in 1888 and which she claimed was directed by a vision from God, to "declare Christ and his law to be the true basis of government, and the supreme authority, in national as in individual life." But the WCTU did not present the only threat in this quarter. Other groups, such as the Prohibition Party and the National Reform Association, were attempting to pass Sunday rest laws. In 1884 at the Third Plenary Council in Baltimore, Pope Leo XIII issued an order for "all Catholics to do all in their power to cause the constitution of the States and legislature to be modeled on the principles of the true church," and in 1888 issued an encyclical, *On the Nature of Human Liberty,* in which he "disproved" the principle of separation of church and state.

Gage felt it was time to form her own organization, the Woman's National Liberal Union (WNLU), dedicated to maintaining separation of church and state and fighting religious fundamentalism. The WNLU brought together a broad coalition of freethinkers, anarchists, suffragists, and prison reformers such as Josephine Cables Aldrich, William F. Aldrich, Helen Gardener, Susan Wixon, Mathilde Wendt, Voltairine de Cleyre, Clara Foltz, Laura de Force Gordon, Elliott Coues, Reverend Olympia Brown, and Belva Lockwood. Gage published one edition of a newspaper, *The Liberal Thinker,* and held a convention in February of 1890 in Washington, D.C. Unable to raise enough money to sustain the WNLU, however, she returned to writing her masterpiece, the book that she called her "major life-work."

Woman, Church and State, is one of the most important documents of nineteenth-century feminism, offering a scathing attack of Christianity and a radically new view of history from a feminist perspective. Gage took the notion of Christianity having elevated women's status and flipped it. In accordance with many scholars in the emerging field of anthropology, she concluded that prior to Christianity, women had enjoyed a position of prominence in ancient civilizations, being worshiped as goddesses in heaven and respected as life-givers and equal partners on earth. Women's subordination, she pointed out, began with the advent of Christianity and its solidification into a patriarchal religion. Gage challenged the assumption, still held today, that women

Gage's home in Fayetteville, New York (photograph by L. Frank Baum; Special Collections Research Center, Syracuse University Library)

were gradually developing and becoming the equals of men. Instead, she asserted that women's equal, sometimes superior, status had been stolen by a patriarchal society basing its authority on a male god and teaching female subordination and inferiority as a means to continue the theft and hide the evidence. For this reason Gage felt it of the utmost importance to name the unknown heroines from the past and teach her fellow suffragists about the extraordinary achievements of women throughout history despite oppression.

Woman, Church and State is startling and courageous, revealing, among other things, that the church had debated whether women had souls and came to blame women as the source of evil; that the imposition of celibacy in the Middle Ages led to abuse of women and children by priests; that the hunt for witches was a female genocide; and that institutionalized Christianity sanctioned for centuries women being robbed of their earnings, their children, their bodies, and their intellectual freedom. Gage wrote,

> Slavery and prostitution; persecutions for heresy; the inquisition with its six hundred modes of torture; the destruction of learning; the oppression of science; the systematized betrayal of confiding innocence; the recognized and unrecognized polygamy of man; the denial to woman of a right to herself, her thought, her wages, her children, to a share in the government which rules her, to an equal part in religious institutions—all these and a myriad more, are parts of what is known as Christian civilization.

Such comments prompted feminist philosopher Mary Daly to write nearly a century later:

Her great work, *Woman, Church and State,* is as timely as it was at the date of its original publication in 1893. Gage is one of the great foresisters of contemporary feminists. In her writing, she transcends the boundaries of time and becomes our contemporary. The qualities which make this possible are the depth of her daring and the amazing scope of her analysis. She made the connections which others feared to make. She prophesied, and she named the enemy. Consequently, of course, her stature has never been acknowledged (Foreword to *Woman, Church, and State,* Persephone Press, 1980).

The great tragedy of Gage being written out of history is that *Woman, Church and State* was virtually unknown to twentieth-century feminists, who had to reinvent her theories. Dale Spender writes in *Women of Ideas and What Men Have Done to Them:*

> It is one of the greatest tragic ironies that this woman who understood so much about the process, who put such energy into exposing and subverting it, should herself be the one to "disappear," should have her work wiped away. Could it be that she was the most dangerous? . . . . it seems to me that she, more than any other woman of the past (with the exception of Mary Beard, 1946), identified and understood the process of the denial of woman's existence, the theft of women's being, in a male-dominated society.

For the last decade of her life, Gage spent winters visiting her children and grandchildren, who had moved away from Fayetteville. Her favorite destination was the home of her youngest daughter, Maud, and Maud's husband, L. Frank Baum, who had grown up in Syracuse. Gage initially opposed Maud dropping out of Cornell University to marry Baum but realized that she had raised a strong-minded daughter who was thinking for herself. Gage hosted their wedding in her front parlor. Gage and Baum grew to become quite close. She became one of Baum's intellectual mentors, opening up a world of new ideas to him. She introduced him to theosophy, which exerted a significant influence on Baum's fourteen Oz books and other writing. In fact, Gage suggested that Baum write down some of the fantastic stories that he loved to tell children, and thus she helped transform him from a bankrupt forty-year-old to a successful and prolific author. *The Wonderful Wizard of Oz,* published in 1900, became one of the most beloved and best-known stories of all time.

Gage's ideas pervade much of Baum's work, especially the world of Oz, where Baum creates a feminist utopia for his mother-in-law. While main characters like the Scarecrow and the Tin Woodman recur frequently, three females rank as the most important characters: Dorothy, of course, the plucky girl from Kansas who eventually decides to live in Oz forever; Ozma, a girl princess introduced in the second book, the rightful ruler of Oz; and Glinda, a witch who uses her powers only for good, and whom Dorothy and Ozma call upon for aid whenever they need powerful magic.

Gage died at Maud and Frank's home in Chicago on 18 March 1898, an outsider to an increasingly conservative movement that sought to distance itself from her radicalism. Gage's contributions were minimized and ignored in the reminiscences, biographies, and official histories written by Stanton, Anthony, and Harper. Since Gage's children were living far from New York, the center of the suffrage movement, and she did not leave an autobiography or diary of her own, no one publicly questioned the history presented by Stanton and Anthony, who outlived Gage by several years. Historians and writers have accepted their version of the past and repeated it over and over.

During the first half of the twentieth century, only a few people knew Gage's name, and fewer still understood her importance. The truth remained in the primary documents of the movement and in the letters and scrapbooks that Gage instructed her family to keep. In 1973 Sally Roesch Wagner met Gage's granddaughter, Matilda Jewell Gage, the guardian of these materials, and Wagner assumed the task of returning Gage to her proper place in history. Wagner has spent the years since then collecting Gage's writings and amassing evidence to support her contention that not only was Gage a major leader of the woman suffrage movement, but that knowledge of Gage and her criticism of the church is essential for understanding women's history. Furthermore, Gage's work still has much to offer on questions of human rights, freedom from religion, and other critical issues that the world faces in the twenty-first century.

Wagner and a network of Gage enthusiasts, including many descendants, created the not-for-profit Matilda Joslyn Gage Foundation in 2000 with the mission of promoting an increased understanding of Gage's life and work. As executive director, Wagner oversees a national and local team of advisers, volunteers, and researchers. The foundation publishes Gage's writings, creates educational programming and curriculum, plans conferences, sends speakers into the community, and welcomes visitors to Gage's home. The Gage Foundation bought her house in Fayetteville in 2002, and efforts are under way to restore and preserve the home for future generations. Because Gage lived in the house for more than forty years and did most of her writing there, the Gage Home is one of the most important women's history sites in the nation. It is also a federal- and state-recognized Underground Railroad site and the only women's-history site that includes information about the Haudenosaunee influence. Open to the public, it stands as an icon for the Freethought movement.

Matilda Joslyn Gage is buried in Fayetteville Cemetery, near her home, under her motto: "There is a word sweeter than mother, home, or heaven; that word is liberty."

Biographies:

Barbara S. Rivette, *Fayetteville's First Woman Voter: Matilda Joslyn Gage* (Fayetteville, N.Y.: League of Women Voters, 1970);

Sally Roesch Wagner, "Matilda Joslyn Gage (1826–1898): Suffragist and Freethinker," in *Women Public Speakers in the United States, 1800–1925: A Bio-Critical Sourcebook,* edited by Karlyn Kohrs Campbell (Westport, Conn.: Greenwood Press, 1993);

Wagner, *Matilda Joslyn Gage: She Who Holds the Sky* (Aberdeen, S. Dak.: Sky Carrier Press, 1998);

Wagner, Introduction and afterword in *Woman, Church and State, Modern Readers Edition* by Gage (Aberdeen, S.Dak.: Sky Carrier Press, 1998);

Leila R. Brammer, *Excluded from Suffrage History: Matilda Joslyn Gage, Nineteenth Century American Feminist,* (Westport, Conn.: Greenwood Press, 2000);

References:

L. Frank Baum, *The Annotated Wizard of Oz, Centennial Edition,* edited with an introduction and notes by Michael Patrick Hearn (New York: Norton, 2000);

Mary Daly, *Gyn/Ecology: The Metaethics of Radical Feminism* (Boston: Beacon, 1978);

Annie Laurie Gaylor, ed., *Women without Superstition: "No Gods–No Masters:" The Collected Writings of Women Freethinkers of the Nineteenth and Twentieth Centuries* (Madison, Wis.: Freedom from Religion Foundation, 1997);

Dale Spender, *Women of Ideas and What Men Have Done to Them* (London: Routledge, 1982);

Lynne Spender, "Matilda Joslyn Gage: Active Intellectual," *Feminist Theorists: Three Centuries of Key Women Thinkers,* edited by Dale Spender (New York: Pantheon, 1983), pp. 137–145;

Sally Roesch Wagner, *Sisters in Spirit: Haudenosaunee (Iroquois) Influence on Early American Feminists* (Summertown, Tenn.: Native Voices, 2001);

Wagner, *A Time of Protest: Suffragists Challenge the Republic 1870–1887,* (Aberdeen, S. Dak.: Sky Carrier Press, 1992);

Wagner, *The Wonderful Mother of Oz* (Fayetteville, N.Y.: Matilda Joslyn Gage Foundation, 2003).

Papers:

The major collection of Matilda Joslyn Gage's papers and one of her scrapbooks are housed in the Schlesinger Library at Harvard University. Four of Gage's scrapbooks and the National Woman Suffrage Association papers are at the Library of Congress, Washington, D.C.

Marcus Garvey

(17 August 1887 – 10 June 1940)

Andrew J. Waskey

Dalton State College

BOOKS: *Aims and Objects of Movement for Solution of Negro Problem Outlined* (New York: Universal Negro Improvement Association, 1924);

Selections from the Poetic Meditations of Marcus Garvey (New York: Amy Jacques Garvey, 1927);

The Tragedy of White Injustice (New York: Amy Jacques Garvey, 1927);

The Poetical Works of Marcus Garvey, edited by Tony Martin (Dover, Mass.: Majority Press, 1983);

Message to the People: The Course of African Philosophy, edited by Martin (Dover, Mass.: Majority Press, 1986).

Editions and Collections: *The Philosophy and Opinions of Marcus Garvey; or, Africa for the Africans,* 2 volumes, edited by Amy Jacques Garvey (New York: Universal Publishing House, 1923, 1925);

The Blackman (Kingston, Jamaica: Blackman Publishing, 1939); republished as *The Black Man* (London: Black Man Publishing, 1939);

Garvey and Garveyism, edited by A. J. Garvey (Kingston, Jamaica, 1963; New York: Octagon, 1978);

Marcus Garvey and the Vision of Africa, edited by A. J. Garvey and John H. Clarke (New York: Random House, 1974);

More Philosophy and Opinions of Marcus Garvey, edited by A. J. Garvey and E. U. Essien-Udom (London: Cass, 1977)—includes *The Philosophy and Opinions of Marcus Garvey;*

The Marcus Garvey and Universal Negro Improvement Association Papers, edited by Robert A. Hill, 10 volumes (Berkeley: University of California Press, 1983–2006);

Marcus Garvey: Life & Lessons, edited by Hill and Barbara Bair (Berkeley: University of California Press, 1987);

Marcus Garvey, Man of Vision and Action: His Life, Ideology, and Work, edited by Linda S. Jimison (Indianapolis: LifeStar Enterprises, 1995).

Marcus Garvey is best known as the founder of the Universal Negro Improvement Association (UNIA) and the leader of the back-to-Africa movement in the United

Marcus Garvey (from E. David Cronon, Black Moses: The Story of Marcus Garvey and the Universal Negro Improvement Association, *1969; Thomas Cooper Library, University of South Carolina)*

States between 1916 and 1927. Garvey advocated racial separatism and black empowerment, especially in economic and cultural matters. Much of his writing focused on reinterpreting human history through the lens of racist propaganda. He viewed all information, including art, as having a propagandistic component, and in his writings he tried to make his followers more critical and discriminating consumers of information.

Marcus Mosiah Garvey was born on 17 August 1887 in St. Ann's Bay, Jamaica, a village on the north coast of the island. He was the eleventh child of Marcus and Sarah Garvey. Only he and Indiana, an older sister, lived into adulthood. Garvey's father was descended from the Maroons, the fierce and independent Africans who escaped from their British enslavers during the colonial times of the seventeenth and eighteenth centuries, and Garvey's family was keenly conscious of this heritage.

Marcus's father worked as a stonemason, but only occasionally when forced by economic needs. The rest of the time he secluded himself in his home study and read from his library of books and magazines. The learning, combined with the stubbornness of the senior Garvey, almost proved the undoing of the family. For twenty years Mr. Garvey received a newspaper from a publisher but was never billed for it. He assumed that it was a gift. When the publisher died, however, the executor of the estate billed him. He refused to pay and was hauled into court, where he was ordered to pay. He still refused. Part of the Garvey property was seized to pay for the debt and the court costs. Other legal actions cost the Garvey family all but the small plot on which their home stood. Sarah Garvey, unlike her husband, was known for her kindness and hardworking approach to life. The daughter of a farming family, she owned a plot of land with a brother. She used the income from its crops along with her baking to provide most of the family's income.

Though not wealthy, the Garveys were more prosperous than most blacks on the island. Most of the island's wealth was in the hands of whites or some of the "coloreds" who were of mixed African and European parentage or ancestry. The Garveys' nearest neighbors were white, and Marcus's early childhood was spent playing with white children. This relationship delayed his first experience of racial prejudice until his teenage years. At puberty he was racially separated from his childhood playmates, both female and male. The experience taught him that he would have to fight to attain a place of dignity in the world.

Marcus's education was in the local grammar school and with private tutors. He also read from his father's library. At the age of fifteen he left school to work full-time for a printer. His godfather, an educated man, extended Marcus's education with the old books, newspapers, and magazines that filled the back room of the printing shop. When he turned eighteen years old in 1905, Marcus moved to Kingston to work in an uncle's printing business. He learned enough in two years to become a master printer and a foreman at one of Jamaica's largest businesses. The knowledge he acquired of printing and publishing proved useful when he later started a series of newspapers and journals as media outlets for his organizations.

The streets of Kingston were Garvey's school of politics. Political ideas of the day were often debated passionately on the sidewalks or in local spots. In these informal debates he saw a rough form of public speaking used to declaim on current events and issues. Garvey's Kingston experience also taught him about the realities and inequities of Jamaica's racial practices, leaving him more than dissatisfied with the status quo. He became acutely aware that blacks had little power to achieve a better distribution of the goods and honors of Jamaican society. Garvey became interested in public speaking and added it to his course of study. He began to visit local churches in order to observe the oratorical styles of Kingston's best preachers. He then practiced their techniques in front of a mirror using lessons from his schoolbooks and passed on what he learned to other young people.

On 14 January 1907 a major earthquake struck Jamaica. Much of Kingston burned in the aftershocks. The destruction caused major shortages of food and other necessities. The impact upon the poor, most of whom were black, was catastrophic. The laborers and the poor soon were reduced by the dramatic spike in prices to near starvation. In response the city's workers, including laborers at the printing company where Garvey worked, went on strike. Garvey, though as a foreman not a union member, joined the strikers as a leader. His company's management offered him a wage increase to keep working during the strike, but he refused it.

The strike was a failure. The union's treasurer absconded with the strike fund, and the printing company was able to replace the strikers with other blacks content to work for low wages. Garvey drew from this experience the conclusion that workers' organizations were not ideal for ending social problems. This situation was especially true on an island where large numbers of unemployed laborers were desperate for work and readily available for exploitation. Shortly afterward Garvey began working at the government printing office.

In 1909 he became politically active when he joined the National Club. Organized by a local lawyer, the club claimed as members people who were involved in the struggle to mitigate the national problems that the British rulers of Jamaica chose to ignore or refused to solve. The National Club campaigned for political candidates. Its members also published a newspaper, *Our Own,* which Garvey helped produce. He tried as well to publish his own periodical, *Garvey's Watchman;* however, it failed.

The docks of Kingston Bay were filled with ships from around the world. Conversations with sailors describing their adventures inspired him with the urge to travel. In order to support his political and organizational activities Garvey determined that he needed

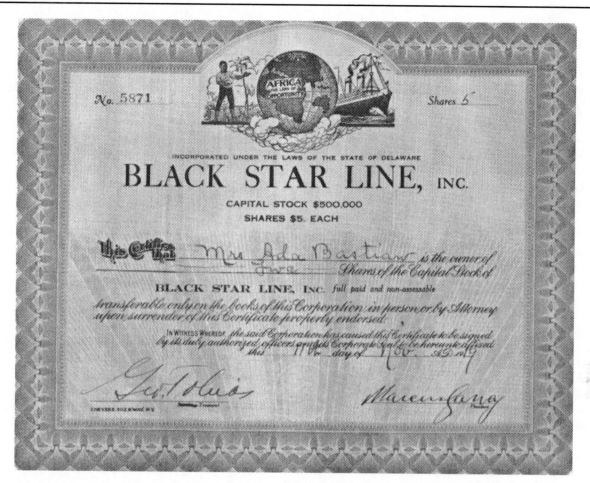

Early stock certificate for Garvey's black-owned shipping business (from The Marcus Garvey and Universal Negro Improvement Association Papers, *volume 2, edited by Robert A. Hill, 1983; Thomas Cooper Library, University of South Carolina)*

funds in greater amounts than he could hope to garner on Jamaica. So, in 1910 Garvey left Jamaica for Costa Rica. His goal was to earn enough money to continue the work of gaining political rights for blacks he had begun in Jamaica. His plans were disrupted when he observed the harsh conditions that confronted the poor in Latin America.

Garvey took a job with the United Fruit Company as a time keeper; however, he could not escape his preoccupation with the plight of the workers and the poor. He found that the wages of many of the black West Indians vanished into the pockets of thieves of various stripes. Indignant, he began a campaign to improve wages and working conditions. He gathered information to document the unhealthy and dangerous conditions that the black West Indians endured and presented it to the British consulate in Puerto Limon. The indifference of the consul convinced him that the British government would not help because it did not value the lives of black men.

Garvey remained in Puerto Limon to organize the laborers on the docks. He began another newspaper, *La Nacionale* (The National), as an organ to agitate for workers' rights. He realized that his efforts were doomed to failure because little political activism could be expected from illiterate men who were often too busy simply surviving. Garvey traveled to Nicaragua, Colombia, Venezuela, and other Latin American nations, finding in each country that the West Indian migrant laborers were exploited and given little opportunity besides hard labor. In Panama, for example, the United States Army was building the Panama Canal with great numbers of blacks from the West Indies in deadly malarial working conditions for poor pay. His appeals to the local British consulates for relief were ignored or rebuffed. In 1912, sick with malaria and harassed by government authorities as a troublemaker, he returned to Jamaica, where he soon recovered his health and organized a delegation to appeal, without success, to the governor of Jamaica for aid.

Rebuffed, Garvey moved to London, where he found work on the London docks. From conversations with black sailors he learned much about the discrimination against blacks around the world. At night he attended Birkbeck College, where he took classes in law and philosophy. He also read about African history and Western political philosophy in London's libraries. He found encouragement in the discovery that African kingdoms and civilizations had existed in the past. He learned that European domination of Africa and much of the world was justified on the ground of Europeans' claims that they provided a civilizing and Christianizing force. London was the center of political activity involving the British Empire, and Garvey found many like himself, who had come from the colonies to study and to promote their visions of political justice.

The Pan-Africa movement, which held that all blacks were a single people and that Africa was their homeland, was founded in the late 1800s. Its members advocated a back-to-Africa movement. Garvey found the ideas and members of this movement compelling. In 1913 he met and began working with Druse Mohammed Ali, the Egyptian publisher of the *African Times and Orient Review,* dedicated to fighting for the rights of native peoples in African and Asian colonies. The job allowed Garvey to continue his education. He published one article in the journal in which he voiced a demand for massive political involvement in Jamaican government by blacks.

Several months later Garvey took a vacation to travel across Europe. After returning to London he made an effort to visit several English cities. In the midst of his travels he came upon a copy of Booker T. Washington's *Up from Slavery* (1901). Washington's ideas had a major impact upon Garvey. Opposing public protest because he believed that the times were not right and that protests would only provoke hostilities between whites and blacks, Washington advocated the idea that blacks should work hard, save their money, and improve themselves with education. These ideas helped Garvey unify his vision of the world, and he saw that blacks had a way to achieve independence.

With his mission in life clarified, Garvey left England. He returned to Jamaica on 15 July 1914. In Kingston he quickly gathered together the people he had previously known and formed the Universal Negro Improvement Association and African Communities League. The title was soon reduced to the Universal Negro Improvement Association. Garvey was chosen as president. UNIA's mission was to unite all blacks of Africa and the African diaspora, to free Africa from colonial rule, and to afford blacks material and spiritual dignity. Locally the goals were to join Jamaica's blacks into a movement of racial pride, to promote universal education, and to promote economic development. Garvey saw UNIA as the engine for driving black protests against their conditions and for achieving their liberation.

UNIA required mobilization and funding. At first the funding came from the membership dues, and the people mobilized into the movement were volunteers. Neither proved sufficient, so Garvey traveled as the chief recruiter through the small towns and villages of Jamaica, seeking donations and recruits. To gain recruits UNIA began promoting education and selling health insurance. Garvey began preaching the ideas of black self-improvement that he had learned from Washington. He was able to use his own life story to tell of his advancement to a higher level in society than dock worker, because he had learned from the books of his grandfather and father.

Garvey promoted the UNIA through debates, classes, lectures, speaking contests, adult-education classes, educational entertainment, and religious meetings. He also called for the spread of educational opportunity for Jamaica's black community, demanding more schools and the opening of higher educational opportunities to them as well. The grand model for his vision was the Tuskegee Institute in Tuskegee, Alabama, where both George Washington Carver and Washington had taught. To establish a similar school in Jamaica became one of UNIA's goals.

Garvey's activities and his vision of educational improvement caught the attention of Jamaica's white leadership. Many of the progressive-minded among them, along with the leadership of the Anglican Church, provided financial support for his educational program. They parted with him, however, in some of his teachings—that when whites in Europe were heathen savages and naked cannibals, blacks in Africa were the creators of a superior civilization, for example.

Garvey's political vision was based on real political equality, but he imagined that blacks would derive the greatest advantage from maintaining a racially separate society. Such a society, he imagined, would quickly bring Jamaica's huge black majority into political power. His most vocal opponents came from Jamaica's colored population. They were usually better educated and wealthier than most blacks. They usually identified themselves with the whites, although they were denied any political power. They were also most threatened by the political vision of two separate societies Garvey espoused. Customarily educated blacks like Garvey married into the colored class and broke their ties with the black laboring class. Garvey's refusal to renounce the poor he sought to lead soon led to harsh attacks upon UNIA and Garvey himself. He found the experience painful, for the colored higher classes produced

THE BLACK STAR LINE?

IF NOT, PLEASE DO SO TO-DAY

The S. S. "FREDERICK DOUGLASS"

Is afloat and has made a successful trip to Central America and the West Indies

Help Float The "PHYLLIS WHEATLEY" On 28th February, 1920

She will sail for Africa

BUY YOUR SHARES AT

BLACK STAR LINE, Inc.

56 W. 135th St.   **New York City**

Advertisement seeking support for Garvey's company (from Tony Sewell, Garvey's Children: The Legacy of Marcus Garvey, *1990; Thomas Cooper Library, University of South Carolina)*

many educated people who could have provided the resources and leadership for advancing UNIA's program.

By 1915 UNIA had made little headway against colored opposition. The war in Europe was distracting whites so that funds for a Jamaican Tuskegee Institute were no longer available. Garvey decided to go to Tuskegee in Alabama to seek help for a fund-raising tour, but, he learned that Washington had just died, so he went instead to New York City and began a new phase of the work of UNIA.

Garvey arrived in the United States on 23 March 1916. He found African Americans ready to listen to his message of ethnic pride and self-improvement. The ground had already been prepared by American black leaders. In New York City, Harlem was becoming a cultural center for African Americans. It was also the center of an emerging black protest movement. For the first few months of his stay Garvey worked as a printer. As in Kingston, he spent his spare time on the streets listening to people and outlining his program of racial solidarity. At first he met with curiosity but little success. Nonetheless, he saved his money to finance an American speaking tour of major cities with large black populations.

Garvey traveled around the United States speaking of his experiences in the Caribbean and in Latin America. He also listened to the views of American black leaders on their history in America and on their current problems, which included a growing legalized program of racial segregation through jim crow laws to keep blacks and whites separate in most aspects of life and even in the cemeteries after death. In addition, Garvey found that with the end of European immigration caused by the war in Europe, northern factories needed labor that was being supplied by black laborers from the rural South. The increases in wages and opportunities had provided cause for hope, but in their northbound migration blacks had, in many cases, exchanged the poverty of the rural South for urban poverty in the North.

Garvey's travels across America in 1916 and 1917 enriched his understanding of the country's black community. The key to upward mobility, he declared, was self-improvement. No handouts were to be expected, but self-sufficiency would be universally respected, even if opposed by many. He was now able to speak a message that appealed to American blacks in a positive way. He had shaped his message into one that was both local and yet universal in vision.

Returning to Harlem in the late spring of 1917, Garvey attended a meeting at which Hubert Harrison, a militant black protest leader, was speaking on 12 June. Spotting Garvey in the audience, Harrison introduced

him to the crowd as the Jamaican leader of UNIA. After Harrison finished his speech, he gave the floor to Garvey. When Garvey explained his program for black improvement, his talk drew cheers and warm applause; it was his first successful speech in New York.

Garvey soon aided a local group in founding a New York chapter of UNIA. He was ready to return to Jamaica when local politicians tried to grab control of the chapter and it was disbanded. Garvey decided to remain in New York and to locate the headquarters of UNIA there. The large and relatively wealthy population of blacks in America made it the natural center for UNIA, which he reorganized, installing himself as president.

To reach the masses Garvey began publishing a weekly newspaper, *Negro World*. At its peak, circulation numbered sixty thousand copies. Distributed across America, throughout the Caribbean, and in both Europe and Africa, it had an enormous impact upon many future black leaders. Jomo Kenyatta, president of Kenya (1964–1978), reported that as a young man he had been inspired by reading copies of *Negro World*. The UNIA motto–"One God, One Aim, One Destiny"–ran across the masthead. *Negro World* described the activities of UNIA in detail. In long editorials Garvey explained and promoted his ideas. He also wrote inspirational profiles describing the successes of black leaders.

As interest in UNIA grew, so did membership, and Garvey's travels intensified. Usually he made two speeches each day, always extemporaneously. When traveling he learned about local conditions and tailored his message accordingly. By 1919 UNIA claimed a membership of two million members in thirty chapters on several continents. Some scholars have disputed UNIA's membership claims as inflated; others have set the number of supporters as high as eight million, whether paying dues or not.

Early in 1919 Garvey started a shipping business, the Black Star Line. The idea of a black-owned company that showcased black accomplishments greatly excited the black community. Stock notices appeared in *Negro World*. Eventually, more than $600,000 worth of stock was purchased to capitalize the line. Garvey also started the Negro Factories Corporation to own and operate businesses in Harlem, including a chain of grocery stories, clothing stores, laundries, a doll factory, restaurants, and other businesses.

By 1919 blacks returning from service during World War I found that their wartime service had little effect on racial discrimination in the United States. Returning white veterans claimed jobs held by blacks during the war; race riots occurred in the United States during the summer of 1919; membership in the Ku Klux Klan increased significantly between 1918 and

1920, in part as a backlash against immigrants. African Americans had supported the war effort loyally, and African American soldiers were praised for their honorable service, but after the war many American blacks despaired of ever attaining racial justice. In this context, Garvey and his UNIA message of universal black unity appealed to millions. His cry of "Up you mighty race" began to be mixed with other approaches to cultivating black pride. He claimed that whites were merely the usurpers and imitators of an earlier superior black civilization. He also encouraged African Americans to stop worshiping a white God and to instead pray to a divine being who was black. Pictures of a white Jesus and white angels in many black homes annoyed Garvey. He urged black parents to give their children black dolls rather than white ones. He also decried the practice of using hair straighteners, skin-bleaching products, and other cosmetics that made people of color look more like whites.

Garvey used UNIA funds to purchase a large auditorium in Harlem to serve as organization headquarters. He renamed it Liberty Hall, a name given to similar auditoriums owned by other chapters of UNIA. In the process Garvey provoked many critics and made some enemies, black and white. His critics included black intellectuals who considered his message crude. Some officials of UNIA went public with complaints against him. Other critics included black clergy who felt that their flocks were being stolen. Editors of competing newspapers and politicians who felt threatened also opposed UNIA. In October 1919 a disgruntled former employee shot Garvey in his New York office. The assailant, George Tyler, claimed that UNIA (i.e., Garvey) owed him $25. Tyler was arrested and died in jail under mysterious circumstances. The assault silenced Garvey's critics while his growing supporters cheered all the louder. On 25 December 1919 Garvey married Amy Ashwood, a UNIA secretary.

Some federal officials saw Garvey as a dangerous radical. J. Edgar Hoover, head of the Department of Justice Bureau of Investigation, the predecessor to the Federal Bureau of Investigation, began investigating him in 1919 at the request of members of the National Association for the Advancement of Colored People (NAACP). The State Department monitored the various UNIA units around the world and found that European powers also had an interest in silencing Garvey.

In August 1920 Garvey staged his most dramatic event, the First International Convention on the Negro Peoples of the World. It opened on 1 August with due solemnity in religious services and silent marches of delegates and UNIA members. The next day a parade marched along Harlem's Lenox Avenue. Conscious of dramatic effect, Garvey had already hired James Van Der Zee, then a rising photographer, to take publicity photographs for UNIA. Garvey himself rode in an open car in a uniform wearing a plumed hat. Many people were astonished to see an army of UNIA organizations marching as African legions, Black Cross nurses, and many other groups including the officers and crew of the Black Star Line. Marching groups carried signs and banners proclaiming their messages of liberty or self-determination.

On the night of 2 August the convention met in Madison Square Garden. Of all the speeches delivered, the grandest was Garvey's. He declared to the European powers that Africa was for Africans and that they were coming to take it all back. A provisional government of Africa was chosen, and Garvey was elected as its president. The new nation was given a flag of red, green, and black. The black was for the color of its people; green was for the lush vegetation of Africa; and red for the color of the blood shed to make its people free. The convention issued a "Declaration of the Rights of the Negro Peoples of the World," which specified fifty-four rights to which African citizens were entitled and due in every country of the world. It also declared 31 August to be an international holiday for blacks. The four-week convention was the high-water mark of Garvey's career.

The second convention in 1921 was less successful than the first. At the end of it, however, Garvey got the black church that he wanted. A friend, George Alexander McGuire, was able to organize the African Orthodox Church. On 28 September 1921, Garvey was ordained as a bishop in a church with a black Jesus and a black God. At its peak, membership numbered around 250,000. Not long afterward, his plan to locate UNIA in an African homeland came to an end. Suspicious of Garvey's motives, the president of Liberia rejected his request for territory for UNIA members.

Financial troubles brought an end to the Black Star Line. It had raised large sums of money, but poor management and simple theft destroyed it. Garvey was not attentive as a businessman, and many of the investors regarded the Black Star Line as more of a propaganda showpiece than as a moneymaking enterprise. The Black Star Line ceased operation after repeated failed efforts to make money with cheap, decrepit ships. Some investors, unhappy with the financial results, claimed that they had been victims of fraud. In January 1922 the federal government charged Garvey and several other company officials with mail fraud.

On 15 June 1922 Garvey divorced his wife and shortly afterward married Amy Jacques. The divorce and marriage were denounced widely in the black community. In August 1922 a new group, Friends of Negro Freedom, came to New York to harass the meeting of

Garvey's second wife, Amy Jacques Garvey (from Rupert Lewis,
Marcus Garvey: Anti-Colonial Champion, *1987;*
Thomas Cooper Library, University of South Carolina)

the third UNIA convention. Street fights erupted between the two groups, and on 15 January 1923, eight leaders in the black community sent a letter to United States Attorney General Harry M. Daugherty, urging him to bring Garvey to trial on the mail-fraud charges. The trial began on 21 March 1923.

Garvey's attempts to force the judge, Julian Mack, an NAACP supporter and contributor, to recuse himself were rebuffed. Garvey's fears of a conspiracy against him were not groundless; however, they caused him first to dismiss his African American attorney and to attempt his own defense, and then to hire a white lawyer who was able to secure an acquittal for the other three defendants but not for Garvey. Many observers felt the guilty verdict was more a judgment against Garvey himself than his actions. On 21 June 1923 Garvey received the maximum sentence of a $1,000 fine and five years in prison. His attorneys immediately appealed.

While out on bail during his appeal, Garvey began a new steamship company, the Black Cross Navigation and Trading Company. This company also ended in failure because it was run too much as a propaganda instrument rather than as an economic asset. On 2 February 1925 the appellate court upheld Garvey's conviction, and three days later he surrendered to federal marshals to begin serving his sentence in Atlanta. In March the United States Supreme Court affirmed the decision of the appellate court. In Atlanta, Garvey was assigned to duty in the prison library. He spent his time reading and writing poetry. He also tried to conduct UNIA business from his cell. His wife struggled to hold the organization together in his absence. Many in the black community believed that his conviction was unjust. Even some of his former enemies seemed to support the view that a black man could not get a fair trial in the United States. Garvey's supporters in UNIA sent telegrams, letters, and petitions demanding the release of their leader. Finally it was determined that few, if any, of the blacks who had bought the stock in the Black Star Line believed that they had been defrauded. The alleged victims saw Garvey's imprisonment not as a protection against a dangerous criminal but as an attack on their race. In response to pressure from the African American community, President Calvin Coolidge commuted Garvey's sentence on 18 November 1927. He was released and immediately deported to Jamaica.

In the United States his movement began to deteriorate without his personal presence. Meanwhile, others put his ideas to use. Elijah Poole, soon to become Elijah Muhammad of the Nation of Islam, and many others used Garvey's ideas about black enterprise and black racial superiority to establish their own organizations. In 1929 UNIA's convention was held in Kingston, Jamaica. Garvey's attempt to relocate the headquarters of UNIA to his place of residence along with his accusations that UNIA officials failed to support him during his legal troubles led to a split in the organization. Garvey then renamed his organization the Parent Body of the Universal Negro Improvement Association.

In September 1929 Garvey formed the People's Political Party, promising reform, especially in the judiciary. He did win seats on local councils, but his party was not a success. In 1930 he wrote a play called *The Coronation of an African King*. At the end of that year he published a brief statement in his journal *The Black Man* about the coronation of Ethiopia's Haile Selassie I that many Jamaican adherents of the Rastafarian religion regarded as a prophecy: in it he quoted Psalms 68:31 and hailed the emperor as the new hope of Africa and the world against European domination. Leonard Howell, one of Garvey's followers, became a founder of Rastafarianism, whose name derives from one of Haile Selassie's titles, Ras Tafari. Garvey did not believe the emperor was divine, however, and sharply criticized him in following years.

In 1935 Garvey and his family (including his two sons, Marcus, born 1930, and Julius, born 1933) left Jamaica for London, where he hoped to revitalize his movement. He was deeply saddened by Benito Mussolini's conquest of Ethiopia (October 1935 to May 1936), and in *The Black Man* he called upon blacks everywhere to fight against it. Expensive to produce and distribute, the issues of *The Black Man* dwindled as the years went by. To recruit the younger generation Garvey organized the School of African Philosophy, based on twenty-two leadership lessons, and presented them at a UNIA conference in Canada in August 1937. Once he returned to London, only eight students took the correspondence course. In 1938 Amy Garvey took the two boys back to Jamaica because the English weather was too hard on them. Garvey remained behind. *The Black Man*'s last issue was published in June 1939.

In 1940 Garvey suffered a stroke. Partially paralyzed and refusing to heed his physicians, he soldiered on in England. Both his physical and financial conditions continued to decline. The end came on 10 June 1940, in a cottage in West Kensington. Despite his wish to be buried in Jamaica, he was interred in England. In 1964 Garvey's remains were returned to Jamaica with a hero's welcome. He had never visited Africa, but during the period of the Civil Rights Movement in the United States and in various African colonial liberation movements that grew throughout the twentieth century, young leaders found his ideas inspiring.

As Garvey had considered himself a leader and a trainer of leaders, in his lifetime he directed most of his efforts toward running newspapers, arranging funding, organizing groups and conventions, and inculcating his target groups with his message of racial empowerment. Most of Garvey's work was not available in other than fragmentary form until late in the twentieth century; his wife collected some of his work for publication before and after his death, but these materials remained rare until relatively recently. His newspaper articles, essays, and speeches have been variously collected, although these compilations tend to be uneven and unsystematic, and often misleading.

A master propagandist whom some have characterized as Machiavellian, Garvey had keen insight into the cultural processes through which ideas and stories became established as "fact" in people's minds. He saw that to loosen the hold of accepted ideas upon the black population, he had to offer an alternate version of history that spoke more to their experience. In a time when most African Americans and other peoples of African descent had directly experienced brutality and injustice from white people, Garvey still had to work to convince his audience that their subjection was part of a larger history. In *The Tragedy of White Injustice* (1927) Garvey offered a rereading of Western civilization as the triumph of a mutant race of murderers and bandits marauding their way around the globe, devaluing older civilizations and destroying whatever stood in their way. He revisited this theme many times, urging his students to improve their knowledge of history and the human sciences, to study the history of the English language, even to buy a set of *Encyclopaedia Britannica*.

Marcus Garvey argued that African Americans must become masters of the existing body of knowledge so that they might "turn the tables on" whites and white supremacy. Above all, he states in the opening of *Message to the People: The Course of African Philosophy* (1986), literacy includes source evaluation, an understanding of the place, time, and interests that have gone into the production of a text. He urged his readers to regard every form of information as propaganda and to regard it with a critical eye. He cultivated an awareness of cultural bias, and, along with many Harlem Renaissance writers, he argued that African Americans must create an Afrocentric counterpropaganda to establish in their own minds and in the minds of the general public the value of their race as a source of wisdom and beauty.

Bibliographies:

Lenwood G. Davis and Janet L. Sims, *Marcus Garvey: An Annotated Bibliography* (Westport, Conn.: Greenwood Press, 1980);

Marcus Mosiah Garvey, 1887–1940: An Annotated List of Materials in the National Library of Jamaica (Kingston, Jamaica, 1987).

References:

E. David Cronon, *Black Moses: The Story of Marcus Garvey and the Universal Negro Improvement Association* (Madison: University of Wisconsin Press, 1955; republished, 1969);

Cronon, ed., *Marcus Garvey* (Englewood Cliffs, N.J.: Prentice-Hall, 1973);

John Hope Franklin and August Meier, *Black Leaders of the Twentieth Century* (Urbana: University of Illinois Press, 1982);

Robert A. Hill, ed., *The Marcus Garvey and Universal Negro Improvement Association Papers* website, 2003 <http://adh.sc.edu/mg/mg-table.html> (accessed 24 July 2008);

Mary Lawler, *Marcus Garvey: Black Nationalist Leader* (New York: Chelsea House Publishers, 1988);

Rupert Lewis, *Marcus Garvey: Anti-Colonial Champion* (London: Karia Press, 1987; Trenton, N.J.: Africa World Press, 1988);

Tony Martin, *Race First: The Ideological and Organizational Struggle of Marcus Garvey and the Universal Negro Improvement Association* (Dover, Mass.: Majority Press, 1986);

Tony Sewell, *Garvey's Children: The Legacy of Marcus Garvey* (Trenton, N.J.: Africa World Press, 1990);

Judith Stein, *The World of Marcus Garvey: Race and Class in Modern Society* (Baton Rouge: Louisiana State University Press, 1986);

William L. Van Deburg, *Modern Black Nationalism: From Marcus Garvey to Louis Farrakhan* (New York: New York University Press, 1997);

Sitamon Mubaraka Youssef, *Marcus Garvey: The F.B.I. Investigation Files* (Trenton, N.J.: Africa World Press, 1998).

Papers:
Marcus Garvey's personal papers are spread around many locations in several countries. Among the more important repositories are the National Library of Jamaica; the Schomburg Center for Research in Black Culture in Harlem, New York; the Fisk University Library in Nashville, Tennessee; and the National Records and Archive Service, Washington, D.C.

Moses Harman
(12 October 1830 – 30 January 1910)

Rebecca Tolley-Stokes
East Tennessee State University

BOOKS: *The Next Revolution: Or, Woman's Emancipation from Sex Slavery: Four Pamphlets* (Valley Falls, Kans.: Lucifer Publishing, 1890);

Digging for Bedrock. Campmeeting Talks, Observations and Experiences (Valley Falls, Kans.: Lucifer Publishing, 1890);

The Kansas Fight for the Free Press: The Four Indicted Articles (Valley Falls, Kans.: Lucifer Publishing, 1899);

Love in Freedom (Chicago: Moses Harman Publishing, 1900);

Institutional Marriage (Chicago: Light Bearer Library, 1901);

Right To Be Born Well Most Important of all Human Rights (Chicago: Light Bearer Library, 1905);

A Free Man's Creed: Discussion of Love in Freedom as Opposed to Institutional Marriage (Los Angeles, 1908).

SELECTED PERIODICAL PUBLICATIONS–
UNCOLLECTED: "Practical Anarchism," *Lucifer,* January 8, 1886;

"Our Object," *Lucifer,* April 9, 1886;

"The Chicago Riots," *Lucifer,* May 7, 1886;

"Anarchism Again," *Lucifer,* March 19, 1886;

"The Lesson of Chicago," *Lucifer,* May 14, 1886;

"The Statute," *Lucifer,* July 1, 1887;

"Another Centennial," *Lucifer,* August 26, 1887;

"God in Politics," *Lucifer,* November 18, 1887;

"Liberty and Licentiousness," *Lucifer,* February 8, 1889;

"The Sovereignty of Woman," *Lucifer,* February 8, 1889;

"Labor Exchange," *Lucifer,* September 23, 1893;

"Knowledge the Only Savior," *Lucifer,* June 5, 1896;

"Letter From the Editor," *Lucifer,* June 5, 1896;

"Criminology," *Lucifer,* July 17, 1896;

"Our New Humanity," *Lucifer,* July 17, 1896;

"Convention Notes," *Lucifer,* July 24, 1896;

"Mt. Pleasant Park," *Lucifer,* August 4, 1896;

"A Few More St. Louis Notes," *Lucifer,* August 7, 1896;

"Shall It Be War," *Lucifer,* August 7, 1896;

"At Camp Brady," *Lucifer,* August 14, 1896;

"Wrongs of Women," *Lucifer,* August 14, 1896;

Moses Harman (Kansas State Historical Society)

"Another Week at Camp Brady," *Lucifer,* August 21, 1896;

"Farewell to Camp Brady," *Lucifer,* August 28, 1896;

"Natural Food," *Lucifer,* September 11, 1896;

"Who Are the Lawbreakers," *Lucifer,* September 11, 1896;

"Current Comment," *Lucifer,* September 18, 1896;

"Co-operative College of Citizenship," *Lucifer,* September 25, 1896;

"Motherhood in Freedom," *Lucifer,* September 25, 1896;

"A New Field of Colonization," *Lucifer,* September 25, 1896;

"Near the Other Side," *Lucifer,* October 2, 1896;

"Our New Humanity," *Lucifer,* October 9, 1896;

"The Campaign of Education," *Lucifer,* November 13, 1896;

"Inequality in Divorce," *Lucifer,* 1896;

"What Children Should Be Taught," *Lucifer,* 1896;

"Freedom of Choice, the Foundation Principle," *Lucifer,* February 24, 1897;

"A Free Man's Creed," *Lucifer,* April 7, 1897;

"The Gospel of Discontent," *Lucifer,* April 7, 1897;

"The Money Value of a Wife," *Lucifer,* 1897;

"The Population Question," *Lucifer,* 1897;

"The True Life of Sex," *Lucifer,* 1897;

"The Emotions of Childhood," *Lucifer,* 1898;

"Love the Universal Law," *Lucifer,* 1898;

"Hear All Sides," *Lucifer,* March 16, 1898;

"From My Point of View," *Lucifer,* September 24, 1898;

"The New Feudalism," *Lucifer,* July 15, 1899;

"The Question of Women's Dress," *Lucifer,* 1899;

"The Population and Economic Question," *Lucifer,* 1899;

"A Plea for Sexual Reform," *Lucifer,* 1900;

"Are Children Human Beings?" *Lucifer,* 1900;

"Pre-Nuptial and Post-Nuptial Contracts," *Lucifer,* 1900;

"Continence or Abstinence," *Lucifer,* June 2, 1900;

"Autobiographical," *Lucifer,* September 15, 1900;

"Politics," *Lucifer,* December 22, 1900;

"Where We Are At *Lucifer,*" *Lucifer,* June 8, 1901;

"What is a Sensible Marriage Law?" *Lucifer,* 1901;

"Children's Rights," *Lucifer,* 1901;

"Militarism, Nationalism, Imperialism," *Lucifer,* May 8, 1902;

"The Coming Sexualism," *Lucifer,* 1902;

"The Meaning of the Press Censorship," *Lucifer,* 1902;

"Slavery In and Out of Legal Marriage," *Lucifer,* 1903;

"The Fall of Nations through Marriage," *Lucifer,* 1903;

"The Free Woman's Choice," *Lucifer,* 1903;

"Friendships Between Men and Women," *Lucifer,* 1904;

"The Right To Be Born Well," *Lucifer,* 1904;

"The Fugitive Wife," *Lucifer,* 1904;

"Book Reviews," *Lucifer,* January 1, 1905;

"Limited Marriages," *Lucifer,* January 1, 1905;

"New Year's Greetings," *Lucifer,* January 1, 1905;

"Book Review of Dr. Hardcastle's Sex-Life Science," *Lucifer,* January 19, 1905;

"The Outlook," *Lucifer,* January 19, 1905;

"The Socialist View," January 19, 1905;

"American Postal Inquisition at Work," *Lucifer,* February 16, 1905;

"Impurity of Divorce Suppression," *Lucifer,* February 16, 1905;

"*Lucifer*'s Symposium," *Lucifer,* February 16, 1905;

"Under the Harrow Once More," *Lucifer,* March 2, 1905;

"Another Edition Confiscated," *Lucifer,* July 6, 1905;

"Elected For A Fourth Term," *Lucifer,* July 6, 1905;

"What of The Future," *Lucifer,* July 6, 1905;

"What Our Exchanges Say About It," *Lucifer,* July 6, 1905;

"*Lucifer*'s Quarter-Centennial," *Lucifer,* July 20, 1905;

"Present Status of *Lucifer*," *Lucifer,* July 20, 1905 ;

"The Right To Be Born Well," *Lucifer,* July 20, 1905;

"Francis Wright," *Lucifer,* August 3, 1905;

"Going Backward," *Lucifer,* August 3, 1905;

"Watchdogs and Their Masters," *Lucifer,* August 3, 1905;

"What Some of Our British Cousins Think of Us," *Lucifer,* August 3, 1905;

"Individualism or Collectivism—Which or Both," *Lucifer,* August 18, 1905;

"Literature of Protest," *Lucifer,* November 9, 1905;

"The Tempest in New York," *Lucifer,* November 9, 1905;

"The Significance of Divorce," *Lucifer,* 1905;

"Postal Censorship in the United States," *Lucifer,* 1905;

"Why Free Speech is Necessary," *Lucifer,* 1906;

"When Divorce is a Blessing," *Lucifer,* 1906;

"Should Women Demand Pay for Being Mothers?" *Lucifer,* 1906;

"Letter From the Editor," *Lucifer,* July 22, 1906;

"Letter From the Editor," *Lucifer,* September 2, 1906 ;

"Letter From the Editor," *Lucifer,* November 29, 1906 ;

"More Letters From the Editor," *Lucifer,* November 29, 1906;

"Interest in Eugenics Increasing," *Lucifer,* 1907;

"Test Case on Obscenity," *Lucifer,* 1907;

"Love and Socialism," *Lucifer,* 1907;

"Socialism and the Christian Church," *Lucifer,* 1907.

MAJOR POSITIONS HELD: *Valley Falls Liberal,* editor 1880–1883;

Lucifer the Light-Bearer, editor 1883–1890 (Valley Falls, Kans.), 1890–1896 (Topeka, Kans.), 1896–1907 (Chicago, Ill.);

The American Journal of Eugenics, editor 1907–1910.

Moses Harman's newspaper *Lucifer the Light-Bearer* provided a forum for free thought and sex radicalism in the late nineteenth century, and he is most remembered for his battles for freedom of speech when the federal government suppressed his newspaper for obscenity. At the time, *Lucifer the Light-Bearer* was the only publication dedicated to sexual liberty for women. Harman's ideas of free love and free thought informed every essay, every article, every letter, and every book he wrote. His policy of accepting explicitness in the publication was unusual for the time and garnered him several prison terms. One of the most radical men of his time, Harman was not the first man to champion women's liberation or to promote the idea of free love, but his ideas were so divorced from the norm that he became a curiosity and must be numbered among early feminists.

Moses Harman was born on 12 October 1830 in Pendleton County, Virginia (now West Virginia) to Job and Nancy Harman. Job Harman was a farmer and land speculator, and the family moved again, through Ohio and Indiana, before settling in Missouri during Moses's first decade of life. Primarily self-taught due to his nomadic childhood, the young Harman borrowed books from friends and neighbors as he could. At twelve, an accident kept him bedridden for months. He spent the time reading. By age sixteen Harman acquired enough knowledge to work as a subscription teacher. At eighteen, his family scrimped so that he could attend Arcadia Methodist Seminary in Arcadia, Missouri. About the same time he was licensed to preach by the Methodist Episcopal Church, South. He earned money for tuition and books by tutoring his wealthy classmates and graduated in 1851.

Harman also studied at the St. Louis Normal School but soon received teaching assignments and began traveling the Midwest. As head of the high school at Warsaw, Missouri, Harman met members of the community and became acquainted with the local Unitarian Universalist community, with whom he shared broadened worldviews and antislavery sentiment. His antislavery beliefs were at odds with the Southern Methodist Church, and by 1860 he strayed from the dogma of his youth and claimed farming as his occupation. At least a decade prior to the outbreak of the Civil War, disagreements about the practice of slaveholding incited violence along the Missouri-Kansas border; it was dangerous to speak plainly against slavery. When the townsfolk of Crawford County learned Harman's abolitionist leanings, they met and voted to run him out of town.

Like most men of his generation, Harman experienced the Civil War as a turning point in his life. Twice he tried to enlist with the Union, but the army would not take him due to residual lameness incurred from the childhood injury. Regardless, Confederate guerilla incursions against his community on the Missouri border fueled his ire, and he helped organize the Thirty-Second Regiment of Missouri Volunteers stationed at Rolla. The volatility of the Civil War changed his community into a highly charged area in which free speech hazarded hanging. In 1863 Harman became Leasburg's first teacher.

On 25 July 1866 Harman married Susan Scheuck. Prior to their marriage they entered a personal contract that pledged voluntary standards of conduct based on love rather than duty. Their first child,

George, was born in 1867, and a daughter, Lillian, was born in 1869. Both Susan and their third child died during childbirth in 1877. Their deaths caused Harman to question his faith and belief in the afterlife. In the years immediately following their deaths, his agnostic viewpoint germinated into a broader set of beliefs about social policy. Social reform soon consumed his thoughts, and he left the ministry altogether.

In June 1879 Harman moved his family to Delaware Township (Jefferson County), Kansas, and gained a teaching post. He married Isabel Hiser of Valley Falls, Kansas. His recently transformed beliefs made themselves manifest in his activities in the Valley Falls Liberal League and the local free-thought organization. In November 1880 Harman and A. J. Searl of Valley Falls began co-editing the Valley Falls *Liberal,* a mouthpiece of the Liberal League.

As a freethinker Harman held unconventional opinions about divorce, marriage, childrearing, and religion. He believed that all social and political structures needed reform and that people should be allowed to think for themselves without the interference of hierarchical structures and organizations. Harman's philosophy was essentially anarchistic; he agreed with the philosophy of anarchism that Emma Goldman later articulated, but at the time he balked at affiliating himself with any movement or organization. At the root of his beliefs lay his conviction of the wrongness of the sexual slavery of women. Women, he believed, were enslaved by the institution of marriage, which was condoned or required by the state. He felt neither religion nor secular government should regulate sexual relations. Harman's beliefs placed him in opposition to the Comstock Act passed on 3 March 1873. The Act's originator, Andrew Comstock, believed that obscenity was the root cause of the country's social problems and that the free-love movement inspired those engaged in distributing obscenity. Comstock thought free lovers had a sexual disorder.

Searl and Harman solicited reader response to their writing, which mocked the local clergy. Published monthly, the four-page paper was free, but subscribers were asked to pay a modest fee of fifty cents per year. When they renamed the paper the *Kansas Liberal* in September 1881, Harman became responsible for the paper's content as Searl stepped down. Around this time, Harman cooled his invective against the church and clergy and turned his efforts toward reform. The paper's controversial articles focusing on ending the sexual slavery of women, spiritualism versus materialism, and Unitarianism. The paper's offices moved to Lawrence for six months in 1882 where Annie L. Diggs assisted Harman with editing, but the *Liberal* returned

Flag for Harman's newspaper, a forum for free thought and sex radicalism (Thomas Cooper Library, University of South Carolina)

to Valley Falls in September 1882 after a clash over the prohibition question erupted.

Harman's views, which always opposed restrictions upon personal freedom, were in the minority among activists in the women's suffrage and free-thought movements. Without peer in his advocacy of women's self-determination, Harman thought women had a natural right to control the conditions of their motherhood, stressed the biological destiny of women as a sign of their moral superiority, and supported the dominion of women in the home and family. He recognized that women would never have political independence until they could earn money and thus earn respect. This was not possible because their best years were devoted to child bearing and raising.

In 1883 Harman dropped the publication's reference to Kansas and changed the title to *Lucifer the Light-Bearer* because the ideas in the paper appealed to people across the United States and heralded the dawning of a new day. Another change he made was divorcing the paper from the Liberal League. *Lucifer* now belonged to its contributors and its editor. Harman's co-editor was Edwin Cox Walker, a book dealer and journalist who shared Harman's ideals. This change in organization attested to his belief in the abolition of paternalism, which he believed was the cause of all social problems. Harman dated the issues of the paper with his own calendar that began with the execution of the astronomer Giordano Bruno in 1601. Bruno questioned church doctrine (specifically, he said that the universe was infinite, which called into question the distinct boundary the Church Fathers imagined between God and the material world), and he was burned at the stake. In the new calendar the letters E.M., meaning Era of Man, followed year dates.

The scope of *Lucifer* was broad. Articles spanned an extended array of progressive and radical causes with which Harman was allied. Harman criticized the government and self-identified as an anarchist, preferring government from within rather than from without. He wrote editorials couched in extreme language about human rights but believed that peace and reform were attainable via education and information, not the violence of revolution. Harman supported labor and covered strikes and labor stories within the pages of *Lucifer*. In the early weeks of May 1886 Harman responded to the Haymarket Tragedy with "The Chicago Riots" and "The Lesson of Chicago." Harman scolded the anarchists for their reliance upon violence and reminded readers that the editor constantly warned labor organizations that shedding blood and rioting puts labor in the wrong. In the latter article, Harman admitted confusion about the events but declared that free speech and Socialist strikers were on trial in Chicago.

Like its earlier incarnation, *Lucifer* included essays and articles that ridiculed the local clergy in Harman's community. Issues in *Lucifer* were riddled with controversy as contributors held open discussions about women's sexual slavery and issues of hygiene and education. Harman ran advertisements for books and pamphlets on the topics of marriage and sex instruction that drew a largely female readership. Before long *Lucifer* became an open forum for any discussion of body parts and birth control. By 1886 Harman instituted his "free word" policy whereby he refused to edit explicit language in any correspondence of letters to the editor that he printed in *Lucifer*. Concurrently Angela and Ezra Heywood, who published a radical monthly called *The Word: A*

Monthly Journal of Reform (1872–1892), adopted the same policy, originating from Stephen Pearl Andrews, a radical reformer.

On 20 September 1886 Harman officiated at the marriage of his daughter, Lillian, to Walker, who sometime prior to that date divorced his wife, Laura V. Walker and left their children to her care. The ceremony united the two in a secular union of mutual autonomy. Harman's stepson, W. F. Hiser, filed a complaint with the Justice of the Peace in Jefferson County that the pair were living together without being legally wed. A warrant was issued for the arrest of Lillian Harman and E. C. Walker. The judge at Oskaloosa set bail at $1,000 and set a trial date. Harman and Walker remained in jail until October, when the trial opened. Radicals of their acquaintance believed the couple was prosecuted to suppress the free love and anarchist content of Lucifer, and the case drew national attention. Both were judged guilty on 20 October 1886; Walker served seventy-five days in jail and Lillian forty-five days. They remained in jail after serving their time, because they refused to pay court costs. Both appealed the case on 4 March 1887, but the Kansas Supreme Court upheld the guilty verdict, declaring that it was the state's duty reasonably to regulate marriages within its jurisdiction. Further, the couple must legally marry or face further charges, but Harman was allowed to retain her maiden name.

On 23 February 1887, in the midst of Lillian Harman's trial, the staff of Lucifer was arrested for the publication of three letters. The most notorious of the three was the so-called Markland letter, which attested in graphic terms to the realities of forced sexual intercourse within marriage. Wesley G. Markland was an anarchist residing in Sherwood (Franklin County), Tennessee, who originally received the letter and forwarded it to Harman. It appeared in Lucifer on 18 June 1886; its content described a wife's difficulty as her husband forced sex upon her person post-operatively, thus tearing the stitches from her incision. The second letter lodged a protest against the availability of contraceptives, and the third clearly tested the obscenity laws by revealing a couple's self-confessed sexual improprieties. Harman was one of many publishers, writers, and journalists who ran afoul of the Comstock Laws, which targeted "obscenity" sent through the U.S. mail.

In 1888 Lillian Harman and Walker resigned from Lucifer because they disagreed with Harman's editorial policies. They published Fair Play in Valley Falls beginning that year until 1891 when the subscription was transferred to Liberty. Walker later published books under the imprint Fair Play Publishing Company in New York. Reprinted from articles previously published in Lucifer, The Next Revolution: Or, Woman's Emancipation from Sex Slavery: Four Pamphlets (1890) covered the details of Harman's obscenity case and the subsequent arrest of J. B. Caldwell, the editor of Christian Life, on obscenity charges for promoting sexual intercourse for procreation only. Additionally, Caldwell's critics denounced him for his public defense of Harman's actions. Harman outlined his editorial policy and offered the facts of his persecution and the proceedings of his trial based upon his publication of the O'Neill letter, or "A Physicians Testimony," which described the doctor's experience of attending women who experienced rape within their marriages. Harman was prosecuted for publication of this item in Lucifer, yet Ezra Heywood printed it in The Word without incident.

Sentenced to five years in the Kansas State Penitentiary on 20 April 1890, Harman served several months before being released on appeal. He moved the Lucifer offices to Topeka, Kansas, later that year. The next year he was sentenced to one year for publication of the O'Neill letter. In March 1891 his case was dismissed due to a technical error. Publication of Lucifer continued during Harman's incarceration, with Lillian at its helm; Walker and George Harman assisted in her endeavors. Harman's legal troubles lasted almost a decade and provided precedents for later court decisions regarding obscenity. He was re-sentenced in June 1895 and released from prison in April 1896. Harman moved Lucifer's offices from Kansas to Chicago, Illinois, then, and the first issue of Lucifer published in the city was dated 8 May 1896.

On 13 October 1897 Harman appeared at a public event, one of several speakers who raised money for imprisoned editors of the Firebrand, an anarchist journal; other speakers included Max Baginski, Lucy Parsons, and Goldman. Harman and Goldman did not formally meet until the next year when Goldman visited Chicago the week of 20 March 1898, and they discussed women's emancipation. In 1898 Harman left the editing and publication issues to his staff and traveled across the country lecturing on free thought and acquiring subscribers for Lucifer. Financial support was always a problem. Many readers were dismayed by his beliefs, and they distanced themselves from him by withdrawing backing. The proceeds of his retrospective account of the obscenity case, The Kansas Fight for the Free Press: The Four Indicted Articles (1899), helped support him a little longer.

By 1899 when The Kansas Fight for the Free Press: The Four Indicted Articles was published, Harman had returned to Valley Falls. The first paragraph of the publication dated 12 October 1889 states that Harman, Walker, and George Harman were about to be tried in the U.S. District Court for the District of Kansas on a charge of improper use of the U.S. Mail Service. Both

Harmans and Walker were cited for publishing and distributing four obscene articles in *Lucifer*. In the interest of justice Harman republished the articles in *The Kansas Fight for the Free Press: The Four Indicted Articles,* because the U.S. Mail Service confiscated newspaper issues containing the articles and subscribers were unable to judge for themselves the merits of the case.

Published in their original order, and as Harman states, their relative importance, the items in question include "The Markland Letter"; "Mrs. Whitehead to Elmina," by Celia Whitehead; "Comments on Chavannes Article" by Elmira Correspondent; and "Family Secrets" by Uncle Tom. Harman argued that the issue at the heart of the indictment was civil rights and that he refused to surrender his fundamental right to freedom of expression and speech. "Mrs. Whitehead to Elmina" deals with preventing conception. The letter's author takes issue with an opinion expressed by Elmina D. Slenker that preventing conception was of primary interest to men and women of the day. Slenker had advocated that contraceptives be issued freely to every woman. Whitehead claimed that if such a thing happened, the language of the law would tell women that they "are the lawful prey of the sexual passions of men." She believed the issue was sexual slavery. Whitehead's concern was that if women were provided with contraceptives, then they would lose their main reason for refusing the sexual demands of their husbands, thus debasing them in perpetuity. She added that childbearing was not the only cause of damage to women's health, however; she knew plenty of barren women whose bodies bore the brunt of their brutish husband's sexual demands.

"Comments on Chavannes Article" responded to a practice of non-orgasmic sexual relations (Dianism) mentioned in Albert Chavannes's 10 December letter to *Lucifer*. The author states that he or she had not seen an article opposed to Dianism. The writer compares two such systems whose expositors claim that sexual emissions waste materials that should have been used to seed future generations. The author advocates male continence and said that sexual organs should be used only for procreative purposes.

"Family Secrets" lays out the story of a man called Isaac Dodson and his wife who believed in the prophecy of William Miller, a Baptist preacher and reformer who gave the year of Christ's return as 1843. "Family Secrets" describes how the married couple prepared themselves for the Second Coming by admitting their domestic secrets to one another. The account includes a reproduction of their dialogue. The husband commands his wife to go first. She obliges by informing him that he was not the father of their son William and names one of their neighbors as the father. Then she

claims that their daughter Mary is not his issue either and named another man in the community. Finally she reveals that their youngest son, Johnny, is not his biological son either. The man calls upon the Lord to take him then, as he is ready to leave the temporal world. Advertisements announcing the availability of the several titles for purchase concluded the pamphlet.

Digging for Bedrock. Campmeeting Talks, Observations and Experiences (1900), summarizes Harman's experiences at the Mount Pleasant Park camp meeting near Clinton, Iowa. Upon his return to Valley Falls from the meeting, he writes that several letters from readers asked that he share what he learned. Harman reveals his learning in a roundabout way. First he asks the reader's forbearance while he reprints an article written some weeks ago for *Lucifer* columns. The article, "Personal and Impersonal," gives an idea of Harman's mentality, aims, and purposes in life. He writes of fighting the good fight, which for him was winning his natural right to "tell naked truths in a nakedly honest and straightforward way." He referenced the courage of Bruno and the unveiling of a monument to the martyred astronomer in Rome. Likening himself to Bruno as one who stood alone, the world against him, Harman champions liberty's cause via passive resistance and despises the despotism of militarism and violence.

On the book's fourth page Harman brings up his present problems: the ongoing conflict between *Lucifer* and the Comstock Act. He declares the battle of and for principles rather than persons, and acknowledges the role of *Lucifer* as antagonist in the fight. Harman admits that he allowed anti-Comstock matter to monopolize the periodical's pages for several years. This new book summarizes the ideas he developed through the years of legal battles and prison time and reveals the direction he wants to take for the future.

By way of transition Harman responds to two letters to *Lucifer*. The first suggested that shock was a good strategy for jolting people out of their theological superstitions. Harman agrees, mentioning medical anecdotes about electric shocks being good for the body as well as shocking the body back to normal after it reached a state of hypothermia. The second letter advised Harman that the best way to burst the bondage of fear is to speak loudly and plainly. Harman applauds Helen Williams for her advice and declares that senseless prohibition of words and knowledge steals liberty from the people. In a section titled "Conditions," Harman develops the thesis that "life forces are dependent upon conditions for results." He discusses omnipotent forces meeting insurmountable objects and deems them both absurd by suggesting that they are imagined and not real. Next Harman relates the history of the planet as a continual struggle against unfavorable conditions. He writes at length about Nature and repeats himself in the following paragraph to stress human struggles against Nature as adaptive. Harman references the theories of Charles Darwin and Thomas Huxley and connects those theories of survival of the fittest, differentiation, and natural selection to human struggles against Nature.

Harman asks the reader to bear with him as he makes brief applications or illustrations. First he discusses the body's natural process of healing itself should a patch of skin be torn from a hand. Without conscious effect, Harman, or any human for that matter, need not guide the process of healing, for it was an example of favorable conditions making for a successful adaptation. Next Harman asks the reader to imagine that his hand was cut or torn off completely, bones and all. With conditions changed so drastically, Nature is changed and fails without man's intervention in repairing and saving the limb. The man is saved though natural selection and survival of the fittest because human intelligence, in the form of a physician, supplements Nature's forces. A last illustration, one Harman calls pivotal, is the man with the deformed limb. He speaks of his own lameness and how his encounter with gravity left one side weaker when his fall from a tree at age twelve injured his femur. Harman illustrates the importance of using the facts of our own experiences and immediate observations in the search for fundamental principles. Harman then turns to geology, delighted with what the study of the ages tell us about the lesson of Universal Nature.

In pages nine through twelve Harman argues in short paragraphs that humans must work with Nature and not against her. Looking to the Greeks with admiration, he attributes their success to their rapport with nature and their adulation of the nude form in their works of art and in their sporting events. Mutual attraction in the form of Madame Oxygen and Monsieur Hydrogen, he notes, comes together without permission from church or state and results in sparkling water. When Oxygen and Hydrogen part they have no need of divorce or intervention from church or state. Harman suggests that this natural process extend to humankind. Harman indicates that by natural selection and survival of the fittest, the Greek race attained perfection. But then it ceased. Harman notes the Greeks were celebrated for their love of freedom and freedom in love. The cessation of perfection in humankind he pinpoints via a study of history. Harman states that the Greeks lost their perfection when they departed from the leadings of nature. He attributes this to luxury and artificial modes of living and relegated human perfection to an earlier, simpler time. Additionally, he thinks war destroyed high Grecian standards of manhood and womanhood.

Harman argues that the most valuable product of any land is its people. Subsequent to classical Greece, attention to industrialization, transportation, and animal husbandry—so-called civilization—diverted energies from the betterment of the human race. In his own century many organizations, institutions, asylums, prisons, and reformatories tried to improve and repair humankind, but Harman believes they were too late. Successful efforts to reform the human race, he argues, should begin with the mother of the unborn child, for there corrections can be effected. He uses the figure of building a house to explain his point. A successful builder looks first at the foundation and to the soundness and durability of his materials. In propagation of the human race, however, Harman complains that people concern themselves very little with the most important outcome, men and women of the future; instead they leave these matters to chance, and then "the human crop of to day is not an improvement on those sown and raised two or three thousand years ago." In this argument readers can see the origins of his interest in eugenics.

After that Harman outlines the essential conditions for the creation of a well-rounded manhood and of noble womanhood. Again drawing from nature, Harman recommends good soil and good seed. Good maternity is most important for it represents both soil and seed in his scheme; man is second in importance. Harman acknowledges women's right to the ballot and to participation in civic affairs, but he insists that based upon biological or "natural" law, superior childbearing is women's most important role. Harman reiterates: to have a race of human beings born so well that there be no need to be born again, women must be supplied with the very best possible conditions in their work as the architect of humankind.

Harman argues against the idea of husband and wife having one name, one purse, and one bed because this arrangement places the man at the head of the family and essentially dissolves the existence of the woman and absorbs her individuality into that of the husband. He likens the relationship between husband and wife to that between master and slave. He applauds men who do not abuse their power, but reminds the reader that the possession of power provides a temptation to abuse it. Harman reminds the reader "how frail, how shortsightedly selfish most men are," and concluded that such abuse was common. The surrender of a woman's surname in marriage, he writes, is the first of many occasions on which the woman will defer, or surrender, to her husband. Next comes the surrender of her purse. Woman without a means of self-support is doomed to economic slavery. Such a state debases her condition and her self-respect. Her lessened self-esteem and independence correlate with the debasement of her offspring. Attempts to procure money from her husband may lead a woman into deceptive practices which Harman believes might mark her unborn child with that tendency and disposition.

Harman deems the "one bed" condition as the worst of the three. He deplores the man who may have a reputation beyond suspicion in the greater world, but at home conducts himself reprehensibly toward his wife in their bed. Women need protection from the law that insists they bow to the whims of the nuptial arrangement. Harman's concern is not really for the woman so much as for her unborn child. He writes that "if debasement in the one bed affected none but herself the case would be bad enough," but this wrongdoing may be transmitted to the legacy of future generations.

He questions whether a remedy for these ills exists. The popular marriage code of "one name, one purse, and one bed," he thinks, creates mental and moral dwarfs, imbeciles, and abortions. The church provides no help in the matter for it preaches that women should practice self-sacrifice and submit to and obey their husbands. Harman indicts the state as the church's servant in supporting and upholding these tenets. The conclusion of *Digging for Bedrock* begins with Harman's summary of married women's legal rights across the nation. He remarks that he cannot call to mind one instance of a legal decision being made in favor of a woman whose husband abused her sexually. He says he intended to write more in this series of articles but was imprisoned and thought it best to present the public with these fragments; he planned to continue along this vein in a subsequent pamphlet.

The end matter of *Digging for Bedrock* continues another two pages. "Voices from Past Ages and Echoes From the Present" includes quotations from Alexander Carlyle's "Letter to John," John Locke's *Letters Concerning Toleration* (1689), John Milton's *Areopagitica* (1644), and Henry Thomas Buckle's two-volume *History of Civilization in England* (1857, 1861). Like *The Kansas Fight for the Free Press: The Four Indicted Articles,* the last pages of the pamphlet advertise other publications published by or sold by *Lucifer* and form a suggested reading list for those interested in the subject of the pamphlet.

Harman's next publication, *Love in Freedom* (1900), was inspired by untimely deaths of Samuel P. Putnam and May L. Collins. Both of Boston, Massachusets, Putnam was president of the American Secular Union and Collins a writer and lecturer within the Free-Thought Movement. Originally a long essay printed in *Freethought Magazine, Love in Freedom* explains Harman's creed in three articles: Freedom, Love, and Wisdom. Harman offers this trinity as a substitute for the "Father,

Son, and Holy Spirit." He explains that names are misleading and, although he expresses the same thoughts as free lovers, that most people were unable to explore meaning beyond labels. A few pages are devoted to Freedom, and Harman lists his vision or ideal of equal freedom for every human. Freedom of choice in matters of food, drink, clothing, books, and amusements tops the list before he moves on to sex companionship, which he deems the most important choice of all. Love and Wisdom each get a paragraph: Love unites, purifies, uplifts and glorifies the human race, and Wisdom is essential, for without it, he writes, Freedom and Love are not enough. Harman's belief in that trinity dissolves his regard for marriage, which he believes destroys freedom, compels slavery, and offers few positive benefits to recommend it.

Beginning on page twelve Harman departs from the trinity and makes arguments against marriage, organized into these subheadings: "Opposes Truth," "Opposes Justice," "Opposes Purity," "Compels Prostitution," "Evolution and Marriage," "Supplementary," "Legalizes Rape," "Love's Greatest Enemy," "An Unequal Love," "The Type of Government," "Siamese Twins," and "Addenda." Harman argues that marriage opposes truth by virtue of its essential dishonesty; married couples lie to each other, to themselves, and project a deceitful conception of the institution. Additionally marriage is unjust to women, because it legally deprives them of ownership and control of their own labor, body, and offspring. Purity is inseparable from love in a sex-companionship, yet love is not essential to purity in the marital state. Marriage compels prostitution because the institution itself is impure. Harman surmises that marriage has evolved into a mere contract, and he declares that a mistake because the law places the woman subordinate to her husband.

The supplementary subheading alerts the reader to the article's condensed form, due to the publisher's space restrictions, and of Harman's intent to insert the previously unpublished material at this point. Cautioning his audience that he speaks only for himself on this particular day and time, not promising to hold the same views tomorrow. Acknowledging his mercurial nature, Harman elaborates on his indictments against marriage, which legalizes rape, and how the law fails to acknowledge the possibility of rape. Harman explores the rationale behind marriage as tacit consent to sexual relations and explains how women's participation in the marital contract is akin to prostitution. Further, he sees marriage as love's greatest enemy because marriage is bondage; love cannot exist where slavery reigns. Harman opposes marriage because it was an unequal yoke that placed a greater burden upon the female; he illustrates this with examples from the history of marriage, as recorded from the Bible through Shakespeare. Sharing the same belief as Robert Ingersoll, "The Great Agnostic," that families are a self-governing organization needing little interference from outside, Harman quotes from Ingersoll's lecture "Liberty for Man, Woman and Child" in support of his tenets. He explains a further opposition to marriage based upon how government and church join forces in perpetuating this status relationship. Objecting mostly to the complicity of church and state, which the First Amendment of the United States Constitution restricts, Harman suggests that marriage serves to supply both entities with submissive slaves and that wives serve mandated duty as breeders. The abolition of marriage, he thinks, would precede the abolition of church and state. In the addenda Harman closes by stating that he does not base his indictment of institutional marriage upon his own experiences. He recalls that his married life was not exceptionally unfortunate but that he did not find all that he hoped to from the arrangement. In the end, Harman counts himself fortunate compared to most men. His observations of marriage, spanning a period of more than half a century, provide the basis from which he analyzed the institution and formulated an unbiased opinion. Husbands and wives with whom he boarded during his years as a teacher confided their marital woes to him, and he also drew from his counseling experience as a justice of the peace and Methodist minister. Furthermore, Harman continues, he avoided reading the works of Rousseau, Byron, Shelley, Thomas Paine, Voltaire, Bolingbroke, and other "infidel writers," as he calls them, because he did not want people to suggest that he did not think for himself; thus, his opinions were solely his own.

After the addenda Harman returns to his new preoccupation with eugenics, and he writes about the conscience of the beasts with an eye toward "race preservation and perpetuity of type." He draws from the work of Edward Payson Evans, *Evolutional Ethics and Animal Psychology* (1898), to demonstrate the role monogamy played in the reproduction of genotype among storks and ravens. Harman suggested that "perfection of type has been reached through conflict, and by survival of the stronger and braver, and not through faithful devotion to a mate first accepted" and concluded that human pair bonding practices more closely resembling that of the other animals would result in an autonomous preservation of racial type because offspring would benefit from the care of both parents.

Next Harman introduces an essay from his Light-Bearer library on social evolution on the human plane. The essay describes the geologic evolution of the earth and its animals and posits that evolutionary progress of man has moved in cycles based on the evidence of

Harman's daughter, Lillian. He performed her 1886 marriage to his Lucifer *co-editor, Edwin Cox Walker, and the couple was jailed for being illegally wed (from Hal D. Sears,* The Sex Radicals: Free Love in High Victorian America, *1977; Thomas Cooper Library, University of South Carolina).*

remains of higher cultures that no longer existed. Harman believes in the moral superiority of earlier times when women divorced with ease and chose the best specimens of manhood without problem. Harman attributes Greece's production of more men of genius than any other area to that society's egalitarianism and what he thought was its elevated status of women. Harman held Greece as an ideal, a "high-water-mark" in the human race's evolution and heralded the advent of a second high-water mark after a lapse of twenty centuries via the suffrage movement in the United States. Harman cites Frances Elizabeth Willard, Susan B. Anthony, Voltairine de Cleyre, and Susan Wixon as being at the forefront of the movement.

In the next-to-last section of *Love in Freedom* Harman references a sex strike and likens it to a labor strike wherein either the strikers or the autocracy must settle. Harman concludes that the human race, with its suffering, anguish, conflict, and loss, is far from the realization of the revolution he imagined. Believing that the new regime should elevate women and love so that a race above the "troglodytic ape" would flourish, Harman advocates the complete reorganization of social and economic systems. He lauds the cooperative home as an example of the new forms of living that might emerge from such a change. In conclusion Harman imagines a world that replaces the monogamous model with individualism, self-ownership, and women's rights in the realm of mate selection and birth control.

Although his ideas changed slightly over the years, Harman could not escape the censorship issue. In May 1905 Harman was tried again on obscenity charges for publishing and mailing two articles in *Lucifer*, "The Fatherhood Question" and "More Thoughts on Sexology." The first argued that women be allowed to choose the best conditions for procreation and the latter defended sexual education for women. Harman was sentenced to one year of hard labor. He was seventy-five. While Harman served his sentence at Joliet Prison, his weekly letter from the editor communicated his thanks to *Lucifer's* readers. The warden restricted the number of outgoing letters Harman wrote, but he was well liked by prison guards and his fellow inmates; they wrote letters on his behalf regarding his positive influence upon them. He mentioned the titles of magazines he received for the month, the books in the prison library, and Jack London's powerful pen; Harman read *Son of a Wolf* (1900) and *Sea Wolf: Tales of the Far North* (1904) in August 1906. He reminded readers of the meaning behind Lucifer's name, urged them to read dictionaries, and commented that George, his son, brought fresh fruit and papers to him on his visits. Harman was overjoyed when he received the delayed letters Goldman sent him from Detroit.

Regardless, his next publication again connected the issues of censorship and eugenics. *The Right To Be Born Well* (1905) was reprinted and expanded from an article of that title Harman had written and published in *Lucifer* on 20 July 1905. Spurred in part by the June 1905 mail fraud and obscenity trial of Dr. Alice B. Stockham, a feminist physician, homeopath, and birth-control advocate, the book contains Harman's thoughts on the government's suppression of basic hygienic information. Stockham, the author of several books, including *Tokology: A Book for Every Woman* (1890) and *Karezza: Ethics of Marriage* (1896), was one of the first marriage advisers in the United States to advocate that men and women abstain from orgasm during sexual intercourse, a practice similar to Tantra. She published *The Wedding Night,* a sexual instruction pamphlet, and ran afoul of the Comstock Law. Feeling affinity with Stockham, Harman supported her case and publicized her troubles via *Lucifer.*

In *The Right To Be Born Well* Harman addresses the government's suppression of information but focuses more on arguments about the sacredness of mother-

hood and its incipient requirement that a woman own herself and make independent decisions. He includes in those decisions the choice to bear children, for children born against the mother's will are not well born. Mothers of unwanted children cannot show natural affection for their offspring, he maintains, nor can they raise children to their full potential as productive humans. Sex relations themselves have much to do with the production of a well-born child. Humans born from the act of rape or coercive intercourse of any kind he believes are immediately marked as deficient. Circling back to his support for Stockham, Harman underscores the importance of basic knowledge of human anatomy and the reproductive system. Without such knowledge, women and men might accidentally create an inferior child, thus contributing to the decline of the human race. Harman admonishes physicians for withholding information about physiology and the hygiene of sex from thousands of women. He recommends a program of sex education for adults and children. Harman champions knowledge as a child's birthright, arguing that children should be encouraged to seek answers, to ask any question imaginable. Further, children should be acquainted with the mechanics of reproduction, the sex act, and birth. Harman recommends that blackboard illustrations of the reproductive system serve as teaching aids and states that the subject is appropriate for mixed groups.

Harman again advances the idea that the superior role of women should be reflected in social arrangements surrounding propagation. He reveres women as enshrining in their physical organisms the "creatory" of every new human being. Consequently any negative experiences a mother suffers during pregnancy, he believes, adversely affect her child's intelligence, personality, and ability to survive in the world. Harman rallies women to guard the interests of the unborn child and seeks to imbue them with a sense of responsibility for their children. Like most free thinkers and free lovers, Harman denounces abortion because of its violent nature. Instead he sketches conditions under which woman could do best the work he believes she was made for: child bearing and child rearing. He encourages primary education for women so that they will not infringe upon the rights of their unborn children; he focuses upon the importance of living up to an ideal of perfect motherhood, because only in perfect motherhood could society create the perfect child who never needed reforming. In an implicit criticism of Christian churches, Harman reasons that in his ideal world children would be so well born the first time that they need not be born again.

Harman changed the title of his periodical from *Lucifer* to *The American Journal of Eugenics* in June 1907 and moved the journal's editorial offices to Los Angeles two years later. There he expected the publication to thrive once removed from the restrictive values of the Midwest. He published *The American Journal of Eugenics* until his death on 30 January 1910, after which Goldman's magazine *Mother Earth* took over distribution.

Many more-famous radicals including George Bernard Shaw wrote memorials of Harman after his death. Although Harman was well known and regarded by journalists of his time, not all approved of his tactics. His grasp of many biological and scientific matters upon which his arguments depended was not strong. His life and work fell into obscurity. Praise for his defense of the First Amendment overshadowed the subject matter on which he concentrated the bulk of his writing. His journalism has received no critical analysis. His association with eugenics later made him a distasteful subject, and his emphasis on the biological destiny of women prevented the sympathy of post-1970s women's-movement scholars or advocates of the sexual revolution. At the beginning of the twenty-first century his writings are scarce and available only on microfilm or in special collections. Nevertheless, as scholarship about non-communist anarchism by such writers as Madeleine Stern, Hal D. Sears, Martin Blatt, Margaret Marsh, and Wendy McElroy has covered more territory, while at the same time scholars such as Linda Gordon, Estelle Freedman, and John D'Emilio have expanded the study of sexuality and reproductive history, Harman's name has begun to appear more often in accounts of his time. The meaning of his writerly legacy has yet to be determined, but he has secured a place in histories of nineteenth-century reform.

References:

Aaron K. Ketchell, "Contesting Tradition and Combating Intolerance: A History of Freethought in Kansas," *Great Plains Quarterly,* 20 (2000): 281–295;

William O. Reichert, *Partisans of Freedom: A Study in American Anarchism* (Bowling Green, Ohio: Bowling Green University Popular Press, 1976);

Hal D. Sears, *The Sex Radicals: Free Love in High Victorian America* (Lawrence: Regents Press of Kansas, 1977);

William Lemore West, "The Moses Harman Story," *Kansas Historical Quarterly,* 37 (1971): 41–63.

Papers:

The primary location of Moses Harman's papers is the Western Historical Manuscripts Collection at Ellis Library in Columbia, Missouri. Harman's correspondence with Herman Kuehn, Joseph Labadie, and William Denton survives in the Labadie Collection, Harlan Hatcher Special Collections Library at the University of Michigan.

Nat Hentoff

(10 June 1925 –   )

Hester L. Furey
The Art Institute of Atlanta

BOOKS: *The Jazz Life* (New York: Dial Press, 1961);

Peace Agitator: The Story of A. J. Muste (New York: Macmillan, 1963);

The New Equality (New York: Viking, 1964);

Call the Keeper (New York: Viking, 1966);

Our Children Are Dying (New York: Viking, 1966);

A Doctor among the Addicts (Chicago: Rand McNally, 1967);

Onwards! (New York: Simon & Schuster, 1967);

A Political Life: The Education of John V. Lindsay (New York: Knopf, 1969);

State Secrets: Police Surveillance in America, by Paul Cowan, Nick Egleson, and Hentoff, with Barbara Herbert and Robert Wall (New York: Holt, Rinehart & Winston, 1974);

Jazz Is (New York: Random House, 1976);

A Helsinki Record: Free Speech in the United States, with Aryeh Neier (New York: U.S. Helsinki Watch Committee, 1980);

Blues for Charlie Darwin (New York: Morrow, 1982);

The 1984 Calendar: An American History, with Tim Keefe and Howard Levine (Rockville, Md.: Point Blank Press, 1983);

The Man from Internal Affairs (New York: Mysterious Press, 1985);

Boston Boy (New York: Knopf, 1986);

The Indivisible Fight for Life (Chicago: Americans United for Life, 1987);

John Cardinal O'Connor: At the Storm Center of a Changing American Catholic Church (New York: Scribners, 1988);

Our Diminishing Protections (Tucson: University of Arizona, 1997);

Speaking Freely: A Memoir (New York: Knopf, 1997);

Living the Bill of Rights: How to Be an Authentic American (New York: HarperCollins, 1998);

The Trials of Lenny Bruce: the Fall and Rise of an American Icon, with Ronald K. Collins and David M. Skover (Naperville, Ill: Sourcebooks MediaFusion, 2002);

Nat Hentoff (from the dust jacket for John Cardinal O'Connor: At the Storm Center of a Changing American Catholic Church, *1988; Richland County Public Library)*

The War on the Bill of Rights and the Gathering Resistance (New York: Seven Stories Press, 2003);

Insisting on Life (New York: Ad Hoc Committee in Defense of Life, Human Life Foundation, 2005).

Editions and Collections: *Does Anybody Give a Damn?: Nat Hentoff on Education* (New York: Knopf, 1977);

Free Speech for Me But Not for Thee: How the American Left and Right Relentlessly Censor Each Other (New York: HarperCollins, 1992);

Listen to the Stories: Nat Hentoff on Jazz and Country Music (New York: HarperCollins, 1995);

The Nat Hentoff Reader (New York: Da Capo Press, 2001);

Boston Boy: Growing Up with Jazz and Other Rebellious Passions (Philadelphia: Paul Dry Books, 2001);

American Music Is (New York: Da Capo Press, 2004).

OTHER: *Hear Me Talking to Ya: The Story of Jazz by the Men Who Made It,* edited by Hentoff, with Nat Shapiro (New York: Rinehart, 1955);

The Jazz Makers, edited by Hentoff, with Shapiro (New York: Rinehart, 1957);

Jazz: New Perspectives on the History of Jazz by Twelve of the World's Foremost Jazz Critics and Scholars, edited by Hentoff, with Albert McCarthy (New York: Rinehart, 1959);

Dennis Stock, *Jazz Street,* introduction and commentary by Hentoff (Garden City, N.Y.: Doubleday, 1960);

The Essays of A. J. Muste, edited by Hentoff (Indianapolis: Bobbs-Merrill, 1967);

"Beyond Civil Rights: A Reply to the Coalitionists" in Jules Chametzky, comp., *Black & White in American Culture; An Anthology from the* Massachusetts Review (Amherst: University of Massachusetts Press, 1969);

Colin MacInnes, *The London Novels,* introduction by Hentoff (New York: Farrar, Straus & Giroux, 1969);

Black Anti-Semitism and Jewish Racism, edited, with an introduction, by Hentoff (New York: Schocken, 1970);

"The Cold Society" and "Them and Us: Are Peace Protests Self Therapy" in Robert Disch, comp., *Hard Rains: Conflict and Conscience in America* (Englewood Cliffs, N.J.: Prentice-Hall, 1970);

"Leon Thomas: Spirits Known and Unknown" and "Archie Shepp: the Way Ahead" in Pauline Rivelli, comp., *The Black Giants* (later republished as *Giants of Black Music*) (New York: Da Capo Press, 1970);

Stephanie Spinner, *Rock is Beautiful: an Anthology of American Lyrics,* 1953–1968, introduction by Hentoff (New York: Dell, 1970);

Henry David Thoreau, *Walden, and Other Writings,* introduction by Hentoff (Garden City, N.Y.: Doubleday, 1970);

Charles A. Thrall and Jerold M. Starr, *Technology, Power, and Social Change,* "Symposium on Technology and Humanism" includes contributions by Hentoff (Lexington, Mass.: Lexington Books, 1972);

"The New Journalist" in Ronald Gross and Paul Osterman, *The New Professionals* (New York: Simon & Schuster, 1972);

"Paying Dues: Changes in the Jazz Life" in Charles Nanry, comp., *American Music: from Storyville to Woodstock* (New Brunswick, N.J.: Transaction Books, 1972);

The Legacy of Paul Goodman, with Gloria Channon et al. *Change* 4 (Winter 1972/1973);

My [pseudonym of Morton Leonard Yanow], *Observations From the Treadmill,* foreword by Hentoff (New York: Viking Press, 1973);

Surveillance, Dataveillance, and Personal Freedoms; Use and Abuse of Information Technology; a Symposium Edited by the Staff of the Columbia Human Rights Law Review, foreword by Hentoff (Fair Lawn, N.J.: R. E. Burdick, 1973);

Antonio Frasconi, *Frasconi: Against the Grain; the Woodcuts of Antonio Frasconi,* introduction by Hentoff (New York: Macmillan, 1974);

"Yiddish Survivals in the New Comedy" in Abraham Chapman, comp., *Jewish-American Literature: an Anthology of Fiction, Poetry, Autobiography, and Criticism* (New York: New American Library, 1974);

Alvin H. Goldstein, *The Unquiet Death of Julius and Ethel Rosenberg,* introduction by Hentoff (New York: Lawrence Hill, 1975);

Dick Moores, *Gasoline Alley,* introduction by Hentoff (New York: Avon Books, 1976);

"Personal Liberty and Education: a Commentary" in Monroe D. Cohen, *Personal Liberty and Education* (New York: Citation Press, 1976);

Irwin A. Hyman and James H. Wise, *Corporal Punishment in American Education: Readings in History, Practice, and Alternatives,* preface by Hentoff (Philadelphia: Temple University Press, 1979);

The Jazz Makers: Essays on the Greats of Jazz, edited by Hentoff, with Shapiro (New York: Da Capo Press, 1979);

"Jazz in the Twenties: Garvin Bushnell" and "An Afternoon with Miles Davis" in Martin T. Williams, *Jazz Panorama: From the Pages of the Jazz Review* (New York: Da Capo Press, 1979);

Pauline Rivelli, editor, *Giants of Black Music,* introduction by Hentoff (New York: Da Capo Press, 1980);

"Man Who Was Convicted of Reading a Book" in William A. Katz, *Library Lit 11, the Best of 1980* (Metuchen, N.J.: Scarecrow Press, 1981);

Max Gordon, *Live at the Village Vanguard,* introduction by Hentoff (New York: Da Capo Press, 1982);

Haig A. Bosmajian, *Censorship, Libraries, and the Law,* foreword by Hentoff (New York: Neal-Schuman, 1983);

Jazzmen, edited by Frederick Ramsey, introduction by Hentoff (New York: Limelight Editions, 1985);

Dom Cerulli et al., *The Jazz Word,* new introduction by Hentoff (New York: Da Capo Press, 1987; reprint of Crowell-Crolier Press ed. from 1962);

Jazz Giants, edited by K. Abe, introduction by Hentoff (New York: Watson-Guptill Publications, 1988);

"Presumption of Guilt" in Richard Curry Orr, *Freedom at Risk: Secrecy, Censorship, and Repression in the 1980s* (Philadelphia: Temple University Press, 1988);

"Anonymous Children, Diminished Adults" in Frank J. Macchiarola and Alan Gartner, *Caring for America's Children* (New York: Academy of Political Science, 1989);

Donald R. Gallo, comp. and ed., *Speaking for Ourselves: Autobiographical Sketches by Notable Authors of Books for Young Adults,* Volume 1, includes a contribution by Hentoff (Urbana, Illinois: National Council of Teachers of English, 1990);

Craig McGregor, *Bob Dylan: the Early Years, a Retrospective,* new preface by Hentoff (New York: Da Capo Press, 1990; reprint of 1972 ed.);

Robert Laurence Barry and Gerard V. Bradley, *Set No Limits: a Rebuttal to Daniel Callahan's Proposal to Limit Health Care for the Elderly,* prologue by Hentoff (Urbana: University of Illinois Press, 1991);

David Mall, *When Life and Choice Collide: Essays on Rhetoric and Abortion,* introduction by Hentoff (Libertyville, Ill.: Kairos Books, 1994);

"Justice Brennan and His Alumni" in *Law Clerks: the Transformation of the Judiciary* (Andover: Massachusetts School of Law at Amherst, 1995);

Mark Twain, *Tom Sawyer Abroad,* introduction by Hentoff (New York: Oxford University Press, 1996);

"Search and Seizure: Fragile Liberty" in E. Joshua Rosenkranz and Bernard Schwartz, *Reason and Passion: Justice Brennan's Enduring Influence* (New York: Norton, 1997);

"Should This Student Have Been Expelled?" in Santi Buscemi and Charlotte Smith, *75 Readings: An Anthology* (New York: McGraw-Hill, 1997);

Cliff Eastwood et al., *Clint Eastwood: Interviews,* includes an interview by Hentoff (Jackson: University Press of Mississippi, 1999);

"Introduction to Lenny Bruce" in Jo Bonney, *Extreme Exposure: An Anthology of Solo Performance Texts from the Twentieth Century* (New York: Theatre Communications Group, 2000);

"Duty to Die?" in John Hardwig et al., editors, *Is There a Duty to Die?, and Other Essays in Bioethics* (New York: Routledge, 2000);

Ralph Beston, *Remembering Bix: A Memoir of the Jazz Age,* introduction by Hentoff (New York: Da Capo Press, 2000);

"Hate Crime Laws Threaten Equal Protection" in Tamara L. Roleff, *Hate Crimes* (San Diego: Greenhaven Press, 2001);

Gene Lees, *You Can't Steal a Gift: Dizzy, Clark, Milt, and Nat,* foreword by Hentoff (New Haven: Yale University Press, 2001);

"The Jazz Life Behind the Scenes: Phil Stern, Norman Granz, and the Nonpareil Players," in *Phil Stern: A Life's Work* (New York: Powerhouse Books, 2003);

"Affirmative Action Ignores Genuine Diversity" in Mary E. Williams, *Racism* (San Diego: Greenhaven Press, 2004);

"The Death Penalty Does Not Deter Murder" in James D. Torr, *Crime and Criminals: Opposing Viewpoints* (San Diego: Greenhaven Press, 2004);

"L. E. Tanner, *The Jazz Image: Masters of Jazz Photography,* introduction by Hentoff (New York: Abrams, 2006);

Barbara Olshansky, *Democracy Detained: Secret, Unconstitutional Practice in the U.S. War on Terror,* foreword by Hentoff (New York: Seven Stories Press, 2007).

Juvenile Books: *Jazz Country* (New York: Harper & Row, 1965);

I'm Really Dragged But Nothing Gets Me Down (New York: Simon & Schuster, 1968);

Journey into Jazz (New York: Coward-McCann, 1968);

In the Country of Ourselves (New York: Simon & Schuster, 1971);

This School is Driving Me Crazy: a Novel (New York: Delacorte, 1976);

Does This School Have Corporal Punishment? (New York: Delacorte, 1981);

The Day They Came to Arrest the Book: a Novel (New York: Delacorte, 1982);

American Heroes: In and Out of School (New York: Delacorte, 1987);

The First Freedom: the Tumultuous History of Free Speech in America (New York: Delacorte, 1988);

Alison's Trumpet and Other Stories: Short Stories by Hentoff, Jean Davies Okimoto, et al. (New York: Scholastic, 1999).

SELECTED PERIODICAL PUBLICATIONS–UNCOLLECTED: "The Diminishing of John Ashcroft," *Village Voice,* 12 February 2004;

"Fred Korematsu v. George W. Bush: No Law Protects Them, No Court May Hear Their Pleas," *Village Voice,* 19 February 2004;

"The Rumsfeld-Bush Legal Black Hole: Powers Formerly Reserved Only for Kings," *Village Voice,* 27 February 2004;

"What Did Rumsfeld Know?" *Village Voice,* 4 January 2005;

"Rabbis Against Torture: Invoking Centuries of Jewish Law, Hundreds of American Rabbis Confront Bush," *Village Voice,* 16 July 2006;

"Supreme Court Obscenity: Imprisoned by the Supreme Court, Ralph Ginzburg and the the First Amendment Survived," *Village Voice,* 21 July 2006.

Nat Hentoff's career developed through three phases. He first became famous as a radio and print commentator on jazz music during the 1950s; by the

1960s he began to write with more concentration in the field of civil rights and politics; and by the 1980s he was recognized as one of the nation's most prominent participants in debates about civil liberties, surprising and often annoying audiences with an amalgamation of ideas from the Left and the Right. Hentoff has written in a variety of genres and addressed a full range of audiences with children's books, adult fiction, studies of political figures, polemics, cultural studies, liner notes for musical recordings, and mass media entertainment columns.

Nathan Irving Hentoff was born in Boston, Massachusetts, on 10 June 1925, the oldest child of Simon and Lena (née Katzenberg) Hentoff, Russian Jewish immigrants who lived in the Roxbury district of Boston. Simon Hentoff worked as a haberdasher and traveling salesman; Lena Hentoff worked occasionally as a department store cashier. The senior Hentoff had his own store, but it failed during the Great Depression. At age ten Hentoff entered Boston Latin School, a prestigious school emphasizing academics. He had to travel some distance to get to school, and on one of his daily commutes first encountered jazz music, which became a consuming passion, second only to his enthusiasm for the books he found at the public library. His sister Janet was born in 1935. Hentoff took his first job at eleven, helping a neighborhood fruit peddler, and made his bar mitzvah at age thirteen despite having been invited to discontinue Hebrew school during the year. Afterward he abandoned religious observance but retained deep emotional ties with the type of Jewish-ghetto culture that spread to the United States from Europe in the first half of the twentieth century, and he credits his experience in that setting with shaping his identity as a political and cultural outsider. He took clarinet lessons and adored *chazzaners* and *klezmorim,* whom he regards still as the Jewish equivalents of bluesmen.

As a pre-teenager he read broadly in Boston's daily newspapers and made a scrapbook of clippings with his commentary on each of the stories. He grew up under the influence of a leftist sensibility and organized co-workers at a candy store at age fifteen, but rebuffed the attempts of his barber to recruit him for the Communist Young People's League and eventually alienated many of his boyhood friends with his criticism of the Soviet Union's intolerance of political dissent. At age seventeen Hentoff read Arthur Koestler's *Darkness at Noon* (first published in English in 1941), which "immunized me from then on against any variant, anywhere in the world, of the credo that . . . 'the only moral criterion we recognize is that of social utility'" (*Boston Boy*). His friends responded to his challenges with the assertion that Koestler was a "fascist," and Hentoff later summarized the interaction: "They gave

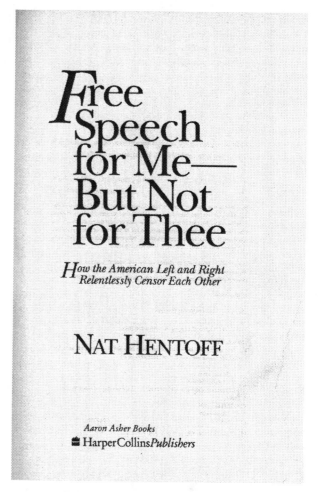

Title page for Hentoff's 1992 collection of his Village Voice *articles about censorship (Richland County Public Library)*

up on me politically. . . . As for me, I decided that when you know exactly what someone is going to say in answer to every single question you ask, you ought to put your nickel in some other machine" (*Boston Boy*).

Hentoff took his first newswriting job at age fifteen, working as an unpaid reporter on *Boston City Reporter,* a paper published by Frances Sweeney to fight political corruption. After graduating from Boston Latin he attended Northeastern University. In the next few years, Hentoff's education took place in three very different locations: at Northeastern, at the Savoy Café, and at Boston's WMEX radio station. At the Savoy, Hentoff acquired a new layer of culture: he became a fixture in the world of jazz. Later he commented that "behind the closed doors of the Savoy, I felt more at home than anywhere else I had ever been, including home" (*Boston Boy,* p. 122).

In June 1944 his friend and former boss Frances Sweeney died of a heart attack at age thirty-six. Hentoff moved away from home that year–he was nineteen–and rented a small apartment in Back Bay from another frequenter of the Savoy. He became close friends with many musicians–notably Duke Ellington and Ben Webster–and the characters who haunted the café. He admired Lester Young from a distance. After sets he joined musicians in after-hours bars and diners and marveled at their openness in conversation with him.

Working as a writer and, in his junior year, editor in chief, for the student newspaper stimulated in Hentoff a lifelong interest in freedom of the press. He held journalists George Seldes and I. F. Stone in highest esteem. Imitating Ralph Ingersoll's innovative newspaper *P. M.*, the Northeastern writers provoked the university president into giving them a choice between narrowing the paper's focus to campus activities and finding another extracurricular activity. They chose to leave the paper.

Hentoff's association with Boston's WMEX radio station began during World War II. A co-worker from his candy-store days who worked there as an announcer urged him to come in for an audition, saying the station was short of help because of the war. Hentoff avoided the draft with a 4-F rating because of botched surgeries on his left arm when he was young and began to work for WMEX, starting first in the sports department. His regular jazz program from 1944 to 1953 featured music and interviews with musicians.

He graduated summa cum laude from Northeastern in 1945, winning the President's Letter, the highest academic honor given by the university, and attended graduate school in American literature at Harvard University, beginning in 1946. In the late 1940s he taught a course at the Samuel Adams School for Social Studies on the history of jazz. He was married for eight months in 1950 to Miriam Fonda Sargent, a Savoy Café regular whom he had dated for six years. By then he worked nights at the radio station, and she worked days at a state mental hospital, preparing for a career in psychiatry. The marriage dissolved by mutual consent.

Hentoff had begun delivering nightly broadcasts from Storeyville, a Boston club owned by jazz impresario George Wien. This enabled him to remain in contact with musicians including Ellington, Sidney Bechet, and Paul Desmond, most of whom appeared on his show at one time or another. Despite the growing popularity of these broadcasts, Hentoff managed to annoy his boss by organizing a union among the station's employees, dressing unconventionally in a leather jacket with no tie, and reading leftist periodicals openly. He won a Fulbright Fellowship in 1950 to study at the Sorbonne, and he took a year's leave of absence from the station. In Paris, he abandoned the idea of a career in academics and explored the jazz scene instead.

Upon his return to the United States in 1951, Hentoff resumed his job at WMEX and began to write a column for *Down Beat,* the most respected jazz magazine of the day. When the column proved successful, he accepted an offer to become an editor of *Down Beat* and moved to New York. On 2 September 1954 he married Trudi Bernstein, a painter introduced to him by Paul Desmond. They later had two daughters, Jessica and Miranda.

In 1957 he was fired for his direct action approach to persuading *Down Beat*'s management to hire African Americans: he simply hired a young African American woman to be an administrative assistant. After briefly struggling to find freelance work, he began to write social criticism, contributing articles to Max Ascoli's paper, *The Reporter,* where he began to investigate the growing Black Muslim movement and met Malcolm X. He also wrote, gratis at first, for the *Village Voice,* which had begun publication in 1956 and was still a small paper without an established audience, addressing a broad range of nonmusical topics. Eventually, he negotiated a pay rate of $10 per column.

In the late 1950s Hentoff's interest in education issues led to invitations as a paid speaker at education conferences. He also worked in the late 1950s with CBS-TV's contentious producer-director Robert Herridge, and the two collaborated on filming highly successful jazz performances for television, most notably the December 1957 television show called *The Sound of Jazz* which captured the last time Billie Holiday and Lester Young, long estranged, performed together.

Maintaining his contacts with the music community, Hentoff co-edited three collections in the late 1950s, *Hear Me Talking to Ya: The Story of Jazz by the Men Who Made It* (1955), *The Jazz Makers* (1957) with Nat Shapiro, and *Jazz: New Perspectives on the History of Jazz by Twelve of the World's Foremost Jazz Critics and Scholars* (1959) with Albert McCarthy. From the beginning, Hentoff's writing, even about music, assumed a contrarian character. In his contribution to *Jazz: New Perspectives on the History of Jazz by Twelve of the World's Foremost Jazz Critics and Scholars,* he takes on the rising discourse about the "respectability" of jazz, noting that acceptance among people who reject and pathologize the conditions out of which jazz music grows is not necessarily good for the music or musicians. During the same period Hentoff had the good fortune to work for a while in the music recording business, first in arranging some sessions for Les Koenig's Contemporary Records. Soon afterward he headed a small label, Candid Records. The label survived a year. One of his accomplishments in that position was organizing the recordings on *Newport Rebels,* a series of sessions conducted to protest what he called the "growing commercialism of the Newport Jazz Festival" *(Speaking Freely)*. From 1959 to 1960 Hentoff also wrote for *Jazz Review,* of which he was a founding editor. During that time, he and Bernstein divorced in early August 1959, and he married Margot Goodman, a writer for the *Village Voice,* on 15 August. In 1960 their son Nicholas was born, and Hentoff began his first juvenile novel, *Jazz Country* (1965). He began to write for *The New Yorker* that year as well–beginning a long relationship that generated book-length treatments of social policy and legal topics, several of which he dedicated to his editor, William Shawn.

Social justice, antiwar activism, and the Civil Rights Movement were increasingly common topics of Hentoff's jouralism during the 1960s. In 1962 Hentoff contributed the lead item, "The Blues of Blacks and Whites," for the first issue of *Eros,* a journal edited by Ralph Ginzburg that lasted only four issues before publication was aborted when it was found to be obscene. Hentoff's first two books of the decade grew from his interest in social issues. The first was *Peace Agitator: The Story of A. J. Muste* (1963); the other, *The New Equality* (1964), offers micro-analyses of problems the Civil Rights Movement faced early in the decade.

The most coherent and comprehensive account of Hentoff's relationship to the Civil Rights Movement and its leaders appears in the essays of *The New Equality,* published the year his son Thomas was born. United by themes of education and leadership, the essays in the collection provide a reliable account of the multilayered struggles within the Civil Rights Movement. Appropriately, the prologue chronicles the events of a February 1964 CORE leadership training institute in Nyack, New York, underscoring the need for such training but the improbability of progress given the young people's desire to engage immediately in the many actions of the day. Of the early civil rights leaders, Hentoff preferred Bayard Rustin, the coordinator of the 28 August 1963 March on Washington for Jobs and Justice at which Martin Luther King Jr. made his "I Have a Dream" speech. In subsequent essays Hentoff traces arguments among civil rights workers and African Americans in general regarding their ultimate goal: separatism or integration.

Other essays in the book address the topics of black pride and black rage that figured prominently in the media following publication of James Baldwin's *The Fire Next Time* (1963). Responding to Baldwin's forthright statements concerning black rage, Hentoff points out the poverty of white counsel to African Americans about "self-improvement" as he analyzes the relationship of crime to race, poverty, and lack of education. Discussing the difficulties confronting even well-intentioned white liberals who want to aid the Civil Rights Movement, he challenges whites who feel tempted to interpret race-based anger among blacks as a sign of essential evil or bad faith with a bald discussion of how little whites know about black life. He also points out that organization against discrimination has been proven to drive down the crime rate in black neighborhoods. Other essays discuss the shifting definition of what it has meant to be a moderate, applying those lessons to racial politics. Following Baldwin's lead, Hentoff discusses the conflicted feelings of upwardly mobile African Americans, in which dissociation, contempt, and guilt mixed in equal parts, noting that the middle class was disproportionately represented among youth leadership in the movement. Laying out the arguments for and against affirmative action with particular application to unions, Hentoff concludes that "it is both too late and too soon to be color-blind."

Next he takes on the urban renewal projects that were supposed to reduce substandard housing in northern cities at the end of the Great Migration but instead pushed African Americans into what Hentoff calls "the creeping ghetto." He argues that merely legal change will not suffice to undo the damages of segregation, because the growth of the middle class after World War II did not, as a rule, include African Americans. Decades of racially discriminatory lending resulted in African Americans being confined to aging public housing as their white counterparts moved away. In the final section of the book he discusses promising avenues of organizational approach to change.

Hentoff reflected on several occasions that his way began to diverge from other liberals during 1965 when he was a member of a delegation sent to meet with Adlai Stevenson at the United Nations: Hentoff, Dwight Macdonald, Harvey Swados, A. J. Muste, David McReynolds, and Paul Goodman were charged with the task of asking Stevenson, as the "resounding spokesman for principled liberalism," to resign from his position and lead the nation in protest against participation in the war in Vietnam. Stevenson's charismatic yet evasive response so disaffected Hentoff that he identifies the encounter as the "experience . . . that began to change how I defined myself politically" *(Speaking Freely)*. He was also affected by a series of increasingly negative encounters with Black Power leaders, culminating in a 1966 fundraiser at which Stokely Carmichael made an anti-Semitic remark so regrettable that Hentoff felt compelled to ask his wife to omit it from her account of the event. In retrospect, Hentoff felt he had been wrong to protect Carmichael's image.

As Hentoff's writing tackled broader topics, he became more prolific. He published in the *Chronicle of Higher Education, Village Voice, The New Yorker, Playboy* (a controversial and hilarious 1965 interview with Bob Dylan), and other national publications. He revisited

*Dust jacket for Hentoff's 2003 collection of political essays
(Richland County Public Library)*

and could create in-depth portraits. Usually these studies began as *New Yorker* articles. During the decade he completed almost a book a year in addition to journalistic writing, juvenile literature, and liner notes for musical recordings.

A Political Life: The Education of John V. Lindsay (1969) reveals much of Hentoff's own political development, covering almost ten years. Hentoff goes on record as a critic of the Kennedy administration, criticizing the president's Cuban policy, civil rights record, and his brother's apparent disregard, while attorney general, for civil liberties. The Republican Lindsay, by contrast, is described as a man of integrity as Hentoff outlines his confrontations with the knotty problems presented by his own party, machine politics, organized labor, and average citizens of New York. Hentoff records Lindsay's dilemmas sympathetically although the two did not see eye to eye on every issue, particularly with regard to the 1968 sanitation workers' strike when the mayor refused to back the unions, what Hentoff considered police riots at Columbia that year, and police brutality in general.

The anecdotes—covering Lindsay's fraught relationship with various antagonists and allies—seem almost impressionistic at first glance, but closer analysis reveals that Hentoff richly layered the stories with statistical and general information. Hentoff creates a detail-packed portrait of a city caught between the party-politics-based antagonism of the governor, the emergent Civil Rights Movement—itself fighting on every front—the resistance to change by entrenched institutional powers such as the police department and the various labor unions, and a growing number of welfare recipients, which "doubled from 1965 to 1968," making up a tenth of the city's population and numbering one million by the beginning of 1969 (*Political Life,* p. 228).

Many times Hentoff has dismissed his reputation as a spokesman on social issues, saying that people regard him as an expert and invite him to speak at conferences simply because he published a *Village Voice* article on a topic; however, the books he published during the 1960s demonstrate an undeniable competence on questions touching on race, education, labor, law, and politics at every level. Two factors combine to create this effect: his ability to converse with people of all social levels, despite his frequent claim of being an outsider, and his compulsion to dig deeply into a story to enlarge his understanding of the various conflicts and players.

In 1970 a House Committee on Internal Security report included Hentoff on a list of sixty-five radical speakers whose presence on college campuses the committee chair, Richard Ichord, considered inflammatory, and *The New York Times* published the list without ques-

the theme of racially segregated education in a 1966 book, *Our Children Are Dying,* in which he closely examined the educational practices of a Harlem public-school principal and educational philosopher, Dr. Elliott Shapiro. A 1968 *Playboy* article, "The War on Dissent," featured criticism of J. Edgar Hoover, the longtime head of Federal Bureau of Investigation (FBI). Hentoff's first book for children, *Jazz Country,* won the *New York Herald Tribune*'s Children's Spring Book Festival Award, the Nancy Bloch Award, and the Woodward Park School Award. He wrote nine books of fiction and nonfiction for young people.

During the 1960s Hentoff was also able to devote more investigative and writing time to the study of political "mavericks" such as New York Representative and Mayor John Lindsay and John Cardinal O'Connor. Using the same methods he had employed with jazz musicians, Hentoff immersed himself in the world of these leaders, interviewing them and their co-workers at all levels many times until he gained their confidence

tion in its 15 October issue. The American Civil Liberties Union filed a case charging an intrusion on First Amendment rights, *Nat Hentoff et al. v. Richard H. Ichord et al.,* in federal court of the District of Columbia. When the case was decided in the plaintiffs' favor, the House responded with a resolution authorizing the report. In April 1971 the FBI sent agents to call on Hentoff at his office because he was one of the journalists who had received packages of secret files from the Citizens' Committee to Investigate the FBI. He refused to turn over the files. These experiences influenced Hentoff's contribution to *State Secrets: Police Surveillance in America* (1974), in which he pulled together excerpts from essays published in *Playboy,* focusing in particular on the growth of electronic surveillance and calling for lawsuits to establish precedents clearly defining limits on uses of the new technology and linking those limits to the Bill of Rights. In 1973 Northeastern University awarded him a University Medal to honor his achievements in journalism.

Though Hentoff prepared to write his life story in 1979 by ordering his FBI file under the Freedom of Information Act, many of his most combative years lay ahead of him. In 1982 he signed a *New York Times* advertisement condemning Israel's invasion of Lebanon and was pronounced "satanic" by a self-appointed tribunal of rabbis in Massachusetts. Louis Farrakhan's followers labeled Hentoff "the antichrist." *The Day They Came to Arrest the Book,* a young adult novel he published that year, stages debates that regularly feature in perennial attempts to ban Mark Twain's novel *Adventures of Huckleberry Finn* (1885).

Hentoff returned to the subject of censorship in *Free Speech for Me but Not for Thee* (1992), a collection consisting primarily of *Village Voice* essays from the 1980s. These essays address the growing support for censorship of speech and press that characterized both sides of the political spectrum during the decade, as expressed, for example, in the Meese Commission's crackdown during the Nixon administration on pornography with the cooperation of feminists Catharine Mackinnon and Andrea Dworkin. Earlier Mackinnon had been instrumental in drafting city ordinances equating possession of pornography with violent crimes against women, and many college campuses had begun to establish codes governing both speech about race and sexual conduct. Hentoff opened the essay addressing these issues with a quotation from the Bible that met every one of Mackinnon's criteria for defining a text as pornography. During this period Hentoff's contentious combination of libertarian positions on civil liberties and pro-life position including advocacy of social welfare programs earned him many other enemies, some of whom took the trouble to leave death threats with his

messages at work. In 1985 his alma mater awarded him an honorary doctorate of laws at its commencement ceremony.

In 1986 he published the first of two autobiographical books, *Boston Boy,* reminiscent of his studies of the Civil Rights Movement and John Lindsay. Hentoff's writing style tends toward the episodic, but this volume is tightly unified, braiding the three threads that run throughout all of his work since the 1960s: Jewishness, jazz, and the Bill of Rights. Despite rampant anti-Semitism in the Boston area, particularly during the 1940s, Hentoff remembers the political scene of his youth as "joyful." Some pieces in the book were recycled, the affectionate and humorous portrayals of former Massachusetts governor James Michael Curley and his sometime political rival Clem Norton, for example.

In 1988, in part responding to the confusion of his opponents regarding his pro-life position, Hentoff published *John Cardinal O'Connor: At the Storm Center of a Changing American Catholic Church,* a book of essays reflecting upon his relationship with the archbishop of New York since the 1960s. The mood of the book recalls Hentoff's portrait of John Lindsay, and Hentoff has often compared the two figures, saying they inspired him by choosing principles over party lines. His account of his first meeting with his subject featured O'Connor shouting on the telephone that Catholic hospitals would not, on his watch, bust unions. Another meeting describes O'Connor challenging a meeting full of New York State politicians as an advocate for the poor.

In 1995, shortly following Hentoff's involuntary retirement from *The New Yorker,* the National Press Foundation gave him an award for lifetime contributions to journalism. At the awards dinner Meg Greenfield, who had recruited Hentoff to write the "Sweet Land of Liberty" column for the *Post* in 1985, introduced him with the observation that "he puts on his skunk suit and heads off to the garden party, week after week, again and again" (*Speaking Freely,* p. 291). In 1997 Hentoff published his second volume of his life story, *Speaking Freely,* a loosely connected series of reminiscences ranging freely among individuals of interest in his life, beginning with Malcolm X.

Hentoff takes pride in being "beyond category," a phrase Duke Ellington used to designate the highest level of achievement among musicians. When not writing journalism, Hentoff develops essays using a signature movement that operates like music: he enlarges on a theme in a circular manner, using motifs and refrains, moving backward and forward in time to establish a mood, a tone. In *Speaking Freely,* for example, he unfolds his identity, explaining how he reached a given conclusion through various moments of reflection, meditating in short chapters on the characters who influenced his thinking by engaging him in dialogues or whose life stories are exemplary of some virtue he admires. Hentoff included a chapter in this book reflecting on his children's chosen professions: two are lawyers, one is a musician, and one is a circus performer. Rarely does he mention family matters. He praises his wife's writing and makes a running joke of the fact that they disagree about abortion.

The best example of Hentoff's style of development from *Speaking Freely* appears in his explanation of his conversion to a pro-life position. Beginning halfway through the book, Hentoff makes a series of passes through the topic over the course of five chapters. Essentially, he argues that "there is much more to abortion than abortion itself," pointing to the system of legal precedents by which the legality of the procedure normalizes what he sees as other–avoidable–forms of refusal to protect the helpless (p. 174). Hentoff reports with some amusement that his presence has not always been welcome among pro-life groups, as he fundamentally disagrees with many of their positions on social-welfare programs (he supported the federally funded Women, Infants, and Children and other programs that offered a safety net to impoverished young mothers, which were eliminated by President Ronald Reagan) and disapproves of the death penalty.

The Nat Hentoff Reader appeared in 2001, including essays that span four decades of work. In 2003 Hentoff published another collection of political essays, *The War on the Bill of Rights and the Gathering Resistance*. Already Hentoff has gone on record as being disappointed with every presidential administration since 1960. In the 1990s he scorned President Bill Clinton as an abuser of women, but the Bush administration has earned the bulk of his direct criticism for its sustained multiple attacks on civil liberties, especially since the terrorist attacks of 11 September 2001. The essays advance a twofold argument, peppered with references to George Orwell's writings on totalitarianism, that Americans must educate themselves about their history and regard their top levels of leadership–particularly wartime presidents, their non-elected appointees who in fact rule the nation, and the supreme courts who support their interpretations of law–with a healthy dose of skepticism if they are to retain their constitutional rights. Using references not just to the framers of the Constitution but to other activists of the revolutionary era including the Sons of Liberty, Hentoff reminds Americans that their heritage has not been one of blind obedience or even giving government officials the benefit of the doubt. The book provides a valuable chronicle, replete with names, dates, cases, and bills, of the activities of the

attorney general's office and quotations from the justices of the supreme court indicating their willingness, contrary to earlier courts, to rubber-stamp intrusions on citizens' constitutional rights.

Hentoff's 2004 *American Music Is* establishes a completely different tone and mood. The collection comprises compact disc reviews and biographical shorts about blues, jazz, country, and folk musicians that appeared originally in the *Wall Street Journal* and *Jazz News* between 1988 and 2003. The ephemeral disguise of the pieces collected might tempt an audience to underestimate their significance. Tellingly, however, Hentoff opens the volume with a review of a 2001 exhibit at the Martin Luther King Jr. Center in Atlanta, Georgia, of lynching, using Billie Holiday and Abel Meeropol's "Strange Fruit" as a device of lyric synthesis to accompany the horrific visual displays of broken, charred bodies. One brief essay gives a taste of Hentoff's lifelong love affair with African American music, and as the reviews progress, note upon note, rhythm upon rhythm, the depth of that love commands reverence.

Appropriately, he closes the book with a reflection on Jewish equivalents of blues and jazz–the music of cantors and *klezmorim*–whose "cries to God" underscore two important facts. First, as Zora Neale Hurston, Ntozake Shange, and others have noted, music and dance act as the repository of emotional memories, the only cultural archive for the dispossessed because they can carry it in their bodies when all else has been stripped away. Second, the only access to this archive lies in the life of the body. As Hurston explained in her essay "Spirituals and Neo-Spirituals," this type of music, defined less by outward style markers than by function, derives its significance not from its product value but from the subjective experience of the participant in the moment–it exists, as Hentoff's title suggests, in the present. American people's music has been, in its finer moments, just such a primal cry to God, Hentoff argues, a communication of the immediacy of divine presence in people and in the world, in the moment.

Nat Hentoff has been criticized for being too topical, but his biographical and autobiographical writings demonstrate that he can produce long, coherent work. He is, above all, a journalist, however, and journalists write about events of the moment. The hundreds of columns and ephemeral pieces he has produced over the years provide a relentless and invaluable micro-history of the interstices of race, legal theory, local politics, and culture over the last half of the twentieth century. True to form, Hentoff has adapted to the Internet and posts columns there for *Jewish World Review* and

Jazznotes.com. Many of his *Village Voice* columns are also available on the World Wide Web, and the Public Broadcasting System and National Public Radio have posted audio clips from Hentoff as well. Hentoff is a member of Authors' League of America, American Federation of Television and Radio Artists, Reporters Committee for Freedom of the Press (member of steering committee), PEN (member of Freedom to Write Committee), and the New York Civil Liberties Union. In January 2004 he became the first writer to be named as a Jazz Master by the National Endowment for the Arts.

References:

"Civil Liberties and Jazz–Past, Present, and Future: A Conversation with Journalist Nat Hentoff" [12 Interviews] *Jerry Jazz Musician,* 6 October 2005 <http://www.jerryjazzmusician.com/mainHTML.cfm?page=nathentoff.html>;

John W. Whitehead, "Why We Are Americans: An Interview with Nat Hentoff," *Oldspeak, An Online Journal Devoted to Intellectual Freedom,* 18 September 2002 <http://www.rutherford.org/Oldspeak/Articles/Interviews/hentoff.html> (viewed 6 August 2008).

Karl Hess

(25 May 1923 – 22 April 1994)

Brian Doherty

BOOKS: *In a Cause That Will Triumph: The Goldwater Campaign and the Future of Conservatism* (New York: Doubleday, 1967);

The End of the Draft, by Hess and Thomas Reeves (New York: Random House, 1970);

Dear America (New York: Morrow, 1975);

Neighborhood Power: The New Localism, by Hess and David Morris (Boston: Beacon Press, 1975);

Community Technology (New York: Harper & Row, 1979);

A Common Sense Strategy for Survivalists (Alexandria, Va.: Kephart Communications, 1981);

Mostly on the Edge: An Autobiography (Amherst, N.Y.: Prometheus Books, 1999).

SELECTED PERIODICAL PUBLICATIONS–UNCOLLECTED: "Should You Own a Gun?" *American Mercury,* 84 (April 1957): 54–60;

"The Death of Politics," *Playboy* (March 1969);

"Barry Goldwater: An Open Letter to My Friend," *Ramparts,* 8 (November 1974): 55–57;

"The System Has Failed," *Penthouse* (August 1974);

"Whiffs of Change," *Progressive,* 28 (November 1974): 55–57;

"America Has a Crisis of Scale–Not Leadership," *Los Angeles Times,* 20 May 1975, p. C7;

"Living Right (and Left)," *Washington Post,* 19 October 1975;

"What Happened to Conservatism?" *Libertarian Review* (May/June 1976);

"Abolish the Corporation!" *Business and Society Review* (Spring 1978);

"Contradictions of a Conservative," *Inquiry* (10 December 1979);

"Anarchism without Hyphens," *dandelion* (Spring 1980);

"Elitism in Defense of Virtue is No Vice," *Liberty* (January 1990);

"Tools vs. Philosophy," *Liberty,* 4 (July 1991): 51–52.

Karl Hess (from the dust jacket for Dear America, *1975; Richland County Public Library)*

Karl Hess's radicalism bridged the gaps between varied American political tendencies. While those dedicated to by-the-book ideological consistency might, and often did, see the twists and turns of Hess's intellectual career as indicating a lack of a core identity, a dearth of intellectual seriousness, Hess himself saw the best in the three tendencies in which he was at various times a major figure–conservatism, leftism, and libertarianism–as of a piece: a belief in localized democracy and the freedom it allowed; a belief in the value of keeping any concentrations of power, whether in the state or in the market, as limited and constrained as possible; a belief in self-sufficiency, and in the benefits and possibilities of technology as a tool of both personal and community empowerment.

Through all his ideological and institutional turns and shifting allegiances, Hess wrote that he was proud of one thing: that he had never been a liberal, in the modern American sense. To Hess that meant he had never been a believer in a state, or any institution, that took upon itself the task of controlling and organizing, even for supposedly benevolent purposes, the lives and freely chosen institutional arrangements of individuals and small, local, independent communities.

Hess was born on 25 May 1923. His father was Carl Hess, a millionaire of Philippine descent; his mother was born Thelma Snyder. Hess was born in the United States but was taken while an infant to the Philippines, where his father's wealthy family lived. His father was serially unfaithful to Hess's mother; tiring of this, she left the senior Hess and took young Carl Jr. back with her to Washington, D.C.

She took no alimony from her estranged husband, and worked to support herself and her son as a switchboard operator and later apartment manager. Hess was unhappy with his father's treatment of his mother, and changed the spelling of his first name to "Karl" in order to distance himself from an unwanted paternal heritage. But Hess, a windmill-tilting romantic himself, did enjoy telling the family legend of how his father eventually died during the Japanese occupation of the Philippines during World War II: beheaded for ignoring an order from a Japanese soldier to interrupt a card game.

Hess credited his mother for imbuing him early with a firm independence of mind and spirit. When he was embarrassed as a child walking ill-clothed through a fancy hotel, she lectured him publicly on the unimportance of what other people thought of him. She also encouraged his love of reading by refusing to answer any question that she thought he could find the answer to himself through a printed source.

By age fifteen, Hess had already dropped out of school. He evaded truancy authorities by simultaneously enrolling in two different area high schools and then filling out transfer forms at each to the other one. He got his first journalism job, at Washington, D.C.-area radio station WOL, through the influence of a friend of his mother's who lived in the apartment house she managed. He lost this job when he was ticketed for driving without a license–he was still too young to have one–on a work-related mission. A day later, he got his first newspaper job at the *Alexandria Gazette*. He attempted to enlist in the army during WWII, but was discharged for lying about his medical records. He had failed to mention various tropical diseases he'd suffered while in the Philippines as an infant.

During Hess's early career as a newspaperman he found employment at many different publications in various capacities during the first half of the 1940s, including the *Washington Star*, *Alexandria Gazette*, and *Washington Times-Herald*. He recalled being fired from the *Washington Daily News* for refusing to write a laudatory obituary for Franklin Delano Roosevelt. Hess regarded the New Deal as an example of the centralization of decision-making and power in one unified state apparatus, and he was already strongly opposed to such a social system.

Hess entered magazine journalism after being fired from the *Daily News*, with stints as editor of *Aviation News* (1945–1947) and then as religion editor of *Pathfinder* (1947–1949). During the late 1940s he also began occasional speechwriting and ghostwriting for politicians and became a writer for the Republican National Committee. In this period anticommunism became his prime obsession, and he wrote a column on the topic for *Pathfinder*. Hess had become attracted to what he saw the Republican Party as standing for in the immediate post–World War II era: individualism, anti-imperialism, and a dedication to the interests of small businessmen.

In 1946 Hess married Yvonne Barbara Cahoon, whom he met while they were both working at the *Washington Star*. Their first child, Karl Hess IV (who later used the name Karl Hess Jr. professionally) was born in 1947; their second, Eric, in 1960. In 1950 Hess started work as press editor at *Newsweek*. His anticommunism cost him his job there; he was fired in 1954 for signing an advertisement defending Senator Joseph McCarthy, with his professional affiliation listed against his employer's wishes. Hess plunged into full-time professional anticommunism after that, writing for and editing the newsletter *Counterattack*, dedicated to publicizing the communist affiliations of public figures, from 1954 to 1956.

Hess's anticommunism was more than just a journalistic concern; he also, often in collaboration with his fellow anticommunist *Newsweek* staffer, right-wing journalist Ralph de Toledano, sought involvement in direct action against communism, in both America and Cuba. Hess collected guns and napalm (given him gratis by Dow Chemicals when he flashed his *Newsweek* credentials and claimed he was conducting gardening experiments) to aid a pre-Castro attempt by Carlos Hevia, a former president of Cuba, to overthrow Fulgencio Batista. In the early 1950s Hess himself rode in a plane over Havana and dropped anti-Batista pamphlets (though he neglected to unwrap the bundle of paper). This coup attempt was squashed, and Hevia was arrested. Hess knew through the FBI connections of his friend, former communist turned anticommunist crusader Whittaker Chambers, that the FBI was aware of his involvement in the coup attempt, which was a violation of U.S. law; he was not prosecuted, however. Hess also met with a lawyer for noted mobster Frank Costello. Hess hoped to talk the lawyer into inducing Costello to use mob resources and men to intercept and steal cash payoffs the Soviet Union made to American communists. Deciding, under the influence of Chambers's anticommunist book *Witness* (1952), that a firm religious base was the only antidote for communism, Hess made a brief attempt at becoming a Roman Catholic in the 1950s.

Hess then moved into corporate speechwriting at the Champion Paper Company, based in Ohio, where he worked from 1958–1961. He credited his experience at Champion with teaching him, by negative example, the value of workplace democracy and worker management over traditional top-down capitalist management styles. He found standard American management techniques were merely hamstringing productivity and dampening worker autonomy and creativity. While Hess was at Champion, one of his bosses who was a former deputy secretary of defense under Eisenhower lent Hess's writing services to the Republican Party; thus he helped compose the 1960 party platform. This involvement in internal Republican politics led him to a job at a Republican-leaning policy think tank, the American Enterprise Institute (AEI), whose president, William Baroody, became leader of Senator Barry Goldwater's brain trust when Goldwater ran for president in 1964.

AEI lent Hess's speechwriting talents to the Goldwater campaign. Subsequently Hess became a valued member of Goldwater's inner circle, traveling most of the campaign year with the candidate. In a campaign whose fate seemed to most observers sealed before it even began, Hess later noted he was the only member of Goldwater's own team who genuinely believed all the way up through election night their candidate would win. After Goldwater's crushing defeat, he and anyone associated with him were considered persona non grata within the Republican Party. Hess, though, did not abandon his belief in his old boss, either in the aftermath of his staggering loss or in the aftermath of Hess's very public shift, within four years, to an ideological stance that seemed in many ways the opposite of Goldwater's crusty Western traditionalist conservatism and heated anticommunism. *In a Cause that Will Triumph,* Hess's first book, published in 1967 (though internal evidence, including reference to the 1966 election as in the future, shows it was completed much earlier), was a detailed defense of Goldwater and Goldwaterism.

While Hess's reputation as the radical libertarian in the Goldwater camp has led many to assume, and to repeat the story, that Hess wrote the most famous and notorious line in Goldwater's acceptance speech at the 1964 Republican convention in San Francisco—

"Extremism in the defense of liberty is no vice, and moderation in the pursuit of justice is no virtue"–Hess clearly stated in this book, and elsewhere, that another Goldwater speechwriter, Harry Jaffa, was responsible for those words. Hess argued, though he later changed his mind, that Goldwater was not in fact the anti-government extremist that his enemies within the Republican Party and the press accused him of being. Hess insisted that Goldwater did not really want to eliminate the income tax and social security completely, as some of his enemies accused, and defended the senator's militaristic stance toward international communism.

Still, Hess's connections with Goldwater made him largely unemployable within the party and its attendant institutions in the years after the 1964 election. That, combined with growing problems in his relationship with his wife, led to an ideological midlife crisis of sorts for Hess. But the real trigger in his change from right-wing careerism to left-wing radicalism and then libertarianism came, fittingly for a thinker who credited the power of tools over ideas, with his purchase of a motorcycle. Hess found that his mere decision to ride a vehicle commonly considered outside the pale of a middle-class Washington apparatchik and suburban family man alienated him further from the world he had inhabited professionally and personally, thrusting him into communities of friends, associates, and eventually lovers that leaned more leftward. The motorcycle, and the way his friends, neighbors, and wife reacted to it so negatively–"even though I wore proper suits and ties while riding the thing"–led Hess to start "thinking about how little the sensual and personal are permitted in modern middle-class lives" *(Dear America).* As he switched to an even bigger motorcycle, he wrote, "That great, roaring, nasty thing must seem like an erotic invader in the quiet suburbs. It trails fantasies of leather-jacketed violence, of crazy goings-on in wild groves and ramshackle houses."

Marcus Raskin and Richard Barnet, the directors of the new-left think tank, the Institute for Policy Studies (IPS) in Washington, D.C., recognized some themes in Goldwater's thought that intersected new-left concerns, mostly in terms of decentralizing some of the power of the federal government. In the mid 1960s they invited Hess to give a seminar at IPS on Goldwater's inherent radicalism. This relationship led Hess to a full-time staff position at IPS from 1968 to 1970, as he began to see even more overlap between his changing ideology and that of the IPS. For example, Hess, after exposure to his new colleagues' arguments, turned from his previous belief that international communism required a firm military response from the United States.

Hess divorced his first wife, Yvonne Cahoon, in 1965 and with his future wife Therese Machotka began living a semi-communal-style life on a houseboat, *The Tranquil*, in the Anacostia River, as part of a larger community in which, as Hess wrote, "about fifty people shared all the chores of community housekeeping" and "shared work projects, ranging from boat repairs to light metal construction to dock construction" (*Dear America*). Hess had begun welding, both as hobby and occasional profession. His budding libertarianism grew when their floating community was disbanded by the government, which decided that living in that boatyard was forbidden by law—although the yachts in which the wealthy lived nearby remained undisturbed.

Hess at that point represented an unusual type: the former hardcore right-winger turned hardcore leftist. By 1968, his reputation as an apostate from the right was already spreading; he was still, however, writing the occasional speech and newspaper column clandestinely for his old friend Goldwater, in one case persuading the famously arch-conservative senator to point out that he had much in common with "the anarchist wing of SDS [Students for a Democratic Society]" (*Dear America*). Two years later, Hess ran into Goldwater while participating in an anti-war protest on Capital Hill; the Arizona senator asked his old friend to give him a call as soon as he was free, despite Hess's fears that Goldwater's staff would not appreciate the scruffy anti-war protestor appearing in his office. Through his turn to the radical left Hess maintained his deep personal affection and respect for Goldwater, even opining that he didn't know anyone who would make a finer member of the radical terror group the Weather Underground than Goldwater.

Hess discovered in 1968 that he was not the only one who saw connections between the values of the old right wing and the New Left, especially in its emphasis on personal empowerment over central state control. He read an article in *Ramparts* magazine in 1968 by another old rightist who had made a new left turn, the economist and political philosopher Murray Rothbard, one of the founding fathers of modern American libertarianism. Rothbard called himself an anarcho-capitalist: he believed that all human needs, including those of adjudication and defense, could and ought to be met by free-market transactions in a world of total private property. Hess was thrilled by this Rothbardian synthesis, and became a good friend and occasional visiting member of his New York City intellectual salon.

In 1968 Hess became the Washington editor of Rothbard's newsletter of commentary on politics and culture, *The Libertarian Forum* (which was launched in 1968 under the title *The Libertarian*). Soon afterward Hess showed up at the Young America Foundation's Labor Day weekend 1969 convention in St. Louis and gave an unscheduled speech at the St. Louis Arch,

drawing away nearly a quarter of the YAF attendees to hear his alternate arguments which attempted to recast the message of the convention from "Sock it to the Left" to "Sock it to the State." The result was the departure of libertarian and anarchist wings of YAF—the latter led by Karl's son, Karl Hess IV (later Karl Hess).

The hundreds of departed YAF members inspired by Hess began the first national libertarian student-membership organization, the Society for Individual Liberty, and also helped feed the ferment of small-press publications advocating libertarianism that arose in the wake of the libertarian departure from YAF. The national attention that ferment brought to the nascent mass libertarian movement (which was celebrated in a *New York Times Sunday Magazine* cover story in January 1971) could be largely credited to Hess's direct inspiration, not just through his guerilla appearance at the YAF convention, but through a long essay he published in *Playboy* in 1969 called "The Death of Politics" that spread a largely anarcho-capitalist message to a large popular audience.

In that *Playboy* article Hess attacked supposedly radical activism during the late 1960s, both right and left, as being in fact reactionary because of its very political nature: instead, he argued that true radicalism in the current context had to be a libertarian radicalism, built on "the view that each man is the absolute owner of his life, to use and dispose of as he sees fit; that all man's social actions should be voluntary; and that respect for every other man's similar and equal ownership of life and, by extension, the property and fruits of that life, is the ethical basis of a humane and open society." He also in the article paints his old patron Goldwater as more radical than Tom Hayden, since Hayden, Hess says, "wants to bulldoze his way into the establishment" while Goldwater "says he wants, in effect, to topple it, to forever end its power to advantage or disadvantage anyone."

Hess was far more enthusiastic about new-left street activism than was the more culturally conservative Rothbard. Their working relationship came to an abrupt end after Hess, as Rothbard saw it, disrupted a conference of libertarian scholars Rothbard helped organize in New York over Columbus Day weekend in 1969; Hess encouraged most of the crowd to stop talking and join him in an antiwar march on Fort Dix. Rothbard and Hess also clashed over Hess's admiration for the Black Panthers and Rothbard's public condemnation of them. Hess's eventual departure from the masthead of *Libertarian Forum* was so abrupt that his name was blotted out by hand on copies of the 1 May 1970 issue.

Hess had begun affecting the sartorial style of a Castro manqué, military fatigues and berets, combined

Dear America

A former top conservative thinker, Goldwater speech-writer, Nixon/Ford ghost-writer, and now left-wing libertarian tells how common-sense Americans can create a participatory democracy, manage their own affairs, sustain a wonderful standard of living, and exist in peace with nature and the world

by Karl Hess

Dust jacket for the first of Hess's two memoirs, published in 1975 (Richland County Public Library)

with the street-fighting rhetoric of the student radicals of the time. His opposition to the Vietnam War grew so strong that he expressed it for a while by wearing a ring made from metal from a shot-down American helicopter in Vietnam—a move he later grew to regret, as it seemed to express untoward glee over the death of a countryman who was not necessarily personally responsible for the policies of the nation that had sent him to Vietnam.

In 1970 Hess, in collaboration with Thomas Reeves and under the aegis of the National Council to Repeal the Draft, published *The End of the Draft,* a book that linked opposition to the draft to opposition to the overweening life and death power of the modern nation-state in general. Displaying his fresh anarchism, Hess argued that the root evil of conscription lay in its placement of the values and needs of the state above the rights and liberties of the individual. The book pointed out that at its very root the nation-state embodied this mistaken view of the proper relationship between the individual and the government. But Hess's pragmatic side showed through as well. The book argued not only that the draft represented a moral wrong, but that "the draft is a more costly and less efficient means of providing manpower than a volunteer force" representing "a net decline in real output because draftees' productivity in the civilian labor market exceeds that required to be a soldier" and that "the draft produces higher turnover and attendant training costs within the military itself" *(The End of the Draft).*

In 1975 Hess published the first of his two memoirs, *Dear America.* It presents his most leftist side: in it he condemns "corporate capitalism" as "an act of theft . . . through which a very few live very high off the work, invention, and creativity of very many others . . . the Grand Larceny of our particular time in history" *(Dear America).* Hess was still enough of a libertarian to condemn the income tax as the beam supporting the weight of the American Leviathan, and to declare that it must go, but simultaneously still enough of a leftist to call for local takeovers of absentee-owned factories or housing.

He wrote in *Dear America* of his decision, in his early libertarian days, to stop paying taxes, and to tell the Internal Revenue Service so. The decision came, he said, not out of any particular ideological revelation, but out of the experience of an IRS audit in which he "suddenly found myself . . . in a face-to-face, significant confrontation with actual, not theoretical, bureaucrats and . . . at a point where I could actually take an action . . . rather than just strike a rhetorical pose" *(Dear America).* Along with his 1040 form in 1969, he enclosed a note reading, in part, "The Federal government of the United States of America today is guilty of exactly every sort of infringement, abuse, and denial stated as intolerable by the Declaration of Independence. I cannot, in conscience, sanction that government by the payment of taxes" *(The Libertarian,* 1 May 1969). The IRS struck back by imposing a 100 percent lien on his income, which drove him out of the conventional salaried job market for the rest of his life. "Refusing to pay taxes is not a laughing matter," he later noted in his second autobiography. "It has cost me a mint of money, left me pretty much destitute, and caused a terrible amount of trouble for my family and for other friends" *(Mostly on the Edge).*

Also in 1975, arising from his work with IPS, Hess produced *Neighborhood Power,* in collaboration with David Morris. The book presented an analysis and defense of the ways in which neighborhoods and communities on the smallest level could more effectively meet their own needs, both economic and social, than can big city governments or the federal government. The authors called not for the capture of existing political power, but empowerment through creating local institutions to meet local needs, from culture and media to health care to food co-ops to credit unions.

Hess's libertarianism resonated even through this IPS work; he stressed that neighborhoods needed to understand that government in and of itself is inherently unproductive. It has at its command only the resources it takes from citizens through taxes or inflation. The book concluded with a discussion that led not only to Hess's next book, but also to the next phase of his life in Adams Morgan, his neighborhood in the District of Columbia.

"Community technology" became the theme of Hess's life in the mid 1970s: an attempt to meet the needs for food and power as much as possible through techniques under the control of small neighborhoods. In pursuit of actualizing these ideas, he tried to turn his Adams Morgan neighborhood into a functioning experiment in local technological and agricultural self-sufficiency. Hydroponic gardens sprouted on rooftops; machine shops were opened to the neighborhood kids; trout breeding occurred in tanks in row house basements. But the experiment did not last long. He found it impossible to get any support even from city government for any of the projects; as he wrote in his second memoir, *Mostly on the Edge,* "they would give some a social worker, others a pass to the hospital, money, or food stamps. The only thing they would never give is the capacity to produce wealth locally" *(Mostly on the Edge).* He felt he and his neighbors had proved that even urban communities could be self-sufficient in food with the rooftop garden and trout breeding techniques they developed, but by the summer of 1975 he and his wife had become disillusioned with the experiment. After one too many break-ins to their home, and too many neighborhood kids who wanted "a job" (that is, a source of income) rather than meaningful work to do, he abandoned the neighborhood and the city. He and Therese relocated to a solar-powered home they built themselves on the Opequon River near Kearneysville, West Virginia, where they lived the rest of his life.

As they prepared to leave D.C., Hess learned another lesson regarding the value of words as opposed to the value of tools:

> We had, of course, several thousand books, institute-type books mostly on political science which look terribly impressive on walls but which few people, including myself, ever read in their entirety. We decided to offer them in trade for books that might actually be of use to us in West Virginia. We didn't get a single nibble on our offer. So, we then offered to swap them for tools. We advertised on bulletin boards and in the local newspaper our desire to trade a set of politically correct books for a good set of socket wrenches. Nothing. The market had made its decision: The col-

lective political wisdom of the ages was not worth a good set of forged-steel hand tools *(Mostly on the Edge).*

Because of his ongoing legal problems with the IRS, Hess found it best to earn as little aboveboard income as possible in the last decade or so of his life. He had begun metal sculpting both for artistic expression and for income in his first leftist phase in the late 1960s, and he continued to practice that art. He and Therese also refinished and sold furniture at Eastern Market in Washington, D.C., in the first half of the 1980s. During this period he also received occasional short-term university appointments, including one as artist-in-residence at the University of Illinois at Champaign-Urbana from 1979–1983, and as "radical in residence" at Warren Wilson College in Swananoa, North Carolina, in 1980. He continued advocacy for locally controlled small technologies as a member from 1978 to 1980 of both a U.S. congressional Appropriate Technology Task Force and the West Virginia Governor's Advisory Committee on Appropriate Technology.

Hess's unique ideological positioning and curious status as a rural small-tech anarchist who had written speeches for the most notoriously "reactionary" politician of the postwar era earned him the attention of a pair of documentary filmmakers, Peter Ladue and Roland Halle, who made a short film about Hess, *Toward Liberty,* which won an Academy Award for Best Short Documentary in 1981.

Hess had befriended right-wing publisher Robert Kephart in the early 1970s, and along with Murray Rothbard helped convert him to anarcho-capitalism. Kephart became a publisher of hard-money newsletters throughout the 1970s and 1980s that helped create, inform, and energize the rising American subcultures of "goldbugs" and survivalists, who thought that government mismanagement of the currency was sure to lead to an economic crisis and possible collapse in which ownership of gold, and possession of survival supplies and skills, would be essential. From 1981–1985 Hess edited for Kephart a survivalist newsletter, *Surviving Tomorrow.*

Hess returned to official libertarian activism in the 1980s, becoming editor of the Libertarian Party's newspaper, *LP News,* from 1986 to 1989. He also became an early contributing editor to the libertarian movement "in-reach" journal *Liberty,* launched in 1987– a magazine dedicated to discussion and debate internal to the libertarian movement, not to explaining libertarianism to the outside world, or converting readers to a libertarian viewpoint. Most of his short-form journalism from 1987–1994 appeared in its pages. Hess also launched a mostly paper Libertarian Party campaign for governor of West Virginia in 1992.

Hess experienced various heart troubles for most of the last decade of his life, with an aortic valve replacement in 1985 and a heart transplant in August 1992. This limited his productivity as writer and sculptor. His last major writing project, a second autobiography, was published posthumously in 1999 as *Mostly on the Edge*. The final version of the book was based on many hours of taped interviews with Hess conducted by libertarian sociologist and controversialist Charles Murray, author of groundbreaking books on the welfare state (*Losing Ground,* 1984) and the importance of IQ, including considerations of the links between IQ and race (*The Bell Curve,* 1994). Although Hess is listed as its sole author, the final manuscript was completed by his son Karl, credited as editor of the book. Karl Hess Jr. had by then become a leading libertarian thinker in the field of environmentalism, applying libertarian lessons about property and incentives to environmental problems. Hess's widow Therese, and Charles Murray's wife Catherine Murray, assisted Karl Hess Jr. in completing the manuscript.

Karl Hess died on 22 April 1994. Hess's days as a minor celebrity of sorts, profiled in both *The New York Times* and *The Washington Post* Sunday magazines, were long over. But his death did not go unnoticed even outside the libertarian movement in which he remained a beloved culture hero. In the *New Republic* Hess was eulogized as a better kind of libertarian, one who "believed in the visible hand of the craftsman, not in the invisible hand of the market" (John Judis, "After You've Gone: Three Wise Men," *New Republic,* April 1994).

Hess is most remembered as a libertarian, and it is by that movement that he is most honored. Most conservatives could never forgive Hess his flirtations with leftist radicalism in the late 1960s, and the left ultimately could find little use for his attachment to small-scale private property and free markets as key to a vibrant, rich, and humane social order. But the colorful and charismatic Hess remains a heroic legend to the libertarian movement, and through his Goldwater connections one of its few, highly valued links to real political legitimacy. His decades of trouble with the IRS also made him a beloved martyr to them, as he was the only prominent intellectual who actually acted on the movement's anti-tax principles and suffered for it. Hess's particular style of libertarian activism came to be known and appreciated within the movement as "living liberty" rather than merely writing and thinking about it. The libertarian supper club in Los Angeles is named after Hess in honor of this.

But Hess always remained a distinct figure, too complicated to be fit snugly under any ideological umbrella. The libertarian movement in which Hess participated for the last two and a half decades of his life comprised, largely, ideologues and political activists inspired by ideologues. Hess was resolutely anti-ideological and for the most part antipolitical, if being political indicates a belief that electoral politics promote social change.

"What really changes our world and the way we live in it are devices and innovations," Hess wrote. "If you want to know what is happening in a society at any point, look at the tools—not the rhetoric, not the books, not the philosophy. If a tool is available you can bet somebody is going to use it, and if it works well you can be certain the world will never be the same again. The free market, for example, is such a tool. Wherever there is unfettered commerce, ordinary people thrive" (*Mostly on the Edge*).

That particular understanding of what free markets mean connected Hess's market-libertarianism with his leftism: a concern with the well-being of the average person and a commitment to achieving that well-being. Hess wrote that he saw liberty as

> the freedom to move beyond the pompous preaching of an opinion to the simple practice of affiliation and engagement. I see in it the creative spark and the productive energy of doing, thinking people who make the tools that change the world . . . I have learned the more free people are to pursue the artistry of their lives, to combine together to build their neighborhoods, and to make and market things, the better are their material lives and the more able are they to pursue their individual happiness (*Mostly on the Edge*).

Although almost all of Hess's writings are out of print, through the people he influenced, both as writer and as friend, Hess's name has retained valuable currency in the libertarian movement, and his memory has been kept alive within it. Hess was once asked what it takes to be the perfect anarchist. Being a good friend, a good lover, and a good neighbor, he replied. Wouldn't "resistance to authority" be the defining characteristic, he was asked; is that all it takes? "What did you expect?" Hess countered. "A lot of rules?"

References:

David Deleon, "The American as Anarchist: Social Criticism in the 1960s," *American Quarterly,* 25, 5 (December 1973): 516–537;

Brian Doherty, *Radicals for Capitalism: A Freewheeling History of the Modern American Libertarian Movement* (New York: Public Affairs, 1971);

John Judis, "After You've Gone: Three Wise Men," *New Republic,* April 1994;

Jerome Tuccille, *It Usually Begins with Ayn Rand* (New York: Stein & Day, 1971).

Robert G. Ingersoll

(11 August 1833 – 21 July 1899)

Matt Sailor
Georgia State University

BOOKS: *The Gods, and Other Lectures* (Peoria, Ill.: C. P. Farrell, 1874);

The Ghosts, and Other Lectures (Washington, D.C.: C. P. Farrell, 1878);

Hell (New York: E. McCormack, 1878);

The Old and the New (New York: Truth Seeker, 1878);

Some Mistakes of Moses (Washington, D. C.: C. P. Farrell, 1879);

Flight of the Shadows (Bristol, England: W. H. Morris, 188-?);

A Review of the Sugar Question (Washington, D.C.: T. McGill, 188-?);

Farm Life in America (London: Freethought Publishing, 1880);

Free Speech and an Honest Ballot (Chicago: C. P. Farrell, 1880);

What Must We Do To Be Saved? (Washington, D.C.: C. P. Farrell, 1880);

Great Speeches of Col. R. G. Ingersoll (Chicago: Rhodes & McClure, 1881);

Six Interviews with Robert G. Ingersoll on Six Sermons by DeWitt Talmage, D.D. (Washington, D.C., 1882);

Civil Rights Speech (New York: C. P. Farrell, 1883);

Ingersoll Catechised (Washington, D.C.: C. P. Farrell, 1884);

Orthodoxy (Washington, D.C.: C. P. Farrell, 1884);

Prose-Poems and Selections from the Writings and Sayings of Robert G. Ingersoll (New York: C. P. Farrell, 1884);

Blasphemy (London: Progressive Publishing, 1885);

The Christian Religion (New York: C. P. Farrell, 1886);

Lay Sermon on the Labor Question (New York: C. P. Farrell, 1886);

Live Topics (London: Progressive Publishing, 1886);

Ingersoll on McGlynn (New York: Truth Seeker, 1887);

The Field-Ingersoll Discussion (New York: North American Review, 1888);

The Household of Faith (London: Progressive Publishing, 1888);

Ingersoll-Gladstone Controversy on Christianity (New York: C. P. Farrell, 1888);

Robert G. Ingersoll (frontispiece for The Works of Robert G. Ingersoll, *volume 7, edited by Clinton P. Farrell, Dresden Edition, 1902; University of California Libraries)*

Repairing the Idols (London: Progressive Publishing, 1888);

The Trial of C. B. Reynolds for Blasphemy (New York: C. P. Farrell, 1888);

A Tribute to Roscoe Conkling (New York: C. P. Farrell, 1888);

The Limitations of Toleration (New York: C. P. Farrell, 1889);

A Wooden God (New York: C. P. Farrell, 1889);

Bible Idolatry (New York: Truth Seeker, 1890);

Crimes Against Criminals (New York: C. P. Farrell, 1890);

Liberty in Literature (New York: Truth Seeker, 1890);

Tolstoi and the "Kreutzer Sonata" (London: Progressive Publishing, 1890);

Christ and Miracles (London: Freethought Publishing, 1891);

Creeds and Spirituality (London: Progressive Publishing, 1891);

Shakespeare (New York: C. P. Farrell, 1891);

Difficulties of Belief (London: R. Forder, 1892);

Ernest Renan and Jesus Christ (London: R. Forder, 1892);

Ingersollia. Gems of Thought from the Lectures, Speeches, and Conversations of Col. Robert G. Ingersoll (Chicago: G. E. Wilson, 1892);

The Three Philanthropists (London: Progressive Publishing, 1892);

About the Holy Bible (New York: C. P. Farrell, 1894);

Abraham Lincoln (New York: C. P. Farrell, 1894);

Declaration of Independence and A Vision of War (New York: C. P. Farrell, 1895);

Is Suicide A Sin? (New York: C. P. Farrell, 1895);

Liberty of Man, Woman, and Child (New York: C. P. Farrell, 1895);

Myth and Miracle (New York: C. P. Farrell, 1895);

Patriotic Addresses (New York: C. P. Farrell, 1895);

Some Interrogation Points (New York: Commonwealth, 1895);

Some Reasons Why (New York: C. P. Farrell, 1895);

Voltaire (New York: C. P. Farrell, 1895);

Which Way? (New York: C. P. Farrell, 1895);

The Foundations of Faith (New York: C. P. Farrell, 1896);

How To Reform Mankind (New York: C. P. Farrell, 1896);

Writings of Robert G. Ingersoll (New York: C. P. Farrell, 1896);

Essays and Criticisms (New York: C. P. Farrell, 1897);

Individuality (New York: C. P. Farrell, 1897);

A Thanksgiving Sermon (New York: C. P. Farrell, 1897);

The Truth (New York: C. P. Farrell, 1897);

Why I Am an Agnostic (New York: C. P. Farrell, 1897);

Rome or Reason (New York: C. P. Farrell, 1898);

Superstition (New York: C. P. Farrell, 1898);

A Few Reasons for Doubting the Inspiration of the Bible (New York: Truth Seeker, 1899);

Address Before the New York Unitarian Club (New York: Truth Seeker, 1899);

The Devil (New York: C. P. Farrell, 1899);

Faith that Surely Wanes (New York: Truth Seeker, 1899);

God in the Constitution (New York: Truth Seeker, 1899);

Great Infidels (New York: C. P. Farrell, 1899);

The Great Ingersoll Controversy (New York: C. P. Farrell, 1899);

Inaugural Address (New York: C. P. Farrell, 1899);

My Reviewers Reviewed (New York: C. P. Farrell, 1899);

Progress and What Is Religion? (New York: C. P. Farrell, 1899);

Robert Burns (New York: C. P. Farrell, 1899);

Thomas Paine (New York: C. P. Farrell, 1899);

To the Indianapolis Clergy (New York: C. P. Farrell, 1899);

The Works of Robert G. Ingersoll, 12 volumes, edited by Clinton P. Farrell (New York: C. P. Farrell, 1900; republished, Dresden edition, 1902);

A Look Backward and a Prophecy (New York: C. P. Farrell, 1901);

Bible Not a Moral Guide (New York: C. P. Farrell, 1903);

Gold Speech (New York: C. P. Farrell, 1903);

Hard Times and the Way Out (New York: C. P. Farrell, 1903);

The Oath Question (New York: C. P. Farrell, 1903);

Stage and Pulpit (New York: C. P. Farrell, 1903);

To The Clergy (New York: C. P. Farrell, 1903);

Tribute to His Brother (New York: C. P. Farrell, 1903);

The Truth of History (New York: C. P. Farrell, 1903);

Vindication of Thomas Paine (New York: C. P. Farrell, 1903);

Children of the Stage (New York: New York Anti-Vivisection Society, 1910);

Heretics and Heresies (New York: C. P. Farrell, 1910);

Humboldt and Heretics and Heresies (New York: C. P. Farrell, 1910);

Fifty Great Selections, Lectures, Tributes, After Dinner Speeches and Essays . . . (New York: C. P. Farrell, 1920);

The Letters of Robert G. Ingersoll, edited, with a biographical introduction, by Eva Ingersoll Wakefield (New York: Philosophical Library, 1951);

The Trial of C. B. Reynolds: Robert G. Ingersoll's Address to the Jury, edited, with an introduction, by Madalyn Murray O'Hair (Austin, Tex.: American Atheist Press, 1986).

OTHER: Van Buren Denslow, *Modern Thinkers Principally Upon Social Science: What They Think, and Why,* introduction by Ingersoll (Chicago: Belford, Clarke, 1880);

Helen H. Gardener, *Men, Women and Gods and Other Lectures,* introduction by Ingersoll (New York: Truth Seeker, 1885);

The Barbarous Decision of The United States Supreme Court, Declaring the Civil Rights Act Unconstitutional . . . Also, the Powerful Speeches of Hon. Frederick Douglass and Col. Robert G. Ingersoll (Atlanta: Bishop H. M. Turner, 1893).

A political orator and lecturer on social issues, Robert Green Ingersoll came to prominence in America after a crowd-stirring speech nominating Senator James G. Blaine for president at the 1876 Republican National Convention in Cincinnati. Although Blaine lost the nomination to future president Rutherford B. Hayes, the charismatic rhetorical style of Ingersoll's "Plumed Knight Speech" captured the interest and imagination of the country, instantly transforming the Illinois lawyer into a national figure. Ingersoll never held a national political office; rather, he toured the country for years as the Republican Party's most effective and beloved stump speaker. Ingersoll was most famous (and in some circles infamous), however, for his fiery denunciations of organized religion, which he delivered at public and private engagements across the country until just before his death in 1899. Undoubtedly the most famous individual of his generation to question openly the existence of God, Ingersoll often confounded his orthodox counterparts not only with the sound logical basis of his humorous and persuasive lectures, but with his charming personality, embrace of family values, and remarkable generosity, all characteristics generally believed at that time to be the exclusive preserve of believers. A devout humanist, Ingersoll worshipped reason in place of God, believing adamantly that America and humanity at large could be truly free only after rejecting what he called the "superstition" of religious belief and pursuing unencumbered intellectual freedom and scientific innovation.

Dresden, New York, was the site of Robert Green Ingersoll's birth on 11 August 1833, but he did not remain there for long. The last of five children born to the Reverend John "Priest" Ingersoll and Mary Ingersoll, he was subjected to constant uprooting and resettling early in his life due to his father's work as an evangelical preacher. More concerned with making a home for his family in heaven than on earth, John Ingersoll moved his family from town to town, conducting revivals and bringing converts to the faith, leaving an impression on many with the potency of his sermons. Though the Reverend Ingersoll's way of life was common among ministers during America's Second Great Awakening, he differed from many of his colleagues in one important respect: he was an ardent abolitionist, a fact that alienated him from many of his contemporaries and compromised his credibility (and even his safety) with many audiences. John Ingersoll's flair for speaking and his willingness to express unpopular opinions clearly made an impression on young Ingersoll. Mary Ingersoll was an active abolitionist who read Voltaire and Thomas Paine. Because she died in 1835, her influence on her youngest son's development was limited.

Illustration from Ingersoll's first book, The Gods, and Other Lectures, *1874 (New York Public Library)*

Ingersoll's education strictly focused on the religious, consisting of his father's biblical instruction and the occasional enrollment in a small rural schoolhouse. Reverend Ingersoll beat his children regularly for misbehavior, but Robert Ingersoll's rebellious nature earned him considerably more beatings than his siblings and classmates. This insolence probably stemmed from the boy's early rejection of his father's orthodoxy. Many years later, in a popular lecture, Ingersoll ruefully reminisced about the monotonous, depressing Sundays spent in church and at home, humorously referring to the Sabbath as a day "too good for a child to enjoy himself." As much as he resented his father's oppressive religiosity, Ingersoll acknowledged the reverend's deep love for his children, understanding that his rigidity stemmed from a sincere fear of damnation. By the time John Ingersoll died in 1859, he had actually come to embrace the Universalist doctrine of universal forgiveness and salvation. He even came to accept his son Robert's religious skepticism.

Ingersoll spent the first twenty years of his life relatively aimlessly, staying loyally by his father on his travels across the country, unable to find a path that truly satisfied him. In 1853 Ingersoll began working toward becoming a lawyer, a profession that would define much of his life. He turned to the law largely on the advice of his brother Ebenezer (Ebon), who until his untimely death in 1879 remained Ingersoll's closest friend, confidant, and adviser, sharing many of his ideas and philosophies. Along with his brother, Ingersoll studied widely in the law library of a charitable Illinois lawyer, hoping to earn a sizable income working within the legal system. The Ingersoll brothers passed the bar together in December of 1854 and left for Shawneetown, Illinois, to start their legal practice. The brothers initially took jobs as legal clerks, but soon made enough money from the practice to support themselves. By 1858 they outgrew Shawneetown and moved on to Peoria, the second largest city in Illinois at the time. There the brothers prospered, largely due to their representation of prominent railroad corporations whose expansion created huge amounts of litigation.

In 1860 Ingersoll's local prominence as a respected lawyer and the oratorical finesse that he had developed at the bar inspired the Democrats of Illinois to nominate him for congress in the Fifth District. The campaign was typically brutal for the time period, with both sides using speeches and the press to disparage not only the politics of the opponent, but his character and sometimes his physical appearance. Most notable about the campaign, which ended in a loss for Ingersoll, was the debate at Galesburg, where Ingersoll boldly spoke out against the evils of slavery and the Fugitive Slave Law. For a Democrat this was a dangerous political decision. Ingersoll demonstrated early on his strength of will in declaring his deepest convictions in spite of the consequences or opinions of others.

When the Civil War broke out, Ingersoll offered his services to the Union government. Ingersoll quickly assembled the Eleventh Illinois Cavalry, over which he was appointed colonel. The Eleventh shipped out early in 1862, but not before Ingersoll found time to marry Eva Parker on 13 February 1862. The two had met in connection with a criminal trial and fell in love almost immediately. Parker had been raised in a household of rationalists; consequently, she was a "woman without superstition," as Ingersoll once put it. He admired her greatly, and she eventually had a great influence on the progression of his thought.

Colonel Ingersoll led the Eleventh Illinois through some pivotal battles in the war, including the Battle of Shiloh, but after only nine months of command he, along with the remains of his regiment, were captured by General Nathan Bedford Forrest. Popular

anecdotes at the time attributed Ingersoll's release to his deft use of rhetorical skill, but the circumstances of the colonel's parole were unremarkable, and after three months of awaiting orders from his commanders he resigned his commission. Ingersoll served with distinction, being promoted to Chief of Cavalry of the Union Army prior to his capture and turning down a position as a brigadier general. Overall, however, Ingersoll did not care much for service in the armed forces. Although not a strict pacifist, he disliked the rhetoric that served to glorify war, and his contempt for authority and blind allegiance did not improve with experience in the chain of command.

Before the Civil War Ingersoll had been a loyal Democrat. He abhorred slavery, but he believed in the popular argument that the federal government had no power to decide "state's rights" issues. During the war he wholeheartedly supported President Lincoln and criticized fellow Democrats who opposed the Emancipation Proclamation, accusing them of endangering the war effort. As the war continued, however, his politics gradually began to change. Given Ingersoll's obsession with individual freedom, it follows logically that he came to identify with the party that promised freedom to all men. In 1864, Ebon Ingersoll ran for the seat in the Fifth Congressional District of Illinois, the same seat that his younger brother had lost four years earlier. He ran as a Republican. Shortly thereafter Robert Ingersoll joined the Republican Party as well; he served as his brother's campaign manager, speaking widely across the district in favor of Ebon Clark Ingersoll, Abraham Lincoln, and the Republican Party. Ebon Ingersoll won the election. Throughout Congressman Ingersoll's career in Washington, his younger brother served as his closest adviser, helping him plan every decision of his political career through lengthy correspondence.

On 14 May 1866 Robert Ingersoll spoke in Peoria; the subject of his lecture was "Progress." Ingersoll had been addressing audiences for years, but most of his speeches up until this time had been of a purely political nature, stump speeches in support of himself or other political candidates. "Progress" was the first of the many original lectures that Ingersoll delivered which systematically analyzed historical, sociological, and philosophical issues. In the lecture he gave a brief, incomplete history of some of the great thinkers of Western civilization and discussed the church's suppression of their ideas. Essentially, he described a history in which the church enforces religious absolutes rooted in antiquated superstitions that impede all attempts to expand the scope of understanding, since new knowledge always challenges preconceived notions. He offered as examples the practice of witch trials, the miscalculations of the sixth-century orthodox geographer

Cosmas, and the biblical justifications once used for slavery in the Americas. Ingersoll concludes that only through continual innovation in science and technology can humanity improve its condition. While not as developed rhetorically as later lectures, "Progress" represents Ingersoll's first attempt at expressing themes he explored for the rest of his career.

But Ingersoll was not yet ready to begin lecturing full-time; he still had his eye on a political office. During the summer of 1866 he spoke widely on behalf of his brother's re-election campaign, and in 1867 his involvement in Illinois politics was finally rewarded when he received the appointment of attorney general for the state. He did not after all enjoy the position, which kept him away from his wife and his two daughters, Maud and Eva, aged four and three respectively when Ingersoll took the office. Additionally, Ingersoll had loftier political ambitions than attorney general, which he revealed when he announced his candidacy for governor of Illinois early in 1868. Though he expected wide support for his bid, the state convention in Peoria proved a disappointment for Ingersoll when John M. Palmer (who had not formally announced his candidacy) took the nomination. Without his own campaign to manage, Ingersoll turned outside Illinois, traveling to Maine to speak on behalf of Senator James G. Blaine. The stint in Maine, along with a subsequent tour of Indiana, gave Ingersoll his first taste of wider acclaim as an orator; his stirring rhetoric received attention from newspapers across the country.

When he returned to Peoria, fellow Illinoisans received Ingersoll warmly, proud of the success of their native son. Though many suggested that he would be the perfect candidate for senator, Ingersoll's experience running for governor turned him away from political aspirations. Instead, he decided to concentrate on his legal practice and spend time at home with his family. Ingersoll valued family highly, and in many of his lectures throughout the years he stressed the paramount importance of the institution. Because of his deep affection for his wife and daughters, Ingersoll's views on women's rights and domestic issues were progressive for his time. He despised discipline, treating his family with compassion and proudly admitting that he indulged their every desire. He gave them full access to family money and involved them in the decision making of the household. His domestic practices influenced his politics. In 1870 Ingersoll spoke alongside Susan B. Anthony at a convention to create a Women's Suffrage Association in Peoria. He continued to play an active part in the association after its inception.

He stopped short of pursuing a national office, but Ingersoll's love of home and family did not prevent him from lecturing frequently within his home state. In

September of 1869 he delivered a tribute to Alexander von Humboldt at a ceremony dedicating a statue in honor of the great German naturalist in Cincinnati. Ostensibly a tribute to the great man, "Humboldt" assails the prevailing religious assumptions of Ingersoll's time, and scholars consider it his first serious lecture in the iconoclastic mode. "Progress" expresses iconoclastic ideas, but not until "Humboldt" did Ingersoll make the statement that "all religions are inconsistent with mental freedom." In "Progress" Ingersoll concentrates more on the negative effects of institutions on intellectual development, but in "Humboldt" he unequivocally asserts that religions are an evil, preventing man from achieving the most important virtue: progress. The lecture celebrates the scientist's efforts to help humankind understand the rational nature of the world. Enumerating Humboldt's accomplishments, Ingersoll uses repetition of the chorus "The Universe is Governed by Law" to underscore the lecture's central theme.

During the next seven years Ingersoll spent his time practicing law and lobbying for various railroad corporations. The large income he derived from this he supplemented with his frequent speeches for Free Thought events around Illinois. In 1874 he published his first book, *The Gods, and Other Lectures,* which collected the iconoclastic speeches he had been making around the state, including "The Gods," "Humboldt," "Thomas Paine," "Individuality," and "Heretics and Heresies." These lectures all center on Ingersoll's recurrent themes of religious authority and superstitious belief curtailing humanity's ability to achieve a state of true intellectual and mental freedom. "Thomas Paine" explores the life of the American revolutionary, who later in life challenged the religious orthodoxy with his book *The Age of Reason* (1794). Paine figures as Ingersoll's ideal human, striving to let only the dictates of reason govern his mind, dedicating his life to the intellectual and physical freedom of others. "Individuality" explores the importance of that characteristic to the thriving of humanity and democracy. "Heretics and Heresies" follows in the vein of "Progress" and provides a celebratory history of some of the great heretical thinkers.

The focal point of Ingersoll's first volume is the title oration, "The Gods," which names humanity as God's creator. Ingersoll explicated the logical fallacies behind the creation myth of the book of Genesis in detail. He also explored the logical failings of the Christian Gospels and dismantled the arguments that many religious thinkers of his time used to justify the existence of God. The crux of the lecture is the use of principles of physics to argue that a creator God cannot be possible. He argued that, since matter cannot be created

Ingersoll with his grandchildren, Eva and Robert Ingersoll-Brown (from The Works of Robert G. Ingersoll, volume 8, edited by Clinton P. Farrell, Dresden Edition, 1902; University of California Libraries)

or destroyed, God would not have been able to create anything unless he used pieces of himself. He also refuted in biblical terms the possibility of God's infinite nature. He explained why the absence of an intelligent God does not detract from the order and beauty of the universe and added historical notes and anecdotes to supplement his assertions.

In 1876 Ingersoll was chosen to deliver a speech nominating Senator Blaine for president at the Republican National Convention in Cincinnati. Ingersoll gladly made the speech; he had befriended Blaine on his first national speaking tour in 1868 when he spoke to support the senator in Maine. The resultant "Speech Nominating Blaine," delivered on 15 June 1876, created an uproar the likes of which few had ever seen at a political convention. Also known as "The Plumed Knight Speech," the address in Cincinnati presented Blaine, who had recently been mired in a scandal on Capitol Hill, as a shining knight of virtue, the only man capable of leading the Republican Party and the United States into the future. Ingersoll's steady cadence, climactic phrasing, and rhetorical power sent the audience into a frenzy, cheering and applauding so vigorously that the meeting was eventually adjourned. The speech is still considered one of the most significant convention speeches of the era. Although the convention adjourned

for the day immediately following "The Plumed Knight Speech," sapping Blaine's momentum and costing him the nomination, the speech gave Ingersoll instant fame.

Ingersoll had received attention from the press in the past; however, most of this coverage consisted of brief regional summaries or announcements for his political speeches. His performance at the Cincinnati Convention garnered him national media attention and turned Robert G. Ingersoll into a household name. Almost every newspaper in the country had something to say about the newly famous orator, and Ingersoll used this to his advantage and that of the Republican Party, quickly embarking on one of the cross-country speaking tours that would dominate the rest of his life. Speaking on behalf of Hayes and other Republicans in Maine, New England, and the Midwest, Ingersoll drew immense crowds numbering at times in the tens of thousands. At a time when political speeches and oratory were a popular source of entertainment, Ingersoll had become a national phenomenon. Despite his dedication to the party and his immense popularity, however, his controversial views on religion ultimately cost him a federal appointment, a fact that Ingersoll resented deeply.

Not the type to dwell on disappointments, Ingersoll in April 1877 set about planning his first nationwide lecture tour, serving as his own manager. His newfound popularity proved lucrative; his average of three lectures a week each earned him anywhere from $200 to $2,400, depending on the seating capacity of the lecture hall. Not only could he make a respectable living from the lecture receipts, but he required a full-time clerk to process the numerous speaking invitations he received. In addition to his existing repertoire, he introduced three new lectures on this national tour: first "The Liberty of Man, Woman, and Child," and "The Ghosts," and in June "My Reviewers Reviewed." In the latter, Ingersoll applied his systematic logic to a painstaking evisceration of the common rebuttals that journalists, scholars, and religious leaders made of his iconoclastic lectures.

In "Liberty," Ingersoll analyzed the various methods by which men, women, and children have been enslaved mentally and physically. He also directly attacked those he saw as responsible for that slavery. He explored the various ways that religious authorities have enslaved man inside his mind, preventing him from achieving the intellectual freedom that Ingersoll regarded as vital to the democratic system. Although this portion repeats and rewords many of the themes from earlier lectures such as "The Gods," "Humboldt," and "Heretics and Heresies," the specific concept of slavery versus the goal of liberation sets itself apart from some of the more systematic treatments of religion in those lectures. The liberty of woman portion illuminates Ingersoll's feminist ideas, an aspect of his character often overshadowed by his vocal agnosticism. He elaborated on his feelings of respect and admiration for women, and his contempt for the kinds of men who keep them from achieving happiness and fulfillment either in marriage or in society at large. In the final section he argues that children should be allowed to enjoy the purity of their childhood, observing that children are often treated as second-class citizens by their domineering fathers while they should be allowed to play, explore, and experience life. This lecture illuminates not only Ingersoll's political and philosophical beliefs, but his views of the family, which he saw as important in the fulfillment of the ultimate goal of personal happiness.

His lecture "The Ghosts" rewords some of the ideas of "Progress" and "The Gods," but takes a more poetic approach, operating as almost a eulogy to the superstitions of the past. A well-reasoned treatise on religion's role in the development of humankind, the lecture exhibits some of Ingersoll's rhetorical development since his earlier works. Central to the thesis is the idea that people have relied since the dawn of civilization upon supernatural explanations for phenomena they do not understand. Ingersoll continually blamed

"The Ghosts" for their manipulation of mankind, addressing them directly as the true enemy, urging the listener to "let the ghosts go. We will worship them no more." According to his reasoning, since science and technology whittle down the world of the unknown by greater degrees every day, the ghosts become more obsolete as time passes, and in the future, people need not resort to such superstitions at all.

At the conclusion of that first national tour, Ingersoll and family moved from Illinois to Washington, D.C., where they occupied a house on Lafayette Square near the White House. There Ingersoll resumed his legal practice and involved himself in the Washington social scene, opening the house to frequent gatherings of the family's large and eclectic group of friends. Ingersoll did not rest long, however, and took another national tour from late 1878 to early 1879. During this period he added the lectures "Some Mistakes of Moses," "Hard Times and the Way Out," and "Robert Burns" to his repertoire. "Hard Times and the Way Out" constitutes Ingersoll's response to Marxism. Ingersoll remained throughout his life an economic conservative. In "Hard Times" he supported the capitalist system, claiming that hard work would suffice to release workers from the threat of poverty. He also argued to maintain the gold standard in American currency. "Robert Burns" is the first of several literary lectures. Although it provides a solid analysis of Burns's work, the lecture offers little in the way of new insight into the poet and was less popular than Ingersoll's more iconoclastic orations.

In "Some Mistakes of Moses," Ingersoll gave the Pentateuch the same treatment that he gave the book of Genesis in "The Gods." Opening with an introduction explaining his motivation to free America's schools, political systems, and citizens from the imperative to support religious ideas and institutions, he went on to deny the usefulness of the Bible as an historical work. Having quickly discredited Moses as the author of the books, for the sake of argument he operated as if he had not done so. He then enumerated the days of creation, using basic scientific logic as a means of denying their veracity. Ingersoll continued through the early parts of the Bible from the expulsion from the Garden of Eden, to the Great Flood, to the Tower of Babel, discrediting their viability as historical fact and their presentation of a moral code worth following. In conclusion, Ingersoll presented a rhetorical masterstroke in a list of all of the "mistakes of Moses," composing one massive sentence that spans several pages in the collected volume.

When Ingersoll returned from his nationwide tour of 1878–1879, the first event to confront him was the death on 31 May of his brother, Ebenezer. The loss devastated Ingersoll. Delivering the eulogy at the memorial service he burst into tears, almost unable to continue. Ingersoll's words at the funeral expressed his great sadness at the finality of the death. He did, however, reference the remote possibility of a life after death, stating that "in the night of death hope sees a star." Although he routinely denied the logical possibility of God's existence in his lectures, he occasionally made a comment similar to this one, admitting the possibility of some unknown element in the universe.

Ingersoll participated in activism as well as oratory during this period. Concurrently with his speaking tours of the late 1870s, he became involved with the National Liberal League, an organization which sought to secularize government and society completely. In 1877 the league chose Ingersoll as its vice president, and he served for several years, even offering his legal services free of charge to D. M. Bennett in the "Truth Seeker" publisher's famous trial on charges of publishing sacrilegious materials. Bennett also served prominently in the National Liberal League, and Ingersoll's defense of the publisher illustrated the lawyer's dedication to the causes espoused by the group. Ingersoll led the league in forming the National Liberal Party with other groups in September 1879. He left the party shortly afterward when it adopted a resolution to pursue the overturning of the Comstock obscenity laws; he believed obscene materials were not protected by freedom of speech. The National Liberal Party did not survive long after Ingersoll's departure.

Finished with third parties, Ingersoll returned to the Republican fold in time for the election of 1880, again making widespread political speeches in favor of the party's candidates. All of Ingersoll's engagements during the campaign cycle drew the immense crowds to which he had grown accustomed on his lecture tours, and the newspapers took notice as well, deriding or glorifying the orator along party lines. Democratic publications execrated him as an obese heathen while Republican papers praised his joviality and peerless command of the language. When James Garfield won the presidency, the two Washington neighbors became fast friends. President Garfield gave Ingersoll the nickname "Royal Bob" for his generous nature and stately bearing, a name that stuck with the orator for the rest of his life. Ingersoll saw the president on the morning of his assassination and sat at his bedside as his condition worsened.

Before and after the election of 1880, Ingersoll introduced the lectures "Some Reasons Why," "The Great Infidels," and "What Must We Do To Be Saved?" to his continually growing arsenal. In "Some Reasons Why" Ingersoll enumerated his reasons for not believing in Christianity as a doctrine. He included the wars Christian nations have started, fealty to God, doubt in the inspiration of the Bible, poor treatment of women by most Christians, the cruelty of God in the Old Testament and many other reasons. This lecture is one of Ingersoll's most plainly stated and easiest to understand. "The Great Infidels" reiterates and expands upon the ideas found in "Heretics and Heresies" and "The Ghosts," adds more examples of freethinkers who have helped society and offers more details on the discussion of how men created their gods.

In "What Must We Do To Be Saved?" Ingersoll endeavored to use the New Testament's Gospels to discover what a person must do to receive salvation. Submitting to a premise he does not actually accept in order to prove a point (as in "Some Mistakes of Moses"), Ingersoll assumed the Gospels to be inspired and investigated them for advice that Jesus gave on achieving immortality. He found that Jesus mostly advised good works, kindness toward others, and a strong character. Nowhere, Ingersoll maintained, does Jesus require belief that he is the son of God or acceptance of the Christian religion and the infallibility of the Bible. Ingersoll wrote off the passages in John regarding salvation as being written years later by figures in the church, and not representing Jesus' advice, noting that the other Gospels do not corroborate this viewpoint. At the end of the lecture, Ingersoll listed the different sects of Christianity and explained what they demand of an individual to be saved, claiming that these creeds are incompatible with the actual teachings of Jesus, focusing inordinately on damnation and the inherent evil of man.

After the tour which introduced "What Must We Do To Be Saved?" Ingersoll limited his lecturing in favor of dedicating time to his legal practice. He spent much of 1881 and 1882 as the defense attorney in the famous Star Route trial, which examined a Republican Party scandal involving the awarding of mail contracts in the West. Ingersoll won an acquittal for the defendant, thanks more to his rhetorical finesse than the apparent innocence of his client. He also engaged in several heated print debates with leading orthodox thinkers in the early 1880s. *The North American Review* published one such debate between August 1881 and February 1882, beginning with an article by Ingersoll entitled "Is All of the Bible Inspired?" which summarized many of the arguments employed in his antibiblical lectures. Jeremiah S. Black, a prominent Democrat and a Christian, replied to Ingersoll with an article that insulted the agnostic's ideas and person, calling Ingersoll vain and fat. The debate continued with another article by Ingersoll and a rejoinder by a Yale scholar, capturing the attention of many Americans and boosting circulation of *The North American Review*. The maga-

"Walston," Ingersoll's home in Dobbs Ferry, New York, where he died on 21 July 1899 (from The Works of Robert G. Ingersoll, volume 11, edited by Clinton P. Farrell, Dresden Edition, 1902; University of California Libraries)

zine held a similar debate again in 1887, with Ingersoll representing the agnostic's side.

By this time Ingersoll had become accustomed to public criticisms of his character and his beliefs. In 1882, Reverend DeWitt Talmage of the Brooklyn Tabernacle delivered a series of anti-Ingersoll sermons, aiming to counter all of the agnostic's arguments against the infallibility of the Bible. While Ingersoll received such treatment in countless sermons across the country during his lifetime, he chose to respond to this challenge, replying with six interviews and a series of three lectures which he called the "Talmagian Catechism" and delivered in a limited engagement around the New England area. This vocal negative response to Ingersoll's iconoclastic ideas continued in 1884 and 1885; many detractors distributed religious leaflets countering Ingersoll's arguments at lecture halls. Some townships and cities even threatened to bring legal charges against Ingersoll under the terms of obsolete (but still enforceable) blasphemy laws dating back to the colonial period. None of this cowed Ingersoll or abated his influence in

the slightest; in 1885 he was elected president of the American Secular Union.

In 1885 Ingersoll and family moved to New York, where they quickly adapted to the cosmopolitan lifestyle, becoming frequent patrons of the arts and charming prominent city residents at their weekly get-togethers. A throat ailment kept Ingersoll away from the lecture circuit until 1891, but he kept busy with various legal duties in the meantime. Between 1885 and 1889 he engaged in frequent anti-trust litigation against financier Jay Gould. Representing several different clients, Ingersoll beat Gould every time. Although Ingersoll ardently supported capitalism, he did not discard all ideas of fairness or take ideas of free enterprise to an extreme, and he thought Gould's aggressive expansion of influence and power dangerous. Aside from the Gould cases, Ingersoll lent his legal knowledge to Charles B. Reynolds, a New Jersey preacher on trial for blasphemy. Though Ingersoll spoke emotionally to the jury, he could not change the legality of the issue; the statute did define Reynolds's actions as blasphemous, and he was convicted.

Ingersoll began lecturing again in 1891, adding "Shakespeare," a lecture on literary analysis, to the rotation. Like his lecture on Burns, "Shakespeare" was less popular with audiences who came to hear fiery agnostic oratory. The routine of lecturing, practicing law, and spending time at home continued for Ingersoll; he added "Abraham Lincoln," "Voltaire," and "About the Holy Bible" to his repertoire in 1894. Like most of his other lectures praising famous figures, "Lincoln" and "Voltaire" summarize and glorify the feats of their subjects and incorporate them into Ingersoll's moral code of pursuing the physical and intellectual liberation of all humankind. "About the Holy Bible," one of Ingersoll's most ambitious lectures, aims to disprove the belief that the Bible is inspired by God. Opening with explanations of the true origins of the Bible, he explored the real and supposed authors of Old Testament books, the non-Biblical origins of various stories, and why the philosophies espoused by the Bible should not be followed by citizens of a modern society. "About the Holy Bible" combines the ideas of "What Must We Do To Be Saved?" and "Some Mistakes of Moses" to create one comprehensive argument challenging the doctrine of divine inspiration.

The election of 1896 brought Ingersoll back to the political stump in support of Republican presidential candidate William McKinley. In McKinley, Ingersoll saw strength, honesty, and integrity unparalleled since Garfield. In 1896 Ingersoll gave the Republican answer to William Jennings Bryan's "Cross of Gold" rhetoric; he explained the evils of free silver, arguing that only an America with a reliable gold standard could hope to maintain a strong, growing economy. This stance, and his support of a strong protectionist tariff, alienated Ingersoll from the populists and progressives who usually supported him, including his own American Secular Union. Ingersoll greeted McKinley's victory with enthusiasm, but a small cerebral hemorrhage that he suffered during a lecture in New York foretold health problems. A medical examination revealed that he suffered from heart disease.

This diagnosis did not stop him, however; he continued to lecture across the country, reducing his hectic schedule only slightly. Throughout the last three and a half years of his life, Ingersoll toured the country from New England to the West to the South, composing five new lectures. Ingersoll introduced both "The Truth" and "A Thanksgiving Sermon" in 1897. Both follow the familiar Ingersoll formula of explaining the failure of the Christian churches throughout history to allow for the intellectual development of humankind. The latter is modified slightly to give thanks to those few who dared to help humanity progress. In 1898 "Superstition" also explored themes familiar to his audiences, but treats the concept of superstition specifically, examining its role in history and the many forms it has taken. First delivered in 1889, "The Devil" provides an in-depth exploration of the titular figure's role in the Christian mythology, examining how he had been used to frighten and tame the masses, and arguing that the Christian faith relies more on the devil than on God.

On 21 July 1899 Ingersoll woke up around 1:00 A.M. with chest pains at his home, "Walston," in Dobbs Ferry, New York. He slept fitfully until later in the morning, when he went downstairs to sit on the porch, waiting for the pain to subside. He died before the doctor could make a call to the house. His last words, "I am better now," were the same as those of his brother Ebon, who had died twenty years earlier. In lieu of a conventional funeral, a small group of family and close friends gathered together a few days later and read from his works. Ingersoll was buried in Arlington National Cemetery. Following his death the newspapers of America published tributes to the great orator. In 1900, Ingersoll's loyal publisher, his brother-in-law Clinton P. Farrell, printed *The Works of Robert G. Ingersoll*, a remarkably inclusive set of twelve volumes that features all of Ingersoll's lectures, many of his political speeches, his periodical writing, newspaper interviews, and other materials. His letters were compiled by his granddaughter and published in 1951.

Robert G. Ingersoll stood as one of the greatest orators of his generation. Boldly ahead of his time, he fearlessly espoused controversial beliefs, most notably agnosticism. But Ingersoll had other progressive viewpoints as well: he favored equality for women, children, and ethnic minorities, spoke compassionately about suicide, saw alcoholism as a disease rather than a sin, opposed vivisection and favored animal rights, saw criminals as victims of circumstance, and opposed capital punishment. Avowedly conservative economically and regarding issues of family, he nonetheless strongly influenced many of the radical thinkers and activists of succeeding generations, including such figures as Eugene Debs, Mark Twain, Andrew Carnegie, Clarence Darrow, and Walt Whitman. His work was widely translated into German, Japanese, and other languages. Most of his lectures have not lost their potency over the years. His criticisms of religions and his arguments against Christian theology remain controversial, and the debates that generated them have not been resolved. The volatility of his ideas may explain why most of his works remain out of print. Nevertheless, his contributions to radical thinking in the United States cannot be denied.

Biographies:

Herman E. Kittredge, *A Biographical Appreciation of Robert G. Ingersoll* (New York: C. P. Farrell, 1911);

Isaac Newton Baker, *An Intimate View of Col. Robert G. Ingersoll* (New York: C. P. Farrell, 1920);

Cameron Rogers, *Colonel Bob Ingersoll: A Biographical Narrative of the Great American Orator and Agnostic* (Garden City, N. Y.: Doubleday, Page, 1927);

C. H. Cramer, *Royal Bob: The Life of Robert G. Ingersoll* (Indianapolis: Bobbs-Merrill, 1952);

Orvin Larson, *American Infidel: Robert G. Ingersoll, A Biography* (New York: Citadel, 1962);

David D. Anderson, *Robert Ingersoll* (New York: Twayne, 1972);

Frank Smith, *Robert G. Ingersoll: A Life* (Buffalo, N.Y.: Prometheus, 1990).

References:

Susan Jacoby, *Freethinkers: A History of American Secularism* (New York: Holt, 2004);

Edgar DeWitt Jones, *Lords Of Speech; Portraits Of Fifteen American Orators* (Chicago & New York: Willett, Clark, 1937);

Gordon Stein, *Robert G. Ingersoll: A Checklist* (Kent, Ohio: Kent State University Press, 1969).

Papers:

The Ingersoll family papers are at the University of Iowa Library, Iowa City. Manuscripts and relevant materials reside in the Library of Congress. The Peoria Public Library in Peoria, Illinois, and the Illinois State Historical Society Library in Springfield, Illinois, also contain Ingersoll-related materials.

Mary E. Marcy
(8 May 1877 – 8 December 1922)

Hester L. Furey
The Art Institute of Atlanta

BOOKS AND PAMPHLETS: *A Satire on Civilization and Other Fables* (Chicago: Donohue, 1900);

Out of the Dump: A Story of Organized Charity, illustrated by Ralph Chaplin (Chicago: Charles H. Kerr, 1908);

Shop Talks on Economics (Chicago: Charles H. Kerr, 1911; Glasgow: Socialist Labour Press, 1922);

Breaking up the Home (Chicago: Charles H. Kerr, 1912);

Wages in Mexican Money (Chicago: Charles H. Kerr, 1912);

Whom Do You Work For? (Chicago: Charles H. Kerr, 1912);

Why Catholic Workers Should Be Socialists (Chicago: Charles H. Kerr, 1914);

How the Farmer Can Get His (Chicago: Charles H. Kerr, 1916);

Stories of the Cave People (Chicago: Charles H. Kerr, 1917);

Women as Sex Vendors; or, Why Women Are Conservative (Being a View of the Economic Status of Women), by Marcy and Roscoe B. Tobias (Chicago: Charles H. Kerr, 1918);

Industrial Autocracy (Chicago: Charles H. Kerr, 1919);

The Right to Strike (Chicago: Charles H. Kerr, 1920);

Open the Factories (Chicago: Charles H. Kerr, 1921);

A Free Union: A One-Act Drama of "Free Love" (Chicago: Charles H. Kerr, 1921);

Rhymes of Early Jungle Folk (Chicago: Charles H. Kerr, 1922);

You Have No Country! Workers' Struggle against War: Articles from the International Socialist Review, *1914–1917,* edited by Franklin Rosemont (Chicago: Charles H. Kerr, 1984).

Editions and Collections: *The Tongue of Angels: The Mary Marcy Reader,* edited by Frederick C. Giffin (Selinsgrove, Pa.: Susquehanna University Press, 1988; London & Cranbury, N.J.: Associated University Presses, 1988).

OTHER: Bruce Rogers, ed., *Debs: His Life, Writings, and Speeches; with a Department of Appreciations,* third edi-

Mary E. Marcy (from You Have No Country! Workers' Struggle against War, *1984; Thomas Cooper Library, University of South Carolina)*

tion, introduction by Marcy (Chicago: Charles H. Kerr, 1908);

Socialist playing cards, by Marcy and Ralph Chaplin, verses by Marcy (Chicago: Charles H. Kerr, 1908);

J. Howard Moore, *The Law of Biogenesis: Being Two Lessons on the Origin of Human Nature,* introduction by Marcy (Chicago: Charles H. Kerr, 1911);

"If Socialism Came," "The Fate of the College Graduate," and "It's Up to You!" in *Socialist Dialogues and Recitations,* edited by Josephine R. Cole and Grace Silver (Chicago: Charles H. Kerr, 1913), pp. 55–59;

"Our Real Enemy," in *Chicago Race Riots,* edited by Harrison George (Chicago: Great Western Publishing, 1919), pp. 4–6;

"My God" and "Song of the Swamp," in *Mary Marcy,* by Jack Carney (Chicago: Charles H. Kerr, 1923), pp. 13–14.

SELECTED PERIODICAL PUBLICATIONS–UNCOLLECTED: "Letters of a Pork Packer's Stenographer," *International Socialist Review,* 5 (August 1904); (September 1904): 175–178; (November 1904): 296–303; (December 1904): 363–369; (January 1905): 418–423;

"A Felicitan Fair," *International Socialist Review,* 6 (June 1906): 729–730;

"The Blanktown Man," *Industrial Union Bulletin* (27 May 1907): 2;

"Our Leader," *Industrial Union Bulletin* (16 November 1907): 2;

"A Pickpocket," *International Socialist Review,* 9 (March 1909): 669–673;

"Ladylike Men," *Solidarity* (18 December 1909);

"The Night Before Christmas: A Monologue," *International Socialist Review,* 10 (December 1909): 490–493;

"The Awakening of China," *International Socialist Review,* 10 (January 1910): 632–635;

"Progress in China," *International Socialist Review,* 10 (February 1910): 689–691;

"A Strike in the 'Model Village,'" *International Socialist Review,* 10 (February 1910): 699–701;

"The Cause of Rising Prices," *International Socialist Review,* 10 (March 1910): 769–774;

"Efficiency the Test," *New York Call* (8 May 1910);

"The Milwaukee Victory," *International Socialist Review,* 10 (May 1910): 991–992;

"Economic Determinism and the Sacred Cows," *International Socialist Review,* 10 (June 1910): 1063–1064;

"The Boys on the Grand Trunk," *International Socialist Review,* 11 (September 1910): 161–163;

"The Near-Socialist," *International Socialist Review,* 11 (October 1910): 215–216;

"Can a Socialist Serve 'All the People'?" *International Socialist Review,* 12 (September 1911): 150–151;

"The Busy Silkworm," *International Socialist Review,* 12 (October 1911): 222–226;

"The World-Wide Revolt," *International Socialist Review,* 12 (November 1911): 261–265;

"What Will Become of Your Children?" *International Socialist Review,* 12 (February 1912): 473–474;

"The Battle for Bread at Lawrence," *International Socialist Review,* 12 (March 1912): 532–543;

"One Big Union Wins at Lawrence," *International Socialist Review,* 12 (April 1912): 613–630;

"The Passing of the Turkish Harem," *International Socialist Review,* 12 (May 1912): 765–767;

"One Hundred Years Ago," *International Socialist Review,* 12 (June 1912): 837–843;

"Things Doing in the Cement Industry," *International Socialist Review,* 13 (July 1912): 58–60;

"Through the Jungle by Rail," *International Socialist Review,* 13 (November 1912): 415–416;

"Morals in Rubber," *International Socialist Review,* 13 (December 1912): 466–469;

"Changing China," *International Socialist Review,* 13 (January 1913): 528–532;

"The New York Garment Workers," *International Socialist Review,* 13 (February 1913): 583–588;

"Hard Times and How to Stop Them," *International Socialist Review,* 13 (March 1913): 654–655.

"A Straw Man," *International Socialist Review,* 13 (March 1913): 691;

"The White Flag Agreement Brigade," *International Socialist Review,* 13 (April 1913): 760–762;

"The Germans in Turkey," *International Socialist Review,* 13 (June 1913): 871–874;

"Help for West Virginia," *International Socialist Review,* 13 (June 1913): 895;

"The Hatfield Whitewash," *International Socialist Review,* 14 (July 1913): 54–55;

"The March of the Machine," *International Socialist Review,* 14 (September 1913): 147–149;

"The Paterson Strike," *International Socialist Review,* 14 (September 1913): 177–178;

"The Food Destroyers," *International Socialist Review,* 14 (November 1913): 267–268;

"The Advancement of the Canning Industry," *International Socialist Review,* 14 (December 1913): 351–355;

"Helen Keller's New Book," *International Socialist Review,* 14 (December 1913): 350;

"Competing with the Machine," *International Socialist Review,* 14 (January 1914): 400–402;

"Nine Sharpshooters," *International Socialist Review,* 14 (February 1914): 462–463;

"China and Standard Oil," *International Socialist Review,* 14 (April 1914): 594–596;

"How Capitalists Solve the Problem of the Unemployed," *International Socialist Review,* 14 (May 1914): 648–650;

"Whose War Is This?" *International Socialist Review*, 14 (June 1914): 729–731;

"Auto Car Making," *International Socialist Review*, 15 (January 1915): 406–412;

"Machines That Have Made History," *International Socialist Review*, 15 (March 1915): 530–536;

"Plenty of Jobs," *International Socialist Review*, 15 (April 1915): 618–620;

"The Power of the Railroad Boys," *International Socialist Review*, 15 (May 1915): 669–671;

"Why You Should Be a Socialist," *International Socialist Review*, 15 (May 1915): 700–702;

"Morals and War Babies," *International Socialist Review*, 15 (June 1915): 719–723;

"Your Great Adventure," *International Socialist Review*, 16 (July 1915): 43–46;

"A Revolutionary Strike without Leaders," *International Socialist Review*, 16 (August 1915): 73–74;

"What You Have to Sell," *International Socialist Review*, 16 (September 1915): 141–143;

"Direct Action," *International Socialist Review*, 16 (September 1915): 179–180;

"The Class Struggle," *International Socialist Review*, 16 (October 1915): 206–208;

"The Goose and the Golden Egg," *International Socialist Review*, 16 (February 1916): 494–495;

"Power," *International Socialist Review*, 16 (May 1916): 691–692;

"One Way of Trimming the Farmer," *International Socialist Review*, 17 (July 1916): 37–40;

"They Belong Inside!" *International Socialist Review*, 17 (September 1916): 146–148;

"Hamstringing the Unions," *International Socialist Review*, 17 (October 1916): 226–227;

"Who Pays the Taxes?" *International Socialist Review*, 17 (November 1916): 294–296;

"Marxian Economics," *International Socialist Review*, 17 (January 1917): 418–420; (February 1917): 489–491; (March 1917): 552–554; (April 1917): 621–624;

"Why Not Register Them All?" *International Socialist Review*, 18 (August 1917): 87–88;

"A Month of Lawlessness," *International Socialist Review*, 18 (September 1917): 154–157;

"German Socialists in Russia," *International Socialist Review*, 18 (October 1917): 216–217;

"Economic Power," *International Socialist Review*, 18 (February 1918): 401–405;

"The IWW Convention," *Liberator*, 2 (July 1919): 10–12;

"The Passing of Cripple Creek," *One Big Union Monthly*, 2 (April 1920): 25;

"The Spendthrift Workers," *One Big Union Monthly*, 2 (August 1920): 58–59;

"Run-Away Slaves," *Industrial Pioneer*, 1 (July 1921): 23;

"Economic Determinism," *Industrial Pioneer*, 1 (September 1921): 9–10;

"The Barbo Fair," *Industrial Pioneer*, 1 (May 1923): 5–6.

In her lifetime Mary E. Marcy ranked as one of the best-known public figures of the American radical Left. As the editor of the *International Socialist Review* during the decade between 1908 and 1918, she wrote articles addressing almost every issue of concern to the Left. Workers who wrote to her reported that they felt they knew her personally, and some of them addressed her in correspondence as "sister." Many of them had used her *Shop Talks on Economics*—which has been translated into many languages and sold over two million copies between its first publication in 1911 and second publication in 1922—as a textbook in the early stages of their labor education. Marcy possessed an extraordinary gift for rendering complex concepts in language that the common person could understand. She read broadly in the sciences, geographic and cultural studies, and industrial trade journals, and many of her articles summarized longer reading selections. Her work received some favorable notice outside the labor movement; H. L. Mencken gave her two positive reviews. Her career was entwined with that of her closest friends: William "Big Bill" Haywood, the charismatic leader of the Industrial Workers of the World, and Charles H. Kerr, the socialist publisher of the *International Socialist Review (ISR)*. When Marcy died in 1922, Eugene V. Debs wrote to her husband that she was "the brainiest woman" of the American Left (quoted in Jack Carney, *Mary Marcy*, 1923). Her friend and artistic collaborator Ralph Chaplin remembered her as "the spark plug" of the *ISR* circle (*Wobbly: the Rough and Tumble Story of an American Radical*, 1948).

In private life Marcy held many secrets, beginning with her origins. By most accounts she was born Mary Edna Tobias on 8 May 1877, the eldest of three children, to working-class parents. In sworn testimony in probate court after her death, however, her husband said that there were six siblings, three of whom died in childhood; the surviving children were separated for some time into different households so that the extended family could support them. Based on a memorial pamphlet published after her death, some scholars have repeated the story that Marcy and her family were from Belleville, Illinois. Sally Miller, an historian of women in the U.S. socialist movement, has noted that St. Clair county records do not support this narrative; nor does the census. A publicity leaflet Charles H. Kerr produced for Marcy's second book, *Out of the Dump: A Story of Organized Charity* (1908), stated that Marcy had lived in Chicago most of her life, and her transcript from the University of Chicago records that she earned a diploma from Evanston High School.

After she finished high school, Tobias supported herself and her younger siblings, Roscoe "Toby" Burdette and Hazel Inez, by working as a telephone switchboard operator for $9.00 per week. At night she studied stenography and eventually found secretarial work. Mary Tobias was discharged from her position at an American flag manufacturer's firm for wearing a button supporting William Jennings Bryan for president in 1896. Clarence Darrow, whom Tobias apparently met at the Chicago Single Tax Club, appealed to his friend, George Burman Foster, a faculty member in the theology department of the recently established University of Chicago, and together they helped Tobias secure a position as secretary for university president William Rainey Harper. Tobias moved in the same social circles until the end of her life.

The 1900 census recorded Mary and Roscoe Tobias living in a boardinghouse in Chicago, and Inez married to Philip Stephens and living in New Trier. Mary Tobias gave "stenographer" as her occupation; Toby was a color proofer. That year Tobias published her first book, *A Satire On Civilization and Other Fables,* under the byline "Miss M. E. Tobias, of the Chicago Single Tax Club." Donohue Brothers of Chicago published a limited run of the book, of which a single copy, at Brown University, is known to survive. The book is dedicated to Toby. Markedly influenced by the Bible and German folktales, *A Satire on Civilization* includes moralizing allegories and fables and inspirational verse, concluding with a play supporting the Single Tax movement, "The Drama of Ten Laboring Men and Eight Jobs." Her job at the university allowed Tobias to attend classes tuition free, and in 1901 she took liberal arts courses, including some classes with John Dewey, but she did not earn a degree. In the same period, Tobias met Kerr, who operated a leftist publishing house in Chicago. Kerr believed his personal mission was to educate the public about radical political causes.

Tobias married Leslie H. Marcy in late 1901, and the couple moved to Kansas City, Missouri. She found employment as the secretary to the treasurer of Armour, a meatpacking company, where she remained from 1902 to 1905. She joined the Socialist Party of America in 1903, two years after its founding in the United States. Beginning in August 1904, Kerr began to publish Marcy's "Letters of a Pork Packer's Stenographer" in the *ISR.* The series established Marcy's signature style of storytelling, counterpointing the corporate public-relations version of events with the insider's account. It ran from August 1904 to January 1905, prior to the publication that year of Upton Sinclair's more famous treatment of the subject in *The Jungle.*

Charles H. Kerr, publisher and close friend of Mary Marcy and her husband (from Allen Ruff, "We Called Each Other Comrade": Charles H. Kerr and Company, Radical Publishers, *1997; Thomas Cooper Library, University of South Carolina)*

Marcy's articles were a success for the *ISR,* but they led to the loss of her job. In April 1905 she was summoned to testify in the Chicago Beef Trust Trials, and her testimony received notice in the Chicago newspapers and in *The New York Times.*

After she left Armour, Marcy returned to Kansas City and began to work with the Associated Charities, a privately funded, semiprofessional social-welfare organization that had branches in many cities at the time. Roger Baldwin had connections to its work in St. Louis beginning in 1906. Shortly, events transpired in Chicago that eventually caused her permanent return. A group of radicals founded the Industrial Workers of the World (IWW) there in June–July of 1905, and Marcy's brother, Toby, as well as *ISR* writers Frank Bohn and Robert Rives LaMonte, numbered among its early associates. The IWW was an offshoot of the radical and sometimes violent Western Federation of Miners, amalgamated with populists, anarchists, and former Knights of Labor, and dominated by the culture of the disaffected, itinerant, often homeless, but cheerful men who frequented hobo jungles and Chicago's Bughouse Square. The organization arose as a radical faction of the Socialist Party, advocating direct action and economic rather than political change.

In Kansas City, Armour threatened to cease contributions to the Associated Charities if she were not dismissed. She retained her position, but almost immediately she began to work on *Out of the Dump*, an exposé of the "scientific charity" exercised by her new employer. "The Dump" was the name of the slum neighborhoods in Marcy's book, the only place affordable to the poor whose lives she described. Invariably the slums were the hazardously run-down and toxic rental properties of the same men who employed the poor at ruinously low wages and gave donations to the charity organizations to avoid criticism of their business practices.

Out of the Dump purports to be fiction but uses the same technique as "Letters from a Pork Packer's Stenographer." It delivers the insights of a social worker whose point of view has been shaped by an earlier experience: she was herself a recipient of public charity after her father died in a factory accident and her mother was incapacitated by exhaustion and illness. Her brother turned to crime in a desperate attempt to make the mother's last days more comfortable. The narrator tries at first to care for her younger siblings with the help of neighbors, particularly the hard-drinking but kind and pragmatic Granny Nome, who cheerfully tends families not her own. This neighbor teaches the narrator and the younger siblings to beg and counsels them always to lie to the police and stay away from charity workers. Marcy counterpoints the struggles of those labeled the "undeserving" poor with the leisure and comfort of a wealthy family for whom the narrator works after charity workers investigate and break up her family.

Out of the Dump details the elaborate ruses the poor used to survive and then, when absolutely necessary, to receive assistance while maintaining minimal contact with controlling and intrusive social workers. Eventually the story evolves into a critique of the profit system. Its conclusion is romantic in a double sense: a wealthy young man becomes interested in the narrator and facilitates her brother's release from jail. The brother converts to socialism in jail. The book may be—like "Letters of a Pork Packer's Stenographer" and *A Free Union*—a fictionalized account of Marcy's personal struggles. Her brother, Toby, spent six months in jail for counterfeiting at some point before 1907. To the end of her life Marcy identified with what she called "the foundlings" in her poem "My God." The book suggests that Marcy's sympathy with the homeless men of the

IWW and the itinerant soapbox speakers of Bughouse Square was not intellectual, but came from a shared experience of forced dependence upon and resentment of the upper classes. Her work offered recurring glimpses of the human face of the criminal underworld.

Marcy's first publication in an IWW newspaper appeared in the spring of 1907; "The Blanktown Man" was her first public criticism of socialism, although she remained in the party for another ten years. Kerr began to serialize *Out of the Dump* in the *ISR* in the summer of that year. While Marcy developed her new book and the IWW emerged as a contentious and polarizing force within the Socialist Party, Kerr's working relationship with the editor of the *ISR*, Algie Simons, had declined. Although very close when they began their association, their political views and their visions for the *ISR* eventually diverged to the point that all friendship was lost. Initially the two had tailored the publication to their target audience of educated insiders on the Left. Over time, however, Kerr moved more to the radical Left and favored syndicalism, a radical self-emancipation of the workers; Simons supported "scientific" and doctrinaire socialism, and became part of the party's conservative, reformist wing that tried to work within existing laws and political processes. Mary Marcy's poem "Our Leader" in the November 1907 issue offered a sardonic commentary on college graduates who nobly offered to lead the workers; without specifying names, Marcy noted that they were replaceable. In any case, Kerr dismissed Simons effective January 1908. Noting that he would rather "please the workers than the college professors," Kerr edited the *ISR* himself briefly.

Soon Kerr persuaded the Marcys to move back to Chicago to work for the *ISR*. Leslie Marcy took possession of five shares of Kerr stock from B. F. Underwood in January, and in February he bought $250 worth of stock. In August, Kerr made Mary Marcy the secretary of the company. He had already taken steps to give the publication a broader appeal, establishing a "News and Views" section so that readers had a space to make their voices heard. Using a $1,000 grant from Eugene Dietzen, he lengthened the *Review* from sixty to eighty pages and began to vary the content, incorporating more illustrations and photographs. Circulation climbed from three thousand to twenty-seven thousand between February 1908 and June 1910 and reached a peak of just over forty thousand in early 1912. Kerr retained the title of editor for the duration of the *Review*'s existence, and by December 1908 Mary Marcy held the title of lead associate editor.

Marcy's editorial approach differed significantly from Simons's in two ways. Fiscally, she was an excellent businesswoman and generated promotional schemes to improve the *Review*'s circulation. Marcy did most of the day-to-day editing work, kept the books, and, according to the published business reports, was the only employee of the cooperative other than Kerr himself to draw a salary. At first, like Kerr, she voluntarily accepted less than her contracted salary to keep the magazine out of financial trouble. Marcy maintained a personal correspondence with readers and was tireless in her efforts to promote the publishing house and keep it financially solvent.

In these early years at Kerr, Marcy also demonstrated her support for what she called "socialism in overalls." Politically, she continued the work Kerr had already begun toward aligning the *ISR* with the left wing of the Socialist Party, which at that time still included the Industrial Workers of the World and its controversial leader, Haywood, who in 1906 was tried for murder of the governor of Idaho and defended by Clarence Darrow. When Haywood came back to Chicago after his acquittal in 1907, he and Mary Marcy became so close that Chaplin later recalled her as Haywood's "lifelong friend." The Kerr group expanded to include radical economist Frank Bohn, poet and artist Chaplin, Haywood, and Irish radicals such as James Connolly (who met Kerr at the 1908 IWW convention in Chicago) and Jim Larkin.

The Marcys and Haywood became especially friendly with Chaplin, who illustrated Kerr's edition of *Out of the Dump*. In April 1908 Mary and Leslie Marcy and Chaplin created a set of Socialist playing cards. She wrote comical verses; Chaplin illustrated them. Chaplin later recalled this work as the most fun he had working for Kerr. A writer in the *Nation* noted wryly that "To-day the *International Socialist Review* of Chicago advertises an artistic pack of socialist playing cards on which John D. Rockefeller is the King of Spades. . . . We do not know how socialists amused themselves in earlier days, but chances are that play was looked upon as somewhat inconsistent with true Marxian zeal" (27 May 1909). Of 3,000 produced, only one set of the cards, in a private collection, is known to survive. Also in early 1909 Marcy's *Stories of the Cave People* began to appear in serial form in the *ISR*.

Although Mary Marcy's health was never good and several times, beginning in April 1909, the *Review* reported that she had been hospitalized, she found the years before World War I relatively happy ones. A series of trivia questions running in the *Review* included "who is the merriest woman in the movement? Mary E. Marcy." The *Review* flourished, and she received a raise in monthly salary from $75 to $90 by March 1910. Also, Marcy was able to provide some legitimate employment for her artistic but wayward brother, who had won a scholarship to the Art Institute, but alter-

nated between ungratifying work and crime. In the 1910s he worked at several jobs, including promotional work for the *ISR*. Occasionally his sister published his work; "Spot Knocking" (December 1915), for example, offers a comic view of the emerging world of photograph alteration, in which Ralph Chaplin and his wife, Edith, also worked. Leslie Marcy represented the company at various Socialist Party events around the Midwest and held a seat on the board of directors for Kerr beginning in 1910. Together the Marcys had a monthly income of about $160, above average for the time.

The next few years proved eventful and contentious, as Marcy and her colleagues fielded conflicts on several different levels. In the first decade of the twentieth century, the Socialist Party developed a broad, loosely defined, far-reaching membership throughout the United States. For a while it seemed the Socialist Party was becoming more radical, but between 1911 and 1912, mirroring the situation of European socialists, tension grew between the radical left wing and the conservative wing of the party. The conservatives had stronger ties to German Socialists. The radicals tended to be more closely aligned with syndicalism–British, French, Dutch, or American, in the form of the Industrial Workers of the World. Their disagreements centered on the issue of political versus economic action, the more conservative members advocating working through existing power structures, promoting Socialist candidates for governmental positions, and gradual reform rather than "direct action," or working toward total revolution. Later, the two groups disagreed over World War I, as well.

At the *ISR* this conflict had several consequences: In 1910 Haywood represented American socialists at the International Socialist Congress in Copenhagen, and when he came back to the United States, he began a lecture bureau operating out of the *ISR* office. Kerr published Haywood and Bohn's pamphlet, *Industrial Socialism* (1911), which many conservative socialists found objectionable. Haywood's ties to the *ISR* became stronger just as opposition to the IWW heightened within the Socialist Party, with the result that as Haywood and the IWW were expelled from the party for advocating direct action and sabotage, the national executive board of the party launched an investigation of the business practices of the *ISR*. The *ISR* circle tried without success to consolidate some strength within the party. In 1911 the Marcys, Kerr, Haywood, and Bohn urged Theodore Debs to run as the replacement for disgraced J. Mahlon Barnes as the secretary-treasurer of the Socialist Party and thereby preserve the power of the left wing. Debs refused because he considered his role as the traveling caretaker of his brother Eugene more important.

JULY, 1915   The   PRICE TEN CENTS

INTERNATIONAL SOCIALIST REVIEW

"A Mere Scrap of Paper"

Whenever Labor Chooses to Regard It as Such.

Cover for an issue of the Socialist journal published by Kerr, for which Marcy served as "Lead Associate Editor" from 1908 until her death (from You Have No Country! Workers' Struggle against the War, 1984; Thomas Cooper Library, University of South Carolina)

A related dispute erupted in the same period over the question of whether the Socialists and the AFL should attempt to form a labor party in the United States. William English Walling first argued against it in the *ISR* in March 1909. The following month Robert Hunter published a rebuttal. Subsequently the *ISR* published a letter Simons had sent to Walling implying that the national executive committee stood ready to rule the party along what it considered doctrinaire lines, regardless of the wishes of the membership, and stating that he personally approved the example of the British Labour Party and thought an amalgamation of the Socialist Party and the AFL might well produce a similar phenomenon in the United States. Simons was not re-elected to the national executive board of the party at the next election.

The party then investigated the *ISR* for heterodoxy and for questionable business practices. The *ISR* opened its books to the party and began to publish its financial reports, clearing itself of all allegations of

financial irregularity, but in 1912 the Socialist Party expelled its radical wing, including Haywood and the IWW. The Kerr group responded by publishing Karl Marx's *Eighteenth Brumaire of Louis Napoleon,* translated by Daniel DeLeon, who led the party's rival group, the Socialist Labor Party (SLP). The *ISR* editors also devoted many pages to the support of radical syndicalism. The leadership of the IWW frequently published there or provided inside information on strikes to *ISR* writers, and the Kerr group began to exhibit more influence from a group of Dutch radicals that included Anton Pannekoek, Herman Gorter, and S. J. Rutgers. Hunter, foremost among the *ISR*'s accusers, later published a book called *Violence in the Labor Movement* (1914) attacking Haywood and the IWW. Marcy dismissed that book as based on straw-man arguments, and argued that Hunter's criticism was misdirected.

At the same time, Marcy experienced her greatest risks, successes, and highest overall production levels as a writer. After Ralph and Edith Chaplin moved to Mexico in 1909, Mary Marcy received unanimous support to fill Ralph Chaplin's seat on the board of the publishing company. Marcy began to write antiwar editorials that began with opposition to U.S. intervention in the Mexican Revolution and later blended seamlessly into opposition to U.S. participation in the European war. Marcy had begun her "Beginner's Course in Socialism and the Economics of Karl Marx" in November 1910. The same month her first story under the pseudonym Jack Morton appeared: "The Story of Rubber in the Congo." The next month, "Capital in Guatemala" continued the Jack Morton series, focusing for a time on individual commodities; in January 1911, "Where Furs Come From" added a new twist.

At other times Marcy wrote studies of world capitalism under her own name (in "Morals in Rubber" and "Things Doing in the Cement Industry," for example); presumably she began to use a pseudonym so that the *Review* would not seem overladen with her work. In addition, she often wrote editorials signed only MEM, or unsigned but credited to MEM or Edna Tobias in the table of contents. "James Morton" advocated the use of birth control in "Fewer and Better Children" in 1914; Mary Marcy published "Morals and War Babies" in June 1915. Marcy took no pains to disguise her voice.

Using a pen name became more common at the *ISR* over the next few years; probably the most famous writer whose work appeared in its pages under a pseudonym was Carl Sandburg, who wrote under such bylines as "Jack Phillips" and "Henry Hegenburg." As the *ISR* became longer and included more work by a variety of writers, Marcy used "Jack Morton" less. Leslie Marcy also contributed stories to the *Review* from time to time or represented the firm at state conventions of the Socialist Party. In 1911 his name began to appear in the list of associate editors; in June 1911 *ISR* reported that he had been very ill but was back at work.

The year 1912 was a watershed for the radical Left, and for Marcy. In January Haywood traveled to Lawrence, Massachusetts when striking mill workers requested the IWW to lead their strike, and this furnished Marcy with the opportunity to write her longest and best-known *Review* essay, "The Battle for Bread at Lawrence." The strike was notable for the fact that twenty thousand unorganized workers without a common language spontaneously struck after their wages were cut the price of three loaves of bread because the state of Massachusetts had passed legislation limiting the workweek of women and children to 54 hours. The mill owners speeded up machinery to keep production levels the same and cut wages. The workers were already so poor that they rented out their beds during the daytime to workers from the night shift and could not afford proper clothing for their children; they could

not accept a pay cut. Marcy's essay appeared in the March 1912 *ISR,* and it stands as the most succinct, detailed, and comprehensive contemporary source on the strike.

The *ISR* reached a peak of more than forty thousand copies sold for that issue. In May, Marcy contributed an article on "The Passing of the Turkish Harem," discussing the history of institutionalized polygamy and interpreting the practice from the perspective of economics, anticipating some of the arguments she later made more fully in *Women as Sex Vendors* (1918). Also in 1911, Kerr collected Marcy's lessons on economics into her most famous small book, *Shop Talks on Economics.* In early 1913 Marcy followed up on the Lawrence story with a piece on the New York Garment Workers' strike. Several of Marcy's inspirational pieces were included in Cole and Silver's edition of *Socialist Dialogues and Recitations* that year. Marcy's brother also began to become more involved in the business and attended board meetings in 1914 and 1915. In January 1915 Leslie Marcy became the vice president of the company. On 14 August 1915 Mary Marcy paid cash for a house located near Rosehill Cemetery, only a few blocks from the place she had lived while a student at University of Chicago. Charles Kerr, who since his divorce had lived in a series of boardinghouses, moved in with the Marcys.

Kenneth Rexroth's *An Autobiographical Novel* (1966) provides some glimpses of Marcy as part of the dynamic Chicago intellectual environment of the 1910s. She had extended connections to the artistic and political circles on the South Side of Chicago that had begun during her years at the University of Chicago. Rexroth remembered meeting her with Bill Haywood at a salon at Esther Czerny's house, and her friends almost without exception frequented Jacob Loeb's "evenings." J. Howard Moore and other members of the Jackson Park circle she knew from the University of Chicago vegetarian club or through Darrow, Moore's brother-in-law. Marcy's closest links, however, were with the IWW and the itinerant male subculture at the core of its Western membership. Thomas Bogard, an IWW organizer, recalled that she and Kerr introduced him to the IWW's Vincent St. John ("the Saint"). Mid-decade the Kerr group helped establish the Radical Bookshop, run by Lillian Udell and later by Theron Cooper (who changed its name to Walden Books in the 1920s). Shortly afterward the Kerr group helped Jack Jones—an IWW member and reknowned saboteur—and Irish revolutionary Jim Larkin establish the Dil Pickle Club, a venue for radical debate and entertainment. Kerr, the Marcys, and other associates of the *ISR* frequented Bughouse Square, a radical soapbox, open-air venue across the street from what is now the Newberry Library, Chinese restaurants and other establishments offering vegetarian fare, and the bohemian marketplace at the Masonic Temple.

Despite the acrimony among socialists in the preceding years, Marcy continued her membership in the Socialist Party, and while she spoke forthrightly against the war that she and others foresaw would involve the United States, she tried to avoid growing factionalism on the Left. In early 1917, for example, she wrote to Raymond Fanning that the *ISR* could not use his article on "The Party's Future," because with the impending entry of the United States into the war, the editors did not want to concentrate on faultfinding within the party. Jack Carney reflects that "it seemed she had been appointed to keep the radicals from destroying themselves."

In April 1917 the United States formally entered World War I, and Marcy left the Socialist Party when it issued statements supporting the war. In the second half of 1917 the U.S. Post Office began to declare issues of the *ISR* unfit for the mail. Marcy's brother was arrested in the summer when an electrician discovered a package of dynamite outside his door in Battle Creek, Michigan, but the Justice Department released him after a day of questioning. The editors of the *ISR* proceeded with caution, reprinting selections from Socialist classics and the founding fathers. When the September 1917 issue of the *ISR* was suppressed, Kerr sent out copies of his translation that year of Paul Lafargue's *The Right to Be Lazy*, with letters explaining the substitution. In October a massive indictment placed virtually all of the IWW leadership in jail. In December, Kerr finally published Marcy's *Stories of the Cave People* as a book after the series ran for a second time in the *Review*, and Marcy began to publish in other places, mostly IWW newspapers.

In February 1918 Marcy contributed her last essay, "Economic Power," to what proved to be the final issue of *ISR*. Marcy and Kerr put together a couple of *Labor Scrapbooks* to send to subscribers in the months of March and May, sending Kerr pamphlets in other months. Surviving texts by Marcy seem frantically optimistic and out of keeping with the actual events in her life. She wrote to Eugene Debs that "this article by Cahn ["The Collapse of Capitalism"] simply keeps me in a fever. . . . there is not enough gold to back up the paper money. The capitalists are doomed." The *ISR* circle struggled to maintain a normal life. By 1918 Toby held the position of office manager. In March 1918 Marcy wrote to Debs that Kerr had been sick for some time and that the three of them—Kerr and the Marcys—intended to go away for a vacation for about ten days. During the summer of 1918 Marcy joined the Industrial Workers of the World.

Many of Marcy's closest friends—Chaplin, Debs, and hundreds of IWW members—were in prison. Those who remained free were in exile or fighting among themselves about politics. The Justice Department raided the Marcys' home while Kerr was there. Mary Marcy's health had never been good, and she struggled with illness. She read and corrected proofs for Sen. Katayama's 1918 book *The Labor Movement in Japan* and speculated privately in a letter to Bertha Rutgers that she might have to look for a new job. Leslie Marcy was arrested and held forty-eight hours for selling Kerr publications at a Socialist Party convention in Canton, Ohio, in June 1918.

Marcy's major publications from the period, particularly *Women as Sex Vendors; or, Why Women Are Conservative (Being a View of the Economic Status of Women)*, written with her brother and published by Kerr in 1918, strongly suggest problems with her personal relationships and some degree of self-hatred. Marcy and Tobias advance the argument that women tend to political conservatism because their status is that of a parasite class, dependent upon the existing system, however exploitative. Referring to Friedrich Engels, they compare women's situation to that of small businessmen: the small business owner more frequently suffers under capitalism than benefits from it; yet he defends the system because he has a small stake in it, and therefore he identifies with big capitalists, hoping to become one. In the same way, women as small monopolists can always survive in an exploitative system by prostitution—either literal, or, in Marcy and Tobias's view, legally, in marriage. Both might have more to gain from a restructuring of society than from maintaining the status quo, but they are averse to the risk and cling to their small measure of security within the familiar system. This book received widespread notice, with a favorable review from the Marxist E. Belfort Bax in *Justice* (19 December 1918) and a more humorous treatment by Eleanor Kilmer Sceva in the *Bookman* (April 1919). Sceva quipped that the book could have been called "Helpful Hints to Homeless Girls" and describes its assembled points as "the most remarkable ideas about the present status of women that have ever passed the censor."

In early 1919 Marcy and others at the *ISR* participated in a letter-writing campaign to various European political activists, urging unanimous support for amnesty for all political prisoners, including U.S. dissidents, immediately on the signing of the peace treaty. Specifically, they were interested in seeing Haywood and Debs freed from prison. At the same time Haywood's friends were trying to convince the court to allow the IWW prisoners out on bond pending appeal. Together Toby Tobias and Kerr gave about $3,000 for the IWW defense fund, and in 1919 Marcy mortgaged a house she owned to join Socialist millionaire William Bross Lloyd in raising bail money for Haywood, who was released in late summer that year.

In the summer of 1919, Kerr and Leslie Marcy came under surveillance by the Department of Justice Bureau of Investigation, later called the FBI. The bureau kept files on the Marcys and Kerr, but the investigations amounted to little except a reprimand for the investigating officer, who according to his superior lacked "a discriminating knowledge of socialism." In any case the group destroyed some of its own records– the Walden-Kerr-Moore families destroyed even their personal correspondence in these years–to avoid incriminating anyone. At the same time, Chicago experienced race riots. IWW member Harrison George put together a book of essays called *Race Riot,* and Mary Marcy contributed a brief essay called "The Real Enemy" that opened the collection.

In September 1919 Marcy circulated a leaflet, "A Revolutionary Party," to the Chicago meetings of the Socialist, Communist, and Communist Labor Parties, begging them to unite against the common enemy. Privately she predicted to the Chaplins that the emerging Soviet Union would be just another state, seeking its own preservation above all else. No copies of the leaflet are known to have survived, but Gregory Zinoviev, chairman of the Comintern, responded to its arguments, mentioning Marcy by name, in "Comintern Open Letter to the IWW, 1920." On 1 January 1920 federal agents and Chicago police again raided the IWW headquarters in Chicago. Haywood was in town staying with the Marcys, who helped him hide in subsequent weeks.

In 1920 *Shop Talks in English* was translated into Chinese; in the coming decade most of Kerr's remaining business came from groups in postimperial China. By June 1920, when the census was taken, Mary Marcy and Inez were staying at Kerr's property at the single-tax colony in Fairhope, Alabama, on the eastern shore of Mobile Bay. There Marcy met Wharton Esherick, a woodblock print artist, who had come in 1919 to teach art at the Fairhope Alternative School run by Marietta Johnson. In a return to the preoccupations of her early publishing days, Marcy began to collaborate with Esherick, compiling into a book some of the rhyming verse she had composed to teach neighborhood children about evolution. The result, *Rhymes of Early Jungle Folk* (1922), like *Stories of the Cave People,* derived loosely from the theories of one of Kerr's Socialist Classics, Lewis Henry Morgan's *Ancient Society* (1877). It was Esherick's first book and Marcy's last. Some sources allege that the Marcys divorced during this time, but probate records from the State of Illinois indicate that no divorce occurred.

Title page for Marcy's last book, her 1922 volume intended to teach children about evolution (San Francisco State University Library)

Haywood disappeared from public view during February and much of March 1921. In late March, anticipating the IWW's appeal, he jumped bail and fled to Russia, reassuring his compatriots that the Bolsheviks would reimburse them for the loss. The appeal was denied in April, and all but a few of the remaining IWW men returned to prison. In June a mainstream news source alleged that Haywood had cabled he was coming back, but he did not, and no money from the Russian government was forthcoming. Several Americans including Lewis Gannett, David Karsner, and Max Eastman traveled to Moscow and published interviews with Haywood. In October, Roger Baldwin of the American Civil Liberties Union wrote to Haywood that the real-estate bond proceedings had begun, and he called Haywood's flight "an act of bad faith and worse tactics" the letter remained hidden in the Soviet Union's Comintern archive until the early 1990s, when Western scholars were admitted to the library there for the first time and the papers of the Communist Party of the United States were microfilmed).

Marcy continued to publish in IWW periodicals, especially the *Industrial Pioneer.* Kerr visited Marcy and her sister a few times, escorting them back to Chicago just before Christmas 1921. During that year Marcy wrote an enigmatic play that she dedicated to Inez. Titled *A Free Union: A One-Act Drama of "Free Love,"* the play depicts a bohemian household whose prominently displayed motto is "Personal Liberty is the God of this Shrine." At least one member of the household's experience does not uphold this sentiment, however. Humboldt, an artist, has been working in commercial illustration to support his female friend, Sonia Borowski, and her sponging object of devotion, a bohemian "poet" named Owen. Too preoccupied with artistic activities to work, Owen eats at Humboldt's expense, takes Humboldt's lady friend out with Humboldt's money, and "borrows" Humboldt's clothes and cigarettes. Humboldt decides he has had enough of being "free" to support this couple and would like to have a slightly more conventional life with a young woman named Jean, whose affections are not so confusing. Sonia discovers his plan and throws a temper tantrum, declaring that Humboldt "belongs" to her, threatening to take poison, and ultimately insisting that if Humboldt wants to be married he must marry her. He leaves half his money and sneaks away while she rants.

According to Carney, the play was staged twice before 1923, probably by the Radical Bookshop Players or at the Dil Pickle Club, and it may have been staged again at the Dil Pickle in the 1920s and 1930s. The piece can be read many different ways. For example, the story can function as an allegory of class struggle—with the "humbled" deciding he's had enough of supporting "borrow-ski" and "owin,'" just as Marcy and her comrades believed the working class should cease supporting capitalist society with its labor. During the 1913–1914 Balkan Wars in Europe, John Reed made a similar gesture in an allegorical story called "The Rights of Small Nations" that Marcy published in the *Review* in January 1916. Also, as the main female character does not appear in a very positive light, the play can function as a continuation of the argument Marcy began in *Women as Sex Vendors.*

Because Marcy herself lived in a bohemian household with two men and did in fact take poison, as Sonia threatens, readers can interpret the play as a dramatic rendering of Marcy's internal dialogues about her situation. The cynicism with which Marcy skewers the values of bohemian life and accepts the costs of "free love" plays as at once bitter and hilarious, and would certainly have pleased the denizens of Bughouse Square and the Dil Pickle because they themselves knew the lifestyle so well. Sonia calls Humboldt "a clod" for thinking too much of earning a living and praises Owen as an exemplar of the well-lived life. When she exclaims

over the fact that some nights Owen spent entirely outside, walking and watching the stars, Humboldt says, wearily and knowingly, "Because he hadn't a place to sleep. I know." In the formative days of public relations and "positive spin," the IWW offered immediate critiques of the language with which those occupying the top levels of social power attempted to cast exploitative actions in a good light. Marcy was the first IWW writer to turn her gaze on the self and personal relationships.

The postwar years were hard on the women of the radical Left. Marcy's closest counterpart among European radicals, Rosa Luxemburg, was killed by a military mob after her release from prison in January 1919; her body was not discovered until June 1919. Emma Goldman was deported; Kate O'Hare did time in prison; Elizabeth Gurley Flynn had a nervous breakdown from which she took almost ten years to recover; Mary Heaton Vorse became addicted to morphine when Robert Minor became a communist and abandoned her while she was hospitalized after a miscarriage. Even May Walden (Kerr's wife from circa 1891 to 1904), out of public view in the near wilderness of Gainesville, Florida, wrote to her daughter that she kept a lethal dose of morphine hidden in her trunk during these years.

Rhymes of the Early Jungle Folk was published in November 1922. According to Carney, she later wrote an article, never published, titled "Shall Any Political Party Control the Unions?" arguing, as Rosa Luxemburg had to the displeasure of Lenin, that socialism must be the result of worker self-emancipation and cannot be instituted by a state. On 4 December 1922 Marcy ingested Paris Green, a pesticide. Leslie Marcy took her to Henrotin Hospital, telling medical staff she had mistaken the substance for medicinal salts, and Kerr told his daughter the same at first but later admitted that the act was intentional. She died on 8 December. In accordance with her wishes there was no funeral, and she was cremated at Graceland Cemetery in Chicago. Two weeks later Kerr walked out absentmindedly into traffic and was struck by a truck, sustaining minor injuries. Following the January 1923 meeting of the board of the publishing company, Kerr engaged Carney, the editor of a Duluth newspaper called *The Truth,* to write a memorial of Marcy's life, which Kerr published. Wharton Esherick created a woodblock print for the pamphlet, *Mary Marcy.*

Varying accounts explain why so little documentation of Marcy's personal life survived. The circumstances of her death were such that many who knew her felt it best never to mention her in public again, and thus Carney's minimal narrative stood unquestioned for almost a century. Marcy's old friend Ralph Chaplin was the single exception. His disaffection from the communist Left allowed him to state directly in his 1948 memoir, *Wobbly,* that he believed Marcy had made a tremendous sacrifice for the cause and that he found Haywood's lack of gratitude toward Marcy appalling. Most accounts of Marcy's suicide follow his lead in stating that she lost her home because Haywood jumped bail, but real-estate and probate records show that Marcy did not lose the home in Bowmanville. A fire in a much-touted fireproof office building a few years after her death destroyed many of the Kerr Company documents from the era of her management, including, presumably, the book of correspondence that she alone had kept since 1908.

Walden always believed and wrote repeatedly in her private papers that Marcy was in love with Bill Haywood. All of his other intimate companions–Jessie Ashley, Nevada Jane Haywood, and Minnie Wyman–had died in the two years before Haywood left the country, and possibly Marcy believed she would join him in Russia. Walden's account is tinged with jealousy, however, and together with errors–she joked that Marcy had taken a product called "Rough on Rats"–her bias lessens the usefulness of the information, in the absence of any sort of verification.

The Kerr circle told their friends that the Justice Department had seized many of Marcy's personal and professional papers in the Red Scare raids shortly after World War I. The Bureau of Investigation did keep the Kerr group under surveillance for a short time, but although documents in the National Archives attest to the fact that meticulous records were kept in preparation for lawsuits, the Bureau of Investigation made no documentation of a raid on either the Marcy home or the Kerr office and, in apparent violation of their customary practice of preparing to present evidence in a court of law, prepared no catalogue of papers seized. The agents in charge of the case seemed to know little about the Kerr group. An operative from the Bureau did break into the Kerr office in 1918, but the items he took–a company catalogue and some pamphlets–earned him only a reprimand. The Chicago police, who kept few records before the 1930s, might have staged the raid, or the Kerr group might have destroyed its own papers.

Kerr and Leslie Marcy continued to live together after Mary Marcy's death. Kerr developed a relationship with Mary Marcy's sister, Inez Stephens, who moved in with them in 1923. His daughter had already written to her mother that she believed Stephens would "start in where Mrs. Marcy left off" (Katharine Kerr Moore to May Walden, 29 December 1922). As Mary Marcy died without a will, Leslie Marcy inherited her estate; Kerr was the executor. The estate included the

house, less than $1,000, and five shares of Armour stock worth $100 each.

Without Kerr's active promotion, Marcy's work was all but forgotten. After her death, insiders on the Left knew Marcy strictly as a pamphleteer; but her pamphlets do not accurately represent her written contributions to the radical Left or the significance of her writing presence while she lived. Although her *Shop Talks in Economics* remained a staple of worker education groups, writers of histories and memoirs of the period tended to reproduce the sectarian politics Marcy abhorred, and she did not fit neatly into those narratives. When federal authorities investigated her circle, agents focused on her male companions. Scholars of socialism in the years following her death ignored her as well, finding the *ISR* of Algie Simons more to their taste. Feminist scholars devoted cursory attention to Marcy, if they mentioned her at all. Mari Jo Buhle, for example, makes reference to Marcy only as a critic of the socialist feminist movement. Although Marcy did not write exclusively about women's issues, from first to last her work addressed problems women faced.

In the 1980s, when the field of cultural studies began to open, Mary Marcy's work began to resurface. About the same time, the Newberry Library purchased the papers of May Walden and Katharine Kerr Moore and the Charles H. Kerr Company archives. In 1984 Franklin Rosemont of the Kerr firm produced a small book of Marcy's antiwar editorials from the *ISR*. In 1988 Frederick C. Giffen put together a collection of her work titled *The Tongue of Angels*. In the 1990s scholars of social movements began to notice Marcy and remark on her work's significance within the history of the left, although few scholars other than Miller and Rosemont have yet read her work in depth.

Letters:

J. Robert Constantine, ed., *Letters of Eugene V. Debs,* 3 volumes, includes letters from Marcy (Urbana: University of Illinois Press, 1990).

References:

Peter Carlson, *Roughneck: The Life and Times of Big Bill Haywood* (New York: Norton, 1983);

Jack Carney, *Mary Marcy* (Chicago: Charles H. Kerr, 1923);

Ralph Chaplin, *Wobbly: The Rough and Tumble Story of an American Radical* (Chicago: University of Chicago Press, 1948);

Sally Miller, "A Voice of the Party Left: The Intellectual Odyssey of Mary E. Marcy," in *Race, Ethnicity, and Gender in Early Twentieth-Century American Socialism,* edited by Miller (New York: Garland, 1996), pp. 119–146;

Kenneth Rexroth, *An Autobiographical Novel* (Garden City, N.Y.: Doubleday, 1966);

Franklin Rosemont, ed., *The Rise and Fall of the Dil Pickle: Jazz-Age Chicago's Wildest and Most Outrageously Creative Hobohemian Nightspot* (Chicago: Charles H. Kerr, 2004);

Allen Ruff, "Mary Marcy," in *Women Building Chicago, 1790–1990: A Biographical Dictionary,* edited by Rima Lunin Schultz and Adele Hast (Bloomington: Indiana University Press, 2001);

Ruff, *"We Called Each Other Comrade": Charles H. Kerr and Company, Radical Publishers* (Urbana: University of Illinois Press, 1997);

U.S. Military Intelligence Reports: Surveillance of Radicals in the United States, 1917–1941, 34 Microfilm Reels (Fredericksburg, Md.: University Publications of America, 1984);

Henry Wessells, "The Book Illustrations of Wharton Esherick," the Avram Davidson Website <http://www.avramdavidson.org/esherick.htm> (accessed 14 August 2008).

Papers:

Some letters from Mary E. Marcy survive in the Eugene V. Debs Papers, Indiana State University, and were published in a collection of letters edited by Robert J. Constantine. A few Marcy letters survive in the Kerr and IWW investigation records of the FBI and the Justice Department at the National Archives in College Park, Maryland. Some have been reproduced in microfilmed U.S. Military Intelligence Reports. Some of Marcy's annotated copies of socialist books and a few unsigned letters are located in the Charles H. Kerr Archive at the Newberry Library in Chicago.

H. L. Mitchell

(14 June 1906 – 1 August 1989)

Lynn Murray
The Art Institute of Atlanta

BOOKS: *The Plight of the Sharecropper,* by Mitchell and Clay East (New York: League for Industrial Democracy, 1934);

The Disinherited Speak: Letters from Sharecroppers (New York: Workers Defense League and Southern Tenant Farmers' Union, 1937);

Mean Things Happening in This Land: The Life and Times of H. L. Mitchell, Co-Founder of the Southern Tenant Farmers Union (Montclair, N.H.: Allanheld, Omun, 1979);

Roll the Union On: A Pictorial History of the Southern Tenant Farmers' Union (Chicago: Charles H. Kerr, 1987).

OTHER: *The Southern Tenet Farmers' Union Papers, 1934– 1970* (Glen Rock, N.J.: Microfilming Corporation of America, 1971);

The Green Rising, 1910–1977: A Supplement to the Southern Tenant Farmers' Union Papers. (Glen Rock, N.J.: Microfilming Corporation of America, 1978).

At an abandoned schoolhouse on a July night in 1934 H. L. Mitchell was present at an unlikely meeting of seven black and eleven white sharecroppers. The eighteen men had come to discuss their grievances against Arkansas landlords who had evicted hundreds of sharecropping families in the wake of the Agricultural Adjustment Act (AAA) of 1933, a New Deal program that paid landowners to reduce cotton crops by one-third. The labor union that grew out of that initial meeting eventually claimed thirty thousand members in seven Southern states and ignited a decade of race and labor radicalism on the cotton plantations of the Mississippi Delta. Mitchell entered a room heated by anger at dishonest landlords, frustration with a volatile cotton market, and distrust of New Deal agricultural policies to help organize what came to be known as the Southern Tenant Farmers' Union (STFU). This groundbreaking interracial union, guided by Mitchell, who served as its executive secretary from 1934 to 1939 and from 1941 to 1944, employed a crusading, nineteenth-century-style populism and prefigured the protest tac-

tics of the Civil Rights Movement of the 1950s and 1960s. H. L. Mitchell is best known for his role founding and guiding the STFU. His life was characterized by an unwavering faith in socialist ideals and a passionate advocacy for the rights of sharecroppers, agricultural workers, and the rural poor.

Harry Leland ("Mitch") Mitchell was born in Halls, Tennessee, in 1906 to James A. Mitchell, an itinerant Baptist preacher and barber, and Maude Stanfield Mitchell, a descendent of the earliest settlers of Halls. In his 1979 autobiography Mitchell recalls that his father was often absent and the family suffered financially, but his mother was known for her charity to the railroad workers and hobos who could find a hot meal in her kitchen near the tracks. Although Mitchell's playmates included both black and white children, at a young age he saw the ugly side of racism in the South. At eleven Mitchell witnessed the lynching of Lignon Scott, a black delivery man accused of raping a white woman. A crowd of more than five hundred arrived in Dyersburg, Tennessee, many, like Mitchell, taking a special excursion train to the event. Mitchell later described the lynching as nauseating and speculated that the experience helped shape the course of his life.

Between the ages of eight and twenty, Mitchell worked as a field hand picking strawberries in the spring and cotton in the fall, sold newspapers, and even tried his hand at bootlegging during Prohibition. Mitchell writes that he became a Socialist in "Moscow–Tennessee, that is" where his family lived during the 1920 presidential campaign. Although he was too young to vote, Mitchell supported Eugene V. Debs, the Socialist Party candidate and began to read Haldeman-Julius's Little Blue Books, which condensed the writings of such thinkers as Plato, Karl Marx, and Will Durant. He returned to Halls to finish high school, proclaiming himself "an atheist, an evolutionist, and a socialist" (*Happening in This Land: Mean Things*). By his own account Mitchell was not much of a student, but his classmates and teachers recalled his enthusiasm for reading about and debating leftist ideas.

H. L. Mitchell (from Donald H. Grubbs, Cry from the Cotton: The Southern Tenant Farmers' Union
and the New Deal, *1971; Thomas Cooper Library, University of South Carolina)*

Mitchell married Lyndell Carmack, a teacher and the daughter of a prosperous farmer outside Halls, on 26 December 1926. The couple lived briefly with the Carmack family and made a sharecrop (clearing $187.00 in 1927) before moving to Tyronza, Arkansas, where Mitchell's father had opened a barbershop. In the back of the barbershop Mitchell started a dry-cleaning business that soon expanded to the storefront next door. He came to know the planters and the sharecroppers throughout the region as he traveled through the countryside drumming up cleaning business from both rich and poor. In Tyronza Mitchell met Clay East, the owner of the filling station next door and, later, the town constable. East shared Mitchell's interest in socialism and helped organize and protect the STFU, once narrowly avoiding being lynched by an angry mob. The two men were vocal radicals and a curiosity to the town's residents who called their end of the street "little Red Square." Both Mitchell and East became active in socialist politics after the 1932 presidential election, and together they made a survey of the working conditions of three hundred sharecropping families. The information they gathered was later used in a pamphlet called *The Plight of the Sharecropper* (1934) with an introduction by Norman Thomas. In 1934 Mitchell served as state secretary of the Arkansas Socialist Party, which had a membership of fewer than one thousand. East and Mitchell brought Thomas,

Socialist Party candidate for president in 1928 and 1932, to Arkansas to meet with displaced tenants in February 1934. Mitchell credits Thomas with the initial idea to organize sharecroppers to fight evictions and to obtain a fair share of government payments for restricting cotton production. Mitchell called Thomas the godfather of STFU.

East and Mitchell were both present at the initial meeting of sharecroppers in July 1934 when the important decision was made to form a single interracial union of sharecroppers rather than two separate unions segregated by race. In his 1936 book *Revolt among the Sharecroppers* Howard Kester, a minister who worked closely with Mitchell in the STFU, writes that Issac Shaw, a black veteran of an earlier attempt to unionize farm workers, rose and argued the point this way: "The same chain that holds my people holds your people too. If we're chained together on the outside we ought to stay chained together in the union." The STFU adopted a resolution, drafted by Kester, making it officially an interracial organization with nonviolence as one of its basic precepts. Black and white sharecroppers, tenant farmers, and wage laborers were all invited to join.

The union's main goals were to raise awareness of the crisis in cotton farming and to provide relief to tenant farmers and sharecroppers suffering as a result of the Agricultural Adjustment Act. By the mid 1930s more than half of all Southern farms were occupied by tenants. Sharecroppers, who lacked basic equipment as well as capital, accounted for one fourth of the white tenants and more than half of the black tenants. Tenant families numbered eight and a half million, about one out of every four Southerners. A sharecropper was extended credit in the spring and summer to buy supplies for his crop and family; after the fall harvest, he split the proceeds with the landlord, who also collected interest on the debt and payment for goods charged in the plantation store. Usually the sharecropper was left with a scant profit, or, more often, he carried debt over to the next year. Mitchell likened sharecropping to a latter-day slavery, with avaricious plantation owners who employed cruel "riding bosses" in the role of overseers. By the 1930s, several factors further stressed the tenant system. In addition to the AAA, the Great Depression and a volatile cotton market created a climate in which tenant farmers were receptive to the STFU's radical ideas about race and labor organizing. Conservative Southerners, fearful of the union's growing power, formed groups of "nightriders" to terrorize and intimidate union members. The winter of 1934 grew violent with sharecroppers threatened, beaten, and whipped; union meetings broken up; and families evicted or their contracts broken. As Kester writes in *Revolt Among the Sharecroppers,* "to the sharecroppers their struggle was a holy crusade for freedom and justice. The planters looked upon the rising of the sharecroppers as the most serious threat on the horizon to their predatory system. They looked upon the Southern Tenant Farmers' Union with loathing and fear because it threatened their very existence." Kester saw the clashes between landowners and union members as so dangerous in those days that he wore a necklace containing a cyanide capsule, a present fashioned by his friend Dr. George Washington Carver.

Soon after its incorporation, the STFU authorized a committee of representatives to travel to Washington in January of 1935 to meet with Secretary of Agriculture Henry Wallace. The parity payments issued to landowners under the AAA had become an incentive to eliminate excess labor from cotton plantations, and Mitchell was a member of a five-man, biracial delegation determined to bring the interests of tenants and sharecroppers to the secretary's attention. After the meeting, Wallace appointed a special investigator to visit Arkansas and study the effects of the AAA on sharecroppers, giving hope to Mitchell and the union. Ultimately, the commission's report, believed to show widespread abuses in the system, was suppressed. The initial success of the delegation, however, helped union organizing efforts, and by early 1935 the union had ten thousand members in eighty locals. In the summer of 1935 the STFU organized its first strike, in which workers simply stayed away from work. Although the strike did not initiate bargaining between sharecroppers and landowners, it raised the payment for cotton and helped further organization efforts. By the end of 1935, the union had nearly twenty-five thousand members.

As the union grew in size, violence against union members increased and internal conflicts developed within the STFU. Mitchell relished a good fight and chronicled with zest his confrontations with landlords, riding bosses, and law enforcement. In one fiery speech to a crowd of fifteen hundred sharecroppers Mitchell blasted the Ku Klux Klan: "If any bunch of sons of bitches with their heads in pillow cases come to my house, they are going to get the hell shot out of them" (*Roll the Union On,* 1987). Mitchell feared, however, for the safety of his family, which had grown to include a son, Harry Leland Jr., and a daughter, Joyce. A third child, Samuel Howard, was born in 1936. Citizens of Tyronza boycotted the businesses of Mitchell and East, and both eventually closed their doors. Mitchell moved his family and the headquarters of the STFU to Memphis in early 1935. The year was filled with trials, both for the union and for Mitchell personally. Mitchell survived two attempts to take his life. While he delivered a speech, a follower of a union faction that wanted to segregate black and white members fired shots at him from behind the podium. The second attempt was made by Walter Moskop, an STFU member, who emptied a pistol at Mitchell when Mitchell visited Commonwealth College in Arkansas. Mitchell attributed the plot to communist infiltrators in the union. Neither would-be assassin was ever charged, arrested, or tried. But, Mitchell writes, "workingclass justice prevailed" (*Roll the Union On*).

Despite conflicts among its leaders, the union's grassroots power was growing. In response to planters who announced they would lower payments for cotton, the union organized a strike of cotton pickers in the fall of 1935, many of whom were successful in obtaining higher payments. A strike in 1936 was less successful, but the union, with the American Civil Liberties Union (ACLU) and the Workers Defense League, managed to break the reign of terror by getting a peonage conviction in federal court of an Arkansas deputy sheriff who held thirteen STFU members and sentenced them to work on his plantation. John L. Handcox, troubadour of the STFU, memorialized the strike in his song "Roll the Union On":

It was nineteen hundred and thirty six
And on the 18th day of May
When the STFU pulled a strike
That troubled the planters on their thrones.

The planters they all became troubled,
Not knowing what 'twas all about,
But they said, "One thing I'm sure we can do,
That's scare them sharecroppers out."

We're gonna roll, we're gonna roll,
We're gonna roll the Union on;
We're gonna roll, we're gonna roll,
We're gonna roll the Union on *(Roll the Union On)*.

Mitchell took the title of his 1979 autobiography, *Mean Things Happening in This Land,* from another of Handcox's protest songs.

From his base in Memphis, Mitchell sought to raise the union's profile and bring the plight of the sharecropper to the attention of government officials, members of the political parties, and union sympathizers across the country. At the Democratic Convention of 1936 Mitchell secured a place for a representative of the STFU on the President's Committee on Farm Tenancy. The President's Committee eventually became the Farm Security Administration (FSA), an agency created, in Mitchell's words, "to undo some of the evils of the New Deal in Agriculture" *(Roll the Union On)*. The union helped evicted Arkansas sharecroppers form the interracial Delta Cooperative Farm in Rochdale, Mississippi, which became a model for the FSA. Other public awareness projects included an annual National Sharecroppers Week, celebrated in many large cities and featuring fund-raisers with nationally known artists, writers, and musicians. In April 1937 the STFU with the Workers Defense League published a pamphlet titled *The Disinherited Speak: Letters from Sharecroppers.* Divided into such subject areas as "Life on the Plantation," "Violation of Civil Liberties," and "In the Union There Is Strength," the unedited letters, most addressed to STFU Secretary Mitchell, reveal the hardships of tenant farming and the hope the union provided.

The STFU sought an affiliation with the Congress of Industrial Organizations (CIO) in 1937 to expand its organization and increase funding. The STFU joined with cannery workers in the United Cannery, Agriculture, Packing and Allied Workers of America (UCAPAWA). From the start, the relationship between the STFU and the CIO was a difficult one. The STFU lacked an infrastructure at the local level to comply with CIO bureaucracy; many STFU members had never paid dues or formally signed membership roles. Mitchell and others also feared the Communists in the UCAPAWA were plotting to take over the union. Just after the Missouri Highway Demonstration in January of 1939, perhaps the most spectacular protest involving the STFU, the union severed its ties with the UCAPAWA-CIO.

The STFU had been successful in getting an order that specified that government subsidy checks would be sent directly to tenant farmers, a small victory for the union. But landlords in Missouri retaliated by giving their tenants a choice: either become wage laborers or leave the plantation. The Missouri Highway Demonstration occurred when twelve hundred evicted families camped out on public highways in protest. The event attracted national attention, and Mitchell, who was in Washington at the time, met with Eleanor Roosevelt in the White House to discuss relief measures for the protesters. The STFU proposed that the government establish a cooperative farming community and build homes for the evicted sharecroppers. Within a year, nearly six hundred homes were built on federal land and rented to homeless families in a project known as the Delmo Farm Labor Homes. At the end of World War II, when the federal government ordered all FSA housing projects dismantled, the STFU used its lobbying power in Washington to form a corporation to buy the homes and sell them at low interest rates to their occupants.

The coming of World War II, the mechanization of the cotton industry, and the shifting character of relief agencies such as the FSA changed the focus of the STFU in the 1940s from tenant farmers to migrant workers. Mitchell left his role as secretary of the STFU in 1939 amidst a scandal involving his affair with an STFU secretary. In his time away from the union Mitchell worked as a consultant for the National Youth Administration, and, briefly, as an organizer for the International Ladies Garment Workers Union. Mitchell was reelected secretary of the STFU in 1941 and held the position until 1944, when he was elected president of the National Farm Labor Union (NFLU), the successor of the STFU. During the war years, Mitchell and the union worked to provide temporary harvesting jobs in western states for unemployed Southern farm workers. The union also flew several hundred black female college students to summer jobs in Northern canning factories. In August 1946 the NFLU became an affiliate of the American Federation of Labor (AFL). When the AFL merged with the CIO in 1956, the group changed its name to the National Agricultural Workers Union (NAWU).

The NFLU moved its headquarters from Memphis to Washington in early 1948. Lyndell Mitchell chose to remain with the children in Memphis, and the couple's marriage, strained by distance and Mitchell's infidelities, ended in divorce. In 1951 H. L. Mitchell married Dorothy Dowe, an Alabama native who had worked with him in the STFU and was elected secretary-treasurer of the NFLU in 1945. Together Mitchell and Dowe ran "Washington's smallest lobby" from 1948 to

1960 *(Mean Things)*. Labor organizer and writer Ernesto Galarza describes their operation this way: "While the President of the nation's poorest national union hounded and harassed and haunted the various establishments on behalf of farm laborers, Dorothy kept order in the organizational housekeeping." Although Mitchell was far removed from union field work in Washington, as president of the NFLU he initiated an organizing project on California farms and ranches. The efforts of organizers Galarza and Hank Hasiwar led to a nationally publicized strike in late 1947 against the Di Giorgio Fruit Corporation, a packinghouse and winery in Kern County with thirteen hundred employees. Eleven hundred union workers went on a strike that lasted more than two years and produced one of the longest-lasting picket lines in American labor history. Although the strike did not end in victory for the workers, it brought attention to the issue of importation of illegal labor from Mexico and led President Truman, at Mitchell's urging, to appoint a Presidential Commission on Migratory Labor in American Agriculture. Mitchell served on the Department of Labor's Committee on Farm Labor and, from 1948 to 1958, as a worker-member of the Federal Advisory Council of the Bureau of Employment Security, Department of Labor.

One of Mitchell's main objectives in moving the union to Washington was to convince the AFL leadership to mount a large-scale organizing campaign of agricultural workers. After much lobbying, Mitchell finally realized his dream in 1958. The AFL-CIO financed an organizing drive based on the membership rolls of the NAWU. After four slow years, the movement began to grow, Cesar Chavez eventually assumed leadership, and the United Farm Workers of America was born. Mitchell writes in *Roll the Union On* that "the Southern Tenant Farmers' Union, and its successor organizations, had been the forerunner, fighting many battles over many years and paving the way for Cesar Chavez and the United Farm Workers." Mitchell adds that Chavez got his first union card from the NFLU and that H. L. Mitchell's signature was on the back.

In 1960 the NAWU was in financial trouble, so the agricultural workers in the AFL-CIO merged with the Amalgamated Meat Cutters and Butcher Workmen. Mitchell, with no national union to run, returned to the South, "low man on the totem pole," to organize for the Amalgamated Meat Cutters *(Mean Things)*. Quickly discovering that much had changed on the cotton plantations of Arkansas over the last twelve years, Mitchell headed for Louisiana, where he worked on behalf of rice mill workers, sugarcane plantation workers, and menhaden fishermen dubbed by Mitchell "sharecroppers of the sea" *(Mean Things)*. Mitchell also began the project that would occupy the rest of his years: record-

Mean Things Happening in This Land

The Life and Times of H. L. Mitchell
Co-Founder of the
Southern Tenant Farmers Union

by H. L. MITCHELL
Foreword by Michael Harrington

Allanheld, Osmun MONTCLAIR

Title page for Mitchell's 1979 autobiography (Thomas Cooper Library, University of South Carolina)

ing his memoirs, first through oral history interviews and later in a book. In the early days of the STFU, Mitchell had, at the urging of Kester, saved every document that came into and went out of the union's office, a practice he continued throughout his career. The collection Mitchell amassed documents the crisis in agricultural labor, as well as Mitchell's talent for using both public and private channels to promote the work of the union and the cause of agricultural workers.

On retirement from union organizing in 1973, H. L. and Dorothy Mitchell moved to Montgomery, Alabama. Mitchell, however, continued his involvement in union activities. He kept the memory of the STFU alive by organizing reunions and anniversary celebrations. The STFU papers, which are held in the Southern Historical Collection of the University of North Carolina at Chapel Hill, were microfilmed, and Mitchell embarked once again on the work of promoting the

STFU, this time to students and historians of labor and the agrarian South. Mitchell traveled the country speaking on college campuses and selling copies of the sixty-reel microfilm edition of the *Southern Tenant Farmers Union Papers, 1934–1970*. The collection includes letters from sharecroppers about their day-to-day trials, union business, correspondence of the officers, and copies of official publications of the STFU and its successors, including *The S.T.F.U. News, The Sharecroppers Voice, The Farm Worker, The Tenant Farmer, Farm Labor News,* and *The Agricultural Unionist.* A second microfilm collection, *The Green Rising, 1910–1977: A Supplement to the Southern Tenant Farmers Union Papers* was released in 1977. Mitchell also began work on his autobiography, *Mean Things Happening in This Land.* The book chronicles Mitchell's eventful life, which was always deeply intertwined with the lives of tenants, sharecroppers, and agricultural laborers, as well as the unions, activists, and agencies that aided them. A second book, *Roll the Union On: A Pictorial History of the Southern Tenant Farmers' Union,* was published in 1987, two years before Mitchell's death, and served as the basis for the concurrently distributed documentary film, *Our Land Too: The Legacy of the STFU. Roll the Union On* is based on Mitchell's earlier book, with photographs and his shortened versions of the significant events in the farm labor movement. In the first years of the twenty-first century the Southern Historical Association established the H. L. Mitchell Award to recognize distinguished books about the history of the Southern working class.

Mitchell's importance derives not from the books he wrote but rather from his untiring determination to bring attention to the plight of the sharecropper and to better the lives of American agricultural workers. He was a powerful communicator in the populist tradition who spent much of his working life influencing people's ideas–whether in makeshift union meeting halls or the paneled offices of the powerful. In his foreword to *Mean Things Happening in This Land* labor historian Michael Harrington writes: "Reading this book is like having a conversation with history; not the history of presidents and princes, but the history of those who do the dying." In both his books Mitchell sums up his life's work with these words: "I have always believed that it was my job, no matter where I was, to expose injustice, to stir up controversy among complacent people. I believe that if 'mean things' are brought to light, then something may eventually be done to correct them."

References:

"Biographical Sketch," in *A Guide to the Collection: The Green Rising, 1910–1977: A Supplement to the Southern Tenant Farmers Union Papers* (Glen Rock, N.J.: Microfilming Corporation of America, 1978);

Mark Fannin, *Labor's Promised Land: Radical Visions of Gender, Race, and Religion in the South* (Knoxville: University of Tennessee Press, 2003);

Donald H. Grubbs, *Cry from the Cotton: The Southern Tenant Farmers' Union and the New Deal* (Chapel Hill: University of North Carolina Press, 1971);

Howard Kester, *Revolt among the Sharecroppers* (New York: Arno Press & the New York Times, 1969, reprint);

Mark Naison, *The Southern Tenants Farmers' Union and the CIO* (Boston: New England Free Press, 1968);

Daniel Singal, *Guide to the Microfilm Edition of the Southern Tenants Farmers Union Papers, 1934–1970* (Glen Rock, N.J.: Microfilming Corporation of America, 1971);

George Brown Tindall, *The Emergence of the New South, 1913–1945* (Baton Rouge: Louisiana State University Press, 1967).

Papers:

The papers of H. L. Mitchell, the STFU and its successor organizations are in the Southern Historical Collection at the University of North Carolina at Chapel Hill. Much material is also widely available in the microfilm collections *Archives of the Rural Poor: The STFU Papers, 1934–1970* and *The Green Rising, 1910–1977: A Supplement to the Southern Tenant Farmers Union Papers.* Additional H. L. Mitchell correspondence, newsletters, and ephemera are available in the Charles H. Kerr Company Archives at the Newberry Library in Chicago. Cornell University's Industrial and Labor Relations Library also owns important files of material on the STFU in its Manuscript and Oral History Collections.

J. Howard Moore

(4 December 1862 – 17 June 1916)

Donna L. Davey

New York University

BOOKS: *A Race of Somnambulists* (Mount Lebanon, N.Y.: The Lebanon Press, 1890?);

Why I Am a Vegetarian: An Address Delivered before the Chicago Vegetarian Society (Chicago: Press of Purdy Pub., 1895);

America's Apostasy (Chicago: Ward Waugh, 1899);

Better-World Philosophy: A Sociological Synthesis (Chicago: Ward Waugh, 1899);

The Universal Kinship (Chicago: Charles H. Kerr, 1906; London: Humanitarian League, 1906);

The New Ethics (London: Ernest Bell, 1907; revised edition, Chicago: Samuel A. Bloch, The Bookman, 1909);

Humane Teaching in Schools (London: Animals' Friend Society, 1911);

The Care of Illegitimate Children in Chicago (Chicago: Juvenile Protective Association of Chicago, 1912);

Ethics and Education (London: Bell, 1912);

Ethics of School Life: A Lesson Given at the Crane Technical High School, Chicago, in accordance with the law requiring the teaching of morals in the public schools in Illinois (London: Bell, 1912);

High School Ethics (Book One) (London: Bell, 1912);

The Law of Biogenesis: Being Two Lessons on the Origin of Human Nature (Chicago: Charles H. Kerr, 1914);

Savage Survivals (Chicago: Charles H. Kerr, 1916; London: Watts, 1918);

Fermented Beverages: Their Effects on Mankind (London: Harrison, 1919).

Edition and Collection: *The Universal Kinship,* edited, with an introduction, by Charles Magel (Fontwell, Sussex, England: Centaur Press, 1992).

OTHER: "Tending toward 'A Celestial Civilization,'" in *To-day's Problems and Their Solution: 150 Messages of Hope and Cheer by 150 Able Writers,* edited by Henry E. Allen (Chicago: Trade Union Book Concern, 1910);

"Discovering Darwin," in *Proceedings of the International Anti-Vivisection and Animal Protection Congress Held at Washington, D.C., December 8th to 11th, 1913* (New York: Tudor Press, 1913).

SELECTED PERIODICAL PUBLICATIONS-UNCOLLECTED: "Meat Not Needed as a Food," *Chicago Daily Tribune,* 29 April 1895, p. 4;

"Clerical Sportsmen," *Chicago Vegetarian,* 3 (November 1898): 5–6;

"The Psychical Kinship of Man and the Other Animals," *Humane Review* (July 1900): 121;

"How Vegetarians Observe the Golden Rule," *The Vegetarian and Our Fellow Creatures* (15 August 1901): 295–297;

"Our Debt to the Quadruped," *Humane Review* (April 1902): 32;

"Treatment, Real and Ideal, of Animals," *Chicago Daily Tribune,* 15 August 1909, p. B5;

"Evidences of Relationship: I. Man-Like Apes; "II. Monkeys" (p. 51–52); "III. Dogs; IV. Ants," *Our Dumb Animals* (August 1914): 33–34, 51–52, 69–70, 87;

"The Source of Religion," *International Socialist Review,* 16 (June 1916): 726–727.

Teacher, writer, and orator J. Howard Moore was a fervent advocate for animal rights. Firmly committed to Darwin's scientific theory of evolution, Moore made the connection between evolution and humanitarian ethics his life's work. Over the course of twenty-one years he wrote seven books, numerous pamphlets and articles, and delivered frequent addresses on animal rights, vegetarianism, socialism, prohibition, women's suffrage, and ethics. Moore sought to instill compassion in his contemporaries—to move them to recognize that ethical considerations extend to animals as well as humans. Moore's philosophy centered on the premise that evolution proved the kinship and solidarity of all sentient beings, and therefore one must reject categorically the anthropocentrism that puts humans at the center of the universe and makes animals their utilitarian subjects. Moore lamented, often with moral indignation, that man was too selfish and unimaginative to realize that the Golden Rule applies to all feeling creatures, not just to other humans. But Moore's deep empathy for his animal kin also left him fragile and despondent

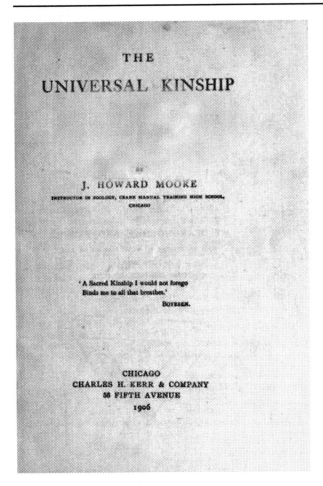

THE

UNIVERSAL KINSHIP

BY

J. HOWARD MOORE

INSTRUCTOR IN ZOOLOGY, CRANE MANUAL TRAINING HIGH SCHOOL,
CHICAGO

'A Sacred Kinship I would not forego
Binds me to all that breathes.'

BOYESEN.

CHICAGO
CHARLES H. KERR & COMPANY
56 FIFTH AVENUE
1906

Title page for Moore's best-known book, a treatise on the interrelationship of all sentient beings (Robarts Research Library, University of Toronto)

that humans had not evolved far enough to recognize this. This despair ultimately led to his suicide. Nevertheless, in his writings, Moore held out the hope that the human race would eventually evolve ethically as it had physically—that one day humans would treat animals kindly and not as just another resource at their disposal. Scholars consider his 1906 book, *The Universal Kinship,* a classic humanitarian work.

John Howard Moore was born in Linden, Missouri, on 4 December 1862. He was a son of William A. and Mary (Barger) Moore and the eldest of their six children. Moore grew up in a household that practiced Christianity and learned through it the anthropocentric belief that God made human beings to rule the earth and thus entitled them to exploit nature and all beings in it as they saw fit for their own use and enjoyment. While he was growing up on the farm in Missouri that he called an Eden, with its stream, flowers, and rolling green hills, Moore liked to hunt. Everyone he knew hunted, and he never heard any objections to it. Moore

later reflected in a collection of lectures, *High School Ethics (Book One)* (1912), that he and his community believed "that was what 'animals' were for—to be treated just as we wanted to treat them."

Moore attended Oskaloosa College in Iowa from 1880 to 1884. The influence of an education in science and Charles Darwin's new theory of evolution transformed Moore's thinking, and as a young man he denounced the religion of his youth in favor of a biocentric ethic in which all forms of life have intrinsic value. In particular he expressed disgust at the clergy's participation in and sanction of what he saw as cruel and barbaric blood sports. For Moore, Darwin's theory made possible a science-based ethic that recognized the worth of animals apart from their service to humans as beasts of burden and sources of food. Little is known about the next ten years of his life except that Moore became a vegetarian for ethical reasons around 1886.

Between 1890 and 1893 Moore lectured in Missouri, Kansas, and Iowa. His indignation at man's barbarous abuse of animals for food, blood sport, and fashion, a recurrent theme throughout his work, provided the subject of his first publication, the pamphlet *A Race of Somnambulists,* probably published in 1890. "Human nature is nowhere so hideous and the conscience is nowhere so profoundly asleep, as in their ruthless disregard for the life and happiness of the animal world," Moore asserts there. He describes Thanksgiving as a day of gluttony and merciless, indiscriminate killing tournaments, of crimes "unparalleled on the face of the earth." Yet, as in other works, Moore concludes with a hopeful vision of the day when people will come to see the malevolence of such customs, and treat animals with kindness. He hopes that man will evolve socially and morally so that "the same sentiment of sympathy and fraternity that broke the black man's manacles and is to-day melting the white woman's chains, will to-morrow emancipate the sorrel horse and the heifer."

In 1894 Moore entered the University of Chicago. He became a socialist while at the university and was vice president of the Prohibition Club. He joined the Vegetarian Eating Club organized in April 1894, serving as president in 1895, and then "purveyor" in 1896. His interests gave him occasion to sharpen his oratory skills, which he developed throughout his life as a teacher and in frequent speeches that were often printed and sold as pamphlets or given away free as "pass ons." Moore spoke on the benefits of vegetarianism, the cruelty of wearing fur, the superiority of Socialist candidates up for election, and the atrocities of hunting, war, and alcohol consumption, among other topics. His passion for these causes infused him with eloquence, and he cultivated a dramatic rhetorical style that earned him wide attention.

In 1895 Moore gave an address, "Why I Am a Vegetarian," before the Chicago Vegetarian Society. Later the address was printed by two publishers and serialized in four installments in *The Chicago Vegetarian* in 1897. In the address Moore sets forth his simple rationale for not eating meat: "I never want happiness that gives another pain." In this address, as in his other writings and lectures, Moore argues for universal solidarity for all sentient beings. He tells his audience that he wants to change their minds about eating meat, a task he acknowledges is too ambitious for a single lecture. He describes the horror and sadness he feels when others engage in the "barbarous, blood-sucking practices" of eating meat and connects this behavior to every other form of exploitation in which the "interests, lives, or welfares of some beings [are usurped] for the whim or convenience of others." Moore believed ethics should apply to all beings and implored his audience to adopt principles of universal courtesy and love for all beings. Favorable reviews of the published versions of this address appeared in *The Phrenological Journal of Science and Health* in May 1899 and September 1900.

A month after that address, on 4 April 1895, the University of Chicago Prohibition Club held its annual oratory contest in the school's Cobb Lecture Hall and Moore took first honors with his address "The Scourge of the Republic" over competitors John L. Hoyt, who spoke on "Liberty," and James P. White, who spoke on "The Ministry and Politics." Moore represented the University of Chicago at the State Prohibition oratorical contest held on 18 April 1895 in Wheaton, Illinois, where he also won top honors. Later that month, he wrote a letter to the editor of the *Chicago Daily Tribune* extolling the virtues of a non-meat diet for both health and ethical reasons. He was convinced that a person would readily become accustomed to a vegetarian diet a few weeks after trying it and that meat eating would gradually seem not only an unnatural habit, but also a disgusting and horrible spectacle. Moore noted that vegetarianism carried health benefits for humans, but that he became a vegetarian "for the benefit of the creatures [he] would otherwise gnaw" rather than for himself (29 April 1895).

Three months later a writer of the *Chicago Daily Tribune* described Moore as the "champion Prohibition orator in the United States." The newspaper's short profile said of Moore, "He thinks it is as wicked to eat meat as to drink liquor. He believes in woman suffrage, has curly hair and soulful eyes, declares that this country is the land of the boss and the home of the sot, but hopes to change all that by a frequent delivery of his prize oration, 'The Scourge of the Republic.' He is full of youthful enthusiasm" (4 August 1895). When the Vegetarian Society of Chicago held its inaugural holiday banquet at the Great Northern Hotel on 28 December 1895, Moore attended along with such luminaries as defense lawyer Clarence S. Darrow, who became Moore's brother-in-law three years later, and the presidents of the Chicago, New York, and American Vegetarian societies. Vegetarians were among the food reformers whose ranks were increasing across America at the end of the nineteenth century. Fruitarians, grainarians, nutarians, and other non-meat eaters all promoted the benefits of their special diets. Moore was one of several individuals profiled along with Darrow and Frances L. Duseneberry, editor of the *Women's News,* in a *Chicago Tribune* article on the thriving vegetarian community in Chicago (20 September 1896).

In 1898 Moore began teaching ethics and zoology at the Crane Manual Technical High School in Chicago, a post he held for the rest of his life, even as he also taught at other Chicago schools and wrote and spoke extensively on the subjects that mattered most to him. Teaching was an appropriate career choice for Moore since he believed that only through education could humans hope to evolve beyond their existing barbaric social state to a higher consciousness.

A year later Moore published his first major work, *Better-World Philosophy: A Sociological Synthesis,* to reviews that, though mixed, nearly uniformly singled out his bold, forceful style and intensity of opinion. Some called him pessimistic, but Moore was fraught with a nearly desperate longing to change the way people saw the world. *Better-World Philosophy* explains his belief in the interconnectedness of all beings and argues that sentience makes ethics possible. Since animals feel, he reasoned, ethics should rightly be extended to them. *Better-World Philosophy* details the altruistic social ideal, explaining the evolution of human beings away from anthropocentrism, and expressing the hope that, following the logic of Darwinian theory, natural selection will eventually weed out undesirable elements and lead eventually to a cooperative, altruistic society for all sentient beings. Moore cautions against thoughtless procreation and argues in favor of eugenics, a movement popular at the time that supported the improvement of hereditary qualities through controlled breeding. He insists that the revision of human nature from egoism towards altruism should begin with the teaching in childhood that one should love all other beings as he loves himself. After reviewing *Better-World Philosophy,* Henry S. Salt, the respected English humanitarian and author of the seminal 1892 *Animals' Rights Considered in Relation to Social Progress,* began a regular correspondence with Moore that grew into a warm friendship.

In 1900 Moore was teaching at the Calumet High School in Illinois when he wrote to the Chicago Board of Education to complain about Republican political clubs using Washington's and Lincoln's birthdays as occasions "for the inculcation of military and imperialistic sentiment among children." He deplored the use of political propaganda to foster the fighting instinct in children, which he believed should be strenuously curbed instead. He complained in his letter about using war heroes as role models and lamented the fact that schools did not offer children alternative visions of greatness.

In July 1900 Moore published "The Psychical Kinship of Man and the Other Animals" in *Humane Review,* a journal produced in London by Salt. The article develops an early version of the second section of his best-known work, *The Universal Kinship,* which he completed six years later. In the earlier text Moore argues that man overestimates "himself, his virtues, capabilities, importance, and destiny" and is grossly mistaken in his belief that he ranks superior to other species. Rather, Moore contends, Darwin's theory of evolution confirms that man shares a common ancestry with all other animals. Even without knowledge of this past, Moore insists, a person relying on observation alone could reasonably conclude that animals have souls and experience joys and sorrows just as humans do. And he decries killing for the sake of killing, as a pastime. This article is a milestone in Moore's growth as a dedicated champion of animal rights and spokesman for the voiceless.

Moore assails man's mistreatment of the animals that contributed to the rise of civilization in "Our Debt to the Quadruped," also published in the *Humane Review* (April 1902). Despite the faithful services rendered by the horse, the camel, the donkey, and the ox, Moore writes, their "lives are drained of everything that makes life worth living, and into them are poured instead all the anguish of prolonged crucifixion . . . doomed to a round of grinding wretchedness and toil such as only machines with no desire for happiness and no capacity for despair would ever voluntarily enter upon." Moore expresses his vision for justice and reciprocity with these "associated beings" so that they are treated by man "not as objects of pillage, but as beings with rights and feelings, and capabilities of happiness and misery, like himself." Such is the only conduct befitting a civilized race, he maintains.

While Moore was an instructor in zoology at the Crane Manual Training High School (also referred to as the Crane Technical High School) in Chicago, he completed *The Universal Kinship.* The Charles H. Kerr Publishing Company published the book in 1906 as part of its International Library of Social Science series. In this book Moore discusses the physical, psychical, and ethical facets of human relationships with the other members of the animal kingdom, explains his position that *all* beings have rights, and asserts that people

should follow the Golden Rule to do unto other beings as they would have done unto themselves. "*The Universal Kinship,*" Moore wrote, "means the kinship of all the inhabitants of the planet Earth." Favorable reviews appeared in *Advocate of Peace,* the writer finding the book sound on scholarly grounds and well written, and in *Current Literature,* which echoed praise for the book as "the most important vindication of humanitarian principles that has appeared for many years" (October 1906). Writing in the *American Anthropologist,* J. R. Swanton commends the book's utility toward kinder treatment of animals, but criticizes Moore for ignoring the real differences between man and such animals as the tiger, centipede, and rat (October–December 1906). Mark Twain, who received a letter from Moore with a copy of *The Universal Kinship,* wrote back on 2 February 1907 with appreciation that the "book has furnished me several days of deep pleasure and satisfaction" and remarked that in the matter of morals humans have gone backward from their reptilian ancestors. Years later, Salt called *The Universal Kinship* "the best book ever written in the humanitarian cause." A review of the 1916 edition of *The Universal Kinship* in *The American Journal of Sociology* praises the work for providing the lay reader with a wealth of general information on evolution and "in a readable, somewhat poetical style an exposition of the thesis that all life is one," while at the same time pointing out that scientists might find the writer does not have "an exacting and critical spirit" (March 1917).

Socialist publisher Kerr published all of Moore's books except the ethics titles. May Walden Kerr, wife of the publisher and an active socialist who wrote and spoke about the movement, became one of Moore's closest friends. The Kerrs divorced in 1904, but May Walden and Moore corresponded with each other over the years, and occasionally the Moores vacationed with Walden and her daughter, Katherine. In his letters to her, as in his letters to Henry Salt, Moore spoke often of his love of nature. His letters to Walden were filled mostly with passages on the wonders of the outdoors and reminiscences of time spent in the undeveloped world enjoying the sights, smells, and beauty of nature.

Moore caused a sensation at the November 1906 convention of the American Humane Association in Chicago with his address, "The Cost of a Skin." In this speech he denounced the fashion of wearing fur and feathers. A front-page article in the *Chicago Daily Tribune* described the reaction of attendees at the dramatic speech in which Moore declared, "Nobody but a barbarian would adorn her head with the carcass of a bird or the heads of grinning weasels. Such things appeal only to the vulgarian. Such a woman is about as attractive as if adorned with a string of dried skulls. She excites pity, for she is a murderess" (16 November 1906). Enthusiastic applause from some and stony silence from others in the audience characterized Moore's reception. Two women left the hall before the talk was over, another burst into tears, and the husband of a woman wearing a black fur boa rose to defend the practice. Moore condemned fur as a savage and unnecessary luxury and called its proponents "conscienceless and inhumane." He lamented a world that would condone such atrocity and told his audience, "When I think that in this day of advanced education and supposed refinement brutalities such as are necessary to secure the furs of these little animals are practiced I am heartily ashamed of the race to which I belong." "The Cost of A Skin" appears as chapter 5 of Moore's book *The New Ethics* (1907) and was also published separately as part of the "A.F. [Animals' Friend] Pamphlet Series" by the Animals' Friend Society of London. Two years after the furor at the American Humane Association convention, Moore delivered the lecture again after the annual business meeting of the Woodlawn's Woman's Club on 4 February 1908.

The problem of how to expand ethics in a manner that seems appropriate given the biological revelations of Charles Darwin's theory of evolution provides the unifying focus of *The New Ethics*, published to wide acclaim. Moore acknowledges the difficulties inherent in revising anthropocentric opinions that have been generations in the making but contends that both individuals and societies grow and evolve. Since all great truths were once scorned and ridiculed, Moore is confident that humans will evolve out of the comfortable selfishness that keeps them savage. Moore was puzzled that *The Jungle* (1906), Upton Sinclair's sensational novel about the horrors of the meatpacking industry, failed to spark any significant public outrage over the suffering of the animals in the filthy plants.

A review of *The New Ethics* in *Health* (August 1909) said of Moore, "the sub-human species never had a more sincere and ardent friend." The reviewers wish that the book could "be placed in the hands of every thinking adult in the world." The reviewer noted that Moore does not seem aware of the latest writings and research of botanists J. Oswinsky, Harold Wager, and Gottlieb Haberlandt who attributed souls, the sense of sight, and reason to plants, respectively.

Writing was difficult for Moore. In a letter to Salt he said that he found prose composition "unnatural and . . . a good deal like 'sweating blood.'" He reflected that "unless I am driven by terrible feelings or convictions, I am inclined to go on and do nothing. I hate writing. It is the greatest hardship of my life. It seems to me I might be reasonably happy if I weren't everlastingly nagged

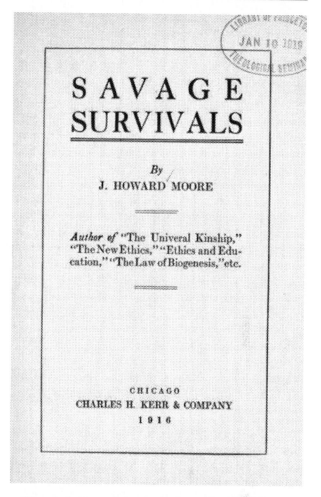

SAVAGE SURVIVALS

By
J. HOWARD MOORE

Author of "The Univeral Kinship,"
"The New Ethics," "Ethics and Education," "The Law of Biogenesis," etc.

CHICAGO
CHARLES H. KERR & COMPANY
1916

Title page for Moore's collection of sixty-three lectures he delivered at Crane Technical High School (Princeton Theological Seminary Library)

by the obligation to perpetrate literary things on people" *(Universal Kinship)*.

On 25 October 1908 Moore delivered a speech before the Young People's Socialist League in support of Eugene V. Debs's run for the U.S. presidency as the Socialist Party candidate. As reported in the *Chicago Daily Tribune*, Moore claimed that Debs would jail the millionaires instead of their victims, who were currently filling the prisons. He argued that the greatest hope for socialism lay with young people and asserted that university students had minds that were the most receptive to socialist propaganda (26 October 1908).

Two months later, in an op-ed essay for the *Chicago Daily Tribune* (15 April 1909) titled "Treatment, Real and Ideal, of Animals," Moore restated his respect for the "great four-footed races" and credited their labor with making many of man's greatest achievements possible. Moore reiterated his disagreement with the anthropocentric view of animals and conveyed his ideal wherein they would co-exist with the human "as associates, not as slaves or machines, as his best friends and most faithful and valuable allies." The animals in turn would come to regard man "as their true guide and benefactor."

In 1909 Illinois passed a law requiring the teaching of morals for thirty minutes every week in all public schools in the state. Unlike many other educators, Moore rejoiced at the news and began to write materials and curriculum in support of the change. Early in 1910, after two terms in the White House, Theodore Roosevelt set off across Africa on a hunting exhibition to bring back to the people of America samples of the beasts of the wild. This prompted an outraged Moore to denounce the former president in especially strong terms in a passionate speech quoted fifty years later in the *Chicago Daily Tribune*. Moore called Roosevelt's expedition "a disgrace to humanity" and argued that Roosevelt had "done more to dehumanize society than all the humane societies can do in years to bring it out of its present savage state" (24 May 1960). *Current Literature* quoted Moore as saying the former president was "obsessed with a desire to kill," and should be condemned for the inhumane expedition which Moore called "a pure exercise in butchery" (April 1910).

In a series of lectures before the Socialist League and Young People's Socialist League in Chicago in the fall of 1910, Moore addressed his recurring themes of the nascent state of human ethical development and the need for rigorous education and rethinking of common assumptions. Later Moore collected these in his *Ethics and Education* (1912). He cared so deeply about the treatment of his fellow creatures that he worked to the point of exhaustion in his efforts to enlighten mankind about the stalled evolution of human ethics. On 25 March 1911 Moore wrote to his friend Salt from Alabama, describing his depression and breakdown from overwork. He tells Salt that the five books he wrote during the previous sixteen or seventeen years "may never amount to much, but I have given an immense amount of work to their production" (*Universal Kinship*). Yet, Moore desperately clung to the belief that ethical education would eventually have an impact. In 1911 Moore published an eight-page pamphlet, *Humane Teaching in Schools,* in which he insists that "The teaching of the correct relation of human beings to each other and of human beings to the other inhabitants of this planet should have a prominent place in every course of instruction designed for human young" (*Humane Teaching in Schools*). Moore crisply asserts that teachers will glean personal satisfaction from mastering a new curriculum and insists that morals, sympathy, and humanitarianism can be taught.

Around 1911 Moore underwent an abdominal operation from which he suffered illness and pain for the next five years. Moore later wrote in *Ethics and Education* about the debilitating effects of ill health on the soul, the mind, and the moral character, and contended that it is impossible for anyone to be a completely moral being when he is not well. He found his own depression, mentioned in his letters to Salt, a great burden. In 1912, while teaching ethics at Crane Technical High School, Moore wrote *Ethics and Education* to assist other teachers struggling with the new requirement that they teach ethics in school. In the book, he concisely reviews his philosophy on the nature of human ethics, explains the function of evolution in the process of moral development, and addresses the physical, vocational, intellectual, and ethical anxiety inherent in such an education. Moore's compulsion to educate people to move beyond the assumptions inherited from previous, unenlightened generations, and to develop in them an awareness that extends ethics to all sentient beings, though diluted, still resonates. He fervently calls for teachers to work to instill compassion, sympathy, imagination, and altruism in all. He revisits Roosevelt's hunting atrocities and cites the public's approval of the former president's trip as sound evidence for his claim that humanity is in an early stage of development but that it could continue to grow and develop a higher moral character.

Ethics and Education was published amid controversy when inflammatory excerpts attacking marriage and the courts were published in the bulletin of the Schoolmaster's Club of Chicago prior to the book's publication. Moore calls marriage "prehistoric" and says judges and lawyers rely on tradition instead of determining what is reasonable and just. Moore defended himself in an interview in the *Chicago Daily Tribune* and invited the board of education to investigate him for his views. He said he would have worded the passages more strongly had his publisher not objected. Moore said that he wrote the book for adults, not children, and insisted that adults should be spoken to with candor. He said that he gave his pupils careful instruction in ethics, not his personal views. Moore added, "I believe Crane is more advanced in the teaching of morals to children than any other school in the world. Our school is the pioneer in the movement" (29 February 1912).

The next year Moore followed *Ethics and Education* with the first volume of ethics lessons given at Crane as *High School Ethics (Book One)*. He intended the work as the first of four books in a four-year high-school course on both theoretical and practical ethics. The lessons address such varied topics as the place and meaning of ethics; the ethics of school life; the spirit of sport; the care and treatment of pets; the source of sealskin, ivory and other animal-derived goods; the rights of women; traits of the ideal character and habits that help; and birds. Moore's fundamental belief that humans have not yet evolved optimal moral consciousness and must be taught ethics in order to develop empathy for other feeling beings permeates these lessons.

In a 1913 speech to the International Anti-Vivisection and Animal Protection Congress in Washington, Moore praised Darwin's doctrine of evolution as "the most important idea so far discovered by the human mind." He assailed anthropocentricism as the fundamental impediment to humanitarianism and cited the innate selfishness and lack of curiosity of humans as supplemental hindrances. He noted that although Darwin's *Origin of Species* (1859) had fully negated anthropocentrism, the belief persisted. The widely held view that the lives of innocent animals are worth less than human life and that this justifies vivisection was, he thought, simply the latest manifestation of that belief. As he saw it, vivisectors inflict monstrous suffering on the helpless in the name of science, but, in Moore's value scale, kindness and sympathy are always more important than scientific knowledge. He believed that the capacity to imagine the suffering of others is a fundamental moral trait.

Between 1913 and 1914, the Chicago Board of Education moved to stop teaching sex hygiene in its schools, a move that Moore opposed. He was a scientist by training and also a practical man who viewed the human body as a machine. He believed students needed to be taught the physiological facts of human reproduction and wrote to the board of education on 5 January 1914 to urge it to allow the classes to continue. As reported in the *Chicago Daily Tribune* (6 January 1914) Moore expressed his hope "that if the present board failed to keep up instruction in sex hygiene another board, with a clearer, more up to date understanding of its duty, will take the step." Shortly thereafter, the *Chicago Daily Tribune* reported that the trustees of the school board had voted to abandon the instruction of "personal purity" in the Illinois schools (8 January 1914). Eight years later, the board reversed itself and allowed sex hygiene to be taught in the public schools (9 November 1922).

Published in 1914, *The Law of Biogenesis: Being Two Lessons on the Origin of Human Nature* comprised lectures Moore had developed at Crane Technical High School. The thirty-three discourses, introduced by Mary Marcy (1877–1922), radical writer and editor of the *International Socialist Review,* consider the physical and mental aspects of biogenesis—how each living creature repeats the evolutionary development of its primal ancestors. The reviewer for *Life* described the book as an "authoritative yet primer-simple summary of the matter . . . at once interesting reading and conducive to an educated outlook" (18 March 1915).

Moore also published a series of four articles in *Our Dumb Animals,* a publication of the Massachusetts Society for the Prevention of Cruelty to Animals, in 1914. Under the heading "Evidences of Relationship" Moore profiles four species in separate sections: man-like apes, monkeys, dogs, and ants. In a down-to-earth tone without the rhetorical flourishes and ardor that characterize his polemical writing, the zoology instructor describes in affectionate detail the exceedingly human traits of these familiar creatures. The articles show a gentler side of Moore and suggest a patient, well-informed, and gifted classroom teacher.

Like many of his friends who were Edward Bellamy enthusiasts, Moore believed in the importance of wilderness preservation. And like some of his socialist friends, including Kerr, he bought land in Alabama, near Mobile Bay, although it is not clear that Moore's purchase was part of the single-tax alternative community there. In a letter to Salt, written on his birthday in 1914, Moore gleefully describes making the final payment on his "blessed" acres in Alabama.

> I shall have 116½ acres there of the loveliest wild woods of pine, poplar, gum, beech, live oak, magnolia, and holly. I have one holly tree that is over a foot in diameter—and magnolias like sawlogs. In my will I will say "My Alabama acres are to be kept as they are forever—as a sanctuary for the wild things and a play place for men" (*Universal Kinship*)

Moore describes the undeveloped land as being away from everything, and teeming with wildlife. In the letter he says, "I can dream there all day and never see any one—except the red birds and squirrels, and great turtles dozing in the sun and the fishes and the great cranes circling above and hear the occasional grunt of an alligator. . . . I have about a mile of water front—river and brook!"

The *International Socialist Review* began publishing excerpts from Moore's work early in 1915 and continued to do so for the next three years. *Savage Survivals,* published in 1916, is a compilation of sixty-three lectures given by Moore at Crane Technical High School. Part of a larger course of lectures on ethics, the volume comprises five sections exploring first the origins and survival of domesticated animals in the wild followed by an exploration of man's savage ancestry and an ethical analysis of those traits that survive in civilized man. The text is accompanied by twenty-seven illustrations by Roy Olson and L. F. Simmons. F. Stuart Chapin's review in *The American Journal of Sociology* (March 1917, 693) describes the book as "an excellent presentation of the concepts of organic and social evolution adapted to the intelligence of children" and a well-developed treatise on the modern idea of prehistoric human evolution.

At the same time, Chapin contends that some of the underlying anthropological research is obsolete.

On 17 June 1916, leaving a note for his wife, whom he always called "Tess," the fifty-three-year-old Moore went to the wooded island in Jackson Park, near his home in Chicago, and took his own life with a gunshot to the head. The note read:

> The long struggle is ended. I must pass away. Goodby. O, men are so cold and hard and half-conscious toward their suffering fellows. Nobody understands. O, my mother! And, O, my little girl! What will become of you? And the poor four footed! May the long years be merciful!
>
> Take me to my river. There, where the wild birds sing and the waters go on and on, alone, in my groves, forever.
>
> O, Tess! Forgive me! O, forgive me, please!

Moore's death was ruled a suicide during a temporary fit of insanity. Darrow delivered a moving address at Moore's funeral in which he praised his brother-in-law's kindness, his love of nature, and his ceaseless devotion to enlightening others throughout his life. Darrow said, "John Howard Moore was a fool, one of those rare and devoted fools, who thought that his words and life could help a world that will not listen and cannot see, and therefore does not feel" (*Universal Kinship*). A brief essay noting his passing appeared in the August 1916 *International Socialist Review,* written by Louis Vineburg, who had met Moore during his lecture series for the Young People's Socialist League. Salt remembers Moore affectionately in his memoir, *Company I Have Kept* (1930), saying that although they had never met in person, Moore was "one of the truest and tenderest of friends, himself prone at times to despondency, as his letters show, yet never failing in his support and encouragement of others and all humane efforts, especially in the cause of 'the poor four-footed,' as he referred to the oppressed animals in the last message he ever wrote."

After Moore's death, some radical publications, including the various papers of the Industrial Workers of the World, began to excerpt his work, in particular *Savage Survivals*. Not long after his death, *Savage Survivals* and *Law of Biogenesis* were translated into Croatian, and *Savage Survivals* was later translated into Chinese. Despite his innovative, evolution-based rationale for extending ethics to all sentient beings and his contribution to humanitarian scholarship with the influential and compelling book, *The Universal Kinship,* Moore was largely overlooked until 1992, when Charles Magel

edited a new edition of *The Universal Kinship* that includes four of Moore's letters to Salt, Darrow's obituary, and a summary of the extant biographical information on Moore. Since then, Moore has been the subject of Greg Novak's 2004 dissertation, "Toward a Comprehensive Ethic," and has received brief profiles in reference titles on animal rights, but scant other attention.

J. Howard Moore was a sensitive creature who dedicated himself to ending the suffering of others in the world. His surrender to his own suffering was a tragic blow for the humanitarian cause and the animals he sought to protect. But Moore's message was ultimately hopeful. Because he concurred with Darwin's scientific theory of evolution, Moore believed that humans would be capable of evolving towards greater ethical treatment of their fellow sentient beings. The preface to *The Universal Kinship* closes with these words: "The time will come when the sentiments of these pages will not be hailed by two or three, and ridiculed or ignored by the rest; they will represent Public Opinion and Law" (*Universal Kinship*). Eventually, Moore believed, humankind would evolve to recognize the kinship of all beings, and the world would finally become a civilized and humane place. The recurring themes of Moore's works are today the foundation of the modern animal-rights movement.

References:

Roderick Frazier Nash, *The Rights of Nature: A History of Environmental Ethics* (Madison: University of Wisconsin Press, 1989);

Allen Ruff, *We Called Each Other Comrade: Charles H. Kerr and Company, Radical Publishers* (Urbana: University of Illinois Press, 1997);

Henry S. Salt, *Animals' Rights Considered in Relation to Social Progress* (New York: Macmillan, 1894);

Salt, *Company I Have Kept* (London: Allen & Unwin, 1930);

Kerry S. Walters and Lisa Portmess, eds., *Ethical Vegetarianism* (Albany: State University of New York Press, 1999).

Papers:

Letters of J. Howard Moore are in the Clarence Darrow Papers, Newberry Library, Chicago; May Walden Kerr Papers, Newberry Library; and his letters to Henry Salt are in the private collection of Blanche Chase and Mary Simonson, Chicago. Letters to Jennie Darrow Moore and at least one letter by J. Howard Moore are in the Karl Kelchner Darrow Papers, Neils Bohr Library, American Institute of Physics, College Park, Maryland.

Ralph Nader

(27 February 1934 –   )

Sarah Trachtenberg

BOOKS: *Unsafe at Any Speed; The Designed-in Dangers of the American Automobile* (New York: Grossman, 1965);

Vanishing Air: The Ralph Nader Study Group Report on Air Pollution, by Nader, John C. Esposito, and Larry J. Silverman (New York: Grossman, 1970);

The Interstate Commerce Omission: The Public Interest and the ICC; The Ralph Nader Study Group Report on the Interstate Commerce Commission and Transportation, by Nader and Robert C. Fellmeth (New York: Grossman, 1970);

Action for a Change: A Student's Manual for Public Interest Organizing, by Nader, Donald Ross, Brent English, and Joseph Highland (New York: Grossman, 1971);

Beware (New York: Law-Arts, 1971);

Water Wasteland; Ralph Nader's Study Group Report on Water Pollution, by Nader, David Zwick, and Marcy Benstock (New York: Grossman, 1971);

What to Do with Your Bad Car: An Action Manual for Lemon Owners, by Nader, Lowell Dodge, and Ralf Hotchkiss (New York: Grossman, 1971);

Whistle Blowing: The Report of the Conference on Professional Responsibility, by Nader, Peter J. Petkas, and Kate Blackwell (New York: Grossman, 1972);

Bitter Wages: Ralph Nader's Study Group Report on Disease and Injury on the Job, by Nader, Joseph A. Page, and Mary-Win O'Brien (New York: Grossman, 1973);

The Discarded Army: Veterans after Vietnam; The Nader Report on Vietnam Veterans and the Veterans' Administration, by Nader and Paul Starr, with assistance from James F. Henry and Raymond P. Bonner (New York: Charterhouse, 1973);

The Monopoly Makers; Ralph Nader's Study Group Report on Regulation and Competition, by Nader and Mark Green (New York: Grossman, 1973);

You and Your Pension (New York: Grossman, 1973);

Paper Plantation: Ralph Nader's Study Group Report on the Pulp and Paper Industry in Maine, by Nader and William C. Osborn (New York: Grossman, 1974);

Ralph Nader (from Kevin Graham, Ralph Nader: Battling for Democracy, *2000; Richland County Public Library)*

Working on the System: A Comprehensive Manual for Citizen Access to Federal Agencies, by Nader and James R. Michael (New York: Basic Books, 1974);

Environment Committees: A Study of the House and Senate Interior, Agriculture, and Science Committees, by Nader and Peter Schuck (New York: Grossman, 1975);

Revenue Committees: A Study of the House Ways & Means & Senate Finance Committees & the House & Senate Appropriations Committees (New York: Grossman, 1975);

Commerce Committees: A Study of the House & Senate Commerce Committees, by Nader and Schuck (New York: Grossman, 1975);

Judiciary Committees: A Study of the House and Senate Judiciary Committees, by Nader and Schuck (New York: Viking Penguin, 1975);

The Menace of Atomic Energy, by Nader and John Abbots (New York: Norton, 1977);

The Lemon Book: Auto Rights, by Nader, Clarence Ditlow, and Joyce Kinnard (Ottawa, Ill.: Caroline House, 1980);

Ralph Nader Presents a Citizens' Guide to Lobbying, by Nader and Marc Caplan (New York: Dembner, 1983);

The Big Boys: Power and Position in American Business, by Nader, William Taylor, and Andrew Moore (New York: Pantheon, 1986);

The Home Book: A Guide to Safety, Security, and Savings in the Home. Selected Readings, by Nader and Elizabeth Hax (Washington, D.C.: Center for Study of Responsive Law, 1989);

Winning the Insurance Game: The Complete Consumer's Guide to Saving Money, by Nader and Wesley J. Smith; foreword by J. Robert Hunter (New York: Knightsbridge, 1990);

Spices of Life: The Well-Being Handbook for Older Adults, by Nader and the Center for Study of Responsive Law (Washington, D.C.: Center for Study of Responsive Law, 1990);

The Stimulation Effect: Proceedings of a National Conference on the Uses of Government Procurement Leverage to Benefit Taxpayers, Consumers, and the Environment, May 23–24, 1988, Embassy Row Hotel, Washington, by Nader, Jessica Cowan, and Steven Gold (Washington, D.C.: Center for Study of Responsive Law, 1990);

Canada Firsts, by Nader, Nadia Millerton, and Duff Conacher (Toronto: McClelland & Stewart, 1992);

Frugal Shopper, by Nader and Smith (Washington, D.C.: Center for Study of Responsive Law, 1992);

The Case Against Free Trade: GATT, NAFTA, and the Globalization of Corporate Power, by Nader et al. (San Francisco: Earth Island, 1993);

Collision Course: The Truth About Airline Safety, by Nader and Smith (Blue Ridge Summit, Pa.: Tab, 1994);

Frugal Shopper Checklist Book (Washington, D.C.: Center for Study of Responsive Law, 1995);

No Contest: Corporate Lawyers and the Perversion of Justice in America, by Nader and Smith (New York: Random House, 1996);

Children First: A Parent's Guide to Fighting Corporate Predators (Washington, D.C.: Corporate Accountability Research Group, 1996);

Ralph Nader's Practicing Democracy 1997: A Guide to Student Action, by Nader and Katherine Isaac (New York: St. Martin's Press, 1997);

Cutting Corporate Welfare (New York: Seven Stories, 2000);

Crashing the Party: How to Tell the Truth and Still Run for President (New York: Thomas Dunne, 2002);

The Good Fight: Declare Your Independence & Close the Democracy Gap (New York: Regan, 2004);

Civic Arousal: Addressed to Citizens of America (New York: Regan, 2004).

Editions and Collections: *The Ralph Nader Reader* (New York: Seven Stories, 2000);

In Pursuit of Justice: Collected Writings 2000–2003 (New York: Seven Stories, 2004).

OTHER: "Ombudsman for State Governments," in *The Ombudsman: Civic Defender,* edited by Donald C. Rowat (London: Allen & Unwin, 1968);

Edward Finch Cox, Robert C. Fellmeth, and John E. Schulz, *The Nader Report on The Federal Trade Commission,* preface by Nader (New York: R.W. Baron, 1969);

James M. Fallows, *The Water Lords: Ralph Nader's Study Group Report on Industry and Environmental Crisis in Savannah, Georgia,* introduction by Nader (New York: Grossman, 1971);

Claire Townsend, *Old Age: The Last Segregation,* introduction by Nader (New York: Grossman, 1971);

Mark J. Green, Beverly C. Moore, Jr., and Bruce Wasserstein, *The Closed Enterprise System: Ralph Nader's Study Group Report on Antitrust Enforcement,* introduction by Nader (New York: Grossman, 1972);

Consumer and Corporate Accountability, edited by Nader and Jean Carper (New York: Harcourt Brace Jovanovich, 1973);

Corporate Power in America, edited by Nader and Green (New York: Grossman, 1973);

James Phelan and Robert Pozen, *The Company State,* introduction by Nader (New York: Grossman, 1973);

David Leinsdorf and Donald Etra, *Citibank: Ralph Nader's Study Group Report on First National City Bank,* foreword by Nader (New York: Grossman, 1973);

Donald K. Ross, *Public Citizen's Action Manual,* introduction by Nader (New York: Grossman, 1973);

Franklin D. Chu and Sharland Trotter, *The Madness Establishment: Ralph Nader's Study Group Report on the National Institute of Mental Health,* introduction by Nader (New York: Grossman, 1974);

Taming the Giant Corporation, edited by Nader, Green, and Joel Seligman (New York: Norton, 1976);

Verdicts on Lawyers, edited by Nader and Green (New York: Crowell, 1976);

Mark J. Green, *The Other Government: The Unseen Power of Washington Lawyers,* introduction by Nader (New York: Norton, 1978);

Green, *Who Runs Congress?* contribution by Ralph Nader and Bruce Rosenthal (New York: Bantam, 1979);

Who's Poisoning America: Corporate Polluters and Their Victims in the Chemical Age, edited by Nader, Ronald

Brownstein, and John Richards (San Francisco: Sierra Club, 1981);

Eating Clean: Food Safety and the Chemical Harvest, edited by Nader and Michael Fortun (Washington, D.C.: Center for Study of Responsive Law, 1982);

"The Consumer Movement Looks Ahead" in *Beyond Reagan: Alternatives for the '80s,* edited by Alan Gartner, Golin Greer, and Frank Riessman (New York: Harper & Row, 1984);

Carl J. Mayer and George A. Riley, *Public Domain, Private Dominion: A History of Public Mineral Policy in America,* introduction by Nader (San Francisco: Sierra Club, 1985);

Kelly Griffin, *More Action for Change,* introduction by Nader (New York: Dembner, 1987);

Francis Cerra Whittelsey, *Why Women Pay More: How to Avoid Marketplace Perils,* introduction by Nader (Washington, D.C.: Center for Study of Responsive Law, 1993);

Martin Teitel and Kimberly A. Watson, *Genetically Engineered Food: Changing the Nature of Nature: What You Need To Know To Protect Yourself, Your Family, and Our Planet,* foreword by Nader (Rochester, Vt.: Park Street, 1999);

Russell Mokhiber and Robert Weissman, *Corporate Predators: The Hunt for Mega-Profits and the Attack on Democracy,* introduction by Nader (Monroe, Me.: Common Courage, 1999).

SELECTED PERIODICAL PUBLICATIONS–UNCOLLECTED: "The Commonwealth Status of Puerto Rico," *Harvard Law Record* (13 December 1956);

"Legislative Neglect Keeps Migrant Workers Mired in Asiatic-Type Poverty," *Harvard Law Record* (10 April 1958);

"Do Third Parties Have A Chance?" *Harvard Law Record* (9 October 1958);

"The American Automobile–Designed for Death?" *Harvard Law Record* (11 December 1958);

"The Safe Car You Can't Buy," *Nation,* 188 (11 April 1959): 310–312;

"Business is Deserting America," *American Mercury,* 90 (March 1960): 25–28;

"Grand Old Man of the Law," *Reader's Digest* (February 1961): 163–168;

"Blue-Law Blues," *Nation,* 192 (10 June 1961): 499–500;

"An Answer to Administrative Abuse," *Harvard Law Record* (20 December 1962);

"An Ombudsman for the U.S.?" *Christian Science Monitor,* 1 April 1963, p. 18;

"Fashion or Safety: Detroit Makes Your Choice," *Nation,* 197 (12 October 1963): 214–215;

"Patent Laws Prime Sources to Secure Safety; Auto Design to Reduce Highway Deaths," *Trial* (January 1965);

"Profits vs. Engineering: The Corvair Story," *Nation,* 201 (1 November 1965): 295–300;

"Safer Cars: Time for Decision," *Consumer Reports* (April 1966): 194–197;

"Seven Safety Features Cars Need Most," *Science Digest* (August 1966): 75–79;

"Business Crime," *New Republic* (1 July 1967): 7–8;

"We're Still in the Jungle," *New Republic* (15 July 1967): 11–12;

"Inventions and Their Uses," *New Republic* (22 July 1967): 32–34;

"Watch that Hamburger," *New Republic* (19 August 1967): 15–16;

"X-Ray Exposures," *New Republic* (2 September 1967): 11–12;

"Automobile Design and the Judicial Process," *California Law Review,* 55 (1967);

"Something Fishy," *New Republic* (6 January 1968): 19–21;

"They're Still Breathing," *New Republic* (3 February 1968): 15;

"Lo, the Poor Indian," *New Republic* (30 March 1968): 14–15;

"Infernal, Eternal, Internal Combustion Engine," *New Republic* (27 April 1968): 7–8;

"Wake Up America, Unsafe X Rays," *Ladies' Home Journal,* 85 (May 1968): 126–127, 137;

"Safety on the Job," by Nader and Jerome Gordon, *New Republic* (15 June 1968): 23–25;

"Consumer Protection and Corporate Disclosure," *Business Today* (Autumn 1968);

"The Great American Gyp," *New York Review of Books* (21 November 1968);

"The Hidden Executives," *Business Today* (Winter 1968): 51;

"Protecting the Consumer; Toward a Just Economy," *Current* (December 1968): 15–24;

"Violence of Omission," *Nation,* 208 (10 February 1969): 166–167;

"The Distorted Priorities," *Business Today* (Spring 1969): 17;

"Corporate Crime," *Business Today* (Summer 1969): 48;

"Yes, It Is Safe to Fly, But Is It Safe to Crash?" *Holiday* (July 1969): 56–57, 93;

"Who Runs the GSA?" *Business Today* (Autumn 1969): 25;

"Crumbling of the Old Order: Law Schools and Law Firms," *New Republic* (11 October 1969): 20–23;

"Danger in Toyland," *Ladies' Home Journal,* 86 (November 1969): 80, 167–168, 170;

"Swiss Cheese," *New Republic* (22 November 1969): 11–12;

"Freedom from Information," *Harvard Law Review* (1 January 1970): 14;

"Yablonski's Unfinished Business," *Nation*, 210 (26 January 1970): 70–71;

"Why They Should Tell You the Octane Rating of the Gasoline You Buy," *Popular Science*, 196 (April 1970): 54–55;

"The Profits in Pollution," *Progressive* (April 1970): 19–22;

"The Corporate Colleges," *Business Today* (Summer 1970): 61;

"Micro-Tyrannies," *Business Today* (Autumn 1970): 24;

"The Professional Responsibilities of a Professional Society," *American Institute of Planners Newsletter* (November 1970);

"Ralph Nader's Most Shocking Exposé," *Ladies' Home Journal*, 88 (March 1971): 98, 176–179;

"Brown Lung: The Cotton-Mill Killer," *Nation*, 212 (15 March 1971): 335–337;

"The Dossier Invades the Home," *Saturday Review* (17 April 1971);

"The Professional Responsibility of Executives," *Newsletter of the Association of Master of Business Administration Executives* (May 1971);

"The Burned Children: 4000 Fatal Fabric Fires," *New Republic* (3 July 1971): 19–21;

"We Need a New Kind of Patriotism," *Life*, 71 (9 July 1971): 4;

"Making Congress Work," *New Republic* (21 August 1971): 19–21;

"A Citizen's Guide to the American Economy," *New York Review of Books*, 17 (2 September 1971);

"Deceptive Package–Nixon's Economic Sales Pitch," *New Republic* (4 September 1971): 15–17;

"In the Public Interest: Student Activists," *New Republic* (19 February 1972): 10–11;

"In the Public Interest: The Property-Tax Gyp," *New Republic* (4 March 1972): 11–12;

"In the Public Interest: Chartering Corporations," *New Republic* (11 March 1972): 9;

"Don't Eat That Dog," *New Republic* (18 March 1972): 12–13;

"What Do You Drink?" *New Republic* (8 April 1972): 8–9;

"Freezing Consumers," *New Republic* (15 April 1972): 12–13;

"Coddling Corporations: Crime in the Suites," by Nader and Green, *New Republic* (29 April 1972): 17–21;

"In the Public Interest: Falling-Apart Houses," (27 May 1972): 11;

"Paying to Be Heard," by Nader, David Sanford, Eliot Marshall, and Leah Young, *New Republic* (19 August 1972): 8;

"Nader and No-Fault," *New Republic* (9 September 1972): 13–14;

"Tainted Meat," *New Republic* (2 December 1972): 9–10;

"Brighteners," *New Republic* (27 January 1973): 14;

"Thalidomide Children," *New Republic* (10 February 1973): 10–11;

"GM's Mind Pollution," *New Republic* (3 March 1973): 9;

"I Think I Can't . . . " *New Republic* (10 March 1973): 10–11;

"The Light That Fails," *New Republic* (17 March 1973): 12–13;

"It's a Gas," *New Republic* (12 May 1973): 16–17;

"The Car in Your Future," *New Republic* (19 May 1973): 11–12;

"Uncollected Taxes," *New Republic* (6 October 1973): 10–11;

"Who Rules the Giant Corporation?" by Nader, Green, and Seligman, *Business and Society Review* (Summer 1976): 40–48;

"How to Recognize Capitalists and Corporatists," *Washington Star* (14 January 1978);

"Is Bigness Bad for Business?" by Nader and Green, *Business and Society Review* (Summer 1979): 20–24;

"Corporate Power in America," *Nation*, 230 (29 March 1980): 365–367;

"Reforming Corporate Governance," *California Management Review*, 26 (Summer 1984): 126–133;

"Must Candidates Avoid Free TV?" *New York Times*, 8 October 1984, p. A19;

"Knowledge Helps Citizens, Secrecy Helps Bureaucrats," *New Statesman* (10 January 1986): 12–13;

"Nader's Favors," *New Republic* (10 February 1986): 6;

"Let's Put the Audience on the Air," *Chicago Tribune*, 27 May 1987, p. 11;

"Corporations Are Not Persons," by Nader and Carl J. Mayer, *New York Times*, 9 April 1988, p. 31;

"The Assault on Injured Victims' Rights," *Denver University Law Review: Tort Reform Symposium Issue*, 64 (1988);

"Run the Government Like the Best American Corporations," *Harvard Business Review*, 66 (November/December 1988): 81–87;

"Corporate Welfare State Is on a Roll," *Los Angeles Times*, 5 March 1990, p. B7;

"Uncle Sam's Corporate Lawyers," by Nader and Wesley Smith, *Washington Monthly* (May 1990): 26–27;

"How to Put the Punch Back in Politics," *Mother Jones*, 15 (July/August 1990): 24–27;

"No More Bailouts!" *Mother Jones*, 15 (September/October 1990): 22–23;

"Leadership and the Law," *Hofstra Law Review* (Spring 1991);

"Rip-Off, Inc." *Mother Jones,* 16 (May/June 1991): 16–17;

"Off-Track," by Nader and Michael Waldman, *New Republic* (3 June 1991): 15–17;

"Children: Toward Their Civic Skills and Civic Involvement," *Social Education,* 56 (April/May 1992): 212–214;

"Breaking out of the Two-Party Rut," *Nation,* 255 (20–27 July 1992): 98–101;

"How Clinton Can Build Democracy," *Nation,* 255 (30 November 1992): 649;

"Looting the Medicine Chest: How Bristol-Myers Squibb Made Off with the Public's Cancer Research," by Nader and James Love, *Progressive* (February 1993): 26–28;

"Democratic Revolution in an Age of Autocracy," *Boston Review* (March/April 1993);

"NAFTA vs. Democracy," *Multinational Monitor* (October 1993);

"A Pull-Down Trade Agreement: Global Corporations Push WTO Declaration of Independence," *Charleston Gazette,* 18 July 1994: p. 5A;

"WTO Means Rule by Unaccountable Tribunals," *Wall Street Journal,* 17 August 1994, P. A12;

"Trade in Secrets," *Washington Post,* 6 October 1994, A31;

"Reject This Flawed Treaty," *USA Today,* 22 November 1994, p. A10;

"Beware the History Books," *Progressive* (April 1995): 26–27;

"Tort 'Reform' Would Aid Wrongdoers," *San Francisco Examiner,* 21 April 1995;

"Bank Mergers Skip Along, Right Past the Customers," *New York Times,* 12 November 1995, p. F11;

"Ralph Nader on Tort Reform," *Legal Times* (1995);

"U.S. Companies Should Pledge Allegiance," *Washington Times,* 4 June 1996;

"The Greens and the Presidency: A Voice, not an Echo," *Nation,* 263 (8 July 1996): 18–19;

"TV News Failing in Its Mission," *Charleston Gazette,* 23 August 1996, p. P5A;

"It's Time to End Corporate Welfare As We Know It," *Earth Island Journal* (Fall 1996);

"Perspective on the Presidential Race: A Way out of the Corporatist Grip," *Los Angeles Times,* 29 October 1996, p. B7;

"Digital Democracy in Action," *Forbes,* 158 (2 December 1996): 48;

"Opinion," *Student Lawyer* (December 1997);

"A Response to Robert W. McChesney's Proposals for Media Reform," *Boston Review* (Summer 1998);

"Why Microsoft Must Be Stopped," by Nader and Love, *Computer World* (9 November 1998): 33;

"Supersonic Brain Shredder," *Forbes* (30 November 1998);

"Overcoming the Oligarchy," *Progressive* (January 1999): 58;

"Socialism for the Rich," *New York Times,* 15 May 1999, p. A17;

"Microradio Opening the Airwaves for More Democracy," *Albany Times Union,* 17 July 1999, p. A7;

"Perspectives on Federal Spending: Build On, Repair What We Have," *Los Angeles Times,* 27 July 1999, p. 7;

"Unsafe at Any Altitude," *Conde Nast Traveler* (September 1999): 122–126;

"Banking Jackpot," *Washington Post,* 5 November 1999, p. A33;

"Toughen up the Rules of the Sky," by Nader and Paul Hudson, *New York Times,* 6 November 1999, p. A17;

"Judging Microsoft: It's a Blow to Real Monopoly," by Nader and Love, *New York Daily News,* 9 November 1999, p. 33;

"The Democrats Bow to the Megabanks," *Progressive* (January 2000): 24;

"Public Is Not Served by Media's Refusal to Ask Specific Questions," *Knight Ridder/Tribune News Service* (1 February 2000);

"Medicare Nightmare," *San Francisco Bay Guardian,* 25 July 2001;

"Adding Insult to Injury," *San Francisco Bay Guardian,* 1 August 2001;

"Playing with Numbers," *San Francisco Bay Guardian,* 8 August 2001;

"Organizing the People: The One Sure Way to Defeat Enronism," *American Prospect* (25 March 2002): 18–19;

"After Enron," *Progressive* (March 2002): 18;

"Corporate Socialism Thursday," *Washington Post,* 18 July 2002, p. A29;

"Make the Recall Count," *Los Angeles Times,* 12 August 2003, p. B15.

The leading consumer-rights advocate in the United States, Ralph Nader first achieved fame when he drew attention to negligence and irresponsibility in the automotive industry. More recently he has attracted the public's attention by running for president of the United States outside the two-party system. Consistently he has spearheaded health, safety, and consumer movements since the beginning of his career, focusing on issues as diverse as air pollution, the beauty industry, and medication for people living with AIDS. *Time* magazine, which numbered Nader among the one hun-

Nader testifying on automobile safety before the Senate Government Operations Subcommittee, 22 March 1966 (from Nancy Bowen, Ralph Nader: Man with a Mission, 2002; Richland County Public Library)

dred most influential Americans of the twentieth century, called him "America's toughest customer."

Ralph Nader was born on 27 February 1934 in Winsted, Connecticut. The youngest of four children, he had one brother, Shafeek, and two sisters, Laura and Claire. His parents, Nathra and Rose Nader, emigrated from Lebanon, and their children grew up speaking both English and Arabic. Nathra Nader, who had to support his family from a young age owing to his father's death, came to the United States in 1912; he went back to Lebanon to marry Rose Bouziane, a teacher, in 1924, and returned to the United States with his wife. The couple owned a bakery and restaurant and were concerned with the duties of citizens in a democracy, instilling in their youngest son an interest in justice and the law; he set a goal for himself to be a lawyer for the people and a "full-time citizen."

The family had frequent political discussions at the dinner table and embraced the idea that one person can cause social change. Outside his family, Nader recalls that his early influences included muckraking books such as Upton Sinclair's *The Jungle* (1906), an exposé of the meatpacking industry and the conditions in which its employees worked, and Ida Tarbell's *The History of the Standard Oil Company* (1904), about corruption and monopoly in the early days of the oil industry. He was also influenced by Stuart Chase's *Your Money's Worth* (1927), about testing advertising claims, Helen Keller's autobiography (1903), and F. J. Schlink and

Arthur Kallet's *100,000,000 Guinea Pigs: Dangers in Everyday Foods, Drugs and Cosmetics* (1933), a book that gave rise to Consumers Union, publishers of the magazine *Consumer Reports*.

As a child Ralph Nader was studious; he listened to court hearings as a youngster and pored over the *Congressional Record* in high school. After graduating with honors from the Gilbert School in Winsted, Connecticut in 1951, he attended Princeton University, majoring in Far East politics and languages (primarily Russian and Chinese). He entered Princeton's Woodrow Wilson School of International Affairs during his sophomore year, majoring in government and economics. He traveled to Lebanon to research his paper "Some of the Problems in the Economic Development of Lebanon."

As an undergraduate Nader initiated what he later considered his first major undertaking: a campaign to ban campus use of the pesticide DDT, which he realized was killing birds. His crusade met with skepticism from his fellow students, who reasoned that if the chemical were dangerous the faculty would have mentioned it. This incident taught Nader a valuable lesson about how average citizens blindly trust bureaucracy to protect them and thus fail to ask questions. Another pivotal college experience occurred when hitchhiking (one of his frugalities). Nader witnessed several car accidents, including one in which an infant was gruesomely injured due to a faulty glove-compartment door. This memory spurred his auto safety campaign. Nader graduated from Princeton magna cum laude in 1955 and was elected to Phi Beta Kappa. Although his professors urged him to earn a doctoral degree, Nader had not forgotten his dream of being a "people's lawyer" and went to law school.

Upon entering Harvard Law School in 1955, Nader joined the staff of *The Record,* the school's independent newspaper, where his first byline appeared on a piece criticizing capital punishment. He was later elected editor-in-chief of *The Record* and encouraged investigative journalism, until his peers voted him down. Nader was not a model student in law school; he tested the boundaries of acceptability by skipping class or, in one case, attending class wearing a bathrobe. The summer after his first year, he visited Native American reservations in the West, inspired in part by his sister Laura, an anthropologist specializing in Native American culture. He wrote in *The Record* about his experiences visiting the reservations and described the shock he felt at the exploitative conditions, for which his sister's experience had not prepared him. In 1955 Nader's interest was sparked by an article classmate Harold Katz wrote "Liability of Automobile Manufacturers for Unsafe Design of Passenger Cars," in the *Harvard Law Review,* which Nader later edited. Nader spent his last year in law school studying auto safety and wrote his final paper for a course on the topic. He graduated with honors in 1958, served in the U.S. Army Reserve for six months as a cook, and in 1959 set up his own small legal practice in Hartford, Connecticut. Owing to his writing and research projects he never took a case.

During the next two decades Nader did not directly participate in the civil rights or peace movements because other people of political significance were involved with those causes, whereas very few progressives at that time focused on the safety of everyday life. As he later pointed out, unsafe automobiles killed more people than the war in Vietnam. When a critic mentioned his lack of involvement in civil rights, Nader responded: "What is more intimately involved with civil rights and poverty than the invisible violence of the corporations? Who do you think gets cheated, diseased, crippled and generally screwed if not the minorities and the poor?" *(Citizen Nader)*.

Writing for *The Nation,* a magazine dedicated to challenging political and social problems and promoting what the editors call "unconventional wisdom," he published an article in April 1959 analyzing unsafe practices in the automotive industry, called "The Safe Car You Can't Buy." He argued there that the U.S. automobile industry designed cars with appearance and marketing in mind while neglecting safety features. The article caught the attention of Senator and Assistant Labor Secretary Daniel Moynihan. The senator concurred with Nader that Katz's earlier stance had been correct: auto accidents were attributable not solely to driver error, but often to design flaws in cars. Moynihan soon published a similar article, "Epidemic on the Highways," in *The Reporter* (1959).

In 1961 Nader traveled to Scandinavia to learn more about the ombudsman system. From 1961 to 1963 he lectured at the University of Hartford on government and history. He also traveled during those years as a freelance journalist, going to places such as the U.S.S.R., Latin America, Europe, and Africa. He wrote for *The Atlantic Monthly,* the *Christian Science Monitor,* and *Reader's Digest.* In 1963 Nader hitchhiked to Washington, D.C., where he took a consulting job with the U.S. Department of Labor, did freelance writing, and worked as an unpaid adviser to Senator Abraham Ribicoff's subcommittee on safety standards in the automotive industry. Senator Moynihan invited Nader to join his planning staff in 1964 to work on highway safety policies. In 1965 after thorough research, Nader completed "A Report on the Context, Condition, and Recommended Direction of Federal Activity in Highway Safety." His suggestion to create a federal highway transportation agency was implemented, and his first book, *Unsafe at Any Speed: The Designed-in Dangers of the*

American Automobile (1965), followed. Disgruntled former employees of the industry proved to be his best sources. Few mainstream publications agreed to review the book for fear of alienating their automobile advertisers. Nevertheless, the book became a best-seller and radically changed industry regulation.

Former Ford Motor Company president Robert MacNamara had proven in a company analysis a decade earlier that automobile fatalities could be significantly reduced through the use of seat belts and other safer-design features such as padded dashboards. Still, many consumers and automobile manufacturers considered seat belts and safety features optional. *Unsafe at Any Speed* confronted the automobile industry about its products and brought large-scale attention to the issue for the first time in America. The Chevrolet Corvair, the car most criticized in *Unsafe at Any Speed,* provided a prime example of unsafe characteristics engineered into the design of a car for the sake of style and marketability. Nader's criticism of the Corvair centered on such limitations as its suspension system, which demanded a very specific tire pressure to insure the car's stability. He called the Corvair "one of the greatest acts of industrial irresponsibility in the present century" *(Citizen Nader).* In 1966 Nader won a special citation in journalism from the Nieman Fellows at Harvard Award for his book.

General Motors (GM), the main target of *Unsafe at Any Speed,* first tried to quiet Nader by offering him a job, thereby allowing him to change things from the inside; he saw this as a bribe and refused. GM fought back in public-relations arenas, maintaining that drivers, not automotive design, caused most car accidents, or at least that its own cars were no less safe than those of other manufacturers. In an era when corporations were unaccustomed to criticism, GM went to great lengths to discredit Nader, intimidating him, having him followed and even going as far as hiring women to try to seduce him in order to provide GM with blackmail material. They especially investigated his private life. Nader believed that he was under surveillance, but his friends told him he was paranoid. Journalist James Ridgeway, another investigator of auto safety design, exposed GM's corruption and its investigation of Nader in *New Republic.* Following the article's publication, Nader sued GM in 1966 for invasion of privacy and won a settlement. He used the money to fund consumer groups.

Nader testified in the 1966 hearing resulting from *Unsafe at Any Speed* before the Senate Subcommittee on Executive Reorganization of the Committee on Government Operations. During a televised hearing, GM chief executive officer James Roche publicly apologized for harassing and following Nader. The hearing propelled Nader to the status of folk hero and *Unsafe at Any*

Speed to the top of best-seller lists. The incident was hailed as a David-and-Goliath story and inspired activists around the country. The automotive industry reshaped the safety features of its products. In 1966, President Lyndon Johnson regulated automobile design by signing the National Traffic and Motor Vehicle Safety Act, which reduced the automobile industry's discretion about the safe design of its products.

Fresh from the success of *Unsafe at Any Speed,* Nader set out to expose other issues of consumer safety and corporate neglect. Between 1966 and 1969, based on research he referred to as "documenting . . . intuitions," Nader's work helped apprehend perpetrators of unsafe practices in the meatpacking industry, coal mines, natural gas, and other industries. In 1967, he wrote and published articles in the *New Republic* about the meatpacking industry's lack of safety standards, "Watch That Hamburger" and "We're Still in the Jungle." The publicity these articles generated initiated tougher legislation, including the Wholesome Meat Act of 1967 and the Wholesome Poultry Act of 1968. The Wholesome Meat Act regulated labeling as well as many health and hygiene issues involved in meat processing, including cleanliness of the workers, facilities, and equipment. It was the first new legislation regulating meat processing since the 1907 Federal Meat Inspection Act that followed upon publication of *The Jungle.* The 1967 act surpassed existing legislation in that it governed meat sold within the state of processing, whereas the 1907 act applied only to meat sold across state lines. During the process leading up to the passage of the Wholesome Meat Act, Aled P. Davies, vice president of the American Meat Institute, who represented his industry, spoke for many of Nader's frustrated opponents when he said of Nader, "there's no point in taking him on when he's right" *(Citizen Nader).*

Nader stopped eating hot dogs and prefabricated lunch meat after his research into the meatpacking industry. Known for practicing what he preached, he also stopped smoking because he acknowledged the link between tobacco consumption and cancer. He had sold the only car he ever owned while he was a student, believing that car ownership had gotten out of hand. He never bought another car, as he thought people would interpret his action as an endorsement.

Beginning in 1967 Nader wrote extensively for the *New Republic,* strategically timing his articles to coincide with upcoming legislation or hearings. In general, he tried to ignite the interest of other journalists in issues he believed were being ignored. In 1967 the U.S. Junior Chamber of Commerce named Nader as one of the ten most outstanding young men of the year. That same year he returned to lecture at Princeton University. Nader's *New Republic* article, "X-Ray Exposures"

(1967), addressed different standards of X-ray technology then in use for Caucasian and African American patients. He found that typically the latter received twice the dosage based on the misguided theory that stronger rays were needed to penetrate darker skin and that the stronger rays caused health repercussions. Although the American Dental Association denied these allegations, Nader and other reporters presented the case to Congress, which passed the Radiation Control for Health and Safety Act of 1968 in response.

In 1968 the cover of *Newsweek* featured Nader depicted in a suit of armor. He founded a team of lawyers and researchers, the Center for Study of Responsive Law, to study and expose negligence, corruption, abuse, and other hazards in industry and corporations. He also became the editor of a new muckraking magazine, *Mayday,* started by Ridgeway. The research group took Nader's concerns into new lines of inquiry. It began that year to investigate the Federal Trade Commission (FTC), a bureaucracy founded in 1914 to protect the rights of consumers. FTC representatives became elusive when the young lawyers questioned them and released information only when researchers threatened to sue them under the Freedom of Information Act. FTC chairman Paul Rand Dixon physically threw Nader associate John Schulz out of his office when Dixon found the interviewer's questions too intrusive. In the resulting 1968 hearing, Nader's team testified. Senator Ribicoff praised Nader and the other authors for uncovering corruption in the FTC, which the press had failed to do. The American Bar Association launched its own investigation of the FTC with similar findings. The FTC was revamped as a result of the attention, and President Nixon replaced Dixon with Caspar Weinberger.

Returning to a concern he had first addressed in a 1966 speech to the American Society of Safety Engineers, Nader testified before a subcommittee in 1968 on natural-gas pipeline safety after a rupture in a Louisiana pipeline caused the deaths of seventeen people. This investigation culminated in the passage of the Natural Gas Pipeline Safety Act of 1968 to correct the hazards of dangerous and out-of-date pipelines. As often happened when his activism contributed to legislation, Nader was dissatisfied with the act. It did not carry criminal charges for those responsible, or those who broke the provisions of the act, whom he believed guilty of homicide by negligence. He noted that representatives of the industry in question dominated the committee set up to enforce the act, a criticism of U.S. enforcement mechanisms he repeated throughout his career.

By 1969 many young crusaders sought work as part of the research group journalist William Greider called "Nader's Raiders." The term proved popular, although Nader himself thought it belittling. Many of the young lawyers on his team were Caucasians who had been squeezed out of the Civil Rights Movement. Nader selected about two hundred young lawyers and law students out of thousands of applicants from prestigious programs, and they saw themselves as truly making a difference. Raider Mark Green said, "Where else could a guy my age have the impact I have?" *(Nader: the People's Lawyer)*. Due to modest funding of his research, Nader was not able to pay his researchers, but he gave them leadership opportunities and rewarded them with bylines and the ability to develop reputations and expertise. Most were genuinely concerned with the causes, and their devotion to public service through research inspired them to join with Nader in launching broad-spectrum attacks on corruption in government, unsafe conditions of everyday life, and environmental dangers including workplace safety.

Also in 1969 Nader continued the research he had begun with the X-ray studies; this time he investigated faulty hospital equipment and found that an average of twelve thousand patients annually were electrocuted in hospital accidents. He petitioned to ban tobacco smoking on commercial flights. Nader subsequently played an integral role in founding the Environmental Protection Agency, the Occupational Safety and Health Administration, and the Consumer Product Safety Commission.

In 1969 members of the United Mine Workers of America (UMWA) met with Nader to discuss failings and corruption in their industry. Dozens of workers had been killed in an accident, and UMWA leader Tony Boyle responded by praising the company's safety record. Nader had already denounced the UMWA for gross lack of responsibility. With his help, one of the complainants, Joseph Yablonski, agreed to run for head of the union. Nader's assistance proved no match for corruption in this case. Due to fraud, Yablonski lost the election to Boyle; Yablonski was then murdered along with his family after he called for an investigation of the election.

In 1970 Green joined Nader in launching the Nader Study Group on Antitrust Law Enforcement. Robert Fellmeth and other Raiders investigated the Interstate Commerce Commission (ICC) set up by Congress to protect public interest in transportation. They produced the report, *The Interstate Commerce Omission: The Public Interest and the ICC* (1970), with a foreword by Nader, and accused the ICC of favoring the transportation industry's interests above those of the public. They alleged that bribes were common. *Vanishing Air* (1970), by John Esposito and Larry Silverman, attacked corporate pollution and the complicity of cor-

rupt politicians. In the foreword Nader accused Senator Edward Muskie of Maine of acting on behalf of industry. Senator Muskie chaired the Subcommittee on Air and Water Pollution and authored the Air Quality Act of 1967. The press did not think Nader's team had made a wise decision in attacking one of its best allies in Congress. *Vanishing Air* received mostly negative attention, as critics viewed its authors as antagonistic and extreme. Muskie and his staff wrote a rebuttal, and even Nader admitted the report might have gone too far. He defended the accuracy of Esposito and Silverman's work, but tried to distance himself from the negative press. Similarly, many viewed Nader as an overly harsh critic when, in 1970, he berated his former ally, Senator Ribicoff, for watering down a consumer-rights bill. Congress and Nader became disenchanted with each other as a result of such incidents.

While Nader involved himself in many causes, auto safety became a permanent point of identification for him. He could not be pacified by legislation and other measures that did not measure up to his standards. He tended to see issues in rigid terms and viewed with distaste the compromises so common in Congress because he felt they diluted the effectiveness of legislation. He received some vindication when, after a huge decline in sales, GM took the Corvair off the market in 1969, and a study by the Highway Safety Research Center of the University of North Carolina confirmed Nader's *Unsafe at Any Speed* findings in 1971. Continuing the fight for auto safety, Nader in 1970 set up a non-profit organization called the Center for Auto Safety. He also contributed to another book on the subject: *What To Do with Your Bad Car: An Action Manual for Lemon Owners* by Lowell Dodge and Ralf Hotchkiss (1971). *What To Do with Your Bad Car* published letters of complaint from disgruntled car owners as well as interviews with engineers and mechanics; it gave advice on how to pressure dealers and manufacturers after the unwitting purchase of a bad car. The book achieved commercial success but was not highly regarded.

Still, Nader's vision remained broad. He established the group Public Citizen in 1971 to reform the political system, specifically the two-party system in American politics and the dependence of Democratic and Republican candidates on large donations to their parties from wealthy individuals. Public Citizen also supported political reform with regard to consumer rights, public health and safety, and other causes. In 1971 he founded the Aviation Consumer Action Project. He confronted the textile industry for its unsafe working environments, citing the high incidence of brown lung among its employees in his article "Brown Lung: The Cotton-Mill Killer" *(The Nation,* March 1971). One of Nader's researchers, James Turner, pub-

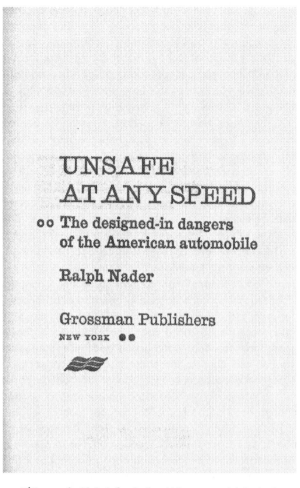

Title page for Nader's first book, which won a special citation in journalism from the Nieman Fellows at Harvard (Richland County Public Library)

lished *The Chemical Feast* (1971), exposing negligence in the Food and Drug Administration (FDA) and finding most advertised foods it approved unwholesome. Turner wrote that FDA directors' interests in the drug industry made unbiased decisions impossible and thereby rendered consumers vulnerable. The book was a best-seller, and *Time* magazine observed that it might be the "most devastating critique of a U.S. government agency ever issued" (*Time,* "Up Against the Wall, FDA!," 20 April 1970). *Politics of Land* (1971) by Robert C. Fellmeth first tackled the issue of corporate consumption of land in California at the taxpayers' expense. In the same year Nader wrote *Beware,* about consumer protection, accidents, and prevention. He received the Max Berg Award from the David and Minnie Berg Foundation, honoring those who made a significant contribution to the quality of human life. The award was named for David Berg's brother, a World War II hero who saved Jews from concentration camps.

Gore Vidal wrote an article for *Esquire* magazine in June 1971 recommending Nader for president.

In 1971 Nader founded the Corporate Accountability Research Group, directed by Mark Green, to investigate antitrust legislation and how it was affected by corporate power. Research for *Water Wasteland,* by Raiders David Zwick and Marcy Benstock (1971) took the authors to some of the most polluted bodies of water in America, and again placed Nader in the position of seeming to antagonize Senator Muskie. Brandywine Creek in Indiana and Maine's Androscoggin River (near Senator Muskie's home) provided the case studies that allowed Zwick and Benstock to expose the industries responsible for dumping pollutants—namely the Oxford Paper Company of Rumford, Maine—enumerate the health risks involved, and detail the lack of response from the government body responsible for oversight, in this case the Federal Water Quality Office. *Water Wasteland* suggested further legislation, but critics responded that the states lacked sufficient financial resources to address the problem. Zwick drafted the bill that became the Clean Water Act, passed in 1972, creating standards of cleanliness and regulating but not eliminating water pollution.

Other Nader-sponsored research reports of the early 1970s include an exposé of the maltreatment of the elderly and of corruption in geriatric care in *Old Age: The Last Segregation* by Claire Townsend (1971) and *Citibank: Ralph Nader's Study Group Report on First National City Bank* by David Leinsdorf and Donald Etra (1973). Nader recruited Townsend from an unlikely source: Miss Porter's School in Farmington, Connecticut, a finishing school for girls from wealthy families whose graduates included Jacqueline Bouvier Kennedy. The publications of Nader-sponsored researchers took on significance because investigative journalism was uncommon at the time, and that not sponsored by Nader did not delve into consumers' rights or safety. Nader tried to set the example that one person could make a difference.

In 1971, Nader's projects developed in a different direction when he co-wrote with Donald Ross *Action for a Change: A Student's Manual for Public Interest Organizing.* They sought to teach students how to form Public Interest Research Groups (PIRGs) and to instruct students on activism. Nader wrote that enough people, resources, and potential existed to bring about social change; the only problem was a lack of awareness about how to organize effectively. Many people wanted to be active in areas such as pollution and consumer injustice, but did not know how to do it. Donald Ross, one of the Raiders, was an expert in the field of student activism, and he and Nader forged the idea of suggesting that students hire professional activism coaches.

The idea first caught on in 1970 at a University of Oregon campus, when Nader and Ross traveled across the country implementing their ideas for campus activism. *Action for Change* resulted from their experiments. Nader wrote that such a manual could probably not have been written earlier, before injustice became so visible that people began to organize in large numbers.

In 1972 Nader sponsored research on the dangerous consequences of using agricultural pesticides; the result was *Sowing the Wind,* by Harrison Wellford. Nader's associates examined the bureaucratic mismanagement of the mental health care system in *The Madness Establishment,* by Franklin D. Chu and Sharland Trotter. After Nader drew attention to the railroad system's routine practice of dumping human excrement on the tracks, the Food and Drug Administration banned the practice in 1972. By this point, Nader and his researchers had completed seventeen books. *Who Runs Congress?* by Mark Green and Michael Calabrese reported findings of the Congress Project, which Nader launched to investigate the 484 members of Congress up for re-election. Although it made the best-seller lists, many critics thought it poorly researched and flawed.

Nader declined to be Democrat George McGovern's running mate in the 1972 presidential election. The New Party asked the activist to run for the office of president. *New Republic* honored Nader in 1972 with its Public Defender Award. As of that year, although he was famous, Nader never commanded more than $150 for an article he wrote for *The New Republic* and often wrote free of charge for a wide array of publications. Nader generally tailors his fee for articles and speeches to what the sponsor can afford. For example, he contributed his column free of charge to the magazine *Business Today,* run by students from Princeton.

Green also spearheaded the research of the 1972 book *The Closed Enterprise System* about antitrust law enforcement. The research group found that antitrust law was not well enforced and recommended forming a new agency for antitrust issues, but to no effect. Nonetheless the book reached number one on the *New York Times* best-seller list. In 1973 Nader established the organization Congress Watch, a consumer-interests watchdog. Nader and Green collaborated closely on many organizations and publications focusing on antitrust laws and corporate responsibility: the books *The Monopoly Makers* (1973) and *Corporate Power in America* (edited by Nader and Green, 1973), a collection of essays about business abuses; the article "Who Rules the Giant Corporation" in *Business and Society Review* (1976); and *Taming the Giant Corporation: How the Largest Corporations Control Our Lives* (with co-author Joel Seligman, 1976), a development from "Who Rules the Giant Corporation" in which they proposed a consumers' and citizens' bill

of rights on the grounds that the government did not always step in to protect citizens. They recommended, among other reforms, to have federal instead of state-regulated corporations. Many readers considered this bold, unprecedented proposal too radical. The corporate world in particular likened Nader's proposals to fascism. Popular interest in Nader continued, however, and inspired two book-length debunkings: Ralph de Toledano's book, *Hit and Run: The Rise—and Fall?—of Ralph Nader* (1975), and former Raider David Sanford's *Me and Ralph: Is Nader Unsafe for America?* (1976), depicted Nader as just another politician with an agenda.

Nader returned to the issue of public land and development in his contribution to Peter Gruenstein and John Hanrahan's *Lost Frontier: The Marketing of Alaska* (1977). In the introduction, he writes:

> The choices of economic development are choices of the kind of society that will evolve. . . . Pipelines have impacts on the wilderness and the cities, on alcoholism and welfare, on corruption and inflation, as any boom-to-bust project would produce . . . fisheries might mean small business. Agriculture means numerous farmholders; minerals mean a few multinational corporations *(Lost Frontier)*.

Lost Frontier depicted Alaska as one of the most valuable parts of the United States. The authors discuss geological resources such as oil and coal, as well as the environmental and social consequences of tapping those resources. On such large-scale issues Nader did not find liberal administrations any more satisfying than the previous ones. In 1977 Nader campaigned for the Consumer Protection Agency and blamed President Jimmy Carter for the bill's defeat in 1978.

More than once in the mid to late 1970s, Nader approached mainstream audiences through popular culture, with varying success. He hosted the edgy *Saturday Night Live* (*SNL*) in 1977, using the forum to air his criticisms of the policies of Jimmy Carter, the president-elect of the United States, particularly his energy plan. Nader's new action group, Fight to Advance the Nation's Sports (FANS), opened in 1978 in *Playboy* magazine with the article "Fans: the Sorry Majority," by Nader and Peter Gruenstein, proposing a fans' bill of rights, citing grievances such as overpriced tickets and poor facilities. FANS became a laughing matter and faded into obscurity. Nader hosted *SNL* several more times over the years and made numerous television appearances including *The Oprah Winfrey Show* and *The Phil Donahue Show,* as well as children's programs such as *Sesame Street.*

Beginning with President Ronald Reagan's administration in 1980, Nader and his colleagues in the organizations he had founded began to come under attack. When the administration weakened the Occupational Health and Safety Act (OSHA), undermining legislation for which Nader lobbied in 1970, Nader sued in *Public Citizen Health Research Group v. Tyson*. In 1988 Public Citizen was successful in imposing higher standards in OSHA with regard to cancer-causing chemicals. Nader revisited the subject of auto safety in *The Lemon Book: Auto Rights* (1980). *The Lemon Book* served as a manual for car owners and included advice on buying, driving, maintenance, and consumer awareness. This book instigated state lemon laws. The second edition of the book took note of these changes, and in the third, Nader's introduction recommends new legislation. Nader's later allegations against the industry included the arguments that Volkswagens, and small cars in general, could not withstand impacts well, and that used Volkswagens were being reconditioned and sold as new cars.

In 1982 he founded Essential Information, which encouraged citizenship and activism on a grassroots level; Trial Lawyers for Public Justice; and, in 1983, Buyers Up, a Washington, D.C. organization of heating-oil customers seeking price controls. In 1984 Nader presented his views on the Reagan administration to the National Press Club in Washington. In the address, "The Megacorporate World of Ronald Reagan" he declared that the president was "building a government of the Exxons, by the General Motors, and for the DuPonts" *(Ralph Nader Reader)*. Reagan's policies, in short, opposed Nader's own objective of limiting corporate influence on the government and putting more power in the hands of ordinary citizens. In the 1980s, Nader and his team focused more on the desirability of Americans controlling their resources, particularly those collectively owned, because they were paid for by taxes. The theme of destruction of taxpayer-owned land for the benefit of private business came up again in a book Nader sponsored, *Public Domain, Private Dominion: A History of Public Mineral Policy in America* (1985), by Carl J. Mayer and George A. Riley. Nader wrote in the book's introduction that institutions constructed to protect America's land and natural resources, such as the Interior Department's Bureau of Land Management, the Forest Service, the National Park Service, and the U.S. Fish and Wildlife Service, had counterproductive practices and lax regulations that actually caused the destruction of the environment. The turning political tide and growing hostility to regulation prompted Michael Kinsey, editor of *The New Republic,* to chide Nader's detractors, "In all statistical probability, at least several dozen of you who are reading this issue of *TNR* would be dead today if Nader had not invented the issue of auto safety" (9 December 1985).

In 1986, attempting to pitch to changed public sentiments, Nader wrote *The Big Boys: Power and Position in American Business* with William Taylor and Andrew Moore, interviewing corporate leaders for their personalities, management styles, and policies. Some critics considered the book insightful, but generally it received poor reviews and little press. Nader developed Bell's palsy that year, and went into temporary seclusion when his brother, Shafeek, died. Later that year he campaigned for Proposition 103 in California. The success of the proposition forced insurance companies to reimburse their customers more than a billion dollars in excessive premiums. Nader returned to his alma mater, Princeton, in 1989 to speak to students about activism, an idea that developed into Princeton Project, a nonprofit organization to support Princeton affiliates in their activist efforts. In the interest of citizens having control over what their taxes pay for, a concept challenged in the era of Reagan and Bush privatization, Nader founded the Taxpayer Assets Project in 1989 to identify areas of mismanaged taxpayer property and resources.

Nader's parents wrote *It Happened in the Kitchen: Recipes for Food and Thought* (1991) musing on the place of food in family cohesion and describing their experiences as Middle Eastern immigrants in America. They noted that they intended their restaurant, the Highland Arms, as a meeting place for the community to "feed the body and the mind." The next year Nader first ran for the office of president as a noncandidate, mostly as a form of protest and to draw attention to his causes. In 1992 he spelled out his suggestions to the candidates in the presidential election, "The Concord Principles: An Agenda for a New Initiatory Democracy" (published in *The Ralph Nader Reader*), ten principles that ran from citizens' control of public assets to protecting the rights of voters, among other issues. Nader's article "How Clinton Can Build Democracy" (1992) indicates that Bill Clinton's electoral victory in 1992 inspired some confidence after the previous administration's antagonism. In it Nader recommended that the president place more power in the hands of citizens to make democracy work, which he thought likely based on Clinton's proposed economic policies and stated goal of "putting people first." Whatever sense of optimism the victory inspired did not last long, however, and he soon added a new dimension to his critique of government nonresponsiveness to the needs of citizens. He began to analyze the problems of the two-party system with "Breaking Out of the Two-Party Rut" (*The Nation*, 20 July 1992), about how the entire presidential election process operates to resist making any positive changes.

He continued to work on consumer rights, albeit in new arenas, as this stage of his career unfolded.

Nader and James Love co-authored an antimonopoly article for *The Progressive,* "Looting the Medicine Chest: How Bristol-Myers Squibb Made Off with the Public's Cancer Research" (February 1993). In this piece Nader and Love allege that Bristol-Myers Squibb, the drug company, tried to monopolize the market for Taxol, an experimental yet promising cancer drug, despite the fact that the drug had gone into the public domain. Nader and Love write: "Such a deal! The taxpayers pay for the invention of a promising treatment for cancer and then give a marketing monopoly to one company, completely with a free or nearly free supply of the primary ingredient. And then the company's role is to agree to sell it back to us" (*Ralph Nader Reader*). In 1994 Nader and Wesley J. Smith explored airline safety with his book *Collision Course: The Truth About Airline Safety,* and he began a series of attacks on another monopoly power, Microsoft, which was defending an antitrust suit.

In 1996 Nader ran for president as the candidate of the Green Party, whose political agenda is to empower people and not corporations, and to protect the physical environment. He chose as his running mate Winona LaDuke, a Harvard-educated Native American community-rights activist, economist, and author. LaDuke, a member of the Ojibway tribe in Minnesota, was, at age thirty-six, already hailed by *Time* magazine as one of America's forthcoming leaders based on her work with the White Earth Project. She nursed her third child on the campaign trail. Nader produced several publications about the election, among them "The Greens and the Presidency: A Voice, not an Echo" (*The Nation,* 8 July 1996). A month before the 1996 election, *The Los Angeles Times* published Nader's article, "Perspectives on the Presidential Race: A Way Out of the Corporatist Grip," in which he argued that negative ad campaigns and the general shallowness of the presidential election led Americans to feel that they had to choose between the lesser of two evils, which in turn caused voter apathy.

Nader started writing the syndicated column "In the Public Interest" in the *San Francisco Bay Guardian* in 1998. He expressed his concern about the announcement that *Sesame Street* on the Public Broadcast System (PBS) would be "sponsored" by the Discovery Zone, an indoor playground manufacturer. In an interview, Nader accused the show and its sponsor of exploiting impressionable children. "It's sad that even Sesame Street is turning into a delivery vehicle for advertisers to pitch to our children," he said, referring to PBS as being, for many Americans, the last bastion of broadcasting free from commercial interests (Commercial Alert, online source, 6 October 1998). Noting that the Microsoft case from 1994 was settled out of court, in 1998 Nader suggested that the government set an example by leading a boycott of Microsoft products. That year, he and Love wrote "Why Microsoft Must Be Stopped" for *Computerworld.* Nader was concerned not just that Microsoft attempted to dominate the market unfairly, but that the company sought to make what were in his view inferior products a default setting for users of software. In 1999 the two writers also collaborated on "Judging Microsoft: It's a Blow to Real Monopoly."

With the book *Cutting Corporate Welfare* (2000), Nader addressed a theme that had begun to develop on the Left during the Reagan years—that mainstream rhetoric censured poor and working-class people who were financially needy and depicted them as parasitic for seeking relief in the form of welfare, while the government diverted phenomenal amounts of money into the coffers of large corporations. Nader argued that the businesses, not individuals on welfare, absorbed more than their fair share of social and financial resources and pointed out that although the public found it easy to blame poor people for tax increases and national debt, they were not truly responsible for them. He had written on this theme earlier in 1996 for *Earth Island Journal* with his article "It's Time to End Corporate Welfare As We Know It." He lamented as well that the bureaucracies created to regulate business by such measures as prohibiting child labor and creating health and safety standards had much less funding and fewer resources than did the corporations in question. Nor was he content to stop here. In *Children First: A Parents Guide to Fighting Corporate Predators* (1996), Nader observed the spike in marketing to children and called it "corporate child abuse."

Nader ran for president again with LaDuke in 2000 as a candidate of the Green Party. He considered his previous races for president largely symbolic, and not until 2000 did he take his campaign seriously, making more than token appearances on behalf of his bid for the office. His announcement of candidacy in the Green Party in 2000 stated that he was running for office to fight plutocracy and abuses of economic power, which he saw as threats to democracy. While he was ineligible to participate in the presidential debates, his campaign drew wide support from liberals who had become alienated from the Democrats. His rallies on the campaign trail featured celebrities such as Pearl Jam's Eddie Vedder and folksinger Iris Dement. The 2000 election turned out to be one of the closest in U.S. history, and many Democrats blamed Nader, whose ticket won three million, or less than 3 percent of total votes, for taking away crucial votes from their candidate Al Gore and allowing Republican George W. Bush to win the race. His opponents called this the "spoiler effect."

*Title page for Nader's book about consumer protection that led Gore
Vidal to recommend in* Esquire *magazine that he run for president
(Coleman Karesh Law Library, University of South Carolina)*

*Crashing the Party: How to Tell the Truth and Still Run for
President* was published in 2002, a memoir of Nader's 2000
bid for the office. In it he responds to critics of his candidacy. In the first chapter, *Business as Usual*, he points out
that most congressional districts are one-party: a Republican or Democratic candidate for the House usually wins
by a large margin with little opposition, or in the end, basically unopposed. He writes that while he had been raised
to be socially conscious without any allegiance to a party,
he saw how gradually the government became more influenced by business; he ran for president to break this cycle.
He recalls that while on the campaign trail, he encountered
many people who wondered why he ran when he knew he
would not win or why he ran when he knew that vote-
splitting would help elect Bush. Nader responds that his
priority was creating new progressive politics in America,
and Gore's loss to Bush was Gore's own responsibility,
since the then vice president had every advantage over
Bush. Subsequently Nader produced "The Democrats

Bow to the Megabanks" (2000) for *Progressive* and "Make
the Recall Count" (2003) for *The Los Angeles Times.* Most of
his recent works contain the theory that Democrats and
Republicans are fundamentally the same (pro-corporate
rather than representing the interests of their constituents).

In addition to the antagonism Nader faced from
the Left, the administration of George W. Bush also
posed many obstacles to Nader's goal of keeping government separate and free of corporate interests, since
the president himself and many members of his administration made their careers in industry and retained
those ties once in office. For example, in 2002 Enron,
an energy company with close ties to both Presidents
Bush, was involved in a scandal involving gross financial impropriety and for a time evaded accountability
because of lack of government scrutiny. Nader held this
as an example of the seriousness of corporate crime in
his articles "After Enron" published in *Progressive* and
"Organizing the People: The One Sure Way to Defeat
Enronism" in *American Prospect.*

Nader again ran for president as an independent
in 2004, despite concerns of vote-splitting, mostly
voiced by Democrats. Nader stated that he would not
back down from the race because he would not abandon the issue of removing U.S. armed forces from Iraq.
He selected Peter Miguel Camejo, an activist who ran
for the office of governor of California in 2002, for his
running mate; having received 1 percent of total votes,
they lost the 2004 presidential election to President
George W. Bush. During this election Nader criticized
filmmaker and former employee Michael Moore for
perpetuating the problem of negative campaigning and
propaganda with his documentary *Fahrenheit 911.*
Moore continued to support Nader as a presidential
candidate in upcoming years, however, seeing himself
as carrying on Nader's mission in his allegations against
President Bush.

In 2004, Nader's book *The Good Fight: Declare Your
Independence & Close the Democracy Gap* was published. In
this retrospective Nader writes about the spoiler effect
and addresses the fears of Democrats and even his own
proponents that his presence on the ballot would propel
Bush to victory. Nader argues that American voters had
the right to more choices, especially since the two-party
system did not offer a real challenge to abuses of power
in the status quo. Nader discusses wide-ranging social
problems—disease, poverty, environmental destruction,
and hunger—making such recommendations as routine
DNA testing to exonerate innocent people wrongly
accused of crimes in order to improve the criminal justice system. Nader then defends his contention that the
bipartisan system is defunct. For example, Nader notes
that Bush supported tort reform, making it more difficult for plaintiffs to collect the damages that they

needed, because the big companies who were usually the defendants made more contributions to his campaign for election. The wealthy have so raised the stakes and consolidated power over the electoral system, particularly at the national level, that promising candidates often cannot enter political races because they lack the funding or connections. Thus the system favors incumbents, leaving the two parties virtually unchallenged. In Nader's view, the system has become very difficult to break into and change.

Notably *The Good Fight* is not simply a self-promotion for Nader as the ideal presidential candidate. His prose is often tongue-in-cheek. He does not paint a picture of George W. Bush as the cause of all evil and himself as the deliverer who would set America straight; more accurately, he offers an honest assessment of common problems and how the political system exacerbates them. The book issues a call to activism to a somewhat jaded populace. In 2004, Nader also published *In Pursuit of Justice,* a collection of over a hundred of his writings from 2000 to 2003. On the same lines of *The Good Fight,* the articles in *In Pursuit of Justice* address many different aspects of political and corporate responsibility.

Since the beginning of his career, Nader has earned his share of critics across the political spectrum. Corporate interests have long accused him of interfering with the free-enterprise system; Ronald Reagan, for example, said that enforcing seat belts in cars cost consumers their freedom. With his typical blunt wit, Nader responded that it indeed cost them their freedom—to go through the windshield. He later noted in *Crashing the Party* that the fatality rate from auto crashes fell from 5.6 deaths per hundred million vehicle miles in 1966 to 1.6 in the year 2000. Meanwhile, liberal-leaning individuals accused him of drawing attention away from more important issues, such as antiracism activism or identity politics. Critics of all stripes describe him as sanctimonious or overly critical.

Nader lives and works in Washington, D.C. and lectures frequently. He has never married. Known for his frugality despite considerable assets, he has given most of his money to worthy causes. All of his siblings became high achievers and worked in fields emphasizing social conscience. Shafeek Nader became a community activist and founded Northwestern Connecticut Community College; after his death, his siblings cre-

ated the Shafeek Nader Trust for the Community Interest to perpetuate his values. Laura Nader became a professor of anthropology at the University of California at Berkeley; she spoke out against the war in Iraq and wrote extensively on political dogma. Claire Nader headed the Shafeek Nader Trust for the Community Interest and wrote about science and technology in developing countries.

Nader aspired early in life to be a lawyer of the people. Having written, edited or co-written more than twenty-four books and countless articles and having founded or helped to found dozens of watchdog and citizens' rights groups, he has been a tireless and prolific activist. Even when he was not running for president, his lecture circuit resembled that of a presidential candidate. His persistence in demanding safety in cars as well as in other commonplace products and situations has saved many lives. By focusing attention on society's harmful assumptions and its less visible hazards, Nader set himself apart from other sources of information, even investigative journalism. His research and exposés contained recommendations, usually in the form of proposed legislation, to correct the problems to which he directed attention.

In August 2008 Ralph Nader announced his fifth candidacy for president of the United States, stating: "We need to get more challenges of McCain and Obama to open up the debates, using Google, Yahoo, independent media. One network needs to break away from their slavish relaying of these parallel interviews they call debates."

Biographies:

Robert F. Buckhorn, *Nader: The People's Lawyer* (Englewood Cliffs, N.J.: Prentice-Hall, 1972);

Charles McCarry, *Citizen Nader* (New York: Saturday Review Press, 1972);

Patricia Cronin Marcello, *Ralph Nader: A Biography* (Westport, Conn.: Greenwood Press, 2004).

References:

David Sanford, *Me and Ralph: Is Nader Unsafe for America?* (New York: Simon & Schuster, 1976);

Ralph de Toledano, *Hit & Run: The Rise—and Fall?—of Ralph Nader* (New York: Arlington House, 1975).

Albert R. Parsons

(24 June 1848 – 11 November 1887)

Matthew Sherman
Saint Louis University

BOOKS: *To the Workingmen of America,* by Parsons, Johann Most, August Spies, Victor Drury, and Joseph J. Reifgraber (Chicago: Bureau of Information, I.W.P.A., 1883);

Appeal to the People of America (Chicago: Lucy E. Parsons, 1887);

Anarchism: Its Philosophy and Scientific Basis as Defined by Some of Its Apostles (Chicago: Mrs. A. R. Parsons, 1887).

SELECTED PERIODICAL PUBLICATIONS–UNCOLLECTED: "Chicago Labor Unions," *National Socialist* (18 May 1878);

"The Progress of the Labor Movement," *Labor Standard* (18 August 1878): 4;

"Die Greenbader und die Sozialiften," *Vorbote,* 7 (8 May 1880);

"Labor vs. Capital," *Journal of United Labor,* 4 (July 1883): 531–532;

"The International," *Truth,* 2 (17 November 1883);

"Chattel and Wage Slavery," *Truth* 3 (October 1884);

"The Autobiography of Albert Parsons," *Knights of Labor,* 1 (16 October 1886);

"The Autobiography of Albert Parsons," *Knights of Labor,* 1 (23 October 1886).

Albert R. Parsons, most noted for his trial and subsequent execution following the bombing at Haymarket Square in Chicago, Illinois, on 4 May 1886, was also an ardent advocate of the working class, a social revolutionary, and an effective speaker and writer. From the end of the Civil War until his execution, Parsons fought for the rights of former slaves and laborers by using constant political action and agitation. His concern for the working class led him to adopt radical political ideologies, including Radical Republicanism, socialism, and anarchism, which he articulated in many speeches at labor and political meetings. Parsons also expressed his political views in newspapers and journals committed to labor and radical politics. He edited three newspapers devoted to the same causes.

From Lucy E. Parsons, Life of Albert R. Parsons with a Brief History of the Labor Movement in America, *1889; University Library, University of Illinois Urbana-Champaign*

Born on 24 June 1848 to Samuel and Elizabeth (née Tompkins) Parsons in Montgomery, Alabama, Albert Richard Parsons was proud of his family's heritage in American society. His father's family had arrived at Narragansett Bay from England in 1632, and two relatives of his mother participated in the American Revolution. Samuel Parsons, the owner of a shoe and leather factory, was a philanthropist involved in the temperance movement in the South. His mother devoted herself to the care of her ten children and died when Parsons was two years old. When his father died in 1853, Parsons found himself under the care of his brother, William Henry Parsons, in Texas. After living with his brother for six years, in 1859 Parsons moved in with his sister, Mrs. A. J. Byrd, who lived in Waco, Texas. Parsons moved to Galveston, Texas, one year later, when he was twelve, to work as an apprentice for the *Galveston Daily News.* Parsons's first experience in the newspaper industry came to an end at the outbreak of the American Civil War in 1861. Drawn to the thrill of battle and adventure, he broke his apprenticeship and joined the local Confederate militia in Waco at the age of thirteen. Following his brief stint with the "Lone Star Greys," he enlisted with an artillery company at Fort Sabine in Texas, where his brother Richard Parsons was stationed as a company commander. Parsons's term ended with the artillery company twelve months later, and he joined his brother W. H. Parsons who commanded the Fourth Regiment Volunteer Texas Cavalry near the Mississippi and Red Rivers. Parsons served as a scout and distinguished himself in several engagements. At the war's end, he traveled back home to Waco and bartered his mule for forty acres of corn. When the corn was ready to harvest, he hired several former slaves to help; it was the first time they had earned money. Consequently, he enrolled at Waco (now Baylor) University with the money he made from selling the corn, but he left after a few months of study and found employment at a printing office in Waco.

After a couple of years' experience in printing newspapers, Parsons founded and edited *The Spectator* in 1868. This event, in many ways, represented a defining moment in his life. No longer a teenager or under the guidance of his elders, Parsons embarked on his own business venture in the newspaper industry, holding the first of many editorial positions. More important, the establishment of *The Spectator* signaled Parsons's rejection of his Confederate past and his first use of a newspaper to express his political viewpoint. In *The Spectator,* Parsons supported the Thirteenth, Fourteenth, and Fifteenth Amendments, which freed and established rights for former slaves. This viewpoint ran contrary to public opinion in Texas and earned Parsons the disdain of many of his former associates. Nonetheless, he championed Radical Republican reconstruction until the political climate forced him to close down his paper within a year. With no means of income, Parsons joined the *Houston Daily Telegraph,* a Republican paper, as a correspondent based in Waco. Working for the *Daily Telegraph* provided him with an opportunity to express his views, albeit from a somewhat tempered viewpoint.

While traveling in northwestern Texas for the *Daily Telegraph* in 1870, Parsons met Lucy Eldine Gathings, a woman of Mexican and African American heritage. Their ensuing relationship became the source of criticism from his friends and neighbors. Nevertheless, Parsons and Gathings maintained a relationship when he was appointed as assistant assessor of the U.S. Internal Revenue Service in Texas in 1870. One year later, Parsons was elected to the Texas state senate as a secretary and was later selected to serve as the chief deputy collector of the U.S. Internal Revenue Service in Austin, Texas. In addition to his governmental position, Parsons also was employed as a militia officer at the Texas Office of Public Instruction, protecting former slaves from the Ku Klux Klan. By 1873, however, his career in Texas politics ended when the Republican Party lost power in the Texas legislature. Following this change in governmental structure, he, now living conjugally with Lucy Gathings (his claim that they were married in 1871 or 1872 in Austin is dubious), returned to journalism, writing as a correspondent for the *Texas Agriculturist.* This position afforded him the opportunity to leave Texas when he and several other editors and writers were offered a tour of the north. Among the cities that Parsons visited was Chicago, where he decided to settle.

Chicago presented Parsons and his wife with an experience different from that in Texas. He readily found work as a substitute typesetter with the Chicago *Inter-Ocean* and joined his first labor union, Typographical Union No. 16. Later, he found full-time employment during the Panic of 1873 with the *Chicago Times,* where he worked for four years. While Chicago provided Parsons with a home and employment, the ongoing labor problems and poverty in Chicago were crucial in developing his political ideology. In 1874 a controversy involving the Chicago Relief and Aid Society, established to raise funds for those affected by the 1871 fire, sparked Parsons's interest in labor issues. Though the society distributed small amounts of money to distressed families in 1874, the amount barely covered basic needs. Consequently, many among the working class and the poor claimed that the board members of the society used the money to advance their own interests.

After investigating these claims for himself, Parsons concluded that their charges were justified and that the plight of the working class in Chicago was similar to that of the African Americans he had tried to protect in Texas. He resolved, therefore, to explore possible solutions to the labor crisis and economic inequity. He discovered the ideas of socialism and communism. Intrigued by these political ideologies, he communicated with some of Chicago's communists and socialists and read Karl Marx, Friedrich Engels, and writers of similar views. When he joined the Social Democratic Party of America in 1875, Parsons had wholly converted to socialism. The next year, he attended a meeting of organized laborers at Pittsburgh, where the Social Democratic Party of America formed a united front with the Workingmen's Party of the United States (WP). The merger inspired Parsons, and he resolved no longer to remain an observer of the labor movement but to become one of the movement's most active participants. He joined the Knights of Labor (KOL) at a meeting of workingmen at Indianapolis, Indiana, in 1876 and entered the race for clerk of Cook County in spring 1877. He lost the election, but not his zeal for the labor movement. The Great Railway Strike in the summer of that same year only fueled his activity.

Asked to address a group of thirty thousand laborers on 21 July 1877 during the strike, Parsons encouraged the audience to join the WP so the government, rather than large conglomerates intent on exploiting the working class, could control the means of production. His speech elicited equally strong responses from his audience, his employers at the *Chicago Times,* and Chicago's city officials. The following day, Parsons learned that he had lost his job at the *Times.* Later that day he was escorted to the office of Chief of Police Hickey, who questioned his motives in addressing the group of working men and possibly causing more problems for the city. Parsons responded that the men in control of the government and the business class had caused the working-class discontent. In the days following his encounter with Hickey, the strike grew in intensity and eventually culminated in a general strike across the nation, later known as the Great Upheaval. It affected the lives of everyone involved, including Parsons, who subsequently was blacklisted by the newspaper industry for two years. Two years of unemployment deepened his disdain for capitalism and fueled his involvement in radical politics.

Several of Parsons's writings in the spring and summer of 1878 illustrate the energy he devoted to the cause of the labor movement. Writing in May for *The National Socialist,* based in Cincinnati, Ohio, Parsons reported that the labor unions of Chicago adopted the Declaration of Principles and Objectives of the International Labor Union of America (ILU), which stressed the importance of an eight-hour workday to alleviate the suffering of the working class. In August of that same year, his article "The Progress of the Labor Movement in Chicago," in *The Labor Standard,* argued that an eight-hour workday opened the door for better wages and working conditions. Parsons also believed that a reduction of hours was necessary for the survival of the labor movement. "The Trade Unions lack but one real

thing to make them a *real* benefit," Parsons maintained, "and that one thing is a *common issue,* and that issue is a *reduction of the hours of labor,* until all have employment." Essentially, Parsons argued that unions should focus on the single issue of hours to provide employment for all workers. Until then, the suffering of the unemployed would continue and the new social order would be postponed. Parsons threaded this idea into many speeches that he delivered to workers. In addition to this form of advocacy, he was elected to prominent positions in organizations promoting an eight-hour workday, including the ILU and the Chicago Eight-Hour League (CEHL).

While Parsons's work supporting the eight-hour day occupied much of his time during the summer of 1878, he remained active in the affairs of the WP as well. He was elected as a delegate to that year's national convention in Newark, New Jersey, where the delegates renamed the party the Socialistic Labor Party (SLP). Following the national convention, Parsons attended a Chicago SLP meeting at Ogden's Grove. There he reached a crucial point in his career as a radical writer when he was chosen as the assistant editor for *The Socialist,* a weekly publication for Chicago's SLP. Frank Hirth, a German carpenter who formerly edited *Vorbote,* served as the editor. The "mission" of *The Socialist,* as the editors proclaimed in the inaugural issue of the weekly on 14 September 1878, was to provide workingmen with a "journal that shall not only give expression of their deeply felt discontent regarding their economic and social repression" but would also "duly expose and stigmatize the prevailing piracy practiced upon honest labor." *The Socialist* adhered to these principles and discussed relevant issues local and national for many Chicago workers. Parsons contributed several articles. The editors and some contributors of *The Socialist* never signed their articles; nevertheless, Parsons's imprint is clearly identifiable in articles comparing slavery to wage labor, assessing progress in the labor movement, and arguing the primacy of the eight-hour workday in a progressive agenda for labor.

Parsons's activities with the SLP extended beyond his responsibilities for *The Socialist.* In March of 1879 the SLP invited Parsons to speak at an event celebrating the Revolution of 1848 and the Paris Commune of 1871. At the largest labor meeting in Chicago's history to that date, Parsons reassured his audience that the SLP sought to change workers' conditions. In July 1879 Parsons became the editor of *The Socialist* after the national executive committee of the party fired Hirth. The paper ceased publication in August due to funding problems, yet Parsons remained a critical member of the SLP. His ability to speak, write effectively, and involve himself in party activities later earned him the presidential nomination at the Allegheny City convention in December 1879. He turned down the offer, pointing out that he did not meet the constitutional age requirement of thirty-five. During this time, Parsons also continued working for the CEHL, and in January 1880 he traveled to Washington, D.C., for a conference on the subject of working hours. After the delegates passed a resolution, Parsons, with several other representatives, lobbied Congress for two weeks to approve an eight-hour law similar to the National Eight-Hour Law passed in 1868, part of the post–Civil War Republican Party agenda, which affected only laborers, mechanics, and workingmen contracted or employed by the government. Parsons and the CEHL's efforts to obtain similar legislation proved futile.

Frustrated and disheartened by this failure, Parsons returned home to face further frustration with the SLP. After the SLP suffered heavy losses in the election of 1880 and thousands of members withdrew from the organization, a deep division occurred within the ranks of the party. During the 1880 election, the national committee of the SLP attempted to head off a collapse by uniting with the Greenback Party (GP), which was formed in 1873 and advocated the printing of paper money to remedy the financial crisis of that year. Initially, Parsons appeared open to the idea of a GP and SLP alliance and attended the GP's convention as a representative for the SLP in Chicago. Much to his chagrin, as he explained in his 8 May 1880 *Vorbote* article "Die Greenbader und die Sozialiften" (The Greenbacker and the Socialist), the proposal adopted by the Greenbackers had only a few references to labor issues. Parsons felt unable to support a union between the SLP and GP because the platform ignored workers. Consequently, he renounced his membership in the party and started to question the efficacy of the ballot box in obtaining reform. "The ballot box," Parsons contends in his autobiography published in the *Knights of Labor* in 1886, "could not be made an index to record the popular will until the existing debasing, impoverishing, and enslaving industrial conditions were first altered." The government had the power to change inequities of the polls, he maintains, but the capitalists of society controlled government with money and influence; therefore, government was a "force of despotism, an invasion of man's natural right to liberty." By 1881 Parsons, like many others, had abandoned socialism as a viable solution and turned toward anarchism.

Although Parsons converted to anarchism and joined the Revolutionary Socialistic Party (RSP) in 1881, he was forced to accept some aspects of the capitalist system in which he lived. Without a permanent job and the ability to provide for his wife and two children, Lula Eda and Albert R. Parsons Jr., Parsons

moved to Hartford, Connecticut, in January 1883 to edit a relatively new publication, *The Connecticut Farmer,* which reported on political issues affecting Connecticut citizens and focused on farm-related subjects: making butter, planting crops, crop prices, stock care, and remedies for the illnesses of farm animals. This position proved uncongenial for Parsons, who had devoted most of his adult life to political and social reform. He still found ways to weave his own political ideals into the newspaper. In Parsons's first issue as editor in January, he related to his readers that the paper "will give discriminating but generous support to every organization" committed to the cause of farmers and "will boldly attack and persistently follow to the end every evil which, in its judgment threatens the farmers of the State" (6 January 1883). Indeed, Parsons devoted himself to protecting the interests of all workers, including farmers.

While Parsons edited *The Connecticut Farmer,* he continued writing for labor journals. In July 1883 Parsons published an article titled "Labor v. Capital" in *The Journal of United Labor,* the monthly publication of the KOL. Mostly a report on the meeting of the Trades Assembly, a Chicago organization of labor representatives, the article expresses Parsons's belief that the resolutions adopted by the organization presented a "remedy" for all workingmen. Shortly after the publication of this article, Parsons left his position at *The Connecticut Farmer* to join his wife and family, who had remained in Chicago. During the next years in Chicago, Parsons became one of the most influential ideologues of American anarchism.

In October 1883 Parsons traveled to Pittsburgh, Pennsylvania, for a conference to revitalize the RSP, founded two years previously in Chicago. Perhaps the most important event to that date for the evolution of anarchism in the United States, the Pittsburgh Congress brought together delegates from twenty-six cities to discuss a plan of action to unite the various groups of social revolutionaries, trade unions, and the working class. As a delegate from Chicago, Parsons played a critical role at the conference. He energized the delegates with stirring speeches and served on the five-person committee that drafted a manifesto for the organization. While Parsons did not contribute as much as Johann Most, the noted anarchist who organized the Pittsburgh Congress, his influence in the manifesto is evident. Especially in his later writings, Parsons often connected the principles of anarchism to the American Revolution, the Declaration of Independence, and the writings of Thomas Jefferson. The manifesto, titled *To the Workingmen of America* (1883), echoed the line from the Declaration of Independence that states, "it is their right, it is their duty to throw off such government and provide new guards for their future security." Then, the authors ask, "do not the necessities of our present time compel us to re-assert their declaration?" The authors of the statement, like the founding fathers, believed they had a right and responsibility to usher in the new revolution and to overthrow the capitalist class that exploited the working class. Moreover, as the leaders of the revolution they would become the protectors of that new society to prevent other "abuses and usurpations" by despots. Given Parsons's pride in his family's heritage dating back to the Revolution, these references clearly had personal meaning for him. But more important, such references also represented an attempt by anarchist groups to claim the moral authority of American historical documents, pointing to texts that the public revered to justify their own actions and beliefs.

After validating its claims with reference to the Declaration of Independence, the committee proposed several goals to assuage the suffering of the working class. First the present social conditions and ruling class must be overthrown. Then a society that provided equal production and free exchange of goods would replace the capitalistic society. With the foundation of liberty established, the people of that society, including women and members of different races, would receive free, secular education. The governance of this society, the committee proclaimed, would be maintained by free contracts between independent communes and people.

To the Workingmen of America, published in several languages including English, German, French, and Yiddish, succinctly summarized anarchist principles: it heavily emphasized equality and rejected political leadership as a desirable institution. The congress underscored this point by changing the name of the organization from the RSP to the International Working People's Association (IWPA). Parsons reported in the San Francisco–based paper *Truth* on 17 November 1883 that the congress and the creation of the new organization represented major developments in achieving the social revolution. Parsons delivered several speeches promoting the organization that year. Almost exactly one year later, he was elected as the editor of *The Alarm,* the weekly paper published by the IWPA.

Editing *The Alarm* was perhaps Parsons's greatest literary achievement. The publication presented him with a ready outlet to articulate his opinions in a weekly publication, and it provided him with his first steady job since his typesetting position at the *Chicago Times.* The money he earned from *The Alarm,* however, was too meager to support his family, so he and Lucy Parsons opened a sewing shop underneath their apartment. Nevertheless, Parsons effectively managed the requirements of *The Alarm,* which was distributed nationwide. Moreover, the office of *The Alarm* served as a gathering point for the Chicago anarchists and as a distribution center for other literature by prominent anarchists including Most, Petr Kropotkin, and Mikhail Bakunin. With such an array of anarchist material available, *The Alarm,* with a masthead declaring "Workingmen of All Countries, Unite," became an important source of information regarding the ideology of anarchism and reported on current issues affecting subscribers. Three articles that Parsons wrote in 1885 best represent his style in this period.

The 18 April 1885 issue of *The Alarm* featured an example of Parsons's obsession with engaging in an intellectual debate over the ideology of anarchism. Responding to a minister's question on the goals of anarchists, Parsons quips that they only want liberty. Liberty provided an opportunity, Parsons maintains, to escape the repressive power of the law. Workers, he further argues, who accounted for the majority of the population, did not have the means to control the product of their labor. Hence, the working class was only an advanced form of slave laborers. Parsons had used this argument earlier. In an article titled "Chattel and Wage Slavery" published in *Truth* in October 1884, Parsons also compared slave labor to the conditions met by industrial workers. Therefore, he resolves in *The Alarm* article, "Let each man be a law unto himself, for . . . where all are equally free to do right, none dare then do wrong." He revisited this argument numerous times during his tenure at *The Alarm,* especially on the occasion of the Fourth of July.

In "July 4, 1776," in the 27 June 1885 issue of *The Alarm,* Parsons argues for the importance of celebrating Independence Day. In a move similar to the references to the Declaration of Independence in *To the Workingmen of America,* he attempts in this article to validate the goals of the anarchists. Unlike the statement adopted at the Pittsburgh Congress, however, Parsons's position more pointedly emphasizes using force to overthrow the ruling class. As the founders of the nation "took arms and vindicated their manhood; so must we," Parsons argues. Additionally, he contends, "By force our ancestors liberated themselves from political servitude; so also must we, their children." His belief that using arms might become necessary grew more fixed as he perceived social and industrial problems worsening.

Parsons became especially concerned at this time about the treatment of women in industry. In "White Slaves!" published for the 22 August 1885 edition of *The Alarm,* Parsons eloquently evaluates the conditions faced by a group of seamstresses on strike at a shirt factory. First, Parsons recounts the invention of the sewing machine and praises its potential service to the American worker. Still, Parsons argues, the wonders of the sewing machine could not ameliorate the circumstances of the women working at the shirt factory, because they did not receive a meaningful wage and had to work sixty hours per week. Nor, he argues, will proposed legislation to reduce the time women work provide a solution to the problem. The government allowed such conditions to develop and was unlikely to make progressive laws because women could not even vote. Since women cannot control the laws that affect their conditions at work, Parsons concludes that the only answer was to abolish government, the creator of all laws.

While editing *The Alarm,* Parsons also maintained a rigorous speaking schedule. On 1 May 1886, he traveled to Cincinnati, Ohio, to address a labor organization on the rights of workers and the importance of the eight-hour system. He returned home to Chicago on 4 May and helped organize a meeting to obtain an eight-hour workday for the seamstresses of Chicago. On the same evening, three thousand laborers rallied at Haymarket Square to protest the killing of six workers by the police at the McCormick Reaper Workers. Parsons went to the meeting of seamstresses prepared to speak on the eight-hour system, but he received an urgent request to talk at the Haymarket Square meeting. Parsons, who never turned down an opportunity for a larger audience, went to Haymarket Square and delivered the speech that he had prepared for the group of seamstresses. He urged his audience to support the eight-hour movement and join labor unions. After speaking for an hour, Parsons walked with his family to a social hall one block away. As he and his family waited, Parsons recalls in his autobiography, they saw a flash of light and heard several pistol shots. In addition to civilian casualties, sixty-seven policemen were wounded, one of whom was killed at the scene and six of whom died later. Fearful of the repercussions of the bombing and his obvious role in the anarchist and labor movements, Parsons fled to Waukesha, Wisconsin, and worked as a carpenter and painter at a hotel. He learned after a few weeks in Wisconsin that the Chicago police had indicted him and seven others for murder, conspiracy, and unlawful assembly. After hiding in Wisconsin for seven weeks, on 21 June Parsons walked into a Chicago courtroom as the trial commenced, declaring his innocence. Within a matter of hours of his surrender and arraignment, he was taken to the Cook County jail.

The trial of the eight anarchists was the most notable legal battle in late-nineteenth-century American history. Every major newspaper in the United States covered the trial on a daily basis, and observers filled the courtroom every day. More important, the trial represented a climatic point in the contest between two unequal political and social ideologies that had festered

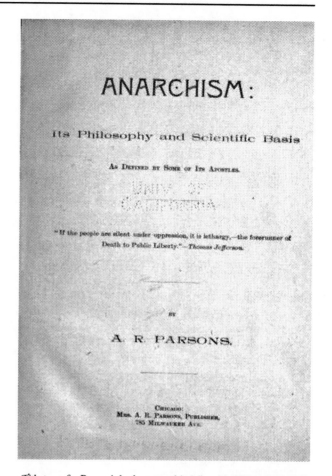

Title page for Parsons's book composed in jail and published by his wife after his execution (University of California Libraries)

since the Great Upheaval of 1877. The actual proceedings of the trial, lasting from 21 June to 20 August 1886, involved a series of witnesses on both sides that had varying interpretations of the events at the Haymarket meeting. The array of witnesses ultimately complicated the trial and confused the jurors. The alibis of the defendants were credible. State Attorney Julius Grinnell was unable to prove conclusively the charges of murder and conspiracy, and so he focused on establishing the revolutionary nature of anarchism. He read passages from anarchist publications such as *The Alarm,* put the surgeons of injured police officers on the witness stand, and showed anarchist bomb-making equipment to the jurors. The defense never recovered from such emotional appeals, and the jury found all of the defendants guilty on 20 August. The jury, as required by Illinois law, also decided upon punishment for the accused. Parsons, along with six other defendants, received a sentence of death. Oscar Neebe was sentenced to fifteen years of prison. Two months later, Parsons's attorney, Captain William Black, petitioned for another trial with Judge Joseph E. Gary, who refused Black's appeal but agreed to allow the defendants to issue final statements from October 7 to 9. Parsons was the last to speak. He restated his innocence before the court, defined anarchism, and denounced capitalism as the slavemaster of laborers. At the end of Parsons's harangue, Judge Gary issued his final statement and set Parsons's and the other defendants' date of execution for 3 December. As Parsons waited to die, he wrote his most influential publications.

Shortly after the trial Parsons published his autobiography in two separate October issues of the *Knights of Labor*. Vividly written and arranged chronologically for the most part, the pieces serve as a critical tool in understanding Parsons's ideological development. He relates his entire life and points out critical moments that shaped his understanding of American politics and society. While his political evolution provides the main theme of the autobiography, a subtle undercurrent appears throughout the publication that connects it to his earlier writings. Most of Parsons's contemporaries believed that anarchists were mostly immigrants from Eastern Europe who imported a foreign ideology into the United States. For the first time for a large reading audience, Parsons dispels this myth by pointing to his family heritage. Similarly, he emphasizes the relation of anarchism to the founding of the United States, ending his autobiography with a passage from the Declaration of Independence.

In response to a failed appeal to the Illinois Supreme Court, Parsons wrote *Appeal to the People of America*, which his wife published on 21 September 1887. In the *Appeal*, Parsons reaffirms his claim that he was innocent of the charges and was not responsible for inciting the individual who did throw the bomb. Parsons states that he would refuse any "vain" attempts for clemency or further appeals to the "capitalist" courts. He believed that such cries for mercy would only prove that he was guilty. His readers, Parsons states, could decide his guilt or innocence based on the facts he presented. Recognizing his role as a martyr for the anarchist and labor movements, therefore, Parsons was "prepared to die" (*Anarchism: Its Philosophy and Scientific Basis As Defined by Some of Its Apostles*, 1887). Parsons believed that his trial proved that liberty was dead in the United States, and he welcomed death, despite attempts by his friends and loved ones to persuade him to reconsider. Parsons remained adamant and reiterated his views in an open letter to Governor Richard Oglesby on 13 October.

Following Parson's execution on 11 November 1887, his wife published *Anarchism: Its Philosophy and Scientific Basis as Defined by Some of Its Apostles*, which Parsons composed while sitting in his prison cell. Divided into two parts, the book first traces the economic history of the United States from the American Revolution to the Haymarket affair. Parsons also includes an analysis of capitalism and several copious excerpts from Marx's *Das Kapital* and Marx and Engels's *The Communist Manifesto* to stress his argument. Part 2 contains the speeches of the eight anarchists during the last days of the trial, several other viewpoints on anarchism by Most, Krotopkin, and Lucy Parsons, and an appendix. The appendix contains Parsons's *Appeal to the People of America*, his open letter to Governor Oglesby, letters of correspondence, and a statement published as "Law v. Liberty" in *The Alarm* on 3 December 1887, in which he defined anarchism and the importance of liberty.

Albert R. Parsons's development as a radical writer provides a study in the relationships between late-nineteenth-century political dissenters that is central to any basic understanding of labor history in the United States. He was involved in major radical movements in the United States following the Civil War and actively spoke and wrote for those movements in major publications. Through his spoken and written words, Parsons expressed his belief that U.S. society was dysfunctional because it marginalized the working class. This argument was by no means original to Parsons, but his advocacy and sustained effort to achieve a social revolution marked him as a prominent leader in the labor and anarchist movements. The Haymarket bombing ultimately proved the defining moment in Parsons's life. Lucy Parsons made herself the guardian of his literary reputation and kept his memory alive for another half century. In 1889 she published the first biography of Parsons, *The Life of Albert Parsons*, which also included several of his published writings from *The Alarm* and an advertisement for *Anarchism*. She continued to invoke his memory and repeat his arguments when appropriate through her speaking engagements and labor rallies until her death on 7 March 1942. He became an icon for the labor movement for many years following his execution. Publications such as Alan Calmer's 1937 biography, Paul Avrich's 1984 *The Haymarket Tragedy*, and David Roediger and Franklin Rosemont's 1986 *Haymarket Scrapbook*, have also recorded the life and work of Parsons.

Biographies:

Lucy Eldine Parsons, *The Life of Albert R. Parsons* (Chicago: Mrs. Lucy E. Parsons, 1889);

Alan Calmer, *Labor Agitator: The Story of Albert Parsons* (New York: International Publishers, 1937).

References:

Carolyn Ashbaugh, *Lucy Parsons: American Revolutionary* (Chicago: Charles H. Kerr, 1976);

Paul Avrich, *The Haymarket Tragedy* (Princeton: Princeton University Press, 1984);

Avrich, *Anarchist Portraits* (Princeton: Princeton University Press, 1988);

Frederick Buchstein, "The Anarchist Press in American Journalism," *Journalism History,* 1 (Summer 1974);

Henry David, *The History of the Haymarket Affair: A Study in the American Social-Revolutionary and Labor Movements* (New York: Russell & Russell, 1958);

Philip S. Foner, *The Great Labor Uprising of 1877* (New York: Monad Press, 1977);

Michael Johnson, "Albert Parsons: An American Architect of Syndicalism," *Midwest Quarterly,* 2, no. 9 (1968);

Bruce Nelson, *Beyond the Martyrs* (New Brunswick, N.J.: Rutgers University Press, 1988);

William O. Reichert, *Partisans of Freedom: A Study in American Anarchism* (Bowling Green, Ohio: Bowling Green University Popular Press, 1976);

Dave Roediger and Franklin Rosemont, eds., *Haymarket Scrapbook* (Chicago: Charles H. Kerr, 1986);

Carl Smith, *Urban Disorder and the Shape of Belief: The Great Chicago Fire, the Haymarket Bomb, and the Model Town of Pullman* (Chicago: University of Chicago Press, 1995).

Papers:

The majority of Albert R. Parsons's papers are available at the State Historical Society of Wisconsin in Madison, Wisconsin. The Chicago Historical Society contains some of Parsons's correspondence and valuable material on the Haymarket affair. Additionally, significant resources on the trial of Parsons and the other anarchists are available at the Abraham Lincoln Presidential Library in Springfield, Illinois, formerly the Illinois State Historical Library.

Lucy E. Parsons

(1853? – 7 March 1942)

Melissa Moore
Central Michigan University

BOOKS: *To Tramps* (Chicago: International Working People's Association, 1884);

Life of Albert R. Parsons, with Brief History of the Labor Movement in America (Chicago: L. E. Parsons, 1889; augmented reprint, 1903);

The Famous Speeches of the Eight Chicago Anarchists in Court: When Asked if They Had Anything to Say Why Sentence of Death Should Not Be Passed upon Them: October 7, 8, and 9, 1886 (Chicago: L. E. Parsons, 1909).

COLLECTION: Gale Ahrens, ed., *Lucy Parsons: Freedom, Equality, and Solidarity: Writings and Speeches, 1878–1937* (Chicago: Charles H. Kerr, 2003).

OTHER: Albert Parsons, *Anarchism: Its Philosophy and Scientific Basis, as Defined by Some of Its Apostles,* edited by Parsons (Chicago: L. E. Parsons, 1889).

From Life of Albert R. Parsons, with Brief History of the Labor Movement in America, *1889; University Library, University of Illinois Urbana-Champaign*

Lucy E. Parsons remained unwaveringly committed to defending the rights of laborers for more than three-quarters of a century. She attacked capitalist society as an oppressor of working-class people and believed anarchism offered the only solution to the social inequities she witnessed. Parsons used her expressive voice, her rhetorical prowess, her unabashed directness, and her impassioned eloquence to challenge the powers of industry and government and to inspire exploited workers to action. She delivered finely crafted speeches, and she was a popular and prolific columnist in many radical publications. Despite the public prominence and notoriety she gained during her lifetime, historians have long overlooked her significant contributions to the labor movement. Her role as powerful labor agitator and devoted social activist has frequently been subordinated to her role as the widow of Albert R. Parsons, one of the anarchists hanged after the famed Chicago Haymarket incident. Parsons worked closely with her husband for more than a decade before the Haymarket trial, and although she consistently invoked the executions as evidence of a failed social system, she served as a leading radical figure in her own right.

In response to personal questions Parsons typically responded only with the assertion that the anarchist labor movement was greater than any individual. The paucity of details about her private life illustrates her lifelong adherence to this philosophy. Almost nothing is known of her before her 1873 arrival in Chicago and subsequent involvement in labor organizations. Scholars believe that the woman who came to be known as Lucy E. Parsons was born near Waco, Texas, around 1853. Her middle initial presumably stands for either Ella or Eldine; researchers have found signatures with each name. The issue of her name is further complicated by the discovery of documents revealing that Parsons employed several surnames including Carter, Diaz, Gathings, Gonzalez, and Hull. Some historians believe that Parsons was once married to a former slave named Oliver Gathings or Gaithings. It is possible that Parsons herself was born into slavery, and she is generally considered to have had some African American ancestry. In the rare instances that she mentioned her past, however, Parsons claimed to be the daughter of a Mexican woman named Maria del Gather and a Creek man named John Waller, and spoke at times of pride in her Native American roots. After being orphaned as a very young child she lived with her uncle Henry del Gather in Buffalo Creek. In his autobiography Albert Parsons maintains that he met Lucy at del Gather's Ranch in 1869, returning three years later to marry her. William Parsons, Albert's brother, attested that Lucy spoke Spanish fluently. Despite these corroborations, most biographers consider her narrative at least partially fabricated, perhaps for the purpose of protecting her from danger or dishonor in a social climate hostile to African Americans, miscegenation, and women's rights. Ultimately, Parsons' origin and ancestry remain indeterminable.

Lucy and Albert Parsons claimed to have been wed in Austin, Texas in 1871 or 1872. The legality of the marriage is questionable, however, for local officials would have been loathe to sanction the marriage of a woman of color and a white man during a time when the Ku Klux Klan actively committed heinous racial atrocities (some of which Lucy Parsons claimed to have witnessed firsthand). The couple departed from Texas in late 1873 or early 1874 in order to escape rampant prejudice and violence. Albert Parsons, a vocal advocate of racial equality in his political speeches and newspaper articles, had been attacked on several occasions for registering black voters and otherwise cooperating with the federal government in post-Confederate Texas. He had visited Chicago briefly and found it a promising city, so they decided to make it their home.

Moving to Chicago proved a pivotal event in Parsons's life. Almost immediately she and Albert Parsons became members of local trade union organizations. He worked as a journalist and joined the typographical union. He spoke frequently at union meetings, joined the Social Democratic Party, and co-founded the city's chapter of the Knights of Labor. Once introduced to the concepts of socialism, the couple became increasingly radical in their beliefs. They hosted meetings of the Workingmen's Party in their home. The fervent discussion at these gatherings and news of massive labor strikes in the East excited Lucy Parsons. She was not alone in her interest; growing numbers of Chicago's workers assembled to hear speeches against capitalism and in favor of workers' rights. Albert Parsons frequently commanded the platforms at these events, and Lucy Parsons was always in attendance.

After the Great Upheaval wound its way across the country in the summer of 1877, Parsons' responsibilities at home and in the labor movement expanded. Albert Parsons spoke at an event related to the Chicago railroad workers' strike that devolved into a deadly conflict between police and protestors. Consequently, he was fired from his position as printer at the Chicago *Times* and blacklisted from further employment in that field. Simultaneously, Lucy Parsons's involvement in labor issues grew, and in 1879 she published her first of many newspaper pieces. The item appeared in the *Socialist*, the paper of the Socialistic Labor Party edited by Albert Parsons. "A Parody" was a dark verse about poverty, hunger, unemployment, and the oppression of workers in imitation of Lord Byron. Parsons' oratorical career was in its incipient stages as well. She began addressing members of the Working Women's Union and received praise for her skill. The specific content of her speeches to the Working Women's Union has been lost, like many of the specifics regarding the organization, but it likely differed little from the content of the many speeches that ensued.

All of Parsons's accomplishments in 1879 she achieved while pregnant with her first child. Albert Richard Parsons was born on 14 September of that year. Lulu Eda Parsons was born two years later on 20 April 1881. By all accounts the Parsons family was happy, although they, like so many other families of the time, struggled financially. They moved constantly once a year or more often—the entire time they lived together in Chicago. Parsons ran a dressmaking business at their home, and Albert worked in the shop. The parents were deeply engaged in the radical cause and included the young children in the picnics, rallies, and parades that characterized the contemporary labor movement. Both of them hoped to raise the children to be socialist radicals who might continue the work they had begun.

As she watched labor continue to fight against wealthy industrialists and witnessed the worsening condition of the working class in Chicago, Parsons turned to a more revolutionary philosophy. She and her friend

Lizzie Swank gathered facts about the pay of pieceworkers and the increasing numbers of homeless people, and they endorsed the use of violent and destructive means to challenge the capitalist system. In 1881 both Lucy and Albert Parsons left the Socialist Labor Party, and they joined the new International Working People's Association (IWPA) in 1883. The IWPA was more militant, and its members considered themselves anarchists. Parsons was known for her militancy even within the organization. In the inaugural edition of the *Alarm,* the association's newsletter, her front-page editorial announces her position. "To Tramps" was an incendiary piece encouraging the disheartened and suicidal unemployed to dedicate their last moments to the labor struggle by using explosives against the rich. Following a long and sympathetic account of the suffering of the jobless, she urged: "But halt, before you commit this last tragic act in the drama of your simple existence. Stop! Is there nothing you can do to insure those whom you are about to orphan against a like fate?" She advised the "tramps" to employ dynamite so that "you can be assured that you have spoken to these robbers in the only language which they have ever been able to understand, for they have never yet deigned to notice any petition from their slaves that they were not *compelled* to read by the red glare bursting from the cannon's mouths, or that was not handed to them upon the point of the sword" ("To Tramps," *The Alarm,* 4 October 1884). Parsons's article proved a rallying point for both the labor movement and their opposition. It articulated the intense frustration and desperation of the working class as well as the greatest fear of the industrialists. In addition, it made clear the anarchist group's perspective that the aims of labor and industry cannot be reconciled and that capitalism must be abandoned to eliminate the imbalanced class system it produces. After it appeared in *The Alarm* "To Tramps" was published as a pamphlet and distributed on the streets.

The publication of "To Tramps" solidified Parsons's status as a leading figure in the anarchist labor movement. She spoke to labor groups around the city, happily headed processions carrying a red banner, and organized large gatherings of workers for demonstrations. As she gained fame within the labor movement, she gained notoriety in the press. She continued to use *The Alarm* as her own platform, publishing essays like "The Factory Child: Their Wrongs Portrayed and Their Rescue Demanded" and "The Negro: Let Him Leave Politics to the Politician and Prayers to the Preacher." These editorials addressed the diverse social issues of child labor and the lynching of African Americans, but Parsons attributed them both to capitalism and endorsed anarchy as their remedy. Her involvement with *The Alarm* increased when during the summer of 1885 she managed the paper in Albert Parsons's absence. Approximately twenty-one thousand IWPA members were on the circulation list at that time. By 1886, Parsons was active in the eight-hour-day movement, which sought to reduce workers' hours while keeping their pay the same, and the movement won significant victories. Parsons had become immensely influential in labor circles, and she reached many people through her tireless efforts.

The successes of the larger labor movement inspired wealthy conservative citizens to create funds to aid the police force in suppressing all labor demonstrations. Protestors and speakers commonly met with harassment, and several confrontations escalated into deadly assaults. The most notorious conflict between protestors and Chicago police occurred at Haymarket Square on 4 May 1886. A relatively small crowd of two or three thousand gathered to hear several prominent anarchists speak about police attacks on picketers at the McCormick reaper factory. Albert Parsons was among the orators. Near the end of the rally, after the Parsons family had gone to Zepf's Hall, a bomb detonated, and police responded by firing into the crowd. Ultimately seven workers and seven police officers died. Police sought the arrest of many anarchists, including Albert Parsons and others of *The Alarm* circle.

The day following the Haymarket attack Parsons began reacting to the episode. She was arrested and released three times on 5 May, but she worked feverishly between the interruptions. She appealed to IWPA members around the country for contributions toward a defense fund for those arrested in connection with the attack. Her husband had fled Chicago the previous night at the urging of their friends and was hiding in Wisconsin. She communicated with attorneys, dealt with the press, demanded justice for the prisoners, and published her version of the Haymarket events in the 10 May issue of the *Denver Labor Inquirer.* In "The Haymarket Meeting: A Graphic Description of the Attack on that Peaceable Assembly" she called the incident "the shortest, sharpest, and most decisive battle, I believe, on record" (Ahrens). She urged readers to wait for more information before forming opinions; she accused the police of invading her home; and she requested support for the imprisoned men. She believed that only public sympathy for the accused would win their acquittal. Albert Parsons returned and surrendered himself in a Chicago courtroom as the trial commenced on 21 June.

The Haymarket trial lasted for a month and, despite the state's documented inability to establish a link between the bomb and the defendants, the court found the defendants guilty of conspiracy to murder a police officer. Five men, including Albert Parsons, were sentenced to death, while others received prison terms. One of the condemned men committed suicide in his cell before the execution date. Lucy Parsons and her children were evicted from their apartment. She sent the children to stay with friends and worked indefatigably to win public support and raise defense money for the prisoners, hoping the case could be appealed to the Illinois Supreme Court. She lectured throughout the eastern half of the United States, gaining publicity for the case. In Chicago she faced personal attacks as the Texas press, getting wind of the case, rehashed the sordid details of her past and inspired Chicago reporters to do the same. Knights of Labor leader Terence Powderly denounced her. Despite a stay of execution, Parsons was ultimately unsuccessful in her mission to have the court's ruling overturned. After the Supreme Court refused to hear the case, she was arrested for speaking and for distributing a statement written by her husband.

At noon on 11 November 1887 the four men who had been sentenced to death were executed. Parsons had been arrested earlier in the day for attempting to see her husband once more, and she, her children, and Lizzie [formerly Swank] Holmes, were strip-searched and incarcerated during the hanging. At 3:00 P.M. police returned their clothing and allowed them to claim Albert Parsons's body. More than ten thousand visitors came through her apartment in the day before his funeral. The next day some quarter- to one-half million Chicagoans watched as Knights of Labor led the funeral procession of fifteen thousand people to Waldheim cemetery in defiance of Powderly. While Parsons felt proud of her husband's sacrifice, she grieved profoundly after his death. Overwhelmed with sadness and loss, she succumbed to outbursts of hysteria. Even in this time of intense sorrow, however, she worked with Lizzie and William Holmes to complete a compilation of writings on their common cause. On December 10 they published under Albert Parsons's byline *Anarchism: Its Philosophy and Scientific Basis, as Defined by Some of Its Apostles*. Parsons edited the volume, which contained several of her husband's writings, some essays from other anarchists, and an essay of her own. Police confiscated all but three hundred copies of the book. Parsons sold copies of it while walking along the streets of Chicago.

The Pioneer Aid and Support Association formed to provide support for the widows of the Haymarket Martyrs. Parsons received $12 weekly from the Pioneers for the next eight years. The next year her book appeared in a German edition. Not long after the publication of *Anarchism* Parsons directed her attention toward another book. Twice she was arrested for vending copies of *Anarchism*, but police harassment did not

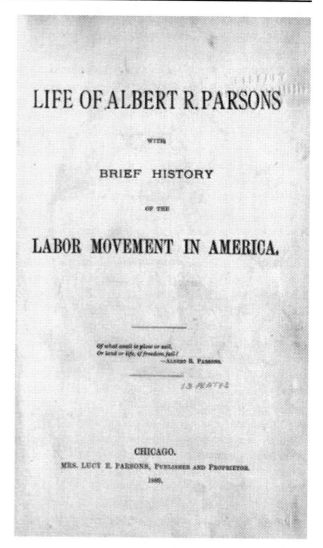

LIFE OF ALBERT R. PARSONS

WITH

BRIEF HISTORY

OF THE

LABOR MOVEMENT IN AMERICA.

CHICAGO.
MRS. LUCY E. PARSONS, PUBLISHER AND PROPRIETOR.

Title page for Parsons's first book, which collected the writings of her husband, one of the Haymarket Martyrs (University Library, University of Illinois Urbana-Champaign)

deter her from the new project. She continued to address audiences at various types of events, even completing a successful speaking tour in Europe in October 1888. She was admired overseas and appeared alongside other famous anarchists such as Petr Kropotkin and William Morris who were influential in Britain. She finished *The Life of Albert R. Parsons, with a Brief History of the Labor Movement in America* in March 1889. This book comprised Albert's writings and letters. In the foreword Parsons described her motivations for publishing the volume and attested to the veracity of the material included. She intended to restore her husband's "sterling integrity as a man" by proving that he was not a criminal, that he was in no way connected to the Haymarket bombing, and that he had always worked on behalf of the suffering and oppressed. In order to convince "the most prejudiced as well as the most liberal minds" of these points, she collected statements from Albert Parsons's ideological adversaries, hoping that these might lend a sense of credibility and objectivity to the text. She aspired to create "a work which might be relied upon as an authority by all future writers upon the matters contained in it." To this end, nothing was "admitted to its pages that is not absolutely correct, so far as it is possible for me to verify it by close scrutiny of all matter treated" (Ahrens).

Dyer D. Lum, who had assumed editorial duties for *The Alarm* after Albert Parsons's death, stopped publishing the newspaper in early 1889, sold the subscription list, and moved away to become Samuel Gompers's secretary, all the time sniping at Parsons. During this year a young German printer named Martin Lacher helped Parsons with the book and eventually moved in with her. He worked for the Pioneer Aid and Support Association. She added *The Life of Albert R. Parsons* to the assortment of books and pamphlets she sold around the city and at speaking engagements. Persisting fascination with the Haymarket trial and waxing poverty and unemployment in Chicago helped with sales. A demonstration had been planned in New York to commemorate the second anniversary of the Haymarket execution, and Parsons wrote to Jo Labadie that she planned to make public appearances en route to that event. She canceled her plans for the tour, however, when her eight-year-old daughter Lulu died of a lymph-system disorder on 13 October 1889.

Parsons carried on with her work. She took note as infighting among movement supporters increased and the policemen who had orchestrated the arrest of the anarchists were one by one expelled from the police force in corruption scandals. In 1891 she took on the editorship of *Freedom, a Revolutionary Anarchist-Communist Monthly*. The foci of the paper were class struggle, revolution, and the suppression of free speech by police, though a broad range of topics was addressed in these terms, including the racial violence that peaked throughout the country that year. In April 1892 Parsons published the article "Southern Lynchings" condemning racial violence in the South and warning that its protraction would lead to revolt. "Brutes, inhuman monsters—you heartless brutes—you whom nature forms by molding you in it" she cautioned the perpetrators, "deceive not yourselves by thinking that another John Brown will not arise" (Ahrens). In the June and August pieces "Ominous Times" and "Rumblings of the Coming Storm" she decried violent attacks on striking workers in Idaho and Pennsylvania and suggested that they augured imminent revolution. Midyear she separated from Lacher after their relationship descended into violence. She brought charges against

him, and he spent a night in jail, but the judge dismissed him with a small fine. Extant issues of *Freedom* reveal that it also addressed women's issues, but it is unclear whether Parsons wrote on the subject for that newspaper.

The election of John P. Altgeld as governor of Illinois in 1892 led to the realization of one of Parsons's most earnest hopes. On 23 June 1893 Governor Altgeld unconditionally pardoned the three men imprisoned for conspiracy in the Haymarket trial. In addition, he published a lengthy document declaring that the trial was based on prejudice and corruption, facts rendering the final verdict unjust. In the seven years since the court's initial ruling Lucy Parsons had attempted to persuade the public of Albert Parsons's innocence, and Altgeld's determination that the guilt lay with the judicial system, not the accused men, proved a significant reward for her efforts. Typically, however, Parsons continued to lead an embattled life. Altgeld had appointed her old friend George Schilling the director of the Illinois Bureau of Labor Statistics, and Parsons was disappointed when he scolded her in a private letter for wasting her energies in aid of "foreigners." She had no intention of abandoning the working-class people to whom she had devoted most of her life, whoever they were, and she showered curses and imprecations on the police at every opportunity, in speeches and in print. The financial panic and rising unemployment and homelessness fueled participation in labor agitation and repeated confrontations with the police. Even Parsons's writing addressed to comrades pelted her readers with unanswered questions and commands.

Around the turn of the century Parsons continued to follow the routine she had established in earlier decades. She spoke wherever her presence was requested. Picketers in Chicago could expect her support on the line, and she sold and distributed anarchist literature on the sidewalks. She became a contributor to the *Rebel*, an anarchist newspaper printed in Boston, in 1895. A fire destroyed her home the following year, but she simply salvaged what she could, offering damaged copies of her books and pamphlets at reduced rates. Although Parsons remained passionately devoted to educating people about anarchism, her philosophy changed. By the close of the nineteenth century she had abandoned the notion that individual terrorist acts could change the capitalist system. She still demanded action, but no longer advocated violent action. More and more she focused on standards of living in the city and building trade unions. She joined Eugene V. Debs's group Social Democracy and met Emma Goldman in June 1897. Later that year Parsons began to write more openly about women's issues, in particular the "free love" debates. Predictably, she clashed with Goldman on that subject. Unlike Goldman, Parsons valued the right to wed the person of her choice, and although she always had male companions, she thought Goldman's public openness about such matters in poor taste.

While Parsons maintained a reputation as an outspoken radical, Albert Parsons Jr. developed into a law-abiding conservative. He attended church regularly and enlisted in the military to fight in the Spanish American War. Parsons, who opposed the war and dissuaded other young men from enlisting, was upset by the decision. In the summer of 1899 she had her son committed to the Illinois Northern Hospital for the Insane, claiming that he had attacked her with a knife. After a brief hearing the court pronounced Albert insane, although the doctor who examined him never diagnosed him with any specific psychological ailment.

As the twentieth century commenced, Parsons was writing about the rising cost of living and the decline of real wages for the publication *Free Society*. Radical publications flourished until the 1901 assassination of President William McKinley. The press and the government made connections between the Haymarket bombing and the assassination. The result was a wave of severe anti-anarchist legislation. Anarchists were denied entrance to the United States and foreign anarchists already within the country were threatened with deportation. *Free Society* collapsed, but Parsons never failed to find a platform from which to share her convictions. With the help of donations Parsons was able to reprint *The Life of Albert R. Parsons*. She had planned a new introduction and supplementary article, but they did not appear in the 1903 reprint. In exchange for monetary contributions from others in the labor movement Parsons did include short biographies of the seven other accused men in the Haymarket case. Carrying the new editions of her book, Parsons embarked on a speaking circuit in the East.

Feeling that no periodical in Chicago represented her philosophy, in 1905 Parsons decided to publish the *Liberator*. For Parsons, all social ills were fundamentally class issues, but class struggle was becoming less important to other anarchists. The paper, therefore, was not successful with intellectuals, although it had a working-class readership. In the *Liberator* Parsons wrote more about women than she had previously. She created a weekly column called "Famous Women in History" in which she offered brief accounts of figures such as Florence Nightingale and Louise Michel. She also endorsed women's reproductive freedom and supported their rights to marry and divorce as they desired. It was another form of economic oppression, she contended, for a woman to rely on men for the essentials of life. In "Woman: Her Evolutionary Development" she called upon women to stop accepting

The Haymarket Monument. The inscription reads "The day will come when our silence will be more powerful than the voices you are throttling today" (from Paul Avrich, An American Anarchist: The Life of Voltairine de Cleyre, 1978; Thomas Cooper Library, University of South Carolina).

lower wages than men. Although she wrote in the *Liberator* about women's oppression, children in factories, crime, and other social problems, she did so in the context of the labor movement. Her central concerns were still to educate workers about anarchy and to inspire them to stand up for their rights. In late June 1905 she attended the meeting to found a new radical union, the Industrial Workers of the World (IWW).

Parsons had traveled widely in her long career, but she made her first journey to the West Coast in 1908. Her reception there encouraged her to broaden her selection of literature for sale. In 1909 she first published *The Famous Speeches of the Eight Chicago Anarchists in Court: When Asked if They Had Anything to Say Why Sentence of Death Should Not Be Passed upon Them: October 7, 8, and 9, 1886*. In the preface to the first edition of *Famous Speeches* Parsons called the volume "an echo from the grave" and suggested that it was "singularly timely, as present-day labor conditions but bear out the real significance and meaning of the prophecies and warnings of these martyrs to the cause of humanity." The new book sold ten thousand copies in two years and helped Parsons to fund the traveling and speaking on which she thrived. Parsons spent most of the next years on the road, traveling to centers of labor conflict or delivering lectures organized by friends. Police records provide the most accurate account of her whereabouts as she moved eagerly from city to city. She was jailed in Los Angeles for selling pamphlets, and she was turned away at the Canadian border. In San Francisco she tried to speak to an audience of the jobless, but she was arrested for inciting riot. Even in the West, Parsons, then about sixty, was deemed a dangerous woman.

In Chicago, Parsons's presence was ubiquitous. She had broad interests, attending meetings of the Anthropological Society, for example, to hear lectures about the growing practice of vaccination against disease. Almost every radical memoir from this period includes at least one Lucy Parsons reference, usually rendered in striking imagery. In June 1912 she attended the funeral of her comrade, Voltairine de Cleyre, bringing a spray of red carnations for her husband's grave at Waldheim. She worked from time to time with IWW groups, but when she led a march of the unemployed in 1915, some felt her domineering personality was out of sync with the IWW credo, succinctly stated by a union member during the Everett massacre: "we ain't got no leaders; we're all leaders."

The last of Parsons's edited books came out in 1915. She printed *Altgeld's Reasons for Pardoning Fielden, Schwab, and Neebe* with an introductory note in which she commended Altgeld for his noble and courageous decision to pardon the men. Nearly thirty years had passed since the trial, but Parsons wanted to make sure that the sacrifices of her husband and his comrades were not forgotten. Albert Parsons Jr., died of tuberculosis on 15 August 1919 after twenty years in the psychiatric hospital. Parsons left no evidence that she ever saw her son after he was admitted to the center. She refused to discuss it, and she kept his ashes at her home.

The 1920s brought disappointment to Parsons. She had dedicated all of her energy to a labor movement she watched unravel during the Red Scare that occurred at the end of World War I. A sense of paranoia pervaded government, and radical activities and organizations were deemed threats to the nation's security. In 1918 The Espionage Act and The Sedition Act became law, and they were used to squelch radical sentiment. Those who had opposed the war or questioned the government's decisions in speech or print faced surveillance, censorship, large fines, expensive trials, long prison terms, and in some cases deportation. The legislation was used to jail hundreds of members of the IWW, to shut down radical publications to which Parsons had long contributed, and to deport radical figures like Emma Goldman. The Palmer Raids, initiated by Attorney General A. Mitchell Palmer in 1920, forced the dissolution of the IWW and polarized the Left, leaving the Workers' Party (later the Communist Party) as the strongest surviving group. With the disbanding of radical leadership and the narrowing of choices, workers lost momentum. Parsons avoided arrest during this chaotic period; nevertheless, she was deeply affected by the changes it wrought. Many of the individuals and organizations with whom she had been aligned were gone.

Parsons continued to devote all of her time to the cause she loved, adapting to the new conditions. She continued to speak anywhere her talents were needed, and she was a visible figure in Chicago for the remainder of her life, eager to share information with any who would listen. She became affiliated with the Communist Party, and she worked for the party's International Labor Defense. Despite her involvement in the Communist Party, she yearned for the fervor she had experienced in her younger days.

Neither Parsons nor the anarchists recovered the power and excitement they had known in the decades preceding World War I, but Parsons continued to contribute to the labor cause until the end of her life. In the 1930s Parsons could still be seen walking Chicago's sidewalks, distributing leaflets, promoting anarchism, even leading marches of the homeless. While she continued with this somewhat old-fashioned practice, she also participated in new radical trends that developed. For instance, she frequented the Dil Pickle Club, a renowned venue for free speech and creativity. During the week, the Dil Pickle hosted a broad variety of artistic and cultural performances, and on Sunday it offered an open forum. Parsons was often listed as a speaker on the forum posters; there she could associate with surviving contemporaries and influence a new generation of radicals. She was usually accompanied by her supportive romantic partner of some years, George Markstall, who assisted her as her eyesight worsened. Parsons never abandoned her conviction that the conditions of working people could be improved and that oppressive capitalist social and economic structures could be overturned.

On 7 March 1942 Parsons died in a house fire. Almost completely blind at the estimated age of eighty-nine, she was unable to exit the burning building. Markstall attempted to rescue her, and he later died of the wounds he incurred. Parsons was buried close to her husband in Waldheim cemetery.

Lucy E. Parsons's career as a social activist spanned six decades. She was a captivating orator and an avid writer of speeches and articles. At every available opportunity she exercised her right to free speech. In her time she was a nationally known labor agitator who inspired workers to unionize and challenge dangerous and unfair labor practices. In the years after her death, recognition of her work decreased. Carolyn Ashbaugh's biography *Lucy Parsons: American Revolutionary,* published in 1976 by the Charles H. Kerr Company, offered the first reminder of her contributions to the labor movement. In 2004 another Kerr publication, *Lucy Parsons: Freedom, Equality, and Solidarity: Writings and Speeches, 1878–1937,* edited by Gale Ahrens, made some of her articles, lectures, and letters accessible. As a woman and a minority Parsons is of interest to the developing discipline of cultural studies. Parsons may secure a place in history equal to her contemporary reputation, although she would not have minded if her name were forgotten as long as her message was recalled.

Biography:

Carolyn Ashbaugh, *Lucy Parsons: American Revolutionary* (Chicago: Charles H. Kerr, 1976).

References:

Gale Ahrens, ed., *Lucy Parsons: Freedom, Equality, and Solidarity: Writings and Speeches, 1878–1937* (Chicago: Charles H. Kerr, 2003);

Paul Avrich, *The Haymarket Tragedy* (Princeton: Princeton University Press, 1984);

Frank O. Beck, *Hobohemia: Emma Goldman, Lucy Parsons, Ben Reitman and Other Agitators and Outsiders in 1920s/30s, Chicago,* edited by Franklin Rosemont (Chicago: Charles H. Kerr, 2000);

Philip Foner, ed., *The Autobiographies of the Haymarket Martyrs* (New York: New York Humanities Press, 1969);

Arlene Meyers, "The Haymarket Affair and Lucy Parsons: 100th Anniversary," in *The Radical Papers,* edited by Dimitrios I. Roussopoulos (New York: Black Rose Books, 1987);

Bruce C. Nelson, *Beyond the Martyrs; A Social History of Chicago's Anarchists, 1870–1890* (New Brunswick, N.J.: Rutgers University Press, 1951).

Terence V. Powderly

(22 January 1849 – 24 June 1924)

Mark A. Noon
Bloomsburg University

BOOKS: *Thirty Years of Labor, 1859 to 1889* (Philadelphia: T. V. Powderly, 1889);

A Little Journey to the Home of Elbert Hubbard (East Aurora, N.Y.: Roycrofters, 1905);

The Path I Trod: The Autobiography of Terence V. Powderly, edited by Harry J. Carman, Henry David, and Paul N. Guthrie (New York: Columbia University Press, 1940).

OTHER: "The Army of the Unemployed," in *The Labor Movement: The Problem of Today,* edited by George McNeill (Boston: A. M. Bridgman, 1887), pp. 575–584;

John Ennis, *The White Slaves of Free America,* contribution by Powderly (Chicago: R. S. Peale, 1888).

SELECTED PERIODICAL PUBLICATIONS– UNCOLLECTED: "The Organization of Labor," *North American Review,* 135 (August 1882): 118–126;

"The Army of the Discontented," *North American Review,* 140 (April 1885): 369–377;

"Strikes and Arbitration," *North American Review,* 142 (May 1886): 502–507;

"The Plea for Eight Hours," *North American Review,* 150 (April 1890): 464–469;

"On Earth Peace, Good Will toward Men," *Cosmopolitan,* 12 (December 1891): 155–160;

"A Knight's View of Labor," *North American Review,* 155 (September 1892): 370–375;

"My Painful Experiences as a Tramp," *American Federationist,* 8 (September 1901): 332;

"Immigration's Menace to the National Health," *North American Review,* 175 (July 1902): 53-60;

"A Man and a Stone: The Same Being a Little Journey with John Siney," *United Mine Workers Journal* (11 May, 18 May, 25 May 1916).

One of labor history's most maligned figures, Terence V. Powderly led the Knights of Labor (KOL) from 1879 to 1893. The organization rose to its pinnacle and

From Thirty Years of Labor, 1859 to 1889, *1890; Robarts Research Library, University of Toronto*

declined into irrelevance under Powderly's tenure as grand-master workman. As a result, he won high praise and became extremely popular, but he also came to be considered inept and self-serving. While much of his writing attempts to answer his critics, his books and articles are a valuable addition to the source literature of the American labor movement, providing important insight into the leading labor federation of the nineteenth century and the struggle to organize workers during the Gilded Age.

Born in the anthracite coal community of Carbondale, Pennsylvania, on 22 January 1849, Terrence Vincent Powderly was the eleventh of twelve children raised by Irish working-class immigrants Terence Powderly and Margary Walsh. Plagued by health problems his entire life, he was a thin, sickly child. A bout with scarlet fever left him deaf in one ear, and he suffered from poor vision and quinsy, a chronic throat condition that led to fevers and abscesses on the tonsils. Due to his physical ailments, he took little interest in sports and, instead, turned to books, spending many evenings with other family members reading before a coal fire. His formal education was brief. He went to a common school in the basement of the Catholic church his family attended. In 1862, at the age of 13, he quit school to begin the same career path as his father—a railroad machinist.

Powderly proved a reliable worker despite his physical difficulties and moved through the ranks as a railroad employee quickly, first working as a switch guard, then as brakeman, and, after a three-year apprenticeship, moving to a position as master machinist. Events in the region gradually guided the young man toward a career as a labor activist. A series of economic recessions and wage struggles following the Civil War slowed the production of anthracite coal in northeastern Pennsylvania, and Powderly was laid off in 1869. In August of that year, he moved from Carbondale to Scranton. Within a month, the young man was deeply affected by a major mining accident that occurred in Avondale, Pennsylvania, approximately fifteen miles south of Scranton. On the morning of 6 September 1869 a coal breaker caught fire. The blaze spread rapidly, and the breaker boys who picked slate from the mined coal and the men working above ground scrambled to safety. The 108 men in the underground workforce were not as fortunate. Not one miner escaped. The mine had only one entrance, and the burning structure blocked it. The blaze raged for several days, and two men were killed in the rescue effort. Powderly was among many who traveled to Avondale after hearing about the disaster. As the bodies were being removed, he heard pioneer labor agitator John Siney denounce the coal operators and their disregard for the safety of their workers. Siney—founder of the first union of anthracite workers, the Workingman's Benevolent Association—called on those gathered on a hillside near the smoldering mine at Avondale to fight to "win fair treatment and justice for living men who risk life and health in their daily toil." Siney's cry for reform profoundly changed Powderly, as he later recalled in his autobiography, *The Path I Trod* (1940):

When on that September day at Avondale I saw the blackened, charred bodies of over one hundred men and boys as they were brought to the surface, when I saw a mother kneel in silent grief to hold the cold, still face of her boy to hers, and when I saw her fall lifeless on his dead body, I experienced a sensation that I have never forgotten. It was such a feeling as comes to me whenever I read of death in the mines or on the railroad. Then when I listened to John Siney I could see Christ in his face and hear a new Sermon on the Mount. I there resolved to do my part, humble though it might be, to improve the condition of those who worked for a living.

Inspired by Siney's activism, Powderly joined the Machinists' and Blacksmiths' International Union in 1871 and worked in the Scranton local as a speaker, organizer, and correspondent. In 1873, he was elected president of the local and also served as its secretary. His personal life took a positive turn in 1872 when he married Hannah Dyer; the young couple faced adversity almost immediately however, when Powderly was blacklisted for his union activity. From 1873 to 1875, he went on the road in search of work, tramping hungry and alone through Pennsylvania, New York, and Canada. His struggles finding employment and his union involvement broadened his awareness of workers' efforts to form national labor unions and promote broad industrial reforms. In 1874, he joined and became a delegate and organizer for the Industrial Brotherhood, a labor society with delegates in over thirty states. Though the Industrial Brotherhood lasted only about two years, in 1874 Powderly took an oath to support what became a much more significant labor association—the Noble and Holy Order of the Knights of Labor.

More of a social-reform organization than a trade union, the KOL supported a broad agenda bordering on utopianism. Founded in 1869 in Philadelphia by Philadelphia tailor Uriah Stephens, the KOL pursued several goals including abolition of the wage system, government regulation of land monopolies, the eight-hour day, the elimination of child labor, a graduated income tax, and equal rights for women. With blacklisting and union repression increasing in the difficult economic times following the Civil War, Stephens opted to pattern the KOL after fraternal orders and secret societies. The new labor organization operated under codes and complex rituals adopted from Freemasonry, and, as a result, it grew slowly with a membership largely limited to workers in eastern Pennsylvania.

Powderly became an official member of the KOL on 6 September 1876. His initiation was a decisive moment in his life, and he became dedicated to expand-

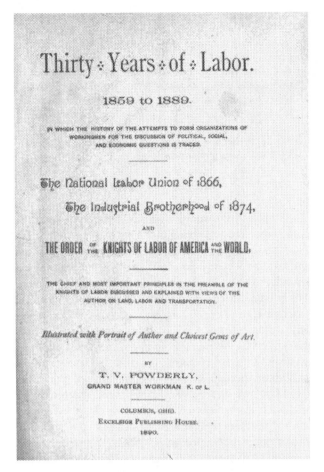

*Title page for Powderly's history of labor unions
(Robarts Research Library, University of Toronto)*

ing the organization's membership. "Prior to my admission to the Knights of Labor I had little time for rest and recreation," Powderly recalled. "After September 6, 1876, I knew no waking hour that I did not devote, in whole or in part, to the upbuilding of the Order" *(The Path I Trod)*. Before the close of the year, he founded and became president of his KOL local, Scranton District Assembly No. 5, and also assumed duties as corresponding secretary of his district assembly. By 1877 he had abandoned the machinist trade and become totally devoted to politics and union activity. The young activist proved to be such an effective organizer that he was elected general grand-master workman (president) in 1879, when Stephens resigned the post to run unsuccessfully for Congress. Powderly also scored a major victory on the local political front. Running on the Greenback-Labor Party ticket, he was elected three times as mayor of Scranton from 1878 to 1884—adding to an already frantic array of duties.

Powderly assumed the KOL presidency at a time of radical changes in America's industrial and social order. Many disgruntled workers—burdened by low

pay, long hours and poor working conditions—were primed for organization. In 1879, the KOL had about ten thousand members. To boost membership, Powderly encouraged members to abandon secrecy and masonic rituals, and he championed a "union open to all." During the 1880s, the organization developed a reputation for inclusiveness. Women were welcomed as members, and, in 1883, African Americans were accepted under segregated locals. Like other early labor organizations, however, the KOL feared the rising tide of immigration and the increased competition for jobs it created for the existing workforce. With Powderly's blessing, the KOL actively campaigned in support of the Chinese Exclusion Act of 1882 and the Contract Labor Law of 1885. Despite its efforts to limit immigrant workers, the KOL continued to grow, bolstered by success in several strikes. The most notable victory came in 1885 in a labor struggle with Jay Gould's Southwestern Railway in 1885. By 1886, the KOL claimed more than 729,000 dues-paying members. The union's growing popularity sparked the interest of the general public and brought Powderly into national prominence.

Considered the spokesperson of American labor in the early 1880s, Powderly became a media sensation. Both the mass and labor press ran his speeches and portraits, and newspaper reporters constantly plagued him for interviews. Baking-powder containers, chewing-tobacco packages and haberdashers' trade cards featured Powderly's name. Children, as well as an Alabama town, were named after him. The labor leader was in great demand. Activists, reformers, politicians, industrialists, and religious leaders sought his opinion about the nation's growing industrial strife. Requests for lectures poured into his office, and, despite his preference to stay at home with his wife in Scranton, he traveled widely and frequently to speak on behalf of labor. When he did make public appearances, contemporaries noted his charisma and refinement. He gradually developed strong oratorical skills and had an extraordinary ability to remember names and faces. His fame also led him to become involved in other causes, most notably Irish and Irish American affairs. Powderly took pride in his ethnic and religious heritage and took leadership positions in the Irish National Land League and the Clan na Gael. Activism in Irish affairs also had its political benefits, making Powderly more popular among the many Irish American workers in northeastern Pennsylvania.

Much of Powderly's time was consumed by responding to letters of enquiry about KOL activities. His assistance was limited to one clerical secretary, and he often had to take up pen and ink and make carbon copies of his replies by himself. When Powderly's widow released his voluminous correspondence to scholars in the 1930s, the collection included between seventy-five thousand and one hundred thousand letters, postcards, and telegrams. In addition, Powderly somehow found the opportunity to respond to requests by editors for articles. He often contributed to journals to reach out to the rank and file. One of his earliest attempts to keep in touch with KOL locals sprinkled across the nation appeared within weeks of his election as grand-master workman. In an independent labor journal based in Philadelphia called *The Trades,* Powderly wrote a series of eight letters providing instructions to workers about union membership and addressing such issues as election of officers, the importance of paying dues, and the importance of attending local meetings. According to the letters, which were published between November 1879 and February 1880, irresponsible members of the KOL frequented saloons, physically abused their wives, and failed to pay their union dues. He urged righteous Knights to make extraordinary sacrifices to ensure that they could pay their dues. Powderly could use language skillfully and stirred the passions of KOL members. Drawing on his working-class background, he developed detailed examples familiar to industrial laborers. He also showed an ability to spell out the KOL position on major labor questions for a wide, general audience by contributing articles to journals such as the *North American Review* and chapters to books such as George McNeill's major compilation, *The Labor Movement: The Problem of Today* (1887).

The year of the Great Upheaval—1886—when the number of strikes and boycotts soared, marked the height of KOL membership as well as the beginning of its decline. When a bomb killed several people at a workers' rally at Haymarket Square, Chicago, on 4 May 1886, a general repression of labor organizations ensued and the public's perception of labor darkened. Capitalists were emboldened, and labor organizations became divided. The KOL then suffered a series of key losses in the wave of strikes and boycotts that were part of the aftershock of the Great Upheaval, most notably the Chicago Stockyard Strike (1886), the New York Central Strike (1890), and the Homestead Steel Strike (1892). The KOL grew weaker yet when cigar maker Samuel Gompers founded the American Federation of Labor (AFL) in 1886. Gompers's fledgling union steadily made inroads into the KOL rank and file. The KOL also suffered from a complex, inadequate bureaucracy; its mix of trades and a web of local, district, and state assemblies made conflicts difficult to resolve. It fell to Powderly to deal with ideological and jurisdictional disputes in the organization and the resulting conten-

tiousness. Despite continued success bringing African Americans and women into the association, membership in the KOL dropped dramatically to about one hundred thousand as the 1890s opened.

Powderly came under attack from all sides—from trade-union members, fellow Knights, employers, reformers, politicians, and clerics. His compromising positions on important issues often dissatisfied KOL members. For example, as grand-master workman he opposed strikes in general and stated that he would authorize one only after "every reasonable means had been resorted to to avert the strike." He based his position, rooted in the long string of failed strikes since the Civil War, primarily on the organization's inability to pay strike benefits to its members.

Other positions were equally controversial. Radicals were angered by Powderly's stand regarding the Haymarket anarchists. Some unions viewed the accused Haymarket men as martyrs and attempted to rally to their support. Powderly, however, believed that the KOL would be tainted with anarchism if he joined the campaign and refused to support the Haymarket clemency campaign to save the convicted defendants in Chicago from the hangman's noose. He writes in *The Path I Trod:*

> I did not hate the condemned men, I did not oppose every man doing what he could to cause the governor to deal leniently with them, and I did not desire their execution as has been said. What I did oppose was committing the Order of the Knights of Labor to the teachings of anarchy.

Through the years he continued to defend his position and remained an outspoken critic of socialism. He was equally unyielding concerning another controversial issue in the Gilded Age—temperance. Many working-class immigrants undoubtedly did not share Powderly's ardent support for temperance organizations. He was particularly outspoken on the subject. He was a teetotaler, and in his youth he joined the major Catholic temperance organization, the Father Theobald Mathew Total Abstinence and Benevolent Union. Although the KOL was an open organization, it denied membership to workers involved in the liquor trades. Powderly formed an alliance with the Women's Christian Temperance Union. His stand on temperance drew its power from the impact that the saloon had on family life, as he records in *The Path I Trod:*

> Let me say that while I was Grand Master Workman I not only did not drink, but would not enter a saloon for fear of encouraging members to do so. . . . I believed, and believe now, that the worst [enemy] to the

workingman is the saloon. It has worked more ruin than any other cause. It has brought desolation to more homes than any other agency. It has starved more children–physically and spiritually–than anything else I ever knew. It has caused the murder of wives, and has driven women to prostitution. . . . I did what I could to cause Knights of Labor and workingmen generally to keep away from the saloon.

Powderly had been among the earliest to attempt to link alcohol abuse with the Molly Maguire episodes in the anthracite coalfields in the 1870s. The wave of violence in counties south of Scranton led to the hanging of twenty Irishmen and had a profound impact on Powderly, who actually met with one of the convicted men in his jail cell before the hangings. As a temperance advocate, Powderly noted that a number of accused Molly Maguires were saloonkeepers, and he argued that violence in the region never would have occurred if area priests had conducted a vigorous campaign against alcohol abuse.

Powderly had an opportunity to elaborate on his ideas when he decided to write an extended account of the KOL, *Thirty Years of Labor, 1859–1889* (1889). According to his preface, the idea for a study of national labor movements in the United States occurred to him in 1886 when industrial conflict "attracted the attention of all classes toward the labor problem" and became the "theme of conversation in public and private." Powderly noted that his manifold duties made it difficult to complete the project and "the time in which the work was done was stolen, here and there, as occasion presented itself to the author." In the initial chapters, he shares his expertise on early labor history and his insight into the formation and eventual decline of the National Labor Union and the Industrial Brotherhood. He sets the opening perimeter of his study as 1859 when the Machinists' and Blacksmiths' Union of Pennsylvania held a convention and adopted a preamble calling for a closer bond between workers of all trades. In that same year, William Sylvis (1828–1869) began efforts to form the National Union of Iron Molders. Eventually, Powderly turns to the main focus of his book, the formation and policies of the KOL.

Powderly quotes generously in *Thirty Years of Labor,* producing a compilation of primary documents including committee reports, letters, minutes from general assemblies, speeches, constitutions, and preambles. He uses these materials to discuss such issues as land agitation, the eight-hour workday, temperance, immigration, anarchism and socialism, and the role of African Americans and women in the labor movement. The book often becomes bogged down in details about the principles of the KOL and its bureaucratic operations. Surprisingly, little insight emerges about the conflicts facing the organization or Powderly's actions in response to them. The conclusion finds Powderly at his most poetic as he proudly describes the good accomplished by the order and looks to the future:

> The full extent of the good that has been done by the Order of the Knights of Labor will never be known. It is not within the bounds of human possibility to detail the many acts that have gone to benefit the millions. One fact attests the value of the Order: Its enemies have attacked it, belied its aims and purposes, and have opposed its advances as they never did those of any organization since the world began. Had the Knights of Labor been weak and unworthy of notice, this would not have been done. . . . The great work is still ahead of us. We must look to the future for what we have been contending for in the past *(Thirty Years of Labor).*

Powderly hoped the book would reenergize the KOL and strengthen his position as leader. It sold poorly and did neither. He blamed its publisher for failing to promote it.

The KOL was in serious decline in the three-year period when the book was written. The loss of membership that began following the Haymarket incident continued. The problems opened the door for his critics, who for years believed Powderly unfit for the office he held. More and more, KOL organizers and the rank and file found the union president vain, arrogant, meddling, and argumentative. More militant, Marxist Knights argued that Powderly had lost contact with workers and was more interested in adulation from employers than service to the membership. By 1892 his allies' support totally evaporated, and in 1893 his opponents inside the organization forced him to resign. The following year he was expelled from the KOL, although he was reinstated in 1900.

Powderly studied law following his resignation. He was admitted to the Pennsylvania bar as an attorney but was unable to establish a successful practice. After aiding the Republican Party as a stump speaker from 1894 to 1896, he was named U.S. commissioner general of immigration in 1897. One of his significant achievements in that post was the institution of the nation's first screening procedures for contagious eye diseases and an improved system for providing medical examination of immigrants. A corruption scandal on Ellis Island prompted President Theodore Roosevelt to remove Powderly from his position in 1902. Powderly later served in a variety of positions in the Department of Labor and the Bureau of Immigration. In 1901 Hannah died, and Powderly mourned for months. Eighteen years later, he married Emma Fickenscher, who had

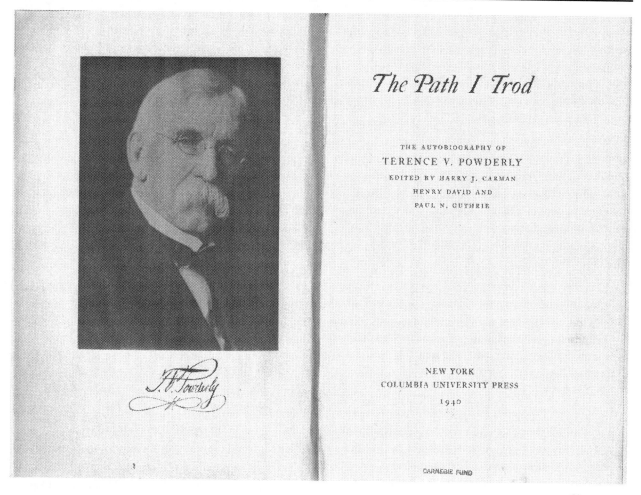

Frontispiece and title page for Powderly's autobiography (Thomas Cooper Library, University of South Carolina)

been his secretary when he led the KOL. He died in Washington, D.C., on 24 June 1924. He was buried in Scranton's Cathedral Cemetery, not far from the grave of another noted labor leader, John Mitchell, president of the United Mine Workers of America and the leader in the anthracite strikes of 1900 and 1902.

Emma Powderly released her husband's papers to scholars a few years before her death in 1940. Researchers learned with surprise that Powderly wrote an autobiography and had apparently worked on it for years. On 22 January 1907 he had written to a friend:

> This is my birthday. I am fifty-eight years young today. Tomorrow I begin to write a partial autobiography. . . . I have not been understood by many and I want to prepare this to leave after me so that I shall be able to give a reason for what I did even tho my lips will be sealed. . . . No one knows what my motives were but me, and I am going to tell why I did certain things so that my real self will be known by those who care to read.

The project had a slow start, and most of the writing occurred between 1914 and 1921. Powderly may have been motivated by hostile assessments of his leadership by labor historians who wrote in the first quarter of the twentieth century, such as William Kirk, Robert Hoxie, and Selig Perlman. The autobiography was edited by Harry J. Carman, Henry David, and Paul N. Guthrie and published posthumously in 1940 by Columbia University Press. In the opening of *The Path I Trod*, Powderly acknowledges that many viewed him unfavorably. The autobiography is an attempt to set the record straight:

> Many of my principal events have become history through pens that took their coloring from friendship, enmity, jealousy, partiality, or prejudice; some of my friends saw in me a demi-god and said so, my enemies, equally as truthful perhaps, from their viewpoint, saw only a demon, and not only said so but kept repeating it. I was not only not good enough to be the former or bad enough to be the latter and tried to strike a mean between such opposites.

To some, the autobiography failed as a history. Craig Phelan describes *The Path I Trod* as "a meandering, self-justifying portrait that has done little to enhance his reputation."

The early chapters of *The Path I Trod* provide vivid details of Powderly's upbringing, his early work experiences in northeastern Pennsylvania, and his conversion to the cause of organized labor. The book is particularly noteworthy for the details about the KOL's organizational methods. Powderly describes in detail membership qualifications, initiation rites, oaths, rituals, and the duties of officers. He also discusses symbols and slogans in detail. For example, a short chapter and appendix is devoted to "the Philosopher's Stone degree" given to Knights who achieved "meritorious conduct in the field of labor." A second appendix documents the "secret circular" read annually at KOL locals and explains the significance of the images in the "Great Seal of Knighthood."

In describing the major events during his years as grand-master workman, Powderly takes an approach similar to the one taken in *Thirty Years of Labor*—quoting heavily from letters, speeches, and union records to justify his decisions. Chapters cover major strikes, prominent personalities he came to know, and his work on behalf of Ireland's Land League. The passing of years and the closing of the KOL's national office in 1917 permitted Powderly to be more open and sincere in his discussion of important issues, particularly in one of the final chapters, "Ecclesiastical Opposition." That part of the book details Powderly's handling of one of the greatest impediments to the KOL—the Catholic Church's objection to secret, oath-bound societies. Many members of the Knights were Catholic; however, bishops frequently sent parishes letters condemning secret societies, and priests threatened to condemn parishioners who did not denounce the fraternal order. As grand-master workman, Powderly worked hard to avoid friction between the KOL and church hierarchy, but he expressed his frustration in *The Path I Trod*:

> Many a priest of the Roman Catholic Church in the day I am speaking of was a tyrant by nature, and his elevation to the priesthood gave him the opportunity to exercise, in a limited way, his tyrannous will. Perched upon a lordly summit from which he brow-beat and berate, he seldom exercised toleration, moderation, or charity in dealing with the poor of his charge.

The autobiography's closing chapter, "Part of My Reward," offers harsh criticism for the nation's business leaders, with Andrew Carnegie cited as a prime example. After describing Carnegie's vast wealth, Powderly argues that to make the money "the sweat and blood of thousands were poured freely forth in steel mill and blast furnace." He then describes in vivid detail the death of a worker in one of Carnegie's plants, and the corporation's abandonment of the dead man's wife and children.

Recent studies of the Knights of Labor continue to point out the failures of Terence V. Powderly during his tenure as grand-master workman; however, he was inducted into the Labor Hall of Fame in 2000. Arguably, the honor was justified. He helped the KOL grow into the largest labor organization of its time, and his efforts on behalf of labor solidarity gave hope to thousands of Gilded Age workers when they faced insurmountable odds.

References:

Herman Bloch, "Terence V. Powderly and Disguised Discrimination," *American Journal of Economics and Sociology,* 33 (1974): 154–160;

Harry J. Carman, "Terence Vincent Powderly–An Appraisal," *Journal of Economic History,* 1 (May 1941): 83–87;

John Common, and others, *History of Labour in the United States,* volume 2 (New York: Macmillan, 1918);

Vincent Falzone, *Terence V. Powderly: Middle Class Reformer* (Washington, D.C.: University Press of America, 1978);

Leon Fink, *Workingman's Democracy: The Knights of Labor and American Politics* (Urbana: University of Illinois Press, 1983);

Gerald Grob, "Terence V. Powderly and the Knights of Labor," *Mid America,* 39 (1957): 39–55;

Robert Hoxie, *Trade Unionism in the United States* (Chicago: University of Chicago Press, 1917);

Sidney Kessler, "The Organization of Negroes in the Knights of Labor," *Journal of Negro History,* 37 (July 1952): 248–250;

Richard Oestreicher, *Solidarity and Fragmentation: Working People and Consciousness in Detroit, 1875–1890* (Urbana: University of Illinois Press, 1986);

Selig Perlman, *A Theory of the Labor Movement* (New York: Macmillan, 1928);

Craig Phelan, *Grand Master Workman: Terence Powderly and the Knights of Labor* (Westport, Conn.: Greenwood Press, 2000);

John A. Turcheneske Jr., *Terence Vincent Powderly Papers, 1864–1937, and John William Hayes Papers, 1880–1921: The Knights of Labor: A Guide to the Microfilm Edition* (Glen Rock, N.J.: Microfilming Corporation of America, 1975);

Kim Voss, *The Making of American Exceptionalism: The Knights of Labor and Class Formation in the Nineteenth*

Century (Ithaca, N.Y.: Cornell University Press, 1993);

Samuel Walker, "Terence V. Powderly, the Knights of Labor and the Temperance Issue," *Societas,* 5 (1975): 279–294;

Norman Ware, *The Labor Movement in the United States, 1860–1895: A Study in Democracy* (New York: Appleton, 1929);

Robert Weir, *Knights Unhorsed: Internal Conflict in a Gilded Age Social Movement* (Detroit: Wayne State University Press, 2000).

Papers:

The papers of Terence V. Powderly–including diaries, scrapbooks, and memorabilia–are held by the Department of Archives and Manuscripts of the Catholic University of America, Washington, D.C.

Adam Clayton Powell Jr.

(29 November 1908 – 4 April 1972)

Claude Hargrove
Fayetteville State University

BOOKS: *Marching Blacks: An Interpretive History of the Rise of the Black Common Man* (New York: Dial, 1945; revised, 1973);

Keep the Faith, Baby! (New York: Trident, 1967);

Adam by Adam: The Autobiography of Adam Clayton Powell, Jr. (New York: Dial, 1971).

OTHER: U.S. Congress, House, *Additional Views of Adam Clayton Powell, Jr., on Minority Report,* 79th Cong., 2nd sess. (Washington, D.C.: Government Printing Office, 1946);

U.S. Congress, House, *The New Image in Education: A Prospectus for the Future by the Chairman of the Committee on Education and Labor,* 87th Cong., 2nd sess. (Washington: Government Printing Office, 1962);

U.S. Congress, House, *Hearings, February 8, 14, 16, 1967,* 90th Cong., 1st sess. (Washington, D.C.: Government Printing Office, 1967).

Adam Clayton Powell Jr., minister, social-justice activist, and member of the U.S. House of Representatives, first became famous by association with his father, the minister of the Abyssinian Baptist Church in Harlem. The younger Powell followed his father's path, actively participating in the church's social-welfare programs in the late 1920s and throughout the Great Depression. The economic crisis caused Powell to involve himself in racial and social-justice causes, particularly those involving jobs for African Americans in New York. He began to be known as a speaker outside the church in these years, and he wrote columns in African American newspapers, one of which he founded and published. In 1937 he took charge of the church, and in 1945 he was elected to the U.S. House of Representatives, becoming the second African American representative elected since Reconstruction. In that role Powell took part in the growing Civil Rights Movement, and a piece of legislation he sponsored made its way into the Civil Rights Act of 1964. He had always been controversial, but in these years he faced a series

Adam Clayton Powell Jr., jokingly showing his Faubus for President pin, 1960 (Charles V. Hamilton, Adam Clayton Powell, Jr.: The Political Biography of an American Dilemma, *1991; Thomas Cooper Library, University of South Carolina)*

of scandals that ended his political career. He wrote his autobiography shortly before his death in 1972.

Powell was born on 29 November 1908 in New Haven, Connecticut, to Adam Clayton Powell and Mattie Fletcher Powell. His sister Blanche was ten years old at the time. Born in 1865 in Virginia, twenty-five days after Robert E. Lee's surrender at Appomattox, the senior Powell was a Baptist minister whose prominence in the Harlem community exerted a strong determining force on the future of his son. His father had worked in West Virginia and Ohio coal mines but unfailingly gambled away most of his money until he experienced a religious conversion at a revival meeting, decided to lead a life of sobriety, and began in 1885 to work as a Baptist minister. Powell Sr. ministered to the congregation of the Abyssinian Baptist Church from its hundredth anniversary year of 1908, shortly after Adam's birth, to 1937, when his only son inherited the pastorate. Abyssinian Baptist was more than a church; it was a powerful force in Harlem for social justice, well respected throughout New York and adjacent states. Powell Sr. built the Abyssinian Baptist Church from a congregation of about sixteen hundred to more than ten thousand, and he helped to establish the social-service mission of the church by erecting a new building, a community house, and a home for the aged.

Adam Powell Jr. grew up in middle-class comfort. Powell Sr. adhered to many of the tenets of Marcus Garvey's belief system, and Powell Jr., at the age of fifteen, joined Garvey's African Nationalist Pioneer Movement. After attending high school at Townsend Harris Hall, Powell had a checkered college career, flunking out of City College of New York after two bad semesters. In the 1920s Harlem, with hundreds of speakeasies, rent parties, and dance halls, was a wild bachelor's delight. Powell spent the modest amount of money he made as a kitchen helper on gambling, women, and liquor.

After Powell's sister Blanche died suddenly of peritonitis in March 1926, his father pushed him back into college, this time at the almost-all-white Colgate University in Hamilton, New York. Powell came from a fair-skinned family. Both his father and his sister had passed on various occasions, as Powell did initially at Colgate, but he was exposed by classmates who found that his father's church was in Harlem. He forthrightly apologized to the handful of other young black male students. In the summers his father insisted that he must work, so Powell found employment in New England resort towns. He still found his way back to the night life of New York City from time to time, and on one such trip he met Isabel Washington, who became his first wife. She was a Catholic from Savannah, Georgia, married, and working as a dancer and actress, none of which recommended her to the senior Powell.

Young Powell had an interest in going to Harvard to study medicine, but with some prodding, he realized that one day his father's well-off church could be his for the asking, so he chose to become a healer of souls instead. Powell was better educated than most civil-

rights activists of his day, but fell short in formal theological study. His real training for the ministry came from hearing thousands of Powell Sr.'s sermons and witnessing many of his good works. His first sermon at his father's church was delivered on Good Friday, 1930, just before his graduation from Colgate. After his graduation trip to Asia and North Africa, Powell briefly took graduate courses at Union Theological Seminary before he completed a master's degree in religious education at Columbia University Teachers' College in 1932. Going to college part-time, he worked as an assistant pastor under his father's supervision and as the business manager of the church. Powell ran a free-food pantry and a job-referral service, and taught literacy classes. As a preacher he cautioned women parishioners, who were mostly domestic servants, to give to the church only what they could afford.

As a leader Adam Powell Jr. inclined toward intolerance of racism, the use of racial rhetoric in denouncing racists, and overly cautious black leaders. His complexion, oratorical skills, natural self-confidence, and quick wit earned Powell a degree of acceptance; but he was regarded with disdain by whites and many black leaders, who generally espoused a philosophy of gradualism as a strategy for challenging racism. Powell was a radical from the start, a lover of both justice and pleasure. He was styled a "militant" by both the white media and conservative African Americans (who feared white backlash in Northern states where they had made some gains).

The firing of five black interns from Harlem Hospital in the spring of 1930 prompted one of Powell's first public acts to promote racial justice. He had already joined his father and members of the National Association for the Advancement of Colored People (NAACP) in taking on the remaining Tammany Hall fixtures who exerted control over the inferior hospital—the only one available for African Americans in the area. The interns claimed their dismissals were due to racial discrimination and asked Powell to represent them. Powell formed a support committee and staged a series of mass rallies to dramatize the issues. The action culminated in Powell leading six thousand blacks to a Board of Estimates meeting at City Hall. While the demonstrators waited in the streets, Powell persuaded the board to reinstate the interns immediately and order a general reform of the hospital. Eventually, the NAACP forced the resignation of a city commissioner over the issue. In 1932 Powell finally convinced his father to allow him to marry Isabel Washington once her divorce was final. She agreed to be baptized and join the church, and they were wed on 8 March 1933. Powell adopted her son, Preston.

When a *New York Post* reporter requested a comment from Powell on the Harlem Riot of 1935, he strongly criticized police brutality and job and housing discrimination in New York City. His remarks elicited wide support in the black community and led him to contribute a regular column, "Soap box," to the *Amsterdam News*. Powell understood that the number-one issue for most people was making a living, and only the lowest paying and least attractive jobs were available to African Americans in Harlem and throughout America. The unemployment and poverty brought about by the Great Depression harmed African Americans particularly. In Atlanta, Georgia, brash white men calling themselves the "Black Shirts" demanded that no African American hold a job until all whites were employed. Jobs traditionally held by blacks began to go to unemployed whites.

In response, Powell began a campaign for jobs on two fronts. "Don't buy where you can't work," he bellowed to the jobless of Harlem, who shopped at the many stores on that thoroughfare, and the command became a slogan. In months the owners of retail stores, pawnshops, restaurants, cleaners, and dozens of other businesses relented and started hiring African Americans in higher-level jobs, as well as traditional ones. Powell then took on a political ally, New York City mayor Fiorello LaGuardia. Powell wanted African Americans placed in city jobs, not just as janitors but as motormen and conductors. The spoils system, maintained by the politicians and the unions, had implicitly banned African Americans from civil-service jobs. The popular "Little Flower," as LaGuardia was called, was reluctant to battle Powell publicly and thus weaken the African American-Democratic Party alliance; he made concessions. Thousands were not hired, but the point was made; African Americans could realistically aspire to desirable jobs.

In 1937 Powell inherited his father's pulpit. The church had about two-dozen full-time and part-time employees with ties to various sectors of the Harlem community and he used the full force of the pulpit for political organizing. Powell forced the vendors of the 1939 World's Fair to hire and promote African American employees. In 1941 he won a city council seat as an independent. In 1938 Shaw University, in Raleigh, North Carolina, awarded Powell an honorary doctorate of divinity.

Powell rejected party loyalty: "I always liked the guy who was nationally a Democrat, locally a Republican, theoretically a Socialist, but practically a Communist." African Americans, Powell reasoned, should not be tied to one party; thus, they could be swing voters with greater political weight. He also formed important alliances with Jewish leaders in the city, in particular

Morris Rosenblatt, who recognized Powell's organizing abilities and often asked him to speak at Zionist rallies, and Stanley Isaacs, with whom Powell drafted housing bills. In 1941 Powell and Mayor LaGuardia endorsed each other and campaigned together. After Powell was elected to the city council that year, he continued to press for civil rights and for jobs for African Americans in public transportation and the city colleges.

The Federal Bureau of Investigation began to monitor Powell in 1942, as his influence dramatically increased. Powell cofounded the *People's Voice* and published it from 1942 to 1946. Leader of the largest African American church in the nation (thirteen thousand members), he was ready to use his political demagoguery and his charisma in defense of African American nationalism. At the time few African Americans were on the faculty of the city-run colleges. Coming to the defense of an African American instructor terminated at the City College of New York because he was a member of the Communist Party, Powell raised the general issue of African American faculty positions with city council and introduced a resolution to eliminate discrimination in the city colleges. A committee of inquiry concluded that the colleges did not discriminate, but Powell's resolution angered many of his white supporters.

Powell's consistent and continuous criticism of the city government also strained relations between him and Mayor LaGuardia, who had come to see Powell as irresponsible and opportunistic. Powell regarded LaGuardia as paternalistic, and other African Americans agreed with him. In July 1943, Detroit exploded in a race riot, requiring the deployment of federal troops. Blacks believed that whites had raped and murdered a black woman and her daughter and then killed them. Whites believed that blacks were randomly assaulting white women. Black and white gangs did the rest with stones and guns stolen from pawn shops. Powell warned LaGuardia and the city council that conditions in Harlem paralleled Detroit and that a race riot seemed likely if measures were not taken to ameliorate the many problems of Harlem.

The next month his prediction proved accurate as Harlem erupted over an incident involving Private Robert Bandy, charged with assaulting a police officer during the arrest of an African American woman. Rumors spread that police officers had killed a black soldier who was trying to protect his mother. Black gangs looted stores and burned buildings. Both the mayor and Powell called for calm, which returned after two days of rioting. Powell praised LaGuardia's handling of the police, keeping casualties at a minimum, and joined the mayor in calling for calm. Subsequently, the state legislature created a new congressional district in Harlem which guaranteed that an African American would be elected to Congress. In 1944 Powell was elected to the seat as a Democrat, though he was a candidate for all three major parties and even had the backing of the Communists. Powell, who served the new district from 1945 until 1971, was the second black to be elected to Congress since Reconstruction. (William Dawson of Chicago was the first black to be elected in the twentieth century to Congress.)

Powell's wife, Isabel Washington Powell, had figured prominently in his campaign for New York City council and in his election to Congress, although she said afterward that she had advised him against politics as a career. As Congressman Powell rose to national celebrity, however, he began to see his wife's background as a hindrance to his career; they separated in late 1944. Even before his divorce was legal, Powell attended official functions in Washington, D.C., in the company of Hazel Dorothy Scott, a pretty, young, and talented jazz and classical pianist and singer with a Julliard education. Born in Trinidad and Tobago and acclaimed as a musical genius by her teachers, she was comfortable among Washington, D.C.'s black privileged class.

Powell's divorce became final in June 1945, two months after his mother died. He married Scott in Stamford, Connecticut, on 1 August 1945, and they established a permanent residence in White Plains, New York. She soon found, however, that Powell's habitual infidelity left her alone and inconsolably miserable. Scott was an established celebrity when Powell met her; she socialized with jazz musicians and had been in movies. After the marriage she continued to live in her own sphere apart from Powell, with a TV show, *The Hazel Scott Show,* Broadway plays, and successful recordings. But she was a critic of Senator Joseph McCarthy and racial segregation; when she was accused of being a Communist sympathizer, her show was cancelled.

Scott never found acceptance at the Abyssinian Baptist Church. Nor did Powell much resemble other African American ministers. He claimed he followed only the teachings of Jesus as embodied in the Gospels, not the entire Bible, because "it is too filled with contradictions" (*Adam Clayton Powell, Jr.: The Political Biography of an American Dilemma,* 1991). Powell did not see a conflict between his transgressions and the basic tenets held by most Christians on moral conduct. He publicly consumed alcohol, smoked, and had adulterous affairs. Powell's interior dimensions were not easy to understand; he was personable and full of energy, but his schedule left little time for deep reflection on religion or politics. Hazel Scott Powell later claimed that her husband suffered from hyperthyroidism, and that this glandular imbalance accounted for his indefatigable vigor in play and work as both congressman and pastor. The image of a tireless and cool Powell was vital to his success as a minister and civil-rights activist.

Title page for Powell's autobiography, published two years before his death (Thomas Cooper Library, University of South Carolina)

In January 1945 Powell began his first term in Congress, immediately launching an assault on traditional Southern customs and their most vocal defenders. This breach of the informal segregation of the Capitol earned him the enmity of Southern congressmen and a reputation for being brash. Congressman Dawson observed the racist customs by carrying his lunch to the Capitol in a paper bag. He opined that he could achieve more for his constituents through quiet and thoughtful demeanor and dialogue. Powell, on the other hand, defied congressional policies that were racist, insisting on ending segregation in the armed forces and public schools. He introduced legislation to outlaw lynching and poll taxes, without success. He fought to prohibit discrimination in housing and employment. Congressman John E. Rankin of Mississippi, a white supremacist, numbered among the first of Powell's new colleagues to feel his wrath; after Rankin made ethnic slurs against Jewish people, Powell called for congressional censure. Rankin announced that he would not sit by Powell in Congress. Powell replied angrily that he shared the sentiment and that Rankin was a fascist fit to sit by the likes of Hitler and Mussolini. Powell readily won the approval of African Americans in Harlem and throughout the nation. Dressing down a Southern racist guaranteed his continuous electoral victories in the Twenty-Second Congressional District. Though the speaker of the House, Sam Rayburn, admonished Powell to observe the U.S. Capitol's segregation etiquette in restaurants, barbershops, and gymnasiums, Powell ground down those mainstays of racism without stint and demanded the seating of African American journalists in the House's press gallery.

These were heady years for Powell. Writers Zora Neale Hurston and Ann Petry worked for his campaign at various times, and the money was pouring in. In 1946 Powell Sr. married Inez Means, who was blonde, fair, and rumored to be white. Powell Jr.'s son, Adam Clayton Powell III ("Skipper"), was born on 17 July 1946, and whatever their other differences, both Powell and Scott were devoted to him. Powell sustained political wounds, however, when he tangled with President Harry S. Truman over the disrespect shown Scott by Bess Truman, whom Powell decried as the "last lady of the land" when she did not give up her membership in the racially discriminatory Daughters of the American Revolution, which had denied Scott the use of Constitution Hall because of her race, just as it had done to Marian Anderson in 1939. President Truman was angered by Powell's comments, made to the national media, and Powell soon found himself marginalized by the president and the Democratic Party. For six years Powell was not invited to the White House. Federal patronage for Harlem was routed through the office of Congressman Dawson.

Powell's pride and impulsiveness limited his ability to help his Harlem constituents until the 1960s, although his behavior continued to win their approval. Given the reality in Washington, Powell's influence was restricted anyway. Racial segregation was the norm; racist epithets still enjoyed casual use in Congress by such Southerners as Theodore Bilbo, James Eastland, and Rankin. Nonetheless, Powell saw himself as a courageous fighter for social justice and racial equality: "I'm the first bad Negro they've had in Congress," he bragged. He made more enemies on Capitol Hill than perhaps any legislator before or since.

Powell's life and times coincided with the momentous events that led to the Civil Rights Movement of the 1950s and 1960s. Although Powell was a prominent and popular representative from Harlem, he was never fully accepted by more-traditional black leaders. In a real sense, Powell stood between two extremes: black nationalists, who wanted self-segregation and possibly a separate nation, and gradualists, who waited for the courts to act or for the hearts of men to change. Powell's approach combined the heated language of revolution with the restraint of nonviolence, but Powell was a foe of racism, not the white race, though some of his critics argued otherwise. In the short term, Congressman Powell's efforts proved more productive in his drive to desegregate the military and the government. In May 1954 the Emperor Haile Selassie of Ethiopia visited Powell's church and awarded him the Gold Cross of Ethiopia for his Depression-era work of relief in Harlem.

From the very beginning of his rise to political power Powell had been pragmatic and cynical, courting Communist support and then snubbing those supporters, pulling strings to keep his adopted son, Preston, out of combat in World War II, and demanding large sums of cash in exchange for speaking engagements and political favors. After Truman froze him out, Powell threw support to the Republicans, especially after his father died in June 1953. In the 1956 presidential election Powell supported Republican Dwight D. Eisenhower. Powell believed that Eisenhower, without the need to satisfy Southern Democrats, would be more progressive than his opponent on civil rights. Powell might have courted the Republican Party for personal reasons—to forestall a Republican-led federal tax-fraud investigation that began in the early 1950s, when several of Powell's aides were convicted of income-tax evasion and rumors circulated that they had also given Powell kickbacks from their salaries.

In the late 1950s he began to face some consequences of his actions over the past decade. In early 1957 Scott left him, moving to Paris with their son. Powell was indicted in 1958 for tax evasion; the trial resulted in a hung jury, and the Justice Department declined to retry him. In late 1959, following surgery to remove a benign tumor from his chest, Powell went to Puerto Rico, where he met Yvette Flores. About the same time he declared war on organized crime when it began to edge out black numbers runners in Harlem. When city police were not responsive enough, Powell began to name names on the floor of the House of Representatives. There he had immunity, but when he repeated the charges as a guest on a television show in March 1960, Esther James, whom he had identified as a "bag woman" for police graft, ultimately was awarded $262,000 after she sued him for defamation and libel. Powell refused to make a settlement, and the case dragged on for eight years. He ignored all seven subpoenas issued in the case.

During the presidential campaign of 1960 he returned to the Democratic Party, at first to support vice-presidential candidate Lyndon Baines Johnson—John F. Kennedy's record on civil rights did not impress him. Later he supported Kennedy, bringing with him many of the African American votes that had gone to Eisenhower in 1956. Powell appeared on the podium with Kennedy at an October 1960 campaign stop in Harlem. Despite the presence of an aging Eleanor Roosevelt, Kennedy made jokes to the effect that Powell probably had more children named after him than Jefferson or Washington, not just because of his statesmanship. Shortly after his divorce became final, Powell returned to Puerto Rico in December and married Flores. He was friendly with Fidel Castro and took his new wife by boat to Cuba to meet him. Their son Adam Diego Powell ("Adamcito") was born in 1961.

Powell's legislative accomplishments were significant during the administrations of Presidents Kennedy and Johnson. The so-called Powell Amendment, a rider on appropriation bills requiring states to desegregate public schools, was, according to Powell himself, his greatest accomplishment. The amendment, in reality crafted by the National Association for the Advancement of Colored People (NAACP), was voted down; however, its concept and Powell's rhetoric helped to shape the ideology of African American goals. The essence of the Powell Amendment finally reached fruition in Title VI of the 1964 Civil Rights Act. Kennedy's presidency coincided with Powell's rise to seniority in the House and the chairmanship of the powerful House Committee on Education and Labor, which controlled a significant portion of the domestic budget. The committee approved more than fifty measures establishing federal programs for minimum-wage increases, education and training for the deaf, Head Start, school lunches, vocational training, student loans, and standards for wages and work hours, as well as aid to elementary and secondary education and public libraries.

During this time Powell's relationships with Martin Luther King Jr. and psychologist Kenneth Clark (whose doll studies were a key component of the NAACP argument in *Brown v. Board of Education*) offered some insight into Powell's character. When King threatened pickets at the Republican convention where Eisenhower was to be nominated, Powell indicated to King that he was prepared to make public the rumors that King was having a homosexual relationship with Bayard Rustin. Powell and Kenneth Clark clashed over the executive directorship of Clark's Harlem Youth Opportunities Unlimited (HARYOU) and Powell's Associated Community Teams (ACT) projects.

In 1965 President Johnson's War on Poverty awarded $110 million to Clark's project; Powell insisted on a merger between ACT and HARYOU. The struggle between the two was long and fiery. When Clark was asked about his relationship with Powell, he said, "I like him. Adam was one of the most honest, corrupt human beings I have ever met. One of the reasons I like Adam is that he had so few illusions." Clark said Powell told him during their conflict, "Ah, Kenneth, stop being a child. If you come along with me, we can split a million bucks" ("Kenneth Clark, Who Helped End Segregation, Dies at 90," *New York Times*, 2 May 2005). Powell's habit of sarcasm and outspokenness gravely wounded him politically. He had no permanent friends; he sided with traditional civil-rights groups and later accused them of being unworthy of the support of African Americans. Such behavior alienated supporters.

Powell's lavish lifestyle and overseas junkets made him a large target for his fellow congressmen and others who wished him misfortune. The more powerful Powell became, the more often his name became associated with scandal. By the mid 1960s his legislative gains could not protect him from the defection of allies and the results of his own corrupt habits. Powell's customary argument against his accusers, "it's because I am black," proved less successful than it had in earlier decades. Attempting to polish his stained image, Powell changed his strategy, portraying himself as a contemplative political leader. His oratory had served him well in the past, and he thought perhaps it would again. He took to the stump: in a Chicago speech entitled "My Life Philosophy," he outlined a program that would move the Civil Rights Movement to its next stage. The speech, actually a position paper as well as an attempt to establish Powell as a thoughtful moderate leader, explained the development of his ideas over the decade. He described what needed to be done to complete the Civil Rights Movement in the latter sixties.

Powell noted that Martin Luther King Jr. had fought segregation, as he had, but what came next in correcting centuries of racism was debatable. Stokely Carmichael and the Black Power Movement were dangerous, he thought, and would cause a white backlash. Powell called instead for "audacious power" through self-assertion, emphasizing the importance of black pride, and demanding more and better jobs for African Americans. Even this attempt at moderation failed, however, when detractors emphasized Powell's comment "that the Negro revolt must change into a black revolution." Powell, justifiably, claimed that without going beyond desegregation and establishing economic and social justice, African American progress would stall and they would remain the "the hewers of wood and carriers of water."

In 1966 a House committee found Powell had improperly placed his wife on his committee's payroll and vacationed in Europe and the Bahamas at committee expense. Powell claimed that he was doing no more than other members of Congress. He further argued that he was being held to a racist double standard. Many of his old foes, including Clark, agreed, but that did not help him. Powell's seniority was a threat to many congressmen who outranked him but were older or would soon retire; others feared Powell at fifty-eight could serve for another decade or longer, or perhaps even become Speaker of the House. Powell finally escaped to Bimini in 1966 with his receptionist, Corinne Huff, a former Miss Ohio.

Powell was risking being sent to prison. Members of the House were happy to investigate him for pocketing congressional employment paychecks to his wife and for taking junkets abroad with female staffers. Conservatives and Southerners saw an opening to do away with the racial agitator and liberal. Powell's liberalism earned him a 100 percent rating by the Americans for Democratic Action, and he was a key player in Kennedy's New Frontier and Johnson's Great Society. Though Johnson reprimanded Powell for not keeping his word about promised legislation in several telephone calls, the president was publicly silent during Powell's troubles. In 1967 a select committee of the House recommended public censure of Powell, stripped him of his committee chairmanship and seniority, and dismissed Huff. The committee also recommended that Powell be fined, but in March the House rejected these proposals and voted 307-to-116 to exclude him from the Congress for the rest of the term.

In 1968 Powell won a special election to fill the vacancy caused by his expulsion, but he did not attempt to take his seat, knowing that Congress would continue to exclude him. In 1969 the U.S. Supreme Court held that although Congress could expel a member, it could not deny a seat to someone duly elected. Powell finally took his seat after an absence of two years, but without seniority and with his pay docked to pay for financial abuses. In 1970 Charles Rangel emerged from a field of several Democratic contestants to defeat Powell. In 1971 Powell completed his autobiography. He died of prostate cancer on 4 April 1972 at the age of 63.

Adam Clayton Powell Jr. lived an astonishing life in the midst of the African American struggle for equality and social justice. To only emphasize his crusade for fair employment, adequate housing, and integrated education in New York City and his congressional record would omit the heart of his political life, however. Powell was a complex individual who seemed unable to compromise or cooperate with friends and political opponents to gain some political benefit. Many

articles and several books have been written about Powell. Some of them point out his shortcomings as congressman and as a clergyman; others praise his courage and steadfast devotion to his Twenty-Second Congressional District of Harlem and to African Americans across the nation. Rangel later said of Powell: "Adam Powell was one of the most effective legislators who ever served in Congress. He was the only idol we had in those days in Harlem. He was audacious and all of us thought when we entered politics that we wanted to be like Adam. God must have sent him, because we'll never see another like him."

The philosophical Powell, while unformed by education or contemplative thought, was experientially shaped by his father's sermons, Garvey's speeches on black nationalism, and ideas of a dozen street-corner orators in Harlem challenging the status quo. Unstructured as this education was, it allowed for a kind of pragmatism that fit well with Powell's innate cynicism and sharp mind. Powell understood sooner than many African Americans the mercilessness of capitalism, the natural rights of all human beings to be equal before the law, the importance of apposite employment in the slums of America, and the necessity of confronting racism and segregation. Like W. E. B. Du Bois and Clark, Powell seemed to reject integration for desegregation. Desegregation did not require, Powell claimed, that African Americans discard cherished values by assimilation into a larger culture. In that sense, he was a kindred spirit to Malcolm X and Stokely Carmichael, who believed that black culture was good enough and surrendering it would be an implicit admission of their people's inferiority to other ethnic groups. Powell had excellent prospects and might have parlayed his rhetorical skills into true political greatness, but his personal limitations in the end proved too great to overcome. His life was the subject of a 2002 documentary created by his sons, entitled *Keep the Faith, Baby!*

References:

"Adam Clayton Powell, Jr.: Black Americans in Congress, 1870–1989," Office of the Historian, U.S. House of Representatives (Washington, D.C.: Government Printing Office, 1991);

Albert N. D. Brooks, "Profile of a Fighter," *Negro History Bulletin,* 20 (May 1957);

Dominic J. Capeci Jr., "From Different Liberal Perspectives: Fiorello La Guardia, Adam Clayton Powell, Jr., and Civil Rights in New York City, 1941–1943," *Journal of Negro History,* 62 (April 1977): 160–173;

Emmett Coleman [Ishmael Reed], ed., *The Rise, Fall, and …? of Adam Clayton Powell* (New York: Bee-Line Books, 1967);

Alexander E. Curtis, *Adam Clayton Powell, Jr.: A Black Political Educator* (New York: ECA, 1983);

Charles V. Hamilton, *Adam Clayton Powell, Jr.: The Political Biography of an American Dilemma* (New York: Atheneum, 1991);

James Haskins, *Adam Clayton Powell: Portrait of a Marching Black* (New York: Dial, 1974);

Wil Haygood, *King of the Cats: The Life and Times of Adam Clayton Powell, Jr.* (Boston: Houghton Mifflin, 1993);

Neil Hickey and Ed Edwin, *Adam Clayton Powell and the Politics of Race* (New York: Fleet, 1965);

Robert E. Jacoubek, *Adam Clayton Powell, Jr.* (New York: Chelsea House, 1988);

Claude Lewis, *Adam Clayton Powell* (Greenwich, Conn.: Fawcett, 1963);

Lawrence J. McAndrews, "The Rise and Fall of the Powell Amendment," *Griot,* 12 (Spring 1993): 52–64;

Kent M. Weeks, *Adam Clayton Powell and the Supreme Court* (New York: Dunellen, 1971).

Papers:

Adam Clayton Powell Jr.'s papers are at the Schomburg Library, New York City. Other collections with significant Powell material include the NAACP Papers, Library of Congress; the American Baptist Historical Society Papers, Rochester, New York; and the papers of various contemporaries in the Municipal Archives, New York City. Powell's file in the archives of the Federal Bureau of Investigation contains the best-known collection of many of his periodical publications.

Jeremy Rifkin

(26 January 1945 –)

James A. Young
Edinboro University

BOOKS: *Own Your Own Job: Economic Democracy for Working Americans,* by Rifkin and Randy Barber (New York: Bantam, 1977);

Who Should Play God? The Artificial Creation of Life and What It Means for the Future of the Human Race, by Rifkin and Ted Howard (New York: Delacorte, 1977);

The North Will Rise Again: Pensions, Politics, and Power in the 1980s, by Rifkin and Barber (Boston: Beacon, 1978);

The Emerging Order: God in the Age of Scarcity, by Rifkin and Howard (New York: Putnam, 1979);

Entropy: A New World View, by Rifkin and Howard (New York: Viking, 1980);

Algeny: A New Word, a New World, by Rifkin and Nicanor Perlas (New York: Viking, 1983);

Declaration of a Heretic (Boston: Routledge & Kegan Paul, 1985);

Time Wars: The Primary Conflict in Human History (New York: Holt, 1987);

Biosphere Politics: A New Consciousness for a New Century (New York: Crown, 1991);

Beyond Beef: The Rise and Fall of the Cattle Culture (New York: Dutton, 1992);

The End of Work: The Decline of the Global Labor Force and the Dawn of the Post-Market Era (New York: Penguin Putnam, 1994, 2004);

The Biotech Century: Harnessing the Gene and Remaking the World (New York: Tarcher/Penguin Putnam, 1998);

The Age of Access: The New Culture of Hypercapitalism, Where All of Life Is a Paid-For Experience (New York: Penguin Putnam, 2000);

The Hydrogen Economy: The Creation of the Worldwide Energy Web and the Redistribution of Power on Earth (New York: Tarcher/Penguin Putnam, 2002);

The European Dream: How Europe's Vision of the Future Is Quietly Eclipsing the American Dream (New York: Tarcher/Penguin Putnam, 2004).

RECORDING: "Into the 21st: The Future of Commerce, Economy, and Culture," read by Rifkin,

Jeremy Rifkin (from the dust jacket for his The European Dream, *2004; Richland County Public Library)*

What is Enlightenment? <http://www.wie.org/bios/jeremy-rifkin.asp>.

OTHER: *How to Commit Revolution—American Style, Bicentennial Declaration: An Anthology* edited by Rifkin and John Rossen (Secaucus, N.J.: Lyle Stuart, 1973);

Common Sense II: The Case against Corporate Tyranny, edited by Rifkin and Rossen (New York: Bantam, 1975);

The Great Bicentennial Debate: History as a Political Weapon, a Record of the Debate between Jeremy Rifkin and Jeffrey

St. John, Held at St. Olaf's College, Minnesota, 1976 (Washington, D.C.: Heritage Foundation, 1976);

The Green Lifestyle Handbook: 1001 Ways to Heal the Earth, edited by Rifkin (New York: Holt, 1990);

Voting Green: Your Complete Environmental Guide to Making Political Choices in the '90s, edited by Rifkin and Carol Grunewald Rifkin (Garden City, N.Y.: Doubleday, 1992).

SELECTED PERIODICAL PUBLICATIONS–
UNCOLLECTED: "The Biotech Century: Playing Ecological Roulette with Mother Nature's Designs," *E: The Environmental Magazine* (May/June 1998) <http://www.emagazine.com/view/?632>;

"Patent Pending," *Mother Jones* (May/June 1998) <http://www.motherjones.com/new/special_reports/1998/05/rifkin.html>;

"Jeremy Rifkin on Dangers of GE Food," *Boston Globe* (7 June 1999), reprinted in <http://www.organicconsumers.org/ge/rifkin6799.cfm>;

"The Perils of the Biotech Century," *New Statesman* (6 September 1999) <http://www.newstatesman.co.uk/199909060007.htm>;

"Another Wolf at Our Door," *Guardian* (24 October 2000) <http://www.guardian.co.uk/Archive/Article/0,4273,4080638,00.html>;

"The Price of Life," *Guardian* (15 November 2000) <http://www.guardian.co.uk/Archive/Article/0,4273,4091302,00.html>;

"Log Off Now: New Technology Was Supposed to Make Our Lives Easier, Not Take Them Over," *Guardian* (26 May 2001) <http://www.guardian.co.uk/Archive/Article/0,4273,4193178,00.html>;

"Dawn of the Hydrogen Economy," *Oil & Gas Investor,* 22 (30 November 2002): 42–44;

"Hydrogen: Empowering the People," *Nation* (5 December 2002) <http://www.thenation.com/doc/20021223/rifkin>;

"The Dawn of the Hydrogen Economy," *Globalist* (10 January 2003) <http://www.theglobalist.com/DBWeb/StoryID.aspx?StoryiD=2738>;

"Dazzled by the Science," *Guardian* (14 January 2003) <http://www.guardian.co.uk/comment/story/0,3604,874312,00.html>;

"Thanks, Mr President: Bush's Actions Are Helping Europe to Fashion a New Sense of Identity," *Guardian* (26 April 2003) <http://www.guardian.co.uk/comment/story/0,3604,943877,00.html>;

"Man and Other Animals," *Guardian* (16 August 2003) <http://www.guardian.co.uk/comment/story/0,3604,1019899,00.html>;

"The European Dream: Building Sustainable Development in a Globally Connected World," *E: The Environmental Magazine* (30 April 2005) <http://www.emagazine.com/view/?2308>;

"American Capitalism vs. European Social Markets," *Spiegel Online* (1 August 2005) <http://www.service.Spiegel.de/cache/international/0,1518,366944,00.html>;

"Sorry, Mr. President, Homilies Won't Stop Hurricanes," *Guardian* (23 September 2005) <http://guardian.co.uk/hurricanes2005/story/0,16546,156714,00.html>;

"An Afternoon with Jeremy Rifkin," *WorldTrans* <http://www.worldtrans.org/whole/rifkin.html>.

Jeremy Rifkin is best known as a maverick figure in the debates about the moral implications of the biotech industry. Like his contemporary Ralph Nader, he began his writing career with conventional training for a man of his class and ideological background, then during the 1960s he diverged radically from the mainstream of liberal thought. He became an aggressive and vocal challenger of the undemocratic power that large institutions and corporations wield over the average citizen in the contexts of marketing, labor, the environment, health, and technology. Believing that these powerful forces exert an undue influence through their ability to control the framing discourses of moral and pragmatic debates, Rifkin committed himself to a lifetime as an advocate for consumers of mass-produced "truth." In particular he has targeted widely received notions of what human efforts count as normality, progress, and intellectualism, as he called upon individuals, communities, and governments to take responsibility for making informed choices about policies and behaviors that will expand or limit the horizons of people in the future. During the course of his development as a writer and activist, he has forged surprising allegiances and enmities.

Rifkin was born to Milton and Vivette Rifkin in Denver, Colorado, on 26 January 1945. His father, Rifkin wrote in *The End of Work* (1994), "understood, better than anyone I know, the workings of the marketplace," while his mother exemplified "the volunteer spirit in American society." Rifkin took a bachelor's degree in economics at the University of Pennsylvania's Wharton School of Business and then a master's degree in international affairs at the Fletcher School of Law and Diplomacy at Tufts University in Massachusetts. He turned from a conventional business career after a stint with Volunteers in Service to America (VISTA) in Harlem during the 1960s and as a result of his growing opposition to the war in Vietnam. In 1967 Rifkin helped to organize the first nationwide protest against that war and helped to found the watchdog Citizens' Commission into U.S. War Crimes in Indochina in 1969. By 1971, when he moved to Washington, D.C., and witnessed the commercially dominated and superficial commemoration planned for the nation's bicentennial, Rifkin set himself against the predominance of corporate values and interests in American culture. He founded the People's Bicentennial Commission.

As head of the People's Bicentennial Commission, Rifkin strove to provide alternatives to the 1976 celebration planned by conservative governmental and corporate authorities. He organized events and activities that emphasized the democratic values embedded in the nation's founding principles: Tom Paine over John Hancock, the Declaration of Independence of 1776 over the Constitution of 1787. Rifkin and the commission staged anticorporate demonstrations, distributing leaflets describing their alternative perspectives, and called at every opportunity for a redistribution of the nation's wealth. Rifkin also published his first works in pursuit of this mission. He and John Rossen collected and edited contributions to *How to Commit Revolution American Style—Bicentennial Declaration: An Anthology,* published in 1973. Rifkin followed two years later, again in conjunction with others, with *Common Sense II: The Case Against Corporate Tyranny.* His rising stature as social critic won recognition from the Heritage Foundation, which published *The Great Bicentennial Debate: History as a Political Weapon, a Record of the Debate between Jeremy Rifkin and Jeffrey St. John, Held at St. Olaf's College, Minnesota, 1976.* In this setting Rifkin introduced his much-repeated thesis that powerful interests use their control of a society's sense of its history to circumscribe people's views of what is possible and thereby to sustain the hegemony of the dominant social groups.

Rifkin's attitudes and activities from the latter 1960s through the mid 1970s foreshadowed his approach to American institutions and ideals into the twenty-first century. Whether the subject under consideration concerned history, the environment, economic justice, biomedical practices, or other matters, Rifkin could be expected to challenge the conventional perspectives and the assumptions that underlay them. He strove to speak truth to power. Attacked by the science-technology-corporate elite and their supporters as an irresponsible gadfly, Rifkin frequently caught the attention of the public and of decision makers with bold assaults on the establishment and its evasion of accountability. To promote his message, Rifkin established the People's Business Commission in 1977, soon to become the Foundation on Economic Trends (FOET), which he financed chiefly in the early days through his prolific publications and his many public appearances. In time FOET came to advise governments, business leaders, labor organizations, educators, and civic leaders on a broad range of emerging scientific, technological, and economic trends around the world. In addition to lead publications by Rifkin and

others, FOET generated seminars and conferences, reports, and position papers. The organization's financial base included support from private foundations, as well as from individuals.

The wide range of Rifkin's interests became evident in 1977. From the bicentennial and other historical concerns, he turned to two other matters. First, in keeping with his earlier focus on American democratic ideals, Rifkin joined with Randy Barber to write *Own Your Own Job: Economic Democracy for Working Americans.* The authors urge workers to develop tactics for controlling economic development at their work sites. Rifkin collaborated the same year with Ted Howard on *Who Should Play God? The Artificial Creation of Life and What It Means for the Future of the Human Race.* Howard and Rifkin challenge conventional notions about the desirability of genetic engineering and voice their concern that advances in biotechnology have begun to outstrip mankind's ability to identify and weigh the positive and negative aspects of such practices as gene transference, cloning, selective breeding and other apparent scientific advancements that provide the ability to affect genetic composition of life-forms. The book, accompanied by Rifkin's lectures and television appearances, established him as a leading opponent of corporate-driven genetic alteration schemes. *Who Should Play God?* also indicated a broadening of Rifkin's focus that came to include a general critique of the Western-initiated idea of progress as it had developed over the previous two hundred or more years, as well as a readiness to question economic and scientific decisions on moral and religious grounds.

In 1978 Rifkin—again in conjunction with Barber—returned to larger, worker-related economic concerns in *The North Will Rise Again: Pensions, Politics and Power in the 1980s.* The authors argue that labor unions constitute the only real power bloc in the United States that is capable of fighting for the rights of working people, much more than "all the Common Causes, Ralph Naders, and public-interest groups together." Despite what they describe as the "ossified and lethargic" union leadership of that time, Rifkin and Barber looked to a "new unionism" that was associated with the Miners for Democracy organization, reform currents in the Teamsters union, and the energy of Ed Sadlowski's dissident campaign for the United Steel Workers presidency to overcome the conservatism and complacency of the labor establishment and the concerted anti-union programs of corporate America. The loss of good-paying union jobs, the authors noted, was being accomplished by the corporate strategy of the "runaway shop," that is, moving work to the largely non-union South or out of the United States entirely. In that connection, they dedicated a portion of the proceeds from the sale of their book to support for the labor boycott of an intensely anti-union Southern textile manufacturer, the J. P. Stevens Company.

The labor challenge, Rifkin and Barber urge, should include union takeover of workers' pension funds and the investment of those funds in what they call "the Greybelt" of declining industrial areas of the East and Midwest. In the workers' pension funds, they argue, lies the means of balancing the pro-Sunbelt bias of federal government grants and contracts and the accompanying investment of private capital in the South and the Southwest, with their cheap labor and tax concessions. Noting that legal impediments obstructed some of their more ambitious suggestions, the authors nonetheless encourage organized labor to save itself and American workers from the fate threatened by capital drain from the industrial heartland. In doing so, they give voice to progressive labor leaders such as International Association of Machinists and Aerospace Workers president William Winpisinger, who argued at the time that "with control over pension funds, we could change the whole course of history."

Rifkin's focus soon shifted again. In continued pursuit of a balanced approach to the uses of science and technology, Rifkin filed a series of lawsuits against the University of California at Berkeley and the National Institutes of Health in opposition to the release of genetically manipulated organisms into the environment. He argued that doing so without knowledge of possible consequences could very likely subject people in the surrounding areas to unknown risks. Rifkin returned on several other occasions to the courts for relief from dangerous practices, but his principal approach to undesirable behavior remained the speeches and publications.

Rifkin underscored the breadth of his concerns with the publication of two books with Howard: *The Emerging Order: God in the Age of Scarcity* (1979), followed by *Entropy: A New World View* (1980). In these works Rifkin and Howard emphasize human responsibility for human survival and the survival of life in general, and Rifkin raises the issue of the covenant between God and man concerning the stewardship of Earth. With *Entropy* in particular, Rifkin calls into question the entire modern concept of progress as received from the Enlightenment Era in the seventeenth century. Humanity's insatiable consumption of the planet's remaining finite energy sources, the authors declare, must give way to the realization that to fend off disaster people must conserve resources and protect the natural environment or face a future of scarcity and, ultimately, stagnation, in accordance with a law in the field of thermodynamics that posits that all matter in the universe is slowing. To effect the needed conservationist ethos, Rifkin holds, people must combine basic changes in attitude with a

Dust jacket for the 2004 edition of Rifkin's 1994 book about the effects of the Information Age (Richland County Public Library)

decentralization of power and a return to labor-intensive economic development.

Rifkin's next book, *Algeny: A New Word, a New World*, with Niconar Perlas, was published in 1983, the year of Rifkin's marriage to attorney Donna Wulkan, an activist on behalf of disabled children. Rifkin and Perlas recruited a diverse coalition of American leaders in opposition to a program of extensive genetic experimentation that gave rise to the new word, *algeny*, a play upon the medieval obsession with *alchemy*, the attempt to create gold from baser metals. Algeny refers in a derogatory way to the modern obsession with creating a higher order of living things from the existing gene pool by means of genetic engineering. Over sixty religious leaders, including the fundamentalist spokesman Reverend Jerry Falwell, signed Rifkin's petition to the U.S. Congress, "Theological Letter Concerning the Moral Arguments against Genetic Engineering of the Human Germline Cells," that is, cells that pass genetic material to descendants. In an interview, Rifkin asserted that once human genetic engineering begins, "there is really no logical place to stop." In *Algeny* Rifkin argues that the Judeo-Christian belief in man's dominion over the earth, rather than the modern concept of progress or secular humanism, fuels the compulsion to control even the genetic aspects of life.

With *Algeny* Rifkin encountered brutal criticism of his work. The chief criticism of *Algeny* came from Stephen Jay Gould, a prominent Harvard University paleontologist, biologist, and historian of science who characterized the book in *Discover* (1985) as "a cleverly constructed tract of anti-intellectual propaganda masquerading as scholarship." In fact, Rifkin, while chiding the Judeo-Christian tradition of humankind's dominion over the planet, attacks the modern scientific community's tradition of Darwinism, noting—as creationists and advocates of "intelligent design" have done—that Darwinism contains unexplainable gaps and may not be the final word on natural history's explanation of the development of life on Earth. As in earlier works, however, Rifkin also questions humankind's capacity to engineer competently the otherwise normal evolutionary processes of genetic development. Rifkin and Perlas question whether life after genetic engineering becomes the norm would amount to a product manufactured to maximize contemporary notions of virtue and necessity.

Undeterred by the pointed criticism of *Algeny*, Rifkin continued to assault the complacent and the conventional. He appeared on radio and television programs and on the lecture circuit. In 1985 he published the little-noted *Declaration of a Heretic*, a brief recapitulation of his thought to date, and a year later he led opposition to the construction of a new biological weapons facility by the Department of Defense. Rifkin and others argued that genetically altered viruses produced in such laboratories could result in a disastrous pandemic. He challenged security measures in existing Department of Defense testing laboratories and provided a "whistle-blower" fund to give support to scientific or military persons who risked jobs and careers by revealing illegal testing of biological weapons.

In his 1987 book, *Time Wars: The Primary Conflict in Human History*, Rifkin recounts a history of time and how people of various eras and cultures have viewed time. He demonstrates that not every culture seeks or has sought to value efficiency, meet deadlines, and reward punctuality. In accomplishing this educational task, of course Rifkin critiques both implicitly and explicitly modern notions of progress and assumptions about the meaning of life. He concludes that the contemporary obsession with speed and efficiency contributes mightily to environmental deterioration and decline. *Time Wars* received mixed reviews.

In his *Biosphere Politics: A New Consciousness for a New Century* (1991) Rifkin turned to history in using the "enclosure movement" of the sixteenth century and after to illustrate dangerous trends in modern thought and action. Rifkin identifies as a turning point the English landed gentry's enclosure of the once-common portions of their land in pursuit of greater income through the raising of animal stock than the subsistence farming of the peasants who had inhabited the land for centuries could offer them. At this time, as he sees it, modern capitalist societies began to reduce the proportion of public or common resources available to all and to increasingly privatize societies' assets. In this volume Rifkin fleshes out the major results of this transition. He recounts the impact of enclosure upon rural life and families, memorialized in Oliver Goldsmith's *The Deserted Village* (1770), the movement's creation of a subsistence-wage workforce for the factories of the nascent Industrial Revolution, as well as highly altered concepts of ownership and privacy in the modern world.

The politics that Rifkin projects toward future alternatives had already been sketched in *The Green Lifestyle Handbook: 1001 Ways to Heal the Earth*, a volume with twenty other contributors that he had edited and published in 1990. In this work, the authors urge readers to "Choose to Eat Low on the Food Chain," to "Boycott," and to undertake "Organic Gardening for a Healthier Planet," among other constructive behaviors. This approach was supplemented in 1992 with *Voting Green: Your Complete Environmental Guide to Making Political Choices in the '90s*, which Rifkin and his second wife, Carol Grunewald Rifkin, edited. *Voting Green* provides a detailed account of the votes cast and policies put forth on environmental issues by hundreds of elected officials. *Voting Green* underscores the collaborative relationship that Rifkin developed in public life with his wife, who was recognized as an animal-rights and environmental advocate and had served as editor of *The Animal Rights Agenda*. The prolific Rifkin also addressed both the individual and the larger scope of problems and potential solutions in that presidential election year by challenging a particular and powerful mainstay of American and Western dietary culture–beef.

In attacking the cattle industry in *Beyond Beef: The Rise and Fall of the Cattle Culture* (1992) Rifkin returns to his focus on environmental questions and the unnecessarily wasteful nature of American social and economic culture. As early as 1987 Rifkin had petitioned the National Institutes of Health to investigate the possibility of a link between the cattle disease bovine immunodeficiency virus (BIV) and AIDS. In *Beyond Beef* Rifkin argues that in terms of resource management few human activities are more wasteful and destructive than the beef-producing industry. Pointing out that Americans grow more grain to feed cattle than to feed people, Rifkin also cites the destruction of Latin American rain forests–the basis of subsistence for Native Americans and the source of many natural medicinal compounds– as a price too high to pay for the consumption of a specific food. He notes as well the high price in heart disease and cancer paid by affluent Americans, Europeans, and Japanese, in particular, for the consumption of beef-laden diets. Citing seventy-two book sources, Rifkin calls upon decision makers to rein in the power of this industry and thereby better preserve the environment as a whole, as well as the health and welfare of specific groups.

Beyond Beef was belittled in the online "Dossier" of the National Center for Public Policy Research, and both positive and negative views of Rifkin's position on the beef industry continued to be published over a decade following the book's debut. Still, in 1994 Rifkin crossed the threshold from activist and popularizer to influential intellectual and expert with his appointment as a fellow of the University of Pennsylvania's Wharton School's Executive Education Program. Thereafter, Rifkin lectured regularly to CEOs and other senior corporate leaders on new trends in science, technology, and environmental considerations. He also continued his college tours and mass-media appearances. Rifkin appeared on ABC's Nightline and Good Morning America, CNN's Crossfire, CBS's Face the Nation, and PBS's The NewsHour with Jim Lehrer. He advised government leaders on both sides of the Atlantic about matters of policy.

Three years of research resulted in Rifkin's next publication, The End of Work: The Decline of the Global Labor Force and the Dawn of the Post-Market Era, in 1994. Rifkin argues that the Information Age creates the third industrial revolution and heralds the possibilities of either freeing people for the first time to pursue lives of fulfillment and leisure or condemning millions to falling living standards while an elite of managers and high-tech workers harvest for themselves the benefits of the new age and the global economy. The author clearly fears that the likelihood of negative consequences outweighs the prospects of a utopian outcome, a conclusion he draws with particular clarity in the chapter "Technology and the Afro-American Experience." Nonetheless, as in earlier efforts, Rifkin urges activism as the appropriate response and ends the book with a challenge: "The future lies in our hands." Not so many of those hands, he repeated in an interview with the Phi Delta Kappan in May 1996, would likely be employed in factory work by year 2020. In addition to enhancing Rifkin's reputation as a stimulating commentator who poses the difficult questions, The End of Work allowed him to establish a lasting publishing relationship with editor Jeremy Tarcher of Penguin Putnam (later Penguin Group) who oversaw Rifkin's book-length publications well into the twenty-first cen-

tury. Tarcher reissued The End of Work, with a foreword by economist Robert Heilbroner, in 2004.

Another four years of research and activism passed before the publication of Rifkin's next book, The Biotech Century: Harnessing the Gene and Remaking the World, for which he credited Carol Grunewald Rifkin's "persistence" in seeing the work to completion. The Biotech Century was to some degree an updated version of Who Should Play God? Developments that Rifkin and Howard had predicted in their 1977 book, such as cloning and transgenic species and more, had occurred by 1998, and their earlier concerns about the potential for genetic discrimination, corporate ownership of gene pools, and the creation of new-life forms seemed urgent. Rifkin returns to the themes of algeny and enclosure, once again criticizing unresponsive scientific, business, and governmental circles for their apparent complacency and reiterating his earlier call for a thorough public discussion of current advances and trends in genetic science. He argues that the confluence of the genetic revolution and the computer revolution creates a powerful "phalanx" of scientific, technological, and commercial interests that require the closest scrutiny because that confluence is "one of the seminal events of our age" that may change humankind fundamentally. At stake, Rifkin asserts, are human values and the ultimate question of the meaning of human life. The biotech revolution raises these questions, he writes, but concludes, characteristically, that "The rest is up to us." Rifkin took his own advice when in 1999 he joined Stuart Newman in legal action to prevent the patenting of a human/chimpanzee hybrid and similar life-forms. A best-selling book in English, The Biotech Century was translated into sixteen other languages.

Rifkin turned once again to the larger economic view in his book The Age of Access: The New Culture of Hypercapitalism, Where All of Life Is a Paid-For Experience (2000). He argues there that the modern capitalist market system of buying and selling properties is on its way to the historical dustbin. Although the economic system waxed in the last few years of the twentieth century, Rifkin points out that markets are giving way to networks, that is, that "Concepts, ideas, and images–not things–are the real items of value in the new economy." Thus, Rifkin contends, companies sell less to one another than previously but pool and share resources, creating giant user networks in which companies co-manage large aspects of each other's businesses. As in the case of office machines, sellers concern themselves less with receiving a high price for goods if they can establish a lasting service relationship with customers, who then need not employ their own machine maintenance workforce. For an expanding number of businesses, Rifkin asserts, the very idea of ownership

JEREMY RIFKIN

BESTSELLING AUTHOR OF *THE END OF WORK*

THE

EUROPEAN

DREAM

HOW EUROPE'S VISION OF
THE FUTURE IS QUIETLY ECLIPSING
THE AMERICAN DREAM

*Dust jacket for Rifkin's 2004 volume about European reactions to the
energy shortage (Richland County Public Library)*

In keeping with *The End of Work,* Rifkin holds that in the Age of Access intelligent machines will increasingly replace people in the manufacturing, agricultural, and basic services areas. He predicts that as little as 5 percent of the current workforce will be needed for traditional industrial production by year 2050, and such new opportunities as exist will emerge as paid cultural work in the commercial world. Others will work "to service cultural needs and desires." Rifkin asserts that the work ethic will be replaced by the play ethic as the paid-for experience becomes an increasing portion of economic activity and civilization's cultural sphere becomes ever more the product of the insatiable commercial sphere, reversing the historical relationship between the cultural base and the derivative commercial sphere. He invites the reader to imagine a society in which all activities outside family relations are paid-for experiences governed by the market rather than by the traditional obligations and expectations created by empathy, solidarity, and the ethos of faiths. This, Rifkin argues, is the crisis of the postmodern world: whether civilization can survive with "a greatly reduced government and cultural sphere and where only the commercial sphere is left as the primary mediator of human life." As with the large questions that Rifkin posed in earlier works, he concludes that the answers will be provided by the world that people will create for themselves in the third millennium.

Rifkin then turned from his questions about the world to be created in the twenty-first century and addressed the problems relating to the modern world's dependence upon fossil-fuel sources. His next foray resulted in the publication of his sixteenth book-length work, *The Hydrogen Economy: The Creation of the Worldwide Energy Web and the Redistribution of Power on Earth,* in 2002. Beginning with the assertion that the road to a secure future lies in lessening the economic dependence upon Middle East oil and ensuring that all peoples can access life-sustaining energy, Rifkin urges a turn away from fossil fuels and toward hydrogen. The author's depiction of the approaching crisis of fossil-fuel production and his optimism concerning the expropriation of virtually omnipresent hydrogen made *The Hydrogen Economy* a best-seller. One outcome of this publication was that Rifkin entered into an advisory relationship with Romano Prodi, president of the European Commission, the governing body of the European Union (EU). In that role Rifkin wrote a strategic memorandum that led to the adoption of the EU's hydrogen conversion plan, a green-based plan to extract hydrogen from sources other than black fossil fuels.

In 2004 Rifkin discussed the European approach to the pending energy shortage in his *The European Dream: How Europe's Vision of the Future Is Quietly Eclipsing*

will appear "limited, even old fashioned," by 2025. In this connection, the author foresees "a very different kind of human being" emerging in a world dominated by asset relationships rather than asset ownership.

Rifkin detected already in 2000 the impact of networked relationships upon consumer choices and cultural developments. Noting that the financial upper fifth of the world's people then spent nearly as much on access to cultural experiences–travel and tourism, theme parks and cities, spectator sporting events, virtual world and games, films and music, gambling, and such–as it spent on the purchase of goods and basic services, Rifkin concludes that humankind is moving toward an "experiences" economy. He finds, correspondingly, that a new operative term has appeared in the business world: lifetime value (LTV) of the customer. This term is defined as the estimated measurement of the monetary value of a person if every minute of his or her life could be commodified. Such commodification of human culture leads, Rifkin argues, to further fundamental changes in employment.

the American Dream. His critique of the American Dream in this text largely extends those ideas presented in his earlier work, emphasizing those qualities—the Judeo-Christian view of mastery over the natural world, the modernist notion that more is better and its stressful consequences, the shrinking of ownership through privatization, and reckless exploitation of people and the earth—that have provided much of the focus of Rifkin's prolific publishing career. The new element in *The European Dream* extends beyond previous critiques of market capitalism and its various apologists. This account offers an alternative to the American vision that appears to be already in motion. Characterizing one of the differences between the United States and Europe as one between "live to work" and "work to live," Rifkin observes that the European model produces even now healthier, better-educated, and longer-lived citizens than does the U.S. system. The European emphasis upon community and quality of life, its value of social democracy and secularism stands in sharp contrast, Rifkin notes, to American individualism, productionism, and religio-patriotism. He also points to the declining credibility of the American Dream, a factor in the statement of one-third of Americans who say that they no longer believe in it.

According to Rifkin's research, Europe has remained competitive with the United States in terms of productivity, while providing a more humane social setting. Further, Europe seems to be approaching the future with a clearer vision than Americans possess. The EU, the author argues, leads the way in supporting the Kyoto Protocol on climate change and has made a commitment to produce 22 percent of its electricity and 12 percent of all energy from renewable sources by the year 2010 and to create a clean hydrogen economy by 2050. Such benchmarks are possible in a society in which the collective good retains a high value and government establishes and remains engaged in public-policy networks, Rifkin reasons. A triple-sector politics involving commerce, government, and civil society replaces the dual-sector economy of the past, with its command-and-control correlation in both government and commerce of the twentieth century. Yet, Jeremy Rifkin does not simply write a paean to postmodern Europe. *The European Dream,* as much of his earlier work, is an attempt to provoke self-examination and

dialogue among Americans and Europeans as a means of striving toward a better world.

While Jeremy Rifkin has attracted critics over the decades, including Gould, he became a major figure in many lands. His books have been widely translated, and he has spoken to audiences at five hundred colleges and universities. In addition to radio and television, Rifkin appears through his monthly column in *The Guardian* in the United Kingdom, in *Die Suddeutsche Zeitung* of Germany, in Italy's *L'Espresso,* Spain's *El Pais,* Denmark's *Information,* Belgium's *Knack, Clarin* of Argentina, and *Ittihad* of the United Arab Emirates. Rifkin audio files were also available through the year 2005 over WIE Unbound, audio broadcast media, which featured his "Into the 21st: The Future of Commerce, the Economy, and Culture." He has been cited in the *National Journal* as one of the 150 most influential people in shaping public policy in the United States. He remains the president of the Foundation on Economic Trends.

Interviews:

Jennifer Byrne, "Jeremy Rifkin Interviewed by Jennifer Byrne," American Broadcasting Company, 3 August 1999 <http://abc.net.au/foreign/interv/rifkin.htm>;

"Harvest of Fear," *Frontline,* Public Broadcasting System, August 2000 <http://www.pbs.org/wgbh/harvest/interviews/rifkin.html>;

Paul Naik, "Biotechnology through the Eyes of an Opponent: The Resistance of Activist Jeremy Rifkin," *Virginia Journal of Law and Technology,* 5 (Spring 2000) <www.vjolt.net/vol5/issue2>;

Amy Otchet, "Jeremy Rifkin: Fears of a Brave New World," *The UNESCO Courier* (September 1998) <http://www.unesco.org/courier/1998_09/uk/dires/txt1.htm>;

Peter Slavin, "The Information Age and Civil Society: An Interview with Jeremy Rifkin," *Phi Delta Kappan,* 77 (May 1996): 607;

Alessandro Torello, "Rifkin: The European Dream, 29 March 2005 <http://www.thetalent.org>.

Biography:

"About Jeremy Rifkin," Foundation on Economic Trends <http://www.foet.org/JeremyRifkin.htm>.

Ernestine L. Rose

(13 January 1810 – 4 August 1892)

Paula Doress-Worters
Brandeis University

PAMPHLETS AND TRACTS: *Speech of Mrs. Rose . . . at the Anniversary Paine Celebration, in New York, Jan. 29, Year of Independence 74th–Christian Era, 1850* (New York, 1850);

A Lecture on Women's Rights Delivered before the People's Sunday Meeting in Cochituate Hall, October 19th, 1851 (Boston: J. P. Mendum, 1851);

Review of Horace Mann's Two Lectures in New York, February 18, 1852 (New York, 1852);

Mrs. E. L. Rose at the Women's Rights Convention Held at Syracuse, September, 1852, Women's Rights Tracts, no. 9 (Syracuse, N.Y.: Masters' Print, 1852);

Address at the 4th National Women's Rights Convention (Cleveland: Gray, Beardsley, Spear, 1854);

Two Addresses Delivered by Mrs. Ernestine L. Rose at the Bible Convention, Held in Hartford (Conn.), in June 1854: Being Her Replies to the Rev. Mr. Turner Accompanied with Comments on the Unreasonable Character of the Bible (Boston: J. P. Mendum, 1888);

A Defence of Atheism: Being a Lecture Delivered in Mercantile Hall, Boston, April 10, 1861 (Boston: J. P. Mendum, 1889).

Collection: *Mistress of Herself: Speeches and Letters of Ernestine L. Rose, Early Women's Rights Leader,* edited by Paula Doress-Worters (New York: Feminist Press of the City University of New York, 2008).

OTHER: "Speech of Mrs. Ernestine L. Rose at Tenth National Women's Rights Convention in New York, May 10, 1860" and "Debate of Mrs. Rose on Divorce Reform Supporting Mrs. Stanton and Opposing Rev. Antoinette Brown Blackwell at Tenth National Women's Rights Convention in New York, May 11, 1860," in *Proceedings of The Tenth National Women's Rights Convention Held at Cooper Institute, New York City,* May 10th and 11th (Boston: Yerrington & Garrison, 1869);

Proceedings of the Meeting of the Loyal Women of the Republic, Held in New York, May 14, 1863, includes speech by Rose (New York: Phair, 1863); republished as *Women in the Life and Time of Abraham Lincoln,* with foreword by

Ernestine L. Rose *(from Carol A. Kolmerten,* The American Life of Ernestine L. Rose, *1999; Thomas Cooper Library, University of South Carolina)*

Daisy Bates (New York: Emma Lazarus Federation, 1963);

"Presidential Address at the 5th National Convention in Philadelphia, October 1854," "Speech on Wills and Inheritance Rights of Married Women in New York State at the New York State Convention in New York City, September, 1853," and "Address to the Woman's Rights State Convention, Rochester, N.Y., November 30 and December 1, 1853," in *History of Woman Suffrage,* volume 1, edited by Elizabeth Cady Stanton, Susan B. Anthony, and Matilda Joslyn Gage (New York: Fowler & Wells, 1881), pp. 376–377, 561–564, 579;

"Debate on Free Love at the 3rd Annual Meeting of the American Equal Rights Association, New York, May 1869" and "Mrs. Rose Moves Change of Name from Equal Rights Association to Woman's Suffrage Association, at the 3rd Annual Meeting of the American Equal Rights Association, New York, May 1869," in *History of Woman Suffrage,* volume 2, edited by Stanton, Anthony, and Gage (New York: Fowler & Wells, 1882), pp. 389, 396–397;

"Letter from London to Susan B. Anthony for the National Woman Suffrage Association Convention in Philadelphia, July 4, 1876," in *History of Woman Suffrage,* volume 3, edited by Stanton, Anthony, and Gage (New York: Fowler & Wells, 1887), pp. 50–51.

SELECTED PERIODICAL PUBLICATIONS–
UNCOLLECTED: "Speech of Ernestine L. Rose," in "Proceedings of The Social Reform Convention, Boston, 1844," *Social Pioneer* (30 May 1844): 73–74;

"Speech of Ernestine L. Rose at the Thomas Paine Anniversary Celebration, New York, January 29, 1850," *Boston Investigator,* 19 (6 March 1850);

"Address at the Anniversary of West Indian Emancipation at Flushing, Long Island, New York, August 4, 1853," *Liberator* (19 August 1853);

"Address to the New England Anti-Slavery Convention May 29-31, 1855," *Liberator,* 25 (8 June 1855);

"The English Divorce Bill," *Boston Investigator,* 27 (21 October 1857): 4;

"England Ruled by a Prayer Book," *Boston Investigator,* 27 (13 January 1858): 1;

"Rights of Married Women," *Boston Investigator,* 29 (11 April 1860): 1;

"The Jews, Ancient and Modern" *Boston Investigator,* 33 (10 February 1864): 315; (17 February 1864): 322; (24 February 1864): 331; (2 March 1864): 339; (9 March 1864): 347; (16 March 1864): 355; (6 April 1864): 379; (13 April 1864): 387.

From the time Ernestine L. Rose arrived in the United States in May of 1836, she exerted a significant influence as an orator and social reformer. Beginning her activism over a decade before the existence of a national women's-rights movement, she was among the first Americans to lecture on women's issues and the first to petition a legislature for women's-rights reforms.

As a freethinker in an increasingly religious age, she courageously opposed conservative clergy and creed-based churches for exerting a stifling effect upon the intellectual freedom of individuals and keeping women in an inferior position. Deeply influenced by the Enlightenment philosophy of natural rights and justice, she believed that truth would emerge from the free exchange of ideas, an ideal that she put into practice by engaging in numerous public debates. She undertook a vigorous life as a lecturer on women's rights, free thought, and abolition, fanning out from New York State to Massachusetts, Pennsylvania, Ohio, and ranging as far away as Michigan, Indiana, and South Carolina, frequently addressing state legislatures as well as the public. Throughout her thirty-three years in America, Rose was always a leading voice for women's rights. Reform colleagues and journalists alike praised Rose as the greatest of the female orators and admired her for her logic, terseness of expression, wit, and fervent delivery.

Ernestine Louise Susmond (or Sigismund) Potowski was born on 13 January 1810 in Piotrkow-Tribulanski in the Lodz province of Poland. Her father, a rabbi, was esteemed for his learning, his wealth, and his community spirit. Potowski's participation in the world of public debate began almost immediately. An intellectually precocious child, she insisted upon learning Hebrew so that she could study the Torah with her father, whom she idolized. With these skills, however, she soon challenged her father's teachings and was labeled a rebel and heretic by her community. After her mother's death, Potowski's father arranged a marriage for his daughter to an older man, with her inheritance promised as dowry. Potowski refused to marry a man whom she did not love and whom she regarded as a master set over her rather than an equal partner. She brought her case to a secular appeals court where she argued successfully for her right to keep her inheritance on the grounds that she had not consented to the marriage contract. At the age of sixteen, with no known preparation, she demonstrated an unusual talent for understanding and utilizing the law as an instrument of justice. After winning her case, she gave most of her recovered inheritance to her father, taking only as much money as she needed to support herself until she found work, and at seventeen she left home to study the modern ideas of the Enlightenment. Her first biographer referred to her as Mlle. Susmond, suggesting that she might have begun to use her mother's surname after breaking off relations with her father.

Arriving at the city gates of Berlin in 1827, Susmond learned that special restrictions governed the settlement of Jews in that city, but that conversion to

Christianity could facilitate her entry. She appealed directly to the king of Prussia, an admirer of Enlightenment thought, on the grounds of universal rights and justice. She received a visa that allowed her to live in Berlin for a limited time. There she lived in a modest room, first earning her living through tutoring, then inventing and marketing a home deodorizing product. She studied comparative religion and "men and laws." Women were not admitted to German universities until 1890, but other resources were available for her self-education, including university seminars held in professors' homes, salons where intellectuals and artists gathered to discuss ideas, and reading rooms where like-minded newspaper readers gathered to discuss politics. Following her stay in Berlin she traveled to Holland, France, and Belgium before settling in England in 1830. She lived there for the next six years.

In London, Rose marketed her home perfumery product and explored the ideas of a variety of reformers. She found herself drawn to the teachings of Robert Owen (1771–1858), a wealthy industrialist turned social reformer. In contrast to the prevailing view that poverty and human misery resulted from sin and vice, Owen taught that environments shape people, and thus he founded planned communities. The Owenites encouraged women to be active participants in their movement. Susmond spoke at trade-union meetings and conventions, perfecting her English and improving her skills of public speaking and debate.

While in London, probably in 1835, Susmond met and married William Ella Rose, a fellow Owenite and freethinker three years her junior. Together they immigrated to the United States and settled on the Lower East Side of New York City, an area of many immigrants with an active freethinker community. They lived in rented rooms over a shop where they supported themselves through William's silversmith craft and Ernestine's sale of colognes. Following her marriage, she used the name of Ernestine L. Rose. Fortunate in her marriage to an equal partner who shared her values and political goals, Ernestine L. Rose was freer than most married women of her time to travel away from home. She lectured widely in the 1830s and 1840s on women and the science of government.

In 1836 she began a petition campaign in support of proposed legislation to reform state laws under which husbands controlled all property of their wives including that brought into a marriage. Rose's early efforts to collect signatures yielded only a handful of names, but she persisted. She traveled ever more widely, lecturing at a time when it was considered immodest for women to address mixed audiences in public, and addressed the New York State Assembly multiple times. She found allies in other parts of the state, first Paulina Wright (Davis) of Utica, and then, in 1840, Elizabeth Cady Stanton, the daughter of an influential state assemblyman. Eventually, they collected thousands of signatures and presented them to the New York State Assembly.

The petition campaign led to the first legislative victory for women's rights. In April 1848, the New York State Assembly passed the first married women's property law in America, a law that was widely adopted by other states. Women's-rights activists accomplished this victory three months prior to the famed Seneca Falls Convention of that summer. Rose did not attend the historic convention organized by Stanton, Lucretia Mott, and other well-known figures. She often lectured in central New York, but she may have missed this regional convention due to pregnancy or illness. During the 1840s, Rose bore, nursed, and lost two children in infancy. She was often ill with the ague, a malaria-like affliction endemic to the Seneca Falls area.

As a woman who had lived in more than three European countries, Rose was more internationalist in her perspective than most American reformers; for her, human rights cut across national boundaries. In her annual speech in 1850 at the freethought movement's Thomas Paine Celebration, she urged Americans, women and men, to support the pro-democracy uprisings spreading across Europe since 1848. She urged offering asylum to displaced European freedom fighters in honor of heroic European allies such as Marquis de Lafayette and Tadeusz Kosciusko, who had supported the American Revolution.

Once the national women's-rights conventions began, Rose played a leading role; she signed calls to conventions, gave major speeches, proposed resolutions, and debated them. At the first such convention in October 1850, at Worcester, Massachusetts, Rose successfully opposed the prevalent idea that women belonged in a separate sphere of domesticity, relying upon men to protect and represent them. She argued that women required access to education to succeed at professions and become independent. The New York Tribune described her extemporaneous argument as eloquent and effective. At the second national convention, again held at Worcester, Rose gave a prepared speech many considered her finest. Interspersed with stories drawn from women's lives, she identified four essentials of women's rights: education; employment; legal rights; and political rights. It became her touring lecture, later reprinted and circulated as a tract.

Rose occasionally engaged in debates with those whom she could not confront in person. For example, when Horace Mann, a member of the United States House of Representatives, presented two lectures in New York on the education of women, Rose was eager to hear the views of the famed education reformer. Disappointed at the banality of his ideas about women, which she regarded as "pandering" to prevailing religious orthodoxy, she wrote a blistering critique of his lectures, *Review of Horace Mann's Two Lectures in New York, February 18, 1852*. This tract provides a rare example of her skill as an essay writer and demonstrates that her preference for the immediacy of the spoken word did not result from any lack of facility in writing in her adopted language.

In September 1852, Rose spoke several times at the third national women's-rights convention at Syracuse, New York. Perhaps because this was a period of heightened attention to ethnicity and immigration, Rose was introduced as "a Polish lady of the Jewish faith." She pointedly reintroduced herself as "a daughter of Poland" and "a child of Israel," asserting that the circumstances of one's birth should be irrelevant to judgments of a person's ideas. Later in the convention, Rose debated a resolution proposed by Reverend Antoinette Brown, one of the first female ministers, to establish biblical authority for women's rights. Rose, concerned that biblical arguments would take up time needed to discuss women's-rights issues, carried the day by arguing that the convention and women's-rights supporters everywhere needed no greater authority than natural rights and justice.

At a public rally on Long Island in 1853, Rose shared a platform with William Lloyd Garrison. She was the only woman speaker at this outdoor abolitionist gathering, one of the few women at that time whose voice was strong enough to be audible in outdoor settings. Rose asked her audience to imagine what it meant to be a slave, lacking the right to choose one's spouse, to protect one's family, to come and go as one wished. This is her earliest extant antislavery speech, but in it Rose recalled a trip to South Carolina in 1844 on which she had been threatened with tar and feathers for speaking out against slavery.

Nor were Rose's controversial speeches always well received by the Northern public. At the Hartford Bible Convention of 1853, convened by freethinkers to critique the Bible, theology students disrupted Rose's speech by turning out the gas lights, prompting Rose to observe: "There are those who prefer darkness to light." Her dramatic closing statement that "women who wish to be equal must trample the Bible under their feet" was widely reported in the press, and the resulting notoriety served at times to undermine her other reform efforts.

In the spring of 1854, shortly after Rose met Susan B. Anthony, who was attending her first women's-rights convention at Syracuse, the two women agreed to tour together. They intended to carry

women's-rights reform south of its area of strength in the northeast to the nation's capital and nearby cities of Baltimore and Alexandria. Rose, as the far-famed orator, was the featured speaker and Anthony the organizer and planner. In Washington, D.C., the chaplain at the Capitol refused Rose use of a speaker's hall on the grounds that she did not belong to a church. Though Rose had addressed many state legislatures, she was not allowed to address the U.S. Congress. She spoke instead at Caruso's restaurant on the education of women. On a subsequent evening, asked about the Fugitive Slave Law, Rose deplored the law's evil influence on the nation as a whole and, like some abolitionist colleagues, suggested that the North secede from the South. Rose and Anthony remained lifelong colleagues and loyal friends.

In October 1854, despite a recurrent lung inflammation, Rose attended that year's national women's-rights convention in Philadelphia and was elected president. Meeting in the city where the nation's founding documents were signed inspired her to speak of the Declaration of Independence. She maintained that the word "man" meant all human beings and that taxation without representation was tyranny. Women were taxed, she argued; therefore, they should be represented. Rose and Anthony resumed their travels in 1855, joined by Reverend Brown. They campaigned throughout central New York State for passage of an expanded married woman's property law that would allow women to keep their own wages and share guardianship of their children.

Exhausted by nearly two decades of activism, attacks by fundamentalist ministers, and more than two years of struggling with a bronchial condition, Rose declared herself "a soldier in need of a furlough." In the spring of 1856, she and William sailed for Europe and traveled for nearly six months. In London, she visited with Robert Owen, a meeting that turned out to be their last before his death in 1858. While in France, Rose met Jenny P. d'Héricourt, a reformer who interviewed her and wrote a short biography published in the French freethought journal, *Revue Philosophique et Religieuse*. Héricourt's account of Rose's life has served as a primary source for subsequent Rose biographers and is especially useful for information about Rose's life prior to coming to the United States.

When Rose addressed the Women's Rights Convention in New York City in November 1856, she brought news of women's rights in England. Devoted to separation of church and state, she wrote a series of scathing letters criticizing church-influenced legislation in England that permitted greater freedom for men than for women in divorce and remarriage. In 1858 Rose attended a gathering in Rutland, Vermont, of freethinkers, abolitionists, spiritualists, women's-rights reformers, and believers in

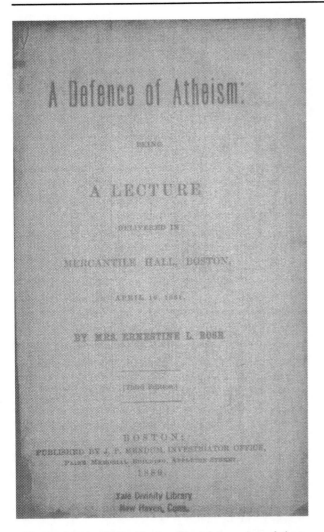

Title page from the 1889 publication of Rose's lecture using evolution to attack the irrationality of the Bible (Yale University Library)

free love. *The New York Times* conflated the latter two issues and accused Rose of promoting free love. Once more Rose became the subject of controversy, but defended her record of advocating equal rights for women and men in marriage. When in 1860 the New York State Assembly finally passed a bill encompassing the long-sought reforms, Rose published a triumphant letter in which she satirized the role of the press as the last to take up the cause of reform or to educate the public.

At the tenth national women's-rights convention in 1860, Elizabeth Cady Stanton introduced a resolution for liberalized divorce laws; specifically, the resolution sought to change the status of marriage to a secular contract. Reverend Antoinette Brown Blackwell countered with an antidivorce resolution on the grounds that marriage was a sacrament and as such could not be dissolved by human intervention. Rose would have preferred that divorce not appear on the agenda that year, so soon after the free love accusation in the press. Yet,

she felt compelled as an Owenite and freethinker to support Stanton on principle. Once more debating Brown Blackwell, Rose argued that true marriage must be voluntary and that therefore divorce must be permitted.

She never shrank from risks, on this or any other topic. At Mercantile Hall in Boston in 1861, Rose gave a lecture entitled *A Defence of Atheism,* in which she used the new science of evolution to demonstrate that the Bible was fantastic and irrational. This speech was reprinted in 1889 as a pamphlet. In 1863, at a national convention of the Loyal Women of the Republic, Rose argued fervently for a war worth fighting and a Union worth saving, one which would free enslaved people in the loyal border states as well as those which had seceded and were not yet under Union control. As abolitionists were not all in favor of war, this position, too, was controversial.

Rose had lived in the United States for nearly thirty years, with relatively little comment on her Jewish roots and minimal involvement in Jewish causes. In 1864, however, Rose responded forcefully to an editorial in the *Boston Investigator* in which Horace Seaver, the editor, deplored the sale of a Universalist church building to a Jewish congregation. He made invidious comparisons between Universalism and Judaism. Highlighting the warlike behavior of the ancient Israelites, Seaver made some highly pejorative remarks about modern Jews, including the wish that Jews would not "spread" in America. In her letter of rebuttal, Rose attacked Seaver for his bigotry and for behaving as a "religionist" rather than as a freethinker. The debate raged on for ten weeks. As a champion of human rights, Rose remained ready to defend any maligned group; however, the passion and tenacity of her defense suggests that Seaver's comments stung, evoking experiences of anti-Semitism growing up in Europe and working as the lone Jew among predominantly Protestant American reformers.

In 1869, after thirty-three years as an actively engaged reformer, Ernestine Rose left the United States with her husband to return to England. Rose left no record of their reasons for leaving. Personal or financial reasons may have contributed to the decision; her letters alluded to the lower cost of living in England. More likely, as an intensely political person, she, like many colleagues, found the splintering of the progressive reform movements following the Civil War distressing. When the Fifteenth Amendment introduced the word "male" into the Constitution for the first time, the decades-long alliance of abolitionists and women's-rights reform fell apart, with unkind and personal remarks on both sides. Then the women's-rights movement itself split into two factions. Lucy Stone's group, with many male women's-rights reformers, agreed with liberals in

Congress that it was "the Negroes' hour" and supported votes for freed African American men while continuing to work on votes for women as a long-range objective. Rose, along with Stanton and Anthony, formed an organization that permitted only women in the leadership and made votes for women the number one priority. Rose argued adamantly that women and African Americans must be enfranchised at the same time.

In England, Rose occasionally spoke and attended meetings. She wrote letters to the women's-rights conventions in America. In 1882, William Rose died suddenly, leaving Ernestine heartbroken and bereft. Rose worried that, growing old alone, she could become vulnerable to proselytizers seeking to publicize deathbed conversions of famous atheists. She implored her closest friends among the English freethinkers to protect her.

She never recanted her views. She died on 4 August 1892 and was buried at Highgate Cemetery in London alongside her husband. George J. Holyoake, leader of the British freethought movement, delivered a graveside eulogy for her. In America, Elizabeth Cady Stanton presented a touching remembrance of Rose at the next women's-rights convention.

When Rose left America in 1869, she received gifts and monetary awards from her grateful contemporaries, a customary way of honoring public figures. Ernestine L. Rose was widely respected as the intellectual voice of the movement; women spoke of "feeling safe" from ridicule when she was on the platform. Her ideas provided a direction for nineteenth-century women's-rights reform and prefigured the feminism of the twentieth and twenty-first centuries. For a time Rose was forgotten, left out of the history of women's rights. On 4 August 2002 a group convened by the Ernestine Rose Society of Brandeis University and joined by members of the Susan B. Anthony House of Rochester, New York, held a ceremony at Highgate Cemetery to dedicate a restored memorial stone for Ernestine and William Rose and to honor Ernestine Rose's life of early and tireless commitment to women's-rights reform.

Biographies:

Jenny P. d'Héricourt, "Madame Rose," *Revue Philosophique et Religieuse,* 5 (1856): 129–139; subsequently republished in English with introduction by Paula Doress-Worters, "Madame Rose: A Life of Ernestine L. Rose as told to Jenny P. d'Héri-

court," *Journal of Women's History,* 15 (Spring 2003): 183–201;

Yuri Suhl, *Ernestine L. Rose and the Battle for Human Rights* (New York: Reynal, 1959);

Suhl, *Ernestine L. Rose: Women's Rights Pioneer* (New York: Biblio Press, 1990);

Carol A. Kolmerten, *The American Life of Ernestine L. Rose* (Syracuse, N.Y.: Syracuse University Press, 1999);

Paula Doress-Worters, ed., *Mistress of Herself: Speeches & Letters of Ernestine L. Rose, Early Women's Rights Leader* (New York: Feminist Press of the City University of New York, 2008).

References:

Sandra J. Berkowitz and Amy Lewis, "Debating Anti-Semitism: Ernestine Rose vs. Horace Seaver in the *Boston Investigator,* 1863–1864," *Communication Quarterly,* 46 (Fall 1998): 457–471;

Ellen Carol DuBois, *Feminism and Suffrage: The Emergence of an Independent Women's Movement in America, 1848–1869* (Ithaca, N.Y. & London: Cornell University Press, 1999);

DuBois, *Elizabeth Cady Stanton/Susan B. Anthony: Correspondence, Writings, Speeches* (Boston: Northeastern University Press, 1992);

Susan Jacoby, *Freethinkers: A History of American Secularism* (New York: Holt, 2004);

Albert Post, *Popular Freethought in America, 1825–1850* (New York: Columbia University Press, 1943);

Elizabeth Cady Stanton, *Eighty Years and More: Reminiscences, 1815–1897,* reprint edition (Boston: Northeastern University Press, 1992).

Elizabeth Cady Stanton, *Eighty Years and More: Reminiscences, 1815–1897,* reprint edition (Boston: Northeastern University Press, 1992);

Stanton, Susan B. Anthony, and Matilda Joslyn Gage, eds., *History of Woman Suffrage* (New York: Fowler & Wells, 1881–1886).

Papers:

Ernestine L. Rose's papers have been lost. Many proceedings of women's-rights conventions may be found in the National American Woman Suffrage Collection of the Library of Congress. Yuri Suhl's papers, including the record of his research on Rose, are at Special Collections, Boston University. A complete run of *The Boston Investigator,* where Rose published most of her letters, is available at the American Antiquarian Society in Worcester, Massachusetts.

Margaret Sanger

(14 September 1879 – 6 September 1966)

Rachel Furey

PAMPHLETS: *What Every Mother Should Know; Or How Six Little Children Were Taught the Truth* (New York: Rabelais, 1914);

Family Limitation (New York, 1914; London: Bakunin, 1920);

Dutch Methods of Birth Control (N.p., 1915);

What Every Girl Should Know (New York, 1915; London: Rose Witcop, 1928).

BOOKS: *Woman and the New Race* (New York: Brentano's, 1920); republished as *The New Motherhood* (London: Cape, 1922);

The Pivot of Civilization (New York: Brentano's, 1922);

Happiness in Marriage (New York: Brentano's, 1926);

What Every Boy and Girl Should Know (New York: Brentano's, 1927);

My Fight for Birth Control (New York: Farrar & Rinehart, 1931; London: Faber & Faber, 1932);

Margaret Sanger: An Autobiography (New York: Norton, 1938; London: Gollancz, 1938);

The Selected Papers of Margaret Sanger, volume 1: *The Woman Rebel 1900–1928* (Urbana: University of Illinois Press, 2003).

PRODUCED SCRIPT: *Birth Control,* by Sanger and Frederick Blossom, Message Feature Film Company, 1917.

OTHER: House Committee on Rules of the House of Representatives, *The Strike at Lawrence, Mass.: Hearings on H.R. 409 and 433.* 62nd Cong., 2nd sess., 2–7 March 1912, H. Doc. 671, H. Doc. 138, serial 6320 (Washington, D.C., 1912): 226–233;

The Case for Birth Control: A Supplementary Brief and Statement of Facts, edited by Sanger (New York: Modern Art Printing, 1917);

Appeals from American Mothers, edited by Sanger (New York: Womans Publishing, 1921);

Birth Control: What It Is, How iI Works, What It Will Do: Proceedings of the First American Birth Control Confer-

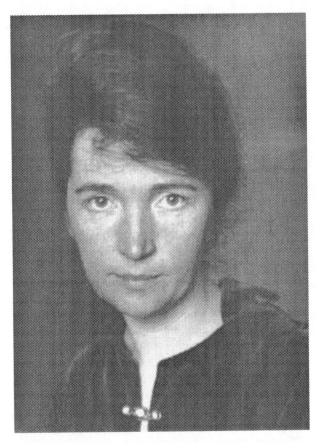

Margaret Sanger (from Edwin Black, War against the Weak: Eugenics and America's Campaign to Create a Master Race, *2003; Thomas Cooper Library, University of South Carolina)*

ence, includes speeches by Sanger (New York: Birth Control Review, 1921), pp. 14–18, 170–174;

"Individual and Family Aspects of Birth Control: President, Mrs. Margaret Sanger," in *Report of the Fifth International Neo-Malthusian and Birth Control Conference; Kingway Hall, London. July 11th to 14th, 1922,* edited by Raymond Pierpont (London: Heinemann, 1922), pp. 30–32;

"The Children's Era," *The Sixth International Neo-Malthusian and Birth Control Conference,* 4 volumes, edited by Sanger (New York: American Birth Control League, 1925–1926), IV: pp. 53–58;

Proceedings of the World Population Conference, Geneva, 1927, edited, with a preface, by Sanger (London: Edward Arnold, 1927);

Motherhood in Bondage, edited by Sanger (New York: Brentano's, 1928);

Laws Concerning Birth Control in the United States, edited by Sanger (New York: Committee on Federal Legislation for Birth Control, 1929);

The Practice of Contraception, edited by Sanger and Hannah M. Stone (Baltimore: Williams & Wilkins, 1931);

"Shall the Citizens of Boston Be Allowed to Discuss Changing Their Laws?" in *A Free Pulpit in Action,* edited by Clarence R. Skinner (New York: Macmillan, 1931), pp. 164–185;

American Conference on Birth Control and National Recovery. Biological and Medical Aspects of Contraception, edited by Sanger (Washington, D.C.: Committee on Federal Legislation for Birth Control, 1934);

"In Perspective," in *A New Day Dawns for Birth Control: Summary of Seven Years Which Led to Legalization and Cleared the Way for an Epoch-Making Advance* (New York: National Committee on Federal Legislation for Birth Control, 1937), pp. 7–13;

"Address by Mrs. Margaret Sanger," in *International Congress on Population and World Resources in Relation to the Family: Proceedings. August 1948, Cheltenham, England* (London: H. K. Lewis, 1948), pp. 85–95.

SELECTED PERIODICAL PUBLICATIONS–UNCOLLECTED: "The Fangs of the Monster at Lawrence," *New York Call,* 15 February 1912, p. 6;

"With the Girls in Hazleton Jail," *New York Call,* 20 April 1913, pp. 6–7;

"The Aim," *Woman Rebel,* 1 (March 1914): 1;

"The New Feminists," *Woman Rebel,* 1 (March 1914): 1–2;

"Marriage," *Woman Rebel,* 1 (April 1914): 16;

"On Picket Duty," *Woman Rebel,* 1 (May 1914): 19;

"Servile Virtues," *Woman Rebel,* 1 (June 1914): 32;

"One Woman's Fight," *Woman Rebel,* 1 (August 1914): 42;

"Where Is Your Power Now?" *Woman Rebel,* 1 (August 1914): 48;

"How to Manufacture Cannon-Fodder," *Woman Rebel,* 1 (September–October 1914): 54;

"Birth Control and the Working Woman," *New York Call,* 25 June 1916, p. 9;

"Portet and Ferrer," *Modern School* (November–December 1916): 136; (January 1917): 157; (February 1917): 184;

"An Open Letter to Judge J. J. McInerney," *Birth Control Review,* 1 (February 1917): 16;

"Clinics, Courts, and Jails," *Birth Control Review,* 2 (April 1918): 3–4;

"London Birth Control Meetings," *Birth Control Review,* 4 (September 1920): 7–8;

"The War against Birth Control," *American Mercury* (June 1924): 231–236;

"The Birth-Control Raid," *New Republic,* 58 (1 May 1929): 305–306;

"Comments on the Pope's Encyclical," *Birth Control Review,* 15 (January 1931): 40–41;

"An Open Letter to Social Workers," *Birth Control Review,* 17 (June 1933): 140–141;

"Birth Control," *State Government* (1 September 1934): 187–190;

"National Security and Birth Control," *Forum and Century,* 93 (March 1935): 139–141;

"The Future of Contraception," *Journal of Contraception,* 2 (January 1937): 3–4;

"Status of Birth Control: 1938," *New Republic,* 94 (20 April 1938): 324–326;

"Birth Control Through the Ages," *Twice a Year,* 5 (Fall–Winter 1940); 6 (Spring–Summer 1941).

Margaret Sanger, nurse, writer, and social activist, is best known as a founding leader of the twentieth-century birth-control movement. Many advocates of women's rights–notably Moses Harman, Ezra Heywood, Emma Goldman, Ben Reitman, and Mary Ware Dennett–distributed information or went to jail for this cause, but Sanger devoted her entire professional life to the issue of making information about contraception available to women so that they might exert greater self-determination. Her work developed contemporaneously with the emerging fields of public health and social science. She made a special study of the laws governing birth-control practices in the United States and several times testified before Congress to support legal reforms. Sanger established and ran three newspapers over the years–the *Woman Rebel, Birth Control Review,* and *Birth Control News.* With her sister, Ethel Byrne, she established the first clinic in the United States to offer women scientifically sound birth-control information, and later she opened what became the first legal birth-control clinic in the United States. Sanger founded and led the organization, the American Birth Control League, that evolved into Planned Parenthood. During World War I, Sanger found support for her work in the international community of birth-control advocates, many of whom were interested in eugenics, a since discredited branch of science concerned with control of human breeding based on the human subject's so-called fitness to reproduce.

Born on 14 September 1879 in Corning, New York, to Michael Hennessy Higgins, a sculptor, and Anne Purcell Higgins, Margaret Louise Higgins was the sixth of eleven children her mother carried to term. Anne Higgins was frail and sickly, her tuberculosis growing worse with each of her eighteen pregnancies. Michael Higgins's pursuit of enlightenment had an impact on the family's already meager wealth during Margaret's early childhood. One winter the family went without fuel after Higgins single-handedly paid for Henry George to give a lecture to the town and bought dinner for all the people who attended. He angered conservative Catholics by inviting Ralph Ingersoll to speak. Higgins's attempt to educate the town left him ostracized and largely without commissions after the town declared a boycott on his labor.

While Higgins insisted that intellectual freedom ranked above providing material wealth for his children, his behavior complicated familial relationships. Several of the children felt closer emotionally to their mother, whereas others resented Higgins for the choices he had made and left home early to earn additional income. Margaret Higgins, more than any of the others, took his side and began to model her behavior and ideas after her father's. The entire family bore the displeasure of the town, and the children often suffered verbal abuse at school. Two weeks before finishing eighth grade, Margaret Higgins decided that she had had enough and dropped out of school. Mary and Nan, the two eldest sisters, who had abandoned hopes of marriage in pursuit of careers at a young age, paid for Margaret's college tuition so that she could continue her education away from the town.

At Claverack College, Higgins refined her skills as an orator and as a leader in feminist discussions. She attended for only three years, after which her father recalled her to take care of her sickly mother, who died on 31 March 1896, leaving the father in charge of the family. Margaret, who had collected medical books in an effort to help her mother, developed an interest in a career in medicine, but stayed at home to help take care of the younger children until a conflict with her father over her dating caused her to leave. A schoolmate from Claverack had her mother arrange for Higgins to attend a nursing school in White Plains, New York.

As a student nurse, Higgins was most interested in the maternity cases that took her out of the oppressive atmosphere of the hospital. Surgeries for her own "tubercular glands" kept her from finishing her nursing certification on time, but by her third year she had delivered several children, as well as assisting at many births. She also began receiving questions about preventing conception from anxious parents who already had too many children. Attending doctors were unwilling to help, so she was forced to tell the parents she did not know how to help them.

In her third year of training Higgins met artist William Sanger at a hospital dance. Their courtship progressed quickly, but trainees were not permitted to marry. After a few months, he delivered an ultimatum: either she would marry him that afternoon, or he would leave her. She agreed but later told her sisters she resented him for it. They were married on 18 August 1902.

Six months after the marriage, Sanger discovered that she was pregnant and must put her career on hold. Their son Stuart was born in November 1903. For the next several years her energies were consumed in recovering from the birth, convalescence after having another flare-up of tuberculosis, and caring for the child as her husband planned and built their new house in the suburbs of New York. They moved into the house in early 1908, and it burned down the first night. Margaret Sanger decided that she would not spend the rest of her life wasting time and energy on material possessions. Still, they moved back into the house six months later, and the next few years passed much as those preceding them; she gave birth to two more children—Grant in July 1908 and Margaret (Peggy) in May 1910—and once again endured a period of enforced bed rest because of tuberculosis. She was advised against having another child.

By this time, the Sangers had been married for a little over eight years, and she began to worry about money. Much of their resources had been used to pay for her medical care and for replacing furniture after the fire. William Sanger was as impulsive about spending as her father had been. Margaret convinced William that she should be allowed to pay for her part of the finances by taking on cases again, and they resolved to move to the city where his mother could take care of the children while they both worked.

As William Sanger had long considered himself a socialist, the married couple joined the Socialist Party (SP) immediately upon their arrival in New York City. Only a few blocks away from SP Local 5, their flat became a meeting place for many party members, including William Sanger's friend and party leader Eugene V. Debs, John Reed, and William Haywood and his sometime companion Jessie Ashley. While William was the Sanger everyone wanted to visit initially, Margaret became more outspoken and drew more attention as time wore on; eventually, by the time they started attending the evenings of Mabel Dodge and met Walter Lippmann and Emma Goldman, Margaret

Sanger had become a favorite among New York radicals.

Throughout 1912, Margaret Sanger kept busy. The entire time that she took cases in the city she also performed various tasks for Local 5, helped with recruitment and organizing for the SP, and even began writing articles for *The New York Call*. Her first few assigned pieces mostly dealt with labor issues, but after a successful impromptu speech in which she discussed women's health issues, *The New York Call* editors decided to allot her a Sunday column in the women's section to discuss health-related topics. "What Every Mother Should Know," her first series about health, provided a detailed yet simple plan for discussing sex honestly with children. The column did not rely upon euphemisms as did other publications at the time; instead Sanger took the popular idea of the birds and the bees and transformed it into a straightforward discussion for beginning sex education as early as the age of four.

Each article, beginning with the first one on the fertilization of plants, emphasized another part of the natural world's reproduction, eventually working up to insects, fish and frogs, birds, and finally mammals and humans, the idea being that one led to the other in terms of questions from children. Plants could introduce children to a very basic understanding of reproduction, and children could be taught about the role of sperm and ovum, then of mate choice, then of forethought in copulation. While many people still referred to sexual organs by various polite terms, Sanger felt this placed too much importance on them and advocated calling every part by its medical name in order to depersonalize sex. Casual naming of organs, both reproductive and nonreproductive, was one of the first habits that got her into trouble with censorship laws of the time. Also, in keeping with her beliefs that sexual education should be strictly biological, she never cited biblical or other religious textual sources but did mention "early man" while detailing the dangers of incest and the evolution of human consciousness in relation to choosing mates. The series of columns essentially provided lesson plans for mothers that were good for the education of their children until the age of six or seven, but it stopped short of being a complete guide to sex education. Sanger stated at the end that she thought it important to save discussions of menstruation (and, by implication, the rest of puberty), venereal diseases, and sexual roles until the child was much older.

After the success of this series, *The New York Call* decided to commission another set of articles from her, picking up where "What Every Mother Should Know" left off. These were dubbed "What Every Girl Should Know" and covered in just a few articles the basics of

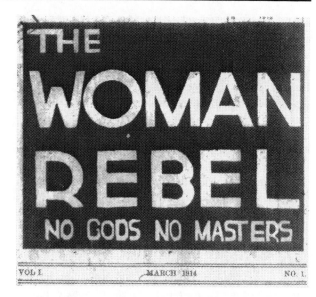

Flag for Sanger's newspaper advocating sex education (Thomas Cooper Library, University of South Carolina)

puberty, sexual impulses, certain consequences of sex (venereal diseases), and Sanger's opinion of masturbation. Sanger and her friends thought this piece was as instructive as the first, and they were surprised to open the paper one Sunday to find that the post office had banned the column. Beneath the headline "What Every Girl Should Know" was simply the word "Nothing!" While the idea of sex education was not offensive to the post office, officials claimed that the words "gonorrhea" and "syphilis" were; her article had been censored for using proper names instead of vague and confusing terminology. This incident began Sanger's battles with the Comstock Law, which had been on the books since 1873.

In January 1912 the strike at Lawrence, Massachusetts, erupted. IWW leaders called in to organize the strikers agreed that since strikers tended to give in to employers' demands more readily if their children were forced to go hungry, they would appeal for aid to the children. Representatives from the Italian quarter of New York said they would temporarily house the children as long as a committee would escort them from Lawrence via train. Haywood, in charge of the strike, nominated Margaret Sanger to lead the committee, citing her experience in both motherhood and medicine. She readily accepted, and she convinced the leadership that each child should be given a physical examination before leaving the state. Once the strike was over, Sanger testified on workers' conditions at the congressional investigation led by Victor Berger. Her meticulous notes on the condition of the children's health and their inadequate clothing shocked many observers at the hearings. In the coldest part of a Massachusetts winter, for example, only 1 or 2 out of some 125 children had any undergarments.

While she spent a lot of time helping her Socialist friends, attending meetings, and writing for publication, Sanger still kept up her nursing duties. Taking maternity cases meant she could plan around her busy schedule to work a few days at a time in the poorer neighborhoods. By 1912 well-to-do women had already begun to deliver children in clinics and hospitals, rather than at home, but the poor could not afford it. Sanger was appalled at what she witnessed on her visits to tenement houses. Married women who had already had given birth to several children begged attending physicians to help them prevent future pregnancies, only to be mocked and told to simply stop having sex. Whereas middle-class women of the time often bought some sort of poison from pharmacists to induce miscarriages, poor women could not afford even that dangerous solution to the problem. Self-induced abortions were rampant, and the ensuing infections brought on from unclean tools and inexperienced hands often took the lives of the women.

In July 1912 Sanger met Sadie Sachs, whom she later credited with having the greatest impact on her life. Sachs's husband, Jake, called Sanger after finding his wife unconscious from a self-induced abortion. When Sanger and the physician arrived, Sachs was near death. After spending a few weeks caring for her, Sanger once again faced the question of how to prevent future conception. She had, by this point, begun suggesting condoms and the withdrawal method, the only two means she knew wealthier families were using, but the lower-class women were desperate for a method by which they could be in control. Sadie Sachs was no different; her doctor had laughed and told her to make her husband sleep on the roof. Sanger's feelings of inadequacy made her stop taking calls from the Sachses asking for further advice until October of the same year when Jake called to inform her that Sadie had once again conceived and tried to end the pregnancy on her own. This time, no one was able to help, and she died.

After these several months of trying to ask acquaintances if they knew of any methods to prevent conception, Sanger became obsessed with the idea of saving women like Sadie Sachs. She appealed for aid from physicians, but they knew as little as she did. Friends did not want to risk their publications by mentioning contraceptives, discussion of which the federal Comstock Law and its state complements specifically banned. Libraries had too few books available on the subject. Despondent, she decided to take her family on vacation to regroup. There she and her husband met Haywood, who was attempting to recover his own

health after the 1913 Paterson strike, and he suggested they travel to France, as it was well known at the time for having the lowest birth rate and highest rate of openly avowed use of contraceptives.

On the way to France, the Sangers stopped in Glasgow so Margaret could work on an article for *The New York Call*. She had derived some hope from hearing that Socialist-run Glasgow had the lowest birth rate of any city, but when she arrived she discovered it had all been a hoax. Glasgow was no better at offering health care to the poor than any other city, and had actually contrived to fix its numbers by pushing poorer families further and further into the suburbs until they were no longer within city limits. The birth rate in the city was low because the general housing was not intended for people with more than two children—once families grew larger, they were forced to move.

Once in France, William Sanger resumed his painting—which he had always preferred to architectural planning—and Margaret Sanger met the editor of *L'Humanité* and several of Haywood's syndicalist friends. Sanger found the birth-control measures she sought readily discussed by French housewives, but the methods proved in many ways disappointing: the French women cited tampons, suppositories, douches, or some combination thereof as their contraceptive methods. They claimed these devices were successful, although Sanger noted that many women still became pregnant—the only difference was that French women who chose to have abortions could obtain them legally, and relatively safely, from physicians. The French received abortions too frequently for the methods to be truly helpful, she thought, but she still felt obliged to share her new knowledge with women in America. At the end of 1913 Sanger decided to return to America and publish her information on the prevention of conception, as well as begin a new publication for lower-income women to promote birth control and women's health issues. William Sanger wanted to remain in France to continue his painting, and they agreed to a temporary separation. Margaret and the children departed on New Year's Eve.

If any one publication defined Sanger's body of work, it was the *Woman Rebel*. Run, written, edited, distributed, and even funded mostly by Sanger's own efforts, the *Woman Rebel* attracted attention before the first issue made it to the post office, partly owing to her notoriety by association with well-known anarchists and socialists, and partly from word of mouth. By the time she was supposed to release the first issue in March 1914, Sanger had several hundred subscribers, as well as offers from unions to use their printing presses and mailing lists and offers from friends for free publicity in their papers. Before Sanger sent out the first issue, she met friends to discuss possible goals and focal points. While trying to come up with a phrase better than "prevention of conception," which seemed to imply total abandonment of giving birth instead of conceiving only after conscientious decision, she hit upon "birth control"–an abbreviation of birth-rate control. Although her opponents later pointed to this phrase as supposed proof that Sanger was trying to control who could conceive and who could not, at the time it seemed to her supporters an appropriate phrase to describe their new movement. At this time, she also formed the National Birth Control League, the first group in America to advocate the promotion of sex education and the distribution of materials related to the prevention of contraception. Sanger herself wrote the editorials and occasionally other articles and used her connections to put together a periodical with an interesting mix of authors. Her regularly featured writers included Olive Schreiner, Helen Keller, Ellen Key, J. Edgar Morgan, Nora Mann, and even Emma Goldman. Others such as Max Eastman, Marion Howard, Voltairine de Cleyre, and Robert F. Pratt contributed occasional pieces as well.

When Margaret Sanger began the *Woman Rebel,* she claimed it would not advocate any "ism" and that all who wanted to submit articles would be welcome. In the very first issue, however, some of her goals indicated that the target audience was mostly extreme liberals. The stated mission was to advocate sex education for everyone, to teach women about preventing conception, to inspire working women to think for themselves, and to provide space for prostitutes to express their opinions about the world. What had originally been intended as an exclusive forum for the promotion of women's-health issues later contained articles condemning Rockefeller and Standard Oil after the Ludlow, Colorado, strike and massacre, Herbert Thorpe's anarchist defense of assassination, and praise of anarchist Becky Edelsohn's hunger strike.

The seventh issue reported that Margaret Sanger had been indicted for publishing obscene material in October 1914. Sanger repeatedly asked what specific words or pieces had gotten her in trouble with the law, but each reply simply contained the same original indictment without clarification. As she had continually avoided promoting individual contraceptive means or even publishing exact material describing the prevention of conception as banned by the Comstock laws, she felt unsure why she was being asked to stand trial. Sanger felt that she had to do something to postpone the trial until she had time to collect her thoughts. She fled to England under the assumed name Bertha Watson, leaving her children behind.

Just before her departure, Sanger decided that if she really must stand trial upon her return regardless of her innocence, she would publish the "obscene" material for which she stood accused. For this purpose, she sent each of the prosecutors and the judge trying her case a copy of her new pet project, *Family Limitation,* a pamphlet detailing several methods for preventing conception and other advice for married couples. She also sent a previously agreed-on signal to her friends around the East coast, and they distributed one hundred thousand copies of the pamphlet as she set sail. Sanger did not consider *Family Limitation* much of a success, but it was later translated into at least twelve languages, sold over ten million copies, and became the one document each couple in the Yucatán, state of Mexico was forced to accept along with a marriage license. Sanger refused to have it copyrighted despite its potential for enormous success, as she hoped poor factory workers could obtain free copies and sell them cheaply to people on the streets as a supplement to their low incomes. As she discovered at a conference two years later, this did happen, so it remains unclear how many copies were unofficially distributed, although some estimates of her friends placed the number at several million more than the official ten million.

Upon her arrival in England, Sanger met Charles and Bessie Drysdale, who ran the Malthusian League. Under their direction she began a rigorous self-study in the British Museum, looking for sources about birth control to use in future papers. Not fully in agreement with the principles of the Malthusian League, she still readily attended its dinners and associated with the members' friends and acquaintances and began to find new supporters for her cause. She met Havelock Ellis, the author of *The Psychology of Sex,* in December 1914 and began an affair with him that lasted several months. Ellis was convinced that Sanger was a terrible writer, but inspired by her sincerity and her determination, he decided to help direct her readings in the British Museum. On his advice she read Malthus's work on the limitation of species based on natural resources, Jeremy Bentham's work on the woman's "sponge," and Francis Place's three methods of birth control: withdrawal; a sheath for the penis made of sheer cloth or animal gut; or sponges, tampons, suppositories, or douches for the woman. Under his guidance, she began to think that birth control was important not just for women's health but also for race improvement and for the adjustment of the overall population based on surrounding resources. During this period, she also learned that one form of contraception never came under attack by censorship laws: the well-advertised condom. As far as she could determine, this was because the device was intended for protecting males

Sanger leaving Brooklyn Court of Special Sessions after arraignment for operating an unauthorized birth-control clinic, January 1917 (from Emily Taft Douglas, Margaret Sanger: Pioneer of the Future, *1970; Thomas Cooper Library, University of South Carolina)*

from venereal disease rather than for protecting women from unwanted pregnancy.

While Margaret Sanger studied in England, one of Anthony Comstock's aides approached William Sanger in his apartment in New York posing as a poor worker looking for a copy of *Family Limitation*. Sanger was skeptical, but, as the man seemed desperate, he gave him his personal copy to keep. The next day the man returned with Comstock and informed Sanger that he was under arrest for the distribution of obscene material. Although Sanger protested and asked to speak with a lawyer, Comstock postponed their arrival at the jail until nightfall when he would be unable to send for legal aid. William Sanger was held without bail. Distraught, he immediately wrote Margaret telling her to stay away until he had been tried, as Comstock did not

seem to care much for fairness. She decided to postpone her return until his trial in fall 1915 was over.

While waiting in England, Sanger wrote three more pamphlets with information similar to that contained within *Family Limitation*. The shipment intended for distribution in America sank aboard the *Lusitania,* however, and as Sanger soon obtained new information about birth control, she never mentioned them again except as a brief aside in her 1938 autobiography. As her affair with Ellis wound down and Sanger faced staying abroad for longer than she had planned, she sought new areas of research in Europe. The Drysdales suggested Holland, known to have the lowest mortality rate, highest rate of legitimate children, and overall good health and stature. Despite qualms that her fake passport might be discovered, and well aware that the war might mean greater trouble at customs if she were caught, Sanger applied for her travel visa and was immediately accepted.

On arriving in Holland, Sanger looked up Aletta Jacobs and Dr. Johannes Rutgers, who were responsible for the first clinics in the world offering contraceptive counsel to women regardless of their reasons for wanting it. Sanger asked Rutgers if she could study with him, and he taught her how to fit women for a new invention called the diaphragm. To Sanger, the diaphragm was a breakthrough that allowed women more control of conception than any other method until that point, but she realized that physicians must be educated in how to fit women properly. During this time she met Marie Stopes, who later became the greatest champion of the birth-control movement in Britain and whose career in some ways paralleled Sanger's. Stopes had tried desperately to find a publisher for her book *Married Love*, recounting her experience in a failed marriage that ended with an annulment and the announcement that she remained a virgin, but its taboo subject put off publishing houses. Sanger helped her publish it in 1918.

In September 1915 Sanger received bad news about her husband's trial and rushed back to America. William Sanger had looked forward to reading his prepared statement of defense, but Judge McInerney had pronounced free speech "rigmarole" and sentenced him without letting him speak. He set the punishment at $150 or thirty days in jail, to be chosen by the defendant. Choosing the latter, Sanger shouted "I would rather be in jail with my self-respect than in your place without it!" As he was escorted from the room, Comstock informed him that he hoped his wife would receive five-years' hard labor for every copy of *Family Limitation* published. Sanger knew about the trial as she stepped off the boat, but she was surprised to discover upon arrival that Comstock had caught a cold during the legal proceedings and died just before her return. Since she knew he had been her main opponent, she hoped the indictment against her might be dropped, but it was not. Lacking funds after her trip to Europe, she began to prepare her defense and apply to her friends for financial backing. She first tried the National Birth Control League, which had taken over her mailing lists since her departure, but the group informed her it did not approve of the inappropriately violent content of some articles she had run in the *Woman Rebel* and was expelling her from membership. Others either disapproved of her previous tactics to gain media attention or simply did not have the means to support her.

Just as Sanger thought she would have to go to trial without legal defense or money to provide for her family in her almost-guaranteed absence in jail, her daughter Peggy became ill while boarding at the Modern School in Stelton, New Jersey. Peggy had contracted an osteomyelitic infection in her leg years earlier, and Sanger attended the girl for three weeks before she died on 6 November 1915. This loss drew media attention to Sanger's case, won her a postponement of the trial, and generated funds raised by poor laborers around the country. It also attracted the attention of lawyers (including Clarence Darrow), who decided this turn of events might help Sanger avoid prosecution, contrary to her wishes. She hoped instead for the laws to be changed and for the judge to drop the charges against her because he realized that what she had done should not be illegal. She decided that the only way to have a proper defense was to represent herself, but after she gave a talk to prominent, wealthy New Yorkers at the Brevoort Hotel, the National Birth Control League concluded that she was worth backing and convinced many others to join in her defense. After seeing the new publicity the morning of the January 1916 trial, the judge quashed her indictment, declaring he did not want to see her become a martyr.

About this time Sanger began an affair with journalist Walter Adolphe Roberts that continued fitfully for a few years, but like all of her other personal relationships, it had little effect on her public life. After her encounter with the courts and the subsequent publicity, Sanger toured the country to promote her views on birth control. Starting with a lecture in Pittsburgh in April, she delivered more than one hundred speeches on the topic. She believed that at least seven situations made birth control necessary: if either parent had a communicable or genetically transferrable disease such as syphilis, epilepsy or even possibly insanity; if the wife were temporarily sick and pregnancy would delay her recovery; if the parents had already given birth to mentally or physically handicapped children; if either husband or wife were too young (her limit being twenty-two for women and twenty-three for men); if the family could not afford another child; if the couple had been married for less than a year, since she felt they needed time to adjust to living together; and if they had just produced a child less than two to three years before.

While on tour, Sanger discovered that *Family Limitation* still circulated among factory workers and other poor laborers. Asking one man to see his copy, she found it severely outdated, so she proposed making a new edition of it. During her speech in Portland, she and several others offered to sell new copies of the pamphlet, which prompted another arrest for selling obscene material. The judge found them all guilty, but he waived the fines for the women and charged the men only $10 each. The trial was a victory as no one had to stay long in jail, but Sanger was forced to cut short her tour and return to New York. There she studied the laws regulating the distribution of materials on birth control. Like those in England, legal methods in America seemed restricted to those that prevented the spread of venereal disease to men or helped to save the life of the woman if she were severely ill or in danger of dying during labor. Also the laws dictated that only physicians could dispense information about such matters. Instead of trying to reach people exclusively through publications, Sanger decided to open her own clinic.

A few physicians volunteered to work with her, but a legal case in which a woman physician was discharged for providing a tubercular woman with a diaphragm convinced Sanger not to put other doctors at risk. She and her sister, Ethel Byrne, decided to oversee the nursing duties in the clinic, where they did not actually fit women for diaphragms but simply estimated the size needed and recommend usage. In October 1916 Sanger opened the first birth-control clinic in the United States in the Brownsville section of Brooklyn, and she notified the district attorney without receiving a reply. Byrne, her assistant/receptionist Fania Mindell, and Sanger saw more than 140 women the first day, and many more who still waited in line at closing promised to return the next day. In addition to taking the basic information for each woman regarding her name and address, they collected statistics on the number of previous pregnancies, miscarriages, abortions, and live births as well as health information on the mother and children.

After the first week, a woman Mindell suspected of being with the police came into the clinic, bought a copy of *What Every Girl Should Know* for more than the normal price, and insisted on listening to Byrne's speech covering how to use a diaphragm. She came back the next day with men to guard the doors as she raided the case files, grabbed the demonstration supplies, and tried to take the names of the women inside the clinic. Sanger told the women to leave and convinced the police they had no right to arrest anyone but herself. She refused to get into the squad car and instead walked in front of it to the Raymond Street jail, with patients protesting all the way. On her release from jail, Sanger held a press conference informing taxpayers in New York they had wasted their money on the jails, as the Raymond Street one could be described only as squalid and filthy. Upon securing bail, she immediately returned to the clinic and began seeing clients again. This time, the police not only raided the clinic but forced her landlord to serve eviction papers. Byrne and Mindell had escaped the raid, but they were charged and served warrants. Sanger hoped for them to be tried

all at once, but they were denied both a joint hearing and the right to a jury trial. Once she learned that her judge was to be the same McInerney who had mistreated William Sanger the year before, she wrote an angry letter asking him to recuse himself as he would be prejudiced against the defendants; he complied, and her case was postponed until January 1917. Jonah J. Goldstein offered his services as her attorney pro bono, and the two became lovers about this time.

Byrne, tried first, defended herself against insinuations that she and her sister had located the clinic in the Jewish quarter because they wanted to do away with Jews, as well as the actual charges brought against her for distributing indecent materials; she was found guilty and sentenced to thirty days in a workhouse. She declared she would follow Becky Edelsohn's example by going on a hunger strike. Because of the publicity and the fact that she quit drinking liquids after the first day, the warden became alarmed and, after a week, decided to make American penal history by force-feeding a woman. Sanger's trial began the day after Warden Lewis started force-feeding Byrne. After the session ended for the day, Sanger rushed to Governor Charles Whitman to see if he would end Byrne's imprisonment. Reluctant to accept his offer for a pardon without first consulting her sister, she went to the workhouse. Byrne's weakened condition convinced Sanger to agree to his terms that Byrne could never work for birth control or flout the laws again. When Sanger wrote *Woman and the New Race* three years later, she praised her sister's protest as the greatest single act of self-sacrifice to alert the public to the importance of the birth-control movement.

Mindell received only a fine for her part in the business. When Sanger received the same sentence as her sister, she was surprised at how brief the imprisonment seemed compared to her expectations. She wrote Byrne from the Queens County Penitentiary that Goldstein sent her baskets of fresh fruit and that women from the workhouse frequently inquired after Ethel's health and wished her well. Determined to use her month in prison for good, she began literacy classes and taught sex hygiene to the women in the adjoining cells, eliciting praise from many of her fellow inmates for her efforts to help the poor. Fred Blossom, her aide and managing editor of her newest publication, *Birth Control Review*, saw that it continued on schedule despite her arrest and imprisonment, so by the time she was released the first issue was already out. The two collaborated in writing a screenplay for a silent movie called *Birth Control* to dramatize the problems of lower- and middle-class women on the Lower East Side of Manhattan.

The *Birth Control Review* drew attention from physicians around the world and became widely popular. At one point it had over more than ten thousand regular subscribers, which meant that Sanger did not have to rely solely on contributions to fund publication. Several months after its initial release, however, problems arose when she and Blossom disagreed over leadership of the paper. Sanger was inarguably the figurehead, but her time spent on the clinic and preparing for trial meant that Blossom had inevitably picked up most of the responsibility for finding readers and meeting printing deadlines. Still, once her other endeavors had ceased, she felt she had a right to direct the paper. After an argument over the advisability of going to war (Sanger took the antiwar position, and Blossom sided with the Germans), Sanger asked him to step down as editor. In retaliation, Blossom fled, taking all of the membership files and funds of *Birth Control Review*—he had been handling Sanger's finances, too—and going into hiding. Sanger spent the next few months trying to obtain copies of her files and suing Blossom. As he had not put several of her largest donations on the books, however, she found it difficult to prove exactly how much he had taken, and his new friends kept Sanger away from him until she gave up the chase. The *Birth Control Review* ceased publication for six months as Sanger desperately tried to find the old subscribers' names and scrape together enough funds to continue. Havelock Ellis offered to contribute to her journal, and her old friend Jessie Ashley took over as managing editor. About that time she received a form of governmental vindication when the American army copied the section on venereal disease from *What Every Girl Should Know,* distributing it as the authoritative text on sexually transmitted diseases. Army officials had copied it anonymously and never gave her credit for it, but she approved nonetheless.

When John Reed was gathering funds to go to Moscow, Sanger bought his house in Truro, Massachusetts. The house served as a vacation home for her sons and also as a means by which she could obtain legal separation from William Sanger, as Massachusetts divorce laws were less strict than those in New York. At the close of 1918 Sanger learned that her tuberculosis, worse ever since her stay in jail, now placed her in grave danger. Unless she made an effort to take a few months off, her doctor warned, she would soon die. Alarmed at the prospect of not being able to stay in New York but determined to start her next work, Sanger took her younger son, Grant, with her to Colorado. They stayed for the next few months, leaving Stuart behind in boarding school.

Woman and the New Race, Sanger's first book, centered mainly on the premise that all problems—wars,

famine, illness, and poor standards of living—derived from women's fertility and the number of people in the world. Sanger argued that these problems could be solved easily with widespread use of birth control. Such a move would, she thought, reduce the number of people, increase the amount of care for each child, increase general health, lower the number of workers, and raise wages (even small wages would go further in small families, she noted). Moreover, women would enjoy physical and sexual benefits once they no longer experienced constant fear of pregnancy. While Ellis disapproved of her writing the book so quickly, he agreed to write the introduction. Finally edited and published in 1920, the book sold almost 250,000 copies.

In the 1920s Sanger remained as productive as before. Her *Birth Control Review* was still published monthly, and she frequently contributed articles about the role of birth control in eugenics, editorials, and even stories about her own travels. Her divorce from Bill Sanger became final in 1920, and she befriended several of the men later linked to her as lovers: H. G. Wells, Hugh de Selincourt, and Harold Child, all of whom had praised her work for many years. She also met J. Noah Slee, the founder of the Three-in-One Oil Company, in 1920. From the first, she saw that he was the exact opposite of Bill Sanger: he was a millionaire, an archconservative in politics, extremely religious, not generally considered an intellectual by her friends, and eighteen years her senior. Regardless, the two were congenial, and he began courting her shortly after they met.

In 1921 the first American Birth Control Conference was held in New York. During the beginning of the conference Sanger decided to disband the defunct National Birth Control League and replace it with a new group: the American Birth Control League (ABCL), later known as Planned Parenthood. She left the group in charge of her journal as she spent the next year in Asia. Once the change was effected, Sanger presided as chair and delivered the welcoming address at the conference, as well as a speech in which she discredited old notions of morality and sin and said a more appropriate moral code would focus on responsibility. One of the last addresses in the conference to be held in the town hall on the same subject was shut down because Catholics protested that it was contrary to public morals.

In 1922 Sanger's second book, *The Pivot of Civilization,* was published, with an introduction by Wells. It expressed many views similar to those in *Woman and the New Race* but linked birth control more directly to the neo-Malthusians, with whom Sanger had kept in contact, and to the eugenics movement. The voice she adopted in the book presented ideas from the perspective of a working-class insider, which some reviewers found odd, but this was a deliberate device to draw in lower-income readers. In this book Sanger declared that the entirety of civilization was based upon the control and guidance of the sexual impulse by birth-control methods. She also blamed the indifference of intellectual leaders in America for the movement's lack of success there compared to its success in England, Europe, and Asia. Sanger also introduced openly her belief that it would be best to suppress the reproduction of the mentally and physically unfit.

The year this book was published, Sanger began an international tour. In 1920 she had made the acquaintance of the Baroness Shidzue Ishimoto, wife of the leader of the Kaizo (Young Reconstruction League) in Japan. They dined together on more than one occasion, and the next year Kaizo invited her to present a lecture in Japan. The other three lecturers invited were Wells, Albert Einstein, and Bertrand Russell. Her youngest son and Slee, who had been courting her for almost two years, accompanied her. Arriving at the Japanese consulate in San Francisco in the beginning of 1922, Sanger discovered that her visa application had been denied. She took a visa for China instead and boarded a boat to Shanghai. Stopping in Honolulu, Sanger made a speech about birth control and began another birth-control league before the ship resumed its course. After a delay, Japanese authorities allowed her to land. They had denied her visa because her lectures were frequently controversial, and Japan still operated under the Dangerous Thought bill, which banned foreign ideas that might be harmful to its indigenous culture, including every idea related to birth control. At first the government said Sanger could visit but not give any speeches, but after mass protests and publicity, they conceded that it might be better to let her go on and quiet the people. She was granted the right to present her ideas, but only if she did not speak of birth control. Sanger used her old speeches, but cited "overpopulation" and "overcrowding" as the problem causing social stresses instead of explicitly saying the problem was the need for birth control.

In addition to the talks, Sanger attended an economic conference in Europe and spent time generating publicity for birth control in China and Korea. This tour directly sparked the Japanese birth-control movement, as Sanger gave more than five hundred interviews, received coverage daily from national papers and monthly magazines, and helped the Kaizo set up a permanent committee to investigate birth control. Later, in her 1938 autobiography, Sanger reflected that though her audiences were almost completely male, she felt satisfied with the impact her visit had made. She also commented on her visits to the red-light districts in Shanghai and Tokyo and the factories in Seoul, deploring the objectification of women and the poor labor conditions of women and children.

On the way back to the United States, Sanger stopped in London for the Fifth International Neo-Malthusian Conference, which changed its name to include the phrase "and Birth Control" in tribute to her. After a successful round of speeches and new introductions to foreign supporters of the birth-control movement, she invited the conference attendees to hold their next meeting in the United States three years later. Shortly after this conference, on 18 September 1922, Sanger married Noah Slee in England. In *My Fight for Birth Control* she mentioned being amused about being able to obtain a divorce and begin a second marriage without detection—the press did not catch on until February 1924. Worrying over the prospect of marrying again, she had written both Wells and Ellis for advice. They told her it was her decision, but that she should not marry unless she was certain Slee would be willing to help her cause.

On her return Sanger had expected to find a new birth-control clinic with an actual physician in charge, the second test to the law. Her friends overseeing the project had been unable to find a physician willing to put his career on the line, however, and many were unwilling to participate in a project that seemed destined only to return Sanger to jail. She took charge in 1923, and began by quietly establishing a research bureau where she only referred women whom she had met to the one doctor willing to work for her. This enterprise became the first legal birth-control clinic in America. After publicly announcing the clinic the second year, she found that she had to expand and hire a new physician. Sanger hired Dr. Hannah Stone to start recommending birth control, and then turned her sights on informing other physicians and improving contraceptive techniques.

Also in 1923 Sanger formed the National Committee on Federal Legislation for Birth Control and served as its president. This was a lobbying organization whose purpose was to repeal the Comstock laws and overthrow legislation outlawing birth control in individual states. At this time Sanger happened upon Dr. James F. Cooper, a former missionary, and engaged him to travel around the country giving lectures for the movement. She applied to the American Birth Control League to pay him a $10,000 annual salary, but the organization had difficulty finding funds. She admitted in her autobiography that she later persuaded Slee to give her the money. Her businessman husband soon proved useful to her cause in other ways. Drs. Stone and Cooper had worked together to create a new, relatively cheap contraceptive chemical to be used with diaphragms (they based the formula on goods Sanger smuggled back from Germany), but they did not know how to properly package it. Additionally, the group found it impossible to ship diaphragms into the country, as the mailing of birth-control methods was still prohibited. Slee helped with both, devising a proper means of packaging and labeling the chemicals for distribution to pharmacies, and then smuggling several thousand diaphragms to a factory in Canada where they were repackaged and sent to New Jersey.

As Linda Gordon has noted, commercial endeavors related to birth control boomed during the Prohibition period. Stone and Cooper's new business began to expand rapidly, but the Slees opted not to become shareholders in its stock, for fear of trouble with the Comstock laws, which remained on the books until the 1930s. Lack of funds made it difficult for Sanger to host the Sixth International Neo-Malthusian and Birth Control Conference in America as promised, and she was unable to pull the *Birth Control Review* out of debt. Applying for donations from wealthy subscribers, she scraped together enough money to pay for the conference. The publicity, as well as the amount of data the conference produced (more than eight hundred articles published) attracted further donations until she was finally debt free. At the conference, many were surprised to hear the data presented by Sanger and Dr. Stone. They had detailed records on each client's personal history, as well as a guide for proper fitting of diaphragms and follow-up information confirming that their birth-control method was the most effective to date. The diaphragm, used with the chemical sold by Stone and Cooper, proved 98 percent effective, compared to the lactic-acid mixture previously used, which was only 92 percent effective.

In 1926 Sanger produced *Happiness in Marriage,* a book mainly concerning the joys of physical passion and the spiritual benefits of a happy marriage. Although Marie Stopes suspected she had stolen the title and premise from her own book years earlier, Sanger was sincerely enamored with her second husband and was intent on answering the letters she received each year from women desperate to achieve an ideal union. The next year, Sanger worked to establish the World Population Conference in Geneva. It attracted twenty-seven nations, and like the International Neo-Malthusian conferences preceding it, managed to draw attention to issues of overpopulation and the methods of preventing it, as well as provide an arena for exchanging valuable medical information.

In June 1928 Margaret Sanger officially resigned as the leader of the ABCL and began to concentrate her energies on lobbying and legal contests. She also published a book that year addressing her daily mail, called

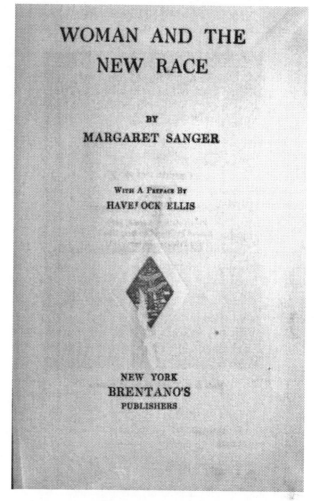

Title page for Sanger's 1920 book describing the social problems caused by women's fertility (Robarts Research Library, University of Toronto)

Motherhood in Bondage. Sanger had for more than a decade been receiving letters by the thousands from desperate women pleading for birth-control information, and while Fred Blossom had still been her aide he had overseen the opening of her mail by volunteers and the beginnings of a collection of what she considered to be the most representative letters. This book grew from those original letters, allowing the people's problems to speak for themselves in a way her previous pieces had not.

The Great Depression brought more acceptance of Sanger's ideas. Birth control was legally established as a medical concern by the end of the decade. Sanger became a greater part of the eugenics movement that was sweeping the nation. She had long advocated the notion that only couples who were both physically and mentally fit should have children, but she began to advocate at this time the segregation of those who were unfit from the rest of the population. In the political atmosphere of the 1930s, many thought such ideas reasonable; for example, few voices objected to the segregation of tuberculosis patients in sanatoriums. Most of the suggested techniques for sexual segregation proved impractical, but Sanger was not alone in suggesting their benefits. Nor was she guilty of the type of eugenics often attributed to her, unlike Stopes, who visited Germany and noted its ethnic cleansing with approval. Sanger was utilitarian but decidedly not racist. Responding to local requests for help, she aided many Asian, Jewish American, and African American communities in developing their own birth-control clinics and leagues. In 1930, for example, she founded a birth-control clinic in Harlem. The clinic was almost entirely staffed by black physicians and nurses, who counseled the population from the surrounding area regardless of race. The clinic enjoyed the support of many prominent people and organizations of the time including W. E. B. Du Bois and the ACLU.

My Fight for Birth Control, Sanger's first autobiography, was published in 1931 when she was fifty-two years old. In it, as in her 1938 autobiography, she focused largely on her efforts in the birth-control movement, with little attention to her personal life. She mentioned her grief over her daughter's death and some details of her marital problems, but both books contained few clear date references. Her romances went unmentioned, even those with the men she married, and she downplayed her experiences in prison. Her friend and biographer Emily Taft Douglas accused Sanger of being more concerned with adept storytelling than with details.

Sanger's writing output dropped in the second half of her life as acceptance of her ideas grew, but she remained active. She led the Birth Control International Information Center starting in 1930 and chaired the Birth Control Council of America beginning in 1937. She launched a second birth-control publication called *Birth Control News* and served as the first chair of the Planned Parenthood Federation of America as it emerged from the old American Birth Control League. Her National Committee on Federal Legislation for Birth Control accomplished its purpose of establishing birth control as a matter for federal, not state or local law, in a 1937 court case, whereupon the organization was dissolved. As her life neared its end, she received many honors, degrees and awards, and during the decade of the 1960s the changing social and political climate brought her a level of public approval she had never sought. Her greatest two triumphs were the legalization of the distribution of the birth-control pill in 1960 (which she helped promote in a series of tours) and the *Griswold v. Connecticut* decision in 1965, which established the right of privacy in marital relations and restricted states from prohibiting counsel with regard to the use of contraception. She died in Tucson, Arizona, on 6 September 1966, knowing that she had achieved her life's goal.

Much has been written about Sanger's work, but little scholarship has focused on her as a writer. As a political activist, she has confused and aggravated scholars. Despite all of her work with the poor, several of her arguments led people to classify her as a conservative and a hypocrite. She was staunchly anti-masturbation, for example, and argued (in keeping with popular and medical opinion of the time) that the practice undermined health and mental stability. This aspect of her thinking provides one example of a lingering religious influence. Another such belief—the one that stimulated her quest for information about contraception—was her reluctance to accept abortion, even under extreme circumstances. Sanger said she despised abortion as an option for desperate women because of her frequent house calls as a nurse to women dying of self-inflicted wounds. (She noted that she quit nursing because of Sadie Sachs's abortions.)

While Sanger argued specifically for birth control and regulation for married couples, most of her sexual life was spent not with her husbands but with other men. She largely escaped criticism for this by downplaying her later relationships except for her second marriage. She was berated by family and friends for not looking after her own children, who grew up with relatives, and William Sanger blamed her for their daughter's death. Over time Sanger received the most censure for her association with eugenics. She at no time supported one race over another, but simply supported having children only if one could afford it. Her arguments for limiting children to the number a family could financially support might be interpreted to mean that the working class should have fewer children than the wealthy, which was not her intent. Later works, such as *The Pivot of Civilization,* begin to transform her early ideas into language more familiar to eugenicists, introducing terms such as "fit" versus "unfit" and broaching discussions of whether mentally and physically defective people should limit their offspring, but as Edwin Black has established, allegations that Sanger was anti-Semitic were baseless.

Whatever objections people may have had to her ideas, Margaret Sanger was the first American to publish the scant information available on the prevention of conception in a scientific setting, and opened the first American birth-control clinic. Additionally, she challenged laws that denied married couples the right to contraceptive devices and counseling, ran several national counsels on the movement, organized birth-control efforts abroad, and maintained a rigorous schedule of lecturing and publishing journal articles throughout much of her adult life.

Bibliography:

Gloria and Ronald Moore, *Margaret Sanger and the Birth Control Movement: A Bibliography 1911–1984* (Metuchen, N.J.: Scarecrow Press, 1986).

Biographies:

Lawrence Lader, *The Margaret Sanger Story and the Fight for Birth Control* (Garden City, N.J.: Doubleday, 1955);

Emily Taft Douglas, *Margaret Sanger: Pioneer of the Future* (New York: Holt, Rinehart & Winston, 1970);

David M. Kennedy, *Birth Control in America: The Career of Margaret Sanger* (New Haven: Yale University Press, 1970);

Madeline Gray, *Margaret Sanger: A Biography of the Champion of Birth Control* (New York: Richard Marek, 1979).

References:

Edwin Black, *War against the Weak: Eugenics and America's Campaign to Create a Master Race* (New York: Four Walls Eight Windows, 2003);

Linda Gordon, *Woman's Body, Woman's Right: A Social History of Birth Control in America* (New York: Grossman, 1976).

Papers:

The bulk of Margaret Sanger's papers are at the Library of Congress. A smaller collection is included in the Sophia Smith Collection, Smith College, Northampton, Massachusetts. Other Sanger-related materials survive in the American Birth Control League Papers, Houghton Library, Harvard University; in the Planned Parenthood Federation of America Papers, Sophia Smith Collection, Smith College; and in the files of the Federal Bureau of Investigation, National Archives, College Park, Maryland. Correspondence from Sanger survives in the papers of many of her contemporaries, including the Upton Sinclair papers, Lilly Library, Indiana University, and the Edward Carpenter Collection, Sheffield Public Library, Great Britain.

Rose Pastor Stokes

(18 July 1879 – 20 June 1933)

Mark A. Noon
Bloomsburg University

BOOKS: *The Woman Who Wouldn't* (New York: Putnam, 1916);

I Belong to the Working Class: The Unfinished Autobiography of Rose Pastor Stokes, edited by Herbert Shapiro and David L. Sterling (Athens: University of Georgia Press, 1992).

TRANSLATION: Morris Rosenfeld, *Songs of Labor and Other Poems,* translated by Stokes and Helena Frank (Boston: Richard G. Badger, 1914).

SELECTED PERIODICAL PUBLICATIONS–
UNCOLLECTED: "Views of a Settlement Worker: A Talk with J. G. Phelps Stokes," *Jewish Daily News* (ca. June–July 1903);

"The Long Day: A Story of Real Life," *Independent,* 59 (16 November 1905): 1169–1170;

"The Conditions of Working Women from the Working Woman's Viewpoint," *Annals of the American Academy of Political and Social Science,* 27 (January–May 1906): 165–175;

"The New Democracy," *Everybody's Magazine,* 14 (May 1906): 607;

"Why Race Suicide with Advancing Civilization?" *Arena,* 41 (February 1909): 191–192;

"The Possibility of Relieving the Monotony of Factory Work," *Playground,* 4 (11 January 1911): 325–328;

"The Slave Driver," *International Socialist Review,* 13 (August 1912): 113;

"Paterson," *The Masses* (November 1913): 11;

"Is It Ever Wrong to Bring a Child into the World?" *The American* (4 January 1916);

"A Confession," *Century,* 95 (December 1917): 457–459;

"A Bolshevik Notes the Spring," *Liberator,* 4 (June 1921): 34;

"We Who Stay," *Liberator,* 4 (June 1921): 22–23;

"Poem," *Literary Digest* (25 June 1921): 69;

"Two Sketches," *Young Worker* (May 1922): 4;

"O Proletariat," *Liberator,* 5 (October 1922): 26;

"At the Fourth Congress," *Liberator,* 6 (February 1923): 21–23;

"A Converted Yankee," *Young Worker* (August 1923): 15;

"Is Woman Suffrage Failing?" *Woman Citizen,* 8 (5 April 1924);

"A Drama in Five Pictures," *Buccaneer,* 1 (January 1925): 6–7;

"The Face," *Theatre Arts Magazine* (February 1926): 86;

"There Are Few Bad Divorces," *Collier's* (13 February 1926): 9, 49;

"The Devil May Care," *Forum,* 75 (June 1926): 952;

"A Child's Heart," *Forum,* 76 (October 1926): 632;

"Lexicographers Take Notice," *Forum,* 79 (May 1928): 797;

"Woolworth Girl," *Forum,* 79 (24 May 1928): 794.

An important forerunner in the advancement of the role of women in the United States, Rose Pastor Stokes was unwavering in her attacks on capitalism as a journalist, public speaker, poet, and playwright. She was the daughter of poor Jewish immigrants, and her extraordinary marriage into New York high society prompted tabloids to label her the "Red Yiddish Cinderella." She never forgot her working-class roots. Her literary endeavors in the early twentieth century embodied a powerful, militant voice in the fight for economic and social reform.

Stokes's experiences with manual labor and working-class issues began when she was young. Born on 18 July 1879 in Augustow, Poland, northeast of Warsaw, she was the child of a couple paired in an arranged marriage, Jacob Wieslander and Hindl Lewin. Her parents divorced within three years of her birth, and her mother relocated to England with her children. Not long after settling in London's East Side, Hindl Lewin married an ineffectual businessman and peddler, Israel Pastor. The struggling family had to turn to their young daughter for help, and Stokes—not yet ten years old—dropped out of school to enter the workforce. Her first job was assisting her mother making black satin bows for shoes. Another job in Stokes's youth sparked her fascination with the stage; she took minor roles in the stage productions at the Princess Theatre, taking

Rose Pastor Stokes with Eugene V. Debs and Max Eastman (from John P. Diggins, Up from Communism, 1975; College of Charleston Libraries)

delight in the costumes and the occasional spoken parts the directors gave her. When she was not working, she enjoyed reading her only book, Charles Lamb's *Tales from Shakespeare* (1807). Perhaps more important, her years in London exposed her to the power of working-class protest. She was among cheering onlookers at marches by striking shoe workers and participated in spirited May Day celebrations at Hyde Park.

The Pastor family continued to face hard times in England, and Israel Pastor felt that better opportunities waited in the United States. The family moved to Cleveland in 1890, and within two days of settling in the city eleven-year-old Rose Pastor started work in a cigar factory. With the exception of very brief stints in a shirtwaist factory and a department store, her main occupation for the next twelve years was rolling cigars. She worked in shops of various sizes, but she mostly toiled in small "buckeyes"—essentially cigar sweatshops in homes where a couple of rooms were jammed with work benches. She found that the monotony of cigar rolling had at least one significant benefit—the job stimulated her interest in verse and singing. Like workers in other crafts, cigar makers turned to songs to lighten the atmosphere; in *I Belong to the Working Class: The Unfinished Autobiography of Rose Pastor Stokes* (1992) Stokes recalls falling into the role of soloist:

These times when the boss went through the loft on his punitive expeditions and left a trail of hot rebelliousness behind him someone would call out: "Sing, Rose, sing!" And I would break into one or another of the many songs I had gathered from various sources:

Tyrants, you cannot compel us!
Doomed is your tyranny.
We'll triumph despite you—we'll triumph.
Till all the world shall be free.

The long shifts, unjust workplace fines, and choking tobacco dust in the buckeyes prompted her to educate herself. Through the efforts of a friend, Pastor obtained a library card. She regularly borrowed books from the local public library and often read by gaslight well into the night. In addition, she found the opportunity to read, memorize, and translate poems while on the job, as she recalls in her autobiography: "I rest the small volume of poetry against my rack, roll a stogie and read as I roll; roll and read, read and roll, and by the end of the day commit the poem to memory. At the sink, where we gather to wash up, I recite it to the workers."

The cigar trade was successfully organized in many parts of the country in the late nineteenth century thanks in part to Jewish immigrant cigar maker Samuel

Gompers. Pastor actively participated in trade organizations at the cigar shops where she worked, and, while on the job, she absorbed ideas about Marxism and socialism exchanged among the workers. As she rolled and trimmed stogies, a co-worker tutored her on the theories of Karl Marx and encouraged her to read the poetry of Percy Bysshe Shelley. Her developing taste in radical literature eventually led to trouble. She was demoted from a supervisory position and received a pay cut after a factory superintendent found in her desk Emile Vandervelde's *Collectivism and Industrial Revolution,* published in 1901 by Charles H. Kerr's socialist publishing house. The experience only stimulated her interest in socialist ideas. Significantly, when she was invited to recite a poem before an organization of aristocratic women in Cleveland, Pastor selected her favorite, Edwin Markham's classic poem of the plight of the exploited laborer, "The Man with the Hoe."

In 1901 Pastor found that her passion for reading and writing could lead her out of the cigar factory. When a neighbor began passing along copies of the *Jewish Daily News* to her family, she scrutinized the articles. One day an advertisement caught her eye. The paper's English-language page carried a notice seeking contributions: IF YOU ARE IN BUSINESS, WRITE A LETTER! DO YOU WORK IN AN OFFICE? WRITE A LETTER! DO YOU WORK IN A FACTORY? WRITE A LETTER! She could not resist the invitation, and during a lunch hour she wrote to the editor and mailed it "in the spirit of a lark." The letter impressed the paper's editor, and he contacted her for more information about herself and her job. He invited her to contribute columns to the *Tageblatt* with working women as her major audience. Pastor felt she was perfectly qualified for the assignment since it offered her the opportunity to act as "'confidential advisor' to dozens of my shopmates." She started writing her first column at eleven o'clock at night and mailed it at four o'clock in the morning. When it was accepted she was overjoyed, and the $2.00 payment gave her an incentive to continue writing. She regularly offered advice to young girls under the pen name "Zelda."

Pastor found it difficult to balance two jobs. After several months, writing the column and working twelve-hour shifts at the cigar factory took their physical toll, and Pastor decided to stop writing in the interest of her health. Readers of the *Jewish Daily News* complained to editors that they missed the columns by "Zelda." In 1903 Pastor was offered an editorial position in New York at the *Tageblatt,* and she accepted. As a full-time editor and writer, she focused her stories primarily on life in the city, moral instruction, and personal relationships. Other assignments called on her to interview prominent figures on the Lower East Side,

including individuals involved in charitable work on behalf of the struggling immigrant population. In July the editor asked her to write the story that would change her life. She was assigned to interview James Graham Phelps Stokes, a wealthy reformer.

Stokes was a member of one of New York's "great families," whose fortunes derived from banking, real estate, insurance, and railways. Born on 18 March 1872, he had enjoyed an excellent education. In 1892 he received a bachelor's degree from Yale's Sheffield Science School. Two years later, he attained an M.D. from Columbia University's College of Physicians and Surgeons. He continued his studies at Columbia, completing a year of graduate studies in political science. He never practiced medicine, nor did he become deeply involved in family business ventures. He did, however, pursue a course that carried on another family tradition—political and social involvement. His father's disapproval prompted him to abandon his plan to become a medical missionary in Africa. Instead, he decided to limit the scope of his charitable work to the United States. He began his social work with the YMCA and then joined the growing social-settlement movement. This reform strategy was based on the premise that the less fortunate would benefit when wealthy, highly educated social workers settled in their midst. Graham learned about settlement-house work by writing a brief study of Hartley House, a social settlement in Manhattan. He then decided to live at one of the nation's first settlement houses, University Settlement, at the corner of Eldridge and Rivington streets. When Pastor was sent to interview Stokes, they met in the University Settlement's clubhouse on the top floor. The article that Pastor wrote, "Views of a Settlement Worker: A Talk with J. G. Phelps Stokes," indicates that she found the highly eligible bachelor admirable. Pastor's first impression prompted her to make comparisons to Abraham Lincoln:

> Mr. Stokes is a deep, strong thinker. His youthful face "takes" by virtue of its frank, earnest and kind expression. . . . Mr. Stokes loves humanity for its own sake and as he speaks on with the sincerity which is the keynote of his character. . . . Mr. Stokes is very tall, and, I believe, six foot of the most thorough democracy. A thoroughbred gentleman, a scholar, and a son of a millionaire, he is a man of the common people, even as Lincoln was. He is a plain man and makes one feel perfectly at ease with him.

Pastor impressed Stokes as well, and he was anxious to see her again. The relationship blossomed, and in April 1905 Stokes held a press conference to announce that they were engaged. A proliferation of news stories resulted, and many headlines drew attention to the couple's religious differences. *The New York Times* announced, "J. G. P. Stokes to Wed Young Jewess." In the months that followed, New York's newspapers ran feature articles about the impending marriage.

On 18 July 1905 hundreds of guests—a mixture of the elite of New York society and inhabitants of the Lower East Side—attended the wedding, which took place at the Brick House, the Stokes country home in Noroton, Connecticut. Anzia Yezierska later drew on her friendship with Rose Pastor Stokes and her familiarity with her marriage to develop the main character in her novel, *Salome of the Tenements* (1922).

After an extended wedding trip to Europe, the newlyweds moved into a nicely furnished flat on the Lower East Side. They continued to be drawn into activities for civic betterment, but they grew disenchanted with moderate reform measures like settlement work. Instead, they became more active in the socialist movement, then entering its high point in America. Socialism had appealed to Rose when she worked in the cigar factories. Graham's interest in socialism dated from 1905 when Upton Sinclair conceived the idea of forming a society for the discussion of socialist ideas on college campuses. When invitations were sent out for the organization meeting of the Intercollegiate Socialist Society (ISS) in 1905, the name of James Graham Phelps Stokes appeared among the list of founders, along with Thomas Wentworth Higginson, Charlotte Perkins Gilman, Clarence Darrow, William English Walling, and Jack London. Graham Stokes succeeded Jack London as president of the ISS in 1907 and retained the post for over a decade. The Stokeses officially applied for membership in the Socialist Party of America (SP) on 1 August 1906, and their subsequent activities earned them a place among the best-known figures in the socialist movement. They often spoke on behalf of the SP and contributed to the cause financially.

Marriage to Stokes gave Rose the opportunity to be selective in her writing endeavors, and she opted to devote her skill to propagandizing for socialism. First, however, she needed to answer her mail. Her celebrity status brought by her rags-to-riches story led to so much correspondence that she needed to hire a secretary to help her handle it. Other quarters made demands for her writing as well. A variety of newspapers and journals sought articles by and about the "Red Yiddish Cinderella." Characteristically, she responded to requests from editors by writing about issues faced by working women. She also wrote a scholarly essay, "The Condition of Working Women from the Working Woman's Viewpoint," in 1906 for the *Annals of the American Academy of Political and Social Science.*

Publications such as *Arena* and *Everybody's Magazine* accepted her poetry, and for the *Jewish Daily Forward* she agreed to write an advice column that was syndicated and picked up by the *Boston American* and *New York Journal.* In 1908 she took on editing duties of the "women's section" or "family page" of the *New York Call.*

A wide circle of writers and activists encouraged Stokes's writing. In this regard, a home outside New York City helped considerably. As a wedding gift from Graham Stokes's mother, the couple received a new home and the island it was built on, Waite's Island, about an hour's train ride from New York, in Stamford, Connecticut. Rose Pastor Stokes changed the name to Caritas Island (*caritas* means "charity" in Latin). The island and its stimulating atmosphere became a favorite place for the couple's friends—writers, artists, socialists, politicians, labor leaders, journalists, and social workers—to meet, organize, and relax. Stokes enjoyed the bohemian scene at her haven on Caritas Island tremendously. She described her feelings about the home to a friend:

> Can you think, dear friend, what all this meant to me who had but yesterday come out of the abyss for the first time in my whole life! . . . God is surely good! My Beloved and I are so grateful.
>
> That is the pause in the summer when one can rest and gather strength and inspiration for the work that lies before. For through it all we do not, cannot forget the suffering world. Injustice of Capitalism; misery of wage-slavery—and again the fight! Socialism! . . . A great, glorious fight. The only thing worth living for in these inspiring days.

Among those who enjoyed the Stokeses' hospitality on Caritas Island were Sinclair, London, Darrow, Walling, Scott Nearing, Elizabeth Gurley Flynn, Leroy Scott, and Courtney Lemon, editor of the *New York Call.* When Maksim Gor'ky came to the United States in 1906 to raise funds and support for the Russian revolutionists, he visited the Stokeses and other socialists at the island.

As Stokes's involvement with the socialist movement increased, she devoted more energy to promoting trade unionism. At the dawn of the twentieth century the United States encountered an unprecedented number of labor conflicts. In *I Belong to the Working Class* she uses military imagery to describe her role in the struggles: "I had thrown myself into strikes with the fury of a true soldier in the ranks of my class." She provided important support for striking shirtwaist makers in the "Uprising of the 20,000" in New York City in 1909–1910. In the early stages of the struggle she volunteered her services at the organizational meeting of the Women's Trade Union League (WTUL). She spoke on behalf of the WTUL at several rallies during the

"Uprising," including the strike's protest rally and march to City Hall. Her participation drew the interest of journalists as employers complained that her presence on the picket lines encouraged strikers.

In subsequent labor struggles Stokes became more deeply involved. The Waiters' Strike of 1912 was an attempt to fight oppressive working conditions at New York City hotels. In this conflict, she served on the strikers' executive committee and handled press relations. The strike was led by the International Hotel Workers' Union and had significant support from the Industrial Workers of the World (IWW). Stokes made speeches before crowds along with IWW leaders. About a year later, she became involved in a much larger strike strongly supported by the IWW, the Paterson Silk Strike of 1913. In this case, she aided the striking silk workers through her literary skills with one of her most praised poems. "Paterson" was published in *The Masses* in November:

> Our folded hands again are at the loom.
> The air
> Is ominous with peace.
> But what we weave you see not through the gloom.
> 'Tis terrible with doom.
> Beware!
> . . . . .
>
> The Warp and Woof of Misery and Defeat
> Take care!
> See how the shuttle goes!
> Our bruisèd hearts with bitter hopes now beat:
> The Shuttle's sure—and *fleet*!

The poem was included in the collection *May Days: An Anthology of Masses-Liberator Verse* (1925), edited by Genevieve Taggard. Even after the silk workers' strike failed, Stokes worked tirelessly for the release of Patrick Quinlan, the IWW activist jailed for inciting a riot during the strike. Working in conjunction with the Free Speech League, she remained committed to winning Quinlan's freedom until 1916, when he was released from prison after serving his term.

Stokes's experiences in labor struggles strengthened her public-speaking skills, and platform speaking claimed more of her time than any other activity. Her style of speaking was spontaneous, with very few references to notes or prepared text. "You forced them to think," wrote Scott Nearing in a letter in which he commented on one of her speaking appearances. Beginning in 1913, the bulk of Stokes's speaking engagements came on tours sponsored by the ISS. Students and faculty at colleges and universities showed considerable interest in socialism during the Progressive Era, and the ISS tours put her on the road for days. The itinerary included mostly visits to college campuses throughout the East and in the Midwest; however, some schools refused her permission to speak on their campuses. The speech she gave most frequently to college students and faculty was titled, "What the Socialists Want and Why They Want It."

Stokes had no regrets that her speaking schedule left little time for writing. In a letter to Sinclair dated 23 March 1911 she indicated that public speaking was an effective method of reaching a varied audience, including the illiterate:

> I covet your joy of being able to crowd so much work into the days, I suppose. If I could work so—but then the platform work would suffer much.
>
> Your "Jungle" may reach the readers, but I have the joy of reaching the earnest men and women who have never so much as heard of your book—who may yet read much some day, because I have reached them with my message.

Despite her enthusiasm for her work, the privations and working conditions in Stokes's youth had a lingering impact on her health that was often evident during her speeches. Occasionally, she would have to take breaks to gather the strength to continue. She was also prone to laryngitis and throat problems. By 1914 Stokes was exhausted, and she was forced to halt her speaking engagements temporarily. In that same year, poor health confined her to bed for a brief period.

Many reformist groups invited Stokes to speak on such issues as birth control, suffrage, war, peace, trade unionism, working conditions, child labor, and capital punishment. Her comments were controversial, and in some instances she risked arrest. A particular speech on birth control offers a significant example. Stokes had been a member of the National Birth Control League since 1915 and served as its financial secretary. On 5 May 1916 she spoke at Carnegie Hall at an event to mark Emma Goldman's release from jail for distributing birth-control information. As she took the podium, she carried slips of paper describing birth control procedures, and while concluding her remarks to the crowd, she proclaimed: "Capitalist society has not succeeded in making me bitter, but it has succeeded in making me unafraid. Therefore, be the penalty what it may, I here frankly offer to give out these slips with the forbidden information to needy wives and mothers who will frankly come and take them." These closing remarks touched off a near riot as a throng rushed the stage to get the information that Stokes offered. She escaped the fracas unharmed, but she was certain that she would be arrested for inciting disorder. Her social position may have prevented her arrest; it proved, however, to be an early example of an act that disturbed members of the Stokes family, who felt, in this instance, that she should apologize for defying the police. She refused.

Ultimately health problems, not the police or concerns about her writing, forced her to halt her speaking schedule. With few exceptions, after her extended illness in 1914 she decided she could best promote socialism through more exclusively sedentary occupations like writing poetry and plays. She had already experienced some success in this area. Her interest in writing poetry had emerged when she was growing up in Cleveland, and she considered herself a poet for the rest of her life. Her early verses had been inspired by her working experiences. A key early example of Stokes's poetry was the seven-stanza "The Song of the Cigar," which detailed the stages of cutting, rolling, and pasting that were part of making a cigar. The opening stanza emphasizes the pressure put on the workers by supervisors:

Cut! cut! cut!
The sumatra as brown as a nut.
The Foreman is looking my way
And I may be docked from my pay.
Cut! cut! cut!

Her poem "The Little Sparrow" had been set to music for voice and piano in 1905. Throughout the rest of her life, Stokes continued to experiment with poetic forms and read widely to improve her skill. She was particularly drawn to the radical themes developed by Walt Whitman as well as the lyrics of Dante Gabriel Rossetti. She welcomed feedback and sent batches of her work to other writers, particularly Lincoln Steffens. She also shared her work with a poet who was one of her closest friends, Olive Tilford Dargan.

After her marriage, Stokes's verses were accepted by several New York papers, including the *Evening Journal, Evening Telegram,* and the *World.* The *New York Call* also published many of her poems from 1908 to 1913, mostly on its women's pages. "Mine" appeared in both the *Call* and *Friends' Intelligencer.* It focused on children entering the workforce, a subject she returned to frequently:

Come little daughter mine into the meadows–
Play while the summer is here.
Winter is chill and abounding in shadows–
My own, my dear.

Go little worker mine into the shadows,–
Work! Adult labor is dear.
Perish the flowers that wait in the meadows–
Whilst Greed waits here.

Dust jacket for Stokes's autobiography, posthumously published in 1992 (Richland County Public Library)

Stokes acknowledged that her poetry was sometimes weakened by its agitational nature. "Propaganda absorbs me utterly," she wrote. With the onset of World War I, her poems took a more militant tone, and her work was not as widely accepted for publication.

Perhaps Stokes's most enduring literary contribution was her role in translating from Yiddish the poems of Morris Rosenfeld. Referred to as the "poet laureate of labor," Rosenfeld wrote poetry focused on conditions faced in New York's garment industry by Eastern European immigrants. His poems were popular with audiences at socialist and union events, and workers in sweatshops, tenement houses, and labor rallies sang them. Highly impressed with Rosenfeld's poetry as well, Stokes had begun translating them during her breaks in the cigar shops, collaborating with a friend from Scotland, Helena Frank. *Songs of Labor and Other Poems* by Morris Rosenfeld was published in 1914. The translations were widely praised in the United States and England both for bringing Rosenfeld's work to an English-speaking audience and retaining the spirit of the Yiddish poet's originals.

Stokes's hiatus from public speaking also provided the opportunity to write plays. Like many leftists of the time, she felt that the theater was an effective venue for projecting working-class struggles. Her dramas depicted workers struggling in society with special attention to the problems faced by women. A dispute focused on the question of plagiarism prevented her first play, *Mary,* from being published or produced. Later, Stokes took the basic idea from *Mary* and developed her first published dramatic text, *The Woman Who Wouldn't.* The play was performed by the Washington Square Players but received more critical attention when it was published in 1916. Its spirited main character, Mary Lacey, a flower maker, refuses to marry although she is pregnant. She no longer loves her fiancé, Joe, who has fallen in love with another woman, and she does not wish to marry simply to provide a father for her unborn child. Mary decides to take on the responsibility of her baby alone and is assisted in her ordeal by only one person, McCarthy, a labor leader. In the end, Mary grows more confident and secure. Before the curtain closes, she decides to become an activist on behalf of labor and the working class. She also vows to raise her daughter as a "woman of tomorrow." The drama mixed Stokes's socialist ideas and her views on working women. It received mixed reviews. Critics generally felt the characters in the play were well developed; however, they noted that the play was weakened by a heavy-handed emphasis on social issues.

Several of Stokes's plays were short, one-act productions. *The Saving of Martin Greer* depicts the unsuccessful suicide attempt of a worker who faces eviction because his low wages are insufficient to pay his rent. Another one-act play, *In April,* brings Lower East Side tenement life into focus. The main character, Annie, is forced to sacrifice love and marriage to her "steady," Tom. The young woman needs to give support to her mother, who is struggling in poverty thanks to her stepfather, Bill, a despicable alcoholic. Many friends and acquaintances viewed *In April* as her best play, and it was performed in little theatres throughout the United States and England. Other theater projects written by Stokes include *On the Day, Chat about People,* and *Squaring the Triangle.*

America's entry into World War I in 1917 and the Russian Revolution later that same year shook and divided radical organizations. The historical events also dramatically changed the course of Stokes's life. Regarding the war, she was in step with her husband and supported the Allied cause. The couple even resigned their membership in the Socialist Party of America because the organization opposed the war. The Bolshevik Revolution in October, however, changed Stokes's position. She felt that events in Russia were a positive sign, and she could no longer support a war that the Bolsheviks, after their seizure of power, were trying to escape. Eventually, her emotional opposition to the war led to a serious clash with the law.

In March 1918 Stokes began a speaking tour of the Midwest. In a speech before the Women's Dining Club in Kansas City, she once again denounced the war and capitalism. A newspaper reporter for the *Kansas City Star* apparently decided to soften her rhetoric, and the story on her speech said she supported the government but opposed the war. She responded with a letter to the editor of the newspaper seeking to correct the garbled story and included the following point: "No government which is for profiteers can also be for the people, and I am for the people while the government is for the profiteers." The government was quick to react. Federal agents interpreted the statement as seditious and a violation of the Espionage Act. This wartime measure called for the prosecution of anyone making "false reports or false statements with the intent to interfere with the operation or success of the military or naval forces of the United States or to promote the success of its enemies." Stokes was arrested on 23 March and found guilty after a hard-fought trial. The sentence was stiff—three concurrent ten-year terms in prison. Her legal team immediately appealed the conviction, which was reversed and remanded for a new trial. The Wilson administration chose not to pursue the case. Stokes avoided serving time in prison. The arrest in Kansas City did little to turn Stokes away from radical politics. When Eugene V. Debs also was tried for violation of the Espionage Act, she was arrested at the trial for applauding one of his statements. She clearly believed that Leninism was the path to a better society, as she participated in the first convention of the Communist Party (CPUSA) in 1919 and served on its Central Executive Committee. A few years later she was arrested for taking part in a Communist Party meeting in Bridgman, Michigan. The case was never brought to trial. In 1922 she played a significant role in the Fourth Congress of the Communist International, held in Moscow. She served as a reporter for the Negro Commission of the Congress, working with the other representatives, Otto Huiswood and Claude McKay.

Stokes continued her involvement with the artistic Left during this time, putting her theatre experience to use as a producer and actress. In 1921 she produced and appeared on stage in Floyd Dell's *King Arthur's Socks* performed at a small East Side theatre; profits went to the International Ladies Garment Workers' Union. Her stage productions brought her to the attention of artists in the developing film industry. Alice Blaché, one of few women directors in the industry at the time, contacted Stokes about writing a screenplay on the subject of birth control. The proposed title for the film was *Shall the Parents Decide?* Stokes's final version of a didactic script included arguments for birth control in almost every scene. The project was ultimately abandoned because Blaché could not find a distributing company willing to promote a movie dealing with the controversial subject.

Stokes's relationship with her husband became strained as she became more involved in the Communist Party. As she moved further to the political Left, Graham Stokes drifted to the Right. He was strongly anti-communist, and he objected when his wife welcomed her political allies into their home. He considered them "ingrate enemies of the United States." Even before she joined the CPUSA, the couple was drifting apart. Following her arrest in Kansas City, Graham Stokes traveled to Missouri to arrange bail for his wife, but he never appeared in court during the trial. They lived apart beginning in 1918, and in 1925 they were divorced. Significantly, she wrote an article in 1926 in *Collier's* magazine calling for the liberalization of divorce laws. The article, titled "There Are Few Bad Divorces," provides a clue about what Stokes felt went wrong in her marriage: "The man whose soul is daily absorbed in the game of making profits or driving hard bargains cannot long retain the spiritual and emotional qualities necessary to a real lover."

Graham Stokes remarried the following year. Following her divorce, Rose fell in love with Jerome Isaac Romaine, a Rumanian immigrant and noted communist theoretician. Though he was almost twenty years her junior, he vigorously courted her, and they were secretly married early in 1927; she kept the name Stokes. Her divorce had been marked by bitterness, as Graham Stokes withdrew monetary support for her family. He even changed the locks on a garage on his property to make it impossible for her to obtain her old possessions without his permission. She and Romaine were frequently poverty-stricken. She returned to writing to ease her financial problems but had limited success, occasionally picking up a few dollars for some articles or poems.

During the late 1920s she became interested in drawing and engraving. Occasionally her small sketches accompanied her literary contributions as illustrations. Her works were often accepted by *Forum,* and she wrote intermittently for the *Daily Worker* from 1927 through 1929. In the same years, she agreed to work on the publication committee for an "anthology of revolutionary poetry," a project supported by Edwin Markham but left unfinished. Marcus Graham (pseudonym of Shemuel Marcus) acknowledged Stokes's help in his 1929 *Anthology of Revolutionary Poetry,* which includes her poem, "The Alarm Clock." Stokes also returned to playing an active role in political and labor campaigns. For example, she worked on behalf of Scott Nearing, who ran as a Communist in the 1928 campaign for governor of New Jersey. She participated in a mass demonstration in December to support a revolution in Haiti. Approximately two thousand protestors participated in the demonstration, and, as police rushed in to break up the rally, a policeman's club struck Stokes. The Hands-Off-Haiti demonstration was among her last.

Stokes was diagnosed with breast cancer in March of 1930. Reports in the press stated that a blow she received from a policeman while protesting caused her cancer; however, Stokes once told a journalist that she had suspected serious health problems since 1924. Following the diagnosis, she spent the next years in a fruitless search for a cure. The main writing project she undertook, in addition to letters, was her autobiography, *I Belong to the Working Class.* Stokes held out hope that the book would provide funds for her medical expenses. As her health grew worse, Stokes traveled to Germany in early 1933 for radiation treatment from a specialist at the University of Frankfurt. In April an estimated five hundred people, including Michael Gold, Anna Strunsky Walling, Tom Mooney, and Sherwood Anderson, attended a testimonial to honor their friend and comrade and raise funds for her medical treatments. Stokes died on 20 June 1933. Her death was widely proclaimed in sympathetic terms in the papers. Reports of her death once again told the story of her rise from poverty to prominence. Many radicals and reformers were deeply saddened by her passing, and moving tributes appeared in the radical press. When Stokes died, she had completed only about two-thirds of her autobiography. Her draft covered her childhood to World War I. Early in 1933, she realized she was not going to be able to finish her memoir, and she contacted her friend, noted novelist and screenwriter Samuel Ornitz, to finish the book as a biography. Ornitz understood Stokes and the immigrant experience in the United States. His novel *Haunch, Paunch, and Jowl* (1923) is a well-written account of immigrant garment workers and labor struggles. Publisher Covici-Friede was also interested in the story of Stokes's life and pressed to get it completed quickly since interest in her was high after her death. Ornitz was committed to working on screenplays, however, and resigned from the project, and it was abandoned. In 1992 the University of Georgia Press published Stokes's unfinished autobiography. Its five chapters, "Childhood in Europe," "Coming to America," "Journalism and Marriage," "Campaigning for Socialism," and "War," take on the tone of a novel. Stokes recalls significant moments in her life in a disjointed fashion, and she adapts a creative, often poetic approach with heavy emphasis on dialogue and concrete detail. Characteristically, the story of her life at times gets bogged down with pages that simply attack capitalism. Still, *I Belong to the Working Class* provides insight into Stokes's personal struggles and achievements as well as a valuable perspective on important moments in political history in the early twentieth century.

After her death, the legacy of Rose Pastor Stokes faded, and her odyssey has generally regarded as an historical footnote. Her many poems were never collected. Yet, during her lifetime, she was arguably the best known of America's radical women, perhaps more famous than such agitators as Emma Goldman, Margaret Sanger, Jane Addams, and Elizabeth Gurley Flynn. Her life and works have received more attention from scholars in recent decades. She remained unafraid in the face of vicious opposition and bravely used her voice and pen on behalf of those hoping for change.

Biography:

Arthur Zipser and Pearl Zipser, *Fire and Grace: The Life of Rose Pastor Stokes* (Athens: University of Georgia Press, 1990).

References:

E.S.M., "The Jewish Mind in These States," *Life,* 71 (20 June 1918): 983;

Lillian Boynes Griffin, "Mrs. J. G. Phelps Stokes at Home," *Harper's Bazaar* (September 1906): 794–799;

Cecyle Neidle, *America's Immigrant Women: Their Contribution to the Development of a Nation from 1609 to the Present* (Boston: Hippocrene, 1975);

"A Practical Exponent of Social Betterment: Mrs. J. G. Phelps-Stokes as a Settlement Worker," *Town and Country* (21 April 1906): 30;

Patrick Renshaw, "Rose of the World: The Pastor-Stokes Marriage and the American Left, 1905–1925," *New York History* (October 1981): 415–438;

Marguerite Young, "Rose Pastor Stokes," *New Masses* (June 1933): 23–24.

Papers:

The Tamiment Collection of the Bobst Library at New York University holds a large collection of Rose Pastor Stokes papers. Another important holding of Rose Pastor Stokes papers is at the Sterling Library of Yale University. Both collections have been microfilmed, and Linda Wrigley compiled a finding guide for the collection at Yale. Stokes correspondence survives in the papers of some of her contemporaries. The James Graham Phelps Stokes Papers are at Columbia University.

Horace Traubel

(19 December 1858 – 8 September 1919)

Kim Urquhart

BOOKS: *Chants Communal* (Boston: Small, Maynard, 1904);

With Walt Whitman in Camden (March 28–July 14, 1888) (Boston: Small, Maynard, 1906; London: Gay & Bird, 1906);

With Walt Whitman in Camden (July 16–October 31 1888) (New York: Appleton, 1908);

Optimos (New York: Huebsch, 1910);

Collects (New York: A. & C. Boni, 1914);

With Walt Whitman in Camden (November 1, 1888–January 20, 1889) (New York: Kennerley, 1915);

With Walt Whitman in Camden (January 21–April 7, 1889), edited by Sculley Bradley (Philadelphia: University of Pennsylvania Press, 1953; London: Geoffrey Cumberlege, 1953);

With Walt Whitman in Camden (April 8–September 14, 1889), edited by Gertrude Traubel (Carbondale: Southern Illinois University Press, 1964);

With Walt Whitman in Camden (September 15, 1889–July 6, 1890), edited by Gertrude Traubel, William White (Carbondale: Southern Illinois University Press, 1982);

With Walt Whitman in Camden (July 7, 1890–February 10, 1891), edited by Jeanne Chapman and Robert MacIsaac (Carbondale: Southern Illinois University Press, 1992);

With Walt Whitman in Camden (February 11, 1891–September 30, 1891), edited by Chapman and MacIsaac (Oregon House, Cal.: W. L. Bentley, 1996);

With Walt Whitman in Camden (October 1, 1891–April 3, 1892), edited by Chapman and MacIsaac (Oregon House, Cal.: W. L. Bentley, 1996).

OTHER: *Camden's Compliment to Walt Whitman, May 30, 1889: Notes, Addresses, Letters, Telegrams,* edited by Traubel (Philadelphia: David McKay, 1889);

At the Graveside of Walt Whitman: Harleigh, Camden, New Jersey, March 30th: and Sprigs of Lilac, edited by Traubel (Philadelphia: Billstein & Son, 1892);

Horace Traubel (frontispiece for Optimos, *1910; University of California Libraries)*

In Re Walt Whitman, edited by Traubel, Maurice Bucke, and Thomas B. Harned (Philadelphia: McKay, 1893);

Homer Davenport, *The Dollar or the Man?* edited by Traubel (Boston: Small, Maynard, 1900);

An American Primer, edited by Traubel (Boston: Small, Maynard, 1904; London: Putnam, 1904);

The Artsman, edited by Traubel (Philadelphia: Rose Valley Press, 1903–1907);

Walt Whitman, *Leaves of Grass and Democratic Vistas,* introduction by Traubel (London: Dent, 1912);

Heart's Gate: Letters between Marsden Hartley and Horace Traubel, 1906–1915 (Highlands, N.C.: Jargon Society, 1982);

"Walt at Bon Echo," in *Walt Whitman's Canada,* edited by Cyril Greenland and John Robert Colombo (Willowdale, Ont.: Hounslow Press, 1992): pp. 194–195.

SELECTED PERIODICAL PUBLICATIONS–
UNCOLLECTED: "Walt Whitman's Birthday, May 31st," *Conservator,* 3 (July 1892): 35;

"Collects," *Conservator,* 5 (April 1894): 17–19;

"Succession," *Conservator,* 5 (June 1894): 57;

"The First Whitman University Course," *Conservator,* 6 (June 1895): 60;

"The Souls of Black Folk," *Conservator,* 14 (May 1903): 43;

"Rose Valley in General," *Artsman,* 1 (Oct. 1903): 25;

"Traubel's Praise For Carpenter's 'Intermediate Sex'," *Conservator,* 23 (February 1913): 188;

"Traubel on 'Drum-Taps'," *Conservator,* 26 (January 1916): 171;

"Traubel on the 'Whitman Literature'," *Conservator,* 27 (June 1916): 60;

"As I Sit at Karsner's Front Window," *Conservator,* 30 (May 1919): 37–38;

"What Walt Whitman Thought of Whitman Celebrations," *Philadelphia Press Sunday Magazine,* 4 May 1919, p. 6.

Horace Traubel, a radical writer from Camden, New Jersey, is best known as the close friend and chronicler of the great poet Walt Whitman. Traubel wrote a nine-volume biography of the end of Whitman's life and headed the Walt Whitman Fellowship until his death in 1919. As a writer, editor, and literary critic, Traubel became a spokesman for American radicalism. While not actually a member of the Socialist Party, he supported its goals and urged collective action through his monthly magazine *The Conservator* and volumes of Whitman-inspired poetry. Traubel was involved with many of the most prominent movements and ideological debates of his era. His socialist leanings put him in contact with critics of the social order, including Helen Keller, Upton Sinclair, and Eugene V. Debs, who described Traubel in 1916 as "one of the supreme liberators and humanitarians of this age . . . not only the pupil of Walt Whitman but the master democrat of his time and the genius incarnate of human love and worldwide brotherhood" (*Horace Traubel: His Life and Works,* 1919).

Horace Logo Traubel was born in Camden, New Jersey, on 19 December 1858. The son of German immigrants, Traubel was the fifth of seven children.

The family first lived in Germantown before settling in Camden near George and Louisa Whitman, the relatives with whom Walt Whitman ultimately came to live following a paralytic stroke in 1873. Traubel attributed his belief in equal political, economic, social, and civil rights to his cultural heritage; his mother, Katherine Grunder Traubel, was a non-observant Christian, and his father, Maurice Traubel, was Jewish. They did not raise their children in a particular religious tradition. Traubel's father rejected his orthodox Jewish upbringing–having once snatched the Talmud out of his own father's hand and thrown it in the fire–and instilled in his son a sense of rebellion and independence. Maurice Traubel worked as a printer, engraver, and lithographer after coming to America and was the parent responsible for his son's middle name of Logo.

By age twelve Horace Traubel ended his formal education and he spent his teenage years learning the printing trade and newspaper business. He first worked as a typesetter, a skill that proved useful throughout his life. By age sixteen he worked as the foreman of the *Camden Evening Visitor* printing office. He then went to work in his father's lithographic shop in Philadelphia, where he refined his skills as a lithographer. Still later Traubel worked as a paymaster in a factory and became the Philadelphia correspondent for the *Boston Commonwealth.* These jobs did not pay much, but he learned from them and improved his writing skills. His most substantial employment during early life was the position of clerk in the Philadelphia Farmers' and Mechanics' Bank, which he held for thirteen years.

The pivotal experience of Traubel's youth came in 1873 when he first made the acquaintance of the poet, Walt Whitman. Whitman had moved to Camden from Washington, D.C., and was recovering at his brother George's Stevens Street home from a stroke and the death of his mother. Whitman was fifty-four, and Traubel was fifteen, yet the two immediately struck up a friendship. Traubel played many roles in the poet's life, from errand boy in his youth to secretary, literary representative, and nurse as Whitman aged. Suffering from depression when he first moved to Camden, Whitman enjoyed chatting with his young neighbor when Traubel was not at his job at the newspaper print shop. Some of the Camden neighbors disapproved of the friendship, but Traubel's open-minded parents encouraged their son's interest. Traubel, like Whitman, read avidly, and the two often had heated front-porch discussions about literature. By his twenties, while working as paymaster and part-time journalist, Traubel visited the poet nearly every day.

The energy Traubel did not devote to Whitman he poured into helping form the Philadelphia Society of Ethical Culture in 1885. As the son of a non-practicing

Jew and a liberal-minded Christian, Traubel found attractive the Ethical Culture movement that embraced all religions as having a common core of theology and ethical moral code. An enthusiastic clubman, he founded the Contemporary Club of Philadelphia in 1886 and served as its secretary and treasurer; he was also an active member of Philadelphia's Penn Club. Later he became interested in the ideas of Henry George and helped found a Single-Tax Club in the Philadelphia area.

In March of 1888, at age thirty, Traubel began keeping an extensive record of his daily conversations in Whitman's Mickle Street home. These daily exchanges, in the last four years of the poet's life, eventually totaled nearly two million words and formed the basis of nine volumes of Whitman chronicles, *With Walt Whitman in Camden* (1906–1996). His visits with Whitman influenced Traubel's political views as the two engaged in debates regarding left-wing politics of the day. Traubel was becoming more involved with radical thought, and he continually urged the poet to admit that one of his best-known works, *Leaves of Grass,* endorsed a socialist agenda. Whitman's *Leaves of Grass* had become a countercultural manifesto for some. Politically, the poet was much more conservative than many of his readers, and Traubel never succeeded in persuading Whitman to claim the movement as his own. Traubel himself was at the time more interested in freedom and individualism than in socialism.

In 1888 Whitman suffered a second stroke, followed by serious illness. In the spring of 1889, a year into documenting his daily visits with Whitman, Traubel organized the first of what became a thirty-year tradition of celebrations in honor of Whitman's birthday (31 May) that continued long after the poet's death. Traubel convinced David McKay, Whitman's Philadelphia publisher, to issue *Camden's Compliment to Walt Whitman,* a record of the event that Traubel edited, documenting aspects such as the guest list of notable Camden residents, and addresses, letters, and telegrams presented to the poet.

In 1890, at the age of thirty-one, Traubel founded *The Conservator,* a journal dedicated to continuing Whitman's literary and social ideals. In *The Conservator,* Traubel found a vehicle to voice his radical social, political, and economic ideas on topics ranging from women's rights to animal rights. He envisioned *The Conservator* as the spiritual voice of the new age, and in 1892 turned it into the unofficial voice of the national Ethical Culture movement. Traubel's biographer David Karsner later remarked of *The Conservator:* "The paper was mostly all Traubel and . . . reflected the optimism of his soul, mirrored the hopes of the oppressed, challenged those that sat upon thrones, championed the

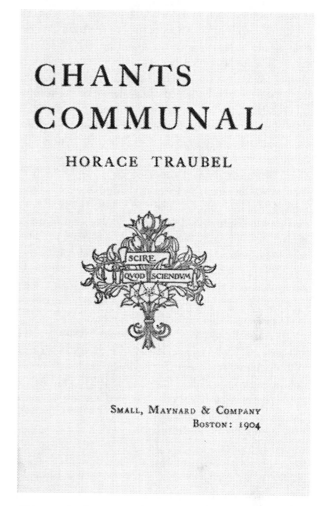

CHANTS COMMUNAL

HORACE TRAUBEL

SCIRE QVOD SCIENDVM

SMALL, MAYNARD & COMPANY
BOSTON: 1904

Title page for Traubel's first volume of verse (New York Public Library)

toilers of the earth, and gave voice to the voiceless" (*Horace Traubel: His Life and Works*). *The Conservator* sold for five cents per copy and was never financially successful. Its continued publication throughout Traubel's lifetime was made possible by the financial support of William F. Gable and Frank Bain, frequent contributors to the magazine. Each issue at first was only eight pages; later the publication grew to sixteen pages with advertisements. Many featured articles were by or about prominent members of the Whitman inner circle. *The Conservator* usually contained a poem by Traubel, almost always an essay on Whitman, Traubel's reviews about books on Whitman, and advertisements for books by and about Whitman. Each issue of *The Conservator* began with Traubel's free-form "Collects" essays, usually targeting capitalist injustice.

Traubel courted Anne Montgomerie, whom he had met at the Philadelphia factory where he was a paymaster and she was a supervisor. Whitman gave their union his blessings, and on 28 May 1891 the couple's wedding ceremony was held in his home. Anne Traubel shared her husband's commitment to the Whitman cause. Throughout their twenty-eight years of marriage she served on the staff of *The Conservator* and continued her husband's work after his death by editing a volume of *With Walt Whitman in Camden*. The newlyweds made their home in Camden, living at different times in various small, two-story brick houses. Their daughter, Gertrude, was born in 1892.

Whitman died of tuberculosis on 26 March of that year, his hand resting on Traubel's. Whitman named Traubel one of his three literary executors, along with Whitman's close friend Dr. Richard Maurice Bucke, and Thomas Biggs Harned, a Camden lawyer who was Traubel's brother-in-law. Traubel commemorated Whitman's death by editing that year *At the Graveside of Walt Whitman: Harleigh, Camden, New Jersey, March 30th [1892]*. In 1893 Bucke, Harned, and Traubel collaborated to produce *In Re Walt Whitman*.

Traubel's son Wallace was born in 1893, named in honor of J. W. Wallace, leader of a group of socialist Whitman admirers from England who had stayed with the Traubels on a visit to Camden in 1891. This association represented Traubel's first step toward forming the international organization of Whitman followers. Ever a supporter of Whitman's work, Traubel helped spread the poet's message to radicals of the day. He founded the national Whitman Fellowship in 1894 and guided it for the next twenty-five years. As secretary/treasurer he set to work establishing chapters in other cities. Under Traubel's leadership, The Walt Whitman Fellowship supported many of the economic and social changes of post-Civil War America, including women's rights, African-American liberation, the Arts and Crafts movement, alternative religions, and socialism. Reflecting its liberal nature, 38 percent of the Fellowhip's original members were women.

Traubel's growing radicalism eventually clashed with the mainly conservative membership of the Philadelphia Ethical Culture Society, and in 1894 he branched off to form his own organization, the Fellowship for Ethical Research. Traubel led the meetings of this group of anarchists, prohibitionists, socialists, and freethinkers, whose views were more congenial with his own. Then, beginning in the mid 1890s, a series of personal losses beset him. First his mother died in February 1895 after a long illness. Then his children came down with scarlet fever. Gertrude recovered, but five-year-old Wallace died on 27 February 1898. Three months later Traubel's father committed suicide. Traubel kept working, and his remaining family eventually became involved in his endeavors. Anne Traubel assumed the role of associate editor of *The Conservator* in

1899, and Gertrude, who was home-schooled, began to work on the journal when she turned fourteen.

By the turn of the century, a socialist movement and culture had begun to flourish in the United States. Traubel's curiosity about socialism continued to grow, sparked by his old friend Wallace's growing involvement in British socialist political programs. By the early 1900s Traubel began to correspond with Eugene Victor Debs, who founded the Socialist Party in 1901 and turned it into one of the most successful third parties in United States history. Much of the socialist movement's success in the United States can be attributed to Debs, a five-time presidential candidate who gained national attention by leading a major railroad strike, serving a subsequent prison sentence, and converting to socialism in 1897. Despite his ties to Debs, Traubel was not a political activist. His brand of socialism was intellectual and emotional.

Traubel developed a complex network of relationships with a broad range of literary, artistic, and political figures. He admired radical reformer Homer Davenport, a cartoonist whose work in the *New York Journal* and elsewhere often mocked the Republican Party and its ties to corporate America. Traubel selected the material for and edited Davenport's *The Dollar or the Man?* (1900). In Traubel's introduction to the book, he remarked upon Davenport's "devotion to the fundamentals of social justice" and said of his illustrations: "his pictures invite battles and tears" ("Art and Heart: Horace Traubel and Homer Davenport").

Traubel's radicalism caused him difficulties. His employers at his long-term bank job threatened to dismiss him unless he gave up his writing and editing of *The Conservator*. Traubel had begun a tradition of opening the magazine with a lengthy essay, usually taking aim at a prominent capitalist. His employers began to pressure him after Traubel published an attack on George Frederick Baer, J. P. Morgan's agent who presided over a Philadelphia-area railroad as well as coal companies that had refused to negotiate with labor unions. The bank wanted to avoid criticism for discharging Traubel based on his radical ideas, so its management resurrected an old rule that no employee of the bank was to conduct an outside business. Traubel could keep his job only if he gave up *The Conservator*. After thirteen years with the bank, Traubel resigned in 1902. He began to live more austerely on the proceeds of his writings and the support of patrons, working solely as a writer and printer.

His time as a wage earner both at the bank and the factory, where he saw the injustices in the life of the working men, gave him an insider's knowledge of the social and industrial problems that he attacked. After leaving the bank, Traubel began contributing to *The*

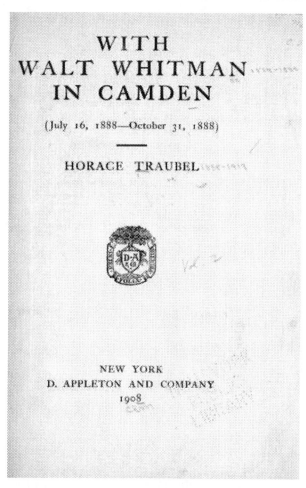

WITH
WALT WHITMAN
IN CAMDEN

(July 16, 1888—October 31, 1888)

HORACE TRAUBEL

NEW YORK
D. APPLETON AND COMPANY
1908

Frontispiece and title page for the second of Traubel's nine volumes of notebooks about his meetings with Whitman (New York Public Library)

Worker, a socialist weekly. By this point, he had earned a reputation for his radical writings. His eccentric style focused almost exclusively on the ideals of love and the people, themes repeated in many variations throughout his life's work. In addition to publishing *The Conservator,* he served for several years on the editorial staff of the Chicago *Unity,* the voice of liberal Unitarianism, as well as writing for the *Boston Index.* He frequently contributed to the literary weekly *Boston Commonwealth,* serving as its Philadelphia correspondent and editorial writer.

In 1903 Traubel helped found Rose Valley, a utopian Arts and Crafts community near Philadelphia. Rose Valley predated most other Arts and Crafts communities in America by several years. Part of a broader reaction to the industrial revolution, the Arts and Crafts movement was a school of design favoring traditional craftsmanship over the mass production gaining momentum through capitalism. Traubel recognized the political potential in this movement, inspired by the

vision that going back to the basics of design and production would ultimately lead to social reform. Traubel's main contribution to the Arts and Crafts period was his development of the Rose Valley Press, where he printed by hand several publications promoting the single-tax community founded in an abandoned mill town by Philadelphia architect William Price. Traubel edited *The Artsman* from 1903 until the Rose Valley experiment folded in 1907. As associate editor, Traubel did most of the writing for *The Artsman,* although it incorporated material from Price and other Rose Valley founders. The thirty-three issues of *The Artsman* document the utopian philosophies and handcrafted products of Rose Valley, including reports on other Arts and Crafts-related activities around the country and abroad. Traubel often interspersed quotes from major figures of the movement throughout its typographically innovative pages; the type style Traubel created in *The Artsman* survived the publication's final issue in 1907. From 1903 forward he issued *The Conservator* under the imprint of the Rose Valley Press.

Traubel's poetry had been featured in various magazines over the years, and in 1904 he published his first book of verse, *Chants Communal*—an oblique rejoinder to Whitman's *Chants Democratic*. Traubel had written the short, free-style pieces included in *Chants Communal* for *The Worker*, the socialist weekly paper that the *New York Call* replaced in 1908. Traubel's newest writing style blended the didacticism of nineteenth-century verse with modernist free-verse style. His effort to win a wider audience with the new writing style of *Chants Communal* met with mixed reviews. Most critics scoffed at it or ignored it altogether, although prominent socialists such as Debs, Clarence Darrow, and Jack London expressed approval. It was translated into German in 1907. In an advertisement at the end of Mildred Bain's biography, *Horace Traubel, Chants Communal* is described as "A collection of inspirational prose pieces fired by revolutionary idealism and instinct with spiritual significance."

Publishing Traubel's record of his daily conversations with Whitman in the last four years of the poet's life proved a monumental effort, and Whitman scholar Gary Schmidgall called it "the most massive oral history project in American letters." The first volume of *With Walt Whitman in Camden* appeared in 1906—fourteen years after Whitman's death—and Traubel saw to completion only three volumes in his lifetime; he died without a publisher for the typescript he had prepared for the fourth volume. In the end, the project filled nine volumes and was completed with the help of Traubel's wife, daughter, and a host of publishers. The final two volumes did not appear until 1996, more than a century after the material had been written. Each volume was carefully edited and includes day-by-day accounts of Whitman's activities, conversations, correspondence, and reports on his failing health and slow death. *With Walt Whitman in Camden* provides significant insight into Whitman's worldviews; yet, the project was—and still is—controversial. Whitman scholars either find the text useful as a rich study of American literary history or question Traubel's accuracy in capturing Whitman's words as he spoke them.

Each morning, Traubel rode the Camden ferry to Philadelphia. From his small office on Chestnut Street he edited *The Conservator*, set type and wrote letters, and met regularly with a group of radicals at a restaurant on Market Street. While riding the Camden ferry in 1909 Traubel suffered an accident that caused the slow decline of his health. A horse knocked him down and trampled on him, crushing his ribs. Nonetheless, Traubel published *Optimos*, a second volume of his verse, in 1910. Like *Chants Communal, Optimos* serves primarily as a guide to all that radicals held sacred at the time. Written in a free-flowing, unrhymed style that mimics *Leaves of Grass,* the collection of poems speaks of social revolt instilled with spiritual idealism, and espouses love, liberty, and the ideal of all races co-existing in harmony. Many early reviewers dismissed it as an imitation. Bain defended the work in *Horace Traubel* (1913), describing *Optimos* as a "brave, strange new book" that had "a selfhood and individuality which cannot, to the intuitive, be confounded with that of any other." She deemed *Optimos* "philosophy in action," calling it "the voice of the protest for justice and human rights." She predicted great recognition for Traubel's *Optimos,* as well as *Chants Communal:* "When it is once realized that these poems are scriptural in their presentation of social issues, they will almost certainly everywhere be used by fighters for freedom as a source of inspiration and guidance."

In 1914 Traubel published another collection of his revolutionary writing under the title *Collects.* Throughout World War I he remained committed to his undying faith in man. He sided with the revolutionary socialists on the war, viewing the struggle from the interests of the working class and observing that it was a war among capitalist powers (Karsner). By the spring of 1914, Traubel's health had become a major concern. The injuries he suffered under the hoof of the horse and a bout with rheumatic fever that left him with a faulty heart valve, combined with the pacifist's personal trauma over the outbreak of World War I, sent his health into rapid decline. In 1917, the night before his daughter's New York wedding, he suffered his first heart attack. In 1918 he survived more heart attacks and a cerebral hemorrhage.

The following year, the Traubels moved to New York City to live near Gertrude, her husband, and their new grandson, Malcolm. Despite his health problems, Traubel attended the one hundredth anniversary celebration of Whitman's birth in 1919. Traubel's subsequent journey to Bon Echo, Canada, for a ceremony celebrating the inscription of Whitman's words and image on a granite cliff, proved his last. He died at Bon Echo on 8 September 1919. On his deathbed, Traubel claimed that Whitman had appeared to him and beckoned him to "come on." ("Traubel, Horace L. [1858–1919]"). Traubel was buried at Harleigh cemetery in Camden, near Whitman's tomb.

Many socialist contemporaries had great faith in Traubel's lasting legacy. Bain called Traubel "the prophet of the new social order," and William English Walling described him as "probably the leading writer in this country, if not in the world, whose work is almost completely saturated with socialism and indeed, grows exclusively out of socialism, in the broader sense of the word." Despite this, Traubel receives only fleeting references in Whitman biographies. Traubel's friends and family, particularly his daughter Gertrude—and the online efforts of Whitman scholars at Rutgers and Duke universities—are largely responsible for preserving his legacy. A classically trained singer and socially concerned intellectual, Gertrude Traubel preserved a portion of the literary heritage of both Traubel and Whitman in the form of family papers, correspondence, notes, and notebooks. In addition to her work with *The Conservator* while her father lived, after his death she supervised a reprint edition of *The Artsman,* edited volumes five and six of *With Walt Whitman in Camden,* and planned a reprint edition of a full run of *The Conservator,* although that project was not completed.

Traubel is regarded as being significant primarily as a biographer of Whitman. Scholars continue to rely on *With Walt Whitman in Camden,* as Traubel introduced Whitman's human side to the world. The timing of this work may have been as influential as the content, as Traubel kept Whitman's memory alive at a critical moment in discussions of national literature. Toward the end of the twentieth century, however, scholars began to study Traubel's own work and to re-evaluate his role in relation to broader cultural changes taking place while he lived. Clearly in his lifetime many readers connected profoundly with Traubel's work and believed that he forged his own identity as a radical and reform writer. His associations among New York radicals and artists reveal much about the period's dynamic synthesis of matters intellectual, political, and artistic. Emma Goldman credited Traubel not only with being the most interesting person to attend her Philadelphia lectures, but for helping her to understand the veneration with which American radicals regarded Debs. Links between Traubel and such figures as Wharton Esherick, Marsden Hartley, and William Carlos Williams also offer promising avenues of study for those interested in the history of American modernism and its effects on the American literary canon.

Biographies:

Mildred Bain, *Horace Traubel* (New York: A. & C. Boni, 1913);

David Karsner, *Horace Traubel: His Life and Works* (New York: Egmont Arens, at the Washington Square Book Shop, 1919).

References:

Guy Davenport, "Endlessly Talking: After a Century, Whitman's Selected Chat," *Harper's Magazine,* 303 (July 2001), pp. 78–82;

Ed Folsom, "Traubel, Horace L. [1858–1919]," <http://www.whitmanarchive.org/disciples/traubel/biography.html> [accessed 3 September 2008];

Frank Harris, *Latest Contemporary Portraits* (New York: Macaulay, 1927);

Justin Kaplan, *Walt Whitman: A Life* (New York: Simon & Schuster, 1980);

Jerome Loving, *Walt Whitman: The Song of Himself* (Berkeley & Los Angeles: University of California Press, 1999);

Carol Masel, "Horace Traubel and J. W. Wallace: Beyond Absence," *Mickle Street Review,* 16 (2004);

William English Walling, *Whitman and Traubel* (New York: Boni, 1916).

Papers:

Horace Traubel and Anne Montgomerie Traubel's papers are in the Library of Congress, Manuscript Division, Washington, D.C. Correspondence, Traubel-related ephemera, and issues of Traubel's periodical publications survive in the following locations: Walt Whitman Collection at Harry Ransom Humanities Research Center, University of Texas at Austin; the Joseph Niver Papers, Special Collections, University of Iowa; the Rose Pastor Stokes Papers, Tamiment Library, New York University; and the Rose Valley Collection, Joseph Downs Collection of Manuscripts and Printed Ephemera, Winterthur Library.

William English Walling

(14 March 1877 – 12 September 1936)

Joan Downs
University of Wisconsin–Whitewater

BOOKS: *Russia's Message: The True World Import of the Revolution* (New York: Doubleday, Page, 1908);

Labor-Union Socialism and Socialist Labor-Unionism (Chicago: Charles H. Kerr, 1912);

Socialism as It Is: A Survey of the World-Wide Revolutionary Movement (New York: Macmillan, 1912);

The Larger Aspects of Socialism (New York: Macmillan, 1913);

Progressivism—and After (New York: Macmillan, 1914);

Whitman and Traubel (New York: A. & C. Boni, 1916);

High-Brow Hearstism: the Peace Agitation of the New Republic (New York: The Globe and Commercial Advertiser, 1917);

Russia's Message: The People Against the Czar (New York: Knopf, 1917);

The German Socialists: Do They Stand for a Democratic Peace? Will They Revolt? (Greenwich, Conn.: 1918);

Addresses by P. U. Kellogg, Samuel Gompers, and W. E. Walling on the British Labor Party's Program of Reconstruction after the War and the Stockholm Conference (New York, 1918);

Sovietism: The A B C of Russian Bolshevism—According to the Bolshevists (New York: Dutton, 1920);

Out of Their Own Mouths: A Revelation and an Indictment of Sovietism, by Walling and Samuel Gompers (New York: Dutton, 1921);

American Labor and American Democracy (New York & London: Harper, 1926);

The Mexican Question: Mexico and American-Mexican Relations under Calles and Obregon (New York: Robins Press, 1927);

Terrorism Under the Cuban Dictatorship: An Exposure of Facts Suppressed by the Press. Here Is the Story as a Basis for Protest to the Cuban Government and for a Demand for a United States Senate Investigation (New York: International Committee for Political Prisoners, 1930);

Our Next Step: A National Economic Policy, with Matthew Woll (New York & London: Harper, 1934);

The Nation's Public School Budget: Read before the National Federation of Settlements (Boston, n.d.).

William English Walling (from James Boylan, Revolutionary Lives: Anna Strunsky and William English Walling, *1998; Thomas Cooper Library, University of South Carolina)*

OTHER: *The Socialists and the War: A Documentary Statement of the Positions of the Socialists of All Countries; with Special Reference to Their Peace Policy,* edited by Walling (New York: Holt, 1915);

The Socialism of Today: A Source-Book of the Present Position and Recent Development of the Socialist and Labor Parties in All Countries, Consisting Mainly of Original Documents, edited by Walling, J. G. Philip Stokes, Jessie Wallace Hughan, Harry W. Laidler, and other members of a committee of the Intercollegiate Socialist Society (New York: Holt, 1916);

State Socialism: Pro and Con; Official Documents and Other Authoritative Selections—Showing the World-Wide Replacement of Private by Governmental Industry before and during the War, edited by Walling and Laidler (New York: Holt, 1917);

Maxim Gorky and others, *The Shield,* introduction by Walling (New York: Knopf, 1917).

SELECTED PERIODICAL PUBLICATIONS–
UNCOLLECTED: "The Dangerous Trades," *New York State Department of Labor Annual Report* (1901): 520–527;

"Child Labor in the North: A Great National Evil," *Ethical Record,* 4 (December 1902–January 1903): 39–42;

"The Mission of Mr. Hearst," *Wilshire's* (April 1903): 28–32;

"Building Trades and the Unions," *World's Work,* 6 (August 1903): 3790–3794;

"Great Cripple Creek Strike," *Independent,* 56 (10 March 1904): 539–548;

"Can Labor Unions Be Destroyed?" *World's Work,* 8 (May 1904): 4755–4758;

"The Movement for Neighborhood Social Halls," *Commons,* 9 (May 1904): 193–198;

"Open Shop Means the Destruction of the Unions," *Independent,* 56 (12 May 1904): 1069–1072;

"The Labor 'Rebellion' in Colorado," *Independent,* 57 (18 August 1904): 376–379;

"New Unionism–the Problem of the Unskilled Worker," *Annals of the American Academy of Political Science,* 24 (September 1904): 296–315;

"Labor Vote," *Independent,* 57 (24 November 1904): 1188–1190;

"A Children's Strike on the East Side," *Charities and the Commons,* 13 (24 December 1904): 305;

"Convention of the American Federation of Labor," *World To-Day,* 8 (January 1905): 89–91;

"What Are Factory Inspectors For?" *Charities and the Commons,* 13 (14 January 1905): 375–377;

"Defeats of Labor," *Independent,* 58 (23 February 1905): 418–422;

"An American Socialism," *International Socialist Review,* 5 (April 1905): 577–584;

"Why American Labor Unions Keep Out of Politics," *Outlook,* 80 (20 May 1905): 183–186;

"What the People of the East Side Do," *University Settlement Studies,* 1 (July 1905): 79–85;

"Revolution in Poland," *Independent,* 59 (2 November 1905): 1040–1042;

"British and American Trade Unionism," *Annals of the American Academy of Political Science,* 26 (November 1905): 721–739;

"Siege of Warsaw," *World To-Day,* 9 (December 1905): 1304–1306;

"Peasant's Revolution," *Independent,* 61 (18 October 1906): 905–910;

"Call to the Young Russians," *Charities and the Commons,* 17 (1 December 1906): 373–376;

"Will the Peasants Act?" *Independent,* 61 (6 December 1906): 1315–1323;

"Ominous Russian Famine," *Charities and the Commons,* 17 (2 February 1907): 785–788;

"How Is It with the Russian Revolution?" *Outlook,* 85 (9 March 1907): 564–567;

"Village against the Czar," *Independent,* 62 (7–14 March 1907): 530–538, 587–594;

"Civil War in Russia," *Independent,* 62 (4 April 1907): 774–779;

"The Evolution of Socialism in Russia," *International Socialist Review,* 8 (July 1907): 42–46;

"Real Russian People at Church," *Independent,* 63 (4 July 1907): 26–32;

"Real Russian People," *Independent,* 63 (26 September 1907): 728–735;

"Power behind the Czar," *Independent,* 64 (19 March 1908): 610–620;

"The Race War in the North," *Independent,* 65 (3 September 1908): 529–534;

"Laborism versus Socialism," *International Socialist Review,* 9 (March 1909): 685–689;

"Science and Human Brotherhood," *Independent,* 66 (17 June 1909): 1318–1327;

"Capitalistic 'Socialism,'" *International Socialist Review,* 10 (November 1911): 303–308;

"Crisis in the Socialist Party," *Independent,* 72 (16 May 1912): 1047–1051;

"Industrial or Revolutionary Unionism?" *New Review,* 1 (11 January 1913): 45–51;

"Belgian Strike," *Survey,* 30 (3 May 1913): 205–206;

"Pragmatism and Socialism," *New Review,* 1 (August 1913): 718–719;

"Why a Socialist Party?" *New Review,* 2 (July 1914): 400–403;

"Socialists and the Great War," *Independent,* 79 (24 August 1914): 268–270;

"British and American Socialists on the War," *New Review,* 2 (September 1914): 512–518;

"The German Socialists and the War," *New Review,* 2 (October 1914): 579–591;

"Socialists and the War," *Harper's Weekly*, 59 (3 October 1914): 319;

"Real Causes of the War," *Harper's Weekly*, 59 (10 October 1914): 346–347;

"Are the German People Unanimously for the War?" *Outlook*, 108 (25 November 1914): 673–678;

"The New Map of Europe," *New Review*, 2 (December 1914): 698–702;

"The Remedy: Anti-Nationalism," *New Review*, 3 (February 1915): 77–83;

"Karl Liebknecht," *Survey*, 34 (3 April 1915): 18–20;

"The Great Illusions," *New Review*, 3 (1 June 1915): 49–50;

"*The Trust of Nations*," *New Review*, 3 (15 August 1915): 184–185;

"The Sure Winner: America," *Masses*, 6 (September 1915): 20;

"Futility of Bourgeois Pacifism," *New Review*, 3 (1 September 1915): 208–209;

"Socialist Attitude toward Peace at Any Price," *New York Times Magazine*, 14 November 1915, p. 19;

"German State Socialism," *Intercollegiate Socialist*, 4 (December 1915–January 1916): 10–13;

"The German Paradise," *Masses*, 8 (June 1916): 20;

"Prospects for Economic Internationalism," *Annals of the American Academy of Political Science*, 68 (November 1916): 10–22;

"A Separation," *Masses*, 9 (May 1917): 14–15;

"No Annexations, No Indemnities," *Independent*, 90 (19 May 1917): 327–328;

"Kaiser's Socialists," *New York Times Magazine* (6 January 1918): 1–2;

"Internationalism and Government Ownership," *Public*, 21 (11 January 1918): 49–52;

"Sowing the Seeds of Bolshevism," *New York Times Magazine*, 21 April 1918, pp. 3–4;

"Russia as the Chief Obstacle to European Rehabilitation: From the Labor Viewpoint," *Annals of the American Academy of Political Science*, 102 (July 1922): 131–137;

"French Radical Support for Ruhr Policy," *Current History Magazine New York Times*, 19 (October 1923): 53–60;

"Program of the British Labor Party," *Current History Magazine New York Times*, 19 (February 1924): 749–757;

"American Labor Leads the World," *American Federationist*, 31 (September 1924): 738–739;

"Labor's Attitude toward a Third Party," *Current History Magazine New York Times*, 21 (October 1924): 32–40;

"Samuel Gompers, the Great Actor," *American Labor World*, 26 (February 1925): 11–12;

"Capitalism or What?" *Bankers Magazine*, 113 (September 1926): 309–311, 327.

William English Walling was a prolific writer whose works developed the themes of socialism, anti-Bolshevism, and labor. His first nationally significant publication, in connection with the Russian Revolution following the Russo-Japanese War of 1905, traced the development of the Socialist Party of America and earned him a reputation as a public-policy expert beginning with the second Wilson presidency, which he served. He was a founding member of several radical organizations including the National Association for the Advancement of Colored People (NAACP), and he named that organization's magazine *The Crisis*. Walling has been described as a socialist who rejected socialism and became a progressive. His work does not fit neatly into any one category, however, nor do his descriptions of the social movements of his time support the conventional definitions. He has been criticized for not adhering to any one point of view or philosophy, but for precisely that reason his work offers invaluable insights about socialism and the labor movements of his day.

Walling was born to Willoughby and Rosalind English Walling in Louisville, Kentucky, on 14 March 1877. The family was wealthy and well connected. During his childhood they moved to Edinburgh, Scotland, for several years, where Willoughby Walling served during the 1880s as the American consul. At age nine, Walling witnessed from his hotel room in London the "Black Monday" revolt of the unemployed, an event that some claimed inspired his inclination to radicalism. Walling was an excellent student, and at age sixteen he enrolled at the University of Chicago. He graduated in 1897 and traveled to London. While there he learned of the English Women's Trade Union League and found the organization so impressive that he later helped to start a similar group in the United States.

In the fall of 1897 Walling briefly attended Harvard Law School and found that he was not attracted to the legal profession. One year later, he returned to graduate school at the University of Chicago, where he earned only two grades out of his ten courses, some of which were taught by Thorstein Veblen. Although he did not complete this course of study either, his years in Chicago influenced his movement toward socialism and reform. For a short time he stayed in a tenement near Jane Addams's Hull House and committed himself to living on the wages of a common laborer. For most of the remainder of his life, however, Walling supported himself not through his own labor but through inheritances and other support from his family. His mother's family provided him with an annual income of $30,000, and he expected to become a millionaire upon the death of an uncle English.

Walling retained a keen interest in the newly emergent body of regulation surrounding the organization of work, workplace conditions, and worker life. From 1899 through 1901 Walling worked as a factory inspector in Chicago. This position, granted by John Riley Tanner, then the governor of Illinois and a distant relative of Walling, ended at the close of Tanner's administration. In October 1901 Walling attended the Fourteenth Annual Convention of the International Association of Factory Inspectors of America in Indianapolis. There he read a conference paper on "The Dangerous Trades" addressing workplace safety, which was already widely regulated in European legislation but only beginning to attract the notice of American lawmakers.

Walling then attempted to set up a project in which he would report in a single volume the nineteen volumes of testimony of the Industrial Commission. Walling seriously underestimated the cost of the project, which he soon dissolved because of its expense. In 1902, recruited by Robert Hunter, a contemporary who had worked for the Chicago Board of Charities, Walling moved to the University Settlement in New York. The settlement was founded on the principle that good could come from university graduates living among, although not necessarily with, the poor. Walling, however, believed that much could be learned from living with the poor. According to his friends from this time period, he scorned the idea of uplift and told his compatriots they had much to learn from the inhabitants of the tenements, although he was conventionally upper-class enough to deplore the influence of the saloon on working-class social life.

In November 1903 Walling attended his first convention of the American Federation of Labor (AFL) in Boston, Massachusetts, marking the beginning of a long and sometimes contentious relationship with the AFL. At the convention, Walling met Mary Kenney O'Sullivan, a unionist and factory worker, and with Jane Addams and Mary McDowell, a Chicago stockyard social worker, they established the National Women's Trade Union League (NWTUL), modeled after the English Women's Trade Union League. The group took as its inspirationAFL founder Samuel Gompers's statement that "what the workingman wants is less charity and more rights" (Stuart, unpublished dissertation). Walling raised funds for the organization, recruited members, and helped establish the headquarters in New York City.

During 1903 and 1904 Walling began to come into his own as a writer, and many of his articles appeared in such journals as the *Independent* and *Ethical*

Record. His benchmark of success, he noted in letters to his father, was to surpass Ray Stannard Baker. Walling's pieces for the Annals of the American Academy of Political Science were often reprinted as small pamphlets, long before he began to be regarded as a policy expert. Two early articles of significance to the labor movement and union organizing were "The Great Cripple Creek Strike" and "The Labor 'Rebellion' in Colorado," both published in the *Independent*. Walling had his first contact with militant unions in Cripple Creek, Colorado, where he visited during the winter of 1903–1904. The mine produced two-thirds of the silver from the state of Colorado. The Western Federation of Miners (WFM) had called a strike there in August 1903. An eight-hour-day law had been on the books in Colorado for some time, but the state supreme court had declared it unconstitutional, and observance throughout the state was mixed. The mine owners wanted to extend the working day to ten hours, which was more in line with the national average of ten to twelve hours per day. Also, the WFM sought to organize the entire trade, not just the one mine. The mine owners formed the anti-union Citizens' Alliance. Governor James H. Peabody decided that the strike was a rebellion and declared martial law. Walling observed that "The military are in Cripple Creek, not to enforce the law, but to break the strike" and concluded that the unions "are fighting a battle for all the unions of the country, and they know that no cause has ever received such a powerful and united support from the working people." The strike was crushed under martial law.

Other important articles from this period were "Child Labor in the North: A Great National Evil," published at the end of 1902, and "A Children's Strike on the East Side," published just before Christmas of 1904. According to the New York State Department of Labor's Annual Report from 1901, roughly a third of children in the state between the ages of five and eighteen (approximately 500,000 of 1.5 million) did not attend school; instead, they worked in street trades and messenger services, did piecework with their families in tenements. About 50,000 were employed as factory hands (Stuart). With Robert Hunter, J. G. Phelps Stokes, V. Everit Macy, Paul M. Warburg, Felix Adler, Jacob Riis, and others, Walling in 1903 founded the New York Child Labor Committee. It was the second such committee in the nation, Alabama having formed the first. Later Walling did fund-raising and ran a publicity campaign for a 1904 strike at the Cohen paperbox factory, where many teenage girls were employed. The girls were protesting the possible implementation of a 10 percent decrease in their wages. Walling wrote an article about it in his capacity as secretary of the Women's Trade Union League of America (WTUL), defending the League's support of the strikers. Walling also attended the 1904 AFL convention and helped coordinate the upcoming 1905 WTUL conference.

Walling's idea that he and others from the upper classes could learn from the immigrants on the East Side turned out to be valid. In January of 1905 a revolt took place in St. Petersburg, Russia, when thousands of the poor, under the leadership of Father Georgii Gapon, sought to petition the czar and were fired upon, resulting in numerous casualties. The event spurred further massacres and became known as "Bloody Sunday." Settlement-house workers were deeply impressed by the silent daylong protest that streamed through their neighborhood, and they began to inform themselves about the political backgrounds of the people they served. Since little information was available in print, they went to cafés and neighborhood parlors to talk to people. This engagement had profound implications for Walling, in both his personal and professional life. By the end of April 1905 he had resigned his various posts, pausing only to sign his name to an organizational call for the new Intercollegiate Socialist Society, and prepared to embark for Russia.

He traveled slowly, making his first stop in London, where he met Ernest Poole, who had been to Russia already. In June they traveled to Paris, where they met French socialists and became acquainted with David Graham Phillips. There Walling encountered Anna Berthe Grunspan, a Russian Jewish immigrant then sixteen or seventeen years old. Walling began a relationship with her. In June, Walling left his friends in the Swiss Alps, and he and Grunspan traveled together to Poland, with Walling having sworn that Grunspan was his wife in order to obtain the necessary passports. There had been an uprising of the Cossacks who attacked and killed Jews at Lodz. Paul Warburg and Jacob Schiff, patrons of the University Settlement, wrote Walling asking him to look into the situation. Also, Grunspan had two brothers waiting for help getting out of Poland. They accomplished both of these goals, and Grunspan and her brothers returned to Paris while Walling remained in Poland writing articles. In late summer of 1905 Walling attempted to sever his connection with Grunspan, who refused to accept his termination of the affair. Walling put a reluctant Grunspan on the train back to Paris and later that year paid her fare to England for training in secretarial skills. This attempt at appeasement failed, for in a few years Grunspan sued Walling for breach of promise.

In New York an organization known as the Friends of Russian Freedom had already invited representatives of the Revolutionary Party to come to the United States to raise money. Anna Strunsky chaired this organization and on its behalf sent out its first pamphlet, which Walling praised in a letter to her. The two had met five years earlier at a Young Socialists' Thanksgiving picnic and talked far into the night. When they renewed their acquaintance in correspondence, he urged her to join him in Geneva. In fall 1905 Strunsky began planning a visit to Russia. Walling moved in December to St. Petersburg, intending to establish a news bureau for the English-speaking world. Anna Strunsky and her sister, Rose, arrived in St. Petersburg in early January 1906. By the end of the month Walling and Strunsky wrote to their families that they were in love. They had not exactly agreed to be married–they had some ideological misgivings–still, knowing their families would insist, they felt they must marry before returning to the United States to avoid a struggle over religious ceremonies.

The St. Petersburg streets were still full of dissent and violence. Walling and Strunsky witnessed a student shot to death by an officer for refusing to rise and sing a patriotic song in a restaurant. Strunsky traveled alone to investigate a massacre of Jews in Homel but failed to produce an article about it. They spent a happy month in Moscow with other American writers before finding that the Strunsky family had suffered great losses in the April 1906 San Francisco earthquake. In May, soon after meeting Tolstoy, they left Moscow for Paris, intending to be married as French citizens. Although Grunspan confronted them immediately, they were married on 28 June 1906 with Rose Strunsky and Jean Longuet, a grandson of Karl Marx, as witnesses. Strunsky continued to use her natal name until the death of their first child. They returned to Russia to study the country and its troubles more broadly, then returned to the United States in November 1906 before setting out again to Europe and to Russia in February 1907.

Walling's connection with the University Settlement had ended because he had absent for so long, but, in his time in New York, Walling had developed significant connections to other radicals and reformers, including the "X Club" and the "A Club." Such clubs generally met in private rooms in restaurants. The "X Club" was founded by W. J. Ghent and included in its membership Lincoln Steffens, Norman Hapgood, Hamilton Holt, John Dewey, James T. Shotwell, Charles Beard, Charles Edward Russell, Morris Hillquit, and Walter Weyl. Walling joined about 1903. When he and Strunsky returned from Russia, they associated with the "A Club," formed in 1905 by many of his colleagues from the Settlement House and Women's Trade Union League. The headquarters of this club was a house in Washington Square where many of them, including Walling, Strunsky, and her sister, Rose, lived communally. The group risked scandal not only by its own liaisons but because it offered shelter to Maxim Gorky when he visited America with a female companion after the 1905 revolution. Later Walling and his wife belonged to the third incarnation of the Liberal Club, which attracted many Greenwich Village radicals.

After leaving their New York friends, Walling and Strunsky stopped first in Italy, where Walling hired Selig Perlman to give Anna Russian-language lessons. (Later Perlman went to University of Wisconsin at Walling's expense.) Then the couple moved to Germany for a meeting of the Second International that included Daniel DeLeon, Bill Haywood, Lenin and Trotsky, Rosa Luxemburg, Mussolini, Jean Jaures, Karl Kautsky, and August Bebel. From there they traveled to Russia, beginning in Odessa and traveling through Moscow to St. Petersburg, where Rose Strunsky took charge of the revolutionary news bureau. The twenty-three-year-old Rose became entangled with revolutionaries to the extent that she was arrested with them, and the police came for Walling and Strunsky next. Walling's relatives used their influence with the American embassy to secure their release and exit visas to Berlin.

In the fall of 1907 the couple settled in Paris, where Strunsky's mother and brother Max, a physician, joined them. On 8 February 1908 their first child, Rosalind, was born but died several days later. Strunsky had begun to chronicle her depression as soon as they were officially married, and she took a long time to recover from the loss of the child. Meanwhile, Walling was intent on completing *Russia's Message: The True World Import of the Revolution,* which was published in 1908. Inez Hayes-Gillmore and Gelett Burgess, Americans living in the Paris Latin Quarter, managed to draw the couple out. Gillmore wrote about them extensively in her diary and later extracted Rose Strunsky's story about the Russian arrests.

Walling's book about Russia was formidable. As James Boylan noted, the book stood in stark contrast to the personal accounts of other American writers who focused only on their own adventures. Walling based the book on hundreds of interviews with Russians from every part of society. His father and uncle argued that he should cut the last two chapters, in which he interpreted his findings in the larger framework of world civilization. He condemned international capitalism for rescuing the czar from a successful revolution. Of more immediate importance for his personal welfare, he had called his uncle Will English's friend, Senator Albert J. Beveridge, "racist" for broad generalizations he had made in writings about Slavs.

Boylan observed that the couple "seemed always to be seeking the new crossroads." They returned to New York, and the next phase of Walling's writing career also drew inspiration from firsthand observation

Walling's wife, Anna Strunsky, June 1906 (James Boylan, Revolutionary Lives: Anna Strunsky and William English Walling, *1998; Thomas Cooper Library, University of South Carolina)*

of mob violence against a minority group. In the summer of 1908 Strunsky and Walling visited his family in Chicago and heard about the riots in Springfield, Illinois. They went to see the situation for themselves. Walling's landmark article, "The Race War in the North," was published in the *Independent* in September. Popular opinion had it that African Americans had started these riots, while Walling and Strunsky laid blame on the white population of Springfield. Walling wrote that the impetus for the riots was the discovery of a Negro in a room with two white girls. Hundreds of whites destroyed black-owned businesses or those of whites thought sympathetic to African Americans. One African American man was lynched for defending his home. Six people died in the violence, and the state of Illinois sent in 3,700 militiamen to keep the peace. Walling and Strunsky interviewed a broad cross-section of the town and Walling wrote, appalled, that it was up to the North to prevent the spread of racial hatred from the South across the entire nation. Walling concludes the article with the injunction, "Yet who realizes the seriousness of the situation, and what large and powerful body of citizens is ready to come to their aid?"

In September the couple returned to New York. Strunsky never completed her Springfield story. She recorded in her diary that their incessant socializing was interfering with her ability to concentrate. This problem worsened as time passed and they had more children. They kept two residences in New York and had several semipermanent guests including Rose Strunsky and Arthur Brisbane. They socialized with J. Graham Phelps and Rose Stokes and with Clarence Darrow when he was in town. They gave lectures in several cities and participated in the Debs presidential campaign. At the same time, Mary White Ovington, a white social worker, enlisted Walling's help in drafting a call for a National Negro Conference to be issued on the anniversary of Lincoln's birth. On 8 February 1909 Strunsky miscarried.

Ovington and Walling recruited an impressive selection of radicals and reformers to head the new organization. Sixty signers agreed to endorse the call, including Ida Wells Barnett and W. E. B. Du Bois. The new organization met at the end of May. The National Association for the Advancement of Colored People grew out of this conference, which three hundred attended. Walling gave an address in which he argued that the Southern racist powers and Northern industrialists could well join forces to oppress all workers, black and white, and he declared "The Negro's only hope is at the same time the sole safeguard of the nation" (Boylan). It became clear over the course of the conference that Du Bois and Walling would push for a more radical organization, whereas *Nation* editor Oswald Garrison Villard would lead a group that attempted to model the NAACP on more conservative reform groups. Immediately afterward Walling and Ovington began corresponding about how best to recruit a much larger group of African American members, and Walling published an article called "Science and Human Brotherhood" that earned him many enemies, including Booker T. Washington. Then Walling and Strunsky took an extended vacation in Europe.

Also in 1909 Grunspan filed her breach-of-promise suit against Walling. The next eighteen months proved difficult for him as he became involved in multi-organizational struggles and prepared for the court case. His physical health went into decline, and some of his contemporaries believed that his mental health suffered, as well. He and Strunsky were upset because their first child had died, and the second pregnancy had resulted in a miscarriage; when she became pregnant again, they attempted to live quietly so that her health would not be jeopardized. He surprised many people by turning his leadership position in the NAACP over to Villard, and he published fewer articles. Some scholars believe his relationship with the organization never recovered from the publicity damage of the Grunspan suit.

In January 1910 Walling became involved in a growing dispute in the Socialist Party. Some conservative members, many believed, intended to form a labor party. Walling was against such a move, reasoning that it would be ineffective on a national level as compared to the organization of trades and collective bargaining with employers. He created a stir with his decision to make public a personal letter to him from A. M. Simons, whom he believed was conspiring with others to rule the party without the consent of its membership. This letter was published in the *International Socialist Review,* January 1910. The most important aspect of the letter was Simons's opinion that the Socialist Party "must be reorganized into a working-class party, fighting every battle of the workers, all the time, and using every weapon."

On receiving this letter the *International Socialist Review* wrote to each member of the national executive committee of the Socialist Party up for re-election and asked whether he supported the merger of the Socialist Party into a labor party. Victor Berger, who later that year was elected to Congress as a Socialist, wrote that he opposed such a merger. Morris Hillquit responded that the question is "purely academic" as there was no labor party in this country. Other members up for re-election, such as B. Berlyn and J. E. Snyder, stated that the Socialist Party was in fact a labor party that supported "the needs and aspirations of the militant working class in their every day struggle." Eugene V. Debs, several times a president of the Socialist Party and later a candidate for the presidency of the United States, wrote that he agreed with Walling and thanked him for bringing this situation to his attention. Despite this controversy, every member of the national executive committee except Simons, was reelected.

On 29 January 1910 Rosamond English Walling was born to Walling and Strunsky. In February 1910 Walling joined the Socialist Party in support of its radical left wing. Walling and Strunsky first met W. E. B. Du Bois in person in 1910 when DuBois came to New York to edit the NAACP's magazine, *The Crisis.* They socialized with him at Rose Pastor Stokes's island home, Caritas, but Du Bois and Walling never felt comfortable with one another, despite their ideological common ground. Villard and Du Bois had a strained, competitive relationship, and Walling was placed in the position of mediating between them although diplomacy was not among his talents. In the fall of 1910 the Wallings, with baby in tow, made a trip to organize for the NAACP, and near the end of that year the first issue of *The Crisis* appeared. The Grunspan suit took up much time of both Walling and Strunsky, who also testified, during the first three months of 1911. Grunspan did not prevail. On 31 December 1911, another daughter, Anna Strunsky Walling, was born.

The years immediately before World War I were productive for Walling. He became an associate editor of the *Masses,* developed a relationship with the new periodical the *New Review,* published in a wide variety of journals, and completed several books. An organization he had helped found in 1905, the Intercollegiate Socialist Society (ISS), elected him to its executive committee, and he served in that position from 1912 to 1918. A small yet complex volume, *Labor-Union Socialism and Socialist Labor-Unionism,* was published in 1912. Walling concludes this ninety-six-page treatise with the statement that "Industrial labor unionism, in large part created by revolutionary Socialists, may be well called Socialist labor unionism." Also in 1912 Walling published a lengthy book, *Socialism as It Is: A Survey of the World-Wide Movement.* Walling describes numerous aspects of socialism and his views of other movements such as reform, labor, and syndicalism. He struggled with the publisher over the length—more than two hundred thousand words—and was so exhausted at the end of the process that he told some correspondents he would not write any more books. He found that he was not finished with the subject, however, and this volume was quickly followed by *The Larger Aspects of Socialism* in 1913. In this book Walling writes that in his *Socialism as It Is* he discussed only the economic and political aspects of socialism while in this subsequent volume he discusses the "intellectual and spiritual side" of socialism. To that end, there are chapters on such topics as "Pragmatism as a Social Philosophy," "The Appeal to Science," and toward the spiritual side, "Socialism and Religion."

In October 1913 Walling and Strunsky's daughter Georgia was born. During the period after the Grunspan suit and before the Great War, while Walling found new publishing opportunities, Strunsky retreated more frequently to the domestic sphere of their country home. She corresponded extensively, including with English, who spent brief periods in the city. Sometimes he helped her arrange to give lectures.

By this time Walling considered himself a publicist. He was not concerned so much with his own reputation as a writer as with the task of informing the public about social and political issues. In his next work, *Progressivism—and After* (1914), Walling writes that he regards socialism as the probable outcome of the progress of the next quarter century but also holds that two social stages must first intervene before socialism

prevails. Walling describes these two stages as "Progressivism," which he also refers to as "State Capitalism," and "State Socialism," which he also calls "Laborism." Walling makes this distinction between the two:

> The central feature of State Capitalism is the development of the small capitalist class and of its control over government. The central feature of State Socialism is the development of a class of more or less privileged wage or salary earners who are either employed directly by the ever-expanding government or owe their superior advantages, in some way or other, to legislation.

Later on in this same volume Walling states that socialism "calls for the abolition of *hereditary privilege*" and "is identical with democracy, especially as it has been understood in America."

Perhaps the most significant aspect of *Progressivism—and After* is one of its appendices, "The American Socialist and the Race Problem." In this appendix, Walling takes another shot at the conservative wing of the party, stating, "at the American Socialist Congress in Chicago (May 1910) more than a third of the delegates favored legislation against Asiatic immigration framed along race lines" and the idea was strongly endorsed by ex-Congressman Victor Berger. Walling continues, "It is the 'reformists' and those inclined to make of the Party a sort of a Labor Party of the British or Australian type who led the restrictionists." Walling thus continues the theme of his earlier article in the *International Socialist Review* (January 1910) that some in the Socialist Party intended to make it into a labor party, and a rearguard one at that.

The outbreak of war in 1914 surprised and tested the American Left. Strunsky participated in peace marches, while Walling mused that the war might have the good effect of overturning the German and Russian monarchies. He wrote to Jack London that "I think it is altogether going to eclipse the French Revolution and have an infinitely greater result for good in all directions" (Boylan). One of three edited collections prepared at the request of the ISS, *The Socialists and the War,* was published in 1915. Perhaps feeling the first tensions that led to his break with socialism and with the ISS, Walling carefully refrained from any argumentation, and thus the book is a collection of original documents, with minimal summaries and analysis.

Strunsky at last published her novel *Violette* in 1915. She had been working on it sporadically since 1905 and received favorable reviews from Max Eastman and her sister Rose, but no one else. As the year progressed, visitors found that the subject of war predominated in their household, and the couple began to have serious differences. Strunsky went on a lecture

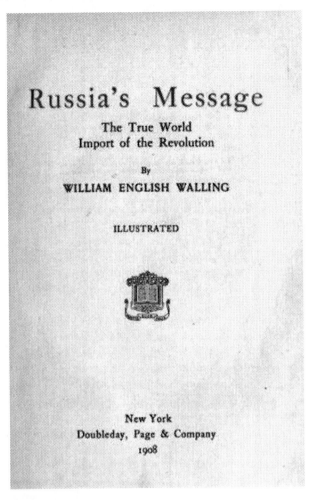

Frontispiece photograph of Tolstoy and title page for Walling's account written after he spent two years in Russia (University of California Libraries)

tour for two weeks in early 1916; when she returned, Walling left for his annual winter vacation with his parents in Florida. Emma Goldman asked Strunsky to speak at a birth-control meeting, and Strunsky, pregnant again at age thirty-nine, fumbled it badly. Walling and Strunsky kept a pleasant correspondence while apart, but during the summer vacation in Nantucket, tensions came to the surface again. While Walling visited his dying father in Chicago in November, leaving Strunsky behind, she received the news that her close friend Jack London had died. Walling's father died early in December, and his son William Hayden was born on 22 December.

Walling was able to complete two projects despite the events of the year. During 1916 *The Socialism of Today* and *Whitman and Traubel* were published. In *The Socialism of Today* Walling joined a committee of the Intercollegiate Socialist Society in collecting in one volume many original documents. Critics of this volume have faulted the editors for relying on documents and offering little

analysis. *Whitman and Traubel,* something of a departure for Walling, collected lectures he had given to the Walt Whitman Society. Walling writes, "Whitman is appreciated as the foremost poet of democracy. He contended from first to last that democracy, the masses of men, were his inspiration–that everything else, no matter how deeply felt, was secondary to that." Walling then quoted Whitman, without attribution, as having stated, "Sometimes, I think, I feel almost sure, Socialism is the next thing coming. I shrink from it in some ways; yet it looks like our only hope." Walling then changed course and criticized Whitman's politics and social philosophy. In this same volume Walling wrote about Whitman's literary executor, the socialist poet Horace Traubel, whose daughter Gertrude was among his and Anna's circle of close friends.

Early in the following year Walling's temper became shorter. He threw a box of crackers and struck Strunsky while she nursed their son. He complained that President Woodrow Wilson was too slow to become involved in the war. In St. Augustine with his mother, he wrote to Strunsky that her support of peace equaled an unforgivable advocacy of German aggression. She wrote back that "You are not a militarist, and I am not a Junker," but essentially "surrendered" to calm him, saying that the German danger to revolutionary Russia compelled an ambivalent sympathy to the Allied cause. Nonetheless, the conflict remained between them, as she clearly portrayed in the same letter: "Ever since Rosalind English was born I have seen everybody as a little baby . . . I have had a mother's tenderness towards the world of men and women. . . . You are more fortunately constituted than I am. You are never divided against yourself. Whatever you think is right and best you have strength for" (Boylan).

In April 1917 Wilson asked Congress to declare war, and it did. Walling broke from the splintering Socialist Party because a substantial fraction of its members opposed war. He began to work with the National Security League that year, contributing the broadside *Germany: A Megalomaniac Nation.* Immediately after the declaration of war, the Socialist Party met in St. Louis, Missouri, and called the declaration of war "a crime against the people of the United States." In May 1917 Walling and Harry W. Laidler collaborated to produce *State Socialism: Pro and Con.* In the introduction Walling and Laidler warn that State Socialism should not be confused with the socialism advocated by the International Socialist movement. At the same time, Wilson attempted to appoint Walling to a commission, charged with persuading Russia to stay in the war. This commission was headed by Elihu Root, secretary of state under President Theodore Roosevelt. In spite of his considerable knowledge of Russia, Walling declined this appointment. Also in 1917 Walling quit the executive committee of the ISS. Walling had a long history of opposition to Morris Hillquit, one of the most popular speakers of the Socialist Party. The ISS's invitation to Hillquit to speak might well have spurred Walling's resignation.

The Bolshevik Revolution in Russia added another dimension of struggle to Walling's writing and personal lives. While the Russian revolutions of 1917 had made it possible for Strunsky to view the Allied cause with some sympathy, Walling found in the Bolshevik Revolution a new set of fronts on which to indulge his newfound taste for battle. In 1918 Walling joined and became secretary of the Social Democratic League (SDL), whose primary purpose was to fight Bolshevism and American dissent. Walling was willing to overlook the SDL's support of "industrial democracy" in order to attain its primary objectives. While he continued to support the war, he began to criticize the Wilson administration for what he saw as its pro-Bolshevik leanings. For example, he understood Wilson's "Fourteen Points," a statement of the conditions for peace generally, as a move to recognize Bolshevism. In March 1918 Strunsky's final pregnancy ended in a miscarriage on her forty-first birthday. The war ended on 11 November 1918.

At the end of 1918 Samuel Gompers and Walling made the first of two visits to Europe as part of Wilson's extended entourage. They remained at least until March 1919 and returned in July to stay through September. While the purpose of the first visit remains unclear, the purpose of the second visit was to attend an international trade-union meeting in Amsterdam and also to observe an international socialist meeting in Lucerne, Switzerland. Strunsky hoped that the end of the war would bring an end to Walling's embattled state of mind, but she was disappointed. He returned each time full of anti-Bolshevik fervor. Meanwhile, many of their old friends fell victim to the Red Scare in the United States, and when Walling supported refusal to seat Victor Berger and other Socialist members who had been democratically elected to the House of Representatives, reproaches began to pour in. John Spargo wrote to the New York *Tribune* to dissociate himself from Walling, and Upton Sinclair wrote to Walling privately urging him to reconsider the extremity of his position. Attorney General Mitchell Palmer and the Republican candidate for president, Warren G. Harding, hardly Bolshevik supporters, had said they thought the Socialists should be seated. Walling's Settlement House friend, Walter Weyl, died in November 1919, but his last essay was a scathing attack on Walling as a man "in love with hate" (Boylan). Strunsky worked on memorials of Jack London that she had begun with a July 1917 essay for the *Masses.* Correspondence between the couple shows that by this time there was much they did not discuss.

Walling published *Sovietism: The A B C of Russian Bolshevism—According to the Bolshevists* in 1920. In this volume Walling states that the Bolsheveki are a "*Sect,* that is an organized movement which believes that it has the only truth and all the truth that is necessary for the social salvation of humanity" and argues that the Bolsheveki are not in the ordinary sense a political party. Again, Walling uses a sort of patchwork of original documents to bolster his argument. The book received little praise, but significantly one who found it likable was Gompers, who asked that Walling rewrite it with Gompers as a co-author. From this request came the book *Out of Their Own Mouths,* published in 1921.

Walling remained uncharacteristically quiet during 1922 and 1923, publishing no new works of significant length. He remained dedicated to discovering hints of Bolshevism anywhere and once accused the *Book*

Review Digest of planting pro-Communist propaganda in libraries. Neither of his biographers, James Boylan nor Jack Stuart, hazards a guess as to the reason for Walling's relative silence. During these years Strunsky was at last able to travel abroad again. She joined Rose for the birth of Rose's baby in Berlin in October 1921, and wrote an article about new birth techniques based on the experience. Strunsky took the children to live in Paris for an extended period beginning in 1922 and lasting into 1923. Strunsky spent some amount of time in these years struggling with Charmian London over Jack London's literary reputation and organizing the roughly one hundred letters he had written Strunsky over the course of their relationship.

In 1924 Walling ran for Congress and was endorsed by the Progressive Party and by the AFL. As he ran in a Republican-dominated district, many of his intimates did not expect him to win, but the election was notable in that Samuel Gompers broke AFL precedent by sending the unions a letter in support of Walling. Critics pointed out that Walling had failed to adhere for any length of time to any one set of beliefs. While Walling was nominated by the Democratic Party, he also listed among his supporters socialists he had roundly criticized in the past. Walling was defeated by an approximately three to one margin.

In 1926 Walling's *American Labor and American Democracy* was published. This volume offers a thorough history of the AFL and chronicles in particular the changing position of the AFL toward endorsement of candidates. Walling's 1924 candidacy marked a radical shift from the previous nonpartisanship of the AFL. Originally the AFL was inclined to support candidates, particularly those for Congress, without regard to political party. As Walling explains, "The American labor movement is absolutely united, then, as to the practicability and the supreme importance of electing progressives to Congress regardless of their party affiliations." However, this ideal of nonpartisanship encountered a particularly stubborn obstacle during presidential elections because of the prevalence of the two-party system in the United States. The AFL endorsed the Democratic candidate for president from 1908 to 1920. In 1924 the AFL seized the opportunity to support a third-party candidate, Robert La Follette of the Progressive Party. A chapter in *American Labor and American Democracy* is "The La Follette Candidacy–A Labor-Progressive Experience." In another chapter, "Bloc vs. Party Government," Walling discusses the value of electing blocs of similarly minded candidates, regardless of party. The volume was translated into several languages.

The Mexican Question: Mexico and American-Mexican Relations under Calles and Obregon was published in 1927. Abandoning all pretext of objective journalism, Walling

candidly states that he asked President Plutarcho Elias Calles of Mexico to review the first ten chapters for accuracy. (Calles was president of Mexico from 1924 to 1928; Alvaro Obregón was president from 1920 to 1924.) Calles affirmed the accuracy of those chapters. Walling also offers the opinion that the clash between President Calles and President Calvin Coolidge originated from a conflict of interests between "Mexican nationalism and American capital." Walling writes that he believes that a solution "depends entirely on the development of a well-informed, aroused, and sympathetic public opinion in this country."

In 1928 Walling became an adviser to Alfred E. Smith, Democratic candidate for president. Walling was architect of the foreign-relations platform of Smith and heard part of his platform stated in Smith's acceptance of the nomination by the Democratic Party. Republican Calvin Coolidge soundly defeated Smith in the November election. The following year Walling supported Fiorello La Guardia in La Guardia's first campaign for mayor of New York. Although La Guardia ran as a Republican, he was well known for his progressive views on such matters as labor reform and opposition to immigration quotas.

At the beginning of the Great Depression, Walling co-wrote with Matthew Woll, vice president of the AFL, *Our Next Step* (1934). Little has been written about this, Walling's last full-length work, nor have scholars had much to say about Walling's decline in productivity during the next few years. Already by the mid 1920s Walling received letters from his brother to the effect that Walling had all but expended his capital and had no income to speak of. The Great Depression also had a deleterious effect upon the Walling-Strunsky household finances. Walling had been disinherited by the uncle whose fortune he expected to inherit when he first married Strunsky. Their children began to leave home, marrying and going away to college. In 1932 Strunsky agreed to a separation. Walling that same year obtained a divorce in Mexico.

Walling accepted the position of executive director of the Labor Chest in late 1935. The purpose of the Labor Chest was to aid refugee unionists in Europe. In June 1936 he sailed to Europe. Walling worked first with the International Labor Organization in Geneva, then in London, and later in Paris, to help form a committee for refugee workers. He hoped and planned to be in Amsterdam on 4 September 1936, to meet with underground opponents of Adolf Hitler, the dictator of Germany. While he succeeded in traveling to Amsterdam, he was unable to keep his appointment because of his declining health. Walling's health deteriorated quickly, and he died of pneumonia on 12 September 1936, in Amsterdam.

Despite all of their trials, Strunsky boarded a ship bound for Europe that evening. After his death she sent out a call to his friends for memorial essays; in 1938 Stackpole published the collection, titled *William English Walling: A Symposium*. It includes contributions from Anna and Simeon Strunsky, Ernest Poole, Jean Longuet, Howard Brubaker, N. I. Stone, Bernard Groethuysen, Charles Edward Russell, Mary White Ovington, Rose Schneiderman, Spencer Miller Jr., Selig Perlman, Gustavus Myers, Matthew Woll, and Raymond Ingersoll. Most of the responses included in the volume were from friends who had known him since his Settlement House days; some had been published already (for example, Russell's obituary that appeared in the November 1936 *Crisis*). Most focus on Walling as an activist, not a writer. After Walling's death, Strunsky came to have some importance as a source of information about the radicalism of her contemporaries. She died on 25 February 1964.

Walling has become an obscure figure, and only two significant studies are devoted to him, *Revolutionary Lives: Anna Strunsky & William English Walling* (1998), by James Boylan, and Jack Meyer Stuart's 1968 dissertation in political science from Columbia University, "William English Walling: A Study in Politics and Ideas." Stuart offers a more coherent and thorough analysis of Walling's writing and relies on interviews with Walling's children, but he makes little effort to relate Walling's intellectual and personal development. Stuart divides Walling's writing career into "pre-war, wartime, and post-war eras." Stuart notes that despite such shortcomings as being "often too anxious to take a position" and thus seeming to change his mind very often, Walling foresaw that unregulated capitalism would be followed, not by socialism as many of his contemporaries thought, but by "an increasingly state-dominated form of welfare capitalism." One of the most important aspects of this study is the degree to which it makes clear that Walling's radicalism relied more on Veblen than on Marx and Engels. Stuart said of Walling, "he would always seek his own way and build his ideology from whatever sources he considered appropriate." Boylan's *Revolutionary Lives* corrects for Stuart's blind spots by making more extensive use of Anna Strunsky's papers as a Walling resource. Walling appears as a quite different writer framed in dialogue with Strunsky.

Another significant source of information about William English Walling are the memoirs of his contemporaries. Charles Edward Russell's *Bare Hands and Stone Walls* (1933), Mary White Ovington's *The Walls Came Tumbling Down* (1947), and Ernest Poole's *The Bridge: My Own Story* (New York 1940) provide substantial information about him. At the very least Walling's writing has value because it illustrates how the brightest and most idealistic Americans of his period digested and incorporated the ideas in circulation during the Progressive Era. Stuart correctly noted that at times Walling's writing could be characterized as "intellectual patchwork," but Walling's quarter-century study of socialism and of labor issues was extensive. Walling's work at best clarifies the commitments and struggles among the various factions of the radical Left—the settlement-house movement and social-work initiatives developed by the upper classes in response to immigrant needs, responses to the revolutionary changes in Russia, varieties of labor organization, the Socialist Party, the Progressive Movement, and the polarizing effects of world war—in the early years of the twentieth century.

References:

James Boylan, *Revolutionary Lives: Anna Strunsky & William English Walling* (Amherst: University of Massachusetts Press, 1998);

Mary White Ovington, *The Walls Came Tumbling Down* (New York: Harcourt, Brace: 1947);

Ernest Poole, *The Bridge: My Own Story* (New York: Macmillan, 1940);

Charles Edward Russell, *Bare Hands and Stone Walls* (New York: Scribners, 1933);

Christine Stansell, *American Moderns: Bohemian New York and the Creation of a New Century* (New York: Metropolitan/Holt, 2000);

William English Walling: A Symposium (New York: Stackpole, 1938).

Papers:

The papers of William English Walling are at the Wisconsin Historical Society. They have been microfilmed and include extensive correspondence with radicals and reformers of his time. There is a Strunsky-Walling Collection at the Bancroft Library, University of California, Berkeley. Anna Strunsky Walling's papers are divided into two major collections at Yale University and the Huntington Library, San Marino, California. Correspondence from Walling survives in the papers of many of his contemporaries, for example the James Graham Phelps Stokes Papers at the Rare Book and Manuscript Library, Columbia University; the Macmillan Company Records at the Rare Book and Manuscript Division, New York Public Library; the Arthur Bullard Papers at the Seeley G. Mudd Manuscript Library, Princeton University; and the Hamilton Holt Papers at Rollins College, Winter Park, Florida.

Josiah Warren

(1798 – 14 April 1874)

James J. Kopp
Lewis & Clark College

BOOKS AND PAMPHLETS: *Introduction to a New Printing Apparatus Adapted to the Wants and Capacities of Private Citizens* (Trenton, Ohio: Josiah Warren, 1836);

Manifesto (New Harmony, Ind.: Josiah Warren, 1841);

A New System of Notation. Intended to Promote the More General Cultivation & More Just Performance of Music (New Harmony, Ind.: J. Warren, 1843);

Letter on Equitable Commerce (New Harmony, Ind.: Warren's Amateur Print, 1844);

Equitable Commerce: A New Development of Principles As Substitutes for Laws and Governments, for the Harmonious Adjustment and Regulation of the Pecuniary, Intellectual, and Moral Intercourse of Mankind Proposed as Elements of New Society (New Harmony, Ind.: J. Warren, 1846);

Practical Details in Equitable Commerce: Showing the Workings, in Actual Experiment, During a Series of Years, of the Social Principles Expounded in the Works called "Equitable Commerce," by the Author of This, and "The Science of Society," by Stephen P. Andrews (New York: Fowler & Wells, 1852);

Written Music Remodeled, and Invested with the Simplicity of an Exact Science . . . A System of Short Hand Accompaniment Introduced (Boston: J. P. Jewett, 1860);

The Principle of Equivalents: A Subject of Immediate and Serious Interest to Both Sexes and All Classes of All Nations (Long Island, N.Y.: J. Warren, 1861);

True Civilization: An Immediate Necessity and the Last Ground of Hope for Mankind. Being the Results and Conclusions of Thirty-Nine Years' Laborious Study and Experiments in Civilization as It Is, and in Different Enterprises for Reconstruction (Boston: J. Warren, 1863);

Response to the Call of the National Labor Union for Essays on the Following Subjects: 1. The Specie Basis Fallacy: 2. Strikes: 3. Co-operation: [etc.] (Boston: 1871);

Political Platform for the Coming Party (Boston: 1871);

Practical Applications of the Elementary Principles of "True Civilization", to the Minute Details of Every Day Life. Being Part III, the Last of the "True Civilization" Series (Princeton, Mass.: J. Warren, 1873).

Josiah Warren (from William Bailie, Josiah Warren—the First American Anarchist, *1906; University of California Libraries)*

SELECTED PERIODICAL PUBLICATIONS–UNCOLLECTED: "To the Friends of the Social System," as "A Late Member of New Harmony," *Western Tiller* (27 July 1827);

"A Letter from Josiah Warren," *Mechanics' Free Press* (10 May 1828): 2;

"To the Friends of Equal Exchange of Labor in the West," *Free Enquirer,* 2 (17 July 1828): 301–302;

"A Few Words to the Pioneers," *Word* (1873);

"The Cost Principle," *Index,* 4 (11 December 1873): 504–505;

"Josiah Warren's Last Letter," *Index,* 5 (28 May 1874): 207–208;

"Labor the Only Ground of Price," *Index,* 5 (28 May 1874): 260–261.

Often identified as America's first anarchist, Josiah Warren had a varied career that encompassed more than his political philosophies. He was an avid inventor, with several patents to his credit, and an accomplished musician, who could have chosen that field as his profession. Warren's writings about philosophical anarchy place him among American radicals and reformers. He based his vision of anarchy on the principles of the sovereignty of the individual and peaceful revolution that grew out of his economic ideas and his communal experiences. These ideas influenced key figures in the rise of philosophical anarchy in America, as well as other reformers.

Warren was born in Boston in 1798, the exact date of his birth unknown. His parents were Josiah Warren Jr. of Little Cambridge (Brighton) and Mary (Polley) Parker of Lynn, Massachusetts. There is some controversy regarding the names of his parents as well as his family connections. Little is known of his upbringing and education other than that he showed musical talent and inclination, playing with his brother George in the "Old Boston Brigade Band." He married Caroline Cutter in 1818 and, seeking to pursue a musical career beyond New England, moved to Cincinnati, Ohio, in 1821 where he became an orchestra leader and a music teacher. Some aspects of his family life were chronicled by his son, George W. Warren, who followed his father's passion for music and became a bandleader. George Warren notes that in 1821 his father invented a lamp for burning lard, to replace the more expensive tallow-burning candles. A patent for the lard lamp was sought in 1823 signed by President John Quincy Adams. As a result of this development, the elder Warren set aside his musical career and established a profitable lamp factory. In 1825 he sold the lamp business to seek a new direction in his life. The ideals of Robert Owen provided this inspiration.

A Welsh manufacturer and reformer, Owen came to the United States to bring his ideals for the New Moral World. Following success at reforms in the industrial mills at New Lanark, Scotland, Owen sought to introduce his scheme for reorganized society in America. To accomplish this he purchased the land owned by the followers of George Rapp who had established a communal society in New Harmony, Indiana. Owen presented his plan at a series of public presentations, including one in Cincinnati, where Warren heard him and made a decision to participate in communal life at New Harmony. With his family he moved from Cincinnati to New Harmony to join many others in what was called Owen's grand experiment. The grand experiment lasted a little over two years, dissolving in 1827, but in its brief history it influenced several individuals who spent time there, including scientist and educator William Maclure, reformer Frances Wright, and Owen's son, Robert Dale Owen. It also marked a critical turning point in the life and beliefs of Josiah Warren. The failure of New Harmony revealed to him the manner in which human happiness and what he called the "emancipation of man" might be achieved. Although Warren left New Harmony in 1827, he continued to have ties to the community and to some of the individuals he met there, including Robert Dale Owen, for the rest of his life.

From the New Harmony experiment Warren learned that any form of communal government based on authoritative leadership would ultimately lead to failure. Hope for any lasting reform, he thought, must be based on complete individual liberty. He also came to realize that any attempt at such a grand reform scheme as at New Harmony must be tested adequately before being offered for widespread adoption. These realizations served as the basis for the development of the principles that would direct his future reform activities and writing. He ranked chief among these the concept of the sovereignty of the individual, and from this he developed theories for economic, social, and political reform.

After leaving New Harmony in 1827, Warren and his family returned to Cincinnati where he further developed his theories and decided to test one that he identified as the cost principle, which grew from the premise that cost is the limit of price. By this Warren understood that the cost of an item would be the actual cost paid by a merchant to a manufacturer or wholesaler plus the cost of the labor involved in buying and reselling the goods. Warren saw cost, however, not just as a monetary construct but as something that incorporated other factors such as "fatigue of body and mind" into the equation of the labor involved in handling goods. Closely tied with this concept is the principle of equity, or more specifically, equity of labor. In his view, different types of labor differentially influenced the cost of an item, an idea reflective of other utilitarian thinkers of the time. John Stuart Mill, who labeled Warren "a remarkable American," noted in his autobiography that he used Warren's phrase "Individual Sovereignty" in his own writings.

Warren later developed his thoughts on these principles in two of his major works, *Equitable Commerce*

(1846) and *True Civilization* (1863), but in 1827 he sought to test this principle, a lesson he learned from the New Harmony experience, before presenting it more widely. He opened a store in May 1827 that he called both the Equity store and the Time Store. The store put into practice Warren's concept that an equal exchange of labor should be included in the cost of any item. Warren's biographer, William Bailie, offers an illustration of this practice:

> A clock hangs in a conspicuous place in the store. In comes the customer to make his purchases. All goods are marked with the price in plain figures, which is their cost price, plus a nominal percentage to cover freight, shrinkage, rent, etc., usually about four cents on the dollar. The purchaser selects what he needs, with not over-much assistance or prompting from the salesman, and pays for the same in lawful money. The time spent by the merchant in waiting upon him is now calculated by reference to the convenient clock, and in payment for this service the customer gives his labor note. . . . The store-keeper thus agreed to exchange his time for an equal amount of the time of those who bought goods of him.

Warren saw this method of commerce as eliminating time wasted by the merchant and the customer in bickering over price; instead, he thought it would develop a sense of mutual respect and confidence between buyer and seller. The idea of the labor note he borrowed from Owen, although Owen had not applied it to any practical situation. Individuals who placed items "on deposit" in the store for sale—a commercial practice with which Owen had also experimented in the Labor Exchange in London—could also use labor notes. In Warren's model, however, store users could place items on deposit only when there was a demand for them, thus eliminating a glutted market (the downfall of Owen's earlier experiment). The initial Equity store in Cincinnati lasted two years and, although it never realized a profit, Warren considered the effort an important step in the development of his ideas.

During this period of the initial Time Store Warren first wrote about his evolving views on society and the means by which it could be reformed. In June and July 1827 he wrote eight communications over the signature "A Late Member of New Harmony" and published them in the *Western Tiller.* He addressed them all "To the Friends of the Social System." The following year "A Letter from Josiah Warren" appeared in *Mechanics' Free Press* (10 May 1828), and a communication "To the Friends of Equal Exchange of Labor in the West" appeared in *The Free Enquirer* (17 July 1828), which Robert Dale Owen and Frances "Fanny" Wright

jointly edited. Warren was beginning to expand his attempts to share his message.

Still, typical of his checkered life, as Warren drafted these communications and supervised the Time Store he continued his involvement with music and in exploring enhanced production methods in printing, a field that he added to his interests. In 1830 he invented a speed press but did not patent it at that time. He returned to improvements in the mechanics of printing repeatedly in the next two decades and printed many of his writing projects using his own press in the 1830s and 1840s as well.

In 1830 another unsuccessful endeavor changed the direction of Warren's ideas and ideals. Robert Dale Owen visited Warren in Cincinnati early that year and convinced Warren to come to New York where the two of them, along with Fanny Wright, might establish an institution devoted to Warren's beliefs in what he was beginning to call equitable commerce. Warren felt emboldened by Owen's confidence in him, and he again left Cincinnati to become involved in a Owen-family experiment. Warren arrived in New York in mid 1830, and in August a communication signed "J.W." appeared in *The Free Enquirer.* Fanny Wright paid special tribute to Warren in an article on "Wealth and Money," published in the 23 October 1830 issue, lauding him for his economic scheme. The lofty plans for the institution Owen had envisioned never materialized, however, so Warren returned to Ohio to resume his own efforts at putting his principles into practice.

The next step in his developing scheme was to expand his equity experiment from the store to a village. In the months following his return from New York, Warren taught himself and his family the skills needed for self-sufficiency in a community, from house construction to spinning. To provide support for these efforts and his family, he again turned to music. During the cholera epidemic of 1832 he provided medical assistance to the many struck down by this disease. Throughout all of this he continued to develop his reform agenda, and in January 1833 he published the first issue of a monthly magazine, *The Peaceful Revolutionist.* Written, printed, and distributed by Warren, this four-page publication brought together his principles of the sovereignty of the individual, equity in labor, and a nonviolent means to achieve a new society. Warren produced five known issues of *The Peaceful Revolutionist*—four in 1833 and one in 1848.

In 1835 Warren's initial attempt to expand his experiments to a village took shape. Appropriately named Equity, this settlement occupied four hundred acres he procured in Tuscarawas County, Ohio. Consistent with his belief in the necessity of testing his experiments on a small scale, Warren included fewer than

Labor note issued by Josiah Warren (from George B. Lockwood, The New Harmony Movement, *1970; Thomas Cooper Library, University of South Carolina)*

twenty individuals in Equity. The efforts to establish the community, however, met obstacles almost as soon as they began. The spot Warren chose for Equity soon proved to be malarial, and the challenges of this disease and others proved too great for the experiment. Although the hardiest of souls remained for two years, Warren abandoned any attempt to make Equity the center of a reform movement.

Following this setback Warren returned to New Harmony, where he spent the next several years. He initially focused on his inventions in printing, including the first continuous sheet press to go into production. The large press was moved by steamboat on a perilous winter voyage from Cincinnati, where he had it built, to Evansville, Indiana. His son, George, who accompanied him on this adventure reports:

> This beautiful machine opened up splendidly, but no sooner had my father returned home than the platen press jammers commenced their anarchistic devilment. They had never seen a press that would print more than four to six copies per minute and they were going to be d—m if any bloody press should take the bread out of their mouths by doing the work in no time. So these scoundrels kept my father in hot water, till one day he engaged some wagons and had the press hauled home and broke up.

Nevertheless, Warren continued to combine his interests in invention and music with further development of his principles of reform, in particular that which he labeled equitable commerce. He opened a second Time Store in New Harmony in 1840, and, similar to the experiment in Cincinnati, this enterprise lasted a relatively brief time, but he considered it another important step in the development of his equity scheme. He produced several more typographical and stereotyping inventions in the early 1840s, and he invented a new system of musical notation that represents harmonic sounds phonetically. He published information on this in *A New System of Notation* in 1843 and later patented this music system.

Warren's most significant contributions came in the latter half of the 1840s. In 1846 he self-published *Equitable Commerce: A New Development of Principles As Substitutes for Laws and Governments, for the Harmonious Adjustment and Regulation of the Pecuniary, Intellectual, and Moral Intercourse of Mankind Proposed as Elements of New Society.* This work brought together the principles he had developed over the nearly twenty years since he left New Harmony. It seemed fitting that this work would be published there. The commerce of which Warren wrote had a broader meaning, as suggested by the lengthy subtitle, with all aspects of human intercourse included in his definition. At the core lay the principles of individuality, the sovereignty of the individual, cost as the limit of labor, and adaptation of supply to demand. *Equitable Commerce* placed Warren on a new standing in a decade that was abundant with reform writers and thinkers.

Soon after the publication of *Equitable Commerce,* Warren saw another opportunity to establish an "equitable village," based on the principles put forth in his new work. In doing so, he assumed the property of a recently failed Fourierist phalanx at Claremont in Ohio, some thirty-five miles from Cincinnati. This commune had begun in 1844; but like many of the efforts to develop intentional communities in the United States in this period following the ideals of Charles Fourier, it lasted a relatively short period before it dissolved. Noting the failure of Owen's New Harmony, Warren pointed out to the remaining inhabitants of the Claremont Phalanx that a communal experiment could never be successful that did not focus on the sovereignty of the individual. This concept was critically important, as well as the observance of all aspects of equitable commerce, and almost all of the communal endeavors of the time overlooked these principles. Just a short distance from Claremont, Warren set up the village of Utopia, sometimes known as Trialville, with several members of the Claremont Phalanx remaining to join Warren's experiment. The village never grew beyond fifteen members, including Warren, but the participants achieved moderate success, building several houses, two stores, and a grist mill. While at Utopia in 1848, Warren attempted to bring out a second volume of *The Peaceful Revolutionist*, but managed to print only one issue. Utopia lasted until 1850 when Warren left the community to seek other ways to share his message.

With a growing interest in his views of individualism and equitable commerce, Warren left Ohio once again in 1850 to move to New York, briefly spending some time in Massachusetts. During this time he increased his public presentations of his ideals in lectures and parlor conversations, developing a following of individuals in the United States and elsewhere. Stephen Pearl Andrews became Warren's principal disciple. Andrews (1812–1886) had varied interests in reform, from abolitionism to perfecting a universal language, but he found the radical individualism of Warren particularly fitting with his developing ideas. Warren and Andrews founded another utopian experiment in 1851 that they named Modern Times. Situated on 750 acres on Long Island about forty miles from New York City, Modern Times was again to be an experiment of an equitable village, putting into practice the principles Warren developed over the previous two decades. Although the settlement never reached the population of one thousand that Warren envisioned, nearly two hundred adherents to Warren's ideals lived at Modern Times at its peak. The increasing popularity of Warren and his beliefs along with the rising number of other reformists and movements and the proximity to New York almost derailed the project shortly after it was started. The press published accusations that Modern Times was a "free love" community and frequently included reports and correspondence related to these accusations. The community also became well known for the quality of entertainment it made available, including frequent opportunities to discuss reformist topics, from abolitionism and abstinence to vegetarianism and women's rights. Modern Times lasted for over a decade and, in terms of relative longevity, was a success. When Warren left Modern Times in 1862, the other reform interests of the inhabitants, along with the impact of the Civil War, had overshadowed the original intent of the community. The name of the village ultimately was changed to Brentwood.

While at Modern Times, Warren continued writing on the principles of equitable commerce, as well as publishing another work on music, but the growing unrest that culminated in the Civil War troubled him. The "peaceful revolutionist" ideals he had espoused for nearly thirty years endured a test with outbreak of hostilities in 1861. Warren wrote frequently in the *Periodical Letter,* a publication he initiated in 1854, of his anti-statist views and the dire consequences of an authoritative political organization. Warren felt that the Civil War validated his criticism of existing society. When he returned to Boston he published what many consider his most important work, *True Civilization: An Immediate Necessity and the Last Ground of Hope for Mankind. Being the Results and Conclusions of Thirty-Nine Years' Laborious Study and Experiments in Civilization as It Is, and in Different Enterprises for Reconstruction* (1863). The focus of this work on the war and the general decline in society that Warren observed placed it in a different category than his earlier writings, which were more philosophical in nature. Although *True Civilization* embodied most of the elements he developed in the previous three and a half decades, it also emphasized more than other works the basic nature of society that must exist to preserve the rights and safety of the individual. Warren felt strongly that such a true civilization must exist without a government that controls the liberties of the individual. He states in *True Civilization:*

> The two great clans are not only *disintegrated,* but hostile; and neighbors, families, and the dearest friends are not only disintegrated, but made enemies to each other from natural and unavoidable differences of opinion and politics, because there is no central idea, no principle known round which they can rally and agree, and in no party has FREEDOM TO DIFFER been practically established as a regulating thought. *Self-sovereignty* is the central idea or principle required.

On the backdrop of the Civil War, Warren made perhaps his strongest statement for philosophical anarchy.

In the final ten years of his life Warren remained in the Boston area. There he continued to write pamphlets, letters, and other short works, most expanding on the principles of equitable commerce and the sovereignty of the individual. He initiated another periodical publication, *The Quarterly Letter,* in 1867, "Devoted Mainly to Showing the Practical Applications and

Progress of 'Equity'." In 1873 he published *Practical Applications of the Elementary Principles of "True Civilization", to the Minute Details of Every Day Life. Being Part III, the Last of the "True Civilization" Series.* By 1873 Warren, succumbing to age and a life of moving repeatedly to pursue his reform objectives, moved in with friends in Princeton, Massachusetts. Even though he was suffering from dropsy, he continued to write until near death, and at least two of his contributions were published in *The Index* in Boston following his death on 14 April 1874. As his son, George, notes:

> Devoting himself to the advancement of civilization, he died in Boston in [1874], having gone through a checkered life, and for many years a fine musician. I never knew him to use profane language or to touch liquor of any kind, or use tobacco in any form. He was strictly temperate in every respect.

"Josiah Warren's Last Letter," written to a friend in July 1873, was published in the 28 May 1874 issue of *The Index.* In the concluding sentences, Warren provides a summary of the development of his views over his lifetime:

> As I have before intimated, I believe it possible to avoid the oppressions of aggressive institutions on the one hand, and the disastrous effects of inexperience on the other. . . . But while I honor the generous sympathies that inspire the widespread and earnest protests against the enslavement of Women, Men and Children in the prevailing aggressive institutions, I take no active part in demolition, as that work is already being done faster than remedies follow.

By the time of Warren's death his work was being carried on by other philosophical anarchists such as Stephen Pearl Andrews, Lysander Spooner, Ezra Heywood, and William B. Greene. Benjamin Tucker, considered the leader of the American anarchist movement up to the rise of Emma Goldman in the late 1800s, also felt Warren's influence, although Tucker was just a college student when Warren died. Soon after Warren's death, however, an increasing influx of European immigrants made an impact on the movement. The native thinkers such as Warren, Andrews, and Tucker had dominated anarchist thought from the 1830s into the 1880s, but more-radical views of the European immigrants began to overshadow the nonviolent elements of philosophical anarchism. The newer radicalism justified acts of violence against the state and its authority, with the German immigrant, Johann Most, as the foremost example. The fact that Most was German and his principal vehicle, *Die Freiheit* (Freedom), appeared in German had an impact on the way the U.S. public viewed anarchism after the 1880s. With the anarchist-led Hay-

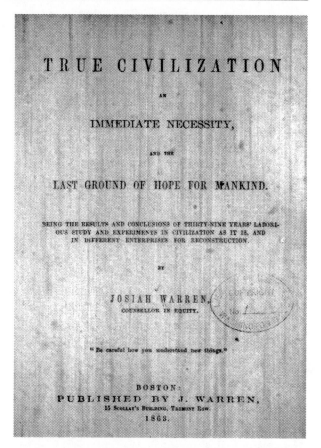

Title page for the work that sums up thirty-nine years of Warren's thought (Library of Congress)

market Riot of 1886 and the attempted assassination of Henry Clay Frick by anarchist Alexander Berkman in 1892, the general public came to associate anarchism automatically with violent actions. When President William McKinley was assassinated by a Polish anarchist, Leon Czolgosz, in 1901, most Americans overlooked the "peaceful revolutionist" ideals of Josiah Warren as "anarchy" became synonymous with "un-American." In 1903 Congress began passing laws to ban all foreign anarchists.

Yet, even at this time, some continued to see the significance of Warren's contributions. One such writer was William Bailie, who wrote the first biography of Warren. Published in 1906 and subtitled *A Sociological Study,* this work examines Warren in the context of "The Anarchist Spirit" and his "Place as a Social Philosopher." Clearly sympathetic to Warren's ideals, Bailie's work still offers an important examination of this often overlooked reformer and writer. Bailie sums up the place of Josiah Warren in the history of anarchism and in his broader contributions: "In accordance with his wish, no headstone marks the spot where he lies. So has it often been: the world's best and noblest quietly act their part, pass off the stage untrumpeted, and their existence is soon forgotten. But the fruits of their good deeds abide, and their influence cannot perish."

Although Josiah Warren's contributions have largely been unheralded, his writings, communal experiments, and even his inventions gave shape in important ways to the developing reform landscape of mid-nineteenth-century America. His beliefs in the sovereignty of the individual and the principle of equitable commerce influenced not only other individualist or philosophical anarchists but found their way into the thought of other reformers, utopian thinkers, and writers of the nineteenth century.

Biographies:

William Bailie, "Josiah Warren," in *The New Harmony Movement,* by George B. Lockwood (New York: Appleton, 1905): pp. 294–306;

Bailie, *Josiah Warren—the First American Anarchist: A Sociological Study* (Boston: Small, Maynard, 1906);

James J. Morton, *Men against the State: The Exposition of Individualist Anarchy in America, 1827–1908* (New York: Libertarian Book Club, 1957).

References:

Ann Caldwell Butler, "Josiah Warren and the Sovereignty of the Individual," *The Journal of Libertarian Studies,* 4 (Fall 1980): 433–448;

Joseph Dorfman, "Philosophical Anarchism," in his *The Economic Mind in American Civilization,* volume 3 (New York: Viking, 1949), pp. 35–42;

Dorfman, "The Philosophical Anarchists: Josiah Warren, Stephen Pearl Andrews," in his *The Economic Mind in American Civilization,* volume 2 (New York: Viking, 1946), pp. 671–678;

Bowman N. Hall, "The Economic Ideas of Josiah Warren, First American Anarchist," *History of Political Economy,* 6 (1974): 95–108;

William Pare, "Equitable Villages in America," *Journal of the Statistical Society of London,* 19 (June 1856): 127–143;

William O. Reichart, "Toward a New Understanding of Anarchism," *Western Political Quarterly,* 20 (December 1967): 856–865;

Roger Wunderlich, *Low Living and High Thinking at Modern Times, New York* (Syracuse, N.Y.: Syracuse University Press, 1992).

Papers:

The Josiah Warren Papers are in the Labadie Collection, University of Michigan Library. These papers include an unpublished account of his life written by his son, George W. Warren (also available at http://faculty.evansville.edu/ck6/bstud/warren.html [accessed 5 September 2008]). The Workingmen's Institute Library at New Harmony, Indiana, has Warren's handwritten notebook with a diary of commentary on the years from 1840 to 1860.

Booker T. Washington

(5 April 1856? – 14 November 1915)

David M. Jones
University of Wisconsin–Eau Claire

BOOKS AND SELECTED PAMPHLETS: *Daily Resolves* (New York: Dutton, 1896);

Home Influences among the Colored People (Baltimore: Maryland Baptist Mission Rooms, 1897);

The Future of the American Negro (Boston: Small, Maynard, 1899);

The Negro and the Signs of Civilization (Tuskegee, Ala.: Normal School Press, 1899);

The Story of My Life and Work (Naperville, Ill. & Toronto: J. L. Nichols, 1900);

Sowing and Reaping (Boston: L. C. Page, 1900);

A New Negro for a New Century (Chicago: American Publishing House, 1900);

Education of the Negro (Albany, N.Y.: J. B. Lyons, 1900);

Keeping in Repair (Tuskegee, Ala.: Extension Bureau, Tuskegee Institute, 1900);

Some European Observations and Experiences (Tuskegee, Ala.: Tuskegee Steam Print, 1900);

Up from Slavery (New York: Doubleday, Page, 1901; London: Thomas Nelson, 1902); republished as *Up from Slavery: An Authoritative Text, Contexts and Composition History, Criticism,* edited by William L. Andrews (New York: Oxford University Press, 2000);

Character Building (New York: Doubleday, Page, 1902; London: Grant Richards, 1902);

The Colored American from Slavery to Honorable Citizenship (Atlanta: J. L. Nichols, 1902);

The Successful Training of the Negro (New York: Doubleday, Page, 1903);

The Work and Influence of Hampton (New York: Lehmaier Press, 1904);

Working with the Hands (New York: Doubleday, Page, 1904; London: Grant Richards, 1904);

Putting the Most into Life (New York: Crowell, 1906);

Twenty-Five Years of Tuskegee (New York: Doubleday, Page, 1906):

The Negro in Business (Boston & Chicago: Hertel, Jenkins, 1907);

Booker T. Washington (from Ray Stannard Baker, Following the Color Line: An Account of Negro Citizenship in the American Democracy, *1908; Robarts Research Library, University of Toronto)*

Frederick Douglass (Philadelphia & London: G. W. Jacobs, 1907);

The Negro in the South, by Washington and W. E. B. Du Bois (Philadelphia & London: G. W. Jacobs, 1907);

The Story of the Negro, 2 volumes (New York: Doubleday, Page, 1909; London: Unwin, 1909);

Some Results of the Armstrong Idea (Hampton, Va.: Hampton Institute Press, 1909);

The New South (Philadelphia: American Academy of Political and Social Science, 1910);

My Larger Education (New York: Doubleday, Page, 1911; London: Hodder & Stoughton, 1911);

Is the Negro Having a Fair Chance? (Tuskegee, Ala.: Tuskegee Institute Steam Press, 1912);

The Man Farthest Down (New York: Doubleday, Page, 1912);

The Story of Slavery (Dansville, N.Y.: F. A. Owen, 1913);

Team Work: Dr. Booker T. Washington's Last Sunday Evening Talk to the Teachers and Students (Tuskegee, Ala.: Tuskegee Normal Institute, 1915).

COLLECTIONS: *Black Belt Diamonds: Gems from the Speeches, Addresses, and Talks to Students of Booker T. Washington* (New York: Fortune & Scott, 1898);

One Hundred Selected Sayings of Booker T. Washington, selected by Julia Skinner (Montgomery, Ala.: Wilson Print Company, 1923);

Selected Speeches of Booker T. Washington, edited by Earnest David Washington (Garden City: Doubleday, Doran, 1932);

The Booker T. Washington Papers, 14 volumes, edited by Louis Harlan and Raymond Smock (Urbana: University of Illinois Press, 1972–1989).

OTHER: *Address Delivered at the Opening of the Atlanta Cotton States and International Exposition* (Atlanta, Ga.: s.n., 1895);

An Address by Booker T. Washington before the Union League Club, February 12, 1897 (Tuskegee, Ala.: Tuskegee Institute Steam Print, 1901);

An Address Given Under the Auspices of the Armstrong Association, Lincoln Day Exercises, at the Madison Square Garden Concert Hall, New York, NY, February 12, 1898 (Tuskegee, Ala.: Tuskegee Steam Print, 1901);

Speech of Prof. Booker T. Washington, Delivered before the Legislature of Virginia, at the Mozart Academy of Music, February 11, 1901, under the Auspices of the Negro Business League (Richmond: Negro Business League of Virginia, 1901);

"Industrial Education for the Negro," in *The Negro Problem: A Series of Articles by Representative Negroes of Today,* edited by Washington (New York: J. Pott, 1903);

Tuskegee and Its People, edited by Emmett J. Scott under Washington's supervision (New York: Appleton, 1905).

While his life and work have generated both admiration and controversy, Booker T. Washington remains a towering figure in the history of American literature and reform movements. He lived fewer than sixty years, but his achievements in the areas of literature, higher education, and American politics are remarkable by any fair standard. His most significant accomplishments include his autobiography, *Up from Slavery* (1901), and the founding of Tuskegee University (1881), an embodiment of a reformist sentiment that inspired the development of historically black colleges and universities across the United States. In these same contexts where Washington found success, however, his opponents vilified him for his hesitancy to criticize the effects of white supremacy directly, as did W. E. B. Du Bois, William Monroe Trotter, Ida B. Wells, and other activists of Washington's day. Regardless, Washington's published writing and private correspondence reveal his resistance to white supremacy through direct (if not always public) action, through his studies of African American participation in religious life, business, and American cultural history, and through his advocacy on behalf of African Americans living in poverty, particularly those living in the most rural quarters of the post–Civil War South. Washington's books convey his idealistic belief in the transformative power of hard work, thrift, cleanliness, and common morality. Such virtues were widely associated with small-town American life in the late nineteenth and early twentieth centuries, and for that reason Washington's work found a large appreciative audience on both sides of the color line.

Birth records are often imprecise for enslaved African Americans, but 5 April 1856 is the likely birth date for Booker Taliaferro Washington. His birth was recorded in a family Bible belonging to James Burroughs, owner of the plantation where Washington was born, near Hale's Ford, Virginia. Washington's mother, Jane, cooked for the plantation. The Burroughs family included fourteen children, seven of whom were still living in the family farmhouse with James Burroughs and his wife, Elizabeth, at the time that Washington was born. Ten slaves also lived on the plantation, including Washington's brother John, his sister Amanda, and his mother. Washington's biological father has not been authoritatively identified, but by all accounts, he was a white man who lived on or around the Burroughs plantation. Biographers have made cases for several men who may have fathered Washington: Thomas Ferguson, a neighbor of the Burroughs who was later named by Washington's daughter as the probable father; Benjamin Hatcher, another neighbor; or any of James Burroughs's five sons who were old enough in 1856 to become a biological parent.

Uncertainty also surrounds the origin of Washington's middle and last names. According to biographers Basil Mathews and Louis Harlan, Washington learned during childhood that Taliaferro was part of his given name, although it was not in common use in his household, and he did not know its origin. The name Taliaferro belonged to a prominent local judge and doctor, neither with any known connection to Jane Burroughs or her family. As far as the source of his last name, Washington reports in *Up from Slavery* that he chose it impulsively when he first attended school, realizing when a teacher called upon him that he was expected to have a first and last name, and Washington was a prominent and respected name for an ex-slave to adopt. His stepfather was Washington Ferguson, a slave to a family who lived near the Burroughs plantation.

The impact of slavery on the family life Washington experienced was undeniable. Exhausted by her duties, his mother had little time to supervise the home. Young Booker maintained a close relationship with his brother, however. In his first autobiography, *The Story of My Life and Work* (1900), Washington describes the single garment he had to wear year-round–a flaxen shirt made of cloth so coarse that it severely irritated the skin even after being "broken in," but nearly unbearable when first worn. Washington owned neither shoes nor a coat to wear during his childhood years in slavery. Washington also describes the beating of his uncle by his master, which included the indignity of witnessing his uncle's nakedness, along with the physical agony and the pleas for mercy the blows produced. Washington's second and best-known autobiography, *Up from Slavery,* includes descriptions of seasons passed in a windowless cabin, with "openings in the side which let in the light, and also the cold, chilly air of winter." The family slept on a dirt floor, and Washington's mother lacked sufficient time for reasonable care or training of her children, much less the resources to procure their formal education, generally unavailable to African Americans under slavery. After seeing a picture of young children in a schoolroom setting, Washington reported later, he "had that feeling that to get into a schoolhouse and study in this way would be about the same as getting into paradise."

The humiliation, pain, and deprivation of slavery left traces in Washington's autobiographical writing, although he also expressed appreciation for the common humanity of the Burroughs family and other slave owners he knew. He wrote respectfully about the death of "Mars' Jim" in 1861, after the plantation patriarch met his end on a Civil War battlefield. The death of Billy Burroughs, "Mars' Billy," also caused a strong reaction among enslaved blacks on the Burroughs plantation, many of them remembering him as an especially kind figure among the Burroughs sons. In *Up from Slavery* Washington stressed the bonds that were part of the master/slave relationship in a way that contrasts with conventional wisdom: "Any one attempting to harm 'young Mistress' or 'old Mistress' during the night

would have had to cross the dead body of the slave to do so." Nonetheless, even in Hale's Ford, patrols, precursors to the night-riding vigilantes that became common after the war, discouraged runaways. Washington's autobiographies suggest that both cruelty and humanity coexisted in black/white relations during slavery, and his public acceptance of social segregation in his later career seems rooted in an insider's view of the antebellum South's contradictory social climate.

Similarly, Washington's family and others living in slavery during the closing years of the Civil War knew both triumph and uncertainty, amid material deprivations and deaths because of war. Just before the close of the war, when he was nine years old, Washington received his first pair of shoes, constructed with wooden platforms for a sole and leather straps for securing the shoes above the foot. They made a clacking sound when he walked. Washington first heard of the Union victory while clad in these makeshift shoes, the former slaves greeting the news with joy, tears, and unexpected dread. To the end of his life, Washington could recall his mother's jubilant tears on that day, followed by the journeys both short and long undertaken by many ex-slaves to ensure that this new liberty was genuine. Before long, however, the sobering challenges of emancipation became clear to all sides. The post-war South had become home to legions of landless, largely uneducated ex-slaves, whose legal and economic rights were denied, ignored, or enforced inconsistently for at least a century afterward. Biographer Basil Mathews imagined the poignant mood on the Burroughs plantation on the fateful first day of emancipation, as the most forthright former slaves went "quietly, almost surreptitiously, in the twilight to the 'big house' to hold quiet consultations" with the Burroughses about their future.

Amid the struggles of Reconstruction, Washington grew into adolescence and young adulthood. Washington witnessed some positive results of regionally based strategies for industrial education. He also noted the examples of several outstanding individuals engaged in charitable work, particularly whites inspired by abolitionist sentiment before the war and eager to contribute to the advancement of African Americans by working as teachers and in institution building in the American South. The moral philosophy Washington expressed through most of his public life grew from the successes he saw in the midst of one of the most contentious eras in our nation's history. His public optimism waned toward the end of his life, as virulent racism seemed to take hold across the country, even into the Progressive Era, a reminder that the Civil War did not resolve the core national problems of racial injustice.

Shortly after the end of the Civil War, Washington's stepfather summoned the family to Malden, West

Washington's first wife, Fannie Smith Washington (from Ray Stannard Baker, Following the Color Line: An Account of Negro Citizenship in the American Democracy, *1908; Robarts Research Library, University of Toronto)*

Virginia, where he had fled during the final chaotic years of the Civil War. After a difficult two-hundred-mile journey made by wagon and on foot, Washington and his family arrived in the run-down community. At his stepfather's urging, Washington immediately found employment in the local salt industries that supplied salt for the pork products of nearby Cincinnati, Ohio. His stepfather confiscated his earnings and hesitated to allow Washington to pursue a primary education, but after repeated entreaties from mother and son, Washington finally won permission to attend a newly opened school in Tinkerville, a predominantly black settlement near Malden. Harlan writes that, as was frequently the case, the local African American community independently operated and funded this modest school, without assistance from the white-run local school board, state, or national sources.

Washington's first school days were spent working from four to nine in the morning at the salt furnace, attending day school, and returning to the furnace for two more hours of work after school. His stepfather abruptly ended this arrangement after a short time, however, and Washington began to work in a nearby coal mine. He was employed as a "trapper," operating the doors to the mineshafts to let in air, mules, and trucks of coal, sometimes becoming lost in the dark interior corridors in the course of his work. He found the work exhausting, but at the mine he happened to overhear a conversation about a college for "colored youth." He learned that the school was in Virginia, although he remained unsure of its exact location. This small bit of information helped sustain Washington's ambition to continue his education beyond primary school.

After one or two years working in the mines, Washington gained employment as a houseboy for the mine owners, Lewis and Viola Ruffner. Lewis Ruffner was a former state legislator and Union general who opposed Virginia's secession and aided in the initial formation of West Virginia as an independent state. Viola Ruffner, a native of Vermont, was an exacting housekeeper whose attention to detail impressed Washington greatly during his employment. She seemed to personify the "New England schoolmarm," a popular though stereotypical image of incorruptible primary-school instructors, often imagined as unmarried and female, determined to make an impact on their pupils. Washington later described Viola Ruffner's commitment to cleanliness, honesty, and care in all things, as a valuable part of his education. In addition to housework chores, Washington sold Viola Ruffner's produce, earning her financial trust and intensifying his belief in the importance of good character when serving others. For four years he remained in the Ruffners' employ, developing an enduring friendship with both husband and wife. Washington's comfortable relationship with Viola Ruffner and later with another transplanted Northerner, General Samuel Armstrong of Hampton Institute, contributed to Washington's ease at working with Northern white politicians in his later life.

Washington witnessed in Malden an increase in Ku Klux Klan activity during Reconstruction. Lewis Ruffner was struck by a brick during his effort to convince the white combatants to disarm during a Klan attack in 1869. The injury left him in critical condition, and Washington came away doubting that the peace could be maintained between the races in that climate.

In 1872 Washington decided to travel east to seek admittance to Hampton Institute in Virginia. Friends who knew of the journey gave him small gifts, and his family helped all they could, but Washington began the journey without sufficient train- or carfare to take him the five hundred miles to the school. He started his journey by railroad and stagecoach, but after a night or two was reduced to walking or taking an occasional wagon ride if offered. He reached Richmond, Virginia, destitute, sleeping under the sidewalk during his first night in a sizable city. The next morning he found work unloading iron at a shipyard, earning enough for meals and small savings. He continued to work in the shipyard for a few days, sleeping outside to preserve money for the remaining eighty-mile journey to Hampton, where he finally arrived on 5 October 1872, in a ragged condition and with fifty cents in his pocket. As a test for admission, a Hampton principal, Mary F. Mackie, asked Washington to sweep the recreation hall, a task he performed to Mackie's approval, after which he was admitted to Hampton as a student. Mackie hired him on as a custodian to help defray the costs of tuition. Throughout his tenure at Hampton, Washington continued to work in this capacity.

Hampton was founded by the American Missionary Association, formerly an abolitionist association based in Boston. The association also founded Fisk University, Atlanta University, and Tougaloo College, among the most important and best-known historically black colleges and universities. The Hampton program focused on skilled crafts, agriculture, and other practical arts, a course of study that came to be known as industrial education. At Hampton, Washington became acquainted with General Samuel Armstrong, the chief administrator, who had served as an officer in the Civil War while in his twenties. In *Up from Slavery,* Washington wrote, "the first time I went into his presence he made the impression upon me of being a perfect man." The personal example of Armstrong's work seems to have led Washington to think seriously about a career in education. A dedicated student and a careful observer of Armstrong's leadership at the institute, Washington learned important lessons about administering charitable organizations, which rely on both a secure philanthropic base and the cultivation of cooperative relationships with local communities. Washington identified with Armstrong's idealistic belief in the importance of education, a sentiment shared by African American communities in the post–Civil War South; he had seen this in his home community of Tinkerville, among those who flocked to the makeshift school he had attended. He witnessed a similar idealism in many of the war veterans who fought for the Union side, and among traveling teachers, white and black, who willingly relocated to faraway rural areas where a position might promise eager pupils, if not a living wage or adequate facilities. All shared a belief in the power of education to transform the lives of recently freed African Americans in the South.

Washington's relationship with Armstrong later reinforced charges of excessive dependence on philanthropic support from white benefactors. Political opponents during Washington's life shared this point of view, and Harlan called attention to Armstrong's apparent belief that African Americans were the biological and cultural inferiors of whites. In an essay written for a collection commemorating the writing of *Up from Slavery* one hundred years after its publication (*Booker T. Washington and Black Progress* [2003], edited by W. Fitzhugh Brundage), Harlan quotes Armstrong's own words to show that he thought the difficulties of African Americans result from "not mere ignorance, but deficiency of character" and conceived of industrial education as a tool to create a work ethic among a people "in the early stages of civilization." Harlan argues more directly that since Washington was the "lifelong disciple of a racist white man," the program of industrial education that Washington developed at Tuskegee carried on this willingness to compromise with the racism of Southern whites.

In any case, Washington absorbed the lessons from such strategies as admitting a student conditionally who appears underprepared and unable to pay the cost for his own education. His work at Hampton also developed his skills as a public speaker. Washington spent the better part of three years at Hampton during his first phase of training, completing his term in 1875, shortly after the death of his mother. Oratory was a common focus among post-secondary training during those years, and Washington participated enthusiastically in the debating clubs at Hampton. His epigrammatic style of speaking and writing began to emerge during those years, aided by the instruction of Natalie Lord in oratory. She and Washington became close friends, taking boat rides together at times and engaging in lengthy discussions. Boating was one of a few approved diversions in a school setting that emphasized rigor in all phases of student life, Hampton administrators believing that a total immersion in scholastic work and moral instruction best prepared students for the enormity of the challenges they faced in a racially discriminating nation.

While his speaking and writing style were nurtured at Hampton with careful study of Shakespearean plays, the King James Bible, and Latin classics, Washington learned much from the more informal Saturday-night debates on public issues sponsored by the "After Supper Club" at the school. His skills included an ability to couch complex and even controversial arguments in a plain style that seemed to issue directly from conventional wisdom. At his commencement, Washington argued that annexing Cuba would cause additional problems of repatriating freed persons. Some remarks in his speech played on the anti-Catholic sentiment that ran throughout American public opinion at the time. The speech won over the audience because Washington made appeals of sympathy to whites who believed in the essential righteousness of Anglo-American culture, despite the virulent racism in social life, as well as appeals to a wider audience through reminders of the sufferings that all Americans endured during the Civil War.

After graduation, Washington returned to Malden, to the acclaim of his neighbors, and taught in the area for three years, a period that extended one year beyond the official end of Reconstruction in 1877. He taught day school as well as night classes for adults needing basic literacy instruction. Through his aid, some of his students, including his brother John, gained admittance to Hampton. During these years, Washington also began a serious courtship with Fannie Smith, whom he had known from childhood.

In 1878 Washington studied for several months at Wayland Seminary, a Baptist theological school in Washington, D.C., that provided African American students an education program more focused on liberal arts than the Hampton industrial model. The seminary was formed shortly after the Civil War, in a building donated through the Freedman's Bureau. Generally in his writing, Washington speaks more unfavorably of his experiences at Wayland Seminary compared to his education at Hampton, although he writes in *The Story of My Life and Work* that "the deep religious spirit which pervaded the atmosphere at Wayland made an impression upon me which I trust will always remain." Washington observed elsewhere that a lack of self-reliance and an emphasis on clothing style at the school indicated to him that Wayland did not prepare students for the practical and moral challenges that awaited in their everyday lives after completing their studies. Washington was clearly unaccustomed to the pace and character of life in a large city as well. Although he encountered several prominent African American political figures and saw Frederick Douglass speak during his stay, Washington criticized what he saw as superficiality and conspicuous consumption among the city residents. He noted with dismay the vice in the city as well.

Before going to Wayland for study, Washington participated as a lobbyist in the statewide debate on which city to designate as the capital of West Virginia, amid opposition to the then-capital of Wheeling as a permanent site. He spoke before predominantly black audiences in support of Charleston, and helped to energize a sizeable turnout for the successful referendum.

After a brief return to Malden in 1879, Washington was thrilled to receive an invitation from Armstrong to teach at Hampton Institute. The invitation to teach at Hampton helped Washington settle on law, the ministry, or education as possible directions for his life's work.

Washington remained at Hampton for two years, engaging in postgraduate study and completing practical experiments in outreach to student populations that in later ages have been described as nontraditional. His responsibilities included work with American Indian students, a task made challenging by language difficulties, general mistrust, and their initial resistance to being taught by an ex-slave. Washington also worked with indigent students in a night-class setting and met with some success. He famously described these students as his "plucky class," many of them sharing the poverty and earnestness that had characterized Washington himself as an entry-level student.

Washington and Fannie Smith married in 1882. That year Armstrong received a letter from school commissioners in Alabama who sought a chief administrator for a new normal (teacher training) school for African Americans in their state. Affronted that the letter called only for a white man to be recommended for the position, Armstrong consulted Washington to see whether he might be interested. Assured that Washington would take the position if offered, Armstrong wrote back recommending him as "a very competent capable mulatto, clear-headed, modest, sensible, polite and a thorough teacher and superior man" (Harlan). A week later, Armstrong read the reply telegram before the whole school: "Booker T. Washington will suit us. Send him at once."

After having some difficulty locating Tuskegee on a map, Washington arrived in the town of some two thousand or so residents in June 1881. Much of his published work describes his personal journey as he went about the task of creating a school that both served the needs of the African American population of the region and would satisfy white Southerners who did not look kindly on any challenge to the white supremacist order, particularly strategies that they feared would make African Americans "uppity," unwilling to fulfill the historic role of wage laborer, or believing themselves the social equals of white men. Initial conditions at Tuskegee did not favor such a task, but Washington's work habits and ingenuity led to some early successes. Arriving in Tuskegee to find that no land or buildings had been set aside for school operations, Washington nevertheless held the first class session "on the fourth of July, 1881, in an old church and a little shanty that was almost ready to fall down from decay" *(The Story of My Life and Work)*. The school's resources included an endowment of $2,000 and a board of commissioners to control its use, but the lack of any books or classroom materials presented an immediate challenge. To help with initial operations, Washington secured some aid through donations and loans from Hampton Institute and credit from a few local merchants to help with shipping and materials costs. His grace in building support from local white leaders also proved crucial to the early success of Tuskegee, giving some reason for his acclaim as a supreme diplomat.

Washington made a quick study of the region, a rural area with an impoverished black population concentrated in the so-called Black Belt. Families often lived in one-room cabins and depended on a sharecropping system for sustenance, though rarely for economic gain. Historian Jacqueline Moore writes that "many of these sharecroppers could not afford to purchase tools and seed, or even food and clothing for their families, until harvest time." Some areas within the Black Belt, including Tuskegee, were not generally served by railroads or convenient to larger towns. In that region and time the ability of families to survive depended not only on a hostile power structure controlled by whites, but also on the cycle of success and failure in cotton farming.

Washington recruited his first class of thirty students locally, some learning of the school from his talks at local black churches. His initial group of students consisted of "mainly those who had been engaged in teaching in the public schools of that vicinity," including both teachers and their former pupils in some cases. *(The Story of My Life and Work)*. Each of Washington's three major autobiographies describes in detail the difficult periods in his work at Tuskegee. Washington worked persistently and creatively to develop a suitable physical plant for the college through the students' own industrial work, patronage, and acquisition. He received a $500 loan from the treasurer at Hampton that he used to acquire a one-hundred-acre farm site for the school, and, with the aid of other gifts, in a few years the college had acquired 2,460 acres of land for its classroom and industrial operations. Through student efforts at brick making and other architectural tasks, several university buildings were constructed, and the student population grew more than fivefold within the first three years.

Tuskegee's growth continued during the 1880s. The school gained national prominence through its distinctive program and the tireless efforts of its founder to serve its students, to develop a mission emphasizing both teacher training and industrial education, and to maintain financial support from multiple sources. For Washington, the decade of the 1880s was personally stressful: his first child, Portia, was born in 1883; his first wife died in 1884; his second wife, Olivia Davidson Washington, who worked extensively with Washington in school administration as well as fund-raising and whom he married in 1885, died in 1889. Washington married for a third time in 1893, to Margaret James Murray, and spent his final years with her.

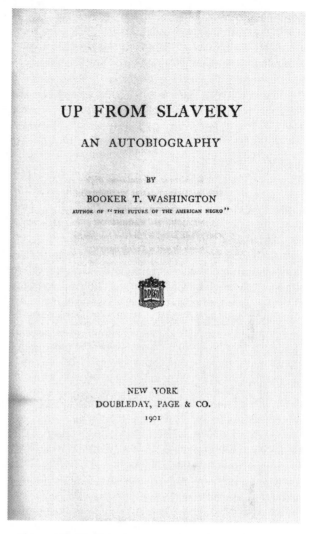

Title page for Washington's second autobiography, which some black intellectuals regarded as accommodationist (Thomas Cooper Library, University of South Carolina)

Washington's first decades at Tuskegee reinforced his belief in the importance of industrial education even for students who might someday engage in professional work. Emma Lou Thornbrough concluded that "his speeches and published writings reveal Washington as a man of a few basic ideas which he constantly reiterated. His fundamental philosophy appears to have crystallized early and to have changed very little. He was a prolific writer, but all his writings say essentially the same thing." His idealized views of industrial education and manual labor usually appear in tandem with arguments about the need for African Americans to accept or at least tolerate current conditions, and for whites—especially the "better class" of whites, including those who were supporters of Tuskegee—to work in a genuine economic partnership with African Americans for "mutual progress." In Washington's view, such an approach was better suited to achieve long-term gains in the status of African Americans than protests in favor of immediate and full human rights and economic justice.

In an article titled "The Awakening of the Negro," published in an 1896 issue of *Atlantic Monthly,* Washington used a brief story to illustrate his philosophy with regard to practical education for African Americans living in poverty: "When a mere boy, I saw a young colored man, who had spent several years in school, sitting in a common cabin in the South, studying a French grammar. I noted the poverty, the untidiness, the want of a system of thrift, that existed about the cabin, notwithstanding his knowledge of French and other academic subjects." Washington repeatedly referred to such images to suggest that the immediate need for a means to make a living and dedication to self-improvement must rank as a higher priority than the forms of liberal learning he saw as esoteric, including in this case foreign language, but also including the arts and music, Greek philosophy, and other specific examples that he names in writing and speeches. While in later texts, including *Tuskegee and Its People* (1905), he suggested that industrial training did not provide the only type of learning African Americans required to advance, Washington consistently argued that immediate needs should take precedence over the "ornamental geegaws of life," a phrase that originally appeared in Washington's historic 1895 speech before the Atlanta Cotton States and International Exposition.

The event, commonly known as the Atlanta Exposition, was organized to generate strategies for revitalizing the economic life of the South, which, still primarily agrarian, had never recovered from the setbacks of the Civil War era. Washington was invited to address the predominantly white conventioneers after he had declined an opportunity to design the "Negro Exhibit," which he felt he could not do effectively amid his duties at Tuskegee. Washington recognized the gravity of this opportunity to address a white audience in the South, an audience of means and institutional influence. Historians have consistently argued that the speech reinforced many conservative assumptions of that audience, most famously with the statement that "In all things that are purely social we can be as separate as the fingers, yet one as the hand in all things essential to mutual progress." Washington's phrasing is strikingly similar to the legal language that appeared a year later in the Supreme Court decision in *Plessy v. Ferguson* upholding racial segregation in all phases of public life, a decision issued the year after the Atlanta speech.

A second memorable and oft-quoted statement from the Atlanta speech also functions as an apt summary of the educational and moral philosophy developed by Washington in his work at Tuskegee and in his writing: "No race can prosper till it learns that there is as much dignity in tilling a field as in writing a poem. It is at the bottom of life we must begin and not the top. Nor should we permit our grievances to overshadow our opportunities." Fine arts receive infrequent commentary in Washington's texts, not so much because he opposed them in any way but because he so single-mindedly addressed himself to the difficult economic situation faced by the majority of African Americans. In this respect, Washington's philosophy seems well adapted to the Gilded Age, a cultural moment at which national rhetoric about the expansion of industry glossed the phenomenon as embodying the fruits of hard work and individualism.

The Atlanta speech met with approval from the audience and was praised in print by many prominent public figures, editorial pages, and even several prominent ex-abolitionists. Historians note that whites reacted more positively to the speech, but a significant amount of thoughtful support as well as criticism came from African American public figures. For example, a few years before he became known as Washington's primary rival, renowned sociologist and African American activist W. E. B. Du Bois wrote to *New York Age* to say that "the Compromise 'might be the basis of a real settlement between whites and blacks in the South, if the South opened up to the Negroes the doors of economic opportunity" (Bauerlein, "Washington, Du Bois, and the Black Future"). At the time, Du Bois was an emerging scholar who had corresponded with Washington and even entertained the notion of joining the staff at Tuskegee. After a decade of collegial relations, Du Bois joined persistent critics of Washington such as Henry Turner, Wells, and Trotter in overt opposition to Washington's philosophy. Du Bois's well-known essay "Of Mr. Booker T. Washington and Others" from *The Souls of Black Folk* (1903), describes Washington's philosophy as "a gospel of Work and Money to such an extent as . . . almost completely to overshadow the higher aims of life."

Critics took Washington to task in particular for his suggestion in the Atlanta speech that "agitation of questions of social equality is the extremest folly, and that progress in the enjoyment of all the privileges that will come to us must be the result of severe and constant struggle rather than of artificial forcing." Washington's critics vigorously opposed this categorical criticism of the protest methods that had energized the abolitionist movement and were being used in anti-lynching campaigns. Critics also emphasized the psychological and financial costs of legal segregation, which touched every part of American life–trade unions, public accommodations, schools, and political institutions, to name a few areas that became battlegrounds in decades to follow. As a counterpoint, Washington's biographers have noted that he opposed segregation directly and often in covert actions, financially supporting legal challenges to grandfather clauses and other unfair voting practices in Louisiana and Alabama. One can also identify in his writing spirited support for the essential dignity of African Americans, a legacy that complements his hands-on work building an institution that became a cultural force despite the polarized racial climate of his era.

Most scholars agree that Washington overestimated the willingness of white leaders in the South to fulfill their end of the bargain described in the Exposition speech–to support fair wages, work, and educational opportunities for African Americans in the South in exchange for continuing a system of segregation that was, in Washington's own words, "purely social." For all the concessions he made, however, Washington had persistent opponents in Southern white communities, including Thomas Dixon, author of *The Clansman* (1905), the inspiration for the 1915 film *Birth of a Nation*. At the height of lynching and Black Codes, a period known to African American historians as the "nadir," opposition to Washington among Southern whites was widespread and grew worse after his social visits to Queen Victoria of England in 1899 and to President Theodore Roosevelt in 1901. Two prominent Southern governors (both elected later to the U.S. Senate), "Pitchfork" Ben Tillman of South Carolina and James Vardaman of Mississippi, acted as the unofficial spokesmen for white supremacists who felt Washington's plans presented a radical challenge to their power. Regardless, Washington maintained a relationship with President Roosevelt that proved helpful in maintaining a positive image and consolidating support for his programs generally.

As a follow-up to the success of building Tuskegee into a vibrant educational institution, the Atlanta speech brought Washington into the national limelight as the most prominent national spokesman on issues of race relations and set the stage for a new thread of criticism related to Washington's leadership style. Many historians have described Washington's network of affiliated organizations, personal associates, and political influence as the "Tuskegee Machine," serving to safeguard his stature as a leader and stifle criticism of his ideas through his institutional connections. Examples of his practice of power politics include financial support for black newspapers (including the influential *New York Age,* led by T.

Thomas Fortune), his founding and critical participation in the National Negro Business League, and his overt and covert opposition in their formative years to the Niagara Movement and the National Association for the Advancement of Colored People–organizations that prominently featured Du Bois as a participant. Also, Washington's national reputation helped him develop a network of contacts and supporters among white national leaders that was unparalleled, equaling or exceeding the influence wielded by Frederick Douglass at the height of his remarkable career. In a climate where, according to one historian, "no meeting or discussion that touched on racial topics was complete without an appearance or a comment by Washington" (Brundage), his uncanny skill at building support through personal contact and his willingness to use hardball tactics to stifle opposition made him a formidable and vilified adversary for the "anti-Bookerites," as Du Bois, Trotter, and others came to be called.

In 1899, four years after the Atlanta speech, Washington published *The Future of the American Negro,* described by Charles Chesnutt as "Washington's first extended utterance in book form." Chesnutt reviewed the text in glowing terms, writing that it "cannot fail to enhance his reputation for ability, wisdom, and patriotism." The introductory section of the book expresses Washington's mature views on industrial education in view of his experiences at Tuskegee and the critical debates that followed the Atlanta Exposition speech. In the first chapter, Washington writes: "When I speak of industrial education . . . I wish it always understood that I mean, as did General Armstrong, the founder of the Hampton Institute, for thorough academic and religious training to go side by side with industrial training. Mere training of the hand without the culture of brain and heart would mean little" *(The Booker T. Washington Papers).* When Washington presented his view on these questions in shorter works, detail and exemplification did not always highlight the nuances of his philosophy, and *The Future of the American Negro* is useful for providing such clarification.

Washington also uses international examples to support the case for industrial training to complement academic work. He notes that "Hayti, Santo Domingo, and Liberia, although among the richest countries in natural resources in the world, are discouraging examples of what must happen to any people who lack industrial or technical training. It is said that in Liberia there are no wagons, wheelbarrows, or public roads, showing very plainly that there is a painful absence of public spirit and thrift" *(The Booker T. Washington Papers).* While Washington never visited Africa and failed to acknowledge the impact of colonialism on the ability of these countries to develop industrially, he raises the salient point that industrial and academic education should complement each other for development to take place and that technological competence and public-spiritedness each might foster the growth of the other.

The Future of the American Negro invited skepticism about Washington's philosophy as well. On questions of internationalism, Du Bois and other opponents questioned Washington's view that African Americans could achieve significant economic success under conditions of inequality, pointing out with reference to his examples that European and American colonialism made it unlikely that development of resources would benefit local populations. Washington also expresses in this text an arguably naive view of Southern jurisprudence and politics of the era, stating that "almost without exception, the governors, the sheriffs, the judges, the juries, and the lawyers are all white men, and they can be trusted, as a rule, to do their duties." Many contrasting points have been made elsewhere establishing unequal treatment in the legal and political systems for African Americans across the South, a case that Washington himself made in other writings. A desire to put the best possible face on conditions of the era—probably an attempt to appeal to multiple audiences—runs in an intriguing and contradictory thread through Washington's writing.

Washington's best-known autobiographies, *The Story of My Life and Work* and *Up from Slavery,* were published in 1900 and 1901. By the time he wrote these texts, Washington was virtually guaranteed a wide audience based on national recognition and support for his strategies of industrial education and disavowals of protest as a strategy for advancement. *Up from Slavery* was published serially in *Outlook* in 1900. Among Washington's many published texts, these two received the most in-depth analysis from literary critics, with *Up from Slavery* outpacing the other in familiarity and critical acclaim. Some critics argue that the two texts might both be described as slave narratives. *The Story of My Life and Work* is the more diffuse book, belonging distinctly to the broader American autobiographical tradition associated with Benjamin Franklin, Frederick Douglass, and Horatio Alger.

The Story of My Life and Work was published by a small company, J. L. Nichols, that specialized in selling books by subscription to African American audiences. Edgar Webber served as Washington's ghostwriter, and after extensive interviews and note taking, Webber prepared a draft manuscript for review by Fortune, who agreed to complete the copyediting while Washington traveled in Europe. Fortune found the manuscript unsatisfactory from the standpoint of both writing style and mechanical errors, some of which were introduced

in the printing process. The publisher, however, had incentive to publish the book quickly to take advantage of the public prominence Washington enjoyed at that moment. So the book was published without full attention to the changes suggested by Fortune, and Washington, according to Charlotte Fitzgerald, "threatened to sue the Nichols firm for full royalties if the targeted market for distribution were not restricted to the South and the subscription audience."

Compared to *Up from Slavery,* Fitzgerald argues, *The Story of My Life and Work* is less a homily highlighting the ability of every citizen to rise in the American system than a compelling personal narrative full of historical details illustrating the impact of slavery and the uneven, often disillusioning journey to better race relations. A fascinating chapter in *The Story of My Life and Work* reprints Washington's letter of protest to Senator Tillman of South Carolina on the eve of a state constitutional convention meeting to disenfranchise African American voters. The passage includes notes of conciliation and challenge as it appeals to Tillman's pride as a Southerner and admonishes him with a universal appeal to the ideal of justice:

> while the hearts of the whole South are centered upon the great city of Atlanta, where Southern people are demonstrating to the world in a practical way that it is the policy of the South to help and not to hinder the Negro—in the midst of all these evidences of good feeling among all races and all sections of the country, I cannot believe that you and your fellow members are engaged in constructing laws that will keep 650,000 of my weak, dependent and unfortunate race in ignorance, poverty and crime. You, honored Senator, are a student of history. Has there ever been a race that was helped by ignorance? Has there ever been a race that was harmed by Christian intelligence?

Judging by his subsequent career, Tillman, a virulent racist, found Washington's appeal unmoving. Nevertheless, Washington's vigorous opposition to the disenfranchisement of African Americans in South Carolina contrasts with the philosophy of passive accommodation associated with him in other contexts. Whether or not Washington's work as a whole allowed white people to ignore racial problems, as Jacqueline Moore argues, *The Story of My Life and Work* shows some of Washington's positive engagement with the struggle to shape race relations at the turn of the century.

Washington's second autobiography, *Up from Slavery,* is widely celebrated as a classic of American literature. Washington provided greater oversight over the editing and publishing process than with *The Story of My Life and Work;* Max Bennett Thrasher, whom Washington acknowledges in his preface, helped outline, draft, and edit the text, according to Andrews. Washington drew inspiration from Frederick Douglass's autobiographical narratives, one of which Washington read while returning from Europe in 1899. Critics generally agree that the personal narrative of *Up from Slavery* is one of its strong points, along with its detailed examination of racial politics in the wake of Reconstruction. Washington beseeches all of his audiences to bear in mind how recently slavery ended as they consider his unlikely success story at Tuskegee, writing that "the laying of [Tuskegee's] corner-stone took place in the heart of the South, in the 'Black Belt,' in the center of that part of our country that was most devoted to slavery, that only sixteen years before no Negro could be taught from books without the teacher receiving the condemnation of the law or of public sentiment." The book proved instrumental in eliciting a new round of financial support for Tuskegee.

The text reinforces the philosophy of industrial education and reiterates Washington's characteristic assessment of race relations in the face of imposing challenges. Regarding industrial education, Washington's primary principle was "that the student shall be so educated that he shall be enabled to meet conditions as exist *now*, in the part of the South where he lives" *(The Booker T. Washington Papers)*. On the more controversial question of how much advancement can be achieved under systemic segregation, Washington maintains that "the individual who can do something that the world wants done will, in the end, make his way regardless of race." *Up from Slavery* exemplifies the strengths of Washington's epigrammatic style as well as the limits of his social analysis. Critics in the past have described Washington as a man of actions, not ideas, and they point to this text to argue there is little new or profound even in his most significant works. The power of his work, however, grows from Washington's understanding that neither ideas nor action alone were sufficient for the transformation of race relations. Washington was venturing into unknown territory by building an educational institution and seeking ways to solve race problems where Reconstruction and the attention of a nation focused on the postwar South could not. Washington's determination to build support for a profitable and harmonious vision of Southern race relations could admit only so much skepticism, at least in his early full-length pieces.

A critical controversy continues to surround Washington's representation of slavery in his autobiographies, because the books describe his experiences as a source of both suffering and inspiration. Some critics have charged that Washington understates the physical and mental suffering produced by slavery. By comparison to the narratives of Frederick Douglass and Harriet Jacobs, probably the two most widely read slave narratives, Washington writes with a forgiving, even charitable tone. This point may best be illustrated with reference to the passage in *Up from Slavery* where Washington refers to his unknown white father as "simply another unfortunate victim of the institution which the Nation unhappily had engrafted upon it at that time." Washington further states that "the black man got nearly as much out of slavery as the white man did," although he clarifies this point by suggesting that African Americans gained work experiences and often experience in trades and crafts through slavery, while many whites lacked industrious habits and critical skills as a result of depending on slavery. Consistently in both his activist work and his writing, Washington desired to highlight cooperation and common humanity between African Americans and whites, and this motivation appears to have outweighed the need to demonstrate the cruelties of the slave system. His autobiographies do depict some of these cruelties, but in such a manner as to emphasize the harm done to both African Americans and whites.

On 30 July 1903, a virulent anti-Bookerite, William Monroe Trotter, publisher of the Boston *Guardian*, confronted Washington at a national meeting of the Negro Business League. During a speech by T. Thomas Fortune, several associates of Trotter interrupted the speech by shouting and advancing on the stage. Others threw cayenne pepper across the stage, making it difficult for Fortune to continue. Trotter's associates continued to shout as Washington took the stage, and after an outbreak of violence that included two stabbings, Trotter and several others were arrested, reducing Washington's speech to "a dispirited rehash of the gospel of thrift" ("Washington, DuBois, and the Black Future").

Working with the Hands (1904) provided an opportunity to rebut some of the persistent charges that his educational program tilted toward the white Southern view on educational methods, specifically the charge that Washington chose industrial education because it offered the least offense to white supremacists. Washington described this book as a sequel to *Up from Slavery;* it received much less critical attention than the first two autobiographical works. Arguably, it is less literary, less centered on creating an authorial persona. By the point at which he published it, Washington had a public stature significant enough to assume an audience familiar with much of his personal history. *Working with the Hands* provides a more detailed treatment of the operation of Tuskegee than did the previous autobiographies. Some of the tenets of industrial education made familiar in early works are revisited in chapters focused on "Welding

Title page for the volume Washington called the sequel to his celebrated
second autobiography (Thomas Cooper Library, University
of South Carolina)

Theory and Practice," "Lessons in Home-Making,"
and "On the Experimental Farm." Under pressure to
show results to both skeptics and potential donors,
Washington notes at the outset that "the effort to
make an industry pay its way should not be made the
aim of first importance. The teaching should be most
emphasized." Washington recognized that education
and training are long-term investments, a message
that he felt only his intense and persistent efforts in
writing and personal appearances could make clear
to potential supporters.

In *Working with the Hands* Washington writes in
more detail also about his interest in the women's-rights
movement, noting that his second wife, Olivia Davidson Washington, had sponsored a women's meeting
during an 1892 conference for black farmers. He also
wrote of the need for a more meaningful role for
women at such a conference, recalling the experiences

of suffragettes, many of whom began their careers as
activists by being denied a voice at anti-slavery meetings. He writes that "in the days of Lucretia Mott, and
the early struggles of Susan B. Anthony, women had no
rights that were worth mentioning, and, notwithstanding the fact that there were many women present at this
first conference, they had little actual place in it." Later,
he speaks of the more prominent role he hopes that
women will play in the future, asking "What can these
poor farmers do with the new ideas, new hopes, new
aspirations, unless the women can be equally inspired
and interested in conferences of their own?"

After *Working with the Hands,* Washington turned
his attention largely to historical topics, producing such
ambitious works of social history as *Frederick Douglass*
(1907) and the two-volume *The Story of the Negro* (1909),
works that have elicited little interest or discussion.
During the same period his singular place as the representative leader of African Americans in the United
States was challenged. Du Bois emerged at the turn of
the century as a powerful intellectual activist who
addressed the lingering problems in race relations more
successfully than did Washington. Du Bois was, at
times, criticized by Washington, as in a personal letter
he sent to Lyman Abbott at *Outlook Magazine.* Washington remarked in the letter, "I do not believe there are
more than two or three hundred colored people of any
prominence or influence who are inclined to follow
such folly as he is the leader of" (Moore). Washington
claimed a much greater following for the Negro Business League, which he headed.

Washington experienced a racial assault on 19
March 1911 that exacerbated the growing disillusionment during his later years. On the Sunday evening
after Washington went to an apartment in New York
occupied exclusively by white residents to seek a donation from a man he had met that evening at a speaking
engagement, Henry Ulrich, a carpenter and proprietor
of the West Side Dog Exchange, attacked him with a
cane, accusing him of lurking about and attempting to
peer into the keyhole of a an apartment where a family
lived whose daughters had been harassed. The assault
and subsequent trial made national news, with Washington's major opponents, including Du Bois and Trotter, writing sympathetically about his suffering during
the ordeal. In the end Ulrich was acquitted of assault
despite evidence that Washington had been brutally
beaten without cause. Immediately after his acquittal,
however, Ulrich was arrested and jailed on a charge of
deserting his family and failure to pay child support.
The publicity from the incident energized Washington's
white-supremacist enemies, including Senator Vardaman and Thomas Dixon.

His health beginning to fail, Washington completed *The Man Farthest Down* in 1912. Dickson D. Bruce views the text as the beginning of a concession on Washington's part that his optimism about the reliability of white officials should be qualified, although Thornbrough interprets the text as an attempt to show that the peasants of Europe had more difficult circumstances to face than African Americans. Stronger evidence of Washington's disillusionment appears in "Is the Negro Having a Fair Chance?" published in *Century* magazine in 1912. After his personal experience in the Ulrich case, Washington reflected that "There are few white lawyers or judges who will not admit privately that it is almost impossible for a Negro to get justice when he has a case against a white man and all the members of the jury are white." The article revives Washington's occasional but impassioned criticism of lynching, noting that "colored people in the South do not feel that innocence offers them security against lynching." Even given his critical stance on these issues, he still states, "I venture to say that there is no example in this history of the people of one race who have had the assistance, the direction, and the sympathy of another race in all its efforts to rise to such an extent as the negro in the United States."

Washington maintained an active schedule until his death at Tuskegee on 14 November 1915. The cause of death remains unclear, but some scholars believe that exhaustion contributed to his demise at fifty-nine. He was buried at Tuskegee.

Booker T. Washington's autobiographical works continue to command attention among critics and general readers, although many are inclined to read only *Up from Slavery*. That book continues to have an energizing effect on contemporary readers, judging from one key example—the predominance of positive assessments of Washington among recent scholars in Brundage's commemorative volume to celebrate the one hundredth anniversary of the publication of *Up from Slavery*, and in critical texts by Houston Baker and Kevern Verney.

Biographies:

Emmett Scott and Lyman Beecher Stowe, *Booker T. Washington: Builder of a Civilization* (Garden City N.Y.: Doubleday, Page, 1916);

Shirley Graham Du Bois, *Booker T. Washington: Educator of Hand, Head, and Heart* (New York: Messner, 1955);

Basil Mathews, *Booker T. Washington: Educator and Interracial Interpreter* (College Park, Md.: McGrath, 1969);

Frederick Drinker, *Booker T. Washington: The Master Mind of a Child of Slavery* (New York: Negro Universities Press, 1970);

Arna Bontemps, *Young Booker: Booker T. Washington's Early Days* (New York: Dodd, Mead, 1972);

Louis Harlan, *Booker T. Washington: The Making of a Black Leader* (New York: Oxford University Press, 1972);

Harlan, *Booker T. Washington: The Wizard of Tuskegee* (New York: Oxford University Press, 1983);

John Perry, *Unshakable Faith: Booker T. Washington and George Washington Carver, a Biography* (Sisters, Ore.: Multnomah, 1999).

References:

Tunde Adeleke, *Booker T. Washington: Interpretive Essays* (Lewiston, N.Y.: E. Mellon Press, 1998);

Houston Baker, *Turning South Again: Re-Reading Booker T.* (Durham, N.C.: Duke University Press, 2001);

Mark Bauerlein, "The Tactical Life of Booker T. Washington," *Chronicle of Higher Education*, 50 (28 November 2003): 12;

Bauerlein, "Washington, DuBois, and the Black Future," *Wilson Quarterly*, 28 (August 2004): 74–86;

Dickson D. Bruce, "Booker T. Washington's *The Man Farthest Down* and the Transformation of Race," *Mississippi Quarterly*, 48 (Spring 1995): 239–253;

W. Fitzhugh Brundage, ed., *Booker T. Washington and Black Progress: Up from Slavery 100 Years Later* (Gainesville: University Press of Florida, 2003);

Kathleen Clark, "Who Made Jim Crow?" review of *Ben Tillman and the Reconstruction of White Supremacy* by Stephen Kantrowitz, *Reviews in American History*, 29 (2001): 238–246;

W. E. B. Du Bois, *The Souls of Black Folk* (New York: New American Library, 1982);

Charlotte Fitzgerald, "*The Story of My Life and Work*: Booker T. Washington's Other Autobiography," *Black Scholar*, 21 (2001): 35–40;

Bob Frost, "The Quiet Force: Booker T. Washington," *Biography*, 4 (July 2000): 102–109;

Donald Gibson, "Strategies and Revisions of Self-Representation in Booker T. Washington's Autobiographies," *American Quarterly*, 45 (September 1993): 370–393;

Louis Harlan and Raymond Smock, *Booker T. Washington in Perspective: Essays of Louis Harlan* (Jackson: University Press of Mississippi, 1988);

August Meier, *Negro Thought in America, 1880–1915; Racial Ideologies in the Age of Booker T. Washington* (Ann Arbor: University of Michigan Press, 1963);

Jacqueline Moore, *Booker T. Washington, W. E. B. DuBois, and the Struggle for Racial Uplift* (Wilmington, Del.: Scholarly Resources, 2003);

Samuel Spencer, *Booker T. Washington and the Negro's Place in American Life* (Boston: Little, Brown, 1955);

Emma Lou Thornbrough, ed., *Booker T. Washington* (Englewood Cliffs, N.J.: Prentice-Hall, 1969);

Kevern Verney, *The Art of the Possible: Booker T. Washington and Black Leadership in the United States, 1881–1925* (New York: Routledge, 2001);

Carla Willard, "Timing Impossible Subjects: The Marketing Style of Booker T. Washington," *American Quarterly,* 53 (2001): 624–669.

Papers:

The Library of Congress in Washington, D.C., and Tuskegee Institute hold the most sizable and significant collections of Booker T. Washington's personal papers. Other sites holding important materials include the National Archives in Washington, D.C., the Schomburg Collection at the New York City Public Library, and Hampton Institute in Hampton, Virginia. For an easily accessible starting point for research, *The Booker T. Washington Papers,* edited by Louis Harlan and Raymond Smock, provides a carefully selected fourteen-volume collection of Washington's speeches, correspondence, and other materials representing about 1 percent of the one million papers available at the Library of Congress. This resource is widely available in print format and is also available online through the University of Illinois Press and the nonprofit organization the History Cooperative.

Appendices

The *Appeal to Reason*

The Industrial Workers of the World

The Modern School Movement

Mother Earth

The *Appeal to Reason*
(1895 – 1922)

Robert J. Fitrakis
Columbus State Community College

A weekly newspaper originating during the Populist Movement of the 1890s to distribute socialist propaganda, *Appeal to Reason* (1895–1922) became, it claimed, the most widely circulated newspaper in the world. Special editions sold more than four million copies, and its weekly subscriber base reached more than 760,000 readers at the height of its popularity. After the creation of the Socialist Party of the United States in 1901, the paper served as its primary publishing outlet. Both reached the apex of their power in 1912. *Appeal to Reason* functioned as much more than a partisan publication of a third party, however. The paper, serving as the flagship of Julius A. Wayland's radical publishing empire, brought together radical labor and political writers, agitators, cartoonists, essayists, and renowned fiction writers. Upton Sinclair originally published his classic *The Jungle* (1906) in its pages. From the small town of Girard, Kansas, the paper forged a national culture among socialists, never repeated in American history. The plainspoken, evangelical tone of the paper transformed hundreds of thousands of former populists into socialists, particularly in the southwest United States.

Perhaps the most powerful socialist institution in American history, the paper's influence began to decline with the suicide of its founder and publisher. Following Wayland's suicide on 10 November 1912, his son Walter took the paper in a less radical direction. The death of Wayland and the paper's new direction led to the departure of many of the old-line editors, including Eugene V. Debs and Fred Warren, as well as a decline in circulation. Its editorial endorsement of a prowar position during World War I further weakened its standing in the radical community. The split between the socialists and communists following the Bolshevik Revolution in 1917 drew away other subscribers and accelerated the paper's decline. The Red Scare in the aftermath of the Great War coupled with changes in ownership and management ended *Appeal to Reason*. The last issue appeared on 4 November 1922. The *Haldeman-Julius Weekly* emerged as its successor.

The editorial line transformed finally from promoting the Cooperative Commonwealth to endorsing individualism and self-help.

The history of *Appeal to Reason* cannot be separated from the story of its founder, Julius Augustus Wayland. Born in Versailles, Indiana, on 26 April 1854, the youngest of seven children, this self-described "One Hoss Editor" provided the vision for his paper's enormous success. Forced into poverty after his father and four siblings died in a cholera epidemic, Wayland had so little education when he took his first job as a journalist that he later admitted he did not know "a noun from a verb" (John Graham). *The Versailles Gazette* hired Wayland when he was sixteen to work as a printer's apprentice. There Wayland used every opportunity to develop his skills as a typesetter and pressman. He worked at various newspapers as an itinerant printer for a few years before returning to Versailles and buying the *Gazette* with a partner in 1872. He bought out his partner in a year and a half. Wayland's early exploits as a radical-Republican newspaper owner and opinionated editor feature prominently in George Allan England's *The Story of the Appeal* (1915).

In 1877 Wayland married Etta Bevan, with whom he subsequently had five children. During the following years he edited several party newspapers and worked at one point as a postmaster, an appointee of the Rutherford B. Hayes administration. In 1882 the Wayland family relocated from the Midwest to Pueblo, Colorado, then a thriving mining town. Undaunted after a small newspaper he started in Pueblo failed, he hung out a shingle as Wayland's One Hoss Print Shop. Throughout his life he made recourse to the "One Hoss" image. Wayland later explained how corporate capitalism was destroying the generalist: "This is the day of concentration and specialties. The world has no place for the jack-of-all-trades—it's the specialist, the man who knows how to do one thing better than everyone else who occupies the center of the stage" (Graham).

Wayland's real moneymaking talent at the time lay not in his skills as a printer but in real-estate speculation. He turned a quick $2,000 profit from his One Hoss Print Shop and immediately bought up more properties in Colorado. By 1893, when he left the state, he held assets that included $80,000 in gold and bonds alone. He used the money to stake a new enterprise: a socialist newspaper. In his autobiography, *Leaves of Life* (1912), published just prior to his death, Wayland attributed his conversion to socialism to a chance conversation in 1890 with William Bradford, an English shoemaker, about railroad strikes. He describes his conversion to socialism as a Saul-on-the-road-to-Damascus experience: "I saw a new light and found what I never knew existed. I closed up my real estate business and devoted my whole energies to the work of trying to get my neighbors to grasp the truth I had learned."

Wayland embraced the utopian socialism of Edward Bellamy's *Looking Backward* (1888) and joined the People's Party and Populist Movement to broadcast his socialist ideology. After leaving Colorado he moved to Greensburg, Indiana, where he published the initial issue of *The Coming Nation,* the predecessor to *Appeal to Reason,* in April 1893. Wayland had his doubts concerning the success of an openly socialist newspaper, yet dreamed of ten thousand copies per week circulation. He planned to subsidize the paper's loss for years, if necessary. As the purveyors of socialism, the Wayland family met with hostility from the majority of the citizens of Greensburg. Still, the paper claimed fourteen thousand subscribers in half a year; three months later, the circulation rose to sixty thousand, making *The Coming Nation* the most widely read socialist publication in the country. Wayland's commentary and reflections dominated the front page of the four-page weekly, its style and tone similar to the later *Appeal to Reason.* Wayland eschewed the more-complex prose of Karl Marx and Friedrich Engels, preferring his own folksy tone and the writings of Laurence Gronlund, the author of *The Cooperative Commonwealth* (1884); John Ruskin; and Bellamy. The preference of *The Coming Nation* for indigenous socialist writings over more-complex continental voices fostered its success. John Graham notes in his anthology, *Yours For The Revolution: The Appeal To Reason, 1895–1922,* that Wayland "placed the new paper directly in the mainstream of the broad Reform movement." *The Coming Nation* addressed both the audiences of the Socialist Labor Party (SLP) and the People's Party, yet found itself sometimes at odds with the hierarchical organization of the SLP. Wayland's policy of ignoring interparty conflicts served his publication well. He focused *The Coming Nation* on spreading the socialist message to an ever-increasing readership, not on which faction or sect had the correct analysis in a left-wing political party.

The hostility of the people of Greensburg on the one hand and the profits of *The Coming Nation* on the other convinced Wayland to undertake an even grander enterprise: a planned, self-sufficient socialist community. He purchased two thousand acres of land north of Tennessee City, Tennessee, and named it the Ruskin Colony. He imagined that his paper would be the central institution of the community, which would include "every convenience that the rich enjoy, permanent employment at wages higher than ever dreamed of by laborers, with all the advantages of good schools, free libraries, natatoriums, gymnasiums, lecture halls and pleasure grounds" (Graham). Moreover, Wayland dreamed that the Ruskin model would inspire similar socialist communities throughout America. On 21 July 1894 the presses stopped in Greensburg and arrived in Ruskin Colony four days later. The primitive conditions of the land purchased for the colony proved unsuitable for many of Wayland's plans. The hastily constructed buildings were hardly upper-class accommodations, and the one hundred colonists immediately began to divide according to political and economic tendencies. Wayland's will to spread socialism proved much greater than his spirit of communitarianism. In July 1895 the Waylands left the Ruskin Colony and *The Coming Nation* behind and headed to Kansas City, Missouri. There, on 6 August 1895, the first issue of *Appeal to Reason* appeared. James R. Green writes in *Grass-Roots Socialism: Radical Movements in the Southwest 1895–1943* that "Few people in the Southwest had heard the Socialist appeal before Julius A. Wayland started his *Appeal to Reason* in 1895."

The four-page weekly's initial reception was less than Wayland expected in comparison to *The Coming Nation.* He found himself back to his One Hoss Shop days—editing, managing, and typesetting his new paper. Wayland left Kansas City, Missouri, for Kansas City, Kansas. He then suspended the operation of the paper and moved it to Girard, a town of 2,500 inhabitants in the southeast corner of the state. The moves were aimed at reducing costs. Mary "Mother" Jones helped Wayland relaunch *Appeal to Reason,* gathering several hundred subscriptions for the new publication. By the end of the first year, the newspaper's circulation stood at 36,000. Its purchase price was minimal: a yearly subscription was 50¢; a club subscription was 25¢; and a three-month trial subscription cost 10¢.

Just prior to the Spanish-American War, the circulation rose to 45,000, but the war frenzy reduced paid subscribers by more than half. Etta Wayland also died of cancer that year. Wayland claimed to be a week away from suspending publication in 1899. When the paper

Top of the front page for the 2 May 1914 issue of the socialist paper then controlled by
managing editor Louis Kopelin (Indiana University Libraries)

fell into desperate economic straits, it would open its pages to advertising, a practice Wayland philosophically opposed. In order to minimize reliance on advertising, the *Appeal to Reason* began a series of subscription contests, awarding prizes, including land, to those who sold the most subscriptions. As Wayland spent more time with his five children, E. W. Dodge took over as the new business manager. The 25 November 1899 issue of the paper—whose circulation was 52,000—announced a subscription contest. The town that sold the most subscriptions would get a "First Class Brass Band" consisting of seventeen instruments, if total circulation reached 75,000.

The sales force also acted as grassroots reporters, peppering *Appeal to Reason* with thousands of reports per week on the economic and political conditions throughout the nation. The *Appeal to Reason* army consisted of people such as S. D. Strong of Lewiston, Idaho, who wrote in the 4 February 1899 issue, "I am 73 years old and blind. God bless you. I wish I could meet you . . . I sent you 12 subs. And think I can send you more later, being old and blind I can't accomplish much. Enclosed find list." The paper created a small fund to exchange copies with other periodicals, and *Appeal to Reason* articles began to be reprinted in thousands of newspapers across the land. The Jonesboro, Arkansas, *Enterprise* praised *Appeal to Reason* as an "outspoken exponent of

the doctrine of socialism. . . . This newspaper discusses issues in a firm, fearless and commendable way" (Graham).

Warren joined the paper in 1900. Born in Arcola, Illinois, he was raised in Rich Hill, Missouri. He and his younger brother Ben had started a Republican newspaper that failed during the 1893 recession. Warren worked as a printer until 1898 when he became editor of the *Bates County Critic*. In his spare time Warren volunteered as the Methodist Sunday-school superintendent. He joined *Appeal to Reason* originally as a printer and later became managing editor. Eugene Debs, later an editor, began his first Socialist Party presidential campaign that same year. The excitement generated by his 1900 campaign gave the paper its political focus. Debs published many of his campaign speeches on the Cooperative Commonwealth there. He polled 97,000 voters, and by the end of the election year *Appeal to Reason* counted 100,000 subscribers.

In April 1901 Wayland married Pearl Hunt, who had worked first at the printing office and later as his housekeeper. He recorded that the cost of their three-week wedding trip totaled $572, but during the same period his paper took in a total of $8,000. Competing socialist editors Herman Titus and Victor Berger published attacks on Wayland alleging that he was driving local papers out of business. The U.S. Post Office sought the first federal suppression of *Appeal to Reason* in 1901. Assistant Postmaster General Edwin C. Madden issued an order denying the paper's right to mail under the inexpensive second-class rate permit, claiming the papers were not going to paid subscribers. Within eight days, 68,000 subscribers signed statements claiming that they had paid for the bundles of paper out of their own pockets, thereby restoring the post-office permit. By 1902 circulation exceeded 150,000.

The growth of the paper during the Wayland-Warren years was phenomenal. By the time Wayland hired Warren, the "One Hoss" persona functioned only as a public-relations device, since the paper had been much too complex and widely distributed to be manageable by one person for a few years. Wayland continued to do much of the writing for the first page, but enough labor items were coming in to require a labor editor, so in 1903 Wayland lured Charles L. Breckon away from the *Chicago Daily Socialist*. Also that year Wayland's niece Josephine Conger began to write a women's column that served as a focal point for women organizers and convention representatives at the 1904 party meeting in Chicago. After a dispute in 1903 between Warren and Breckon, Warren left the paper and resurrected *The Coming Nation,* which drew away many of Wayland's best writers, including Kate Richards O'Hare and cartoonist Ryan Walker. Meanwhile, Wayland hired the Marxist Ernest Untermann, already famous for his translation of leftist classics from the German for the Charles H. Kerr Company, to replace Warren. They published one million copies of a special Populist edition targeting former People's Party supporters. The post office again attempted to block mailing of the edition to non-subscribers. Wayland mailed the edition anyway, thus provoking U.S. government repression.

In October 1903 Wayland's employees struck, in part because of his gift of $1,000 to the Socialist Party. The workers, Socialists themselves, protested working conditions and questioned who owned the paper and its profits. The thousand dollars given to the Socialist Party, they believed, demonstrated that they were not paid full value for their labor, according to Socialist theory. The conflict had been growing for some time. The business strategy of the paper was to keep income high and wages low. Wayland was one of the most significant employers in Girard, and he lived very well. He had promised himself to stop speculating in real estate a few years before, but he had not stopped and his wealth grew. His nonsocialist neighbors gloated in their newspapers about chickens coming home to roost. Wayland's employees had no sympathy from the town, but business leaders appreciated the humor of a socialist being forced to cope with socialism. With all but four of

the fifty workers on strike, the workers formed a union, while Wayland attempted to comply with their wishes that he turn ownership of the paper over to the Socialist Party. The Socialist Party's constitution prohibited publishing a party newspaper, however, and ownership of the paper remained under Wayland's control, a decision some historians blame for its later demise. The strike was settled in one day, with Wayland giving in to all of the union's other demands except those about discharging anyone connected with his family.

Early in 1904 Wayland purchased *The Coming Nation* for $5,000 to bring Warren and his brother back to Girard; Warren took over as managing editor. The Socialist Party and the paper unified around Debs's 1904 presidential campaign. Debs polled more than 400,000 votes with the *Appeal to Reason* acting as his campaign newsletter. This massive increase in socialist voters provided a growing market of readers. Under the united leadership of Wayland and Warren *Appeal to Reason* expanded to eight pages, and many times to twelve. The additional space created room for more essays, cartoons, and literary features.

Late in 1904, Warren contracted with the novelist and muckraker Upton Sinclair, who agreed on a $500 advance to investigate the conditions in Chicago's meatpacking houses. Sinclair immersed himself for seven weeks in the sordid surroundings of the unregulated slaughterhouses. In 1905 Sinclair's serialized, thinly veiled fictional accounts of the unsanitary and brutal industrial practices caused quite a stir and were later published as the best-selling novel *The Jungle*. In Graham's later scholarly assessment of the paper, he notes that "Although the literature took many forms, some forms never appeared. Absent was 'art for art's sake,' self-conscious writing estranged from common experience, and absent as well was literature proposing individual solutions to collective problems." *Appeal to Reason* engaged in the common leftist practice of rewording well-known songs in its pages, such as the following example line to the tune of "The Battle Hymn of the Republic": "I have seen the guilty prosper and the wicked win renown, I have seen the rich oppressor crush the poor man deeply down . . ." (Graham).

In 1906, in one of Debs's most famous polemics, he threatened in *Appeal to Reason* to march on the capitol in Boise, Idaho, and on Washington, D.C., with "a million revolutionists." The threatened march was to express support for Western Federation of Miners' leaders William D. "Big Bill" Haywood and Charles Moyer, both facing death sentences on trumped-up murder charges. *Appeal to Reason* put out a three-million-copy "Rescue" edition publicizing the Haywood-Moyer case. Again, the post office attempted to halt the paper's distribution. With their credentials firmly established as publishers of the foremost radical labor and political newspaper in America, Wayland and Warren hired Debs, the country's best-known Socialist, as a writer and lecturer. In January 1907 Debs arrived in Girard, formally linking the Socialist Party with *Appeal to Reason.* Other radicals felt comfortable in Girard as well. Mother Jones later wrote in her autobiography: "If any place in America could be called my home, his home was mine. Whenever, after a long, dangerous fight, I was weary and felt the need of rest, I went to the home of Fred Warren."

For years *Appeal to Reason* ran articles on how to organize Socialist locals and regularly reported on state- and local-chapter progress. The paper counted 275,000 subscribers in February 1907. In a nonpresidential election year, Debs, Wayland, and Warren were determined to fan the flames of radicalism by improving their reader's sense that they had a voice that mattered. In addition to having distributors double as reporters, they launched Socialist organizers to approach communities through tent meetings, encouraged the formation of clubs and study groups, and offered to provide literature for their discussion. In one of the first targeted mass-mailing campaigns, they sent copies of *Appeal to Reason* to legislators, teachers, and union members. They established a lecture bureau, sending socialist agitators throughout the nation. Admission to speeches could be obtained by purchase of a year's subscription to the paper. It introduced readers to "The First Socialist Lecture Van" in America in the 13 February 1904 issue. Later, the paper gave away a horse-drawn van as a subscription-contest prize. Debs campaigned by train, the Red Special, in the 1908 presidential election. Readers were informed of Debs's location or where the next Socialist tent meetings would be held in the Southwest. One pitch for the radical tent revival read: "Turn the cows out; let the hogs go to the brush; hitch up the mules; tuck the wife and children in the old wagon; throw care to the winds; and go to the camp for a week's pleasure and recreation" (Graham).

The entire Socialist platform was published in the 10 October 1908 issue. Despite the formal alliance between the Socialist Party and *Appeal to Reason,* the presence of 3,000 local party chapters, and 41,000 card-carrying Socialists in thirty-nine states, Debs polled only 420,000 votes in 1908. Congress introduced the Penrose Bill during the campaign year, targeting second-class mail permits for radical publications. Socialist supporters counterattacked, flooding Congress with tens of thousands of protest letters. The bill never made it out of committee. The paper continued to send Debs a weekly paycheck as he campaigned for president.

Dramatic growth in the size of the Socialist Party—its membership tripled between 1908 and 1912—paralleled a massive increase in *Appeal to Reason* subscriptions. A healthy bottom line created heady radical optimism in 1910. The army of reporters and subscription agents numbered about 56,000 by this time. For a brief period the paper ceased accepting commercial advertising, but in September 1910 it began again. In January 1911 the paper began the year with 477,000 subscribers; the number surpassed half a million by May 1912. The paper put together a book called *Who's Who in Socialist America* based upon responses from its 500 best subscription agents. Green offers the most extensive analysis of this text, noting that the volume's entries are almost evenly divided between working-class and middle-class men, demonstrating the broad appeal of the paper and of socialism during these years. Three-quarters of these salesmen reported that reading and private study had led them to socialism; only about 20 percent had belonged to a radical organization before becoming socialists.

An indicator of the newspaper's success is the fact that in 1910 Wayland revived *The Coming Nation* again, this time as a more in-depth, high-quality monthly publication, with Algie Simons from Chicago as editor. Simons had edited the *International Socialist Review* until 1906. Josephine Conger-Kaneko, who had written the women's column for *Appeal to Reason* and had since been married and widowed, launched a new publication, the *Progressive Woman,* at roughly the same time. Wayland and Warren were so confident of their prosperity that they secretly signed a five-year contract awarding Warren a $25,000 annual salary. Warren had also begun to engage in real estate and commodities speculation, and oil was discovered on some of his land in Oklahoma. Wayland began to make almost weekly trips to Amarillo, Texas, where he was buying up corners of the developing business district. Also at this time the two of them began to invest in alternative commercial companies in the area, in particular a manufacturing plant that produced a cereal coffee substitute called Nutrito from 1907 to 1911.

The larger *Appeal to Reason* grew, the more negative attention it garnered from the federal government. In 1907 the paper's turn toward investigative journalism resulted in two episodes of legal trouble for the editors. First, Warren antagonized authorities by countering the kidnap and trial of Haywood and Moyer with the published offer of a $1,000 reward for the capture and return of former gubernatorial candidate William S. Taylor to his home state of Kentucky, which he had fled after being indicted for the murder of a man who had bested him in an election. Warren was charged with soliciting kidnapping and was found guilty and sentenced to six months' hard labor and a $1,500 fine.

Warren, who thought he might have to serve the time at Leavenworth Prison, decided to investigate the prison, and the muckraking article that resulted led to yet more federal indictments for C. L. Phifer, Wayland, and Warren in November 1911. The new indictments charged the men with sending "indecent, filthy, obscene, lewd, and lascivious printed material" through the mail. The article depicted Leavenworth as a thoroughly corrupt institution where officials brutalized prisoners and allowed unnatural sex acts to take place. A federal investigation resulted in the resignation of the warden and the firing of the deputy warden. The *Appeal to Reason* staff were found not guilty in the spring of 1912, but new indictments were issued for obstruction of justice, which included Debs during his historic 1912 presidential campaign. The government charged that the defendants paid a prosecution witness to leave the state. They won acquittal in the second trial in 1913. President William Howard Taft pardoned Warren for the first conviction.

In October 1910, near the end of a year in which Socialists won hundreds of local elections and the party seemed to be doing very well, an explosion at the printing facility of the *Los Angeles Times* killed twenty-one workers. On the front page of *Appeal to Reason* Debs accused the *Times* of causing the violence, because its publisher's virulently anti-union politics were well known; the *Los Angeles Times* was, he said, "the most venomous foe of organized labor in the U.S." (Elliott Shore). Unexploded bombs were found at the publisher's home and at the headquarters of the Manufacturers' Association. In April 1911 union members from the Midwest—the McNamara brothers and Ortie McManigal—were arrested and accused of bombing offices of the *Los Angeles Times* and another place in Los Angeles. The argument of *Appeal to Reason* at this point was that U.S. Steel wanted to break the Bridge and Structural Iron Workers' Union, of which John McNamara was secretary.

For a while the editors at *Appeal to Reason* decided they believed that Harrison Gray Otis, the *Los Angeles Times* publisher, had not only indirectly caused the explosion, as Debs accused, but had planned the entire incident himself and hired operatives to create an explosion using gas leaks. They published a statement to this effect and sent an agent to investigate. After a month the agent seemed to have disappeared, and the editors imagined that he had been kidnapped or harmed. Otis had hired the Burns Detective Agency to investigate the explosion, and the Left expected underhanded tactics from the detectives, including that the defendants would be framed.

Eventually, the McNamaras made a last-minute confession, shocking the movement. The *Appeal to Rea-son* agent, a married man with family in Girard, was proven to have spent the month with his teenage mistress, the daughter of a fellow socialist. Afterward, *Appeal to Reason* offices were repeatedly burglarized; Warren, Wayland, and Simons were attacked with weapons; and the *Los Angeles Times* launched a smear campaign against Wayland claiming his ancestors were involved in arson, child mutilation, and murder. Other stories claimed that Wayland had seduced a fourteen-year-old orphan and taken her to Missouri, where she died during an illegal abortion. Rumors abounded that Wayland would be indicted on federal charges for violating the Mann Act. Other stories concerned the wealth that Wayland and Warren were amassing. In August 1912 Warren tried to play down some of the negative press in this quarter by offering his prospering Missouri zinc mine to the four readers who sent in the largest books of subscriptions to *Appeal to Reason*.

Unlike the inner-city bohemia in which the masses leavened and flourished in New York or the marginal and subversive underworld to which the Kerr circle had substantial connections in Chicago, the socialist culture that developed around *Appeal to Reason* in Girard was conventional and wholesome, embracing many mainstream values. The various revelations and public smears, therefore, on top of the McNamara confession, were damaging—reflected in an almost immediate decline in sales—and demoralizing.

Debs's 1912 presidential vote total, a record 900,000 votes, or 6 percent of all ballots cast, sorely disappointed Wayland, who had anticipated better results and believed that the internal squabbles of the Left following the unaccountable conduct of the newspaper's agent in Los Angeles were in part to blame. Disappointed with the election outcome, under threat of federal indictment, plagued by recurring cancer, depressed over the death of his second wife the previous year and constant vilification in the corporate press, the One Hoss editor ended his life. Painfully shy in personal life and prone to depression, Wayland had written in 1906 of his emotional state in the pages of *Appeal to Reason*: "There have been many dark hours—days and months of them together. I have walked the floor many a night; I have walked the silent woods and lonely railroad tracks with feelings akin to suicide; the rest would be so sweet; what a relief to end it all" (Graham). In the late evening of 10 November 1912, the fifty-eight-year-old Wayland shot himself in the head with a pistol. On a table next to his bed he left a copy of Bellamy's *Looking Backward* with a note tucked into its pages: "The struggle under the competitive system is not worth the effort; let it pass." Debs wrote to Warren from Terre Haute, Indiana, on 19 November 1912,

But it was a great battle and until the news of the tragedy came from Girard I was never in more buoyant spirits in spite of everything else. When that came I was in bed and as Mrs. Debs read the message to me I was so stunned that I could not believe my own senses, and have not yet entirely recovered from it. . . . Wayland is about the last man I would have expected to take the shortcut into the unknown by his own hand. How his heart must have been wrung with agony and his soul torn with despair and desperation before he reached that fatal conclusion! But he had reached the farthest limit of capacity to endure and while we all pity him with all our hearts not one of us may breathe the breath of blame upon him.

What passed away with Wayland was a fighting, uncompromising movement spirit. During the 1912 election year, the *Appeal to Reason* masthead defiantly proclaimed: "When the Appeal suspends it will be when capitalism ends and when the Appeal Army is mustered out of service forever. Until then, we are 'Yours for the Revolution.'" Perhaps a more important factor in determining the paper's outcome was its passing into the hands of the less committed Wayland family. Wayland's son Walter assumed the mantle of publisher, seemingly to honor his father's radical memory. By the summer of 1913, both Warren and Debs had left the paper.

Warren was forced out by the hiring of Louis Kopelin as the new managing editor. Warren's official resignation and removal of his name from the masthead did not come until July 1914, but Kopelin clearly had control of the paper by August 1913. Walter Wayland lacked his father's radical will and vision, functioning in a routine business capacity rather than as a hands-on editor. He did, however, along with Warren, sue various periodicals for printing libelous stories about his father. He won those suits. Nevertheless, the paper quickly shifted in a less militant direction. After Walter Wayland took control of *Appeal to Reason,* its circulation plummeted.

In order to deal with the economic problems brought on by the precipitous decline in readership, Kopelin employed Emmanuel Julius, an East Coast metropolitan writer with little knowledge of the Midwest or Southwest populist traditions. Julius married Marcet Haldeman soon after arriving in Girard. Haldeman was Jane Addams's niece and an heiress to a Girard banking fortune. They used the married name of Haldeman-Julius. They purchased a third of *Appeal to Reason* initially, and eventually the entire paper. Emmanuel Haldeman-Julius proved even less committed to socialism and radicalism than Walter Wayland and seemed to grasp little of the importance of the paper to the socialist movement. Prior to the U.S. entry into

World War I, *Appeal to Reason* aligned itself with the peace movement. Debs wrote in the 11 September 1915 issue that "I am opposed to every war but one; I am for that war with heart and soul, and that is the worldwide war of social revolution." The paper attacked a U.S. Marine Corps recruiting poster that included the words of the Marine Corps hymn. The editorial noted that the marines were out attacking people "from the halls of Montezuma to the shores of Tripoli," and that this was "where our patriotic capitalists could make a profit." The paper published the works of the 1916 Socialist Party presidential candidate and antiwar activist Allan Benson, an obscure Socialist journalist from Michigan until his column in *Appeal to Reason* propelled him to national fame. Benson staunchly opposed U.S. entry into World War I.

Once the United States declared war, however, the old Socialist radicals like Debs were imprisoned under the Espionage Act of 1917, and the government systematically shut down not only radical periodicals but also many mainstream journals that opposed or questioned the war. Haldeman-Julius renamed the paper *The New Appeal* and adopted a prowar, nationalistic editorial policy. All remaining ties to the antiwar Socialist Party were severed. On 6 July 1918 Benson also announced his change of allegiance in a column making public his immediate resignation from the Socialist Party and stating, "I know the government of the United States wages war for neither money nor land, while the government of Germany covets both money and land. . . . I feel that until she will accept a just peace she should be compelled to accept war."

After the war ended, the paper opportunistically moved back into the peace camp and returned to its original name, but it had lost much of its credibility. By 1919 the Socialist Party had shattered into various splinter groups ending its golden era in ideological warfare. Still, Debs managed to pull a million votes from prison in 1920. The American radical movement perceived the paper's editorial shifts as unprincipled and unacceptable, leading to the inevitable death of *Appeal to Reason* in 1922. In its place, the *Haldeman-Julius Weekly* appeared, dedicated to a self-help ideology with the slogan, "By improving one's self the degree of general excellence will be permanently improved." Haldeman-Julius wrote, "The *Haldeman-Julius Weekly,* hitherto known as the *Appeal to Reason,* will carry out a carefully wrought out policy of individual self help through one's own efforts" (Graham). Thus, the nation's greatest Socialist and communitarian newspaper ended by embracing the individualistic philosophy of pulling oneself up by one's own bootstraps. Perhaps no greater summation of the transition from the Progressive Era to the unfettered capitalism of the Roaring Twenties is available.

References:

J. Robert Constantine, ed., *Letters of Eugene V. Debs: Volume I 1874–1912* (Urbana: University of Illinois Press, 1990);

Eugene V. Debs, *Debs: His Life, Writings and Speeches* (Girard, Kans.: Appeal to Reason, 1908);

George Allan England, *The Story of the Appeal* (Ft. Scott, Kans., 1915);

John Graham, *Yours for the Revolution: The Appeal to Reason, 1895–1922* (Lincoln: University of Nebraska Press, 1990);

James R. Green, *Grass-Roots Socialism: Radical Movements in the Southwest 1895–1943* (Baton Rouge: Louisiana State University Press, 1978);

Mary "Mother" Jones, *The Autobiography of Mother Jones* (Chicago: Charles H. Kerr, 1925);

Howard H. Quint, *The Forging of American Socialism* (Columbia: University of South Carolina Press, 1953), pp. 175–199;

Elliott Shore, *Talkin' Socialism: J. A. Wayland and the Role of the Press in American Radicalism, 1890–1910* (Lawrence: University Press of Kansas, 1988);

Julius Augustus Wayland, *Leaves of Life* (Girard, Kans.: Appeal to Reason, 1912).

Papers:

The Fred D. Warren Papers are held at the Archives and Special Collections at the Thomas J. Dodd Research Center, University of Connecticut, Storrs. The J. A. Wayland Collection and the Haldeman-Julius Papers are housed at the Leonard H. Axe Library, Pittsburg State University, Pittsburg, Kansas. This Wayland collection consists of his diaries and correspondence; it also contains *Appeal to Reason* company files and taped interviews with family members, as well as the correspondence of Fred D. Warren. The Library/Archives Division of the Kansas State Historical Society holds what it believes to be a complete set on microfilm of *Appeal to Reason* (8/31/1895–11/4/1922). The Ruskin Settlement Collection, 1893–1901, is a collection of documents from the Ruskin Cooperative Association, the first Marxist-influenced commune in the United States, cofounded by J. A. Wayland. It resides at the Tennessee State Library and Archives in Nashville.

The Industrial Workers of the World (IWW)

(27 June 1905 –)

Edward D. Melillo
Yale University

SELECTED BOOKS BY THE IWW AND ITS MEMBERS: *Proceedings of the First I.W.W. Convention* (New York: New York Labor News Company, 1905); republished as *The Founding Convention of the I.W.W.–Proceedings* (New York: Merit Publishers, 1969);

The Little Red Songbook (Chicago: I.W.W. Publishing Bureau, 1909);

Vincent St. John, *The I.W.W.: History, Structure and Methods* (Chicago: I.W.W. Publishing Bureau, 1917);

George Francis Vanderveer, *Opening Statement of Geo. F. Vanderveer, Counsel for the Defense of One Hundred and One Members of the Industrial Workers of the World, in the Case of the U.S.A. vs. Wm. D. Haywood, et al.* (Chicago: I.W.W. Publishing Bureau, 1918);

Tom Mann, *Tom Mann's Memoirs* (London: Labor Publishing, 1923);

William D. Haywood, *Bill Haywood's Book: The Autobiography of William D. Haywood* (New York: International Publishers, 1929); republished as *Autobiography of Big Bill Haywood* (New York: International Publishers, 1966);

Ralph Chaplin, *Wobbly: The Rough and Tumble Story of an American Radical* (Chicago: University of Chicago Press, 1948);

Ammon Hennacy, *Autobiography of a Catholic Anarchist* (New York: Catholic Worker Books, 1954); revised as *The Book of Ammon* (Salt Lake City: The Author, 1965);

Elizabeth Gurley Flynn, *I Speak My Own Piece: Autobiography of "The Rebel Girl"* (New York: Masses and Mainstream, 1955); republished as *The Rebel Girl: An Autobiography* (New York: International Publishers, 1973);

George Hardy, *Those Stormy Years: Memories of the Fight for Freedom on Five Continents* (London: Laurence & Wishart, 1956);

Haywood, *The I.W.W. Trial* (New York: Arno, 1969);

Fred Thompson and Patrick Murfin, *The I.W.W., Its First Seventy Years, 1905–1975* (Chicago: I.W.W. Publishing Bureau, 1976);

Len DeCaux, *The Living Spirit of the Wobblies* (New York: International Publishers, 1978);

Industrial Workers of the World, *Songs of the Workers to Fan the Flames of Discontent,* thirty-fifth edition (Chicago: I.W.W., 1984);

Henry McGuckin, *Memoirs of a Wobbly* (Chicago: Charles H. Kerr, 1987);

Lorenzo Kom'boa Ervin, *Anarchism and the Black Revolution* (Philadelphia: Monkeywrench Press, 1994).

Editions and Collections: Joseph Hillstrom, *The Songs of Joe Hill,* edited by Barrie Stavis and Frank Harmon (New York: Oak, 1960);

Rebel Voices, an I.W.W. Anthology, edited by Joyce L. Kornbluh (Ann Arbor, Mich.: University of Michigan Press, 1964);

Hillstrom, *The Letters of Joe Hill,* compiled and edited by Philip S. Foner (New York: Oak, 1965);

Helen Keller, *Helen Keller: Her Socialist Years; Writings and Speeches,* edited by Philip S. Foner (New York: International Publishers, 1967);

Fellow Workers and Friends: I.W.W. Free-Speech Fights As Told By Participants (Westport, Conn.: Greenwood Press, 1981);

Ernest Riebe, *Mr. Block,* facsimile edition (Chicago: Charles H. Kerr, 1984);

Solidarity Forever: An Oral History of the IWW, edited by Stewart Bird, Dan Georgakas, and Deborah Shaffer (Chicago: Lake View Press, 1985);

Carlos Cortez, *Wobbly: 80 Years of Rebel Art* (Chicago: Gato Negro Press, 1985);

Dreams and Dilemmas: Elizabeth Gurley Flynn's Writings on Women, edited by Rosalyn Fraad Baxandall (New Brunswick, N.J.: Rutgers University Press, 1986);

Nothing in Common: An Oral History of IWW Strikes, 1972–1992, edited by John Silvano (Cedar Rapids, Iowa: Cedar Publishing, 1999);

The Big Red Songbook, edited by Archie Green and Franklin Rosemont (Chicago: Charles H. Kerr, 2006).

RECORDINGS: *Don't Mourn, Organise! Songs of Labor Songwriter Joe Hill,* Various Artists, *Smithsonian/Folkways Recordings,* 1990;
We Have Fed You All for a Thousand Years, Utah Phillips, Rounder Records, 1993.

The Industrial Workers of the World (IWW) is a revolutionary union movement that began in Chicago in 1905. Its founding members drew upon a distinctive blend of Marxist and anarcho-syndicalist ideas from Europe, combining them with the indigenous American traditions of populism and industrial unionism to create an organization widely known for its ambitious goals, its dynamic repertoire of direct-action tactics, and its unwavering commitment to organizing across the boundaries of race, class, and gender. From the start, its members, commonly known as Wobblies, welcomed all workers, skilled and unskilled, non-whites, immigrants (including Asians), and women, who found opportunity within IWW ranks in an era when other U.S. unions excluded them from participation. During its heyday in the years preceding World War I, the IWW counted well over 100,000 members in its ranks, although the number of workers informally affiliated with the organization may have been several times that figure. Throughout the IWW's first two decades, most North American radicals either joined the IWW ranks or participated in Wobbly-sponsored campaigns for workplace democracy, women's rights, free speech, and a worker-controlled economy. The IWW continues to exist, albeit on a much smaller scale.

Many of the IWW's most enduring contributions to American history have been in the realm of cultural production. Wobbly musicians composed dozens of songs now considered classics of American folk music. IWW artists inspired the contemporary underground cartoon movement. Wobblies invented a host of propaganda-dissemination techniques, while the organization's newspapers built a vast multilingual readership in an era of single-language periodicals. The IWW was at the forefront of the free-speech fight at a time when the federal government presented profound challenges to popular expression. IWW history also shaped American literary production. Great American playwrights and novelists built their narratives around Wobbly figures and events. Additionally, Wobblies have written extensively about their own lives and experiences, and a growing body of historical scholarship on the IWW continues to emerge from academic circles.

On 27 June 1905 more than two hundred socialists, trade unionists, and syndicalists gathered in Brand's Hall on Chicago's north side to launch a revolutionary working-class organization called the Industrial Workers of the World. William "Big Bill"

Haywood, secretary of the Western Federation of Miners, opened the convention with a succinct declaration of the group's radical intentions: "Fellow workers, this is the Continental Congress of the working class. We are here to confederate the workers of this country into a working-class movement that shall have for its purpose the emancipation of the working class from the slave bondage of capitalism." The gathering was a virtual who's who of the North American Left, including: Daniel DeLeon, Socialist Labor Party leader; Eugene V. Debs, leader of the American Socialist Party and organizer of the Pullman Locomotive Strike of 1894; "Mother" Mary Jones, the legendary miners' and childrens' rights activist; Vincent St. John, a well-known organizer of western mine workers; Charles O. Sherman, secretary of the United Metal Workers; A. M. Simons, then editor of the *International Socialist Review;* Lucy Parsons, organizer of the poor and widow of "Haymarket Martyr" Albert Parsons; Father Thomas J. Hagerty, editor of the American Labor Union's *Voice of Labor;* and William E. Trautmann, editor of the United Brewery Workers' German-language newspaper.

This eclectic band of radicals had come together to mount an unprecedented challenge to the elitist craft unionism of Samuel Gompers's American Federation of Labor (AFL). IWW convention participants shared the goal of building a revolutionary working-class organization from which a new social order could emerge. The opening lines of the preamble to the IWW constitution could hardly have presented a more unequivocal indictment of the capitalist wage system:

> The working class and the employing class have nothing in common. There can be no peace as long as hunger and want are found among millions of working people and the few, who make up the employing class, have all the good things in life. Between these two classes a struggle must go on until the workers of the world organize as a class, take possession of the earth and the machinery of production, and abolish the wage system.

IWW members, or "Wobblies," sought to build "One Big Union" to unite all workers and transform society into what they called an "industrial democracy" in which social needs, not the imperatives of profit, would drive production. In their attempt to accomplish this monumental task, the Wobblies relied on a mixture of foreign radical ideology, including Marxism and anarcho-syndicalism, and the homegrown North American tradition of industrial unionism. Workers were to build industrial unions in their workplaces and use these organizing bodies to make gains within the existing factory system until the whole IWW coalition could muster the strength to call a general strike, halting the nation's economic activity. Once this paralysis of production had occurred, workers would demand that industrial unions replace private enterprises and government agencies as the organizing centers of the economy. After this peaceful and democratic revolution had been accomplished in one country, they hoped, it would spread to all nations of the world.

This strategy amounted to a wholesale rejection of the AFL's twenty-five-year-old model of unionism. Gompers and his organization grouped skilled workers into small, compartmentalized units, separated along long-standing craft divisions. The AFL shunned new immigrants, non-whites, and women, preferring instead to build a so-called aristocracy of labor among established male craftsmen. For many years, it discouraged its membership from taking radical positions about public-policy matters, and it dissociated itself from all matters not directly related to the employer/employee relationship at work. In stark contrast, the IWW was all-inclusive in its membership; it was rooted in a utopian vision of the future; and it disapproved of status-based hierarchies.

The early years were marked by a few divisions within the union, but they were based on ideological differences, not identity groups. In 1907 the Western Federation of Miners (WFM) withdrew from the IWW as a backlash against the negative publicity drawn on the WFM when Bill Haywood was accused of participating in a conspiracy to murder the governor of Idaho. In 1908 and 1909 the union splintered as the DeLeon–led Detroit IWW clashed with the rowdy and unpolished Western branches over the issue of whether the IWW should involve itself in politics (DeLeon favored use of the ballot as well as other means) or stick to a purely economic revolution. In 1911 the Socialist Party picked up a thread of the same argument as it considered expelling its radical wing, which included Haywood and the IWW, for advocating direct action, including sabotage, rather than political engagement. In 1912 the radicals were expelled, and antagonism between the IWW and the Socialist Party, at least at the organizational level, continued into the World War I years.

From 1905 to 1920 the IWW had the largest percentage of black workers of any major working-class organization in the United States. In *Anarchism and the Black Revolution* (1994), Lorenzo Kom'boa Ervin estimated that during this fifteen-year period, more than 10 percent of the IWW's membership was black. Only a few years after the IWW's founding convention, racially integrated IWW locals controlled the docks in Philadelphia, the cigar-making trade in Pittsburgh, and a majority of the lumberyards in the South. Wobbly rhetoric matched shop-floor efforts to expand upon these successes. When interviewed by the press, "Big Bill" Haywood declared that the IWW organized all workers; to Haywood and his fellow Wobblies, it "did not make a bit of difference whether he is a Negro or a white man" (quoted in *Rebel Voices: An IWW Anthology*). In keeping with Haywood's promise, several African Americans, such as Philadelphia labor leader Ben Fletcher, became national figures in the IWW movement. Also, IWW members tended to frequent places, such as Chicago's Dil Pickle Club and Bughouse Square or Asian restaurants on the West Coast, where segregation was not observed.

The IWW made similar overtures to Asian Americans. In the early twentieth century, the AFL and its older cousin, the Knights of Labor, excluded Asian Americans from participation in their organizations and presented the unions as the "protectors" of American labor value. In many cases, these unions also favored harsh curbs on Asian immigration to the United States and even supported political measures, such as the Chinese Exclusion Act, to suppress the economic and social rights of these ethnic groups. Diverging from mainstream American labor, the IWW became the first major working-class association to welcome and actively pursue Asian American workers.

Women also played crucial parts in both the IWW's rank-and-file membership and its founding leadership. "Mother" Jones, Elizabeth Gurley Flynn, Lucy Parsons, Helen Keller, Matilda Rabinowitz, and Vera Moller, were just a few of the prominent female IWW organizers in the union's early years. In 1916, the IWW paper, *Solidarity,* ran a special issue on women's rights in which Flynn decried the tragedy that had befallen women in modern society. Men, she declared, had denied women their rights, forced them into domestic servitude, and kept them from obtaining the education they deserved and needed to establish economic independence. As Flynn put it, "Religion, home, and childbearing were their prescribed spheres. Marriage was their career and to be old a lifelong disgrace. Their right to life depended on their sex attraction and the hideous inroads on the moral integrity of women, produced by economic dependence, are deep and subtle."

In several cases women took charge of official IWW publications. In 1905 Lucy Parsons edited *The Liberator,* an IWW paper based in Chicago. Parsons, a descendent of slaves, Creek Indians, and Mexicans, had been an activist and a writer for radical causes since the late 1800s. Her husband, Albert, was among the Haymarket Martyrs, four defendants who were hanged (another committed suicide the night before his scheduled execution) after a controversial guilty verdict for bombing during a labor protest at Chicago's Haymarket Square on 4 May 1886 in which eight policemen were killed. After her husband's death, Parsons devoted

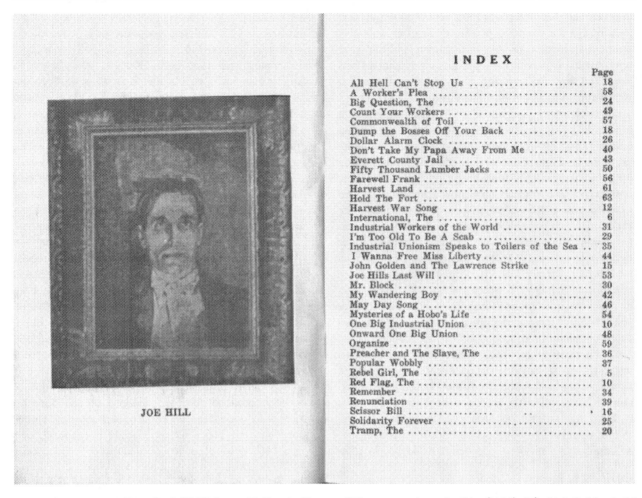

JOE HILL

Pages from I. W. W. Songs: To Fan the Flames of Discontent, *nineteenth edition (1923), "The Little Red Songbook"*
(Collection of Richard Layman)

her life to the struggle for social justice. In 1891 she and fellow activist Lizzie Holmes began editing *Freedom: A Revolutionary Anarchist-Communist Monthly*. Parsons later helped to found the National Committee of the International Labor Defense, an organization that grew out of discussions between James Cannon, a Communist Party leader in the United States, and Haywood, who had fled to Soviet Russia to avoid prison. In the 1930s the organization became famous for offering aid to African Americans, such as the Scottsboro Nine, who had been unjustly accused of rape. In the early 1900s, Parsons used the pages of *The Liberator* to argue her case on a number of crucial women's issues, including a woman's right to divorce, remarriage, and birth control. She also wrote inspirational columns on famous women and working-class history.

The Liberator was just one of scores of Wobbly newspapers and journals to appear in the first quarter of the twentieth century. IWW locals printed more than sixty-six serialized publications between 1909 and 1918. From 1907 to 1909 the Chicago-based *Industrial Union*

Bulletin (IUB) served as the first nationally circulated IWW newsletter. It soon fell out of publication in favor of the popular journals, *Solidarity* and *The Industrial Worker (IW)*. In 1909 *Solidarity* began publication out of New Castle, Pennsylvania, serving as the propaganda organ for the IWW's Eastern branches. Later it moved to Cleveland, where in mid 1916 Ralph Chaplin moved to become the director of IWW publications. Haywood was consolidating his control over the organization and centralizing as many functions as possible in Chicago. In 1917 conflict between Haywood and Ben Williams, the editor of *Solidarity,* came to a head, and Haywood replaced Williams with Chaplin and moved the newspaper to Chicago.

On the other side of the continent, the four-page *IW* covered Western Wobbly news. It was published first in Spokane, then Seattle, from 8 March 1909 to 21 November 1931 and targeted audiences of lumberjacks, miners, farmhands, and hops workers of the Pacific Coast and the Midwest. The *IW* contained a blend of

THE REBEL GIRL

Words and Music by Joe Hill

There are women of many descriptions
   In this queer world, as everyone knows,
Some are living in beautiful mansions,
   And are wearing the finest of clothes.
There are blue blooded queens and princesses,
   Who have charms made of diamonds and pearl;
But the only and thoroughbred lady
   Is the Rebel Girl.

CHORUS
That's the Rebel Girl, that's the Rebel Girl!
To the working class she's a precious pearl.
She brings courage, pride and joy
To the fighting Rebel Boy.
We've had girls before, but we need some more
In the Industrial Workers of the World.
For it's great to fight for freedom
With a Rebel Girl.

Yes, her hands may be hardened from labor,
   And her dress may not be very fine;
But a heart in her bosom is beating
   That is true to her class and her kind.
And the grafters in terror are trembling
   When her spite and defiance she'll hurl;
For the only and thoroughbred lady
   Is the Rebel Girl.

Words and Music of "The Rebel Girl" may be obtained in popular sheet form by applying to I. W. W. Publishing Bureau. Price 25 cents.

5

news regarding Wobbly strikes, song lyrics, political cartoons, book reviews, job postings, announcements of IWW entertainment and fundraising events, advertisements, and obituaries. Job postings in the *IW* imparted detailed information on wage rates and candid critiques of working conditions at job sites. For example, an advertisement in the 15 January 1927 issue contained the following particulars on available work in Washington: "Scenic, Wash–Great Northern R.R. tunnel project is working full force, with A. Guthrie and Company the contractors. The wages on this job are, Miners, $6.40; Muckers, $4.80; Chucktenders, $5.20; and outside laborers, $4.00 per day. Bedding is $0.05 per a day, and Hospital fee is $1 per a month. The board is fair, but sleeping conditions are rotten."

The *IW* also served as a tool for disseminating Wobbly propaganda. Many issues were emblazoned with slogans and mottos intended to awaken the revolutionary fervor of the readership. Phrases such as "Labor produces all wealth," "An injury to one is an injury to all," and "Solidarity is labor's one weapon! Educate, Organize, Emancipate," all originated in the pages of the *IW* and soon found their way onto other

types of IWW propaganda. IWW printers turned out sixty-five thousand copies of each *IW* issue in 1913.

English-speaking workers were not the only audience for these periodicals. In 1920, the IWW general executive board and individual IWW unions published at least fourteen journals in languages other than English. A list of available publications printed that year in *The One Big Union Monthly* advertised magazines in Russian, Hungarian, Spanish, Italian, Bulgarian, Yiddish, Lithuanian, Polish, German, Swedish, and Finnish. Recent immigrants had access to many of the same articles, cartoons, and illustrations featured in the English-language journals, but editors translated the texts and often fine-tuned the cultural meanings of the articles to fit the requirements of each magazine.

In addition to newspapers, the Wobblies employed far more subversive means of transmitting their message across vast distances. One such technique was the use of gum-backed stickerettes about two to four times the size of postage stamps. A package containing one hundred of these so-called silent agitators cost only ten cents. Providing their owner with an arsenal of miniature propaganda posters, the stickerettes ended up on lampposts, tools, bunkhouses, and box-cars. Chicago-born Ralph Chaplin designed many of the stickerettes and noted that "At the peak of the stick-erette campaign it was said that every Boxcar in the country carried with it at least one good argument in favor of joining the I.W.W." The IWW printed three million of these stickerettes in 1917 alone.

Wobbly propaganda, such as the messages emblazoned on the "silent agitators," often highlighted the IWW's "by any means necessary" philosophy of direct action. In practical terms, direct action included a repertory of such techniques as foot-dragging, walkouts, freedom rides, orchestrated mass arrests to fill jails beyond capacity, and outright sabotage of industrial machinery. While such tactics were the subject of much debate and sparked several schisms among the IWW leadership, Wobblies used them to great effect in a series of more than 150 strikes that occurred throughout the country between 1905 and 1917. Some of the most noteworthy of these labor actions were the Nevada miners' strike (1906–1907); the strike at Marston Textile Mill in Skowhegan, Maine (1907); the Pressed Steel Car Company strike at McKees Rocks, Pennsylvania (1909); the Lawrence, Massachusetts, "Bread and Roses" textile strike (1912); the Louisiana and Arkansas lumber workers' strikes (1912–1913); the Patterson, New Jersey, silk workers' strike (1913); the Wheatland Riots at Durst Ranch in Wheatland, California (1913); the ironworkers' strike in the Mesabi Range of northeastern Minnesota (1916); and the Bisbee, Arizona, copper strike (1917). These aggressive labor actions punctuated popular discontent with an era of rising prices, stagnating wages, terrible factory conditions, high unemployment, and devastating depressions.

In addition to leading the fight for material gains in the privatized sphere of the workplace, Wobblies battled to protect the public's rights of free speech and assembly. Despite the fact that these liberties were guaranteed in writing by the First Amendment, in practice they were frequently violated by city police, federal government agents, or hired thugs on the payrolls of corporate bosses who saw the IWW as an alarming threat to capitalist production. In the IWW's early years "soapbox oratory" became the predominant means through which the Wobblies, like other organizations such as the Salvation Army, reached out to migrant workers at railroad stations, hiring halls, and itinerant camps throughout the United States. The practice of standing on a small platform such as a wooden box and speaking to passersby served as the major source of spoken-word news in the age before radio, and it soon became bitterly contested in communities around the country. Wobblies congregated in designated spots to challenge repressive local ordinances against their soap-box drives. Often reading from the U.S. Constitution or the Declaration of Independence while being carted off to the

police station, IWW members purposely crowded jails until the holding facilities were filled beyond capacity.

In Spokane, Fresno, Denver, Kansas City, Duluth, New Castle, San Diego, New Bedford, and Missoula, Wobblies positioned their soapboxes on street corners and began to address the crowds that invariably gathered. All together, Wobblies carried out more than thirty of these free-speech campaigns between 1907 and 1917. Most of these efforts ended in the repeal of the law or ordinance that had outlawed public political oratory, "seditious" speech, or large gatherings. These victories came at a considerable price, however. Several Wobblies died, thousands received severe beatings, and many spent years in prison for their part in campaigns to defend the right to speak freely.

Despite these hardships, many IWW members looked back proudly on the free-speech fights of the early 1900s as one of their organization's key contributions to American civic life. These battles also, they felt, vindicated the IWW's uncompromising tactics. As Wobbly organizer Frank Little later wrote, "The best method of repealing a bad law is to make the officials enforce it." American Civil Liberties Union founder Roger Baldwin joined the IWW briefly after his release from prison for refusing to serve in World War I, and he recalled the IWW free-speech fights as defining battles over basic freedoms of expression. Wobblies managed to recruit famous civil-libertarian attorney Clarence Darrow to their cause, most notably when Haywood and others were kidnapped, taken across state boundaries, and charged with the murder of Idaho governor Frank Steunenberg in 1907. Darrow and his Chicago partner Victor Yarros also volunteered much time to the cause of defending IWW members charged with violation of speech ordinances.

While in jail for their defiant stances, Wobblies drew upon an array of inspirational protest songs composed on the shop floors, fields, tenement houses, and boxcars where they lived or worked. The music and words to many of these tunes eventually found their way into *The Little Red Songbook*. The songbook first emerged as the creation of Wobblies from Spokane, the so-called Overalls Brigade, in 1909. Earlier some locals had published and distributed song cards. West Coast IWW organizer and Socialist Party member J. H. Walsh enlisted help from two migrant harvesters, Harry McClintock and Richard Brazier, in gathering up a representative collection of cards and leaflets on from rallies, meetings, and demonstrations. The trio brought this eclectic assembly of contributions together in *The Little Red Songbook*. During the years following its first publication, the book became a staple at labor events and union halls. It has gone through more than thirty-six editions since 1906 and can still be found at union offices throughout the United States. A comprehensive edition *The Big Red Songbook* (2006), has been assembled by labor historians Archie Green and Franklin Rosemont.

IWW songwriters such as Joe Hill, Ralph Chaplin, Covington Hall, Laura Payne Emerson, and T-Bone Slim often set their lyrics to the music of deep-rooted, emotionally loaded, and easily recognizable hymns and spirituals. In one instance Wobblies replaced a stanza of the hymn "Take It to the Lord in Prayer" with the lines:

Are you poor, forlorn and hungry?
Are there lots of things you lack?
Is your Life made up of misery?
Then dump the bosses off your back.

IWW members, especially in the West, intimately familiar with Christian hymns because so many of the itinerant men had sought food and overnight lodging in mission shelters. Often these charity seekers were forced to sing the songs even when they had paid for soup and a bunk. Chaplin's song "Solidarity Forever," set to the music of "Battle Hymn of the Republic," went on to become the national anthem of American labor. This songwriting practice was rooted in nineteenth-century labor traditions, but IWW songwriters excelled at it.

Many IWW songwriters became well-known figures in the popular-music scene of their day, but only one attained mythical status in American history: Joe Hill. Born in 1879 in Gävle, Sweden, his given name had been Joel Emmanuel Hägglund, but he simplified it to Joseph Hillstrom upon immigrating to the United States in 1902. Eventually he became known simply as "Joe Hill," the hobo songwriter and itinerant worker who traveled throughout North America on rail lines, finding odd jobs and unearthing inspiration for new poems and songs. Hill joined the IWW in 1910. The 1911 edition of *The Little Red Songbook* included his ballad, "The Preacher and the Slave," set to the tune of "In the Sweet By and By" and featuring the following chorus:

You will eat, bye and bye,
In that glorious land above the sky;
Work and pray live on hay,
You'll get pie in the sky when you die.

Author Wallace Stegner later adopted "The Preacher and the Slave" as the title for his novel about the Wobbly songwriter.

Some of Hill's other well-known tunes included: "There Is Power in a Union," "Don't Take My Papa Away from Me," "Casey Jones, the Union Scab," and "The Rebel Girl," which he wrote for the IWW's legendary orator Flynn. While these songs were celebrated in their own day, Hill's tunes eventually found their way into the repertoires of a diverse array of subsequent musicians, including Paul Robeson, Pete Seeger, Joan Baez, Woodie Guthrie, Bob Dylan, Sweet Honey in the Rock, Phil Ochs, Billy Bragg, Utah Phillips, and Ani DiFranco.

Hill also drew cartoons for Wobbly magazines and became an extremely successful organizer for the IWW. While campaigning on behalf of copper workers in Utah during the winter of 1914 Hill was arrested for the murders of grocer John G. Morrison and his seventeen-year-old son, John. After a trial marred by irregularities, an overtly biased court convicted Hill. Labor leaders throughout the country insisted that copper bosses, fearful of a Wobbly-led miners' strike, had framed him. While Hill languished in prison during a string of unsuccessful appeals, support for his exoneration grew to include AFL President Samuel Gompers, the Swedish minister to the United States, and even President Woodrow Wilson. The Utah Supreme Court disagreed with Hill's many allies, however, and at sunrise on 19 November 1915 a firing squad executed Hill in the yard of the Utah State Penitentiary. Massive rallies honoring his life occurred throughout the United States, and his ashes were mailed to locals across the American West for scattering, as he had requested. Others made their way, confiscated by postal officials, into the files of the National Archives. In the wake of his untimely death, Hill became one of America's best-known labor martyrs. In his penultimate letter from prison, Hill had concluded with the Swedish phrase: "Sörj Ej, Organisera!" Its English translation, "Don't Mourn–Organize!" eventually became a motto for the U.S. labor movement. Paul Robeson recorded a moving rendition of the song "I Dreamed I Saw Joe Hill Last Night."

In addition to the cultural contributions of Hill and the IWW's other songwriters, Wobblies left a distinctive legacy of artistic traditions. IWW cartoonists and illustrators were often self-taught and their material was grounded in a "hobo style" of informality, brash humor, and to-the-point imagery. The cartoons of German-born Ernest Riebe, who created the longest-running Wobbly comic, *Mr. Block,* epitomized this unvarnished approach to visual humor. Mr. Block, a gullible working-class fellow, experienced a long series of raucous adventures that usually featured being cheated by capitalist bosses and learning that he should have joined the IWW sooner. Other Wobbly artists, such as Ralph Chaplin, Ern Hanson, C. E. Setzer, and William Henkelman, enlivened the pages of the IWW's journals with their cartoons, producing potent propaganda statements, understandable even to those not fluent in English. The more recent success of IWW artist Carlos Cortez, whose revolutionary linocuts have been exhibited at the Museum of Modern Art in New York, demonstrates that Wobbly traditions have outlasted the organization's phase of precipitous decline in the mid 1920s.

The IWW's losses of membership and strategic power during the decade following World War I resulted from a confluence of factors. First, in the years preceding the war, the government ran a series of aggressive and often violent campaigns targeting the IWW and its members. Most IWW members vociferously protested U.S. entry into World War I, declaring the conflict an imperialist power scramble from which common people and workers had nothing to gain and much to lose. U.S. Justice Department agents used Wobbly opposition to the war as a premise for a massive raid on IWW offices across the country in September 1917. Under the Espionage Act of 1917, IWW members who challenged the government's decision to send U.S. combat troops to Europe were branded as criminal subversives. Officials served warrants for the arrest of more than two hundred men and women in the organization. Almost the entire IWW leadership received federal prison terms of one or two decades and fines as high as $20,000. These harsh sentences were often coupled with severe infringements on the constitutional rights of IWW members to competent legal representation and defense files.

In January 1920, while some Wobblies were out on appeal, federal authorities led another series of raids, including one on the organization's national headquarters in Chicago, confiscating almost all the paperwork of the organization, which was not then available to those who needed it as part of their legal defense. The appeal was denied in April 1921. Several IWW members whose bonds had been set very high, including Haywood, jumped bail and fled to Soviet Russia a month earlier, leaving the union to pay the bonds. One of the group was committed to St. Elizabeth's Hospital for the Insane. The remainder, imprisoned in Leavenworth Penitentiary, splintered into two groups over the terms of their pardon by President Warren G. Harding in 1923.

In addition, self-titled "patriotic leagues," including American Legion-affiliated groups, and employer-sponsored gangs, including operatives of Pinkerton's National Detective Agency, attacked IWW union halls, residences, and meetings with relative impunity. Violent confrontations between right-wing mobs and Wobblies at Everett, Washington (5 November 1916), and Centralia, Washington (11 November 1919), ended in deaths and further escalations of the brutality. At Centralia IWW member Wesley Everest, a veteran in uniform, was lynched by a mob on Armistice Day. This persecution of Wobblies received further judicial support when many states adopted criminal syndicalism laws, designed with the express purpose of destroying the IWW.

The IWW had also laid the foundation for its own decline by training several leaders who switched loyalties and joined the Communist Party from 1919 through the 1930s. Haywood, George Hardy, and many Russian immigrant leaders thought that the Bolshevik Revolution offered the surest way to the world the IWW envisioned, and Russia's new government created the short-lived Siberian mining colony of Kuzbas as a conciliatory gesture to the noncommunist left. Lucy Parsons felt that communist movements in the United States had assumed the revolutionary qualities that the IWW no longer possessed. A schism over tactics erupted during a 1924 IWW convention, precipitating an unbridgeable split in the leadership. Flynn suffered a nervous breakdown after 1925 and took ten years to recover. When her health improved, she joined the Communist Party USA. Chaplin stayed into the 1930s but felt that the organization had gone off track. Other Wobblies parlayed their experience with the labor struggle into prominent roles in the new Congress of Industrial Organizations (CIO), a coalition founded in 1935 by eight international unions in an attempt to push the AFL in a more radical direction. Despite this exodus, the IWW held onto significant membership in the maritime trades, agricultural labor, and mining. The organization formed unions of the unemployed in New York, Chicago, and Portland during the Depression years of the 1930s, and won contract improvements for several thousand workers in Ohio by orchestrating a dozen strikes in plants around Cleveland during the middle of that decade.

IWW influences remained strong in the literary world, as well. Wobblies provided inspiration and subject matter for many of America's great writers, including Jack London, Eugene O'Neill, Upton Sinclair, John Dos Passos, Carl Sandburg, Gary Snyder, E. L. Doctorow, and Wallace Stegner. In James Jones's novel of World War II, *From Here to Eternity* (1951), an old sergeant recounts to a young soldier his memories of the IWW: "You don't remember the Wobblies. You were too young. Or else not even born yet. There has never been anything like them, before or since."

Like many radical institutions and entities in the United States, the IWW enjoyed a renaissance in the 1960s, confirming that a new generation had not forgotten the Wobblies. In 1964 a group of Chicago's young IWW members kept the Wobbly art tradition alive by publishing a successful underground magazine called *The Rebel Worker*. Issues blended Wobbly-inspired class-war humor with surrealist playfulness, using pirated pop-culture icons such as Bugs Bunny and the Incredible

Hulk to mount vivid cartoon critiques of capitalism. At about the same time, Wobbly buttons and IWW pamphlets began to make a showing at Students for a Democratic Society (SDS) rallies and anti-Vietnam War protests. IWW veterans and their direct-action techniques played leading roles in the Civil Rights struggle, as well.

On the academic front, interest in the IWW grew exponentially with the rise of the subfield of social history in the 1960s and 1970s. Joyce L. Kornbluh edited *Rebel Voices, an I.W.W. Anthology* (1964), the most important history of Wobbly culture yet compiled. The following year Philip S. Foner's *History of the Labor Movement in the United States: Volume IV: The Industrial Workers of the World, 1905-1917* offered a detailed Marxist-Stalinist reading of the IWW's history. Melvyn Dubovsky's *We Shall Be All: A History of the Industrial Workers of the World* (1969) has earned a place as the most comprehensive general history of the IWW.

New work on the IWW continues to emerge in stunning quantities. In 1986 Walter P. Reuther Library archivist Dione Miles published *Something in Common—An IWW Bibliography,* an exhaustive compilation of sources by and on the *Wobblies.* Miles assembled over five thousand annotated entries on the IWW, including 235 books that "represent significant works dealing with the IWW." The last two decades of the twentieth century marked an especially rich period in IWW scholarship, culminating in several publications timed for the organization's centennial in 2005. In *Wobblies: A Graphic History* (2005), editors Paul Buhle and Nicole Schulman return to the Wobbly's pioneering artistic format, the cartoon, to recount the IWW's first hundred years.

Despite this prolific output from North American historians, scholars have contended that more work must be done in the field of Wobbly history. Franklin Rosemont, who has been one of the IWW's most committed chroniclers for more than five decades, has recently concluded in *Joe Hill: The IWW and the Making of a Revolutionary Workingclass Counterculture* (2003) that a "first-rate, truly comprehensive history of the IWW is yet to be written." Part of the difficulty of this task, Rosemont stresses, is that the historical record is riddled with holes. The U.S. government confiscated and destroyed IWW records beginning in 1917; other records survive in the National Archives, in the files of the Federal Bureau of Investigation, Justice Department, and Military Intelligence, but finding guides are fragmentary or nonexistent, and no scholar of radicalism has yet attempted to index them.

Several labor libraries, including the Labadie Collection at the University of Michigan in Ann Arbor; the Labor-Management Documentation Center at Cornell University in Ithaca, New York; the Walter P. Reuther Memorial Library at Wayne State University in Detroit; and the University of Arizona Library in Tucson; maintain collections of IWW materials that were not lost to these raids. Other related collections are being more carefully indexed than in the past, and new collections emerge every year that have a bearing on IWW history—for example, the University of Minnesota's law library has purchased the letters of Clarence Darrow, certain to be of use to future scholars of the IWW. The Industrial Workers of the World, currently headquartered in Philadelphia, hosts its own website with materials on IWW history, culture, and current campaigns at <http://www.iww.org>. Also the Charles H. Kerr Publishing Company in Chicago has devoted itself to keeping in print studies and memoirs that fill in details of the milieu in which the IWW arose and throve.

The IWW has left a profound legacy to American culture and society. By showing a reluctant mainstream union movement that workers who had previously been dismissed as unorganizable could be mobilized into a force with powerful striking and bargaining capacities, the IWW left an indelible mark on the character of modern struggles for social justice. This Wobbly spirit of solidarity has also shaped a diverse array of contemporary cultural practices. The IWW's influence can still be found in the graphic arts, fiction writing, folk music, and social movement culture. Although critics of IWW may take issue with the organization's goals and tactics, no one has lately found fault with the Wobblies' unwavering commitment to free speech, dignity, and equality for all Americans.

Bibliography:

Dione Miles, *Something in Common—an IWW Bibliography* (Detroit: Wayne State University Press, 1986).

References:

Leland Bell, "Radicalism and Race: The IWW and the Black Worker," *Journal of Human Relations,* 19 (January 1971): 48–56;

Richard Brazier, "The Story of the I.W.W.'s 'Little Red Songbook,'" *Labor History,* 9 (Winter 1968): 91–105;

Paul F. Brissenden, *The I.W.W.: A Study of American Syndicalism* (New York: Columbia University Press, 1919; revised edition, New York: Russell & Russell, 1957);

John G. Brooks, *American Syndicalism: The I.W.W.* (New York: Macmillan, 1913; revised edition, New York: AMS Press, 1978);

Tony Bubka, "Time to Organize: The IWW Stickerettes," *American West,* 5 (January 1968): 21–22, 25–26;

Paul Buhle, "The Wobblies in Perspective," *Monthly Review,* 22 (June 1970): 44–53;

Buhle and Nicole Schulman, eds., *Wobblies: A Graphic History* (London: Verso, 2005);

Verity Burgman, *Revolutionary Industrial Unionism: The Industrial Workers of the World in Australia* (New York: Cambridge University Press, 1995);

William Cahn, *Lawrence 1912: The Bread and Roses Strike* (New York: Pilgrim Press, 1977);

Frank Cain, *The Wobblies At War: A History of the IWW and the Great War in Australia* (Melbourne: Spectrum, 1994);

Alan Calmer, "The Wobbly in American Literature," *New Masses,* 12 (18 September 1934): 21–22;

Ardis Cameron, *Radicals of the Worst Sort: Laboring Women in Lawrence, Massachusetts, 1860–1912* (Urbana: University of Illinois Press, 1994);

Helen C. Camp, *Iron in Her Soul: Elizabeth Gurley Flynn and the American Left* (Pullman: Washington State University Press, 1995);

Peter Carlson, *Roughneck: The Life and Times of Big Bill Haywood* (New York: Norton, 1983);

David A. Carter, "The Industrial Workers of the World and the Rhetoric of Song," *Quarterly Journal of Speech,* 66, no. 4 (1980): 365–374;

Joseph R. Conlin, *Bread and Roses Too: Studies of the Wobblies* (Westport, Conn.: Greenwood Press, 1969);

Conlin, ed., *At the Point of Production: The Local History of the IWW* (Westport, Conn.: Greenwood Press, 1981);

Bernard A. Cook and James A. Watson, "The Sailors and Marine Transport Workers' 1913 Strike in New Orleans: The AFL and the IWW," *Southern Studies,* 18 (1979): 111–122;

Cletus E. Daniel, "In Defense of the Wheatland Wobblies: A Critical Analysis of the IWW in California," *Labor History,* 19 (Fall 1978): 485–509;

Mike Davis, "The Stop Watch and the Wooden Shoe: Scientific Management and the IWW," *Radical America,* 9 (January–February 1975): 69–95;

Eldridge Foster Dowell, *A History of Criminal Syndicalism Legislation in the United States* (Baltimore: Johns Hopkins University Press, 1939);

Melvyn Dubovsky, *We Shall Be All: A History of the Industrial Workers of the World* (Chicago: Quadrangle, 1969);

Michael H. Ebner, "I Never Died: The Case of Joe Hill v. the Historians," *Labor History,* 12 (Winter 1971): 139–143;

Robert E. Ficken, "The Wobbly Horrors: Pacific Northwest Lumbermen and the Industrial Workers of the World," *Labor History,* 24 (Summer 1983): 325–341;

Philip S. Foner, *History of the Labor Movement in the United States,* volume 4: *The Industrial Workers of the World, 1905–1917* (New York: International Publishers, 1965);

Foner, "The IWW and the Black Worker," *Journal of Negro History,* 55 (January 1970): 45–64;

Hester L. Furey, "IWW Songs as Modernist Poetry," *Journal of the Midwest Language Association,* 34 (Spring 2001): 51–72;

John S. Gambs, *The Decline of the I.W.W.* (New York: Columbia University Press, 1932);

Ronald Genini, "Industrial Workers of the World and Their Fresno Free Speech Fight, 1910–1911," *California Historical Quarterly,* 53 (Summer 1974): 100–114;

Steve Golin, *That Fragile Bridge: The Patterson Silk Strike–1913* (Philadelphia: Temple University Press, 1988);

Archie Green, *Wobblies, Pile Butts, and Other Heroes* (Urbana: University of Illinois Press, 1993);

Greg Hall, *Harvest Wobblies: The Industrial Workers of the World and Agricultural Laborers in the American West, 1905–1930* (Corvalis: Oregon State University Press, 2001);

Rob E. Hanson, *The Great Bisbee IWW Deportation of July 12, 1917* (Bisbee, Ariz.: Signature Press, 1980);

Hanson, ed., *With Drops of Blood; The History of the Industrial Workers of the World: Department of Justice Investigative Files* (Bigfork, Mont.: Signature Press, 1999);

Michael R. Johnson, "The I.W.W. and Wilsonian Democracy," *Science and Society,* 28 (Summer 1964): 257–274;

Howard Kimeldorf, *Battling for American Labor: Wobblies, Craft Workers, and the Making of the Union Movement* (Berkeley: University of California Press, 1999);

Clayton R. Koppes, "The Kansas Trial of the IWW, 1917–1919," *Labor History,* 16 (Summer 1975): 338–358;

Mark Leier, *Where the Fraser River Flows: The IWW in British Columbia* (Vancouver, B.C.: New Star, 1990);

Sidney Lens, "The Wobblies 50 Years Later," *Progressive,* 19 (August 1955): 20–21;

Charles P. LeWarne, "On the Wobbly Train to Fresno," *Labor History,* 14 (Spring 1973): 264–289;

John McClelland, Jr., *Wobbly War: The Centralia Story* (Tacoma: Washington State Historical Society, 1987);

Donald J. McClurg, "The Colorado Coal Strike of 1927–Tactical Leadership of the IWW," *Labor History,* 4 (Winter 1963): 68–92;

Phil Mellinger, "How the IWW Lost Its Western Heartland: Western Labor History Revisited," *Western Historical Quarterly,* 27 (Autumn 1996): 303–324;

George T. Morgan Jr., "The Gospel of Wealth Goes South: John Henry Kirby and Labor's Struggle for Self-Determination, 1901–1916," *Southwestern Historical Quarterly,* 75 (October 1971): 186–197;

Robert K. Murray, "Centralia: An Unfinished Tragedy," *Northwest Review,* 6 (Spring, 1963): 7–18;

Linda Nochlin, "The Patterson Strike Pageant of 1913," *Art in America,* 62 (May–June 1974): 45–53;

James O'Brien, "Wobblies and Draftees: The IWW's Wartime Dilemma, 1917–1918," *Radical America,* 1 (September–October 1967): 6–18;

Bryan D. Palmer, "'Big Bill' Haywood's Defection to Russia and the IWW: Two Letters," *Labor History,* 17 (Spring 1976): 271–278;

David M. Rabban, "The IWW Free Speech Fights and Popular Conceptions of Free Expression before World War I," *Virginia Law Review,* 80 (August 1994): 1055–1158;

Richard A. Rajala, "A Dandy Bunch of Wobblies: Pacific Northwest Loggers and the Industrial Workers of the World, 1900–1930," *Labor History,* 37 (Spring 1996): 205–234;

Merl Reed, "Lumberjacks and Longshoremen: The IWW in Louisiana," *Labor History,* 13 (Winter 1972): 41–59;

Patrick Renshaw, "The IWW and the Red Scare, 1917–24," *Journal of Contemporary History,* 3 (October 1968): 63–72;

Renshaw, *The Wobblies: The Story of Syndicalism in the United States* (Garden City, N.Y.: Doubleday, 1967; London: Eyre & Spottiswoode, 1967);

Franklin Rosemont, *Joe Hill: The IWW and the Making of a Revolutionary Workingclass Counterculture* (Chicago: Charles H. Kerr, 2003);

Ellen Doree Rosen, *A Wobbly Life: IWW Organizer E. F. Doree* (Detroit: Wayne State University Press, 2004);

Daniel Rosenberg, "The IWW and Organization of Asian Workers in Early Twentieth Century America," *Labor History,* 36 (Winter 1995): 77–87;

Salvatore Salerno, *Red November, Black November: Culture and Community in the Industrial Workers of the World* (Albany: State University of New York Press, 1989);

David Saposs, *Left Wing Unionism* (New York: Russell & Russell, 1967);

Ann Schofield, "Rebel Girls and Union Maids: The Woman Question in the Journals of the AFL and IWW, 1905–1920," *Feminist Studies,* 9 (Summer 1983): 335–358;

Jack Scott, *Plunderbund and Proletariat: History of the I.W.W. in B.C.* (Vancouver, B.C.: New Star, 1975);

Nigel Anthony Sellars, *Oil, Wheat & Wobblies: The Industrial Workers of the World in Oklahoma, 1905–1930* (Norman: University of Oklahoma Press, 1998);

William Seraile, "Ben Fletcher, IWW Organizer," *Pennsylvania History,* 46 (July 1979): 213–232;

Rosalie Shanks, "The IWW Free Speech Movement, San Diego, 1912," *Journal of San Diego History,* 19 (1973): 25–33;

Gibbs M. Smith, *Joe Hill* (Salt Lake City: University of Utah Press, 1969);

Robert E. Snyder, "Women, Wobblies, and Workers' Rights: The 1912 Textile Strike in Little Falls, New York," *New York History* 60 (January 1979): 29–57;

Donald G. Sofchalk, "Organized Labor and the Iron Ore Miners of Minnesota, 1907–1936," *Labor History,* 12 (Spring 1971): 214–242;

Wallace Stegner, "Joe Hill, the Wobbly Troubadour," *New Republic,* 118 (5 January 1948): 20–24, 38;

Stegner, "The Case of Joe Hill–Joe Hill: IWW Martyr," *New Republic,* 119 (15 November 1948): 18–20;

Philip Taft, "The Federal Trials of the IWW," *Labor History,* 3 (Winter 1962): 57–91;

Meredith Tax, *The Rising of the Women* (New York: Monthly Review Press, 1980);

Eugene M. Tobin, "Direct Action and Conscience: The 1913 Paterson Strike as Example of the Relationship between Labor Radicals and Liberals," *Labor History,* 20 (Winter, 1979): 73–88;

John C. Townsend, *Running the Gauntlet: Cultural Sources of Violence Against the I.W.W.* (New York: Garland, 1986);

Anne H. Tripp, *The I.W.W. and the Paterson Silk Strike of 1913* (Urbana: University of Illinois Press, 1987);

Ian Turner, *Tom Barker and the I.W.W.* (Canberra: Center for the Study of Labour History, 1965);

Robert L. Tyler. *Rebels of the Woods: The I.W.W. in the Pacific Northwest* (Eugene: University of Oregon Press, 1967);

Irving Werstein, *Pie in the Sky: An American Struggle, the Wobblies and Their Time* (New York: Delacorte, 1969);

Donald E. Winters, *The Soul of the Wobblies: The I.W.W., Religion, and American Culture in the Progressive Era, 1905–1917* (Westport, Conn.: Greenwood Press, 1985);

Roy T. Wortman, *From Syndicalism to Trade Unionism: The IWW in Ohio, 1905–1950* (New York: Garland, 1985);

Sally Zanjani and Guy Luis Rocha, *The Ignoble Conspiracy: Radicalism on Trial in Nevada* (Reno: University of Nevada Press, 1986).

The Modern School Movement

Daniel C. Marston

An educational experiment founded by anarchists, libertarians, socialists, and other freethinkers, the Modern School Movement sought to implement anarchist, free-thought, and libertarian ideas in independent schools throughout Europe and later in the United States between 1901 and the late 1930s. The founders of this movement hoped for a total transformation of society through education. They emphasized self-reliance and freedom of students in direct contrast to the formality and strict discipline in state-sponsored and traditional classrooms of the time. Modern Schools developed primarily to serve children of working-class people as well as children of anarchists and socialists. The founders sought to abolish all forms of coercive authority and develop a new society through the voluntary cooperation of individuals. The movement itself started in the late 1800s, and its original U.S. adherents survived until the 1960s. A small Modern School reunion meets at Rutgers University each year.

The Modern School movement started in France in the late 1800s. Much of the original thinking for the movement came from experimental education techniques outlined in Jean-Jacques Rousseau's *Emile,* published in 1762, but the writings of the English anarchist William Godwin exerted a greater influence. Louise Michel took those ideas and started a school in Montmartre that she described as an alternative to the "soul-destroying institutions, the bourgeois school" (Goldman, *Anarchism and Other Essays*). The typical school of the time set very definite rules, accepted only children from privileged backgrounds—and usually only one sex—and had programs that appealed only to the upper social classes. Notably, high-achieving intellectuals of the period often refused to send their children to state-sponsored schools because the quality of learning was so poor. Like Marie and Pierre Curie or Margaret Mead's parents, those who could afford to educate their children at home or who had access to laboratories and workshops where children could learn from experts chose not to subject the children to educational environments that emphasized obedience and rote memorization instead of stimulating real thought.

Michel's school existed for several years but was closed when she was imprisoned during the Paris Commune of 1871. Later, Paul Robin established a similar larger school in Cempuis near Paris. His school sought out orphans or children from the lower rungs of French society. Robin sought to prove that the children could break out of the social classes of their families if provided with deep understanding, educational stimulation, freedom, exercise, love, and sympathy. In her essay on the Modern School movement, Emma Goldman wrote that Robin "took his children from the streets, the hovels, the orphan and foundry asylums, the reformatories, from all the gray and hideous places where a benevolent society hides its victims in order to pacify its guilty conscience" *(Anarchism and Other Essays)*. The French government later closed Robin's school because he allowed coeducation, then prohibited under French law. Nevertheless, Madeline Vernet and Sebastian Faure soon set up similar schools in other parts of France. These schools emphasized the importance of developing a love of study and learning in children by helping to stimulate interest in their environment and emphasizing the importance of direct investigation and reflection on the results of their investigations. School staff also taught that students should never accept anything on blind faith, including what teachers and school administrators told them. At an international anarchist conference in 1907 Goldman had articulated the anarchist criticism of the typical public school as a "veritable barrack, where the human mind is distilled and manipulated into submission to various social and moral spooks and thus fitted to continue our system of exploitation and oppression" (quoted in Avrich, *The Modern School Movement*). Afterward she visited Faure's school, "The Beehive," and planned to push for the establishment of such schools in the United States.

Francisco Ferrer is the individual whose name appears most frequently in association with the international Modern School movement. Ferrer was exiled to Paris in 1885, along with his wife and children, as punishment for being a supporter of Spanish republican leader Manuel Ruiz Zorrilla. In Paris he first encountered in a significant way the ideas of Robin, Vernet, and Faure. While there he divorced his wife and married a wealthy Parisian teacher who later played a significant role in funding the movement. Using ideas from the French schools, he started the first Modern School in Spain in 1901. He opened the Escuela Moderna, a progressive school in Barcelona, in defiance of the state-run educational system in that country. Virtually the entire system of education in Spain at that time was controlled by the Catholic Church. Ferrer expressed belief in the need for education free from the authority of church and state and sought to develop just such a school. His critical approach to the Church and its involvement in education eventually triggered the strongest opposition leveled against him and the Spanish Modern School movement. But in 1901 the Escuela Moderna was considered very successful, and soon several different branches of the school appeared throughout Spain. Between 1901 and 1909 Ferrer opened 109 Modern Schools, and his followers organized 308 similar schools. Notably, the educational enterprise necessitated the use of a printing press. Ferrer reported printing 150,000 copies of modern texts on subjects such as natural science and sociology.

Although the schools had success, the Spanish government and established powers within Spanish society opposed them. In 1906 Ferrer was accused of involvement in a plot to kill the king of Spain, and as a result all the Modern Schools under his supervision were closed. The evidence exonerating him proved very strong, however, and he was released later that year. In September 1909 Ferrer was arrested again, accused of leading a workers' protest in Barcelona that turned into an open and violent rebellion (later called "Tragic Week"). Anarchists around the world believed that little evidence connected Ferrer directly to the uprising, although the Spanish government reported that it had the accounts of seventy-two witnesses on paper. In a letter from Ferrer to his friend Soledad Villafranca (and quoted by Goldman in her essay on Ferrer) he seems to believe that the evidence will not support the charges and writes "No reason to worry; you know that I am absolutely innocent" (quoted in Goldman, *Anarchism and Other Essays*). Ferrer was found guilty at his trial and was executed by the Spanish government on 13 October 1909. Most of the remaining Modern Schools in Spain were subsequently closed, and this essentially ended the Modern School movement in Spain.

Ferrer's approach to education generated significant support and opposition both in Spain and internationally. Most of the support and criticism occurred in speech rather than on paper. Goldman's "Francisco Ferrer and the Modern School Movement," developed

from a speech given two months after Ferrer's death, provides insights into the way Ferrer's supporters viewed the movement as well as a summary of some of the movement's criticisms by its contemporaries. Two years after Ferrer's death, Goldman, one of the strongest proponents of Ferrer's philosophy, described Ferrer as a man who was strongly motivated to help children grow into "self-reliant, liberty-loving men and women" and who showed concern for the poor and downtrodden of the world. As Goldman saw it, Ferrer tried to help children understand the splendor and wonder of the world, and "in so doing he made it forever impossible for the poisonous weeds of the Catholic Church to take root in the child's mind" (*Anarchism and Other Essays*). One of the criticisms leveled against Ferrer was his atheism, but his supporters did not see it as negating the validity of his views on education. Goldman dismissed nasty gossip about Ferrer's personal life as having been started by representatives of the Catholic Church as a way of discrediting him. Other criticism alleged that Ferrer hated the wealthy and that he (again according to Goldman) "prepared the children to destroy the rich" (*Anarchism and Other Essays*). Ferrer's supporters presented his views as supporting the poor rather than advocating hatred of the rich.

Ferrer's execution generated an outcry from anarchists throughout the world and started an active movement to carry on his work. Within a few years of Ferrer's death, Modern Schools were established in the United States, England, Belgium, Holland, Italy, Germany, Switzerland, Poland, Czechoslovakia, Argentina, Brazil, Mexico, China, and Japan. In the United States a group of anarchists led by Goldman and Alexander Berkman met on 3 June 1910 at the hall of the Harlem Liberal Alliance in New York City to found the Francisco Ferrer Association. The free-thought Thomas Paine Association was well represented within the assembled group, including its newly elected officers. Leonard Abbott was the first president of the association, and William van der Weyde and Dr. E. B. Foote held the same offices, secretary and treasurer, that they did in the Paine Association. Other charter members included Harry Kelly, Alden Freeman, Jack London, Upton Sinclair, Jaime Vidal, and Dr. Charles Andrews, the son of a famous anarchist (Stephen Pearl Andrews). London, Sinclair, Charles Edward Russell, J. G. Phelps Stokes, and Rose Pastor Stokes served on an advisory board, most of them socialists. Hutchins Hapgood and Alden Freemen were liberals from the upper class sympathetic to anarchism. Some single-taxers also contributed significantly to the group as time progressed, most notably Gilbert Roe, Theodore Schroeder, and Bolton Hall. There were twenty-two charter members in all, whose subscriptions raised the group's first funds. The stated objective of the association was "to perpetrate the work and memory of Francisco Ferrer." The group agreed to do that in three ways: they would hold memorial meetings each year on 13 October, the date of his death; they would publish books to honor the education martyr and support his cause; and they would establish Modern Schools throughout the United States.

From the beginning the Modern School movement in the United States included a social component and emphasized the importance of publishing. Alexander Berkman had established the very first Ferrer school in the United States, a radical Sunday school, but it did not survive long. Other members spent the first year raising funds for the Modern Schools and compiling a volume of essays about Ferrer, which Abbott edited and they published in 1910 as *Francisco Ferrer: His Life, Work, and Martyrdom*. Even before the collection was complete, the group had published two small pieces, Ferrer's "The Modern School," translated by Voltairine de Cleyre (a full version was translated by Joseph McCabe and published in London in 1913 as *The Origin and Ideals of the Modern School*), and "The Rational Education of Children" (published as a pamphlet by The Association in 1910), both reprinted from Goldman's monthly journal *Mother Earth*. Also, Harry Kelly and Stewart Kerr began editing a monthly *News Letter* that fall. The group also made distribution of literature about Ferrer and his schools a special project.

In October the Ferrer Association oversaw the organization of memorial meetings in twenty-five U.S. cities. In New York, Cooper Union hosted the largest meeting, with five thousand attendees. That meeting collected $500 for the school fund. The association developed branches around the United States. Following the establishment of the first U.S. Modern School by the Ferrer Association in 1911, Modern Schools sprang up that same year in Chicago and Philadelphia, and then in Detroit, Seattle, Portland, New Jersey, and Salt Lake City by 1915.

Similar schools existed already in the United States prior to 1900, although they were not part of an organized educational movement. Alternative education in the United States is as old as the country itself. Robert Owen had experimented with some ideas in his New Harmony schools that anarchists later considered central, in particular the precept that "the individuality of the child must be sacred" (quoted in Avrich). Josiah Warren had taught classes to boys at Spring Hill, Ohio, so that they might be able to have a trade and earn a living. Many teachers who spent time with the Modern Schools admired the work of Bronson Alcott and Elizabeth Peabody at the Temple School. A closer contemporary of the Modern School was Marietta Johnson's School of Organic Education, located at Fairhope, Alabama, and connected with a single-tax colony there.

Finally, "Sunday schools" were founded across the country by immigrants and employed the native languages of the schools' founders to teach their children ethnically focused history and culture from their places of origin. Some began as radical free-thought schools in response to Johann Most's call, following the 1883 Pittsburgh Congress of the International Working People's Association, for secular education organized to teach scientific rather than religious principles for girls and boys. In *The Modern School Movement: Anarchism and Education in the United States* (1980), Paul Avrich points out that some Sunday schools became radicalized, and in a few cases Modern day schools developed from them. The Socialist Party of America began to become involved in alternative Sunday schools in 1908 because its membership agreed that public schools indoctrinated children with the qualities of competition and aggression rather than with cooperation. Avrich identified twenty-one known Modern Schools and twelve related schools, in most cases run by anarchists. Other schools were organized on a temporary or seasonal basis, with summer retreats to the countryside so that the children might have a respite from the heat and grime of urban areas. Given the Modern Schools' secularist bias, they invariably incurred the displeasure of Roman Catholic clergy in their neighborhoods, although the power of the clergy over everyday life in the United States was in no way comparable to the situation in Spain, where an estimated 70 percent illiteracy rate had prevailed at the time Ferrer opened his first school.

The first Modern School founded by the Ferrer Association in the United States opened in 1911 in New York City, in Greenwich Village. It was called "The Ferrer Center and Modern School," and it combined the functions of a community gathering place, concert hall, theater café, day school for children, and free university. This center served not only as a school for children but also as a popular setting for adults to meet, particularly intellectuals who were interested in the anarchist movement. The children's school was small at first, with only nine pupils including Margaret Sanger's son. Bayard Boyeson took a leave from Columbia University to serve as director for the center and principal of the school. Classes for adults included philosophy, English, and painting, including classes taught by artists Robert Henri and George Bellows. Some of the other famous instructors and lecturers at this center included Clarence Darrow, Lincoln Steffens, Margaret Sanger, and Hapgood.

Later, as it attracted more attention and its programs more attendance, the Ferrer Center moved to

East Twelfth Street, then to Harlem. By the end of its time in New York the Center occupied a building with a basement and three floors. The basement was a recreational area where Hippolyte Havel lived and worked on various publication projects, including an anarchist journal called *Revolt*. The first floor was an adult lecture and concert hall, and the second floor housed the children's day school. On the third floor were apartments the Center rented out, usually to anarchists. This proved a problem in the summer of 1914, when four anarchist tenants–Arthur Caron, Carl Hanson, Marie Chavez, and Charles Berg–who had intended to bomb the Rockefeller mansion accidentally detonated the bomb in their apartment, killing themselves and another renter. In October another suspected anarchist bomb plot in the city brought an intolerable level of pressure on the school, which had already come under federal surveillance. The Ferrer Center stayed in New York until May 1915 when it moved to Stelton, New Jersey, and was subsequently called "The Stelton School and Community."

Another major Modern School in the United States was located in Philadelphia, where a large immigrant anarchist community had arisen and supported cultural institutions such as the Radical Library well before the Ferrer Association's founding. Voltairine de Cleyre, the poet and teacher, lived in the Jewish ghetto there. In October 1910 the Radical Library, led by Joseph Cohen, started a Modern Sunday school. Cohen was a cigar maker and a member of the Jewish fraternal organization called The Workmen's Circle. Within six months the school had sixty children enrolled. Cohen, his wife Sophie, de Cleyre's best friend Mary Hansen, and Hansen's companion George Brown, an English shoemaker, were the teachers. After five years more than a hundred children attended. This school included an adult program with nightly lectures given by an array of local and visiting speakers such as Scott Nearing, Lucy Parsons, and Will Durant. In 1913 Cohen moved to New York to run the Ferrer Center, and a graduate student in philosophy from the University of Pennsylvania, Abe Grosner, took his place. The Philadelphia school never managed to open a day school, but it did create Camp Germinal, a summer camp for children and adults, in neighboring Jamison, Pennsylvania. Both institutions lasted into the 1930s.

The Chicago Francisco Ferrer Club was founded in the summer of 1910, opening a free library and reading room at 1015 South Halsted Street. In October of that year William Nathanson and some friends and family opened a Modern Sunday school with nightly lectures for adults at a home on Twelfth Street. The school opened just as de Cleyre moved to Chicago, and she taught there for a few months but was temperamentally unsuited to the environment, preferring to give private lessons, although she liked to imagine alternative living arrangements including a country boarding school. Also, de Cleyre was terminally ill; she died in 1912. The school did not survive one year. At least two other efforts were made to form a Modern School in Chicago with no success, even from a very promising 1914 Modern School League under the guidance of Robert McConochie, Dr. J. H. Greer, and preacher-turned-socialist William Thurston Brown, who went on to found several other Modern Schools in Salt Lake City, Los Angeles, and Portland.

In the United States, Goldman served as the primary front person and publicity generator for the Modern School movement. In the June 1910 edition of Goldman's radical newspaper *Mother Earth* Leonard Abbott wrote that "Emma Goldman has done more than anyone else to keep alive American interest in the martyred founder of the Modern School" (quoted in Avrich, *The Modern School Movement*). Her 1910 essay "Francisco Ferrer and the Modern School" remains probably the most-referenced work on Ferrer. Her friendship with philosopher John Dewey, then teaching at Columbia University, undoubtedly influenced the association's ideas about education. Goldman's fame, however, sometimes obscures the fact that she had very little to do with the day-to-day operations of any school, even the one in New York.

Those who did operate the New York school hailed more often from the bohemian left of Greenwich Village than from the immigrant-dominated tenements. Many were associated with Columbia University. Alden Freeman, the son of a wealthy oil executive, paid most of the rent and salaries for the first Ferrer Association Modern School and then also raised the funds to move the school to Stelton. The day school's first principal was Bayard Boyesen from Columbia University. Durant later took over for a year as principal in 1912. Leonard Abbott, a writer from a wealthy family and the president of the Ferrer Association, served in an administrative capacity and taught from time to time at the school. The poet Lola Ridge was the school secretary. Durant credited her with his recruitment. Cora Bennett Stephenson was the next principal and lead teacher until Elizabeth and Alexis Ferm arrived in 1920. Jim and Nellie Dick came from a Modern School in England, working first at Stelton and later at Lake Mohegan, N.Y. A Chinese anarchist student of Dewey named Gray Wu worked at Stelton into the 1920s; he later became a dean of Peking University. Pryns Hopkins, another Columbia graduate whose family wealth derived from the Singer Sewing Machine Company, became a benefactor of the Stelton Colony and ran his own Modern School, Boy Land, for six years in Santa Barbara, California.

For many years Modern Schools were the only schools in America that deliberately sought students from working-class families. Although most of the participants in the Modern School movement (including financial supporters and parents who sent their children to the school) were anarchists, freethinkers, or libertarians, support of a particular point of view was not expressly identified as a criterion for admission to or involvement with the schools. Education ranked as the primary purpose of the schools, and a corollary purpose was to develop a radical sensibility among the students. Most founders of the school expressed hope that more class-conscious students would work to shape a society in which all forms of authority were abolished, and voluntary and free cooperation of individuals became the norm. These goals for education formed the primary connections between the schools as a movement, given that all the Modern Schools were independent. The Modern School Association of North America (MSANA) was established in 1916 and met annually on Labor Day weekends at Stelton, but its meetings served as more of a networking and education conference than to provide any sort of governance for the schools. Harry Kelly, a printer and original member of the Ferrer Association who owned one of the adjoining parcels of the Stelton Colony, chaired the MSANA.

The curriculum varied from school to school but in many cases tended to be traditional, including classes in areas such as reading, math, and grammar. School offerings depended upon the talent and knowledge at hand; for example, when Grosner took over the Philadelphia Modern School, he recruited his brother to teach classes in astronomy. The Brooklyn Modern School hired a teacher of Esperanto. Resident writers and artists, such as George Seldes and Rudolf Rocker at the Mohegan school, Hugo Gellert at Stelton, and Havel at the New York Ferrer Center, lent their energies to education and invited their friends to lecture. Some Modern Schools offered classes in etiquette. Even when many of the general subjects were traditional, however, the learning environment differed significantly from the typical school. Freedom and respect for the individual child took precedence much more than in typical schools of the time. Children at the Modern Schools typically chose learning or recreational activities for themselves and decided when they wanted to participate. Classes in painting, drawing, and music were offered for almost all Modern School students. The Modern Schools also offered frequent outings, such as picnics and trips to museums and zoos, as opportunities to expand on classroom experiences. The country schools sometimes kept animals and involved children

in their care. Students at Modern Schools were also provided opportunities on a regular basis to correspond with children of other countries. This last approach was used to help reinforce students' view of themselves as part of a worldwide movement and a global society.

All the Modern Schools emphasized student freedom and learning through experiences. For example, the Stelton School required only two activities of students on a daily basis: they had to attend the morning meeting, which included singing, and each child had to help clean one room in the afternoon. Teachers were encouraged not to impress their views (or any other views for that matter) on the students. Some schools relied upon alternative theories such as those of Marietta Johnson and Elizabeth Ferm that children should not be subjected to any pressure about learning to read before age ten. A few schools involved pupils in decisions made about the schools, anticipating contemporary democratic schools. Arts and crafts appeared in the curriculum as ways to encourage self-expression and self-reliance. At Stelton, for example, children could learn printing, weaving, metalworking, and other skilled trades using equipment at the on-site workshops. Children there were responsible for maintaining the buildings and keeping the labs and tool rooms in order. The development of manual skills, through building and repair projects, formed another common thread throughout the Modern Schools.

The degree to which any rules were implemented and enforced differed from school to school, but each Modern School kept these rules to a minimum compared to more-traditional schools. Most Modern Schools also did not give tests or grades. When asked by the Progressive Education Association in 1927 how Modern Schools determined grade standings, Jim Dick, one of the directors of the Mohegan Modern School, gave a typical response: "by studying each individual child" (quoted in Avrich). Such an approach rested on the assumption that the greater good would be served by students growing to see themselves as active, responsible, voluntary members of society who determined their own paths in life rather than passively following rules and accepting others' judgments. This more open approach to education and educational assessment brought with it some uncertainties, however, that as time passed caused anxieties among parents and possibly even administrators of the Modern School movement. After Dick made his 1927 statement about student assessments, for example, the Mohegan School implemented a more structured curriculum and assessment process for the students within a year, although the new program was still much less structured than other schools of the time. The Dicks returned to Stelton when that happened. In fact, most Modern Schools did

Cover design by Rockwell Kent for a 1917 issue of The Modern School *magazine (Paul Avrich,* The Modern School Movement: Anarchism and Education in the United States, *1980; Thomas Cooper Library, University of South Carolina)*

modify their programs over the years, and the majority of these changes moved clearly in the direction of implementing more-conservative structure and rules.

Durant, though he did not espouse anarchism, embodied the spirit of the Modern Schools and their daily operation. He worked as a teacher at the Modern School and Ferrer Center from 1910 to 1912; he became principal in 1912 and kept that position until mid 1913, when he left for a professorship at Columbia University. The children at the school called him "Will" and tended to have a friendly yet respectful relationship with him. He became known for showing children why

assignments were important rather than forcing them to do assignments. Durant said that he believed the best schools, like the best governments, were the ones that governed least, and he followed through on this philosophy in the operation of the school. He also married one of his teenage students from the Modern School. In their *Dual Autobiography* (1977) Durant and his wife, Ariel, explained that the students at the school were allowed considerable freedom but were not free to do things that would endanger their physical safety (such as walk out into the city streets). In the New Jersey countryside, however, Modern School children spent all day out of doors and were free to ice-skate on the brook that ran through the property or to roam anywhere on the three large parcels that made up the colony.

From 1912 to 1922 the Modern School movement published a magazine called *The Modern School*, which started as a newsletter for parents whose children attended the Modern School in New York. Both the newsletter and the magazine were printed on the handpresses used to teach printing at the school. The poet Ridge served as its first editor, then Columbia University's Carl Zigrosser took over in 1917. In later years the magazine was distributed to parents of students at other Modern Schools as well as to those generally interested in the Modern School movement, and it became a well-respected source of poetry, prose, and art as well as articles about libertarian education. Elizabeth Ferm first published *The Spirit of Freedom in Education* (1919) in serial form in *The Modern School*. Max Weber's poems and woodcuts appeared there, as did articles by Charlotte Perkins Gilman; poems by Horace Traubel, Adolf Wolff, and Harry Kemp; and prose sketches by Manuel Komroff and Konrad Bercovici. All admired William Morris, William Blake, and Walt Whitman and attempted to incorporate these figures' associated styles and spirit into the magazine. Graphics and illustrations for the magazine won the respect of the artistic world and elicited praise of *The Modern School* from many artists and writers of the time (including Hart Crane and Wallace Stevens). Rockwell Kent created a logo for the Modern School Association of North America and a decorative alphabet for the magazine.

The Modern School in New Jersey continued to meet all three original goals of the Francisco Ferrer Association, including the publication of books and periodicals to support the movement and spread ideas congenial to Ferrer's philosophy. Joseph Ishill, an anarchist printer from Romania, taught printing at the Stelton school beginning in 1915 and oversaw the children in their publication of their own magazine, *The Path of Joy*. He printed *The Modern School* using the same handpress. He supported himself by working in New York as a typesetter, and for a short time he and his wife, Rose Freeman, moved back to the city. By September 1918 they decided they missed the country, so they bought a house from Hall in Berkeley Heights, New Jersey, and from there they ran what at first they called The Free Spirit Press but after 1926 became the Oriole Press. Even before he left Stelton, Ishill had begun publishing a series of finely printed private editions, beginning with Oscar Wilde's *Ballad of Reading Gaol* in 1916. He and Rose published anthologies of literature and twice produced literary magazines. From 1919 to 1921 they ran a literary review called *The Free Spirit,* with contributions by Abbott, Durant, and others connected with the

Stelton school. Again in 1926 Ishill produced a magazine with Havel called *Open Vistas*. Inspired by Morris, Ishill also published the work of anarchist poet J. William Lloyd as well as keeping the works of many anarchist and libertarian authors in print.

World War I had a significant impact on Modern Schools and led to their rather rapid decline throughout the world. Many European countries that had Modern Schools were directly involved in the war and had all their educational systems vastly altered or completely shut down during or immediately after the war. Since the Modern Schools were already small and working on very tight budgets, many of them were forced to close because of the war. The unprecedented casualties of the war placed financial strain on families. In the United States, World War I had several effects on the Modern Schools. First, it caused bitter divisions among those involved in the schools. Those who supported the war were denounced and insulted; those who protested against the war were often subjected to varying degrees of persecution for their opposition to the government and its policies. Most anarchists were considered in de facto violation of the Espionage and Sedition Acts, since they advocated the dismantling of government in one form or another. Some went to prison; others committed suicide; some, like Berkman and Goldman, were deported.

Some U.S. Modern Schools continued to function through the 1920s, but, like other alternative cultural institutions and movements, confronted more difficult times during the 1930s. During the Depression many of the working-class parents had to withdraw their children from the schools because of economic difficulties. Because children of working-class parents made up a large percentage of the Modern Schools' student body, many Modern Schools were unable to generate the funds to continue operation. As jobs became harder to find during these years, many parents of Modern School students became concerned that their children did not have access to the educational training needed to find work. Child-labor laws that radicals had sought since the 1890s finally began to take hold in the 1930s, when almost a quarter of the adult workforce was unemployed, and as it became more common for children to go to school rather than work, the education profession consolidated and exerted a formidable influence over normative ideas about schools. The absence of formal grading procedures at many Modern Schools caused concerns for some parents who saw that their children were unable to present concrete data (letter grades, test scores) to show how well they performed at school. The Ferms, at Stelton, had contended with parental tendencies to view education as a means to an end, but even if the parents agreed with the ultimate goals of the Modern Schools' educational philosophy, their practical concerns about how their children would function in a society where jobs became harder to find led many parents to withdraw their children from the schools. A few schools remained open into the 1940s, and the last Modern School closed in the early 1950s. The MSANA stopped meeting in the late 1950s. Ishill was preparing to move to Gainesville, Florida, having been invited by the University of Florida to be its printer in residence, when he died in 1964.

The significance of the Modern School movement has manifested in its legacy and aftereffects more than its direct effect on education during the period in which Modern Schools operated. Since at most only several dozen U.S. Modern Schools operated at any one time in the first half of the twentieth century (out of several thousand schools throughout the country) and since most of the European Modern Schools did not stay open long (Ferrer's Modern Schools, for example, were only open from 1901 to 1909), they did not directly affect mainstream education much at the time. But the approach to education that emphasized student freedom and de-emphasized following rules did have an impact on the students and did continue even after the last Modern School closed. Probably the system of "free schools" that began to be established throughout the United States in the 1960s provides the clearest example of this influence. Many of these schools were developed by people who studied Modern Schools and even by some people who studied as children at Modern Schools. Like Modern Schools, "free schools" employ active methods of learning, encourage pupil participation in decision-making, establish informal relations between pupils and teachers, and encourage creative self-design and independent study. Central concerns of these schools include self-realization of the child and development of all the child's abilities and talents in an atmosphere of spontaneity and freedom. These original "free schools" fostered the use of more open and unstructured approaches to education that continue to develop today among members of Alternative Education Resource Organization, a loose alliance of education professionals, parents, and students from free schools, alternative schools (including public, democratic, Waldorf, and Montessori), as well as homeschoolers, and "unschoolers." Whereas Modern Schools did not directly change education in the United States or Europe, the Modern School movement did set in motion changes that continue to affect contemporary education.

In the 1970s and 1980s Avrich, a historian of anarchism, conducted a series of interviews with surviving members of various radical-left movements in the United States, including many students of the Modern School. The Friends of the Modern School began to meet at Rutgers University in 1973. The organization continues to meet and includes the children and grandchildren of people who worked at Modern Schools. A few former students of Modern Schools attend, and together they compiled an archive of the movement and plan to publish books about it, including books of photographs. Avrich's *Anarchist Voices: An Oral History of Anarchism in America* (1995) includes the testimonies of some Modern School associates.

References:

The Anarchy Archives Website (An Online Research Center on the History and Theory of Anarchism) <http://dwardmac.pitzer.edu/Anarchist_Archives> (accessed 15 August 2008);

Paul Avrich, *Anarchist Voices: An Oral History of Anarchism in America* (Princeton: Princeton University Press, 1995);

Avrich, *The Modern School Movement: Anarchism and Education in the United States* (Princeton: Princeton University Press, 1980);

Murray Bookchin, *The Spanish Anarchists* (Edinburgh: AK Press, 1997);

Will Durant and Ariel Durant, *A Dual Autobiography* (New York: Simon & Schuster, 1977);

Emma Goldman, *Anarchism and Other Essays* (New York: Mother Earth Publishing Association, 1911);

Joseph Ishill, *The Oriole Press: A Bibliography* (Berkeley Heights, N.J.: Oriole Press, 1953);

Alice Wexler, *Emma Goldman in America* (Boston: Beacon, 1984).

Papers:

The Modern School Collection is located in the library of Rutgers University in New Brunswick, New Jersey. Other collections related to the movement include the Joseph Ishill collections of anarchist correspondence and memorabilia at Harvard University and the University of Florida, Gainesville; the Joseph Cohen Papers, the Bund Archives of the Jewish Labor Movement, New York; the Emma Goldman Papers, New York Public Library; the Sadakichi Hartmann Papers, University of California, Riverside; and the Lola Ridge Papers, Smith College.

Mother Earth

(March 1906 – April 1918)

Linnea Goodwin Burwood
State University of New York, Delhi

The anarchist monthly journal *Mother Earth* (March 1906–August 1917) and its successor journal *Mother Earth Bulletin* (October 1917–April 1918) were the most vital English language anarchist journals in America during the early twentieth century. *Mother Earth* was the creation of one of the leading anarchists in the American movement, Emma Goldman. "Red Emma," as she became known, was born in Kovno, Russia, in 1869. She immigrated to the United States with her half sister Helena in 1885, arriving in Rochester, New York. She began working in a clothing factory and married Jacob Kershner, a fellow factory worker. Goldman soon left the loveless union. Still without having learned English or having assimilated to American culture, she moved to New York City in August 1889. Within days she met two of the most influential men in her life, the German anarchist Johann Most and a fellow Russian Jewish immigrant, Alexander Berkman. Her lifelong relationship with the anarchist Berkman was based on their mutual Russian radical background. They admired the nihilist Russians who had fought to reform the autocracy through both propaganda and radical activism. Both believed that the United States was the home of Jeffersonian democracy and became disillusioned by a nation in which capitalist interests had, by the 1890s, subsumed what Goldman and Berkman understood to be the roots of republican virtues. The "judicial murder" of the anarchists in the Chicago Haymarket Riots of 1886 that resulted from a worker movement to win an eight-hour day became a focal point for the immigrant anarchist community. Goldman and Berkman felt drawn to the anarchist movement as expressed in the beliefs of the Haymarket "martyrs" and in the writings of Most, founder of the radical German language newspaper *Die Freiheit* (Freedom).

The extended anarchist movement was a mostly leftist response to the excesses of corporate capitalism, distinct from the Socialist and Populist movements that began in the 1890s. Anarchism, unlike other political movements, was not a united phenomenon and found resonance particularly in certain immigrant communities, most famously among Italians and Jews. The concerns of progressive reforms, industrial unions, women's rights, education, urban reform, poverty, and immigration echoed throughout the varieties of anarchist thought. *Mother Earth,* from its inception in 1906, was never a journal restricted to philosophical anarchism or any other specific ideology. Goldman herself adhered most closely to the collectivist philosophy of Russian anarchist Peter Kropotkin, but she intended from the beginning for her journal to represent all anarchist thought. Within the pages of *Mother Earth* readers could find articles from proponents of collectivist, individualist, communist, and philosophical anarchist ideas. Goldman believed it was more important to inform and instruct the American public in the varieties of political thought within the movement than to propagate her personal political ideology.

The journal was unequivocally the brainchild of Goldman, conceived as a response to the anti-anarchist, nativist attitudes that prevailed in America after a decade of "propaganda by the deed" actions by anarchists both in the United States and in Europe. Throughout Europe during the 1890s, a series of bombings and attempted assassinations, some successful, snaked through France, Spain, Austria, and Italy; anarchists of various stripes took credit for these events. Berkman himself made an attempt, inspired by this tradition (as well as by the tradition of populist violence in Russia even earlier), to kill Henry Clay Frick, general manager of the Carnegie Corporation, during the Homestead Strike of 1892. Berkman shot Frick but failed to kill him, and received a twenty-two-year prison sentence for the attempted murder. Most, Goldman's mentor, lived in the United States because he had been forcibly deported from Germany for his extremist advocacy of terror as a means of achieving political and social change. Goldman attacked Most with a horsewhip when he publicly denounced Berkman in a seeming attempt to save his own skin.

When a disaffected and mentally unbalanced Pole, Leon Czolgosz, assassinated President McKinley in 1901, Goldman became the target of government interest and persecution for her political beliefs. For the following five years she lived in relative obscurity due to the virulent anti-anarchist attitudes in the population. She could gain employment as a nurse and massage therapist only under a pseudonym, E. G. Smith. Goldman realized that most of the population outside the immigrant community did not understand the tenets of anarchism and believed that all anarchists were wild-eyed bomb throwers. She believed that American politics lacked an anarchist voice to add to the spectrum of political debate raging in the country.

Goldman earned the money to start *Mother Earth* from a stint as manager and interpreter for a troupe of Russian actors. With the $250 she earned at this endeavor the journal began. Its original title was *The Open Road,* a reference to a poem by Walt Whitman, who was a favorite author among the anarchist community; however, when threatened by a lawsuit for copyright infringement, Goldman settled on a new title, *Mother Earth.* She decided on the title in spring of 1906 when she observed the rebirth of nature in the greening of the earth. The initial run of the first issue, 3,000 copies, sold in a week, and she and her friends decided on an additional printing of 1,000 copies. Goldman's dream became a reality.

Goldman's opening essay for the inaugural issue in March 1906 explained the purpose of the journal:

> Mother Earth will endeavor to attract and appeal to all those who oppose encroachment on public and individual life. It will appeal to those who strive for something higher, weary of the commonplace; to those who feel the stagnation is a deadweight on the firm and elastic step of progress; to those who breathe freely only in limitless space; to those who long for the tender shade of a new dawn for a humanity free from the dread of want, the dread of starvation in the face of mountainous riches.

Goldman's ideals and commitment to exposing the audience to all anarchist voices provided the only guidelines for articles, poetry, and short stories that were published in the journal throughout its lifetime.

The masthead from March 1906 until July 1907 reflected Goldman's conception of the journal as a "Monthly Magazine Devoted to Social Sciences and Literature." Goldman's busy speaking schedule during 1906 and early 1907, motivated by the financial needs of *Mother Earth,* precluded her personal oversight of the journal. As time passed and editorship changed, the journal reserved fewer pages for artistic anarchism and devoted more space to political, social, and economic issues reflective of the times. Even so, throughout its existence *Mother Earth* contained literary reviews and a books-received column. Scholars have difficulty understanding how articles were chosen for publication or discerning the internal workings of the editorial board because the working papers of the journal, along with subscription lists and correspondence from readers, were confiscated by the federal government when the *Mother Earth* offices and Goldman's home were raided on 16 June 1917 and have never resurfaced. The best source of information about the creation of *Mother Earth* and those involved in its inception remains Goldman's autobiography *Living My Life* (1931), published long after the events it describes.

Goldman chose her former lover, Max Baginski, as the journal's first editor. During Baginski's sixteen-month tenure as editor between March 1906 and July 1907, the pages of *Mother Earth* reflected Goldman's original idea of a journal divided between artistic and social science as these topics related to anarchism. The May 1906 issue included articles about literature, art, and a poem by Walt Whitman, together with discussion pieces on governmental paternalism and the role of liberty in American life. Berkman took over the editorship of the journal in August 1907 shortly after his release from prison, having served fourteen years of his original term.

Berkman continued as editor until April 1915. He was good at his job, and the journal reflected his own commitment to the cause of anarchism; however, he greatly reduced the number of pages that the magazine had given over to literature and artistic issues under Baginski's guidance. In the March 1910 issue, for example, only one article dealt with any topic other than social science. Under Berkman's editorship *Mother Earth* reflected his own interests in labor issues, politics, economics, and social inequities. After Berkman left for San Francisco in January of 1915, Goldman left his name on the contents page as editor until April, when she assumed the editorship herself until August 1917, though the real chores of editing during the last years of *Mother Earth's* existence were divided between Goldman's niece Stella Comyn, her nephew Saxe Commins, and Berkman's then current lover M. Eleanor Fitzgerald. "Fitzie," as she was known to all, had joined the family of *Mother Earth* in 1908 and remained involved with its publication until 1915 when she went with Berkman to San Francisco to aid in his short-lived West Coast anarchist newspaper *The Blast* (January 1916–June 1917).

Despite several changes of address, *Mother Earth* remained a New York City publication based in Manhattan. It began at Goldman's apartment at 210 East 13th Street, although the editorial address was a post office box at Madison Square until January 1907 when Goldman changed the address to 210 East 13th Street.

In January 1911 *Mother Earth* moved to 55 West 28th Street, where it remained until September 1913. In October 1913 the office moved to 74 West 119th Street in Harlem, and in October 1914 to 20 East 125th Street, where it remained until June 1917. *Mother Earth*'s final home for the last two issues in July and August 1917, after the federal marshals had raided its offices, was at 226 Lafayette Street.

Goldman had an editorial board, an inner circle of people she trusted. This group varied throughout the journal's existence but included Voltairine de Cleyre until her death in 1912; Goldman's current or past lovers, men such as Baginski, Berkman, Hippolyte Havel, and Ben Reitman; publisher Leonard Abbott; and printer Harry Kelly. Younger people joined the inner circle with the addition of Fitzgerald and Goldman's niece and nephew. Each of the inner circle members contributed regularly to the pages of *Mother Earth*.

The presentation of the journal remained the same throughout its lifetime. The page size was roughly equivalent to that of a dime novel, but the printing was always of good quality. Unlike those in other journals, the articles in *Mother Earth* appeared in their entirety without the interruption of ads. *Mother Earth* was an anarchist educational tool and serious articles ranging from birth control, trade unionism, the Russian Revolution, education reform, and other topical subjects were presented to stimulate the readers. The average number of pages was sixty from March 1906 until May 1908 when production costs forced a reduction to thirty pages. Occasionally, as in the tenth anniversary issue in March of 1915, the journal expanded to its original size. The journal always sold for ten cents, despite the constant financial needs.

Mother Earth rarely continued articles or short stories from one issue to the next, with a few notable exceptions, such as C. L. James's "Economy as Viewed by an Anarchist," printed in its entirety in the August and September 1911 issues. Goldman believed serial publication discouraged new readers. Though the first six issues included a drawing of a nude woman who had her back to the reader, gazing at the natural world around her, *Mother Earth* included very little artwork; the only political cartoon appeared in October 1912. Occasionally artistically significant covers appeared, including a famous send-up of national and religious imagery by Man Ray.

Under Berkman's editorship *Mother Earth* became the leading English-language anarchist journal in the United States. Berkman had learned English during his fourteen years in jail and ran a small underground anarchist journal, *Prison Blossoms,* during that time. Contentious and uncompromising, he exerted a firm control over *Mother Earth*'s pages during his tenure. One reveal-ing innovation started in the April 1910 issue when Berkman printed definitions of the terms "anarchism," "anarchy," and "anarchist" on the opening page. Anarchism he defined as "the philosophy of a new social order based on liberty unrestricted by man-made law; the theory that all forms of government rest on violence and are therefore wrong and harmful, as well as unnecessary." The glossary expanded in the December 1912 issue to include the terms "free communism" and "direct action." As the readership was expanding and the editorial inner circle believed that its role was to educate the public about the tenets of anarchism, the definitions served to explain the journal's ethos. The definitions appeared in different issues of the journal and rarely in the same place twice.

The tenth anniversary issue in 1915 was filled with articles that celebrated Goldman's achievement and reader-activist testimonials about the difference both *Mother Earth* and the anarchist movement had made in their political understanding. The enlarged issue, although celebratory in nature, allowed Goldman to reflect on initial goals for the journal. She believed *Mother Earth* had fulfilled part of her ambition "to voice untrammeled and unafraid every unpopular cause" and had remained outside the machinations of politics, even those of the anarchist social movement. However, Goldman also believed that the journal had not brought "the revolutionary spirit" of anarchism into the sphere of the creative. She reasoned that "the creative artist himself in America" was not aware of the social struggle that raged all around him, and that therefore the journal could not rely on American writers and artists to understand its purposes. Berkman added to Goldman's sentiments that anarchism was a "social philosophy, a revolutionary tendency, a popular movement" and that *Mother Earth* had successfully given voice to the variety of voices that he believed made up the "Anarchist spirit." This issue demonstrated the variety of anarchist thought of the day with communist, philosophical, and individualist anarchists all lending their voices to the celebration of the journal and anarchism.

Mother Earth included few regular columns. In most issues an "Observations and Comments" column offered short editorials, breaking news stories that dealt with anarchist topics of interest to the editor, and contemporary issues in various urban areas, mainly New York, of interest to *Mother Earth*'s main audience. For example, the June 1916 column opened with a piece on the Irish revolution taking place in Dublin as a call to arms to "all the oppressed of the earth." There followed an assessment of the new pieces of legislation signed into law by Governor Whitman of New York as representing in reality a militarization of the state. The editor explained that the new legislation made it obligatory for

Cover for the first issue of Emma Goldman's anarchist magazine (University of California Libraries)

all schoolchildren and college students to have military training. *Mother Earth* took the position that when the people of New York recognized that the politicians had created a compulsory conscription for men between the ages of eighteen and forty-five, they would rebel. In the same issue a short piece on a New York City Preparedness Day parade pointed out that many of the marchers were forced to participate by their employers and argued that the situation demonstrated the hypocrisy of the government on the issue of militarism. A short provocative piece then discussed a Westinghouse strike that had taken place in Pittsburgh. The anarchist conclusion was that at every juncture when workers rose to demand their share "they were confronted with the hired thugs and murderers of plutocracy." Reports followed on the various trials of anarchists on the West Coast, discussing "evidence" and legal maneuvering of the state.

The last editorial piece in this issue was also typical. It reported on the trial of Ben Reitman, physician, comrade to Goldman since 1908, and birth-control advocate who had handed out birth-control information, which was against the law. The report discussed a Union Square rally where anarchists had collected more than eight thousand signatures demanding access to birth-control information. The editor claimed the legal system was the "coldest anti-social institution" existing and that Reitman's actions had served the best interests of the population. Whenever an anarchist was incarcerated for breaking a law, the pages of the "Observations and Comments" not only championed the cause but also wrote in praise of the individual's spirit and commitment to anarchist principles. An example appeared in the February 1914 issue when Mexican labor anarchists Ricardo and Enrique Magon, Librado Rivera, and Anselmo Figueroa were released from a federal penitentiary after serving eighteen months for farm-labor agitation in California. The journal called the men heroes, who fought "ceaselessly" in the "battle of the disinherited." The final editorial praise was that their courage would inspire the social revolution to come.

In 1907 when Goldman went on her first speaking tour to raise funds for the journal, she began writing a monthly report column of her activities and observations on both the meetings at which she spoke and the various places she visited. The Goldman columns offer enormous insight into the political dialogues of the time and reveal what America looked like, emotionally as well as geographically, between 1907 and 1917. In the May 1908 issue Goldman's notes appeared under the title "En Route" from Los Angeles, California. She described the beauty and peace within the city before describing her encounters with the police, who

interfered with her right to free speech, in the various cities in which she spoke on her way. Goldman sarcastically described her encounters in San Francisco: "No potentate was ever received with greater deference and hospitality." She explained how kind it was of the chief of police to meet her at the train station, take her to her hotel and leave four officers who were instructed "to be close, very close" during her sojourn. Throughout the lifetime of *Mother Earth,* Goldman used her travel-lecture column to give the readers information about the size of and enthusiasm for the anarchist movement in the various cities she visited. The column went by different titles such as "The Joys of Touring" (January 1909), "On the Trail" (monthly from January through July 1911 and again in August and September 1914) and "Adventures in the Desert of American Liberty" (September and November 1909).

From 1907 through 1917 Goldman lectured widely in both the United States and Canada. She always warmly described the people she met or with whom she stayed in various places and always noted the police response as they surveyed her audiences or closed down her lectures. Her column contained information about the number of lectures given, audience size, and the amount of money raised. The lecture circuit grew through the years, and *Mother Earth* always announced tour dates, locations, and lecture topics. The June 1914 issue shows that Goldman delivered eight evening lectures and two afternoon talks between 17 and 24 May. She named the hotels where she would stay and asked comrades to meet her and help arrange more lectures in the state. The lecture tours became the most lucrative source of much-needed revenue to sustain the journal. Lecture titles included subjects as diverse as "Anarchism and Literature," "Limitation of Offspring," and "Social Revolution vs. Social Reform."

The journal ran a subscription appeal almost monthly, sometimes after the "Observations and Comments" columns or inserted after an article and other times as a full-fledged plea for funding, as in February 1910 with the *Mother Earth* Sustaining Fund." These columns contained a strict accounting of all revenue, whether from donations or one of Goldman's lectures, how the revenue was spent, and a general request for funding through either subscription or a donation. The journal needed a constant stream of funds to pay for paper, printing, and postage; it also raised funds for a variety of anarchist causes. Some of the ongoing funding drives provided defense funds for arrested anarchists, such as the June 1916 appeal for the Magon brothers, a Free Speech Fund in the February 1910 issue, or the March 1917 appeal for birth-control trial contributions. *Mother Earth* also hosted balls, masquerades, and concerts for its benefit. The journal ran announcements for events such as the December 1909 Christmas Eve concert and ball to celebrate a "real resurrection" meaning a social revolution, and a November 1906 masquerade ball for people to forget the "troubles of life." Modestly priced tickets could be purchased through the *Mother Earth* office, with all of the proceeds going to many anarchist causes including the journal.

Mother Earth never ran ads for consumer goods. Advertising was confined to the back pages and promoted the sale only of anarchist books or tracts, usually those published by the magazine. In August 1907 ads for pamphlets, essays, and books gave notice of the existence of the Mother Earth Publishing Association; Maxim Gorky's pamphlet "The Masters of Life" and Goldman's "The Tragedy of Women's Emancipation" were the first publications offered for sale in this manner. The list of publications grew over time with an all-star anarchist author list. In December 1909 the author list included Peter Kropotkin, Emile Pouget, Élisée Reclus, William Morris, and de Cleyre. None of the volumes were priced over $1. The May 1913 issue offered the complete works of Frederich Nietzsche at less than $2 per volume. The May 1916 issue offered works by Goldman, Berkman, Max Stirner, Michael Bakunin, Francisco Ferrer, and Margaret Sanger, each for less than $2. The publishing company was an extension of the journal, and many of the authors were part of the *Mother Earth* family or foreign supporters of Goldman's dream. In the November 1907 issue an advertisement appeared offering for sale other anarchist publications from the United States. The list included journals available in English, German, Yiddish, and Italian, information about their publication (whether they appeared weekly or monthly), and the city of their origin.

Mother Earth never boasted a coterie of famous journalists who wrote for it regularly, nor did any of its staff contributors gain much fame. In most cases the writers were not paid for their contributions as the journal was perennially short of funds. Some authors famous in anarchist circles wrote for the journal. The best known contributor was the playwright Eugene O'Neill; both Lincoln Steffens and Upton Sinclair wrote for *Mother Earth*. Many of the contributors were well known to the New York radical audience as the city became the home of anarchism after the Chicago Haymarket Riots of 1886. Some of the more famous American contributors included de Cleyre, Havel, Kelly, Mabel Dodge, and Leonard Abbott. Sanger was a radical but never an avowed anarchist in the tradition of Goldman, as her association with the free-speech movement that *Mother Earth* championed in its pages focused solely on the birth-control movement. Each of the American contributors, whether new to the cause (such as Dodge) or seasoned writers (Cleyre), manifested the ongoing anarchist dialogue that Goldman had envisioned when she first imagined the journal.

Many sympathetic foreign contributors and their ideas made their way into the pages of *Mother Earth* through translation. Some of the most notable Russian radicals of the time—including Leo Tolstoy, Gorky, and Kropotkin—wrote essays, poems, and short stories that appeared in *Mother Earth*. Leo Tolstoy, an avowed pacifist, explained his objection to governmental power in his article "America and Russia" in March 1909, which fit well with the anarchist goal of freedom, especially from the perceived public reliance on government in any form. Gorky, an advocate of social revolution, contributed in translation during his 1906–1907 tour of the United States while he was soliciting funding for a Russian revolutionary movement. During the year he published two stories in *Mother Earth:* "Comrade" in May 1906 and "The Masters of Life" in January 1907. Not an anarchist, Gorky was still radical enough for the pages of *Mother Earth*.

The most respected Russian collectivist anarchist of the day was Kropotkin. A Russian prince, he was also a friend to both Berkman and Goldman. His contributions to *Mother Earth* included the five-part reprint of "Modern Science and Anarchism," which ran from August 1906 through December 1906. Kropotkin's reprints ranged from a letter he wrote to Spanish anarchist educator Ferrer about education reform, appearing as "The Reformed School" in the August 1908 issue, to a review of goals of the participants in "The Commune of Paris" in the May 1912 issue. Kropotkin remained a favorite of the journal until World War I. The November 1914 issue of *Mother Earth* reprinted a Kropotkin letter to the British anarchist journal *Freedom*. In that letter Kropotkin advanced the opinion that the history of Germany since the 1880s had led to the conflagration in Europe and admitted that in that context he believed the war was necessary. *Mother Earth* bristled in reply that workers of all countries are the ones to die in "*all* capitalist wars," focusing instead on the idea that militarism could only be destroyed "by the social revolutionary power of the united international proletariat." The break between *Mother Earth* and the leading Russian voice of anarchism remained until the Russian Revolution in 1917. One of the most famous French radicals of the time was the syndicalist Emile Pouget, whose translated article, "The Basis of Trade Unionism," appeared in the January 1908 issue. Ferrer's article, *"L'Ecole Renovée,"* advocating intellectual freedom in the classroom for students, was translated and republished in the November 1909 issue after Ferrer's execution.

MOTHER EARTH

Vol. IX. September, 1914 No. 7

PRICE 10 CENTS

Cover by Man Ray. The journal was then edited by Alexander Berkman (Paul Avrich, The Modern School Movement: Anarchism and Education in the United States, *1980; Thomas Cooper Library, University of South Carolina).*

The table of contents of *Mother Earth* issues reflected not only the range of anarchist thought but also both local and international concerns, which added to its appeal. The December 1915 issue exemplifies the variety and breadth of the journal. It began with an article by Goldman on the military preparedness movement sweeping the United States. Goldman argued that preparedness was a "plague" and was done at the behest of "politicians and munitions speculators." She advocated revolution against both the state and capitalism in order to do away with war. An article by the British labor radical Tom Mann outlined the direct action campaign for British workers to avoid conscription in the British Army. Mann advocated action against the state as the workers made up the military and they were being sent to the front to kill German workers, who were also conscripted and sent to the front. Two articles dealt with the David Caplan and Matthew Schmidt trial related to the dynamiting of the Los Angeles Times Building the previous September. *Mother Earth* took the

position that Caplan and Schmidt were being tried simply for being anarchists, as they were not present at the explosion. The two men were likened to the Haymarket defendants, and the journal pledged to raise money for their defense. The issue also included an article about the execution of the labor radical Joe Hill in Salt Lake City in the previous month.

Mother Earth championed the movement and alerted readers to the location and nature of the fronts on which anarchists were fighting. In the early years the journal focused on the need to educate the public and called for reader involvement in the various causes undertaken by Goldman and colleagues. The December 1916 issue stressed the urgency of action as the nation moved towards involvement in World War I. The "Observations and Comments" column outlined the problems of the day: lynching of workers in Washington, Minnesota, and California without any justice from the courts; the rebellion of workers in several European countries as a response to the war; the release of an imprisoned leader of the Patterson Silk Workers Strike of 1915; the arrest of Sanger for being a public nuisance by handing out birth-control literature; the beatings of Industrial Workers of the World members by law enforcement officers during a strike in Seattle, Washington; and an acerbic comment about President Wilson's message that all Americans should pray for the war-ravaged peoples of Europe. The issue contained articles about the federal government's attempts to stop union activities along with explanations of the links between capitalism and the war in Europe. There was a reprint of a telegram to Goldman, who was on a lecture tour at the time, from her lawyer Harry Weinberger informing her there would be no jury in her trial for handing out pregnancy-prevention literature in May. Goldman asked the readers for contributions to a defense fund.

By December 1916 anarchists were battling the federal government on most issues as a matter of free speech. The greatest source of anxiety was the march towards war that acted as a catalyst for all *Mother Earth* activities in the remaining eight months of its existence and indeed absorbed the energies of much of the radical left for the next few years. In the April 1917 issue, while several pieces celebrated the revolutionary events taking place in Russia, the main focus remained on the war. As the April and May issues were published before President Wilson's April declaration of war, the June issue was totally devoted to anti-war commentary. Every article dealt with some aspect of war, capitalism, militarism, labor, or the humanitarian needs of the European population. The most virulent articles in the issue dealt with conscription. The Congress enacted a conscription law less than six weeks after a declaration of war. The pages of *Mother Earth* provided a scathing indictment of the government, discussing its use of patriotism, democracy, and the infringement on individual liberties. Goldman used the pages of the journal to speak out against the government's policies, and she and her friends founded the No-Conscription League which they ran from the *Mother Earth* office. The league ran ads for rallies against registering for service as a matter of conscience. Goldman, Berkman, and other anarchists spoke at a No-Conscription League rally on 4 June; the following day the government passed the Selective Service Act, followed on 15 June by the Espionage Act, making it illegal for anyone to speak out against the draft and equating such speech as undermining the United States government. Federal agents raided the offices of *Mother Earth* on 16 June. Both Goldman and Berkman were arrested, files and subscription lists were confiscated, and remaining issues of the journal removed.

Publication of *Mother Earth* continued during the months of July and August through the hard work of Fitzgerald and Comyn. The July issue covered the trial of Goldman and Berkman, their statements at trial in defense of anarchism, and their sentences of two years in federal prison and $10,000 in fines. The issue also contained information about the anti-conscription activities and the bravery of the young men who refused to register for military service. The final issue of *Mother Earth* appeared in August 1917, containing articles by Goldman and Berkman, who were on their way to prison. Both wanted the movement to continue and thanked their friends for support. The main problem for the journal was a lack of subscription lists and, between this and constant government surveillance, the journal was doomed. The August issue was full of news about the war, conscription, Russia's ongoing revolution, arrests of suffragettes, and the attempt by the state of California to extradite Berkman in connection with the San Francisco Preparedness Day bombing in 1916. The final issue contained all the elements that every *Mother Earth* publication had previously included, but the spark was gone, its two leading voices jailed and ostensibly silenced.

The end of *Mother Earth* coincided with the effective end of the anarchist movement in the United States. Although a few issues of *Mother Earth Bulletin* came out between October 1917 and April 1918 while Goldman and Berkman were released on appeal, this periodical publication never had the same power as its predecessor. Goldman went on tour to agitate and raise money, but both local and federal police were watching her every move, and the Post Office confiscated issues. As the government confined the group's ability to maneuver physically and publishing nationally was no longer an option, the days of *Mother Earth Bulletin* were numbered. When Goldman and Berkman were returned to prison, the life was gone from the journal. In April 1918 its final issue was published. Although Fitzgerald and Comyn attempted to carry the anarchist message forward through the Mother Earth Book Shop, federal agents raided it in July 1918 and Goldman's dream ended.

References:

Alexander Berkman and Emma Goldman, *Anarchism on Trial: Speeches of Alexander Berkman and Emma Goldman before the United States District Court in the City of New York, July 1917* (New York: Mother Earth Publishing Association, 1917);

Berkman and Goldman, *Deportation, Its Meaning and Menace: Last Message to the People of America* (Ellis Island, N.Y.: Fitzgerald, 1919);

Berkman and Goldman, *A Fragment of the Prison Experiences of Emma Goldman and Alexander Berkman: In the State Prison at Jefferson City, Mo., and the U.S. Penitentiary Atlanta, Ga., February 1918–October 1919* (New York: Stella Comyn, 1920);

Peter Glassgold, ed., *Anarchy: An Anthology of Emma Goldman's Mother Earth* (Washington, D.C.: Counterpoint, 2001);

Emma Goldman, *Living My Life,* 2 volumes (New York: Knopf, 1931);

Robert Graham, ed., *Anarchism: A Documentary History of Libertarian Ideas* (Montreal: Black Rose Books, 2005);

Mother Earth Bulletin, 12 volumes (New York: Greenwood Reprint Corporation, 1968) [includes both *Mother Earth* and *Mother Earth Bulletin*].

Books for Further Reading

Adamson, Madeleine, and Seth Borgos. *This Mighty Dream: Social Protest Movements in the United States*. Boston: Routledge & Kegan Paul, 1984.

American Social History Project. *Who Built America? Working People and the Nation's Economy, Politics, Culture, and Society*, 2 volumes. New York: Pantheon, 1992.

Anderson, Carlotta R. *All-American Anarchist: Joseph A. Labadie and the Labor Movement*. Detroit, Mich.: Wayne State University Press, 1998.

Avrich, Paul. *Anarchist Portraits*. Princeton: Princeton University Press, 1988.

Avrich. *Anarchist Voices: An Oral History of Anarchism in America*. Princeton: Princeton University Press, 1995.

Avrich. *The Haymarket Tragedy*. Princeton: Princeton University Press, 1984.

Bailey, Robert, Jr. *Radicals in Urban Politics: The Alinsky Approach*. Chicago: University of Chicago Press, 1974.

Bates, Beth Tompkins. *Pullman Porters and the Rise of Protest Politics in Black America, 1925–1945*. Chapel Hill: University of North Carolina Press, 2001.

Beisel, Nicola. *Imperiled Innocents: Anthony Comstock and Family Reproduction in Victorian America*. Princeton: Princeton University Press, 1997.

Beito, David T. *From Mutual Aid to the Welfare State: Fraternal Societies and Social Services, 1890–1967*. Chapel Hill: University of North Carolina Press, 2000.

Bell, Daniel. *Communitarianism and Its Critics*. Oxford: Clarendon Press, 1993.

Bird, Stewart, et al. *Solidarity Forever: An Oral History of the IWW*. Chicago: Lake View Press, 1985.

Black, Edwin. *War Against the Weak: Eugenics and America's Campaign to Create a Master Race*. New York: Four Walls Eight Windows, 2003.

Boylan, Anne M. *The Origins of Women's Activism: New York and Boston, 1797–1840*. Chapel Hill: University of North Carolina Press, 2002.

Brooks, Frank, ed. *The Individualist Anarchists: an Anthology of Liberty (1881–1908)*. New Brunswick: Transaction Publishers, 1994.

Bruns, Roger A. *The Damndest Radical: The Life and World of Ben Reitman, Chicago's Celebrated Social Reformer, Hobo King, and Whorehouse Physician*. Urbana: University of Illinois Press, 1987.

Burns, Stewart. *Social Movements of the 1960s: Searching for Democracy*. Boston: Twayne, 1992.

Chatfield, Charles, and Robert Kleidman. *The American Peace Movement: Ideals and Activism*. New York: Twayne, 1992.

Conlin, Joseph R., ed. *At the Point of Production: the Local History of the I.W.W.* Westport, Conn.: Greenwood Press, 1981.

Davis, Allen F. *Spearheads forReform: The Social Settlements and the Progressive Movement, 1890–1914*. New York: Oxford University Press, 1967.

Dawley, Alan. *Changing the World: American Progressives in War and Revolution*. Princeton: Princeton University Press, 2003.

Dawley. *Struggles for Justice: Social Responsibility and the Liberal State*. Cambridge, Mass. & London: Belknap Press of Harvard University, 1991.

D'Emilio, John, and Estelle B. Freedman. *Intimate Matters: A History of Sexuality in America*, second edition. Chicago: University of Chicago Press, 1997.

De Grazia, Edward. *Girls Lean Back Everywhere: The Law of Obscenity and the Assault on Genius*. New York: Random House, 1992.

DeLeon, David. *The American as Anarchist: Reflections on Indigenous Radicalism*. Baltimore & London: Johns Hopkins University Press, 1978.

Donner, Frank. *Protectors of Privilege: Red Squads and Police Repression in Urban America*. Berkeley: University of California Press, 1990.

Dorn, Jacob, ed.. *Socialism and Christianity in Early 20ᵗʰ Century America*. Westport, Conn.: Greenwood Press, 1998.

Duncombe, Stephen, ed.. *Cultural Resistance Reader*. New York: Verso, 2002.

Echols, Alice. *Daring to Be Bad: Radical Feminism in America 1967–1975*. Minneapolis: University of Minnesota Press, 1989.

Egbert, Donald D., and Stow Parsons, eds. *Socialism and American Life*, 2 volumes. Princeton: Princeton University Press, 1952.

English, Daylanne K. *Unnatural Selections: Eugenics in American Modernism and the Harlem Renaissance*. Chapel Hill: University of North Carolina Press, 2004.

Fellman, Michael. *The Unbounded Frame: Freedom and Community in Nineteenth-Century American Utopianism*. Westport, Conn.: Greenwood Press, 1973.

Falk, Candace, ed. *Emma Goldman: A Documentary History of the American Years*, 2 volumes. Berkeley: University of California Press, 2003–2005.

Fones-Wolf, Ken. *Trade Union Gospel: Christianity and Labor in Industrial Philadelphia, 1865–1915*. Philadelphia: Temple University Press, 1989.

Glassgold, Peter, ed. *Anarchy! An Anthology of Emma Goldman's* Mother Earth. Washington, D.C.: Counterpoint, 2001.

Goldberg, Robert A. *Grassroots Resistance: Social Movements in Twentieth-Century America*. Belmont, Cal.: Wadsworth, 1991.

Gordon, Jacob U. *Black Leadership for Social Change*. Westport, Conn.: Greenwood Press, 2000.

Gordon, Linda. *The Moral Property of Women: A History of Birth Control Politics in America*. Urbana & Chicago: University of Illinois Press, 2002.

Gorman, Paul R. *Left Intellectuals and Popular Culture in Twentieth-Century America*. Chapel Hill: University of North Carolina Press, 1996.

Gorn, Elliott J. *Mother Jones: The Most Dangerous Woman in America*. New York: Hill & Wang, 2001.

Greider, William. *Who Will Tell the People? The Betrayal of American Democracy*. New York: Simon & Schuster, 1992.

Halker, Bucky. *For Democracy, Workers, and God: Labor Song-Poems and Labor Protest, 1865–95*. Urbana: University of Illinois Press, 1991.

Heider, Ulrike. *Anarchism: Left, Right, and Green,* translated by Heider and Danny Lewis. San Francisco: City Lights, 1994.

Height, Dorothy. *Open Wide the Freedom Gates: A Memoir*. New York: PublicAffairs, 2003.

Jacobs, Paul, and Saul Landau. *The New Radicals: A Report With Documents*. New York: Random House, 1966.

Jacoby, Susan. *Freethinkers: A History of American Secularism*. New York: Metropolitan, 2004.

Jones, Margaret C. *Heretics & Hellraisers: Women Contributors to* The Masses, *1911–1917*. Austin: University of Texas Press, 1993.

Kelley, Robin D. G. *Race Rebels: Culture, Politics and the Black Working Class*. New York: Free Press, 1994.

Klein, Marcus. *Foreigners: The Making of American Literature, 1900–1940*. Chicago: University of Chicago Press, 1981.

Kornbluh, Joyce, ed. *Rebel Voices: An IWW Anthology,* expanded edition. Chicago: Charles H. Kerr, 1988.

Lynd, Staughton, ed. *"We Are All Leaders": The Alternative Unionism of the Early 1930s*. Urbana: University of Illinois Press, 1996.

Marchand, C. Roland. *The American Peace Movement and Social Reform, 1898–1918*. Princeton: Princeton University Press, 1972.

Marsh, Margaret. *Anarchist Women 1870–1920*. Philadelphia: Temple University Press, 1981.

Martin, James J. *Men Against the State: The Expositors of Individualist Anarchism in America, 1827–1908*. Colorado Springs, Colo.: Ralph Myles, 1970.

McAdam, Doug, John D. McCarthy, and Mayer N. Zald, eds. *Comparative Perspectives on Social Movements: Political Opportunities, Mobilizing Structures, and Cultural Framings*. Cambridge & New York: Cambridge University Press, 1996.

McAdam. *Political Process and the Development of Black Insurgency, 1930–1970,* second edition. Chicago: University of Chicago Press, 1999.

McElroy, Wendy. *The Debates of Liberty: An Overview of Individualist Anarchism, 1881–1908*. Lanham, Md.: Lexington Books, 2003.

McElroy. *Individualist Feminism of the Nineteenth Century: Collected Writings and Biographical Profiles*. Jefferson, N.C.: McFarland, 2001.

McGrath, Patrick J. *Scientists, Business, and the State, 1890–1960.* Chapel Hill: University of North Carolina Press, 2002.

Miller, Sally M. *Race, Ethnicity, and Gender in Early Twentieth-Century American Socialism.* New York: Garland, 1996.

Monkkonen, Eric, ed., *Walking to Work: Tramps in America, 1790–1935.* Lincoln: University of Nebraska Press, 1984.

Moore, Lawrence. *Religious Outsiders and the Making of Americans.* New York: Oxford University Press, 1986.

Painter, Nell Irwin. *Standing at Armageddon: The United States 1877–1919.* New York: Norton, 1987.

Pivar, David J. *Purity Crusade: Sexual Morality and Social Control, 1868–1900.* Westport, Conn.: Greenwood Press, 1973.

Piven, Frances Fox, and Richard A. Cloward. *Poor People's Movements: Why They Succeed, How They Fail.* New York: Pantheon, 1977.

Pollitt, Katha. *Subject to Debate: Sense and Dissents on Women, Politics, and Culture.* New York: Modern Library, 2001.

Roediger, Dave, and Franklin Rosemont, eds. *Haymarket Scrapbook.* Chicago: Charles H. Kerr, 1986.

Rosemont. *Joe Hill: The IWW and the Making of a Revolutionary Workingclass Counterculture.* Chicago: Charles H. Kerr, 2003.

Rosenzweig, Roy. *Eight Hours for What We Will: Workers and Leisure in an Industrial City, 1870–1920.* New York: Cambridge University Press, 1983.

Ruff, Allen. *"We Called Each Other Comrade": Charles H. Kerr & Company, Radical Publishers.* Urbana: University of Illinois Press, 1997.

Sale, Kirkpatrick. *The Green Revolution: The American Environmental Movement 1962–1992.* New York: Hill & Wang, 1993.

Schultz, Bud, and Ruth Schultz. *It Did Happen Here: Recollections of Political Repression in America.* Berkeley: University of California Press, 1989.

Schwartz, Judith. *Radical Feminists of Heterodoxy: Greenwich Village 1912–1940.* Lebanon, N.H.: New Victoria Publishers, 1982.

Sears, Hal. *The Sex Radicals: Free Love in High Victorian America.* Lawrence: Regents Press of Kansas, 1977.

Shepard, Benjamin, and Ronald Hayduk, eds. *From ACT UP to the WTO: Urban Protest and Community Building in the Era of Globalization.* New York: Verso, 2002.

Shore, Elliott, Ken Fones-Wolf, and James P. Danky, eds. *The German-American Radical Press: The Shaping of a Left Political Culture, 1850–1940.* Urbana: University of Illinois Press, 1992.

Smith-Rosenberg, Caroll. *Disorderly Conduct: Visions of Gender in Victorian America.* New York: Knopf, 1985.

Sochen, June. *The New Woman: Feminism in Greenwich Village, 1910–1920.* New York: Quadrangle Books, 1972.

Stansell, Christine. *American Moderns: Bohemian New York and the Creation of a New Century.* New York: Metropolitan, 2000.

Summers, Martin. *Manliness and Its Discontents: The Black Middle Class and the Transformation of Masculinity, 1900–1930.* Chapel Hill: University of North Carolina Press, 2004.

Tichi, Cecelia. *Exposés and Excess: Muckraking in America, 1900–2000*. Philadelphia: University of Pennsylvania Press, 2004.

Van Deburg, William L. *New Day in Babylon: The Black Power Movement and American Culture, 1965–1975*. Chicago: University of Chicago Press, 1992.

Winter, Thomas. *Making Men, Making Class: The YMCA and Workingmen, 1877–1920*. Chicago: University of Chicago Press, 2002.

Zieger, Robert H. *The CIO, 1935–1955*. Chapel Hill: University of North Carolina Press, 1995.

Zinn, Howard. *The Zinn Reader: Writings on Disobedience and Democracy*. New York: Seven Stories Press, 1997.

Contributors

Sue Boland	*Matilda Joslyn Gage Foundation*
John D. Buenker	*University of Wisconsin–Parkside*
Linnea Goodwin Burwood	*State University of New York, Delhi*
Donna L. Davey	*Tamiment Library, New York University*
Eugenia C. DeLamotte	*Arizona State University*
Brian Doherty	Reason Magazine, *Los Angeles*
Paula Doress-Worters	*Brandeis University*
Joan Downs	*University of Wisconsin–Whitewater*
Robert J. Fitrakis	*Columbus State Community College*
Hester L. Furey	*The Art Institute of Atlanta*
Rachel Furey	*University of California, Santa Cruz*
Edward Austin Hall	
Jessica Handler	*The Art Institute of Atlanta*
Claude Hargrove	*Fayetteville State University*
Jennifer Harrison	
Karen Holleran	
David M. Jones	*University of Wisconsin–Eau Claire*
Kurt R. Kessinger	*EthicsPoint*
James J. Kopp	*Lewis & Clark College*
Stephen Malagodi	*WLRN*
Daniel C. Marston	*Pittsburgh, Pa.*
Edward D. Melillo	*Franklin Marshall College*
Melissa Moore	*Central Michigan University*
Lynn Murray	*The Art Institute of Atlanta*
Mark A. Noon	*Bloomsburg University*
Stephen E. Randoll	*Saint Louis University*
Matt Sailor	*Georgia State University*
Matthew Sherman	*Saint Louis University*
Rebecca Tolley-Stokes	*East Tennessee State University*
Sarah Trachtenberg	*Brookline, Mass.*
Kim Urquhart	*Emory University*
Mark W. Van Wienen	*Northern Illinois University*
Andrew J. Waskey	*Dalton State College*
James A. Young	*Edinboro University*

ISBN-13: 978-0-7876-8163-0
ISBN-10: 0-7876-8163-6